Angel Veneration and Christology

Library of
Early Christology

Larry W. Hurtado
David B. Capes
April D. DeConick
Editors

SERIES INTRODUCTION

Over the past forty years or so, there has been a renewed interest in the origins and early developments of belief in Jesus, many of these studies sometimes referred to as loosely forming a kind of "new religionsgeschichtliche Schule" (new history of religion school). This body of work both resembles and differs from the German scholarship of the original "Schule," particularly in emphasizing more the roots of early Jesus-devotion in the rich and varied Jewish traditions of the Greco-Roman era.

Available from the Library of Early Christology Series

Bousset, Wilhelm. *Kyrios Christos: A History of the Belief in Christ from the Beginnings of Christianity to Irenaeus*

Capes, David B. *Old Testament Yahweh Texts in Paul's Christology*

DeConick, April D. *Seek to See Him: Ascent and Vision Mysticism in the Gospel of Thomas*

Fossum, Jarl E. *The Name of God and the Angel of the Lord: Samaritan and Jewish Concepts of Intermediation and the Origin of Gnosticism*

Gieschen, Charles A.. *Angelomorphic Christology: Antecedents and Early Evidence*

Hengel, Martin. *Between Jesus and Paul: Studies in the Earliest History of Christianity*

Hurtado, Larry W. *Ancient Jewish Monotheism and Early Christian Jesus-Devotion: The Context and Character of Christological Faith*

Juel, Donald H. *Messianic Exegesis: Christological Interpretation of the Old Testament in Early Christianity*

Newman, Carey C. *Paul's Glory-Christology: Tradition and Rhetoric*

Newman, Carey C., James R. Davila, and Gladys S. Lewis, editors. *The Jewish Roots of Christological Monotheism: Papers from the St Andrews Conference on the Historical Origins of the Worship of Jesus*

Segal, Alan F. *The Other Judaisms of Late Antiquity: Second Edition*

Segal, Alan F. *Two Powers in Heaven: Early Rabbinic Reports about Christianity and Gnosticism*

Stuckenbruck, Loren T. *Angel Veneration and Christology: A Study in Early Judaism and in the Christology of the Apocalypse of John*

Angel Veneration and Christology

*A Study in Early Judaism and
in the Christology of the Apocalypse of John*

Loren T. Stuckenbruck

BAYLOR UNIVERSITY PRESS

Published in 1995 by Mohr. Copyright © 1995 J. C. B. Mohr (Paul Siebeck), Tübingen, Germany
Reprinted in 2017 by Baylor University Press, Waco, Texas

All rights reserved. This book may not be reproduced, in whole or in part, in any form (beyond that permitted by copyright law) without the publisher's written permission. This applies particularly to reproductions, translations, microfilms and storage and processing in electronic systems.

Cover design by Savanah N. Landerholm for Baylor University Press

Library of Congress Cataloging-in-Publication Data

Stuckenbruck, Loren T.
    Angel veneration and Christology: a study in early Judaism and in the Christology of the Apocalypse of John / by Loren T. Stuckenbruck
    xviii, 348 p. ; 24 cm.
    Originally published: Tübingen: J. C. B. Mohr, 1995, in series Wissenschaftliche Untersuchungen zum Neuen Testament, 2/70
    ISBN 3-1614-6303-X
    Includes bibliographical references and index.
    1. Jesus Christ—History of doctrines—Early church, ca. 30-600. 2. Bible. Revelation—Criticism, interpretation, etc. 3. Dead Sea Scrolls. 4. Angels—Christianity—History of doctrines—Early church, ca. 30-600. 5. Angels—Judaism—History of doctrines. 6. Angels—Cult. I. Title. II. Series.

  BT198 .S77   1995
    235'.3'09

95162876

Baylor University Press ISBN: 978-1-4813-0798-7 (paper)

Printed in the United States of America on acid-free paper.

PREFACE TO THE REPRINT EDITION

I am grateful, both to Dr. Henning Ziebritzki of Mohr Siebeck Verlag in Tübingen and Dr. Carey Newman of Baylor University Press in Waco, for arranging for the reprint of a book, published in 1995, that I had researched and written as a doctoral thesis during 1992–1993 under the supervision of James H. Charlesworth at Princeton Theological Seminary.

While a large number of articles and monographs have appeared since 1995 on Christology and its Second Temple Jewish context, I do think there are several areas in which this reprint may provide an opportunity to consider aspects of the argument that have either been misunderstood in some quarters or still have something to contribute to current discussions. In the brief space allowed, I would like to mention three matters, two on a smaller scale and one that relates to the thesis as a whole.

First, readers of this volume may find the discussion of "Angelophanic Prohibitions in Jewish and Jewish Christian Wrings" (pp. 75–103) helpful as a way to think about the form-critical background to the development of the phrase "do not fear" into a prohibition alongside its more basic function as comfort. In addition, the significance of the prohibition as an equivalent to the parallel phrase "do not worship" extends beyond angelophanic encounters in and of themselves and opens a window into a common feature of piety that, in particular situations, was concerned with protecting honor that belongs to God (or, as could be implied, to Jesus) alone. Hence the discussions of Joseph's encounter with his brothers in Genesis

50, Peter's refusal to acknowledge the prostration of Cornelius in Acts 10, and the angel of the Lord's emphasis on Jesus at the tomb in Matthew 28 are open to fresh interpretations that yet remain to be worked out in their respective rhetorical and literary contexts. Thus, the section should not be regarded simply as the reworking of a Richard Bauckham's prior treatment of a "refusal tradition" in 1980–1981.

Second, building on an assumption that the refusal by an angel of glorious appearance to be worshiped lies in the background (especially in the fragmentary Apocalypse of Zephaniah), the relationship between the angelophanic Christophany in Revelation 1, which culminates in "do not fear" as an expression of comfort, and the two refusals by the seer John's angelic guide (whose appearance is not described) in chapters 19 and 22 are open to reconsideration. Here I refer to what may be recognized as a perceptively creative split of an angelophany, on the one hand, and a refusal to be worshiped, on the other. This appropriation of pious tradition, not unlike the narrative in Matthew 28, underscored the author's emphasis on Jesus' special position as one worthy of worship alongside God (pp. 257–61).

Third, it is perhaps worth repeating that for the most part, both in this monograph and since, I find myself in essential agreement with Larry Hurtado's well-known view that Jesus' position within the "cultic devotion" of his followers contrasts with the attention given to prominent figures in much of Second Temple Jewish literature. However, even in this study it was not my intention, nor would it be so today, simply to emphasize this contrast while, with Hurtado, maintaining a certain continuity with Jewish apocalyptic tradition. Determining the degree of continuity and the degree of the unprecedented, however much these do hold up, is not as clear-cut as many would like it to be. There is much yet to learn. For example, it may be debated whether terms such as "cultic," (in relation to the likewise slippery expressions "devotion," "veneration," and "worship") or "monotheism" (even as I have applied it in this book) best describe what is at stake in the emerging Christology of Jesus' followers in the first century C.E. Moreover, it may also be debated whether Bauckham's category of "divine identity" and Jesus' inclusion

PREFACE

therein adequately describes what distinguishes emerging Christian tradition within its Second Temple and Mediterranean context. Data available to us does not so easily domesticate, and it is my hope that future studies of Christology will look for new ways to come to terms with this complex, yet promising area of research.

13 May 2017
Loren T. Stuckenbruck
Ludwig Maximilian University of Munich, Germany

For my father,
Earl Roy Stuckenbruck

FOREWORD

This book represents a slightly revised version of a dissertation submitted to the faculty of Princeton Theological Seminary during September of 1993.

I would first like to thank the committee readers of the dissertation, Professors J. Christiaan Beker, Ulrich W. Mauser and James H. Charlesworth (chair) each of whom has contributed to the unfolding of ideas contained here. I shall remain indebted to the learning, criticisms, and patient guidance they have given me. In particular, Professor Charlesworth offered support and insight at pivotal points along the way. It is to him that I owe, to a large extent, my interest in exploring early Jewish traditions and their relation to New Testament writings.

In addition, a basis for this study took shape in the context of dialogue and conversations with several scholars who should be mentioned here. During our two years in Tübingen on a Fulbright Grant (1986-1988), I learned much from Professors Martin Hengel, Otto Betz, and Hans Peter Rüger, as well as from Professor Klaus Beyer in Heidelberg. Professor Hengel graciously recommended the publication of this work in the *WUNT* 2 series.

The specific direction taken in this book was inspired by the reading of articles and monographs by Larry W. Hurtado, Richard Bauckham, and Alan Segal. As the following pages represent an initial attempt to explore an issue vital for religious self-understanding of Jews and Christians in antiquity, I look forward to learning from these and other scholars who share an interest in venerative attitudes and worship in Early Judaism and emerging Christianity.

During the final stages of the dissertation and preparation of this manuscript, I have been surrounded by ideal working conditions at the Christian Albrechts Universität in Kiel, not the least of which has been a consistent show of collegiality and support within the theological faculty and assistance from the library staff headed by Mr. Rolf Langfeldt. A special word of thanks goes to Professor Peter Lampe. During my two years in Kiel, he has been both a tireless source of encouragement and an engaging partner in theological discussion.

My sincere appreciation goes to Mr. Georg Siebeck and Mrs. Ilse König at J.C.B. Mohr (Paul Siebeck) for their counsel and flexibility during the production of this manuscript.

My parents, Earl and Ottie Mearl Stuckenbruck, through their many years of service in ministry and teaching in Germany and the United States, have played an indispensable role in preparing me for theological study and, thus, for this book. It is to my father that this work is dedicated.

Finally, I wish to thank my wife, Lois, who during the course of research, writing, and publication of the book has been a great source of strength. During this time she has helped create a nurturing environment for me and our two children, Nellie and Hanno, in three countries of residence.

Durham, England
1. September, 1994   Loren Stuckenbruck

TABLE OF CONTENTS

Abbreviations XI

PART ONE: INTRODUCTION 1

I. The Problem 3

II. Jewish Concepts and Early Christology:
Continuity and Discontinuity 5

III. "Monotheism": Defining a Theological Construct 15

IV. Scholarly Approaches to Christology in the Apocalypse of John 22
   A. The Apocalypse: Jewish or Christian? 23
   B. Eschatology 26
   C. The Socio-Historical Situation 31
   D. The Symbolic World 35

V. Angelology, Christology, and Monotheism:
An Approach to the Apocalypse of John 42

PART TWO: ANGELIC AND HEAVENLY FIGURES: VENERATION AND MONOTHEISM 45

I. An Accommodation of "Monotheism" in Judaism: The Criterion of
Veneration 47

II. The Venerative Status of Angels 51
   A. Polemical Texts 51
      1. Midrashic Proscriptions in Rabbinic Literature 52
         a. Rabbinic Interpretation of Exodus 2:4,23: Angels and
           Natural Phenomena 56
         b. Other Rabbinic Interdictions 63
           i. *j.Berakhoth* 9:13a-b 63
           ii. *Exodus Rabbah* 32:4 68
           iii. *b.Sanhedrin* 38b 69
           EXCURSUS 72
         c. Summary 73
      2. Angelophanic Prohibitions in Jewish and Jewish-Christ-
ian Writings 75
         a. Bauckham's Study 78
         b. Components of the Angelic Refusal: The Origin and
Development of the Tradition 80
           i. The Seer's Reaction to an Angelophanic Setting 81
           ii. Fear: The Seer's Veneration and the Angel's Pro-
hibition 87
           iii. The Angelic Denial of Superiority over the Seer 92

iv. The Emphasis on God 99
c. Summary 101

3. Alleged Allusions to Angel Worship in New Testament
   Writings and Early Christian Literature 103
   a. Galatians 4:3,8-9 (viz. 3:19-20) 104
   b. Colossians 2:18 111
   c. Hebrews 1:5-2:18 119
   d. Second Century Accusations: *Kerygma Petrou*, Aristides, and Celsus (Origen, *c.Cels.* 1.26; 5.6) 140

4. Summary 146

B. Non-Polemical Sources 149

1. Qumran Documents 150
   a. Purported Evidence 151
   b. "Fellowship" with Angels and Veneration 154
      i. The *Songs of the Sabbath Sacrifice* 156
      ii. 11Q Berakhot 161
   c. Summary 163

2. Other Early Jewish Texts 164
   a. A Doxology in Tobit 11:14-15 164
   b. *Joseph and Aseneth* 14:1-12 and 15:11-12x 168
   c. *Pseudo-Philo* 13:6 170
   d. Angelic Mediation and Prayer: Other Early Jewish Texts 173
      i.   Enochic Literature 174
           (a) *1 Enoch* 9:1-11 174
           (b) *1 Enoch* 15:2 175
           (c) *1 Enoch* 40:6,9 175
           (d) *1 Enoch* 47:1-2 175
           (e) *1 Enoch* 99:3 176
           (f) *1 Enoch* 104:1 176
      ii. *Testaments of the Twelve Patriarchs* 176
           (a) *Testament of Levi* 3:5-7 176
           (b) *Testament of Levi* 5:5-6 176
           (c) *Testament of Dan* 6:2 177
      iii. Other Writings 178
           (a) Tobit 12:12,15 178
           (b) *3 Baruch* 11-16 178
           (c) *Pseudo-Philo* 15:5 178
           (d) *Vita et Adae et Evae* 9:3 178
           (e) *Testament of Solomon* 5:5 179
   e. Summary 179

3. Ἄγγελος Inscriptions in Asia Minor 181
   a. Rheneia (near Delos) 183
   b. Kalecik (Galatia) 185
   c. Eumeneia (Phrygia) 187
   d. Jewish Magical Materials from Asia Minor 188
      i. Cyzicus (ca. 90 mi. north of Pergamum) 190
      ii. The Region of Smyrna 191
      EXCURSUS: Jewish Invocation of Angels in Magical Sources from Antiquity 192

III. Summary 200

A. A Veneration of Angels in Early Judaism? 200

    B. Angelology and Christology 203

PART THREE: ASPECTS OF ANGELOLOGY AND MONOTHEISM IN THE CHRISTOLOGY
OF THE APOCALYPSE OF JOHN 205

I. Introduction 207

II. The Opening Epiphany in Revelation 1:12-20 and Its Relation
to Angelology in the Apocalypse 209

    A. A Traditio-historical Comparison 211

    B. Christ's Divinity: The "Ancient of Days" and the Old Greek
Tradition to Daniel 7:13 213
EXCURSUS 216

    C. Christ as an Angelomorphic Being: The Tradition 218

    D. Christ as an Angelic Being: Affinities Between Angels in
the Apocalypse and the Opening Epiphany 221

        1. The "Voice as the Sound of Many Waters": 14:1-5 and
19:1-8 222

        2. "Clothed" and "Girded at the Breasts with Golden Belts":
The Seven Angels in 15:6 226

        3. "His Face as the Sun" and the "Cloud": The Angel in
10:1-11 229

    E. Christ and the Angels of the Seven Churches 232

        1. The "Angels" of the Seven Churches 234

        2. The Portrayal of Christ in the Letters and the Epiphany 238

III. Revelation 14:6-20: "One like a Son of Man" and the Angels 240

IV. The Refusal Tradition in the Apocalypse of John 245

    A. The Angel in 19:10 and 22:8-9 246

    B. A Double Refusal 249

        1. Revelation 19:9-10 251

        2. Comparison Between Revelation 22:8-9 and 19:10 253

    C. The Refusal Tradition and the Opening Vision of the Apocalypse 257

V. Christology and Monotheism in the Apocalypse 261

PART FOUR: CONCLUSION 267

I. Angels and Monotheistic Devotion 269

II. Traditions Against Worshiping Angels 270

III. A Polemic Against "Worshiping" Angels in the Apocalypse of
John 271

IV. Angelomorphic Christology in the Apocalypse of John 271

V. Christology and Monotheism: A Pattern of Accommodation? 272

Appendix: Texts Form-Critically Compared for the Refusal Tradition 275

Selected Bibliography 284
    I.   Primary Sources and Reference Works 284
   II. Secondary Sources 290

Index of Passages 317

Index of Subjects 341

LIST OF ABBREVIATIONS

1 Chr	1 Chronicles
1 Cor	1 Corinthians
1 En	*1 Enoch*
1 Kgs	1 Kings
1Q21 (=1QTLevi ar)	Ms of *Testament of Levi* from Qumran Cave 1
1Q36	Ms no. 36 from Qumran Cave 1 (*DJD I*, pp. 138-41)
1QapGen	Genesis Apocryphon from Qumran Cave 1
1QH	*Hodayoth* from Qumran Cave 1
1QIsa^a	First copy of Isaiah from Qumran Cave 1
1QM	*Milchamah* from Qumran Cave 1
1QS	*Serek ha-Yahad* from Qumran Cave 1
1QSa	*Serek ha-'edah* from Qumran Cave 1, appendix to 1QS
1QSb	*Berakhoth* from Qumran Cave 1, appendix to 1QS
1 Sam	1 Samuel
2 Bar	*2 Baruch*
2 En	*2 Enoch*
2 Kgs	2 Kings
2QJN	New Jerusalem ms from Qumran Cave 2
2 Sam	2 Samuel
3 Bar	*3 Baruch*
3 En	*3 Enoch*
3 Macc	3 Maccabees
3Q15	Copper Scroll from Qumran Cave 3
4 Ez	*4 Ezra*
4 Macc	*4 Maccabees*
4Q181	Ms no. 181 from Qumran Cave 4 (*DJD V*, pp. 79-80)
4Q186 (=4QCryptic)	Astrological Cryptic Document from Qumran Cave 4
4Q196 (=4QpapTob ar^d)	Fourth copy of Aramaic Tobit from Qumran Cave 4
4Q200 (4QTob heb)	Ms of Hebrew Tobit from Qumran Cave 4
4Q213-214 (4QTLevi ar)	Mss of *Testament of Levi* from Qumran Cave 4
4Q315 (=4QBront)	Zodiacal document from Qumran Cave 4
4Q400-407	Copies of *Shirot 'Olat ha-Shabbat* from Qumran Cave 4
4Q491 (=4QM1)	First copy of *War Scroll* from Qumran Cave 4
4Q511	Ms no. 511 from Qumran Cave 4 (*DJD VII*, pp. 219-62)
4Q534	Birth of Noah ms from Qumran Cave 4
4Q560	Amulet formula from Qumran Cave 4
4QBer (=4Q286)	*Berakhoth* from Qumran Cave 4
4QD^b (=4Q267)	Covenant of Damascus, copy 2 from Qumran Cave 4
4QEn^a (=4Q201)	First copy of *1 Enoch* materials from Qumran Cave 4
4QEn^b (=4Q202)	Second copy of *1 Enoch* materials from Qumran Cave 4
4QFlor (=4Q177)	*Florilegium* from Qumran Cave 4
4QShirShabb (=4Q400-407)	*Shirot 'Olat ha-Shabbat* from Qumran Cave 4
4QTest (=4Q175)	*Testimonia* from Qumran Cave 4
5QJN (=5Q15)	New Jerusalem ms from Qumran Cave 5
11QBer (=11Q14)	*Berakhoth* from Qumran Cave 11
11QJN (=11Q18)	New Jerusalem ms from Qumran Cave 11
11QMelch (=11Q13)	*Melchizedek* text from Qumran Cave 11
11QShirShabb (=11Q17)	*Shirot 'Olat ha-Shabbat* from Qumran Cave 11
11QTemple (=11Q19)	Temple Scroll from Qumran Cave 11
AB	Anchor Bible

ABD	*The Anchor Bible Dictionary* (ed., David N. Freeman)
Abod.Zar.	*'Abodah Zarah*
Abr.	Philo, *De Abrahamo*
AGAJU	Arbeiten zur Geschichte des antiken Judentums und des Urchristentums
Agr.	Philo, *De agricultura*
Agric.	Tacitus, *Agricola*
Akhm	Akhmimic
ALGHJ	Arbeiten zur Literatur und Geschichte des hellenistischen Judentums
AnatSt	*Anatolian Studies*
AnBib	Analecta Biblica
ANRW	Haase, W., and H. Temporini, eds., *Aufstieg und Niedergang der römischen Welt* (eds., W. Haase and H. Temporini)
Ant.	Josephus, *Antiquitates Judaicae*
AOAT	Alter Orient und Altes Testament
AOS	American Oriental Series
AOSoc	American Oriental Society
Apoc.Abr.	*Apocalypse of Abraham*
Apoc.Elij.	*Apocalypse of Elijah*
Apoc.Ezek.	*Apocalypse of Ezekiel*
Apoc.Gosp.Mt.	*Apocryphal Gospel of Matthew*
Apoc.Mos.	*Apocalypse of Moses*
Apoc.Paul	*Apocalypse of Paul*
Apoc.Sedr.	*Apocalypse of Sedrach*
Apoc.Zeph.	*Apocalypse of Zephaniah*
Apol.	Justin Martyr, *Apology*
Apost.Const.	*Apostolic Constitutions*
OT	*The Apocrypha and Pseudepigrapha of the Old Testament* (ed., R.H. Charles)
Aram	Aramaic
ARWAWSond, PapCol	Abhandlungen der Rheinisch-Westfälischen Akademie der Wissenschaften, Sonderreihe Papyrologica Colonniensia
Asc.Isa.	*Ascension of Isaiah*
b. (before rabb. txt.)	Babylonian Talmud
BaHod.	*BaHodesh*
BAS	Biblical Archaeology Society
BCH	*Bulletin de Correspondence Hellénique*
Bell.Jud.	Josephus, *Bellum Iudaicorum*
Ber.	Berakhoth
Ber.R.	Bereshith Rabbah
BETL	Bibliotheca ephemeridum theologicarum lovaniensium
BEvT	Beiträge zur evangelischen Theologie
BIAAnk	British Institute of Archaeology at Ankara
Bib	*Biblica*
BibNot	*Biblische Notizen*
BJFL	*Bulletin of the John Rylands University Library of Manchester*
BJS	Brown Judaic Studies
BTB	*Biblical Theology Bulletin*
BU	Biblische Untersuchungen
BZNW	Beiheft zur *Zeitschrift für die neutestamentliche Wissenschaft*
CBA	Catholic Biblical Association
CBNTS	Coniectanea Biblica, New Testament Series
CBQMS	*Catholic Biblical Quarterly* Monograph Series

c.Cels.	Origen, *contra Celsum*
CD	Covenant of Damascus
C. Gen.	Cairo Geniza
Cher.	Philo, *De cherubim*
CIJ	*Corpus Inscriptionum Judaicorum* (ed., Jean-Baptiste Frey)
CNT	Commentaire du Nouveau Testament
(Cod.) Alex.	Codex Alexandrinus
(Cod.) Sin.	Codex Sinaiticus
(Cod.) Vat.	Codex Vaticanus
Col	Colossians
Comm.Joh.	Origen, *Commentary on John*
Conc	*Concilium*
Conf.ling.	Philo, *De confusione linguarum*
Copt	Coptic
CRINT	Compendia Rerum Iudaicarum ad Novum Testamentum
Dan	Daniel
DBAT	*Dielheimer Blätter zum Alten Testament*
Deb.R.	*Debarim Rabbah*
Dec.	Philo, *De decalogo*
Deut	Deuteronomy
Dial.	Justin Martyr, *Dialogue with Trypho*
DJD (plus Arab. num.)	Discoveries in the Judean Desert Series (plus vol. no.)
DJD (plus Rom. num.)	*Discoveries in the Judean Desert* (plus vol. no.)
Ebr.	Philo, *De ebrietate*
Eccl	Ecclesiastes
EI	*Eretz Israel*
EKKNT	Evangelisch-katholischer Kommentar zum Neuen Testament
EPGM	*The Greek Magical Papyri in Translation* (ed. Hans Dieter Betz)
Ep.Jer.	*Epistle of Jeremiah*
EPRO	Études préliminaires aux religions orientales dans l'Empire Romain
Esth	Esther
Eth	Ethiopic
Ex	Exodus
Exod.R.	*Exodus Rabbah*
ExT	*Expository Times*
Ezek	Ezekiel
FB	Forschung zur Bibel
FRLANT	Forschung zur Religion und Literatur des Alten und Neuen Testaments
Fug.	Philo, *De fuga et inventione*
FZPhTh	*Freiburger Zeitschrift für Philosophie und Theologie*
Gaium	Philo, *Legatio ad Gaium*
Gal	Galatians
GBTh	Gegenwartsfragen biblischer Theologie
GCS	Die griechischen christlichen Schriftsteller der ersten drei Jahrhunderte
Gen	Genesis
Gosp.Pet.	*Gospel of Peter*
Gosp.Th.	*Gospel of Thomas*
GRBS	*Greek, Roman, and Byzantine Studies*
Grk	Greek
Hag	Haggai
Hag.	*Hagigah*

Heb	Hebrew
Hebr	Hebrews
Hekh.	Hekhalot
Hellenica	*Hellenica. Recueil d'Épigraphie de Numismatique et d'Antiquites Grecques* (ed. Louis Robert)
Hermeneia	Heremeia: A Critical and Historical Commentary on the Bible
Hist.	Herodotus, *Historia*
Hist.Rech.	*History of the Rechabites*
Hist.Rom.	Dio Cassius, *Historia Roma*
Hist.Eccl.	Eusebius, *Historia ecclesiastica*
HNT	Handbuch zum Neuen Testament
Hos	Hosea
HSM	Harvard Semitic Monographs
HSS	Harvard Semitic Series
HThKNT	Herders theologischer Kommentar zum Neuen Testament
HTR	*Harvard Theological Review*
HTRHDR	*Harvard Theological Review* Harvard Dissertations in Religion
Hul.	*Hullin*
ICC	International Critical Commentary
IDB	*Interpreter's Dictionary of the Bible* (ed. Georg A. Buttrick)
ieiun.	Tertullian, *De ieiunio*
IEJ	*Israel Exploration Journal*
Int	*Interpretation*
Isa	Isaiah
j. (before rabb. txt.)	Jerusalem Talmud
JAOS	*Journal of the American Oriental Society*
JBL	*Journal of Biblical Literature*
Jer	Jeremiah
Jewish Symbols	*Jewish Symbols in the Greco-Roman Period* (ed. E.R. Goodenough)
JKDAI	Jahresbuch des Kaiserlichen Deutschen Archäologischen Instituts
JÖAI	*Jahreshefte des Österreichischen Archäologischen Institutes in Wien*
Jon	Targum Jonathan
Jos	Joshuah
Jos.	Philo, *De Iosepho*
Jos.Asen.	*Joseph and Aseneth*
JSHRZ	Jüdische Schriften aus hellenistisch-römischer Zeit
JSNT	*Journal for the Study of the New Testament*
JSNTSS	*Journal for the Study of the New Testament*, Supplement Series
JSOT	*Journal for the Study of the Old Testament*
JSOTSS	*Journal for the Study of the Old Testament*, Supplement Series
JSPS	*Journal for the Study of Pseudepigrapha*, Supplement
JSS	*Journal of Jewish Studies*
JStJud	*Journal for the Study of Judaism*
JTS	*Journal of Theological Studies*
JU	Judentum und Umwelt
Jub	*Jubilees*
Jud	*Judaica*
Judg	Judges
Koh.Z.	*Midrash Kohelet Zuta*
Lat	Latin

LBS	The Library of Biblical Studies
LCL	Loeb Classical Library
LD	Lecto divina
Leg.all. 1-3	Philo, *Legum allegoriae* 1-3
Lev	Leviticus
LexThQ	*Lexington Theological Quarterly*
Lk	Luke
LLJC	The Littman Library of Jewish Civilization
LXX	Septuagintal tradition
m. (before rabb. txt.)	Mishnah
Mal	Malachi
Mand.	*Mandates, Shepherd of Hermas*
MasShirShabb	*Shirot 'Olat ha-Shabbat* from Masada
Mek.	*Mekhilta*
MeyerK	H.A.W. Meyer, Kritisch-exegetischer Kommentar über das Neue Testament
Mic	Micah
Midr.Tann.	*Midrash Tannaim*
Midr.Teh.	*Midrash Tehillim*
Migr.	Philo, *De migratione Abrahami*
Mk	Mark
MNTC	Moffatt New Testament Commentary
MPG	J. Migne, ed., Patrologiae graecae
MPL	J. Migne, ed., Patrologiae latinae
Mt	Matthew
ms(s)	manuscript(s)
MT	Masoretic tradition
Mut.Nom.	Philo, *De mutatione nominum*
NCBC	New Century Bible Commentary
NEB	Die Neue Echter Bibel
Neh	Nehemiah
Neof	Targum Neofiti
New Schürer	Emil Schürer, *The history of the Jewish people in the age of Jesus Christ* (eds. Geza Vermes, Martin Goodman, and Fergus Millar)
Nich.Eth.	Aristotle, *Nichomachean Ethics*
NICNT	New International Commentary on the New Testament
NRSV	New Revised Standard Version
NT	*Novum Testamentum*
NTA	*Neutestamentliche Apokryphen* (ed. Wilhelm Schneemelcher)
NTS	*New Testament Studies*
NTT	New Testament Theology
NTT	*Nieuw theologisch Tijdschrift*
Num	Numbers
OBO	Orbis Biblicus et Orientalis
OdesSol	*Odes of Solomon*
Onk	Targum Onkelos
OTL	Old Testament Library
OTP	*The Old Testament Pseudepigrapha* (ed. James H. Charlesworth)
PAM (+ no.)	Palestinian Archeological Museum photograph number
Pan.	Epiphanius, *Panarion*
Paneg.	Pliny the Younger, *Panegyricus*
Par.Jer.	*Paraleipomena Jeremiou*
PCSBR	*Papers for the Chicago Society of Biblical Research*

PGM	Preisendanz, Karl, ed. *Papyri Graecae Magicae. Die Griechischen Zauberpapyri* (ed. Karl Preisendanz)
PMR	James H. Charlesworth, *The Pseudepigrapha and Modern Research with a Supplement*
Pol.	Aristotle, *Politica*
Post.Cain	Philo, *De posteritate Caini*
Praep.Ev.	Eusebius, *Praeparatio evangelica*
Pr.Jos.	*Prayer of Joseph*
Prot.Jas.	*Protoevangelium James*
Prov	Proverbs
Ps(s)	Psalm(s)
PSB	*Princeton Seminary Bulletin*
Ps-Jon	Targum Pseudo-Jonathan
Ps-Philo	*Pseudo-Philo (=Liber Antiquitatum Biblicarum)*
PTA	Papyrologische Texte und Abhandlungen
PVTG	Pseudepigrapha Veteris Testamenti graece
Quaes.Ex. 1-2	Philo, *Quaestiones et solutiones in Exodum 1-2*
Quest.Ez.	*Questions of Ezra*
Quis rer.div.her.	Philo, *Quis rerum divinarum Heres sit*
QuodDeus	Philo, *Quod deus immutabilis sit*
rabb.	rabbinic
RB	*Revue biblique*
Rec.	recension
Ref.	Hippolytus, *Refutatio*
REG	*Revue des Études Grecques*
REJ	*Revue des études juives*
Rev	Revelation
Rev.Elch.	*Revelation of Elchasai*
RevEx	*Review and Expositor*
RHR	*Revue de l'histoire des religions*
R.Hash.	*Rosh ha-Shanah*
RNT	Regensburger Neues Testament
Rom	Romans
RQ	*Revue de Qumran*
RSEHA	*Revue sémitique d'épigraphie et d'histoire ancienne*
Sacr.	Philo, *De sacrificiis Abelis et Caini*
San.	Sanhedrin
SBLDS	Society of Biblical Literature Dissertation Series
SBLMS	Society of Biblical Literature Monograph Series
SBLSBS	Society of Biblical Literature: Sources for Biblical Study
SBLTT, PS	Society of Biblical Literature Texts and Translations, Pseudepigrapha Series
SC	Sources chrétiennes
ScJTh	*Scottish Journal of Theology*
ScrHier	Scripta Hierosolymitana
SCS	Septuagiant and Cognate Studies
SeptGott	Septuaginta Gottingensis
Sg of Sg's	Song of Songs
Shep.Herm.	*Shepherd of Hermas*
ShirShabb	*Shirot 'Olat ha-Shabbat*
SHR	Studies in the History of Religions
Sib.Or.	*Sibylline Oracles*
Sim.	*Similitudes, Shepherd of Hermas*
SJ	Studia Judaica
SJLA	Studies in Judaism in Late Antiquity
Slav	Slavic

SNT	Studien zum Neuen Testament
SNTSMS	Society for New Testament Studies Monograph Series
Somn. 1-2	Philo, *De Somniis* 1-2
SPB	Studia postbiblica
SPCK	Society for the Promotion of Christian Knowledge
Spec.Leg.	Philo, *De specialibus legibus*
ST	*Studia Theologica*
STDJ	Studies on the Texts of the Desert of Judah
Strom.	Clement of Alexandria, *Stromata*
StudNeot	Studia neotestamentica
SUNT	Studien zur Umwelt des Neuen Testaments
Supp.Ep.Gr.	*Supplementum Epigraphicum Graecum*
SuppNT	Supplements to *Novum Testamentum*
SVTP	Studia in Veteris Testamenti pseudepigrapha
Syr	Syriac
t. (before rabb. txt.)	Tosephta
T12P	*Testaments of the Twelve Patriarchs*
T.Abr.	*Testament of Abraham*
Tal	*Talanta*
Tanh.	*Tanhuma*
Tarb	*Tarbiz*
T.Benj.	*Testament of Benjamin*
T.Is.	*Testament of Isaac*
T.Jac.	*Testament of Jacob*
T.Job	*Testament of Job*
T.Levi	*Testament of Levi*
T.Sol.	*Testament of Solomon*
TDNT	*Theological Dictionary of the New Testament* (eds. Gerhard Kittel and Gerhard Friedrich)
TDOT	Botterweck, G. Johannes, Helmer Ringgren, and H.J. Fabry, eds., *Theological Dictionary of the Old Testament* (eds. G. Johannes Botterweck, Helmer Ringgren, and H.J. Fabry)
TED	Translations of Early Documents
TEH	Theologische Existenz heute
Tg.	Targum
ThBer	*Theologische Berichte*
Theod.	Theodotionic tradition
THNT	Theologischer Handkommentar zum Neuen Testament
ThRund	*Theologische Rundschau*
TLQ	*The Lutheran Quarterly*
TLZ	*Theologische Literaturzeitung*
Tob	Tobit
TQ	*Theologische Quartalschrift*
TS	Texts and Studies
TS	*Theological Studies*
TSAJ	Texte und Studien zum antiken Judentum
TU	Texte und Untersuchungen
UNT	Untersuchungen zum Neuen Testament
UTB	Urban-Taschenbücher
VigChr	*Vigiliae Christianae*
Virt.	Philo, *De virtutibus*
Vis.	*Visions, Shepherd of Hermas*
Vit	Suetonius, *Vitae Caesarorum*
Vit.	Josephus, *Vita*
Vit.Ad.Ev.	*Vita Adae et Evae*
Vit.Cont.	Philo, *De vita contemplativa*
Vit.Mos. 1-2	Philo, *De vita Mosis* 1-2

VT	*Vetus Testamentum*
VTS	Vetus Testamentum Supplements
Vulg	Latin Vulgate
WBC	Word Bible Commentary
WMATNT	Wissenschaftliche Monographien zum Alten und Neuen Testament
WThJ	*Westminster Theological Journal*
WUNT	Wissenschaftliche Untersuchungen zum Neuen Testament
Yom.	*Yoma*
Zeph	Zephaniah
ZKG	*Zeitschrift für Kirchengeschichte*
ZNW	*Zeitschrift für die neutestamentliche Wissenschaft*
ZWT	*Zeitschrift für wissenschaftliche Theologie*

PART ONE

INTRODUCTION

I. THE PROBLEM

> And there will be nothing accursed any more, for the throne of God and of the Lamb (ὁ θρόνος τοῦ θεοῦ καὶ τοῦ ἀρνίου) will be (ἐστίν) in it, and his (αὐτοῦ) servants will worship him (αὐτῷ) and see his (αὐτοῦ) face, and his (αὐτοῦ) name (will be) on their foreheads. (Rev 22:3-4)

The above passage illustrates the theological problem to be investigated in relation to the Apocalypse of John. The expression "the throne of God and of the Lamb" may raise the following question: How "monotheistic" is the New Jerusalem of the seer's vision? As scholars have frequently noted, the Apocalypse, more than any other writing in the New Testament, gives expression to an interest in the worship of Jesus alongside God.[1] At the same time, one may wonder whether the singular pronouns in the passage cited were motivated by a concern that the worship of Christ *not* be misunderstood as a compromise of monotheistic faith. To what extent, then, are the figures of "God" and "the Lamb" identified in the Apocalypse and to what extent can we say that they are distinguished? In this respect, what can be learned from the author's simultaneous application to Christ of characteristics traditionally associated with God, on the one hand, and with angelic figures, on the other, as in Revelation 1:13-17 and 14:14-20? While within "Christian" circles the divine position of Christ could be reinforced through expressions associated with God, is it also possible that the appropriation of Jewish angelological traditions reflects lines of development which explain his exalted status as one who may be worshiped? How are angelology, *Christ*-ology, and *the*-ology ultimately related within the author's monotheistic framework? To what extent does the author, who emphasizes elsewhere the importance of worshiping only "God" (22:8-9; also 19:10), nevertheless produce a vision of something like "two powers" in heaven, a notion which later became the object of rabbinic polemics?[2]

---

[1] In addition to the passage cited above, see esp. Rev 5:6-14; 7:9-12; 11:15-18; 12:10-12; 14:1-4; 19:1-16; and 20:6.

[2] For an analysis of the pertinent rabbinic texts, see Alan F. SEGAL, *Two Powers in Heaven. Early Rabbinic Reports About Christianity and Gnosticism* (SJLA, 25; Leiden: Brill, 1977) 33-59; some of these passages are evalu-

These questions and their Jewish background in Greco-Roman antiquity constitute the focus of this study. They call for three distinct, yet interrelated, levels of analysis: history of religions, history of traditions, and exegetical considerations in the Apocalypse. Since the expression "monotheism" has served theologians as a comparative category for classifying Christianity among the world religions, the investigation of possible antecedents will be limited to sources that may help delineate "monotheism" as the author of Revelation understood it.

On the level of history of religions, the questions raised by the Apocalypse revolve around the distinctiveness of early forms of Christian veneration of Christ, as opposed to various forms of religiosity within contemporary Judaism and contiguous cultures (Egyptian, Parthian, Nabatean, Phoenician, Syrian, Greek, and Roman). In contrast to the emphasis during the early part of this century on the formative significance of Hellenistic and Oriental religions for expressions of Christian conviction, a growing number of scholars have attempted more recently to account for Christ's exalted status by appealing to the diverse matrix of contemporary Judaism. This perspective has been accompanied by a tendency to assign significant christological developments not only to later second- and third-generation communities, but especially to groups of devotees during the first two or three decades after Jesus' crucifixion.[3] Studies of this sort, beginning with the strong probability of antecedents to Christology in Early Judaism, have provided a fresh impetus to address a theological problem that continues to confront contemporary interpreters of the New Testament writings: While it seems clear that Christians, unlike much of their environment in which the worship of a plu-

---

ated in Part Two (section II.A.1, pp. 52-75 below. What SEGAL analyzed under the "two powers" heresy constitutes a broader and, for the most part, later problem than the one addressed here. Whereas the polemics against "two powers" in rabbinic literature may have included developed Christologies within "Christian" circles as well as dualistic patterns known through "gnostic" sources, the study here takes its departure on the more specific problem of complementary, angelic beings and the question of whether a veneration of them can be detected within early Jewish literature; see *ibid.*, pp. 265-66.

[3] See esp. the collection of essays by Martin HENGEL, *Between Jesus and Paul. Studies in the Earliest History of Christianity* (Philadelphia: Fortress, 1983); idem, *Der Sohn Gottes. Die Entstehung der Christologie und die jüdisch-hellenistische Religionsgeschichte* (Tübingen: J.C.B. Mohr [Paul Siebeck], 1977²); and the important study of Larry W. HURTADO, *One God, One Lord. Early Christian Devotion and Ancient Jewish Monotheism* (Philadelphia: Fortress, 1988). This development in scholarship has led HENGEL and Jarl E. FOSSUM to speak of a "new" History of Religions School; see n. 23 below.

rality of deities was observed among many religions, retained the notion of "one God," their belief in the exaltation of Christ was apparently regarded by at least some Jews as inconsistent--or even incompatible--with such monotheistic claims. In other words, upon what basis could Christians accommodate a devotion to "one Lord, Jesus Christ" with their belief in "one God, the Father" (1 Cor 8:5-6)?

An explanation for such an accommodation encounters difficulties which emerge more clearly as one considers ways in which scholars have applied early Jewish concepts and motifs in relation to this problem. Thus, before discussing major questions which have arisen in studies of the Christology of the Apocalypse of John and the approach to be followed in this study, it is pertinent to comment on the state of scholarly discussion in two areas: (1) the contribution of early Jewish ideas to convictions among early Christians concerning the exalted Jesus, and (2) problems and prospects related to the usefulness of the term "monotheism" as a category for investigating this contribution.

II. Jewish Concepts and Early Christology: Continuity and Discontinuity

What are some of the factors which gave rise to or shaped a devotion to the exalted Jesus in the first-century Christian communities? In order to reconstruct a plausible scenario, scholars have drawn on *religions-* and *traditionsgeschichtliche* approaches since the late nineteenth century. By focusing on hypotheses of some key figures in early and recent discussion, we shall find ourselves in a better position to propose a further area for investigation and, thereby, to delineate the basic parameters for this study.

Just after the turn of this century, Wilhelm BOUSSET, an influential proponent of the "history of religions school," argued that the worship of Jesus in early Christianity is only explicable by a context in which the strict monotheism of the Old Testament was being significantly compromised.[4]

---

[4] Concerning aspects of Judaism to which early Christian thought fell heir, see esp. the chapter entitled "Der Monotheismus und die den Monotheismus Beschränkenden Unterströmungen," in BOUSSET, with Hugo GRESSMANN, *Die Religion des Judentums im späthellenistischen Zeitalter* (HNT, 21; Tübingen: J.C.B. Mohr [Paul Siebeck], 1926³) 302-357, which concludes as follows: "Wir können das, was hier vor sich gegangen ist und was namentlich in der Theologie des Paulus wirksam wird, eine gewisse Erweichung des Monotheismus nennen, der Jesus selbst fremd gegenübersteht. In der Engellehre, dem Dualismus und

Bousset attributed this development to "paganizing" elements which had meanwhile infiltrated post-exilic Judaism. These elements, which posed a threat to a purer form of monotheism proclaimed by the prophets, included the following: dualistic tendencies as exhibited in apocalyptic writings and growing speculations concerning divine agents, such as angelic and "hypostatic" beings.[5]

By ascribing these ostensible developments in Judaism to pagan influence and by stressing a necessary distinction between Palestinian Judaism, on the one hand, and Hellenism (including Diaspora Judaism), on the other, BOUSSET reasoned that post-exilic Jewish thought must have been infiltrated by a weakened sense of God's presence in the world, a caricature which he further associated with an intensified legalism among pious Jews. Though still generally characteristic of Judaism as a whole, an exclusive devotion to God had

---

der Dämonologie und letztlich in der Hypostasenlehre hat das Judentum dem Christentum ein nicht in jeder Beziehung heilvolles Geschenk gemacht." BOUSSET's classic expression concerning the origins of early cultic worship of Christ is *Kyrios Christos. Geschichte des Christusglaubens von den Anfängen des Christentums bis Irenaeus* (Göttingen: Vandenhoeck & Ruprecht, 1965[5], orig. pub. 1913) and *Jesus der Herr. Nachträge und Auseinandersetzungen zu Kyrios Christos* (Göttingen: Vandenhoeck & Ruprecht, 1916), in which he sharpened his emphasis on a distinction between Palestinian Judaism and Hellenism, the latter of which he concluded played the decisive role in the deification of Jesus.

[5] In positing such a development, BOUSSET was not alone. With respect to the theological significance of angelology, he was dependent on the work of his student, Wilhelm LUEKEN, *Michael* (Göttingen: Vandenhoeck & Ruprecht, 1898) 4-12 (see also p. 166). Furthermore, his assertion of a belief within Second Temple Judaism in independent "hypostatic" beings betrays his debt to his contemporaries such as Ferdinand WEBER, *System der Altsynagogalen Palästinischen Theologie aus Targum, Midrasch, und Talmud* (Leipzig: Dörffling & Franke, 1886); Alfred EDERSHEIM, *The Life and Times of Jesus the Messiah* (2 vols.; Grand Rapids: Eerdmans, 1960[3], repr. from 1890) esp. 2.748-55; and, with respect to Philo's thought, Emil SCHÜRER, *The Literature of the Jewish People in the Time of Jesus*, trans. Peter CHRISTIE and Sophia TAYLOR (New York: Schocken Books, 1972) esp. pp. 371-73. SCHÜRER's understanding of Philo is essentially retained in the *New Schürer* edition, 3.880-85.

The notion of hypostasized beings, as entertained by these scholars, was soon vigorously contested by George Foot MOORE, "Intermediaries in Jewish Theology," *HTR* 15 (1922) 41-85 and "Christian Writers on Judaism," *HTR* 14 (1921) 197-254, esp. pp. 237-41. Nevertheless, the view which links the notions of divine transcendence, a gulf between God and the world, and intermediary figures (as the resulting development) has persisted as an assumption among writers such as D.S. RUSSELL, *The Method and Message of Jewish Apocalyptic 200 B.C.-A.D. 100* (OTL; Philadelphia: Westminster, 1964) 235-49, 257-62 (angelology arose under the influence of Persian thought); H. RINGGREN, *The Faith of Qumran* (Philadelphia: Fortress, 1963) 81; and H.C. KEE, "Testaments of the Twelve Patriarchs," in *OTP*, 1.790 n. d.

receded to the extent that intermediary beings were allowed to function as compensating objects of "cultic" veneration. These considerations led BOUSSET to explain the rise of the "Christ-cultus" on the basis of certain "foreign" elements in Judaism which were threatening to undermine the essential Jewish belief in monotheism.[6] Hence, BOUSSET concluded that the early Christians, in their worship and veneration of Jesus, were putting into effect a ready-made paradigm that was diametrically opposed both to the message of the prophets and the teaching of Jesus.

Both BOUSSET's assumption of an era of "purity" in Judaism and his corresponding historical explanation for the evolution of Christology among early Christians have been justly questioned[7] by scholars, and with increasing frequency since World War II.[8] Among most recent critics, few have opposed the "Boussetian" paradigm as vigorously as Larry W. HURTADO, in his recently published monograph on *One God, One Lord* (1988).[9] HURTADO's critique of BOUS-

---

[6] BOUSSET stressed, in particular, the indebtedness of Jewish preoccupation with intermediary beings to Persian ideas; see *Die Religion des Judentums*, pp. 469-524. Originally for BOUSSET, angelic and hypostatic beings were a means by which Jews sought to overcome polytheistic tendencies of popular religion (by transforming pagan gods into beings which could be subordinated to Israel's God). This attempt to preserve monotheism, however, soon degenerated to the point that, with respect to angelology, BOUSSET could even speak of a "cult" which had penetrated into the lower classes, especially in the Diaspora; *ibid.*, pp. 330 and 343.

[7] The understanding of Second Temple Judaism has evolved significantly during the course of this century. Among the many factors involved, one may mention two of the most important reasons: (1) The application of sociological and anthropological sensitivities, in their stress on formative patterns from an environment as *intrinsic* to the phenomenology of religion, has led to a growing awareness of and empathy toward extraneous influences on Judaism. (2) The discovery and study of documents in Egypt (Elephantine papyri, Oxyrhynchus, Cairo Geniza, Nag Hammadi) and in Palestine (esp. the "Dead Sea Scrolls") have yielded roughly contemporary materials that underscore the diversity of post-exilic and rabbinic Judaism, sometimes even with respect to the religious praxis of observant Jews.

[8] For an overview of these critiques, see esp. HURTADO, "New Testament Christology: A Critique of Bousset's Influence," *TS* 40 (1979) 306-317. Perhaps the most definitive statement against any simple equation of Palestinian Judaism with an unhellenized religiosity is HENGEL's *Judaism and Hellenism*, trans. John BOWDEN (2 vols.; Philadelphia: Fortress, 1974). Though HENGEL's work deals primarily with evidence in the 3rd and 2nd centuries BCE, it has significant implications for the influence of Hellenism in first-century Palestine; see now HENGEL, *The 'Hellenization' of Judaea in the First Century after Christ*, trans. John BOWDEN (Philadelphia/London: Trinity International and SCM, 1989).

[9] See n. 3 above. HURTADO's basic argument was already epitomized in "The Binitarian Shape of Early Christian Devotion and Ancient Jewish Monothe-

SET has two primary components: First, he contends that the distinctive character of early Christian worship evolved out of a Jewish Palestinian setting and not, as BOUSSET suggested, from Hellenism or Diaspora Judaism. Thus, in accordance with the growing scholarly recognition that virtually all forms of Judaism came under the influence of non-Jewish cultures,[10] he locates the rapid growth of Christology after Jesus' death within a Palestinian Jewish milieu.[11] Second, and of particular relevance to this study, HURTADO also draws a clear line of *discontinuity* between Jewish concepts underlying the Palestinian Jesus Movement and the latter's "cultic" veneration of Christ.[12] According to this schema, it is no longer necessary to argue that Jewish monotheism was significantly compromised or accommodated during the Second Temple period.

Whereas HURTADO and BOUSSET would agree in principle that early Christians made use of Jewish ideas to express their convictions about Jesus, they no doubt disagree concerning the extent.[13] Ironically, though BOUSSET is pri-

---

ism," in *SBL 1985 Seminar Papers*, ed. K.H. RICHARDS (Atlanta: Scholars, 1985) 377-91; from HURTADO, see most recently his essay, "What Do We Mean by 'First-Century Jewish Monotheism'?," in *SBL 1993 Seminar Papers*, ed. David LULL (Altanta: Scholars, 1993) 348-68.

[10] For a concise summary of this development, see now "Diversity in Post-biblical Judaism" by Gary G. PORTON, in eds. Robert A. KRAFT and George W.E. NICKELSBURG, *Judaism and Its Modern Interpreters* (Philadelphia/Atlanta: Fortress and Scholars, 1986) 57-80.

[11] HURTADO, *One God, One Lord*, pp. 3-9. In this respect, HURTADO echoes Joseph A. FITZMYER, "The Semitic Background of the New Testament *Kyrios*-Title," in *A Wandering Aramean. Collected Aramaic Essays* (SBLMS, 25; Missoula, MT: Scholars, 1979) 115-42 and HENGEL, "Christology and New Testament Chronology," in *Between Jesus and Paul*, pp. 30-47.

[12] *Ibid.*, pp. 17-39 and "The Binitarian Shape of Early Christian Devotion," in which HURTADO's major theses show the influence of formulations by Harold B. KUHN, "The Angelology of the Non-Canonical Jewish Apocalypses," *JBL* 67 (1948) 217-32: "Angels do not appear to have been objects of veneration ..." (221) and "It appears that at this time there was room within Judaism for great diversity of doctrine [concerning angels], and that its monotheism was in no sense outraged by the popular conception of the existence of a vast multitude of super-human beings" (232). HURTADO has most recently rehearsed this view in "What Do We Mean by 'First-Century Jewish Monotheism'?," in *SBL 1993 Seminar Papers*, ed. David J. LULL (Atlanta: Scholars, 1993) 348-68. HURTADO's thesis seems also reminiscent of MOORE's criticisms of BOUSSET (see "Intermediaries" 62-79 and "Christian Writers" 243-8), though, of course, one of MOORE's main criticisms, unlike HURTADO, was BOUSSET's choice of so-called "unorthodox" sources.

[13] It is important to keep in mind that the comparison which follows is confined to their respective views concerning the role of *Judaism* in early Palestinian Christianity; here we do not address the specific influence of

marily known for his later stress on the debt of pre-Pauline Christianity to Hellenism, he drew a more direct line between Christology and modifications of monotheism within Jewish circles than HURTADO, who instead ascribes the rapid development of devotion to Christ to the teaching of Jesus himself[14] and, especially, to the various worship experiences of his followers.[15]

These different historical reconstructions by HURTADO and BOUSSET, concerned as they were with the continuity and discontinuity of early Christologies with contemporary Judaism, illustrate an as yet unresolved problem in the history of religions. In recent discussion, debate has centered around the nature and function of angelic and other intermediary figures in Jewish thought. HURTADO has certainly not taken an anomalous position in drawing a firm line of discontinuity between the early worship of Jesus and paradigms of devotion inherited from Judaism during the infant stages of "Christianity." Similarly, there are others who emphasize that a christological modification of monotheism occurred primarily within the setting of the early Christian communities; they include Richard BAUCKHAM,[16] Nils A. DAHL,[17] James

---

Hellenistic religion on early Christianity which BOUSSET emphasized in *Kyrios Christos* (see n. 4 above).

[14] BOUSSET, in line with the Protestant "liberalism" of his day, almost entirely left out a discussion of the historical Jesus in *Kyrios Christos*, thereby exonerating Jesus from any religious expressions in his environment which would have posed a threat to monotheism.

[15] See HURTADO's chapter on "The Early Christian Mutation" in *One God, One Lord*, pp. 93-124. His stress on "inner" developments hence tends to overlook the possibility that contemporary Jewish ideas continued to be of significance for the area of devotion to Christ.

[16] "The Worship of Jesus in Apocalyptic Christianity," *NTS* 27 (1980-81) 322-41: "Since the early church remained - or at least professed to remain - faithful to Jewish monotheism, the acknowledgement of Jesus as worthy of worship is a remarkable development" (322); cf. also idem, "Jesus, Worship of," in *ABD*, 3.812-19. BAUCKHAM's own perspective is, however, not entirely onesided; though the Jewish or Christian provenance and date of the *Asc.Isa.* is not clear, a comparison of the Eth, Slav, and Lat versions of this apocalypse with the shorter "Greek Legend" (2:21-22) suggests for him a deliberate rejection of "a form of *Merkabah* mysticism (whether Jewish or Christian is not clear) in which angels were revered and invoked both as obstacles and as aids in the mystical ascent to heaven" ("The Worship of Jesus" 332). See also *ibid.* 338 n. 33, where in discussing rabbinic and Hekhalot texts concerning Metatron, he admits that "the warnings against the danger of this [worshiping Metatron] presuppose that the danger was sometimes realised, though perhaps those who did 'worship' Metatron would not have regarded it as worship."

[17] See DAHL, "Sources of Christological Language," in *Jesus the Christ. The Historical Origins of Christological Doctrine*, ed. Donald H. JUEL (Minneapolis: Fortress, 1991) 113-36, esp. pp. 121 and 131.

D.G. DUNN,[18] R.T. FRANCIS,[19] Martin HENGEL,[20] Paul A. RAINBOW,[21] and Michael THEOBALD.[22]

---

[18] *Christology in the Making* (Philadelphia: Westminster, 1980) 149-62; "Was Christianity a Monotheistic Faith from the Beginning?," *ScJTh* 35 (1981) 303-336. In the latter publication, DUNN finds an exception in Merkabah mysticism, but dismisses its "lasting impact on either Christianity or Judaism," being tolerated within the "redefined monotheism" of the former and rejected within the strict monotheism of the latter (i.e., rabbinic Judaism; p. 334). See further DUNN's essay, "Let John be John," in ed. Peter STUHLMACHER, *Das Evangelium und die Evangelien. Vorträge zum Tübinger Symposium 1982* (WUNT, 28; Tübingen: J.C.B. Mohr [Paul Siebeck], 1983) 322-25. This view is reiterated and elaborated by DUNN in response to HURTADO and ROWLAND (bibl. below) in *The Partings of the Ways* (London/Philadelphia: SCM and Trinity International, 1991) 207-229.

[19] "The Worship of Jesus: A Neglected Factor in Christological Debate?," in *Christ the Lord. Studies in Christology presented to Donald Guthrie*, ed. H.H. ROWDON (Leicester: Inter-Varsity, 1982) 17-36, esp. pp. 24-25.

[20] "Hymns and Christology," in *Between Jesus and Paul*, pp. 78-96; *Der Sohn Gottes*, pp. 90-93: "Grundsätzlich ist zu bedenken, daß es sich hier nicht einfach um die simple Reproduktion älterer jüdischer Hypostasen- und Mittlerspekulationen handeln kann, sondern daß die früheste Christologie ein durchaus originäres Gepräge trägt und letztlich in dem kontingenten Ereignis der Wirksamkeit Jesu, seines Todes und der Auferstehungserscheinungen wurzelt: Der religionsgeschichtliche Vergleich kann nur die Herkunft einzelner Motive, Traditionen, Sprachelemente und Funktionen, nicht dagegen das Phänomen der Entstehung der Christologie als Ganzes erklären" (p. 92). However, in the same work HENGEL does acknowledge the potential significance of "Jewish Hekalot and Merkabah literature for early Christian Christology" (*Der Sohn Gottes*, pp. 137-38 and n. 151). Furthermore, fully aware of the diversity of Early Judaism, he can admit, on the basis of an inscription at Delos, the *Kerygma Petrou*, rabbinic polemics, Hekalot texts, magical papyri, and some NT passages (Col 2:8,18; Gal 3:19 with 4:9), the existence of a "jüdischer Engelskult" in "Der alte und der neue Schürer," *JSS* 35 (1990) 20 (also n. 44) and "Psalm 110 und die Erhöhung des Auferstandenen zur Rechten Gottes," in eds. Cilliers BREYTENBACH and Henning PAULSEN, *Anfänge der Christologie. Festschrift für Ferdinand Hahn* (Göttingen: Vandenhoeck & Ruprecht, 1991) 65 ("Anrufung und Verehrung [of angels] waren streng untersagt, wobei das Verbot [in rabb. lit.] und die jüdische Mystik und Magie zeigen, daß sie doch eine große Rolle spielten"), but does not consider in these publications its possible significance for Christology. Since the term "Kultus" is not defined by HENGEL, it is not clear whether this claim is to be understood as a shift from his previous position; see further "Die Synagogeninschrift von Stobi," *ZNW* 57 (1966) 156 n. 32.

[21] "Jewish Monotheism as the Matrix for New Testament Christology: A Review Article," *NT* 33 (1991) 78-91.

[22] "Gott, Logos und Pneuma," in ed. Hans-Josef KLAUCK, *Monotheismus und Christologie. Zur Gottesfrage im hellenistischen Judentum und im Urchristentum* (Freiburg/Basel/Vienna: Herder, 1992) 41-87; see esp. pp. 46-50 and 56-64.

On the other side, there are many who, despite differences with BOUSSET on other matters, are like BOUSSET inclined to argue that by the beginning of the common era, a speculative interest in angels, other figures, and "hypostatic" beings was enough in place that it could have provided a formative backdrop to early Christian convictions concerning the exalted status of Jesus. Recent discussions which have been variously inclined toward this perspective include studies by Margaret BARKER,[23] Andrew CHESTER,[24] James H. CHARLESWORTH,[25] Ioan P. CULIANU,[26] Jarl E. FOSSUM,[27] Peter HAYMAN,[28] C.R.A.

---

[23] In *The Great Angel. A Study of Israel's Second God* (London: SPCK, 1992). On the limited value of BARKER's wide-ranging presentation, which attempts to understand the worship of Jesus among early Christians as simply a continuation of a belief in ancient Israel of Yahweh as "a second God," see HURTADO, "'First-Century Jewish Monotheism'," pp. 353-54.

[24] "Jewish Messianic Expectations and Mediatorial Figures and Pauline Christology," in *Paulus und das antike Judentum*, eds. Martin HENGEL and Ulrich HECKEL (WUNT, 58; Tübingen: J.C.B. Mohr [Paul Siebeck], 1991) 17-89, esp. pp. 54-55 and 62-65. As evidence for the worship of angels, CHESTER cites *Joseph et Aseneth* and *Vita Adae et Evae* (p. 64); of these, however, only the former text may be relevant (see pp. 168-170, 179-180 below).

[25] CHARLESWORTH, "The Jewish Roots of Christology: The Discovery of the Hypostatic Voice," *ScJTh* 39 (1985) 19-41, esp. p. 35.

[26] "The Angels of the Nations and the Origins of Gnostic Dualism," in eds. R. VAN DEN BROEK and M.J. VERMASEREN, *Studies in Gnosticism and Hellenistic Religions. Festschrift for G. Quispel* (EPRO, 91; Leiden: E.J. Brill, 1981) 78-91. CULIANU rightly distinguishes "*ditheism* (or binitarianism) and *dualism*" (p. 78) and sees in the former a Jewish "pre-Christian" conception which was transformed into the latter through the fusion of the notion of angelic guardians of the nations and a categorical conviction (post-70 CE) of Roman rule as satanic.

[27] "Jewish-Christian Christology and Jewish Mysticism," *VigChr* 37 (1983) 260-87, more comprehensively treated in *The Name of God and the Angel of the Lord* (WUNT, 36; Tübingen: J.C.B. Mohr [Paul Siebeck], 1985), esp. pp. 241- 338. See also "The New *Religionsgeschichtliche Schule*: The Quest for Jewish Christology," *SBL 1991 Seminar Papers*, ed. Eugene H. LOVERING, Jr. (Atlanta: Scholars, 1991) 638-46, in which FOSSUM, following up on a statement made by HENGEL on the cover of HURTADO's *One God, One Lord*, declares the formation of a "new" History of Religions School that, with respect to early Christianity, stresses the Jewish roots of Christology.

[28] "Monotheism - A Misused Word in Jewish Studies?," *JJS* 42 (1991) 1-15. HAYMAN, who makes no distinctions between pre-, post-exilic, and rabbinic Judaism, contends that "monarchism" is more descriptive of Jewish faith; see below.

MORRAY-JONES,[29] Christopher E. ROWLAND,[30] Jane SCHABERG,[31] Alan F. SEGAL,[32] and Pieter W. VAN DER HORST.[33]

Significantly, though scholars within the latter group show some affinity with BOUSSET's basic interest in tracing religio-historical lines of *continuity* for developments in Christology, nowhere do they adopt his "cultus"

---

[29] "Transformational Mysticism in the Apocalyptic-Merkabah Tradition," *JJS* 43 (1992) 1-31, esp. pp. 6-7. MORRAY-JONES follows ROWLAND (see following n.) in stressing an interest among early Jewish apocalyptic circles in the divine *kabod*, whose functions, in order to safeguard God's transcendence, were transferred to independent beings. This development eventually led to "Gnosticism" and "Christianity." MORRAY-JONES thus implies a continuity in praxis between Judaism and Christianity on the basis of mystical speculations concerning the divine throne, a connection which goes hand-in-hand with his derivation of "visionary-mystical traditions" in the Tannaitic period from earlier Apocalyptic sources; see his dissertation, *Merkabah Mysticism and Talmudic Tradition* (Cambridge: Diss., 1988) and, further, his article on "Hekhalot Literature and Talmudic Tradition: Alexander's Three Test Cases," *JStJud* 22 (1991) 139, esp. pp. 3-4 (and n. 10).

[30] *The Influence of the First Chapter of Ezekiel on Judaism and Early Christianity* (Cambridge: Diss., 1975); "The Vision of the Risen Christ in Rev. i.13 ff.: The Debt of an Early Christology to an Aspect of Jewish Angelology," *JTS* 31 (1980) 1-11; *The Open Heaven. A Study of Apocalyptic in Judaism and Early Christianity* (New York: Crossroad, 1982) 100-13; "A Man Clothed in Linen," *JSNT* 24 (1985) 99-110; and his review of SEGAL, *Paul the Convert* in *JJS* 42 (1991) 269-70 (a call to reopen the investigate the indebtedness of early Christology to Jewish apocalyptic and mystical ideas). In *The Open Heaven* ROWLAND refers to a "monotheistic thread" in Jewish beliefs concerning exalted angels, but likewise emphasizes that they were "susceptible of complete misunderstanding" (p. 112) and "could rapidly disintegrate" (p. 113).

[31] "Mark 14.62: Early Christian Merkabah Imagery?," in eds. Joel MARCUS and Marion L. SOARDS, *Apocalyptic and the New Testament. J.L. Martyn Festschrift* (JSNTSS, 24; Sheffield: JSOT, 1989) 69-94.

[32] Though careful to speak of the emergence of Christology in earliest Christian circles as a compromise of monotheism "from the rabbinic perspective," SEGAL nevertheless sees an analogous development in Judaism during the first century. Aside from Christian circles (which SEGAL subsumes under "Judaism"), however, it is difficult to determine just where in Judaism SEGAL would posit such tendencies. See *Two Powers*, pp. 182-219; "Heavenly Ascent in Hellenistic Judaism, Early Christianity and their Environment," in *ANRW*, II.23.2, 1334-94, esp. 1369-77; "Ruler of This World: Attitudes about Mediator Figures," in ed. E.P. SANDERS, *Jewish and Christian Self-Definition* (3 vols.; Philadelphia: Fortress, 1989) 2.245-69 (notes, 403-13), esp. 250; concerning Pauline Christology, *Paul the Convert. The Apostolate and Apostasy of Saul the Pharisee* (New Haven: Yale Univ., 1990) 39-71; and, most recently, "The Risen Christ and Angelic Mediator Figures in Light of Qumran," in ed. James H. CHARLESWORTH, *Jesus and the Dead Sea Scrolls* (Garden City, NY: Doubleday, 1992) 302-328.

[33] "De Joodse toneelschrijver Ezechiel," *NTT* 36 (1982) 97-112 and "Moses' Throne Vision in Ezekiel the Dramatist," *JJS* 34 (1983) 21-29.

terminology in their descriptions of Jewish thought. The absence of such "cult" vocabulary in their works is in clear contrast to its application by HURTADO as a negative criterion for assessing previous and contemporary studies. HURTADO leaves his readers with the impression that he has chosen a category which can be easily dismissed when it comes to possible Jewish antecedents to Christology, but which can nevertheless be adopted as a criterion against which to measure the distinctiveness of the Early Christians' christological convictions. When taking exception to contemporary scholars, then, he seems to link attempts to show modifications in post-exilic Jewish "practice and belief" and "worship"[34] with BOUSSET's claims concerning the development of an angel "cult." Whatever the connotations of terms such as "(cultic) veneration," "(cultic) devotion," "worship," and "cult," their virtual identification by HURTADO betrays a certain ambiguity with respect to what both sides of the discussion are attempting to convey. While HURTADO is not convinced that there are any clear signs in Early Judaism of the worship of intermediaries in a *cultic setting*, there are others who conclude that angelological ideas in Early Judaism reflect a theological development which includes a *certain devotion* to angelic beings as such. The semantics of this discussion does not make clear to the observer whether or not a line is to be drawn between a "cultic worship" of, for example, principal angels and less intense forms of "veneration" of or "devotion" to them,[35] that is, whether that which passes as evidence of "binitarianism" for HURTADO and what others claim as evidence of devotion and veneration to subordinate beings actually refer to the same thing.

If an illumination of the Jewish background for the worship of Jesus requires a clear demonstration that within Judaism there existed *cultic rituals* devoted to the *worship* of hypostases, patriarchs or angelic beings, then it is difficult to dispute HURTADO's stress on discontinuity. If, however, it is possible to speak of a certain *veneration* of such intermediary figures without having to demonstrate the existence of supporting cultic rituals, we may be in a position to speak of certain lines of continuity which account

---

[34] See esp. *One God, One Lord*, pp. 27-39; RAINBOW, "Jewish Monotheism" 83; and THEOBALD, "Gott, Logos und Pneuma," p. 46.

[35] In denying almost any form of angel veneration in Early Judaism, HURTADO seems to demand the presence of a cultic *system*. Therefore, he sets up a position which is easy to counter, without further nuancing his terminology.

for developments[36] which may be related to the worship of Jesus among the early Christians.[37] Thus the problem of whether the motif of divine transcendence in post-exilic Judaism can be interpreted in terms of God's remoteness may need to be distinguished from the question of other beings as possible objects of veneration.

This review of the problem suggests that, as a whole, there is a general indecision concerning the most appropriate way of explaining the religious background for the exalted status of Jesus. The complexity of a religio-historical reconstruction is reflected in the difficult, yet necessary, fusion of two approaches. On the one hand, there is the attempt to describe the *distinctiveness* of early and ongoing Christian thought and practice and, on the other hand, there is the search for *analogues* in the history of religions. However necessary it may be for the study of Christology in Early Christianity, a comparative approach which simultaneously seeks to move in both directions is often fraught with the inherent uncertainty of identifying a given analogy and of determining the degree to which it may or may not explain the phenomenon in question.

The differences outlined between the views associated with HURTADO and those with whom he takes issue on the origins of Christology are further illustrated by scholarly application of the term "monotheism" in connection with Judaism and Early Christianity. In addition, some evaluative comments concerning the use of this expression are appropriate if one is to be aware of its potential pitfalls and if there is to be a certain transparency in our discussion of Jewish literature and the Apocalypse of John.

---

[36] Given our ultimate focus on the Apocalypse, the study to be undertaken will not be restricted to sources that are "pre-Christian." Developments leading up to the end of the first century need to be taken into account as well; it is perhaps during this period that certain problems and conceptions, as expressed within Jewish literature, were assimilated into or paralleled by Christian reflection on the significance of Christ.

[37] In this connection, it may be helpful to distinguish between devotion within a "cultic" setting and devotion as expressed in the context of liturgy. If a "cult" implies a series of rituals organized around a specific deity or group of deities, "liturgy" expresses but a part which, within a "cultic" context, serves the ends of the ritual. This distinction would preserve an essential difference between symbolic ritual and liturgical meditation, while positing a line of continuity between them on the basis of the veneration which both involve. See pp. 156-161 concerning the Qumran *Shirot 'Olat ha-Shabbat*.

III. "Monotheism": Defining a Theological Construct

Biblical scholars have conceived of "monotheism" within both broad and narrow limits. In the former case, it suffices to have "monotheism" refer to the belief in or worship of one, universal god.[38] In the latter, narrower sense, however, the expression is applied in a way that specifically precludes a belief in the existence of other deities.[39] In either case, one's understanding of "monotheism" depends to some degree on how it is contrasted with "polytheism,"[40] concerning which there is more unanimity in definition: the belief in or worship of two or more gods in which, of course, the veneration of one deity does not exclude the worship of another. As is apparent from the discussion below, this understanding of polytheism has left its mark on terms which sometimes have been preferred over "monotheism."

Many scholars, particularly those concerned with problems in Old Testament theology, have recently expressed dissatisfaction with the term.[41] We may

---

[38] See Ulrich W. MAUSER, "One God Alone: A Pillar of Biblical Theology," *PSB* 12 (1991) 255-65, esp. pp. 257-60. Insofar as the existence of other divine beings is not excluded, this definition is termed "relative monotheism" by A. SCHENKER "Der Monotheismus im ersten Gebot, die Stellung der Frau im Sabbatgebot und zwei Sachfragen zum Dekalog," *FZPhTh* 32 (1985) 329-30. This concept is sometimes designated "monolatry"; see, e.g., Manfred H. VOGEL, "Monotheism," in *Encyclopaedia Judaica* (Jerusalem: Keter, 1971) 12. 260-63; Bernhard LANG, "Zur Entstehung des biblischen Monotheismus," *TQ* 166 (1986) 135-42; and Hans HÜBNER, *Biblische Theologie des Neuen Testaments* (Göttingen: Vandenhoeck & Ruprecht, 1990) 1.240-57, though HÜBNER retains "monotheism" when referring to theoretical reflection.

[39] As, e.g., VOGEL ("Monotheism," col. 260) who, in distinguishing between "monotheism" and "monolatry," argued that between the "monotheism" of biblical faith and the plurality of gods in paganism lies an "arithmetical difference" (i.e., *either* more than one god *or* one God). See also LANG, "Zur Entstehung des biblischen Monotheismus," 135-42.

[40] As apparent in essays by Robert CASPAR, "Der Monotheismus des Islams und seine bleibende Bedeutung," *Conc* 21 (1985) 47 and Joseph COMBLIN, "Monotheismus und Volksreligion," *Conc* 21 (1985) 61, who have claimed that an adherence to "monotheism" presupposes the existence of idolatrous religious practices which are subject to critique (e.g., in Islam). Similarly, in a discussion applying language from evolutionary theory, Gerd THEISSEN (*Biblischer Glaube in evolutionärer Sicht* [München: Chr. Kaiser, 1984] 93-110) distinguishes between "syncretistic" (philosophical reduction) and "antipolytheistic" (a protest against "selective" forces of society with ethical implications) forms of monotheism.

[41] See the names listed by David L. PETERSEN in his overview of "monotheism" in Old Testament scholarship in "Israel and Monotheism: The Unfinished Agenda," in eds. Gene M. TUCKER, David L. PETERSEN, and Robert R. WIL-

identify at least three reasons for this attitude: (1) In both nineteenth- and twentieth-century scholarship, the expression often functioned as an influential theological category which was all too readily absorbed into idealistic perspectives. Thus, when scholars attempted historical reconstructions of Israelite religion, post-exilic Judaism and Christianity, they ventured theological judgments in which "monotheism" tended to function as an organizing principle,[42] whether considered as a purer form of religion from which later Judaism ("Spätjudentum") deteriorated,[43] or as the culmination of a long process that began with various forms of polytheism.[44] As a result, the use of the expression is thought to be counterproductive to any effort to be "descriptive." (2) Increasingly, the term itself has been considered inadequate as a way of describing the distinctiveness of Israelite religion and Judaism,[45] owing to important strides made in knowledge about the Ancient Near East and the history of religions approach to biblical writings. (3) Alternate, and presumably more descriptive, expressions have been introduced, such as "henotheism," "monolatry," and "monarchism."

The first two reasons given above for an abstinence from the term "monotheism" are closely related. They illustrate that the expression has often been bound up with some form of theological idealism. This criticism, however, ought not necessarily be translated into a demand that the term be avoided. Its use in relation to philosophical and theological thought and praxis

---

SON, *Canon, Theology, and Old Testament Interpretation* (Philadelphia: Fortress, 1988) 92-107, esp. p. 103 n. 3.

[42] Most conspicuously, Yecheskel KAUFMANN's *The Religion of Israel. From Its Beginnings to the Babylonian Exile*, abridged and translated (from original Heb) by Moshe GREENBERG (Chicago: Univ. of Chicago, 1960), e.g., pp. 63-64 and 227. See also his *History of the Religion of Israel. From the Babylonian Captivity to the End of Prophecy*, translated by C.W. EFROYMSON (New York: Ktav, 1977) 18.

[43] In addition to the bibliography in n. 5 above, see John H. HAYES and Frederick PRUSSNER, *Old Testament Theology. Its History and Development* (Atlanta: John Knox, 1985) 96-97 (D.G.C. VON CÖLLN), 99 (W.M.L. DE WETTE); William F. ALBRIGHT, *From Stone Age to Christianity* (Garden City, NY: Doubleday, 1957); and KAUFMANN, esp. *History of the Religion of Israel*.

[44] See HAYES and PRUSSNER, *Old Testament Theology*, pp. 69 (G.L. BAUER), 102 (J.K.W. VATKE), 131 (J. WELLHAUSEN, R. SMEND, W.O.E. OESTERLEY, and T.H. ROBINSON).

[45] See PETERSEN's brief discussion of monotheism in Old Testament theology in "Israel and Monotheism," especially 92, 104 n. 3 and HAYMAN's contrast between T.C. VRIEZEN and N.P. LEMCHE in "Monotheism - A Misused Word" 1-2. HAYMAN himself contends that "it is hardly ever appropriate to use the term monotheism to describe the Jewish idea of God" (p. 2).

in antiquity does not have to depend on whether only one God was thought to exist or whether there was an exclusive worship of one God in a pure form. What was ideally thought or practiced at a given point in time may not always have coincided with conceptions which were couched in more rigid formulations. Rather, analogous to the expression "polytheism," "monotheism" may be made to represent one end of a continuum of religious ideas and practices. Thus the term, especially in its adjectival form ("monotheistic"), may typify *the extent* to which exponents of a religion claim to be devoted to an exclusive worship of or belief in a universal god.[46]

The third explanation for the disuse of "monotheism" calls attention to other vocabulary which, admittedly, may possess an ultimately greater heuristic value for the investigation of Early Judaism and Christology. Use of the terms "henotheism" and "monolatry" originally arose within attempts to reconstruct stages of development between forms of polytheism and monotheism in ancient and Israelite religion. Whereas "henotheism" denoted a stage of religious development from polytheism to monotheism, "monolatry" was often applied to a stage in which monotheism disintegrates into polytheism.[47] Nevertheless, despite their originally different contexts, they have come to share an almost identical meaning that resembles "monotheism" in the broadest, non-exclusive sense: the worship of a primary deity which allows for belief in the existence of others.[48] Thus with respect to Israelite religion this con-

---

[46] If in this sense, "monotheism" would not have to be descriptive. In this connection it is worth citing the similar position taken by Theodore M. LUDWIG in an excellent discussion of "Monotheism" in *The Encyclopedia of Religion* (New York: Macmillan, 1987), 10.73: "... monotheistic thought focuses especially on the theoretical or verbal dimension of religious experience. When we move to the practical and the social spheres we encounter a variety of phenomena which at times may not be distinctively monotheistic. Worship, law, customs, and social forms may show striking parallels in different religions without regard to the theoretical stance on monotheism, polytheism, or monism. ... The veneration of saints in some sectors of Islam and Christianity appears similar to the veneration of spiritual beings in tradition African religions, but other sectors of Islam and Christianity strongly reject these practices. Thus care needs to be taken in setting up a monotheistic typology, so that religious traditions are not fitted in too tightly, doing damage to the integrity and richness of the particular religion."

[47] For a discussion of these terms, see PETERSEN, "Israel and Monotheism," pp. 97-98.

[48] Thus "Henotheism" and "Monolatry" are cross-referenced as virtual synonyms in *Encyclopedic Dictionary of Religion*, eds. Paul Kevin MEAGHER, Thomas O'BRIEN, and Consuelo Maria AHERNE (Washington, D.C.: Corpus Publications, 1979) 2.1639, 2419.

cept has come to denote generally the devotion to a national or patron god, as opposed to an allegiance toward deities of other nations. Indeed, one advantage of using the terms "henotheism" and "monolatry" to describe Early Judaism and the Palestinian Jesus Movement is their descriptiveness, and hence "realism," with respect to a possible conflict between religious thought and practice. Either expression calls attention to the possibility that one can sometimes distinguish sharply between religious claims and accommodations in praxis of a person or group (from the perspective of anthropology) or between the religious claims and practices of one Jewish group in contrast with those of another (from the perspective of sociology).

The expressions "henotheism" and "monolatry," however, lose much of their usefulness when we consider the specific problem of how first-century religious practices in Judaism were adapted in the worship of Jesus' followers. For one thing, that which the earliest Jewish Christian communities accentuated *as formative tradition* was not so much an allowance for the existence of numerous gods as the accent upon belief in and worship of the one God. A further difficulty is that definitions for "henotheism" and "monolatry" (and, to a lesser extent, for "monotheism") are usually confined to the problem of relationships among *deities*; the problem of how complementary angelic beings are to be understood, though not necessarily precluded by such a framework, remains largely unaddressed. Insofar as the question turns on the veneration of subordinate mediating figures, the term "monotheism," whether broadly or narrowly defined, appears to be more suitable. The image of "the throne of God and of the Lamb," considered within the first-century context of the exaltation of Jesus among first-century followers, approximates more closely the issue of how a deity and subordinate being are related than the question of the relationship between one deity and another. Consequently, if understood as one end of a continuum of ideas, "monotheism"--as a conceptual category--provides a framework in which our problem can be delineated in acute form: Can the worship of or belief in the existence of *only one* supreme being (God) be held along with the worship of a subordinate, allied, figure?[49]

Once monotheism, thus understood, is recognized as a useful category for analysis, the problem remains how narrowly or broadly it may be defined

---

[49] This question, as its formulation suggests, does not presuppose an *a priori* decision concerning the existence or non-existence of other deities. To the extent that, in a given instance, "monotheism" can denote allegiance to one deity *as opposed to* others, it comprehends the meanings attached to the terms "henotheism" and "monolatry."

when considering possible antecedents in Early Judaism and developments in Christology. If HURTADO's conclusions are correct, then the worship of Jesus amounts to a "mutation" which is nevertheless continuous with monotheism. But if developments in early Christology can be understood as continuous with patterns that existed in early Jewish sources, then the "monotheism" operative in Judaism itself requires a broader definition.

In a recent essay on "Monotheism-A Misused Word in Jewish Studies?",[50] HAYMAN has suggested that another term, "monarchism," may be more descriptive of early Israelite religion and Judaism as a whole. For him the word refers to a *dualistic* pattern in which God's heavenly court is made up of a plurality of powerful beings "not always under his control."[51] Initially, this definition appears to coincide with HURTADO's understanding of early Jewish "monotheism" in that the recognition of other heavenly beings is not thought to compromise God as the sole object of worship. But, semantics aside, HAYMAN and HURTADO's conclusions concerning the relationship between "Judaism" and "Christianity" indicate how much their perspectives actually differ. HAYMAN asserts that "monarchism" is a pattern that continues into the Second Temple period from pre-exilic times, a pattern from which the early church's belief in Jesus' divinity hardly deviated.[52] HURTADO, by interpreting the growing interest in angelic hierarchies and "divine agency" in Early Judaism as a continuation of earlier Israelite beliefs in the majesty of God, concludes that a belief in intermediary figures actually served to underscore the Jewish belief in one God[53] and thus posits a chasm between this schema and the "wor-

---

[50] See n. 28 above.

[51] The concept of divine μοναρχία occurs in Jewish literature associated with Egypt, beginning in the late 3rd cent. BCE with ARTAPANUS (of the Egypt. king Chenephres; cited in EUSEBIUS, *Praep.Ev.* 9.27.5), in *Sib.Or.* 3.11 and 704 (of God), 3 Macc 2:2 (of God), and especially in the works of PHILO (e.g. *Spec.Leg.* 1.12,13-31; 2.224; *Dec.* 31,51,61; *Abr.* 98). The use of kingship as a metaphor for monotheistic belief in these texts is discussed by Erik PETERSON, "Der Monotheismus als politisches Problem," in *Theologische Traktate* (München: Kösel, 1951) 49-64. Since the precise definition given by HAYMAN to "monarchism" is not always reflected in these texts, it is perhaps best, in order to avoid confusion, to restrict references to the term to its ancient application.

[52] HAYMAN is, unfortunately, too quick to correlate the notion of angels of the nations (which for him reflects a "dualistic pattern") and the idea of complementary figures, the latter of which need not presuppose the former. Concerning the necessity of such a distinction, see CULIANU, "The Angels of the Nations," pp. 78-79.

[53] *One God, One Lord*, pp. 90-92.

ship" of Christ. Again, as above, this comparison reflects the different intentions behind the words used. Whereas the point of continuity with Judaism for HAYMAN is "belief in the divinity of Jesus,"[54] HURTADO finds distinctiveness in early Christianity by extending this criterion to the area of praxis, that is, to the cultic *worship* of God's divine agent.[55] Accordingly, HURTADO has appropriately insisted that, rather than evaluating the primary sources with an "a *priori* assumption of what monotheism must mean," one should attempt to discover the beliefs and practices of those who professed themselves to be monotheists.[56] In this sense, HURTADO's phenomenologically oriented definition, which leaves ample room for religio-historical and sociological diversity, is more comprehensive.

The attention HURTADO devotes to the area of religious praxis provides an important contribution which, incidentally, reflects the similar stress of BOUSSET on the formative role of the worshiping community for the development of Christology. HURTADO's insistence that an understanding of early Jewish "monotheism" should be informed by a more inductive approach opens the way toward considering the flexibility with which Jews and Christians could use this concept to describe the diverse forms of religion which they espoused. Moreover, HURTADO is correct to doubt that a direct christological development from early Jewish thought would demand more than a mere transference of cognitive patterns of belief, as if one can ignore their impact on religious forms.

And yet, HURTADO's actual *application* of this approach toward "monotheism" falls ultimately short of these aims. Though in his scheme the expression should broadly be made to embrace both the worship of one God in Judaism *and* its "mutation" by Jesus' followers, he applies the term in its strict sense almost exclusively within the context of Early Judaism; for him it is more specifically the expression "binitarianism" (as a sub-category of mono-

---

[54] HAYMAN (*ibid.*, p. 14) does speak of "monotheism," but can only do so by making a distinction between theory and function, both of which refer only to the arena of belief. Thus for him Jewish monotheism in theory meant belief in the existence of one divine being, while in terms of function Jews could believe in the existence of a plurality of divine beings.

[55] BAUCKHAM represents a similar view; see "The Worship of Jesus" 335 and "Jesus, Worship of," col. 813.

[56] See esp. "What Do We Mean by 'First-Century Jewish Monotheism'?," pp. 354-55.

theism) which points out the distinctiveness of the worship of Jesus.[57] The resulting impression is that, with respect to Early Judaism, HURTADO ends up with a definition ("monotheism" in a strict sense) which seems narrower than what his call for a more flexible interpretation otherwise seems to suggest. Despite his valid insistence on the distinctiveness of the worship of Jesus, the question remains whether writers of documents such as the Apocalypse of John would have wanted themselves to be understood as "binitarian."[58] Does this sub-category detract from the flexibility which "monotheism" allows? Once more, given the conceptual function of monotheism outlined above, it is preferable to see how *strict monotheistic claims could be coupled with venerative language associated with other beings* (see Part Two); then--and more in line with the understanding of Jesus' devotees--we may speak of the degree to which a claim to the exclusive worship of the one, universal God continued to be operative in early Christologies.

Having given some indication of the history of religions discussion and having proposed the retention of "monotheism" as conceptually useful, it becomes possible to situate the present study within broader scholarly debate concerning Christology and angelology in the Apocalypse of John and to outline the background, perimeters, and approach to be followed.

---

[57] HURTADO's attempt to preserve this distinction apparently leads him to avoid using milder terms, such as "veneration" in describing Jewish interest in angels.

[58] Just as HURTADO is aware that the concept of "divine agency" is a modern classification, the same may be observed with respect to "binitarianism." The fact that Lars HARTMAN can speak of a firm conviction in the Fourth Gospel concerning the oneness of God despite its "high" Christology, should encourage one to exercise caution from supposing that early Christians would have considered themselves "binitarian," even if it is considered a subcategory of monotheistic belief; see HARTMAN, "Johannine Jesus-Belief and Monotheism," in eds. Lars HARTMANN and Birger OLSSON, *Aspects of Johannine Literature* (CBNTS, 18; Uppsala: Almqvist & Wiksell International, 1987) 85-99.

IV. Scholarly Approaches to Christology in the Apocalypse of John

Studies of Christology in John's Apocalypse have, in a variety of ways, devoted considerable space to the specific titles applied to Jesus.[59] However, it is important to observe that a purely titular approach has only rarely been followed. The reason for this seems clear: An analysis limited to titles alone cannot be expected to provide information that adequately illuminates their function in their respective literary contexts. If the proposed investigation--angelology in relation to monotheistic and christological claims in the Apocalypse--were limited to such an approach, it would involve a linguistic comparison of titles and descriptive phrases, as well as an effort to ascertain how this language may correspond to or depart from other known Jewish and Christian traditions. This methodology, germane as it is to an understanding of Christology, would tend to fall short of addressing particular problems which the document as a whole presents interpreters. With good reason, then, scholars have contextualized "the Christology" of John's Apocalypse

---

[59] For such studies, which discuss the christological titles in the Apocalypse as a whole, see esp. D.M. BECK, "The Christology of the Apocalypse of John," in ed. E.P. BOOTH, *New Testament Studies* (New York/Nashville: Abingdon-Cokesbury, 1942) 253-77; H.W. TRIBBLE, "The Christ of the Apocalypse," *RevEx* 40 (1943) 167-76; D.E. COOK, *The Christology of the Apocalypse* (Duke University: Diss., 1962) esp. pp. 109-58; Traugott HOLTZ, *Die Christologie der Apokalypse des Johannes* (TU, 85; Berlin: Akademie-Verlag, 1972²) esp. pp. 5-26 and *passim*; as treated in Ferdinand HAHN's methodological approach in *Christologische Hoheitstitel. Ihre Geschichte im frühen Christentum* (Göttingen: Vandenhoeck & Ruprecht, 1966³); B.W. RODGERS, *The Christ of the Apocalypse. A Study in the Origin and Nature of the Christology of the Book of Revelation* (The General Theological Seminary: Diss., 1965); J. COMBLIN, *Le Christ dans l'Apocalypse* (Tournai, Belgium: Desclée, 1965); Rudolf SCHNACKENBURG, "Christologie des Neuen Testament," in eds. Johannes FEINER and Magnus LÖHRER, *Mysterium Salutis* 3/1. *Das Christusereignis* (Einsiedeln/Zürich/Köln: Benziger, 1970) 227-388, esp. pp. 367-75; Ulrich B. MÜLLER, *Messias und Menschensohn in Jüdischen Apokalypsen und in der Offenbarung des Johannes* (SNT, 6; Gütersloh: G. Mohn, 1972); Johannes Jacobus ENGELBRECHT, *The Christology of the Revelation to St. John* (in Afrikaans) (University of South Africa: Diss., 1981); Sarah Alexander EDWARDS, "Christological Perspectives in the Book of Revelation," in eds. Robert F. BERKEY and Sarah A. EDWARDS, *Christological Perspectives. Essays in Honor of Harvey K. McArthur* (New York: Pilgrim, 1982) 139-54; Gregory K. BEALE, "The Problem of the Man from the Sea in IV Ezra 13 and its Relation to the Messianic Concept in John's Apocalypse," *NT* 25 (1983) 182-88; Richard Robert CREECH, *Christology and Conflict. A Comparative Study of Two Central Themes in the Johannine Literature and the Apocalypse (Lamb of God, Logos, Ego Eimi, Revelation, I Am)* (Baylor University: Diss., 1984); and D.E. LOHSE, "Wie christlich ist die Offenbarung des Johannes?," *NTS* 34 (1988) 321-38, esp. pp. 328-32.

within the framework of other questions. The most significant of such interpretive issues are identified here as follows: (1) the "Jewish" or "Christian" character of the Apocalypse, (2) the author's eschatology, (3) the socio-historical situation reflected and addressed in the document, and (4) the author's "symbolic world." What follows is a brief outline and evaluation of these issues as they relate to Christology in the Apocalypse. This discussion, in turn, provides the broader interpretive context for this study and will assist in clarifying the substantive and methodological considerations to be taken.

A. The Apocalypse: Jewish or Christian?

Rudolf BULTMANN epitomized the nature of this problem when he concluded that "The Christianity of [the Book of] Revelation has to be termed a weakly Christianized Judaism."[60] However one evaluates BULTMANN's judgment and his criterion for making it,[61] his caricature arises from a question that continues to be vigorously debated, with implications for the Christology of the Apocalypse. This problem has been addressed on several levels of analysis: (1) literary/source criticism, (2) redaction criticism, and (3) the document in its present form.

At the turn of the century, the interpretation of pseudepigraphal and New Testament writings often turned on the assumption that Jewish and Christian concepts could be clearly distinguished. This approach, which had been adopted by numerous interpreters,[62] was exemplified by R.H. CHARLES who, like many of his contemporaries, did not hesitate to resolve inconsistencies in

---

[60] *Theology of the New Testament*, trans. Kendrick GROBEL (New York: Charles Scribner's Sons, 1951 and 1955) 2.173.

[61] For BULTMANN, the "Christian" character of the Apocalypse is apparent only in the certainty of eschatological hope, a motif which thought to be lacking in Jewish apocalypses. Otherwise, the "faith" expressed by the author, in contrast to Paul, has more to do with "faithfulness" (= "works," "pure conduct," and "repentance") and its future rewards than with the radical faith by which one is already "right-wised" into an eschatological tension ("between-ness") inherent in Christian existence; *ibid.*, 2.173-75.

[62] Cf. BOUSSET's overview of the contemporary source-critical analysis of Revelation in *Die Offenbarung Johannes* (Göttingen: Vandenhoeck & Ruprecht, 1906) 108-118 and the synoptic summary in CHARLES, *Studies in the Apocalypse* (Edinburgh: T. & T. Clark, 1913) 185-90. BOUSSET was a proponent of a modification of the literary-critical hypothesis by arguing that the author edited "fragments" from various older works; See further MÜLLER, *Messias und Menschensohn*, pp. 157-67 and Philipp VIELHAUER, *Geschichte der urchristlichen Literatur* (Berlin/New York: Walter de Gruyter, 1978^2) 500-501.

the text of the Apocalypse by positing essentially Jewish sources.[63] Though this method has gradually lost support,[64] some interpreters of the Apocalypse still apply it, while using Christology as a determinative criterion.[65] While the possibility that the author has integrated Jewish material cannot be categorically dismissed, the attempt to posit sources in order to account for the Christology of the document often rests on tenuous assumptions concerning what can and cannot properly belong to a Jewish or (Jewish-) Christian milieu. Thus much of the effort to identify and delineate written sources behind the text has been abandoned in favor of redaction criticism or traditio-historical analysis,[66] both of which correspond to an interest in arguing for the literary unity of the Apocalypse.[67]

---

[63] See, e.g., CHARLES' treatment of Rev 7:1-17 in *The Revelation of St. John* (ICC; New York: Charles Scribner's Sons, 1920) 188-218 and *Studies in the Apocalypse*, pp. 104-118, in which CHARLES regards "absolute universalism" as a criterion by which to distinguish the author's Christian perspective.

[64] This shift of perspective is reflected in the constellation of documents chosen by CHARLES, *APOT*, and CHARLESWORTH, *OTP*, for their respective collections; a discussion documenting this shift is given in CHARLESWORTH, "The Significance of the New Edition of the Old Testament Pseudepigrapha," in ed. M. PHILOLENKO, *La litterature intertestamentaire. Colloque de Strasbourg (17-19 octobre 1983)* (Bibliothèque des Centres d'Études Supérieures Spécialisés; Paris: Presses Universitaires de France, 1985) 11-25, esp. pp. 15-16 and 25-27.

[65] See MÜLLER, *Messias und Menschensohn*, pp. 157-216; J. Massyngberde FORD, *Revelation. Introduction, Translation and Commentary* (AB, 38; Garden City, NY: Doubleday, 1975) 12-19; and esp. the essays by EDWARDS, "Christological Perspectives" and John F. WHEALON, "New Patches on an Old Garment: The Book of Revelation," *BTB* 11 (1981) 54-59.

[66] In this vein, Klaus-Peter JÖRNS, *Das hymnische Evangelium* (SNT, 5; Gütersloh: G. Mohn, 1971), has sought to account for the formation, structure and function of hymnic pieces in the Apocalypse, a study which leads him to some weighty conclusions concerning the relation between Christ and God in the document. Rather than arguing for pre-existing written sources behind the hymns (whether used in synagogues or churches), JÖRNS emphasized that the author composed the hymns while drawing from various traditions which he expanded. JÖRNS concludes that traditions used are theocentric; in many cases, they have been expanded in order to incorporate Christ into the salvific activity of God (cf., e.g., the "and + prep. + Lamb/Christ" clauses in 7:10; 11:15; 12:10; and 22:3). Though the author accords to Christ a central role on behalf of believers, the end product remains theocentric, since it is only God who acts as judge; see pp. 170-75. For a similar approach, but with a different and less carefully worked out conclusion, see David R. CARNEGIE, "Worthy is the Lamb: The Hymns in Revelation," in *Christ the Lord*, pp. 243-56.

[67] See the assessments concerning the state of the question by Elisabeth SCHÜSSLER FIORENZA, "Research Perspectives on the Book of Revelation," in idem, *The Book of Revelation. Justice and Judgment* (Philadelphia: For-

A different turn has been taken by those who have devoted their assessments to the Apocalypse as a whole. To what extent, it has been asked, is the present form of this writing "Jewish" or "Christian" in character? A closely related problem is the relative significance which the author has apportioned to God and to Christ in his theology. We may ask, however, whether posing the question in terms of theo-centricity or Jewishness, on the one hand, or of Christo-centricity or Christian self-understanding, on the other, can be said to account adequately for a presentation of the author's theology.[68] And so, in order to avoid an imbalance of emphasis, most scholars addressing this issue have done so in a manner that resembles a dialectic.[69] The danger inherent in this line of inquiry is thus its tendency to beg the question; the outcome of the analysis is easily made to reflect the way the problem has been posed at the start.[70] For this reason we consider the theological question concerning the Jewish or Christian nature of the document or of its sources as an inadequate place to begin our inquiry. The problem of monotheistic elements in Christology in relation to Jewish thought is more adequately covered in an

---

tress, 1985) 12-32, esp. pp. 15-21 and Frederick David MAZZAFERRI, *The Genre of the Book of Revelation from a Source-critical Perspective* (BZNW, 54; Berlin/New York: Walter de Gruyter, 1989) 8-34.

[68] As with the problem of identifying underlying Jewish sources, an analysis bent on clearly separating and distinguishing theo-centricity from Christo-centricity is misleading. The latter is a concept which, in light of John's Apocalypse, certainly requires qualification. In order to conclude that a document is "Christo-centric," one would, by definition, either have to argue that the picture of God is simply overwhelmed by the portrayal of Christ (so that one cannot speak of God without speaking of Christ) or to qualify the idea in some other way (e.g., in relation to soteriology and ecclesiology).

[69] Thus, e.g., the moment Prigent ("Le temps et le Royaume," in ed. J. LAMBRECHT, *L'Apocalypse johannique et l'Apocalyptique dans le Nouveau Testament* [BETL, 53; Leuven: Univ., 1980] 238 and n. 16) asserts that the Apocalypse is "trés Christocentrique"--since many titles applied to God are transferred to Christ--, he is obliged to acknowledge that this Christo-centricity is built on a "theocentric foundation." Similar examples can be found in many studies of the Apocalypse. A more rigorous attempt to define what is meant by these terms is needed if they are to remain useful for exegetical discussion.

[70] Despite attempts to account for the other emphasis, note the correspondence between the conclusions and questions posed by G.R. BEASLEY-MURRAY, "How Christian is the Book of Revelation?," in ed. Robert BANKS, *Reconciliation and Hope. New Testament Essays on Atonement and Eschatology* (Grand Rapids: Wm. B. Eerdmans, 1974) 275-84; HOLTZ, "Gott in der Apokalypse," in *L'Apocalypse johannique*, 247-65, esp. 238 n.16; P. PRIGENT, "Le temps et le Royaume dans l'Apocalypse," in *ibid.*, pp. 231-45; Karl Martin FISCHER, "Die Christlichkeit der Offenbarung Johannes," *TLZ* 106 (1981) 165-72; M. Eugene BORING, "The Theology of Revelation: 'The Lord Our God the Almighty Reigns'," *Int* 40 (1986) 257-69; and LOHSE, "Wie christlich ist die Offenbarung?"

examination of the author's appropriation and use of traditions to shape his presentation.

B. Eschatology

Once eschatology is allowed to shape an approach to the Christology of John's Apocalypse, the analysis is almost invariably confronted by the task of determining what the author perceives as "already" and "not yet" fulfilled in the figure of Christ.[71] The selection of an eschatological framework which, after all, represents a major theme in the Apocalypse is entirely appropriate. It is reflected not only in the document's theological interpretation of past, contemporary, and future events, but also in its schematic movement from crisis to resolution as worked out in the narrative as a whole. Therefore, the linear element of time, whether made apparent through the author's understanding of history or gleaned from one's perception of the movement of the narrative, cannot be overlooked. For our purposes here, temporality has a bearing on an understanding of the author's theology in that it inhibits one from speaking of, to put it simply, a systematic Christology. In contrast to a "static" portrait of Christ in the Apocalypse, temporality opens up the way toward exploring the document for a dynamic correlation between Christology and eschatology, on the one hand, and between Christology and the unfolding narrative, on the other.[72]

Mere emphasis on linear movement in the Apocalypse, however, can be too one-sided. If cosmological and spatial elements are ignored, it becomes difficult to envision the place which the author has accorded to Christ in his

---

[71] So HOLTZ, *Christologie*, whose approach to Christology in the Apocalypse is structured around the distinction between the present (pp. 27-164) and future function (pp. 166-211) of Christ. SCHNACKENBURG (in "Christologie" 367-75) has adopted this scheme from HOLTZ.

[72] With respect to narrative movement, the Apocalypse of John fits in well with some recent, though diverse, attempts to define "apocalypse" as a genre in ancient literature which speak of apocalypses in terms of literary movement; see especially the studies by David E. AUNE, "The Apocalypse of John and the Problem of Genre," *Semeia* 36 (1986) 65-96, esp. pp. 87-88; Hans Dieter BETZ, "The Problem of Apocalyptic Genre in Greek and Hellenistic Literature: The Case of the Oracle of Trophonius," in ed. David HELLHOLM, *Apocalypticism in the Mediterranean World and the Near East* (Tübingen: J.C.B. Mohr [Paul Siebeck, 1983) 577-97, who applies the term μῦθος; John J. COLLINS, *The Apocalyptic Imagination* (New York: Crossroad, 1987) 4, drawing on earlier publications; and David HELLHOLM, "The Problem of Apocalyptic Genre and the Apocalypse of John," *SBL 1982 Seminar Papers*, ed. K.H. RICHARDS (Chico, CA: Scholars, 1982) 157-98.

construction of reality. The significance of this dimension for apocalyptic writings has in recent years been underscored by the increasing reluctance among scholars to characterize the genre of "apocalypse" merely in terms of eschatology. Since this development affects our approach to the Apocalypse of John, it bears further comment.

Apocalyptic writings have frequently been characterized within an eschatological framework. Paul D. HANSON, for example, has concluded that the essential core of apocalyptic thought consists of a particular eschatology in which there is an expectation of a new cosmos as an antidote to a sense of despair arising from oppressive social conditions.[73] This stress on apocalypticism as a response to crises within historical circumstances has gone hand in glove with the view that apocalyptic thought represents a development of biblical prophetic literature.[74]

A very different view was advanced by Gerhard VON RAD, who claimed that apocalyptic literature was primarily an outgrowth of "sapiental" knowledge, which he termed "the nerve-centre of apocalyptic literature."[75] In reacting against the notion that apocalyptic literature expresses a modification of prophetic eschatology, VON RAD argued that the presence of "figurative discourses" in apocalyptic documents and the identification of the seers as "wise men" (Daniel, Enoch, Ezra) suggests a formative background in wisdom tradition. Understood in this light, eschatological motifs can be said to arise from the broader question concerning the nature of the cosmos. This thesis allowed VON RAD to account for the interest shown by apocalyptic au-

---

[73] Though most of HANSON's work is concerned with the origin of apocalyptic eschatology during the post-exilic period, it provides an ideological basis for his contextualization of apocalyptic literature when it flowered during the late Second Temple period; see *The Dawn of Apocalyptic. The Historical and Sociological Roots of Jewish Apocalyptic Eschatology* (Philadelphia: Fortress, 1975) 11-12 and "Apocalypticism," in *IDB*, Suppl., cols. 28-34.

[74] Ibid. Similar lines of connection with prophecy have been drawn by other scholars who, at the same time, have tried to account for obvious differences; see esp. H.H. ROWLEY, *The Relevance of Apocalyptic. A Study of Jewish and Christian Apocalypses from Daniel to Revelation* (London: Lutterworth, 1947) 13: "... apocalyptic is a child of prophecy, yet diverse from prophecy ..."; D.S. RUSSELL, *The Method and Message of Jewish Apocalyptic* (OTL; Philadelphia: Westminster, 1964) 73-103 and 178-202; and Otto PLÖGER, *Theokratie und Eschatologie* (WMATNT, 2; Neukirchen-Vluyn: Neukirchener, 1968³).

[75] *Old Testament Theology*, trans. D.M.G. STALKER (2 vols.; New York/Hagerstown/San Francisco/London: Harper & Row, 1965) 2.301-308, esp. p. 306; see also idem, *Wisdom in Israel*, trans. James D. MARTIN (London/Nashville/New York: SCM and Abingdon, 1972). As far as literary form is concerned, von Rad considered apocalyptic literature as a *compositum mixtum*.

thors in laws which govern the world; only to this underpinning, according to VON RAD, can one attribute the concern for explanations of natural phenomena and history in the Jewish apocalypses.

Though VON RAD's thesis was severely criticized at the time,[76] modified forms of it, which stress an interrelation between eschatology and wisdom in apocalypses, have subsequently been advocated.[77] ROWLAND, in his attempt to achieve a comprehensive definition, has argued that "apocalyptic" (thought) was primarily concerned with "the revelation of the divine mysteries through visions or some other form of immediate disclosure of heavenly truths."[78] While ROWLAND, with VON RAD, characterizes apocalyptic thought as a form of knowledge, he is nevertheless more apt to consider eschatology as an "important component" of heavenly mysteries.[79] More recently, James C. VANDERKAM has suggested that the concern for comprehensiveness also be applied to our understanding of prophecy. Calling attention to similarities between late biblical prophecy and divination, he argues that it would be misleading to distinguish sharply between the activity of the later prophets and "mantic wisdom."[80] If VANDERKAM's suggestion is correct, then one should imagine a matrix

---

[76] E.g., by P. VIELHAUER and Georg STRECKER, "Apokalypsen und Verwandtes: Einleitung," in *NTA* 2.502; P. VON DER OSTEN-SACKEN, *Die Apokalyptik in ihrem Verhältnis zu Prophetie und Weisheit* (TEH, 157; München: C. Kaiser, 1969) 9-10; Klaus KOCH, *Ratlos vor der Apokalyptik* (Gütersloh: G. Mohn, 1970) 40-46; and later, HANSON, *Dawn of Apocalyptic*, pp. 8-9. The basis for much of this criticism was the absence of eschatology in wisdom tradition.

[77] See esp. J.Z. SMITH, "Wisdom and Apocalyptic," in ed. P.D. HANSON, *Visionaries and Their Apocalypses* (Philadelphia: Fortress, 1983, repr. from 1975) 101-120 (both are scribal phenomena); Michael E. STONE, "Lists of Revealed Things in the Apocalyptic Literature," in eds. F.M. CROSS, W.E. LEMKE and P.D. MILLER, *Magnalia Dei. The Mighty Acts of God. Essays in the Bible and Archaeology in Memory of G. Ernest Wright* (Garden City, NY: Doubleday, 1976) 414-52, esp. pp. 439-43; Michael A. KNIBB, "Prophecy and the Emergence of the Jewish Apocalypses," in eds. R.J. COGGINS, A. PHILLIPS and M.A. KNIBB, *Israel's Prophetic Heritage. Essays in Honour of Peter R. Ackroyd* (Cambridge: Univ., 1982) 155-80 (apocalypses are continuous with prophetic literature, but stand "within a learned tradition"); and ROWLAND, *Open Heaven*.

[78] *Open Heaven*, p. 70.

[79] Ibid., p. 71; see also pp. 28-29, 37-38, and 203-208.

[80] "The Prophetic-Sapiential Origins of Apocalyptic Thought," in eds. James D. MARTIN and Philip R. DAVIES, *A Word in Season. Essays in Honour of William McKane* (JSOTSS, 42; Sheffield: JSOT, 1986) 63-76. VANDERKAM has followed H.P. MÜLLER's distinction between courtly-pedagogical and mantic/divinatory wisdom, the latter of which he argues provided the source of the motifs of determinism, claim to inspiration, symbolic imagery, and pseudonymity in apocalyptic literature; see MÜLLER, "Mantische Weisheit und Apokalyptik," in *Congress Volume, Uppsala, 1971* (VTS, 22; Leiden: Brill, 1972) 268-93.

for apocalyptic literature in which the streams of eschatology and knowledge of the mysteries of the universe were merging.

The importance of this direction of research may be suggested as follows: To the extent that the Apocalypse of John belongs to a particular--that is, apocalyptic--genre of literature in Early Judaism, an understanding of its author's Christology cannot be exhausted by consideration of dimensions of eschatology. With respect to the proposed study, this means that the interaction between Christology and eschatological movement in the horizon of history is complemented by a vertical dimension, that is, the position and function of Christ within the cosmos envisaged by the author.

Furthermore, the recognition of connective elements between apocalypses and certain forms of esoteric knowledge coincides with the recent proliferation of studies of "Merkabah Mysticism" and its antecedents in Early Judaism.[81] The impetus for this wave of scholarship is certainly due to the influential work of Gerschom SCHOLEM in Jewish mysticism[82] and the textual editions and translations being prepared under the direction of Peter SCHÄFER.[83]

---

[81] Most significant are the following studies: Ira CHERNUS, *Mysticism in Rabbinic Judaism. Studies in the History of Midrash* (SJ, 11; Berlin/New York: Walter de Gruyter, 1981); "Visions of God in Merkabah Mysticism," *JStJud* 13 (1983) 123-46; David HALPERIN, *The Merkabah in Rabbinic Literature* (AOS, 62; New Haven: AOSoc, 1980); *The Faces of the Chariot. Early Jewish Responses to Ezekiel's Vision* (TSAJ, 16; J.C.B. Mohr [Paul Siebeck], 1988); Ithamar GRUENWALD, *Apocalyptic and Merkavah Mysticism* (AGAJU, 14; Leiden: Brill, 1980); *From Apocalypticism to Gnosticism. Studies in Apocalypticism, Merkavah Mysticism and Gnosticism* (Frankfurt: Lang, 1988); Peter SCHÄFER, "Engel und Menschen in der Hekhalot-Literatur," *Kairos* 22 (1980) 201-225; "New Testament and Hekhalot Literature: The Journey into Heaven in Paul and in Merkavah Mysticism," *JJS* 35 (1984) 19-35; and "Tradition and Redaction in Hekhalot Literature," *JStJud* 14 (1983) 172-81. For further bibliography, see SEGAL, *Paul the Convert*, pp. 315-16 n.'s 17 and 18.

[82] See esp. his *Major Trends in Jewish Mysticism* (New York: Schocken Books, 1974 repr. 1954³); *Jewish Gnosticism, Merkabah Mysticism, and Talmudic Tradition* (New York: Jew. Theol. Seminary, 1965²). An important review and assessment of SCHOLEM's scholarship is offered by Joseph DAN, *Gershom Scholem and the Mystical Dimension of Jewish History* (New York/London: New York Univ., 1988) esp., for our purposes, the chapter on "The Early Beginnings of Jewish Mysticism," pp. 38-76. Also providing impetus for recent research are studies by H. ODEBERG, *The Hebrew Book of Enoch or Third Enoch* (New York: Ktav, 1973²); Morton SMITH, "Observations on *Hekhaloth Rabbati*," in *Biblical and Other Studies*, v.1: *Studies and Texts*, ed. by A. ALTMANN (Cambridge, Mass.: Harvard Univ., 1963) 142-60; and Alexander ALTMANN, "Sacred Hymns in Hekhaloth Literature," *Melilah* 2 (1946) 1-24.

[83] *Synopse zur Hekhalot-Literatur* (TSAJ, 2; Tübingen: J.C.B. Mohr [Paul Siebeck], 1981); *Übersetzung der Hekhalot-Literatur* (4 vols.; TSAJ, 17, 22, and 29; Tübingen: J.C.B. Mohr [Paul Siebeck]; vol. 2, 1987; vol. 3, 1989; vol. 4, 1991).

Most recently, however, new dimensions have been opened up with the publication of texts from Qumran which demonstrate that the creative exegesis of Ezekiel's vision of the Merkabah, or divine chariot throne, antedates considerably the composition of the Apocalypse of John.[84] The interest of the Qumran documents, broadly speaking, in God's throne within the ideal heavenly world of exemplary worship, divine order and celestial beings overlaps considerably with traditions that are taken over in many apocalyptic writings, including the Apocalypse of John. This link encourages a consideration of the heavenly world as such and a comparison between its function in the document and the way it is portrayed in early Jewish literature, especially those documents which are clearly antecedent to or contemporary with Revelation and, hence, to the later full-blown "Merkabah Mysticism" that flowered in the rabbinic and medieval periods. In this light, the question of the usage of symbolism associated with mediator figures and Christology in early Jewish and Christian circles acquires new significance. It would be fruitful, then, to explore Christology in the Apocalypse through an analysis of the structures of the heavenly world, especially as concerns the symbolic function of the divine throne, on the one hand, and that accorded to angelic beings, on the other.

These considerations suggest that it is misleading to emphasize either the eschatological or cosmological dimensions of John's Apocalypse to the exclusion of the other. Just as movement in time resists the notion of a sys-

---

[84] For editions and more significant discussions of 4Q400-407, the Masada frgt.'s and 11QShirShabb, see John STRUGNELL, "The Angelic Liturgy at Qumran--4QSerek Šîrôt 'Olat Haššabbat," in *Congress Volume: Oxford, 1959* (VTS, 7; Leiden: Brill, 1960) 318-45; Lawrence H. SCHIFFMAN, "Merkavah *Speculation at Qumran*: The 4Q Serekh Shirot 'Olat ha-Shabbat," in eds. Jehuda REINHARZ and Daniel SWETSCHINSKI, *Mystics, Philosophers, and Politicians* (Durham: Duke Univ., 1982) 15-47; Carol NEWSOM and Yigael YADIN, "The Massada Fragment of the Qumran Songs of the Sabbath Sacrifice," *IEJ* 34 (1984) 77-88; NEWSOM, *Songs of the Sabbath Sacrifice: A Critical Edition* (HSS, 27; Atlanta: Scholars, 1985), to be supplemented by Elisha QIMRON, "A Review Article of *Songs of the Sabbath Sacrifices* (sic!): *A Critical Edition*, by Carol Newsom," *HTR* 79 (1986) 349-71; Jean CARMIGNAC, "Roi, Royauté et Royaume dans la Liturgie Angélique," *RQ* 12 (1986) 178-86; Joseph M. BAUMGARTEN, "ShirShabb and Merkabah Traditions," *RQ* 13 (1988) 199-213; and Anna Marie SCHWEMER, "Gott als König in den Sabbatliedern," in eds. M. HENGEL and A.M. SCHWEMER, *Königsherrschaft Gottes und himmlischer Kult im Judentum, Urchristentum und in der hellenistischen Welt* (WUNT, 55; Tübingen: J.C.B. Mohr [Paul Siebeck], 1991) 45-118. For publications of other merkabah materials from Qumran, see D. DIMANT and STRUGNELL, "4Q Second Ezekiel (4Q385)," *RQ* 13 (1988) 45-58 and "The Merkabah Vision in *Second Ezekiel (4Q385 4),*" *RQ* 14 (1990) 331-48. Finally, see 4Q286-287, in preliminary (and rather uncritical) text and translation in Robert EISENMAN and Michael WISE, *The Dead Sea Scrolls Uncovered* (Rockport, Maine: Element Books, 1992), pp. 222-30.

tematic Christology behind the author's assertions, so also a spatial view prevents the author's portrait of the exalted Christ from appearing unconnected and, hence, inexplicable within the context of the document as a whole.

C. The Socio-Historical Situation

Numerous scholars have interpreted christological titles and motifs of the Apocalypse as part of the author's response to a specific social and political crisis facing the Christian communities of Asia Minor during the first century. Particularly germane to the discussion has been the problem of how to interpret christological designations such as μάρτυς (1:5 and 3:14), ἀρνίον (28 times) and κύριος κυρίων (17:14; 19:16) which have traditionally been thought to mirror a context of political persecution[85] during the latter part of the reign of Domitian (81-96 CE).[86] Here Christ (especially as the Lamb) is portrayed in radical contrast to the self-aggrandizing assertions of this emperor (as the second beast in ch. 13) which lay claim to divine status.[87]

---

[85] E.g., see the classical treatments by E. LOHMEYER, *Christuskult und Kaiserkult* (Tübingen: J.C.B. Mohr [Paul Siebeck], 1919) and Ethelbert STAUFFER, *Christ and the Caesars*, trans. K. and R. Gregor SMITH (Philadelphia: Westminster, 1955) 147-91; and, more recently, John GAGER, *Kingdom and Community* (Englewood Cliffs, NJ: Prentice-Hall, 1975) 49-57, esp. pp. 51-53; CARNEGIE, "Worthy is the Lamb," 254-6; SCHÜSSLER FIORENZA, "The Followers of the Lamb: Visionary Rhetoric and Social-Political Situation," in *The Book of Revelation*, pp. 181-203; and Mitchell G. REDDISH, "Martyr Christology in the Apocalypse," *JSNT* 33 (1988) 85-95.

[86] In the 19th century, especially among British scholarship, it was customary to interpret the Apocalypse in relation to a Neronian persecution, a view which no longer has much support; but see John A.T. ROBINSON, *Redating the New Testament* (Philadelphia: Westminster, 1976) 230-31 and ROWLAND, *The Open Heaven*, pp. 403-13. A later date, however, does not preclude the possibility that traditions associated with Nero have been incorporated into the Apocalypse.

Most scholars have ascribed a Domitianic context for the Apocalypse. A balanced treatment arguing for this dating is provided by Adela YARBRO COLLINS, "Dating the Apocalypse of John," *PCSBR* 26 (1981) 33-45 and more fully in "When Was Revelation Written?," in idem, *Crisis and Catharsis: The Power of the Apocalypse* (Philadelphia: Westminster, 1984) 54-83.

[87] Thus GAGER translates LÉVI-STRAUSS's structural interpretation of myth, which functions "to overcome unwelcome contradictions between hope and reality," into a series of opposing symbols (see below). According to this scheme, Christology belongs to the symbols of hope and victory (built from Christian and Jewish traditions) and the Roman cult belongs to the symbols of oppression and despair; see *Kingdom and Community*, p. 52.

It is apparent, however, that two problems, historical and methodological in nature, may be associated with an unquestioning acquiescence to this scenario: (1) On the historical level, it should be noted that scholars are far from agreed concerning the presence and intensity of a persecution of Christians in Asia Minor during Domitian's reign. (2) As for methodology, the contextualization of Christology within the social and political environment raises questions concerning the degree to which appeal to data external to the document can be illuminative without vitiating the author's own message. Both points are examined in what follows.

First, as is increasingly recognized, it is primarily later, post-Domitianic Latin and Christian authors who characterized the period of Domitian's rule as a time of incompetence, persecution, and distress,[88] while evidence from the time of Domitian offers a contrasting picture. More contemporary evidence, such as epigraphy, coins, and biographies of senators, suggests a climate in which the empire, especially Asia Minor, was flourishing economically.[89] Ironically, the inconsistency of the ancient source materials can at times go unheeded among Roman historians whose views concerning the nature and scope of a Domitian persecution seem more to reflect traditional views concerning the Apocalypse of John than on the diverse materials they are more accustomed to scrutinize![90]

This is not to say, however, that the notion of a Domitianic persecution should be classified as no more than a product of vengeful or heroicizing imaginations of PLINY THE YOUNGER (*Paneg.*, 2.3 *passim*), TACITUS (*Agric.* 39-45), SUETONIUS (*Vit* 8 [*Dom.*]), DIO CASSIUS (*Hist.Rom.* 67-68), and EUSEBIUS (*Hist.Eccl.* 3.17-20; 4.26.9).[91] It is difficult to envision how a document re-

---

[88] This point is vigorously emphasized by Leonard L. THOMPSON, "A Sociological Analysis of Tribulation in the Apocalypse of John," *Semeia* 36 (1986) 147-74 and *The Book of Revelation. Apocalypse and Empire* (New York/Oxford: Oxford Univ., 1990) 15-17, where THOMPSON significantly notes that the Roman sources are frequently falsely used as evidence for the persecution of *Christians*.

[89] David MAGIE's thorough treatment of the general situation in Asia Minor during the Flavian dynasty is still regarded as definitive; see his chapter on "Centralization and Prosperity under the Flavians," in *Roman Rule in Asia Minor* (2 vols.; Princeton: Princeton Univ., 1950) 1.566-92, esp. pp. 576-82 (concerning the period of Domitian's rule).

[90] See, for instance, S.R.F. PRICE, *Rituals and Power. The Roman imperial cult in Asia Minor* (Cambridge: Cambridge Univ., 1984) 196-8 and Donald L. JONES, "Christianity and the Roman Imperial Cult," in *ANRW* II.23.2, pp. 1032-35.

[91] Given the tendency in recent discussion to emphasize the literary sources, there remains a need to analyze thoroughly the evidence (numismatic,

plete with the language of beheading (20:4), conquering (2:7,11,17,26; 3:5, 12,21; 5:5; 12:11; 13:7; 15:2; 17:13), pouring out of blood (15:6), reigning (5:10; 20:4,6), and death (2:13; 6:9,11; 12:11; 20:6), even if to some degree proscriptive, *cannot* mirror harsh circumstances among the Christian communities addressed. The question is one of nature and degree. For the sake of exegesis it seems best, then, to speak, at the very least, of a "perceived crisis"[92] which, without a categorical denial of a political persecution in some form, allows the language of the Apocalypse to be explained on the basis of the author's own background, use of traditions, theological perspective, and social factors. The extent to which the Roman hegemony itself can be said to have generated the adverse conditions of those to whom the document was addressed remains an open question.

The second, methodological problem presupposes the first. Difficulties in reconstructing the socio-political context shared by the author and his original readers lead to the question of the sphere in which the language of crisis is to be explained. What is the proper role of historical analogy, or "referential history" in relation to the author's *literary* program? According to Leonard THOMPSON,[93] the effort to account for the language and social circumstances of the Apocalypse by *relying* on contemporary literary, epigraphic, and numismatic sources begs the question. Such an approach assumes that the text, wherever possible, must refer directly to some aspect of the writer's and/or readers' social environment. For example, Colin HEMER claims that the

---

iconographical, architectural, and epigraphic) *from Asia Minor* for a provincial cult of the Roman emperors (especially under the Flavians). A significant step in this direction has recently been taken by Steven John FRIESEN, *Ephesus, Twice Neokoros* (Harvard University: Diss., 1990), who concludes that during Domitian's reign a Temple of Sebastoi in Ephesus was dedicated to the worship of the Flavian emperors (89/90 CE). FRIESEN's assessment should serve as a caution to those who are quick to dismiss an even provincially inspired Domitianic persecution. Moreover, one does well to note the reasoning of the Roman historian Marta SORDI who, after pointing out the problems associated with assuming a persecution of Christians under Domitian, argues that "In order to prove that the persecution never actually happened ... each reference would have to be explained away separately. The sudden calamities which befell the Christian community in Rome (Clement) would have nothing to do with persecution; the references in the Revelation would be either purely eschatological or else a recollection of Nero's persecution; ..."; see SORDI, *The Christians and the Roman Empire* (Norman/London: Univ. of Oklahoma, 1986) 45.

[92] The expression is introduced by YARBRO COLLINS, "The Social Situation - Perceived Crisis," in *Crisis and Catharsis*, pp. 84-110.

[93] *The Book of Revelation*, pp. 202-205, in which THOMPSON directs his critique at to the works of Colin HEMER, *The Letters to the Seven Churches of Asia in Their Local Setting* (JSNTSS, 11; Sheffield: JSOT, 1986) and John COURT, *Myth and History in the Book of Revelation* (Atlanta: John Knox, 1979).

idea of sharing Christ's throne as Christ shares the throne of the Father in Revelation 3:21 would have referred, for author and readers alike, to the Zenoid dynasty of Asia Minor, and pronounces "the general appropriateness" of these words for Laodicea.[94] While the study of social history should provide an important method for illuminating the context of the Apocalypse, the question remains whether it can offer the interpretive key to its language.

Two general considerations suggest that THOMPSON's somewhat negative valuation of interpretation through historical analogy, even if a bit one-sided, should nevertheless be taken seriously. For one thing, if allusions can be found to *diverse* phenomena in the Greco-Roman society, and especially that of Asia Minor, one may rightly ask how far these may be expected to contribute to a reconstruction of the *coherence* of the author's message. In addition, an attempt to isolate historical phenomena behind the symbolism of the Apocalypse does not do justice to what SCHÜSSLER FIORENZA has termed the "evocative power" of symbolism,[95] that is, the multi-valent character of symbols when they are encouched in poetic-mythical language.

For THOMPSON, the "referential" approach has little use, and he opts for a reading of the Apocalypse which stresses the essential *difference* between legitimation through "public discourse" within the sociological context at large and validation through "private discourse" within the Christian community. Consequently, he distinguishes a "boundary" between the message of the author (= "revealed knowledge") and the social structures (= "public knowledge") of the environment.[96] The importance of social history for Revelation is marginalized, since THOMPSON argues that the author adopts a kind of language which *as a whole* and *in itself* amounts to a protest against society at large.[97] From this perspective, the crisis may be understood as "perceived"

---

[94] *The Letters to the Seven Churches*, pp. 205-206. It is important to note that HEMER's historical scrutiny hardly ever allows him to find a perfect "fit" between the author's language and the environment. Thus, HEMER relies on the "cumulative weight" of the evidence; see, e.g., *ibid.*, p. 224 n. 1 concerning the letter to the church at Laodicea.

[95] See, in particular, her discussion of the limitations of historical-critical methodology in *The Book of Revelation*, pp. 20-21.

[96] See *The Book of Revelation*, pp. 171-85, in which THOMPSON employs categories for sociology of knowledge from Peter BERGER to explain this contrast.

[97] See *ibid.*, pp. 194-97, where the social situation of the Christian communities addressed is designated by THOMPSON as "cosmopolitan sectarianism," that is, a situation where a minority "countercommunity" erects strong boundaries against the rest of the world and fosters a strong sense of solidarity among its members.

in the true sense of the word, that is, as a product of a social critique already existent within the author's community. Tensions that are already experienced among the Christian communities of Asia Minor are sharpened when they are filtered through the author's alternative structure, in which Christology plays an important role.[98]

THOMPSON's criticisms should not, however, discourage one from searching out a proper use of a socio-historical approach, without which the interpretation of the Apocalypse is at risk of being one-sided. While it is one thing to expect contemporary and geographically localized data to demonstrate the "appropriateness" of the document within its context, it is yet another to maintain that its message is "plausible" only within a reconstruction of this environment. While THOMPSON stresses the sharp boundaries between the author's conception of reality and that of the validating structures of his surroundings, it ought not be surprising if some of the language in the Apocalypse is found to adopt and adapt symbols held in common with structures the author opposes. Indeed, if such is the case, then a significant part of the author's message, even aspects of his Christology, rests in an analysis of ways these symbols have been taken over, shaped and readjusted. The function(s) of such symbolism need not merely be limited to results attained through a reading of the text on a literary level (see section IV.D below). THOMPSON's reminder of difficulties encountered in reconstructing the external environment through both external sources and allusions of the author may suggest that at least part of what is addressed in the Apocalypse may not be immediately related to the churches' social environment: problems which the author perceived *within the Christian communities themselves*. If this is true --and the inclusion of "letters" to the seven churches certainly lend credibility to such an assumption--, then it may be asked whether varying images applied to the Christology of the Apocalypse (e.g., as a lamb or in angelomorphic terms) can be accounted for by the presence of both "internal" and "external" factors behind the author's attempt at communicating with the intended readers.

D. The Symbolic World

In the last twenty years, considerable attention has been devoted by scholars to the perception of reality in the Apocalypse. This work has impor-

---

[98] *Ibid.*, pp. 187, 189-90.

tant implications for the author's Christology. In this vein, the studies of John GAGER,[99] Elisabeth SCHÜSSLER FIORENZA,[100] and THOMPSON[101] are especially significant and will be presently discussed and evaluated.

GAGER's reconstruction of the symbolic world of the Apocalypse takes its point of departure in LÉVI-STRAUSS's proposed definition for myth: knowledge which brings the conflict between hope and harsh reality to a resolution.[102] For GAGER the Apocalypse, analogous to psycho-analytic therapy, brings to expression tensions that have been repressed by the Christian community on the level of the unconscious. The author provides a "language" through which these conflicts can be identified and uses his network of symbols in proceeding toward a resolution. Christ (as the Lamb), heavenly worship and throne, then, are placed among symbols that signify victory and hope, while others, such as the threatening activity of the beasts and judgment, function as symbols of oppression and despair. These opposing symbols oscillate throughout the document until the narrative culminates in a therapeutic vision of the New Jerusalem (21:1-22:5). The interplay between hope and despair prepares the reader to experience a catharsis that effectuates and reinforces an internalized resolve which declares that social oppression has no claim to finality. In this manner, ultimate reality, which is represented in the Apocalypse as the future, is made present to the reader.[103]

With respect to Christology in the Apocalypse of John, GAGER's approach, creative as it is, has several limitations. First, the structuralist conception of myth raises terms and criteria for analysis which themselves do not occur within the Apocalypse itself. While certain aspects of the author's solution to chaotic incongruities in the world are illuminated, the imposition of psycho-analytical language tends to play down the linguistic signs provided by the author himself. Second, GAGER's treatment of the symbolism of the Apocalypse does not take seriously its eschatology, which he has, in effect, demythologized into a spatial-cognitive framework. The solution is not

---

[99] *Kingdom and Community*.

[100] "The Followers of the Lamb," reprinted as "Visionary Rhetoric and Social-Political Situation" in *The Book of Revelation*, pp. 181-203.

[101] *The Book of Revelation* and "A Sociological Analysis of Tribulation"; see n.66. See also David L. BARR, "The Apocalypse as a Symbolic Transformation of the World: A Literary Analysis," *Int* 38 (1984) 39-50.

[102] See *Kingdom and Community*, p. 55 and Claude LÉVI-STRAUSS, *Structural Anthropology*, trans. Claire JACOBSON and Brooke Grundfest SCHOEPF (New York/London: Basic Books, 1963) 197-203.

[103] *Kingdom and Community*, p. 55.

bound up in time, but can be experienced whenever the Apocalypse is read. Against this function of the document, however, one may question--and rightly, in our opinion--whether the author would have knowingly offered an experience of reigning with Christ on God's throne when, at the same time, he has gone to great lengths to paint the present as a time of crisis. The future, though made present, is, after all, still future to the readers.[104]

Third, while the Apocalypse does oppose, for instance, the Lamb to the beast, other symbols are more ambiguous and cannot be so easily classified as belonging to one side of the conflict or the other. "Destruction and judgment" can evoke despair (so GAGER, referring to Rev 14:8-15:1), but they also express divine vengeance (6:9-17); the symbol "throne" evokes God's ultimate control over the universe (22:1,3), but along the way it can also represent the (albeit, temporary) power given to Satan (2:13) and to the beast (13:2); even the term "angels" can be placed in service of God (7:2-3,11; 8:2; 10:1-10; 14:6-20; 15:1,5; 18:1; 19:17) and Satan (12:7-9). The likelihood that some symbols are put in service of conflicting sides suggests that they may be explored for their function in traditions--as they occur in myths, antecedent literary forms, and the social environment--which the author has taken over. This use of "neutral" symbols, that is, symbols capable of expressing aspects of a world order devoted both to God's and Satan's rule, raises the possibility that the author is engaged in some degree of "redefinition."[105]

SCHÜSSLER FIORENZA, like GAGER, finds in the Apocalypse a network of symbols which were intended to counteract a crisis experienced by the original readers. The scope of the author's "symbolic universe," however, is not as comprehensive as that outlined by GAGER. Since for her the expression has to do with an "alternative" world constructed by the author in order to address the needs of his readers, it does not embrace symbols associated with evil. The author's "symbolic universe," pieced together from mythic and cultic images known primarily, but not exclusively, through Israelite religion, functions to overcome the harsh realities of the present by inviting the reader to participate imaginatively in a reality diametrically opposed to the

---

[104] So SCHÜSSLER FIORENZA, *The Book of Revelation*, pp. 167-68. It seems preferable to speak of a future whose prolepsis is already at work in the present.

[105] James H. CHARLESWORTH, "The Apocalypse of John--Its Theology and Impact on Subsequent Apocalypses," in idem with James R. MUELLER, *The New Testament Apocrypha and Pseudepigrapha* (Metuchen, NJ/London: American Theological Library Association and Scarecrow, 1987) 29, refers more specifically to the author's "redefinition of power."

pagan structures of the Greco-Roman environment. The author's symbolism thus functions as rhetoric. It is calculated to assist the reader in finding meaning in suffering and death and, hence, to inspire Christians to faithful obedience during persecution.[106]

Similar to GAGER, SCHÜSSLER FIORENZA's emphasis on the rhetoric of symbols, exemplified by the contrast between a crisis experienced by the original readers and the alternative world painted by the author, leads to a bifurcation of the symbols themselves, so that some are identified with the powers of evil while others are identified with God and the vindication of the righteous oppressed. Thus whereas throne imagery in the Apocalypse, according to her scheme, would evoke the idea of power in general (whether of the Roman emperor or of God), as rhetoric it is an assurance of God's omnipotence and ultimate victory over forces of oppression. SCHÜSSLER FIORENZA's emphasis on the Apocalypse as a rhetorical work, which presupposes a particular construal of the readers' socio-historical circumstances, leads her away from exploring the multi-valent possibilities of its symbolism.[107] She ends up with an infelicitous division in her analysis, for it is precisely the multivalent character of symbols which makes analogues and correlations possible between the world of experience and the alternate world provided for the readers.[108] Rather than exploring the author's symbolism either as indeterminate and ambiguous or as having one specific rhetorical function, we would propose that an analysis of symbols in the Apocalypse be open to both dimensions. In this way the analysis may allow symbols as inherited from tradition and (perhaps) encountered in the environment to interact with the aims of the author. As we shall see below, this is especially important for the kind of questions being addressed in this study.

THOMPSON's approach to the author's symbolic universe involves, as already discussed, a critique of crisis and deprivation theories which place historical circumstances at the center of interpretation.[109] Since the experiences of Christian communities of Asia Minor during the late first century have to be inferred from scattered literary and epigraphical sources and hy-

---

[106] "Visionary Rhetoric and Social-Political Situation," 192-9.

[107] Ibid., p. 187.

[108] Her analysis, perhaps unintentionally, undermines the possibility that motifs associated with pagan religion or the imperial cult could have had any impact on the seer's language.

[109] See esp. his evaluation of SCHÜSSLER FIORENZA, GAGER and YARBRO COLLINS in *The Book of Revelation*, pp. 205-210.

pothetically reconstructed from various passages in the Apocalypse, an analysis of the author's message ought not begin there. Before anything else, the symbolic structure should be read for its own internal coherence. In contrast to SCHÜSSLER FIORENZA and GAGER, THOMPSON insists that the symbolism of the Apocalypse should not be ultimately regarded as a *response* to circumstances in the readers' environment; the author was seeking to affect his readers' perception of the world rather than choosing language that reflects specific circumstances of their lives. In this vein, THOMPSON's "symbolic universe" is more comprehensive than SCHÜSSLER FIORENZA's "alternative world" which stands apart from and above the "real social world." The political and social realities of the Christian communities form but part of the author's overall program, which concerns Christian existence in its totality.

THOMPSON's positioning of symbolism in relation to understanding the Apocalypse has several advantages. First, his emphasis on a program for thought and behavior that is not a function of social oppression may serve to illustrate the formative significance of traditions which the author used to construct his symbolic universe. While THOMPSON himself focuses primarily on the level of the text and not so much on the problem of received tradition, his approach suggests that if the author intended at all to address effectively the readers' situation with a comprehensive message--whatever the circumstances--, we may expect him to have selected symbols the significance of which could be recognized by his readers. In other words, the rhetorical effect of the symbols would have depended not only on how the symbols are proportioned and prioritized by the author in the document itself but also on the degree to which those symbols related to a shared preunderstanding between the author and his audience.

Second, THOMPSON's critique of categories of social oppression and deprivation as points of departure to explicate the author's message underlines the import of considering the Apocalypse in relation to apocalyptic *literary* traditions of Early Judaism. While many scholars continue to regard documents written from the perspective of apocalyptic eschatology as "crisis" literature,[110] there is reason to question whether the assumption of a socially peripheralized community behind every apocalyptic writing is valid. Despite the impediments faced among specialists of early Jewish literature in coming to

---

[110] This characterization indicates the degree to which literature considered as "apocalypses" can simply be identified with "apocalypticism" as a social movement of the alienated. See HANSON's "Overview of Early Jewish and Christian Apocalypticism" in *The Dawn of Apocalyptic*, pp. 429-44.

some agreement concerning the definition of "apocalypse" as a genre, this should in no way be taken to invalidate the enterprise. Certainly the value of genre criticism ought not be measured in accordance with the extent of unanimity achieved! More importantly, the search for a coherent description of the genre persists because of the common recognition that a number of writings, especially during the late Second Temple period, shared stylistic and material elements which represented a distinct mode of expression. If we grant with HANSON that a particular social position contributed to the origin of apocalyptic literature, what, then, are we to make of apocalyptic writings in which literary conventions appear to have been reapplied? Are we to assume that in each case the social realities of the communities which produced and re-produced apocalyptic writings bore an identical stamp? If not, then it is possible that apocalyptic communities, though at some points in their existence probably subject to some form of marginalization or persecution, may have appropriated apocalyptic language simply because it was an inherited medium of expression. The way social deprivation and the apocalyptic language are often linked may mislead one to expect that once the oppressive circumstances of an immediate crisis come to an end, the apocalyptic medium would no longer be employed. This point alone is suggested by the increasing recognition among scholars that apocalyptic thought and language, indeed "apocalypticism," was not limited to the outcast fringes of society, but flowered among various Jewish (and Christian) groups.[111]

While this line of reasoning is not intended to prejudge the social world behind the Apocalypse, it does assist us in specifying why theological questions in and of themselves, such as the problem to be studied here--i.e. angelology, Christology and monotheistic belief--, are appropriate for our interpretation of the document. For the moment, then, it is important to leave open the question whether the place of Christ in the author's theological and symbolic scheme is merely a function of the situation of the Christian communities as perceived by the author or whether it stems from the author's prophetic attempt to impose a conceptual framework onto his audience.

Third, the comprehensiveness attributed by THOMPSON to the author's symbolic world in the Apocalypse necessitates a view of the symbols and their function which recognizes a degree of fluidity. In order to situate the functions assigned by the author to various symbols, THOMPSON speaks in terms of

---

[111] See, e.g., CHARLESWORTH's summary assessment in "The Apocalypse of John," pp. 23-24, n.'s 19-22.

"boundaries" between them. In applying the expression "metaphor" THOMPSON begins with the notion that the various symbols of the Apocalypse are distinct, and then devotes his analysis to the interrelationships among the symbols in which the lines of demarcation are retained or may be described as "soft" or "blurred." Thus a sharp contrast between Satan and God in the author's presentation does not mean that both camps do not share a common symbolism. For example, both God and Satan have thrones (e.g., 2:13; 4:2), Satan's locusts and the twenty-four elders wear golden crowns (4:4; 9:5), lamb imagery can be associated with the beast (13:11), and the scarlet beast may be described in language similar to that applied to God (viz. 17:8; 1:8; 4:8). In this way, THOMPSON is able to draw attention to the multi-valence of symbols in the Apocalypse and to argue that this flexibility makes it possible for the author to offer a comprehensive view of reality that, as a whole, addresses the circumstances of the Christian communities of Asia Minor.

Though the approach of THOMPSON makes a valuable contribution to the discussion of symbolism in the Apocalypse, his emphasis on the author's conceptual framework in terms of "boundary" does not do justice to the eschatological dimensions of the symbols. Instead, THOMPSON speaks of time in spatial language, referring, for example, to the dawning of the new Jerusalem as an instance of "topographical arrangement in space." This overall outlook-- one which tends to collapse time into one interrelated, spatially-conceived continuum that blurs past, present, and future into an interchangeable reality[112]--diminishes the importance of temporality and affects THOMPSON's construal of Christology in the Apocalypse. His argument that the Christology of the Apocalypse centers around the "irony of kingship through crucifixion" does not, therefore, sufficiently distinguish between the present state of "having conquered" (of Jesus and his followers on the basis of the Christ event) and a future, eschatological conquering which awaits fulfillment.

In summary, the above considerations concerning symbolism in the Apocalypse of John provide us a way of speaking about the function of symbols within the communicative situation between author and readers, and this, without demanding that the symbols themselves comprise an inflexible system of reality. From this point of view, the symbolic, and sometimes fluid language attached by the author to Christ and angelic beings may find a place in our understanding of their respective roles in the author's theology.

---

[112] See *ibid.*, pp. 81 and 84-86.

V. Angelology, Christology, and Monotheism: An Approach to the Apocalypse of John

The above review of recent discussion brings us to the point of outlining the particular approach and, hence, scope of this study. It is not the purpose here to produce another "Christology" of the Apocalypse of John, but rather to illuminate one aspect of Christology as understood by the author and his communities in relation to contemporary Jewish thought. The question addressed in the chapters below is whether and to what degree we may speak of a veneration of angels in early Jewish and Christian sources, and then how (if at all) this motif may have been applied to Christology by the author of the Apocalypse. Is a monotheistic framework threatened at all by the author's Christology? Is the logical tension in the Apocalypse between the worship of Jesus and monotheistic belief unique to Christian circles or are there any antecedents which provided Christians with language to express this conceptual ambivalence? Given the prominence of "monotheism" in the inquiry, special attention is devoted to pertinent traditions as they are preserved in early Jewish documents, while applicable parallels from the Greco-Roman environment will be drawn upon within the exegetical analysis of the Apocalypse.

In our investigation of the Apocalypse, it will be seen that recent dialogue concerning the "symbolic universe" points out one approach by which to understand the author's christological convictions. Consideration of a symbolic network which allows for temporal and spatial rigidity and fluidity opens the way for addressing the relative position of Christ and angels within the author's theological scheme. An assessment of the author's symbolism in relation to Christology, however, should not be confined to or begin with an internal analysis. The dynamics behind the interplay between the author's "symbolic universe" and the world of the readers he addressed require an approach that takes into account the backdrop of formative traditions which they may be assumed to have shared.

Instead of angelic symbolism, it might be argued that an analysis of throne symbolism in the Apocalypse provides a more useful starting point for getting at conceptual tensions posed by Christology for the claim to worship one God. Indeed, the prominence of the term θρόνος and related imagery is undisputable; the term itself appears in seventeen of the twenty-two chapters of the document. Furthermore, as a symbol which is integrally related to the motif of kingship and authority, it evokes a problem integral to the author's message: Who is in charge? In the author's portrait of a conflict between the powers of good and evil, this symbol and the related concept of enthronement figure prominently as features associated with both sides. Finally, the throne is a central power-symbol within the Apocalypse, one around which and from which much of the activity is authorized. The throne in the Apocalypse of John plays a central role in the author's view of the world. It can function as a "boundary" between God and other (allied) beings; in this respect, the language of worship provides the major criterion which determines how the divine throne may be related to the author's respective christological and angelological formulations (7:10-17). And yet, for the author the symbol also gives expression to a fluidity between christological, anthropological (3:21; 20:4), and demonic (2:11; 13:2) categories. Thus though "throne" in the Apocalypse signals a distinction between Christology and angelology, its serves as an inadequate starting point for the analysis. Where Christ, in contrast to "angels," is expressly associated with the enthronement motif (as in 5:6-14; 7:9-17; 22:1,3), the term "throne" is as such not *explicitly* used to reinforce the distinction. Therefore it would seem that the distinguishing function of throne symbolism within the author's Christology depends on the question of how the author has related Christology and angelology to begin with.

This problem constitutes the heart of the following study, which is divided into two parts. The following section (Part Two), in which the position of angelic beings within Judaism receives primary consideration, is devoted to exploring developments in Early Judaism which may illuminate the accommodation of the worship of Jesus to monotheism in the Apocalypse. The final section (Part Three) follows a traditio-historical and exegetical analysis, which is brought to bear on key passages where the author's Christology and claim to monotheism may seem to converge and to conflict.

PART TWO

ANGELIC AND HEAVENLY FIGURES: VENERATION AND MONOTHEISM

I. AN ACCOMMODATION OF "MONOTHEISM" IN JUDAISM:
THE CRITERION OF VENERATION

What were the boundaries of Jewish monotheistic faith? To what extent could the claim that there is one God accommodate the veneration or even worship of another figure? Does the worship of both Jesus and God as represented in the Apocalypse of John reflect a specifically "Christian" development or is it possible to maintain that it evolved from patterns which existed in Jewish tradition?

Since angels in the Apocalypse of John, along with Christ, figure prominently as beings aligned with God and since Christ is sometimes represented with characteristics associated with angels, the purpose of Part Two is to explore the stated problem in relation to angelology within the matrix of early Jewish and Jewish-Christian traditions. Did Jewish interest and belief in angels ever develop into patterns of veneration which were coordinated with the belief in the only God of Israel? Given the diverse genres and viewpoints represented in the ancient sources, one can expect Jewish writers to have expressed the special status of some mediating figures in a variety of ways. The ensuing discussion of this question will involve a dual procedure: the examination of (a) literary and epigraphical texts which have ostensibly furnished evidence for venerative attitudes towards such figures as well as a consideration of (b) religious developments underlying the formation of these traditions.

In his article on "The Worship of Jesus in Apocalyptic Christianity," BAUCKHAM asserts that "worship ... was the real test of monotheistic faith in religious practice."[1] Obviously, it is also the question of worship which occupies and defines the approach taken here. The task at hand is not, however, only a matter of weighing the evidence for and against a postulated "cultic" worship of heavenly beings distinguished from the one God of Israel. The problem is a broader one. It is possible, for instance, that honorific language, even if not intended as a "cultic" form of devotion, was subject to (mis)interpretation by outsiders. Hence, as is argued below, some writers associated angels with venerative language, while taking deliberate measures to avoid

---

[1] "The Worship of Jesus" 322; see also p. 335.

being misunderstood as compromising monotheistic belief.[2] Thus our point of departure is *language* in early Jewish and Jewish-Christian writings *which poses the question of human venerative attitudes or behavior towards angelic figures subordinate to God's purposes*. Whether the sources in question are concerned with scenes of earthly or heavenly worship, whether they contain honorific assertions which presuppose real attitudes of reverence or merely function rhetorically, it is ultimately the reverential language itself which raises questions as to the object, nature, and *extent* of veneration in each given instance. In this way it may be possible to appreciate the variety of postures assumed among early Jewish and Jewish-Christian circles. Further, a more open-ended formulation of the question is advantageous, since a simple denial that a cultic worship of angelic figures existed may risk overlooking ways in which cultic and non-cultic veneration can be understood as overlapping categories.

It should come as no surprise, then, that language thought to suggest the veneration of angelic figures is frequently difficult to interpret. Thus before this criterion can be used with any precision, several comments are in order.

First, as encountered in the texts treated below, the relationship between *literary* (especially non-liturgical) evidence and religious *praxis* is quite often far from clear. It is therefore imperative to consider the form and function of the source material while exploring its significance for ascertaining the worship habits of a particular group or groups.

Second, there is often a problem with how to interpret the nature of a referent in question. It should be asked whether venerative language in some texts is being associated with a real, independent figure or whether, as may be the case in Philonic writings, it merely constitutes a metaphorical way of speaking about God. Though metaphorical language for God may offer some background for and conceptual affinities with the worship of Jesus, it should not

---

[2] On the other hand, the criterion of "veneration" in view here is more specific than the problem of mediating figures with which it is often collapsed; see p. 48 below. For the distinction between posture behind petitionary prayer and worship, see BAUCKHAM, "Jesus, Worship of," p. 813. The mediation of human prayer to God by a heavenly figure was not *in itself* considered a threat to a belief in one God, though the notion of mediation might have led to such; see below, II.B.2.d (pp. 173-179). A focus on language of worship in relation to mediating figures may help define the degree of flexibility in monotheistic belief among early Jewish circles prior to or roughly contemporaneous with the Apocalypse of John (late 1st-early 2nd cent. CE).

necessarily be mistaken for the reverence toward an independent being, much less for an organized ritual that embodied such an attitude. This important distinction, however, does not mean that motifs connected to divine attributes are only of secondary importance. The *language* itself may be fluid, and that which separates philosophic metaphorical categories from a belief in the existence of mythological figures is frequently hard to determine. Even ideas concerning divine attributes, then, may have been adapted in contexts referring to an independent being and hence may eventually have had repercussions in religious praxis.

Third, the broader notion of veneration should neither be isolated from nor simply blended in with traditional motifs which were likewise applied to the figure(s) in question. As far as angelology is concerned, the analysis should therefore not proceed under the assumption that well-known motifs such as classification of angels, angelic mediation of the Torah, the association of angels with God's rule over the nations, angelic mediation of human supplication, interest in heavenly worship of God by angels, or even the invocation of angels, all somehow reflect a veneration of angels among humans. These thematic traditions--that is, factors which may well have been related in one way or another to such a development--will be considered in instances which seem to reflect such connections.

HURTADO, too, has recognized that "worship"--in its cultic sense--functions as a useful criterion for examining the question whether Jews accommodated monotheistic claims. Prior to his discussion of figures associated with "divine agency" in Early Judaism, he devotes an entire chapter to the question of whether or not there was any room in Early (and Rabbinic) Judaism for the "cultic" worship of beings allied to God.[3] However, as will be argued during the course of this study, the results of his analysis can be disputed on several points. For the moment, we note two fundamental problems connected with his approach.

First, as put forth in the discussion above (esp. pp. 20-21), HURTADO proceeds with too narrow a definition for "worship." While he produces a number of arguments to support his thesis that no early Jewish (and rabbinic) sources clearly attest a *cultic* devotion to any figure except God, his defi-

---

[3] "Divine Agency in Ancient Jewish Monotheism," in *One God, One Lord*, pp. 17-39.

nition does not adequately allow for various degrees of veneration.[4] Consequently, in the area of veneration he rules out by definition *a pattern of accommodation* within the framework of early Jewish monotheism through which to explain the worship of Christ, such as in the Apocalypse of John.

Second, HURTADO draws on the Apocalypse of John for examples of "early Christian mutation" and, in this respect, seems to minimize the possibility of the document's debt to ongoing developments within early Jewish tradition.[5] Accordingly, he derives the worship of Jesus in the Apocalypse exclusively from the worshiping life and thought of the early Christian communities. As a consequence, the impression left is that there is little continuity in character between the author's distinctive Christology and motifs which are predominantly attested in Jewish tradition. Admittedly, while HURTADO focuses primarily on the *origins* of devotion to Jesus among the first Christians, the ultimate concern in this study is the appropriation of Jewish tradition in relation to the extent of devotion to Jesus in the Apocalypse of John. However, though earlier "Christian" concepts and experiences were, without doubt, within the author's purview, it does not follow that a possible *formative* influence--through "Christian" exegesis and adaptation of Jewish sources and, perhaps, through early Jewish praxis--should be excluded from consideration. Furthermore, if the Apocalypse reached its final form in the latter part of Domitian's reign, the scope of its religio-historical background need not be limited to the origins of Christology, but ought pro-

---

[4] Thus in what follows we make a necessary distinction between "veneration" and "cultic worship"; see similarly SCHWEMER, "Gott als König in den Sabbatliedern," p. 100 n. 153 and Michael MACH, *Entwicklungsstadien des jüdischen Engelglaubens in vorrabbinischer Zeit* (TSAJ, 34; Tübingen: J.C.B. Mohr [Paul Siebeck], 1992) in his formulation of the issue, as relates to angelology (p. 292): "Von welchem Stadium ab aber hat eine solche Verehrung als Engelkult zu gelten?"
HURTADO's tendency to play down the significance of invocation to angels for religious life in even some Jewish circles (*One God, One Lord*, pp. 28-29) corresponds to his tendency to identify this motif with "cultic" veneration; see also Marcel SIMON, "Remarques sur l'Angélolâtrie Juive au Début de l'Ère Chrétienne," in idem, *Le Christianism antique et son contexte religieux* (WUNT, 23; Tübingen: J.C.B. Mohr [Paul Siebeck], 1981; repr. from 1971) 454 n. 1.

[5] *Ibid.*, pp. 103-104 and 119-22; see also DUNN, *Partings of the Ways*, p. 219. HURTADO acknowledges that the late date of Revelation might undermine the supposition that it reflects the dynamics of the "earlier Christian visionary experiences" (119). Nevertheless, he argues that the document provides evidence for "the sort of experiences that early Christian religious life included, especially in worship gatherings" (120).

perly to embrace components of Jewish thought as they were developing during the course of the first century. The analysis of early Christian tradition cannot preclude continued interaction, albeit sometimes contentious, between traditions of both communities.[6]

Notwithstanding a diversity of scholarly opinion concerning early Jewish attitudes towards divine agents, the following discussion will attempt to weigh the evidence as it pertains to angels. Special attention is given here to the symbolism associated with these figures in search of clues that may elucidate the religious background against which christological traditions in the Apocalypse of John were shaped.

II. The Venerative Status of Angels

The possibility that angels were worshiped by some Jews before and during the first century has been debated by scholars for at least a century. For reasons to be enumerated below, the Jewish and Christian evidence which has played a primary role in this discussion may be broadly classified under two headings: polemical and non-polemical texts. This classication allows us to differentiate between views preserved by "outsiders" and "insiders" and facilitates an awareness of traditio-historical developments within each.

A. Polemical Texts

These sources may be grouped into the following areas: (1) midrashic proscriptions in rabbinic literature, (2) prohibitions in angelophanies narrated in Jewish and Christian documents, and (3) accusations (mostly Christian) which have often been interpreted as allusions to such a practice. Despite their accusatory nature, these traditions are important in two respects. First, they help identify ideas or attitudes associated with angelology which were at least *perceived* as dangerous. Second, they raise the problem of identifying those groups against which, in a given instance, the polemic is being leveled. Certainly, the critical tone of such traditions, often thought to reflect views from an "outside" perspective, requires a critical examination

---

[6] When sufficiently recognized, this point indicates the logical difficulty with limiting comparative material for the Apocalypse of John (or, for that matter, to any writing of the New Testament) to that which is strictly "*pre*-Christian." See now Gabriella BOCCACCINI, *Middle Judaism* (Minneapolis: Augsburg-Fortress, 1991).

which, of course, does not presume either the veracity of the claims made or a continuity between literary argumentation and religious practice. Nevertheless, with respect to rabbinic proscriptions and angelophanic prohibitions, the degree of social distance between opposing "outside" and "inside" groups cannot be easily determined. Hence, one should not ignore the likelihood that behind such polemics there lurks a shared tradition which may help situate the controversy among known religious groups.

1. Midrashic Proscriptions in Rabbinic Literature [7]

A number of passages in rabbinic literature proscribe the veneration of angels through sacrifices, images, petitions, or outright worship.[8] The sig-

---

[7] The passages chosen for analysis are restricted to the motif of censurable veneration where it is explicitly mentioned. It should be stressed that they are not the only midrashic rabbinic texts which emphasize the superiority of God over his מלאך. For example, events associated with the deliverance of Israel from bondage in Egypt, which in one stream of interpretation was associated with an angel (e.g., Num 20:16-וישלח מלאך ויצאנו ממצרים; 1 Chr 21:12-MT מלאך יהוה משחית, LXX ὁ ἄγγελος ὁ ἐξολεθρεύων), are often retold in a way that specifically excludes any role of the angel; so, e.g., in the Passover Haggadah (on Deut 26:8): "'And YHWH brought us out of Egypt': Not by an angel, and not by a seraph, and not by a messenger, but the Holy One, blessed be He, in His glory and by Himself"; see ed. N.N. GLATZER, *The Passover Haggadah* (New York: Schocken Books, 1953) 36. Other rabbinic texts are mentioned in the discussions by Louis FINKELSTEIN, "The Oldest Midrash: Pre-Rabbinic Ideals and Teachings in the Passover Haggadah," *HTR* 31 (1938) 306-309 and J. GOLDIN, "Not by Angel and not by a Messenger," in ed. J. NEUSNER, *Religions in Antiquity: Essays in Memory of Erwin Ramsdell Goodenough* (SHR, 14; Leiden: Brill, 1968) 412-24. A similar concern seems to be expressed in LXX Isa 63:9 (οὐ πρέσβυς οὐδὲ ἄγγελος ἀλλὰ αὐτὸς κύριος); cf. the more ambiguous Heb: לא צר ומלאך פניו הושיעם; צר=either "envoy" (i.e., ציר) or "distress" and לא = either a negative particle or confusion with לו. The Tg. Jon to Isa, which has the verbal form אעית correspond to צר, produces a meaning opposed to the LXX rendering: "...he did not leave them in distress, but an angel sent from before him delivered them."

It is not clear how these passages are related to those which explicitly prohibit the worship of angels; this question would require an investigation on its own. Logically, the former seem to presuppose the dangers expressed by the latter; but whether this is an acceptable criterion for establishing a relative chronology depends on other traditio-historical observations.

[8] Esp. *Mek. de-Rabbi Ishmael, BaḤod.* 6 and 10; *t.Ḥul.* 2:18 (viz. *m. Ḥul.* 2:8; *b.Ḥul.* 40a; *b.Abod.Zar.* 42b and 43a); Tg. Ps-Jon Ex 20:23; *j.Ber.* 9:1 (fol.13a-b; viz. *Midr.Teh.* 4:3 and *b.Yom.* 52a); *Exod.R.* 32:4; *b.Sanh.* 38b; and *b.R.Hash.* 24b. These passages, and others (see n. 13 below), are discussed and partly cited by SCHÄFER in *Rivalität zwischen Engeln und Menschen* (SJ, 8; Berlin: Walter de Gruyter, 1975) pp. 67-72; cf. also W. LUEKEN, *Michael*, pp. 4-12; and A. Lukyn WILLIAMS, "The Cult of Angels at Colossae,"

nificance of these texts for late first-century Judaism is problematic, partly because many of the rabbinic discussions began to take shape in the second century CE and partly because the two major Jewish revolts against Rome (66-70 and 132-135 CE) led to significant adjustments in religious practices which once had centered upon the Temple cult. These texts, however, merit discussion in that they sometimes preserve traditions or reflect trajectories of traditions which can be traced to the Second Temple period, or at least to the period between the revolts. Moreover, it may be asked whether any of the censures of rabbinic texts allow us to infer anything which suggests that some *Jewish circles* during the Tannaitic and Amoraic periods fell heir to and developed the angelologies already espoused in much earlier Jewish writings.[9]

Assessments of these prohibitions have generally steered in one of two directions. Whereas SCHÄFER has concluded that they provide "indirect" yet "clear" testimony to the existence of an "Engelkult" in Judaism during the rabbinic period,[10] HURTADO is much more cautious.[11] HURTADO adduces several

---

JTS 10 (1909) 428-32. Many are also discussed in SEGAL, *Two Powers* and in E. E. URBACH, *The Sages. Their Concepts and Beliefs*, translated by I. ABRAHAMS (Jerusalem: Magness, 1989 repr. 1979²) esp. pp. 135-83.

[9] This is certainly not the only possible explanation for the views of angelic beings opposed by the rabbis. Behind their polemical statements scholars have seen "Gnosticism," "Christianity," Jewish Christianity, and religious syncretism (including magical texts). The focus here is, more specifically, on groups which would have characterized their religiosity as faithful expressions of Judaism. In any case, none of these religious forms can be categorically dismissed as targets of rabbinic polemics, and determinations must be based on the analysis of specific texts.

[10] *Ibid.*, pp. 67 ("das tatsächliche Vorhandensein eines Engelkultes im rabbinischen Judentum") and 72 ("unter ihren [die Rabbinen] eigenen Glaubensgenossen"). SCHÄFER's conclusion is a modification of LUEKEN's even more confident assumption that a polemical tradition, such as found in the *Kerygma Petrou* or rabbinic texts, may be regarded as "ein direktes Zeugnis für Engelverehrung bei den Juden" (*Michael*, p. 5); cf. also CHARLES, *Revelation*, pp. 224-25; E.R. GOODENOUGH, *Jewish Symbols*, 2.146; J. MICHL, "Engel II (jüdisch)," in *Reallexikon für Antike und Christentum* (Stuttgart: Anton Hiersemann, 1962) 5.88; SIMON, "Remarques sur l'Angélolâtrie Juive," p. 454; *Verus Israel. A study of the relations between Christians and Jews in the Roman Empire (135-425)*, translated by H. McKEATING (LLJC; Oxford: Univ., 1986) 345; FOSSUM, *The Name of God*, pp. 193-4; Karl Erich GRÖZINGER, "Engel III. Judentum," in *Theologische Realenzyklopädie* (Berlin/New York: Walter de Gruyter, 1982) 9.586-96, esp. pp. 590, 593-94; Horacio E. LONA, *Die Eschatologie im Kolosser- und Epheserbrief* (FB, 48; Würzburg: Echter, 1984) 206; and MACH, *Entwicklungsstadien*, pp. 298-300.

[11] His critique of SCHÄFER's conclusions from rabbinic texts echoes the assessment already reached by WILLIAMS ("The Cult of Angels" 432) in response to LUEKEN. Nevertheless, WILLIAMS, unlike HURTADO, based his caution towards the rabbinic evidence on the distinction, common among Christian

reasons. First, he notes with SCHÄFER[12] that many of the passages do not focus exclusively on angels but also proscribe the veneration of natural objects such as celestial (sun, moon, planets, stars) and geological elements (mountains, seas, rivers, desert places).[13] However, HURTADO asks rhetorically whether the supposition of an angel cult on the basis of these texts would not also imply that the other items were being worshiped by Jews--a posture which he claims was unthinkable.[14] Second, HURTADO asserts that the rabbis were primarily occupied with scriptural interpretation; on the basis of the texts one can only assert that they were (merely) attempting to specify the meaning of prohibitions in the Decalogue (Ex 20:4,20). Finally, he maintains, without much explanation, that an actual veneration of angels among Jews would have precipitated a more vigorous response within the literature.[15]

The opposing positions of SCHÄFER and HURTADO, though echoing the views of predecessors from the earlier part of this century, are best comprehended in relation to more recent approaches adopted for assessing the presence of merkabah mystical motifs in rabbinic sources. This correlation comes as no surprise, since the interest in and speculation about angelic beings is a prominent feature in the Hekhalot texts which speak about ascents to the divine throne. P.S. ALEXANDER has recently termed the two main approaches to Jewish mysticism as "socio-historical" and "midrashic,"[16] that is, approaches which correspond to emphases on "practical" and "exegetical" forms of mysticism. At the risk of over-simplification, we may observe that these methods, in their extreme forms, are to some degree reflected in the views of SCHÄFER and HURTADO. If SCHÄFER's interpretation of the rabbinic censures was based on a tenuous assumption that indirect allusions of this sort can be construed

---

scholars in the early 20th cent. (cf. the comments on BOUSSET, pp. 4-6 above), between the religious praxis of the "more educated and literary side" (as expressed in early rabbinic literature) and "the popular and lower side" of Judaism, which would have been more open to religious syncretism (429). For him, syncretistic ideas explain the worship of angels mentioned in Col 2:18 (438); in addition, see KUHN, "The Angelology of the Non-Canonical Jewish Apocalypses" 231-32 and Ernst PERCY, *Die Probleme der Kolosser- und Epheserbriefe* (Lund: Gleerup, 1946) 150-51.

[12] Cf. *Rivalität*, p. 72.

[13] Cf. esp. *b.Abod.Zar.* 42b and 43a; Tg. Ps-Jon Ex 20:23; *t.Ḥul.* 2:18; *Midr.Tann.*, pp. 190-91; and *Deb.R.* 2:34. Angels are absent from such lists in *m.Ḥul.* 2:8; *Koh.Z.* p. 107.

[14] *One God, One Lord*, pp. 30-31.

[15] *Ibid.*, p. 31.

[16] ALEXANDER, "3 Enoch and the Talmud," *JStJud* 18 (1987) 41-42.

as evidence for the phenomenon itself,[17] HURTADO proceeds on the even more problematic assumption that the interpretation of scripture, unless shown otherwise, was not related to contemporary currents of religious attitudes and observance.[18] Such literary and historical methods, however, need not be mutually exclusive. Already in volume III.1 of the *New Schürer* (1987), ALEXANDER has independently called for a synthesis which strikes "the right balance."[19]

---

[17] SCHÄFER's presentation of the rabbinic proscriptions in *Rivalität* reflects a stage of analyzing merkabah-related traditions during which the assumptions brought by SCHOLEM to the material were often presumed. However, on the basis of a recent proliferation of literary- and source-critical analyses of merkabah traditions in rabbinic and Hekhalot texts, SCHÄFER seems to have modified his assumption concerning such a connection; see his review of the works of GRUENWALD, HALPERIN, and CHERNUS in "Merkavah Mysticism and Rabbinic Judaism," *JAOS* 104 (1984) 537-41. In the adjustment of his methodology, SCHÄFER belongs to a growing number of scholars who have questioned or called for significant modifications of SCHOLEM's views; see H.E. GAYLORD, "Speculations, Visions, or Sermons," *JStJud* 13 (1982) 187-94 and the bibliography in the following note. A similar shift, though not explicitly in relation to the Tannaim, may be detected in ALEXANDER, whose early optimism for the correlation between "Hekhalot mysticism" and "Talmudic esotericism" (= "orthodoxy") has given way to a more mediating position in which literary analysis is used to derive--and hence to contrast--the former (esp. *3 En*) from the latter; cf. his "The Historical Setting of the Hebrew Book of Enoch," *JJS* 28 (1977) 156-80 and "3 Enoch and the Talmud" 40-68.

The studies of SCHOLEM have, of course, exercised and continue to exercise an enormous influence on how scholars have conceived of the relationship between rabbinic literature and religious practice. In *Major Trends in Jewish Mysticism* and *Jewish Gnosticism, Merkabah Mysticism, and Talmudic Tradition*, he proposed that apocalyptic literature from the Second Temple period and the later Hekhalot literature were linked historically by a tradition of esoteric and visionary mysticism practiced by the Tannaim. According to this hypothesis, the rabbinical texts provide a window into historical reality. This use of the literature is represented, for example, in the following discussions: S. LIEBERMAN, "Mišnat Šir haššīrīm," Appendix D in SCHOLEM, *Jewish Gnosticism*, pp. 118-26; M. SMITH, "Observations on *Hekhalot Rabbati*," pp. 142-60; N. SÉD, "Les Traditions Secrètes et les Disciples de Rabban Yohanan ben Zakkai," *RHR* 184 (1973) 49-66; GRUENWALD, *Apocalyptic and Merkavah Mysticism* (1980); and ROWLAND, *Influence of the First Chapter of Ezekiel* and *Open Heaven* (1982).

[18] HURTADO's views follow along the path of those who have criticized SCHOLEM's integration of religious history (mystical practices) with the literary sources: esp. URBACH, "The Traditions about Merkabah Mysticism in the Tannaitic Period" (in Heb), in eds. E.E. URBACH, R.J. WERBLOWSKY, and C. WINZUBSKI, *Studies in Mysticism and Religion presented to Gershom G. Scholem* (Jerusalem: Magness, 1967) 1-28; HALPERIN, *The Merkabah in Rabbinic Literature* (see also his bibl. on p. 4 n. 25) and *Faces of the Chariot*. See also the publications of SCHÄFER and GAYLORD cited in the previous note.

[19] "3 Enoch and the Talmud" 43; see also "Appendix: 3 Enoch," in the *New Schürer*, 3,1.273-74.

A remaining methodological question is how one moves from the reading of rabbinic materials to hypotheses concerning religious life. Since the polemical statements against veneration of angels are conveyed through a literary medium, it is necessary to find criteria in order to address the problem of historical reconstruction. Thus elements (in prohibitions) not part of a biblical text or anterior interpretive tradition, but which are introduced either *de novo* or from another biblical text, may indicate a censure which responds to a new situation. In addition, texts devoted primarily to problems presented by angelophanies in scripture may provide a basis for fruitful investigation. With these considerations in mind, comments on some of the most relevant passages follow.

a. Rabbinic Interpretation of Exodus 20:4,23: Angels and Natural Phenomena

In a number of cases the scriptural interdictions are applied both to angelic beings and natural phenomena. That they should appear side by side is by no means surprising. As is well known, natural phenomena are identified with angels as early as Psalm 104:4 (רוחות=מלאכי; אש להט=משרתיו), an association possibly taken up in LXX tradition to Deuteronomy 33:2.[20] Furthermore, in earlier writings such as *Jubilees* 2:2 and *1 Enoch* 60:11-22 various kinds of meteorological activity, created by God, could be attributed to the supervision of the angels.[21] This affiliation, however, could also be portrayed negatively. Thus several names of the fallen "watchers" in *1 Enoch* 6:7, 8:3, and 69:2 are etymologically related to manifestations of weather (e.g., 4QEn[a] 6:7-ברקאל, probably "lightning of El"; 4QEn[c]-זיקאל, "comet of God") and

---

[20] Corresponding to the unclear text in the MT (מימינו אשדת למו), which in the Vulgate is rendered as *in dextera eius ignea lex* (< אש דת) *dilexit populos*, the LXX reads ἐκ δεξιῶν αὐτοῦ ἄγγελοι μετ αὐτοῦ. The identification of angels with fire depends on whether the LXX tradition is to be derived from the uncertain אשדת, which would have had to be understood as "fire." As the Latin translation shows, the phrase was interpreted in conjunction with the context of the bestowal of the law (viz. v. 4). Cf. also Hebr 1:7.

[21] See further the discussions in conjunction with Gal 3:19 by Heinrich SCHLIER, *Der Brief an die Galater* (MeyerK, 7/11; Göttingen: Vandenhoeck & Ruprecht, 1951) 109 and Terrance CALLAN, "Pauline Midrash: The Exegetical Background of Gal 3:19b," *JBL* 99 (1980) 551.

geographical entities (e.g., 4QEn^a 6:7-טוריאל, "mountain of God").[22] Despite the possibility that meanings reflected in some of these names do not bear a negative connotation, the warnings against worshiping angels in lists including natural phenomena are not the product of an effort to combat a dualistic view in which evil is derived from angels. There is no indication that these rabbinic texts are referring to fallen angels; whenever mentioned, proper names include almost invariably "Michael" (מיכאל, "who is like God?").[23] In any case, the varied formulations of these scriptural prohibitions reflect a special apprehension against the possibility of worshiping the angels.

Both the Second Commandment (Ex 20:4-5) and the prohibition against fashioning "gods of silver and gold" in Exodus 20:23 are applied to angelic beings. In the *Mekhilta de-Rabbi Ishmael* (*BaḤod.* ch. 6, pp. 242-43[24]), a composite document which preserves traditions going back to the Tannaitic period (2nd cent. CE), an extended list of objects excluded from worship contains a specific condemnation against fashioning an image (דמות) of "angels, cherubim, and ophanim."[25] The censure of worshiping of such beings follows immediately upon a similar one which, without doubt on the basis of the more specific proscription in Deuteronomy 4:19, excludes the imaging of celestial bodies: sun, moon, stars, and planets.[26] In the midrash this order is determined by the scriptural phrase, "that which is in heaven above" (Ex 20:4), which is

---

[22] For detailed studies in which the Aram, Grk, and Eth lists of angels are compared and subjected to etymological analysis, see J.T. MILIK, *The Books of Enoch. Aramaic Fragments of Qumrân Cave 4* (Oxford: Clarendon, 1976) 152-56; Michael A. KNIBB, *The Ethiopic Book of Enoch* (Oxford: Clarendon, 1978) 69-76; Matthew BLACK, "The Twenty Angel Dekadarchs at I Enoch 6,7 and 69,2," *JJS* 33 (1982) 227-35 and idem, *The Book of Enoch or I Enoch* (SVTP, 7; Leiden: Brill, 1985) 118-24.

[23] Thus, contra HURTADO, the analogy between elements of nature and angels is only apparent.

[24] Pp. of *BaḤod.* are given according to the edition of Jacob Z. LAUTERBACH, *Mekilta de-Rabbi Ishmael* (3 vols.; Philadelphia: The Jewish Publication Society of America, 1933-1935) vol. 2.

[25] Perhaps through the influence of Ezek 1:5-21, the cherubim and ophanim are regarded as angelic beings; see further H. BIETENHARD, *Die himmlische Welt im Urchristentum und Spätjudentum* (WUNT, 2; Tübingen: J.C.B. Mohr [Paul Siebeck], 1951) 55-56. The particular danger associated with the living creatures around the divine throne lies in the fact that many rabbis derived the Israelites' worship of the golden calf at Sinai from a vision of the throne at the Red Sea. This connection is discussed by HALPERIN in *Faces of the Chariot.*

[26] "Planets" (מזלים) is lacking in Deut 4:19; 17:3; and Jer 8:2. See 2 Kgs 23:5 ("the sun, the moon, the planets, and all the host of heaven").

bifurcated in its application. Consequently, the term "above" (מִמַּעַל) acquires a distinct meaning:

> As for "that [which] is in heaven" (אֲשֶׁר בַּשָּׁמַיִם) one might think it refers only to sun, moon, stars, and planets? But it says: "Above," meaning, [do] not [make] an image of the angels, [do] not [make] an image of the cherubim, and [do] not [make] an image of the ophanim.[27]

The angels, in conjunction with the cherubim and ophanim associated with the divine throne, are hence not equated with the other items. The possibility of making an image of angels, cherubim and ophanim presupposes that they can be "seen," but in a different context as objects of nature. In this way the midrash, in distinguishing between the locative phrases in the biblical text, singles out the danger of this aspect of image making.

In a further passage of the *Mekhilta* (*BaḤod.* ch. 10, pp. 276-77), Exodus 20:23 is interpreted by R. Ishmael as a prohibition of making an image of angels, cherubim, and ophanim.

> "*You Shall Not Make with Me* (אִתִּי)." R. Ishmael says: "You shall not make an image (דְמוּת) of My servants who serve before Me on high, not an image (דְמוּת) of angels, not an image (דְמוּת) of cherubim, and not an image (דְמוּת) of ophanim."[28]

Here the biblical text, which says nothing about making an "image,"[29] is adjusted to the prohibition of image making (דְמוּת) in the Second Commandment,[30] while its statements about gold and silver are not mentioned. The basis for specifying the angels, cherubim and ophanim was apparently the word אֱלֹהִים (Ex 20:23), which R. Ishmael is said to have rendered in the sense of "divine be-

---

[27] The bracketed words represent adaptations from LAUTERBACH's translation (*Mekilta*, 2.243).

[28] Translation from *ibid.*, p. 276.

[29] Ex 20:23 MT: לֹא תַעֲשׂוּן אִתִּי אֱלֹהֵי כֶסֶף וֵאלֹהֵי זָהָב לֹא תַעֲשׂוּ לָכֶם.

[30] Tg. Ps-Jon contains a version which assimilates more to Ex 20:23: "My people, you children of Israel, do not, in order to worship, make (לָא תַעַבְדוּן לְמִסְגוּד) an image of the sun, and moon, and stars, and planets and angels which serve before me (קֳדָמַי מַלְאֲכַיָּא דִמְשַׁמְּשִׁין); do not make for yourselves gods of silver and gods of gold." A basis for combining vv. 4 and 23 may already be suggested in the LXX tradition of v. 4, which translates the Heb פֶסֶל ("hewn / cut image") with εἴδωλον ("idol" = an image of an alien god); see W. Barnes TATUM, "The LXX Version of the Second Commandment (Ex. 20,3-6 = Deut. 5,7-10): A Polemic Against Idols, not Images," *JStJud* 17 (1986) 177-95.

ings" (or "angels") instead of as pagan "idols" or foreign "gods."[31] Admittedly, the passage as a whole does not put any special emphasis on proscribing the veneration of angels.[32] And yet, the prominence given to the heavenly beings by means of an allusion to the Second Commandment is at least indicative of a conscious application of an exegetical procedure to alleviate such a concern.[33]

Another group of texts related to Exodus 20:4-5 is concerned with sacrifices: m.Ḥullin 2:8, t.Ḥullin 2:18, and the Gemarah in b.Ḥullin 40a. However, in contrast to the Mekhilta passages, the biblical text is not cited but presupposed; instead, the point at issue is halakhic. The preserved forms of this tradition run as follows:

m.Ḥullin 2:8 [34]	t.Ḥullin 2:18 [35]
The one who slaughters in the name of mountains, in the name of hills, in the name of seas, in the name of rivers, in the name of desert places--	The one who slaughters in the name of the sun, in the name of the moon, in the name of stars, in the name of planets, in the name of Michael the prince great of the army,

---

[31] As correctly observed by SCHÄFER, Rivalität, p. 68.

[32] Immediately following the comments attributed to R. Ishmael, a tradition ascribed to R. Nathan construes the ambiguous אתי as a nota accusativi with the 1st person suffix, resulting in a reading which condemns attempts to fashion images of God. The third interpretation of Ex 20:23 is attributed to R. Akiba, who renders אתי as "with me" but not in R. Ishmael's sense of "besides"/"other than." R. Akiba's view, which reads as a warning that Israelites should not treat God (through behavior) as Gentiles treat their gods, provides the point of departure for the remaining section of BaḤod. ch. 10.

[33] Contra PERCY, Probleme, p. 151. Significantly, the Mekhilta (BaḤod. ch. 6, p. 245) transmits a dispute between R. Gamaliel and a Gentile philosopher, whom the former accuses of worshiping "the sun, the moon, the stars and the planets, the mountains and the hills, the springs and the glens, and even human beings." While one cannot conclude from this that there was no angel worship among Gentiles, it appears that the compilers, perhaps even R. Gamaliel, did not deem it necessary to fault them with the veneration of angels. The lack of evidence for Jewish and Christian accusations against pagan angel worship is conspicuous. This, in turn, may suggest that the problem was perceived in terms of its relation to praxis in circles with some connections to Jews and/or Christian groups. The likelihood of this is enhanced by the association of angels with cherubim and ophanim, which reflects the influence of the merkabah tradition in Ezek 1.

[34] Translated from the text in the critical ed. of E. ALBECK, revised by E. ELON, משנה סדרי שישה קדשים סדר (Jerusalem/Tel Aviv: Bailik Institute and Debir, 1958).

[35] The translation is based on the text in the edition of M.S. ZUCKERMANDEL, Tosephta (Jerusalem: Wahrmann Books, 1963).

his slaughtering is invalid (שחיטתו פסולה).	even (-ו) in the name of a small worm--behold, this flesh is sacrifices to the dead (זבחי מתים).

b.Ḥullin 40a (Gemarah) [36]

פסולה אין זבחי מתים לא ורמינהי
השוחט לשום הרים לשום גבעות
לשום נהרות לשום מדברות
לשום חמה ולבנה לשום כוכבים ומזלות
לשום מיכאל השר הגדול
לשום שילשול קטן
הרי אלו זבחי מתים

אמר אביי לא קשיא
הא דאמר לדר הא דאמר לגדא דהר
דיקא נמי דקתני דומיא
דמיכאל שר הגדול

> Gemarah: Not invalid only (but also) sacrifices to the dead. But we will contradict it:
> (Baraita) One who makes sacrifice in the name of mountains, in the name of hills, in the name of rivers, in the name of desert places, in the name of the sun and the moon, in the name of stars and planets, in the name of Michael the great prince, (even) in the name of a small worm--behold, these are sacrifices to the dead.
>   Abaye said: (It is) not difficult. What he said to the mountain is what he said to the deity (גדא) of the mountain. (There is) indeed justification (for this view) since the analogy pertains to Michael the great prince.

The Mishnah and Tosephta traditions, though sharing a common structure,[37] are composed of two different lists of items to which it is forbidden to offer animal sacrifice. The pericope in the Mishnah only lists geological elements, while the Tosephta, except for the "small worm," specifies celestial objects, including "the great prince of hosts Michael." The tradition in the Babylonian Talmud demonstrates, however, that the point of debate underlying these texts is not so much the items listed as the precise status of the rejected

---

[36] The text is taken from the Daniel BOMBERG ms presented in ed. I. EPSTEIN, *Hebrew-English Edition of the Babylonian Talmud* (London: Soncino, 1960-).

[37] Note the common structural elements: (1) introduction of the case of "one who slaughters," followed by (2) a list of forbidden objects of worship through sacrifice, and (3) the final pronouncement.

offering.³⁸ Whereas the Mishnah tradition considers the terrestrial objects in its list "invalid" (פסולה³⁹), the heavenly elements (and the "small worm") in the Tosephta are even more unacceptable;⁴⁰ they are "sacrifices to the dead" (זבחי מתים).⁴¹ The Babylonian Gemarah inquires whether the mishnaic ruling is contradicted by another tradition (Baraita) in which a composite list is given the pronouncement found in the Tosephta.

The relationship among these traditions is not clear. It is impossible to establish whether the Gemarah has combined those of the Mishnah and Tosephta or whether it transmits an antecedent tradition of which the Mishnah and Tosephta formulations were adaptations.⁴² With respect to the angelic figure, however, one may observe that the lists in the Tosephta and Talmud both culminate in the mention of Michael. The weight assigned to the angel, albeit negative, comes to further expression through the contrast drawn between this "great prince" and the "small worm." The explanation attributed to Abaye

---

   ³⁸ Of course, the texts of both the Mishnah and Tosephta agree that only sacrifices offered to God are valid; cf. SCHÄFER, Rivalität, p. 69.

   ³⁹ Though the mishnaic and talmudic passages say nothing about "making an image (פסל)," the term denoting invalidity suggests a word-play with the prohibition (Ex 20:4).

   ⁴⁰ The distinction between earthly and celestial objects apparently derives from the formula בשמים ממעל...בארץ מתחת in Ex 20:4. This would correspond with a further interpretive distinction, in which פסל (see previous note) is applied to terrestrial items and תמונה is taken as a reference to heavenly bodies. Though the substance of the Second Commandment (image making) is not carried over, its structure and wording are assumed.

   ⁴¹ The notion of sacrifice to the dead is, of course, well attested in the Ancient Near East. Along with necromancy, it was strictly forbidden in the biblical texts; see Deut 18:9-12 and esp. 26:14. Concerning the practice in the Ancient Near East, see, e.g., Kathleen KENYON and Thomas A. HOLLAND, Excavations at Jericho vol. 3 (Jerusalem: British School of Archaeology, 1981) esp. pp. 229, 305 and, more recently, Theodor J. LEWIS, Cults of the Dead in Ancient Israel and Ugarit (HSM, 39; Atlanta: Scholars, 1989) 5-98 (including comments on Mesopotamia and Palmyra).

   ⁴² Cf. Ibid. SCHÄFER's own comments proceed on the assumption of the latter possibility, while MACH (Entwicklungsstadien, p. 297) holds to the former. An argument in either direction on linguistic grounds is not determinative. Though the morphology in the Talmud passage reflects a later development than that of the Mishnah or Tosephta (here, e.g., more plene sp., more consistently a u vowel before labial in שום), it remains possible that the language may have been affected by scribal transmission. Moreover, the appearance of "seas" (ימים) in the Mishnah, absent in the Gemarah, does not necessarily disprove the priority of the Baraita. Unless the term was inadvertently omitted in the Talmud, the compilers of the Mishnah may have added it before "rivers" in an earlier tradition to form a parallel construction opposite the topographical elements (mountains, hills).

(Bab. Amor. ca. 280-339 CE) in the Talmud recognizes this emphasis: Sacrificing "in the name of a mountain" is regarded as an "offering to the dead" (and therefore invalid) because of its association with Michael, a connection lacking in the Mishnah. The mention of Michael, which downgrades even further the invalidity of a sacrifice, may express, at least in the Amoraic period, a vigorous polemic against the veneration of this figure. Once again, an angel (or angelic figures), though listed among other phenomena, achieves a conspicuous function in the argument.

This emphasis on angels, when they are associated with natural phenomena, also turns up in another midrashic tradition related to Israel's reception of the Torah at Sinai. According to the kernel of the tradition, which is variously preserved in several texts (*Midr.Tann.*, pp. 190-91[43]; *Deb.R.* 2:34; *Deb.R.*, p. 65[44]; and *Lam.R.* 3:8), Israel and the nations reacted differently to the descent to Sinai by God and the angels. Whereas the nations chose angels (Michael and Gabriel in *Deb.R.*; *Deb.R.* [in LIEBERMAN] adds sun and moon; and *Midr.Tann.* adds sun, moon, stars, planets) to rule over them, Israel is to have chosen the Lord as her "portion" (חלק).[45] While this account of the Sinai covenant marks an attempt to reconcile the privileged status of Israel with the universality of God's rule, it accords angels (and, with less emphasis, heavenly bodies) a certain divine status in relation to other nations. The special danger associated with sacrificing to angels may thus be

---

[43] Pp. in D. HOFFMANN, *Midrasch Tannaim zum Deuteronomium* (Berlin: Poppelauer, 1908-1909).

[44] Pp. according to the edition of LIEBERMAN, *Midrash Debarim Rabbah* (Jerusalem: Wahrmann Books, 1964²).

[45] Cf. LXX Deut 32:8-9; *Jub* 15:31-32; and Sir 17:17--in these texts the actor is God. The tradition is placed within a homiletic midrash on the Shema in Deut 6:4 in conjunction with Sg of Sgs 3:24 ("'The Lord is my portion [חלקי],' said my [Israel's] soul..."). In *Midr.Tann.*, pp. 190-91 and *Deb.R.* 2:34 (see the מדרש רבה, ed. by Moshe A. MIRAKIN [Tel-Aviv: Yavneh, 1967] 11. 50-51) the choice of God by Israel is illustrated by the reception of a king and his entourage upon entry into a city. While some citizens chose the ruler's officials as patrons, the smart one (אחד שהיה פקח) settles for nothing less than the king himself. As in the passage in *Deb.R.*, the medieval Hebrew *Testament of Nephtali* only refers to choosing an angel, but here the tradition is applied to Abraham: "...thus each and every nation chose an angel, and none of them remembered the name of the Holy One, blessed be he. But when Michael spoke to Abraham our father, ...Abraham answered, 'I choose and I select only the one who spoke and the world came into being, who formed me within the inside of my mother's womb ... Him I will select and to him I will cleave, I and my seed forever'"; see CHARLES' collation of the Heb mss in *The Greek Versions of the Testaments of the Twelve Patriarchs* (Oxford: Univ., 1908) 239-44.

related to a dual recognition of their function as rulers over the nations, on the one hand, and their service as messengers from God.[46] Once the former is admitted, an interest in the latter could rather quickly have been associated with idolatry (see II.A.2.b below).

b. Other Rabbinic Interdictions

Second, the traditio-historical independence of strictures against angel worship from censures against idolatry towards natural elements is further suggested by several of the listed passages in which the interpretation of Exodus 20:4 and 20 is not in view. This obtains, for example, in the following texts: *j.Berakhoth* 9:13a-b, *Exodus Rabbah* 32:4, and *b.Sanhedrin* 38b. A brief look at these passages yields further observations.

j.Berakhoth 9:13a-b[47]

> R. Judan said in his own name, "[Someone of] flesh and blood has a patron. When a time of distress (צרה עה) comes to him, he does not go in to him suddenly (פתאום). Instead, he enters and stands at the door of his patron and calls (קורא) to his servant or[48] to a member of his house, and he says, 'Such and such is standing at the entrance to your courtyard.' Perhaps he allows him to enter and perhaps he leaves him outside. But the Holy One, blessed be he, is not

---

[46] In the rabb. passages mentioned above there is no explicit description of these angels as evil; they are understood as subordinate, yet independent, beings. The notion of angelic rule over the nations was early on, of course, subject to more a dualistic interpretation in which a conflict among the angels could be envisaged; so, e.g., Dan 10:13, 20-21. Similarly, see the Jew.-Chr. *Clementine Recognitions* 8.50. But even in the *Recognitions*, the motif is not a product of a dualistic interpretation of the Sinai events; the context is concerned with the fallen angels and the flood. Where the *Recognitions* do speak of the assignment of angels to govern the nations at Sinai (2.52), the emphasis is the inappropriateness of designating these angels (or any other created beings) as "gods"; they are not considered hostile (see Deut 32:8 LXX; Sir 17:17; *1 En* 60:15-21; 89:70-76; *Jub* 35:17; and *Shep.Herm. Vis.* 3.4.1-2). Here again, the danger of compromising monotheistic belief is associated with subordinate beings not explicitly bound up with any dualistic notion of evil.

[47] Translation is based on the collation of eight manuscripts in *Synopse zum Talmud Yerushalmi* I/1-2, eds. Peter SCHÄFER and Hans-Jürgen BECKER (Tübingen: J.C.B. Mohr [Paul Siebeck], 1991) 224-27.

[48] Only *'En Ya'aqov*, collated by SCHÄFER with other manuscripts for the Palestinian Talmud, omits לעבדו; cf. *ibid.*, pp. 224-25.

so. When distress comes upon a man, he should not cry out (לא יצוח[49]) to either Michael or to Gabriel; instead, he should cry out to me, and I will answer him immediately (מיד). That is what is written: 'Everyone who calls (יקרא) on the name of the Lord shall be saved' [Joel 3:5]."

In this passage R. Judan, a fourth-century teacher in the Palestine academy, contests the idea that one should expect to approach God through a mediary. To this end, a negative comparison is drawn with the behavior of a "patron" who is only indirectly accessible. This image, which ultimately goes back to the Persian ideal of kingship, underscores a ruler's majesty, supreme authority, and remoteness from the subjects.[50] In contrast, R. Judan stresses that God may be approached directly and explicitly counsels against appealing initially to either Michael or Gabriel. Though SCHÄFER is correct in noting that the idea of mediation here has its background in the "well-known" motif of angels as bearers of human prayer to God,[51] he does not account for the

---

[49] 'En Ya'aqov: לא תצוח ("you should not cry out").

[50] A close parallel to the image used by R. Judan is found in HERODOTUS (*Hist.* 1.98-99) who describes architectural measures taken by Deioces, the 7th cent. BCE Median king: "Deioces built these walls for himself and around his own palace; the people were to dwell without the wall. And when all was built, it was Deioces first who established the rule that no one should come into the presence of the king, but all should be dealt with by the means of messengers (δι' ἀγγέλων δὲ πάντα χρᾶσθαι); that the king should be seen by no man; and moreover that it should be in particular a disgrace for any to laugh or spit in his presence" (trans. by A.D. GODLEY, *Herodotus* v.1 [LCL; Cambridge, Mass./London: Harvard Univ. and Heinemann, 1966] 131).
It was only a matter of time before this image, further underlined by epithets such as "the Great King" and "King of kings," was taken over in language about divine kingship during the Hellenistic period. See esp. the conscious application of royal Persian imagery to underline the grandeur of deity in AESCHYLUS, *Agamemnon* 43-4 and *Persae* 532-6, 762-4 (Zeus); PS. ARISTOTLE, *de Mundo* 398a-b; and APULEIUS, *Liber de Mundo* 346-351. Concerning the Persian influence on divine kingship from the 3rd cent. BCE on, see Klaus W. MÜLLER's important discussion in "König und Vater," in *Königsherrschaft Gottes und himmlischer Kult*, pp. 37-43.
Lest the analogy be carried too far, this background occasionally made it necessary for, e.g., the author of *2 Enoch*, to argue *minores ad maiores* that the prospect of judgment before "the King of earthly kings" (39:8, Rec. J) is more frightening than even before "an earthly king"; cf. also *2 En* 46:1-3 (Rec. J).

[51] See SCHÄFER, *Rivalität*, pp. 70 and 28-29 (apocryphal and pseudepigraphal literature), 62-64 (rabbinic sources) for selected references. Rabbinic, early and medieval Jewish sources are collected concerning the prominent angel Michael by LUEKEN, *Michael*; see also H.L. STRACK-P. BILLERBECK, *Kommentar zum Neuen Testament aus Talmud und Midrasch* (6 vols.; München: C.H. BECK, 1922-1956) 1.782 and 2.560-61. On the non-rabbinic, early Jewish sources, see section II.B.2.d (pp. 173-179) below.

main point: the polemic itself. The argument of R. Judan brings together two motifs: (1) the (ultimately) Aristotelian critique of Persian monarchy which advocated "beneficence" and "friendship" between a king and his subjects[52] and (2) the application of stereotypes of Persian royalty to God in order to reject the worship of intervening beings between God ("the Great King") and human beings. PHILO's adaptation of the image provides a good example of such a rejection[53] and hence merits discussion below.

Commenting on the First Commandment in *de Declogo*, PHILO draws the following comparison:

> So just as anyone who rendered to the subordinate satraps the honours due to the Great King would have seemed to reach the height not only of unwisdom but of foolhardiness, by bestowing on servants what belonged to their master, in the same way anyone who pays the same tribute to the creatures as to their Maker may be assured that he is the most senseless and unjust of men (sic!) in that he gives equal measure to those who are not equal, ... Let us then reject all such imposture and refrain from worshipping those who by nature are our brothers (τοὺς ἀδελφοὺς φύσει μὴ προσκυνῶμεν), even though they have been given a substance purer and more immortal than ours.... Let us, then, ...acknowledge and honour the one God Who is above all... (*de Dec.* 61, 64, 65; cf. 178).[54]

Whereas R. Judan, as represented in *j.Berakhoth* 9:13a-b, is critical of ideals associated with Persian kingship, PHILO makes positive use of the analogy to advance a similar point: the absolute condemnation of showing reverence to God through subordinates. These different appropriations of royal imagery result in contrasting emphases. In the case of PHILO, Persian ideals supply the basis for appealing to God's majesty and remoteness in order to

---

[52] ARISTOTLE characterized the Persian monarchy as form of "tyranny," that is, a perversion of the institution of kingship (*Nich.Eth.* 8.10.3, φαυλότης γάρ ἐστι μοναρχίας ἡ τυραννίς). ARISTOTLE proposed instead that the ideal kingship should be analogous to forms of household rule (master-slave, father-children, husband-wife). Of particular importance to his critique is the notion of paternal authority (properly understood) which is to be defined by φιλία and εὐεργεσία (*Nich.Eth.* 8.10.4-11.3). The persistence of such regal tyranny is explained by ARISTOTLE on the basis of a stereotype; "the barbarians" and "Asiatics" are "more servile in nature than the Greeks and Europeans" (*Pol.* 3.9.3, τὸ δουλικώτεροι εἶναι τὰ ἤθη φύσει οἱ μὲν βάρβαροι τῶν Ἑλλήνων οἱ δὲ περὶ τὴν Ἀσίαν τῶν περὶ τὴν Εὐρώπην).

[53] As also PS. ARISTOTLE (1st cent. CE).

[54] Trans. by F.H. COLSON, *Philo* (LCL) 7.37-39.

unveil the foolishness of worshiping anything subordinate, an emphasis that stems from his immediate concern to explicate the First Commandment (Ex 20:3). Moreover, the context suggests that PHILO is probably not referring to angels as such, but to heavenly bodies (see *Dec.* 66; 75-76) and thus gives expression to the widespread Jewish condemnation of pagan idolatry.

According the rabbinic tradition R. Judan, however, draws on critiques of God's remoteness in order to stress the accessibility of divine assistance to someone in a time of crisis.[55] The chasm that exists between the "patron" and the needy person is contrasted with the proximity of God to those in dire circumstances. The connotation of grandeur in God's kingship is not dispensed with entirely in the tradition; in a way similar to ARISTOTLE, the image is redefined in order to illustrate that an emergency entitles the petitioner to a privileged position.

This comparison allows two features in *j.Berakhoth* 9:13a-b to emerge more clearly, as they relate to the worship of subordinate beings. The first feature which contrasts with PHILO is, of course, the explicit mention of angels Michael and Gabriel without any obvious allusion to the First Commandment. The analogy initially leads one to expect that Judan's interpretation will have one or both angels perform the same duties as those of the "go-betweens" in the patron's household. Such an expectation is emphatically reversed in the comparison. Second, there is the element of emergency (עת צרה) which is introduced in both parts of the analogy. Just as the person in distress seeks help from his "patron," it is the person in distress who should petition God. At this point the image and its interpretation by R. Judan diverge. While nothing in the passage as a whole forbids the notion of angels functioning as intermediaries for petitions,[56] R. Judan's application is more acute. The less reliable procedure of going *through* angels, itself not rejected, provides the basis to censure going *to* angels for help at all. At times when the need is greatest, direct petition to angels betrays one's doubt in

---

[55] The emphasis on the individual here contrasts with generalizing statements in rabbinic literature concerning Israel's special access to God, a tradition which is found in various forms; cf., e.g., *Midr.Tann.*, pp. 190-91 (to Deut 32:9; see also other texts cited in n. 45 above): unlike the nations, Israel chooses God as patron) and *b.Yom.* 52a (R. Jose: Israel's privileged position is symbolized by the high priest's straight path to the Mercy Seat).

[56] *Contra* WILLIAMS, "The Cult of Angels" 430, whose interpretation implies a complete rejection of the image painted of divine kingship; cf. also HURTADO, *One God, One Lord*, p. 31.

the reliability of God (Joel 3:5). Rather than conveying God's presence, the mediating role of angels can be mistaken as an indicator of God's remoteness. At stake is, then, the correct understanding of God's "patronage." The care taken not to reject this image entirely may imply an effort to resolve an ongoing debate in Palestinian circles in which, on the basis of this image, the proper understanding of angelic mediation was being disputed (see II.B.2 below).

Though the text opposes God's disposition to that of a "patron," the contrast is not carried through completely. Even the critique of R. Judan leaves room for this analogy, with its complement that God has a retinue of heavenly "servants." The customary implications of Persian kingship are modified to make the point that, *when the situation demands it*, the most reliable source of aid comes from *God*. The expectations raised by the analogy, according to which petition to angels would have been a normal means of procedure, suggests that if not in praxis, prayer to, through, or involving prominent angels such as Michael or Gabriel was at least conceived as a more respectful way (as in the Philonic adaptation of the image) of gaining a hearing before God.[57] The words attributed to R. Judan apparently envision a situation in which dire circumstances could lead one to invoke angels directly for help. The polemic, then, seems to be less of an attempt to preclude a hypothetical possibility than, at the very least, the suppression of an attitude which had been and was circulating in relation to Jewish tradition.[58]

---

[57] See the comment in the previous footnote.

[58] A further case in point is worth noting. As long as the term מלאך יהוה could represent alternative language for God, its presence in passages from the Hebrew scriptures posed no difficulty for monotheistic belief. However, once the expression was combined with an angelology that gave independent names to מלאכים or ἄγγελοι, some reinterpretation was required. In the context of invocative prayer, this development is best seen in relation to the three-fold blessing of Ephraim and Manasseh in Gen 48:15-16. In the Heb text (and, similarly, in Grk, Lat, Copt, Syr, Onk, and Neof versions) Jacob calls upon (1) "God before whom my fathers Abraham and Isaac walked", (2) "God who shepherded (הרעה) me from my youth until today," (3) "the angel (המלאך) who redeemed (הגאל) me from all evil (מכל־רע)" to bless (juss., יברך) Joseph's sons. Though most of the translations do not significantly alter the text, the Sam Pentateuch tradition reads the third part with the more metaphorical המלך ("king"), while Tg. Ps-Jon represents המלאך as possessing a likeness comparable to that of Jacob (דמלאכא דומות לי), the latter apparently presupposing the angelic portrayal of Jacob = Israel; cf. Jonathan Z. SMITH, "The Prayer of Joseph," pp. 262-65.

Whatever the intended sense behind המלאך, several interpretive traditions felt it necessary to distinguish clearly between האלהים and המלאך.

Exodus Rabbah 32:4

Another interpretation: *Do not be rebellious against him* (Ex 23:21)--do not confuse me with him and do not make a substitute for me. Perhaps you will say, "Since he is our [angel] prince, we want to serve him and he will forgive us of our evildoing." Not so! He will not forgive you of your evildoing. [He is] not as I, for it is written of me: *"Who forgives guilt and overlooks evildoing"* (Micah 7:8). But he [the angel prince] will not forgive your evildoing! And not only this, but you will be the cause of removing my name from within him, for it says, *"For my name is within him"* (Ex 23:21).[59]

This passage is a midrash on Exodus 23:21. In the scriptural text, God promises to send an angel to guide the Israelites through the wilderness. The people are warned not to rebel against this angel; if they do, they cannot expect to be forgiven, since "my name is in him." For the rabbis this verse raised the problem of whether forgiveness can be obtained through the angel.[60] As has been observed,[61] the verb תַּמֵּר in v.21 (תַּמֵּר, caus. of מָרָה or מָרַד, "to be

---

This is already seen in PHILO (*Leg.All.* 3.172-178) who, in commenting on this passage, argues that it is only appropriate that God's feeding of Jacob is superior to the angel's/Logos's (ἄγγελον ὅς ἐστι λόγος) activity as "healer of ills." A similar comparison, which bears the same emphasis as PHILO, is found drawn in *b.Pes.* 118a and *Ber.R.* 78:1: human sustenance (*Ber.R.*- הפרנסה; *b. Pes.*- מזונות) is more difficult than redemption from evil. Here it is significant to note that the point of emphasis is God's superiority; the inclusion of "the angel" in the invocation is not in itself questioned. See the positive view of angelic mediation of prayer in *b.Sota* 33a, according to which the proper language of prayer is Hebrew (and not Aramaic) since the angels do not know Aramaic.

[59] Translation from *Midrash Rabbah* v.2, eds. H. FREEDMAN and M. SIMON (London: Soncino, 1939). The problem of dating the *Exod.R.* as a whole is discussed, with bibliography, by H.L. STRACK and G. STEMBERGER, *Einleitung in Talmud und Midrasch* (Nördlingen: C.H. Beck, 1982⁷) 284-5. In contrast to the first part of the work, the second (= *parashoth* 15-52), which contains this passage, shows significantly less influence from the Bab. Talmud. Though a systematic linguistic study for a relative dating has yet to be applied to the document, the non-Babylonian form of many traditions in the second part points to a setting in Palestine sometime during the Amoraic period.

[60] This point already seems to have been perceived as a problem by the LXX translator in Ex 21:23, in which the milder ὑποστείληται corresponds to the Heb נשא. The danger of confusion between the angel and God in the interpretation of this passage is reflected in Tg. Neof (fol. 160a), which exchanges the 3rd pers. suffixes with the less objectionable 1st pers.: "...and obey *my* voice, do not rebel against *my* words."

[61] E.g., SCHÄFER, *Rivalität*, p. 71 and S.M. LEHRMAN, *Midrash Rabbah. Exodus* (London: Soncino, 1939) 408 n. 5.

contentious, rebellious") is interpreted on the basis of the root המר (caus., "to change, exchange"). This rendering results in a more innocuous description of the angel's role, namely that (a) the angel sent to guard and accompany the Israelites through the wilderness should not be confused with God and that (b) the angel is *incapable* of forgiving sins, which is the sole prerogative of God. To venerate (פלחה) this angel is to violate the specific purpose with which he was charged.[62]

For the moment, it is important to note that two elements of the pericope, both associated with the angel, are nowhere else in rabbinic literature related to natural phenomena: (1) the *possibility* of forgiveness and (2) the expression of this possibility by an antagonist in the first person.[63] Whatever one makes of the combined mention of angels and natural elements (see above), the language of this and like passages chiefly concerned with angels denote a problem (the veneration of angels) which was perceived as a real threat to the claim to worship one God.

This proposal is enhanced by consideration of a similar passage:

b.Sanhedrin 38b

> R. Naḥman said: "He who is as skilled in refuting the *Minim* as is R. Idith [ms M: R. Idi], let him do so; but not otherwise. Once a *Min* said to R. Idith: 'It is written, *And unto Moses He said, Come up to the Lord* (Ex 24:1). But surely it should have stated, *Come up unto* me!' - It was Metatron [who said that], he replied, whose name is similar to that of his Master, for it is written, *For my name is in him* (Ex 23:21). But if so, [he retorted,] we should worship him! The same passage, however, - replied R. Idith - says: *Be not rebellious against him*, i.e. exchange Me not for him. But if so, why is it stated: *He will not pardon your transgression?* He answered: By our troth [lit.: we hold the belief] we would not accept him even as a messenger, for it is

---

[62] In the context of this midrash, the assignment of a guiding angel (Ex 23:20, "Behold, I send an angel...") is explained as divine punishment for Israel's worship of the golden calf at Sinai (*Exod.R.* 32:1,2,3,7), whereas previously only the Lord had been their guide (Ex 13:21; viz. *Exod.R.* 32:2).

[63] Though one might argue that the first person is merely rhetorical, and therefore refers to an imaginary opponent, such language is conspicuously lacking in the proscriptions involving the Second Commandment (Ex 20:4).

written, *And he said unto Him, If Thy presence go not* etc. (Ex 33:15).[64]

This tradition, attributed to R. Naḥman (late third century), records a debate between a heretic (the *Min*) and a certain R. Idith (middle third century?),[65] whose proficiency at argumentation is singled out as exemplary. In countering the interpretation that Exodus 24:1 refers to two deities[66]--that is, that the biblical text distinguishes between the one speaking to Moses and "the Lord"--, R. Idith cites Exodus 23:21 and, as in *Exodus Rabbah* 32:4, interprets הכר from the root נור. In addition to warning against confusion between the angel (here called "Metatron") and God, he appeals to Moses' refusal in Exodus 33:15 to have the Israelites depart from Sinai without being accompanied by *God's presence* (פניך). The passage ends, then, on a more emphatic note than *Exodus Rabbah* 32:4. Whereas the latter passage still leaves room for the angel of Exodus 23:21 to have a legitimate function as a guide in the wilderness (though it is subject to misinterpretation), the added appeal to Exodus 33:15 in *b.Sanhedrin* 38b undergirds R. Idith's assertion that the angel should not even be considered a messenger (פרוונקא).[67]

Certain elements in *b.Sanhedrin* 38b discourage a confident identification of the *Min* with someone "outside" the parameters of "Jewish circles."[68]

---

[64] Translation in I. EPSTEIN, *Sanhedrin* (Heb-Eng edition of the Babylonian Talmud; London: Soncino, 1987).

[65] The identity and provenance of R. Idith is not known and opinions are divided. URBACH (*The Sages*, pp. 139 and 742 n. 13) assumes that he was from Babylon, while SEGAL (*Two Powers*, p. 68) supposes that R. Naḥman was from Babylon and that R. Idith was from Palestine during the preceding generation. On the hypothesis of a Palestinian provenance for *Exod.R.*, the added details in *b.Sanh.* 38b suggest that URBACH's view is more likely.

[66] This aspect of the passage is discussed in SEGAL, *Two Powers*, pp. 68-71. See further the discussion below.

[67] SEGAL (*Two Powers*, pp. 69-70 n. 31) argues that the choice of this Mandean-Persian loanword (="letter carrier") instead of שליח reflects the rabbis' unwillingness to show any approval towards the concept of angelic mediation. SCHÄFER (*Rivalität*, p. 71), who at this point is more sensitive to the context, maintains that the term disparages the angel's status: i.e. "not even the role of a letter carrier suits the angel."
The sharpened polemic in *b.Sanh.* 38b, traditio-historically considered, thus preserves a form that is later than the form of the tradition found in *Exod.R.* 32:4.

[68] HURTADO's narrow understanding of this phrase--he apparently thinks of "rabbinic" Judaism (*One God, One Lord*, p. 31)--corresponds to his reticence to allow for any form of angelic veneration within Judaism during the Tannaitic and Amoraic periods. This view corresponds to the conclusions of URBACH, "The Traditions about Merkabah Mysticism." Thus it is not unexpec-

This is most immediately apparent in the disclosure of the angel's name, "Metatron," which is *not made by the heretic*, but by R. Idith. Hence the knowledge of a "Metatron"[69] as one in whom God's name resides is represented as

---

ted to find URBACH identifying the heretic in *b.Sanh.* 38b as "a Christian sectarian" (*The Sages*, 139; cf. also pp. 141-50, 742 n. 13).

[69] The origin of the name *Metatron* still lacks a definitive solution. Major recent attempts include the following: (1) After admitting the hypothetical nature of many attempted explanations (cf. H. ODEBERG, *III Enoch* [Cambridge: Univ. of Cambridge, 1928] 125-42), SCHOLEM argues that the name is in fact symbolic and was "formed ... in order to replace the name Yahoel as a *vox mystica*" (*ibid.*, p. 70). Thus the title "Lesser Yaho" (= YHWH), found already in early Gnostic literature, lies behind the heretical pronouncement of Aḥer and Metatron's punishment of "60 fiery lashes" in *b.Ḥag.* 15a; cf. also idem, "Metatron," in *Encyclopaedia Judaica* (Jerusalem: Keter, 1971) 11.1443-46. Important criticisms of this derivation are given by SEGAL (*Two Powers*, pp. 65-66) and URBACH (*The Sages*, pp. 139, 743). Esp. noteworthy is the argument that the numerical equivalent of שדי equals מיטטרון (= 314) and hence may explain Metatron's association with the phrase "my name is in him." (2) It is unclear why URBACH (*The Sages*, p. 139) credits R. Idith with having introduced the name "from the onomasticon current in his Babylonian environment," since elsewhere he suggests the meaning "guide" (743 n. 15), a term derived from the Latin *metator* (as implied in *b.Abod.Zar.* 3b). (3) In "Metatron, the meaning of his name and his functions" (appendix in I. GRUENWALD, *Apocalyptic and Merkavah Mysticism*, pp. 235-41) Saul LIEBERMAN, with GRUENWALD (*ibid.*, p. 141 n. 32), revives the theory rejected by ODEBERG that "Metatron" transliterates a Grk term that had inherited connotations associated with σύνθρονος. LIEBERMAN argues that the sense of the prefixed συν- does not have to imply that one throne is shared; the shift to μετα- is explicable as an attempt to avoid a designation frequently applied to Christ. The difficulty with LIEBERMAN's view is that the term μεταθρόνος is thus far unattested in Grk and, if correct, would have to posit a direct shift from the Grk σύνθρονος to the Heb מיטטרון.

A connection between the name and divine throne, however, should not be waylaid. The mention of Metatron in *b.Sanh.* 38b appears just after a discussion concerning the plural "thrones" in Dan 7:9, one of several biblical texts which *Minim* interpreted as a reference God in the plural. Whereas the tradition ascribed to R. Akiba finds an allusions to a throne of God (=the "Ancient of Days") and a throne of David (one like a son of man), R. Jose applies the plural metaphorically: one throne for justice and the other for mercy. Another teacher, R. Eleazar b. Azariah, has "thrones" refer to the divine throne proper and to a footstool for God's feet. Furthermore, in the BOMBERG Edition of *b.Ḥag.* 15a it is Metatron's "sitting" (ישיבא) which leads "Aḥer," in his *pardes* vision (see following note), to conclude that there are "two heads" (ב' רשויות) in heaven, whereupon Metatron is led forth and punished. Here, it should be noted that ALEXANDER ("3 Enoch and the Talmud" 64-65) and MORRAY-JONES ("Hekhalot Literature and Talmudic Tradition: ALEXANDER's three Test Cases," *JStJud* 22 [1991] 23) consider the BOMBERG recension to be later than those preserved in the manuscripts Vaticanus 134 and Munich 95 which do not single out the motif of "sitting" as determinative. However, if underlying these versions is a suppressed (Aḥer) tradition such as is found in *3 En* 16:1-5--in which Metatron describes himself as "sitting on a great throne"--, as MORRAY-JONES argues, then the signification of the name in relation to the throne gains further credence. See also Wolfgang FAUTH,

tradition held in common by both sides of the dispute. It is only in response to the *Min*'s proposal to worship Metatron (ליה ניפלחו) that R. Idith dismisses any hint of veneration.[70] In view of this designation alone, one would be hard-pressed to suppose that the heretic is a "Christian," "non-Jewish," or merely someone on the outskirts of Judaism. Thus it is likely that an ultimately common tradition behind this passage has undergone redaction through a reshaping and redefining in response to a foregoing conflict.

Excursus

In this sense, SCHOLEM's historical reconstruction of a practical interest in the Merkabah in the Tannaitic period (SCHOLEM, *Major Trends*, p. 43 and *Jewish Gnosticism* throughout), with some modifications, provides a more satisfactory model for explaining the prohibitions against worshiping angels.[71] SCHOLEM's hypothesis, however, should be qualified in at least two points: One is the assumption that language about "ascent" or "descent" to the divine throne originates in a context of *mystical activity*. The other is his characterization of such speculation as "Jewish Gnosticism"; for critical assessments of this identification, see ALEXANDER, "The Historical Setting of the Hebrew Book of Enoch," *JJS* 28 (1977) 156-80; idem, "3 Enoch," in *OTP* 1.250-55; and Ira CHERNUS, *Mysticism in Rabbinic Judaism*, pp. 10-16. Despite these difficulties, SCHOLEM's attempt to take seriously the diversity of post-Second Temple Judaism provides a more realistic point of departure for assessing the particular claim of angel veneration. While speculation concerning the divine throne should not be confused with devotion to angelic beings, it is not inconceivable to suppose that the exegetical interest in the angelophanies of Exodus and heavenly creatures in Ezekiel generated strains in this direction.

David HALPERIN's dismissal of SCHOLEM's position (*The Merkabah in Rabbinic Literature*; cf. *The Faces of the Chariot*, pp. 11-37), for all its thoroughness and proper concern to treat the emerging mysticism as a literary phenomenon, remains unconvincing. The debate concerning mystical strains in the Tannaitic period has revolved around the well-known tradition about the four rabbis who entered a garden (*pardes*). According to HALPERIN, this *pardes*

"Tatrosjah-Totrosjah und Metatron in der jüdischen Merkabah-Mystik," *JStJud* 22 (1991) 83-86. Finally, a common (subsequent) association of Metatron with the divine throne is reflected in the Aram epithet "the great prince of his throne" (אסרא רבא דכורסיה) inscribed on a bowl found in Babylon; see text n. 49.11 in Charles D. ISBELL, *Corpus of the Aramaic Incantation Bowls* (SBLDS, 17; Missoula: SBL and Scholars, 1975) and the variation in 56.12-13 (אסרא רבה דכליה עלמא, "the prince of the entire universe").

[70] At least this much seems clear; but it is unnecessary to go as far as SCHOLEM (*Major Trends*, p. 67) who remarks that "the assumption that the verse in Exodus XXIV, 1 'Ascend to YHWH' refers to Metatron seems to contain an implicit recognition of the latter as the 'lesser Yaho,' which he explicitly becomes in later texts." While Scholem rightly posits an underlying tradition, its date and origin have been subjected to considerable debate (see the previous note).

[71] See n. 17 above.

tradition—variously attested in the Tos. (Ḥag. 2:3-4) and the Pal. (Ḥag. 2:1, 77b) and Bab. (Ḥag. 14b, 15a-b) Talmudim—did not originally refer to a mystical "ascent" to the merkabah. Instead, he argues that it was an allegory concerned with the Torah and its proper application; see also SCHÄFER, "New Testament and Hekhalot Literature" 27-28. HALPERIN explains R. Akiba's *safe departure* from the *pardes* in the original tradition (prooftexted by Sg of Sg's 1:3-4) as a metaphor for death, that is, what the *Mekhilta* (*Shirah* 3) and *Sifre Deut.* (343), referring to the same biblical text, refer to as an entry into the King's "chambers." This tradition, according to HALPERIN, was only later given a "mystical" framework in a "mystical collection" behind the rabbinic accounts. This explanation is hard to substantiate through the comparison. The original *pardes* tradition, constructed out of the elements common to the three versions, has the four men (Ben Azzai, Ben Zoma, Elisha b. Abuyah=Aḥer, and R. Akiba) *enter* a *pardes*. There, upon looking, Ben Azzai died, Ben Zoma went mad, and Elisha b. Abuya cut the young plants. Nothing is said about emerging from the *pardes*, except in the case of Akiba, who not only enters "safely" but also emerges "safely." In other words, the tradition associates death, when it is said to occur, with the entry and not the exit. It is difficult, then, to explain Akiba's *departure* as a metaphor for his martyrdom. The vision in its association with the *entry* is connected with the element of danger. See *1 En* 32:3, the Aram fragment of which, to a greater extent than the later (Grk and Eth) versions, underscores that Enoch's vision of the "garden of truth" does not involve an actual entry: ואהלפת לי פרדס קשט[א] ואחזית מן רחיק. If SCHOLEM is even partly correct, then it is not unreasonable to suppose that within the bounds of rabbinism there must have existed an esoteric mysticism (inherited from apocalyptic tradition) which, in specific cases, could lead to speculation which the rabbis would have regarded heretical. For a similar view, see MORRAY-JONES, *Merkabah Mysticism and Talmudic Tradition* (Cambridge Univ.: Diss., 1988); "Review of Halperin, *The Faces of the Chariot*," *JTS* 41 (1990) 585-89, esp. p. 585; "Hekhalot Literature and Talmudic Tradition" 1-5; and "Transformational Mysticism in the Apocalyptic-Merkabah Tradition" 1-31.

c. Summary

The above review of some of the more significant rabbinic texts yields several traditio-historical observations. First, the proscriptions which explicate the Second Commandment contain various lists: natural phenomena only,[72] natural phenomena and angels, and angels only. The existence of lists excluding either natural phenomena or angels suggests the existence of two originally separate traditions which in some passages have been brought together. Therefore, it would be misleading to conclude with HURTADO that such statements against venerating angels were merely the product of exegesis or that the mention of angels was a later novel element inserted into a previously existing tradition concerned primarily with natural phenomena. Each of these censures seems to have had a pre-history of its own. This differen-

---

[72] See n. 13 above.

tiation in tradition is further underscored by the fact that the angels in view (e.g., Michael), unlike elements of nature customarily associated with idolatry, are perceived as independent beings whose proper function is consistent with God's purposes. Finally, the midrashic arguments which depict the mode of God's rule over Israel and the other nations are formulated in a way that presupposes a prominence of angelic figures vis-à-vis heavenly bodies. The association of angels with God's indirect rule over other nations could easily lead to a further association of angels with pagan idolatry.[73]

Second, this differentiation of traditions makes it likely that the proscription against reverence toward angels was not integrated into explications of the Second Commandment until the Tannaitic period. While traditio-historical considerations suggest that the tradition against venerating angels is older, the *inclusion* of angels in midrashic exegesis of this particular injunction may be a relatively novel development. If so, it is legitimate to ask whether the inclusion of angels is merely the product of exegetical considerations and why the rabbis refer to angels to begin with; these prohibitions could have comprised some sort of dynamic response to developing attitudes towards angels which were perceived as a breach of the Torah. It may well be that the notion of angels as rulers over idolatrous nations explains this inclusion within some of the midrashim on the Second Commandment, while in the *Mekhilta de-Rabbi Ishmael*, on the other hand, speculation concerning beings "above" associated with the divine throne probably underlies the censure. In any case, the rabbinic traditions censuring the worship of angels, however ultimately related to the belief that only God is worthy of worship, cannot simply be explained as a logical explication of the biblical text.

Third, the activity rejected in relation to angels could take the form of invocation (*j.Ber.* 9:13a-b). While the notion of angelic mediation itself is not entirely discarded, the polemic likely took shape within a context of debate in an attempt to sort out a proper understanding. Here, a practice of directly petitioning angels for help could be perceived as a threat to monotheistic belief.

Fourth, it appears that the passages which focus exclusively on the veneration of angelic figures (*j.Ber.* 9:13a-b; *Exod.R.* 32:4; *b.Sanh.* 38b) as-

---

[73] A similar development is suggested by MACH (*Entwicklungsstadien*, p. 298), though in the motifs of image-making and sacrificing to angels he posits more specifically a background in magical practices. Nothing in such general strictures of idolatrous practices, however, specifically indicates such a context.

sume a milieu in which both sides of the debate shared common traditions, such as the names of angels, an interest in explicating the Torah (sometimes in connection with Ezekiel's vision), and an understanding of God in terms of kingship. Though any one of these elements cannot be identified with one religious stream alone, the combination of them (as in b.Sanh. 38b) suggests a concern to curb possible practical ramifications of speculation on the *Ma'aseh Merkabah* within Jewish circles.[74]

Taken together, these considerations add plausibility to the thesis that during the Tannaitic and Amoraic periods there existed among some Jews attitudes and practices which were suspected as posing a threat to monotheistic belief. Of course, these polemical texts do not (a) reveal much concerning the self-understanding of such Jews, that is, whether or not angels were being venerated at all, nor do they (b) represent material which can always be confidently assigned to the first-century CE or before. A more direct approach to these problems, on the basis of ideas preserved in early Jewish and Jewish-Christian traditions, will be attempted in our discussion of further polemical traditions (II.A.2-3) and non-polemical texts (II.B) below.

2. Angelophanic Prohibitions in Jewish and Jewish-Christian Writings

The worship of angels aligned with God is also vigorously rejected in some Jewish and Jewish-Christian documents which do so within the narrative context of an angelophanic encounter. The passages listed below (where possible, with approximate dates of the writing) consist of prohibitions directed against a seer's revering reaction to the presence of an angelic figure (supplied in parentheses):[75]

> Revelation 19:10 and 22:8-9 (end of 1st-cent. CE; 22:8- the angel who showed these things to me");
> *Apocryphal Gospel of Matthew* 3:3 ("an angel of God");
> Tobit 12:16-22 (3rd-2nd cent. BCE[76]; Raphael);

---

[74] Cf. SEGAL, *Two Powers*, p. 265.

[75] See the Appendix for a comparative synopsis of these and form-critically similar passages.

[76] The five mss of Tobit (4 Aram, 1 Heb) from Cave 4 of Qumran leave no doubt concerning an original Semitic composition which, on paleographical grounds, has a *terminus ad quem* in the 1st cent. BCE. The fragments of these mss still await official publication; see already Klaus BEYER, *Die aramäischen Texte vom Toten Meer. Ergänzungsband* (Göttingen: Vandenhoeck & Ruprecht, 1994) 134-47. Two of them (4Q196=papTob ar[a], 4Q200=Tob heb) preserve portions corresponding to 12:16-22; see MILIK, "La patrie de Job," *RB* 73 (1966) 522-30. The extant evidence for this part of Tobit, however, is so

Apocalypse of Zephaniah 6:11-15 (1st-2nd cent. CE; Eremiel);[77]
Ascension of Isaiah 7:18-23 and 8:1-10,15 (2nd cent. CE; 7:2-"a glorious angel");
2 Enoch 1:4-8 (see p.275 n. 1; 1st-2nd cent. CE; "two huge men");
3 Enoch 1:7 ("the princes of the chariot"); 16:1-5 (Metatron); and
Cairo Genizah Hekhalot Fragment "A/2,13-16" (Zehobadyah/ a youth/ Metatron).[78]

In addition there are passages in the New Testament, as well as in later Jewish and Christian writings which, though not always in an angelophanic setting, may well have been formally influenced by this "refusal tradition."[79] Here we may especially note Mark 10:17-18 and parallels ("Good Teacher..."; "Do not call me good; nobody is good except one, God"); Acts 10:25 (Peter's rejection of Cornelius' prostration); *History of the Rechabites* 5:3b-6:3 (a mild reprimand of Zosimus' posture); *Joseph and Aseneth* 14:9-11 (implicit rejection of Aseneth's fearful reaction) and 15:11-12 (esp. the longer recension; refusal to divulge name after Aseneth declares her intention to praise the angelic figure); *2 Enoch* 20:1-3 and 21:2-3; *Apocalypse of Abraham* 11:1-5

---

fragmentary that, unless otherwise indicated, it is necessary to rely on the Grk recensions.

[77] Following the numeration of O.S. WINTERMUTE, "Apocalypse of Zephaniah," in *OTP* 1.509-515. See 9:12-10:9 in G. STEINDORFF's edition of the Akhmimic ms. in *Die Apokalypse des Elias, eine unbekannte Apokalypse und Bruchstücke der Sophonias-Apokalypse* (TU, n.F. 2/3a; Leipzig: Hinrichs, 1899).

In the preceding passage (6:1-10) the seer is twice told not to worship "a great angel" (vv. 8,17) whom he has mistaken for God, "the Lord Almighty" (v. 4-*pchaeis ppantokratōr*; cf. also titles of address in v. 7). The reason for reprimanding the seer here does not require the formal angelophanic refusal; this "great angel," who emerges from seawaves of burning sulfur and pitch, is later identified as "the one who accuses men in the presence of the Lord" (6:17; see 7:9). The formal angelic refusal is reserved for the seer's encounter with Eremiel who is God's emissary.

[78] See the publication by GRUENWALD in *Tarb* 38 (1968) 362 (without a photograph for leaf 2) and the more complete publication by SCHÄFER, *Geniza-Fragmente zur Hekhalot-Literatur* (TSAJ, 6; Tübingen: J.C.B. Mohr (Paul Siebeck), 1984) 97-111 ("T.-S. K 21.95.C"), esp. pp. 104-105 (text and photo) and 111.

[79] This terminology will be applied throughout the ensuing discussion, though one should be aware that a refusal *by an angel* does not strictly characterize each of the encounters enumerated above. In the narrower sense, I apply the term to denote instances in which (an) angelic figure(s) who, while accompanying a visionary, *refuse(s)* an inappropriate show of veneration; in the list above this element only avails in Tob 12:17-18; *Apoc.Zeph.* 6:15; *Asc.Isa.* 8:5; Rev 19:10 and 22:9; and *2 En* 1:8. Common to all the passages, however, is the stern warning during a visionary encounter (in all cases, except Tob and *Apoc.Gosp.Mt.*, during a heavenly ascent) against worshiping an angel, with the (sometimes implicit) corollary that such an attitude should be reserved for God.

(if interpreted with 17:1-2); *Ladder of Jacob* 3; and *Apocalypse of Paul* (see note 81 below). Lastly, it is possible that such a tradition was adapted early on among Christian circles for christological emphasis, as, for instance, in the Matthean redaction of the Transfiguration (17:6-8; cf. Mk. 9:8) and resurrection (28:2-10; cf. Mk. 16:3-8) accounts (see note 136 below).

With respect to ascertaining devotional attitudes among early Jewish and Jewish-Christian groups, the significance of each of the angelophanic refusal texts depends first on a determination of obvious factors such as date and provenance, issues for which precise information is sometimes impossible to obtain. Nevertheless, given the use of this tradition in the Apocalypse of John and its occurrence in several documents dating to the second century CE or earlier, a form-critical analysis exploring questions of origin, form, development, and purpose is not unwarranted and may yield important conclusions for this study.

The literary form under consideration has, until recently, been the object of only scant thoroughgoing examination. The major exception is a seminal study by BAUCKHAM (1981),[80] who may be credited with the first detailed discussion of this tradition,[81] as well as with a cursory analysis of some of the more pertinent pericopes. The ultimate concern of BAUCKHAM's essay is to demonstrate how the refusal of worship by an angel in the *Ascension of Isaiah* and Revelation represents a Christian adaptation of a common, underlying motif also found in earlier, contemporary, and later Jewish and Christian writings. By arguing that this tradition could function rhetorically to safeguard monotheistic worship from a--in his view, mostly potential--danger of an excessive interest in prominent angels, BAUCKHAM has contributed to an understanding of how "high" christological claims among Christian circles could be combined with a claim to be monotheistic. In what follows we shall attempt to go beyond the more immediate aims of BAUCKHAM's study by (a) exploring the traditio-historical roots of this tradition and by (b) asking whether, on this basis, we can make inferences concerning the religious attitudes of any of the circles among which it circulated. Does the form of the prohibition--

---

[80] "The Worship of Jesus," esp. pp. 323-27. Unfortunately, I have not had access to a revised version of this article printed as chapter 4 in a collection of BAUCKHAM's essays, *The Climax of Prophecy: Studies on the Book of Revelation* (Edinburgh: T. & T. Clark, 1992).

[81] For more brief and less comprehensive treatments, see PERCY, *Probleme*, pp. 151-53; WINTERMUTE, "Apocalypse of Zephaniah," pp. 504-505; Martha HIMMELFARB, *Tours of Hell* (Philadelphia: Univ. of Pennsylvania, 1983) 65-66 and 151-56; Pierre PRIGENT, *L'Apocalypse de Saint Jean* (CNT, 14; Geneva: Labor et Fides, 1988) 285-87; and DUNN, *Partings of the Ways*, pp. 218-19.

in either a religiosity presupposed by its development or in a situation-oriented rhetorical function in any of the pertinent writings—betray an effort to counter a religious posture in which angels were actually being venerated?

The traditio-historical aspect of the problem as formulated requires that we devote attention to two further questions: (1) What are the salient features which set this tradition apart from others containing similar elements, and (2) how have the characteristic elements of the tradition acquired their polemical connotation? Since question (1) overlaps somewhat with the focus of BAUCKHAM's study, we begin here with a brief summary of his analysis and conclusions.

a. Bauckham's Study

In addition to Revelation and the *Ascension of Isaiah*, BAUCKHAM identifies an angel refusing worship in Tobit 12:16-22 (for him, "the earliest and mildest version"), the *Apocalypse of Zephaniah* (6:11-15, the Akhmimic Coptic version), the *Apocalypse of Paul* (the Sahidic Coptic version),[82] and the *Apocryphal Gospel of Matthew* 3:3. Of these writings, BAUCKHAM regards Tobit as a whole as pre-Christian and Jewish, considers the *Apocalypse of Zephaniah* as a Jewish document with hardly a conspicuous sign of Christian editing,[83] and

---

[82] Despite similarities with the emphasis in *Asc.Isa.* 7:21-22 on the visionary's ultimate status, this version of the longer *Apoc.Paul* does not actually contain an explicit denunciation of an unwarranted form of angel veneration; see the English trans. by E.A.W. BUDGE in *Miscellaneous Coptic Texts in the Dialect of Upper Egypt* (New York: AMS, 1977, repr. 1915) 1043-1084, esp. p. 1078. The seer (Paul) prostrates himself out of fear when he sees the angelic hosts worshiping God the Father. It is not clear whether the angelic guide's following statement ("Fear not, O Paul") was intended as a genuine reprimand or as words spoken to assuage the visionary's fright. Given the way in which Paul is addressed, it seems that the narrator meant the angel's words as comfort (cf. II.A.2.b.ii, pp. 89-90 below). Therefore, if the refusal tradition has been adapted by the writer of *Apoc.Paul*, it has undergone considerable modification.

[83] Correctly, in contrast to MACH, *Entwicklungsstadien*, pp. 295-96; see also *NTA*, 2.625. This point is esp. noteworthy since the manuscript and citation evidence for the *Apoc.Zeph*. indicates at least a transmission within Christian circles of Egypt: CLEMENT OF ALEXANDRIA, *Strom*. 5.11.77; a Sahidic frag.; and the Akhmimic ms mentioned in n. 77 above, in which it precedes the *Apoc. Elij*. (Christian in its present form). See CHARLESWORTH, *PMR*, pp. 95, 220-23 and M. GOODMAN and G. VERMES in *New Schürer*, 3,2.803-804. Concerning the possibility of Christian elements in *Apoc.Zeph*. 2:1-4 and 10:9, see the perceptive comments of WINTERMUTE, "Apocalypse of Zephaniah," pp. 501, 509-510 n. c, and 515 n. b. In any case, nothing in the angel's rejection of worship in 6:11-15 contains any hint of Christian reworking; it is thus safe to

Polemical Texts: Angelophanic Prohibitions 79

holds the remaining two as late and written by Christian authors.[84] Taken together, these texts comprise for BAUCKHAM "the evidence for the tradition in which an angel refuses worship."[85]

BAUCKHAM calls attention to other passages which he thinks contain other, yet similar, ways of safeguarding against angelolatry. Thus he notes that in the *Ladder of Jacob* 3 the face of the archangel Sariel is declared to be no match for that of God.[86] Further, the tradition preserved in *3 Enoch* 16:2-5--which above (p. 76) has been assigned to the refusal texts--asserts that the declaration of Aḥer, upon beholding Metatron enthroned and beset by an array of ministering angels and heavenly princes, that there are "two powers in heaven," is an irrevocable apostasy.[87] The fallacy of Aḥer's error is then visibly demonstrated; Metatron receives sixty lashes of fire and is coerced to stand (cf. par. *b.Ḥag.* 15a). Finally, in the tradition preserved in Cairo Genizah Hekhalot A/2 lines 13-16--again, included among the refusal texts above (p. 76)--, a writer leaves no doubt that the glorious appearance of "Zehobadyah" is merely derived from God's glory.[88]

---

assume with BAUCKHAM ("The Worship of Jesus" 324) that this section stems from the original (non-Christian Jewish) part of the document. If this view is correct, then *Apoc.Zeph.* becomes a valuable source of understanding angelological ascepts of the *Zeitgeist* within which the Apocalypse of John took shape (see Part Three, section IV.C, pp. 257-261 below).

[84] Concerning the *Apoc.Gosp.Mt.*, see below n. 115 (II.A.2.b.ii). The numerous parallels between the *Apoc.Paul* and the *Apoc.Zeph.*, in light of the former's expansionistic tendencies in some of the motifs shared, indicate a dependence, direct or indirect, of the *Apoc.Paul* upon the latter; see, most recently, the comparison by HIMMELFARB, *Tours of Hell*, pp. 147-51.

[85] "The Worship of Jesus" 326.

[86] Along roughly similar lines, we might note that such a comparison of physical features was placed within Christian tradition in service of Christology, as in the *Gosp. Pet.*, in which the two young men at the tomb are contrasted with the resurrected Lord (10:39-40): "While they [the soldiers] were relating what they had seen [to the centurion and the elders], they again saw three men coming out from the sepulcher, two of them supporting the other one, as cross following them, and the heads of the two *reaching unto heaven* (χωροῦσαν μέχρι τοῦ οὐρανοῦ), but that [the head] of him whom they led by the hand *overpassing the heavens*" (ὑπερβαίνουσαν τοὺς οὐρανούς); see *NTA*, 1.187. The Grk is cited according to Adolf HARNACK's edition in *Bruckstücke des Evangeliums und der Apokalypse des Petrus* (Leipzig: Hinrichs, 1893²).

[87] Preserved in MS Mün. 40; see SCHÄFER, *Synopse*, par. 856: "Return to me, apostate sons, except for Aḥer" (שובו בנים ג'יל בנים/שובבים חוץ אחר). The inclusion of the motifs of the angel's glorious appearance, the seer's reaction, and a rejection of this behavior, corresponding to a monotheistic emphasis on the supremity of the one, transcendent God, provides grounds for considering this passage as an adapted form of the refusal tradition.

[88] To BAUCKHAM's list of similar traditions one might add *Apoc.Abr.*

At the same time, BAUCKHAM observes that the passages just mentioned retain some of the traditional elements marking the angel's refusal of worship. Thus in the *Ladder of Jacob* the seer stresses that although the face of the archangel Sariel was "beautiful and awesome," he "did not fear" his appearance (3:3-5).[89] In *3 Enoch* 16 the privileged enthroned status of Metatron is qualified as only a matter of similitude;[90] the measures taken against Metatron, which in the manuscripts are placed in the mouth of Metatron himself, ensure that "the throne of glory" (כסא הכבוד) belongs only to "the Holy One, blessed be He."[91] Finally, in the fragment from the Cairo Genizah the worship of Metatron is censured with the injunction, "Do not bow down to him!" (1. 14—אל תשתחוה לו).

The discussion by BAUCKHAM suggests that an identification of the refusal tradition in any given instance rests on the presence of one or more of several traditional elements: (1) a seer's reverent posture before an angelic figure, whose prominence is marked by a glorious appearance or special mediating role; (2) the angel's explicit rejection of this posture (e.g., in the statement, "Do not fear/worship [me]!"), sometimes supplemented by the angel's emphasis that the seer is not inferior to him (e.g., "I am not your lord"/"I am a fellow-servant"); and (3) the attempt, usually by the angel, to steer, more properly, the seer's attention to God (e.g., "Worship God!"). Of these elements, (2) comprises the "refusal" itself, while (1) sets the stage and (3) expresses the tradition's monotheistic emphasis.

b. Components of the Angelic Refusal: The Origin and Development of the Tradition

On the basis of the traditional elements in Revelation and the *Ascension of Isaiah*, the evidence culled by BAUCKHAM identifies clearly what at least

---

17:2, in which the guiding angel (Iaoel), whose splendor is earlier (11:1-4) described in language reminiscent of Rev 1:14 and partly borrowed from Dan 7:9, is said to kneel down *with* Abraham and worship.

[89] Here we follow H.G. LUNT's trans. from the Slav version in *OTP*, 2. 408.

[90] Derivative characterizations are frequently given for other prominent angels in *3 En*: see 18:18 (ענפיאל), 24 (שופריאל and סופריאל-mss Vat. 228/4 and Mus.); 24:7a (כרוביאל); 26:7a (סרפיאל); 28:3a (עיריא).

[91] Significantly, the expression "the throne of glory" is in the Hekhalot literature nowhere associated with any figure besides God; see *3 En* 10:1, in which the throne made for Metatron is "a throne *like* the throne of glory" (כסא הכבוד); כסא מעין MS Mün. 40 in SCHÄFER, *Synopse*, par. 894).

seems to have been a circulating *literary tradition* which precluded a veneration of angels. But as the blending of the components of the tradition with other ways of discouraging reverence to angels suggests (e.g., as in the *Ladder of Jacob, Jos.Asen.* 15:11-12x, *Apoc.Abr.* 11:1-5 with 17:1-2, and perhaps the Hekhalot texts), the tradition, in its individual components, was rather fluid and hence easily adapted into various contexts (see pp. 76-77), and quite often into those containing a description of an angel's glorious appearance. The initial impression left is that we have to do with a convergence of motifs which also circulated orally and which, as widespread as it was, expressed a religious sentiment commonly held among Jews during the Greco-Roman period.

This latitude in formal elements could sometimes result in a certain degree of ambiguity. As we shall see below (II.A.2.b.i-iv), each of the traditional components of an angelophanic refusal, both in form and emphasis, could be applied with a variety of nuances. Consequently, in some instances a precise interpretation of the formal elements in an angelophany is difficult to obtain.[92] The complex development of traditional elements behind the refusal tradition accounts in large part for this difficulty. Therefore, a reconstruction of the origin, development, and purpose--that is, the religious function--of the angelophanic refusal tradition must account for the various ways in which the traditional elements were employed. This, in turn, may yield clues which indicate something about the religious conditions under which the tradition arose.

i. The Seer's Reaction to an Angelophanic Setting

As noted above, the seer in the refusal tradition is dissuaded from a posture which the angel regards as an act of worship. Is there a basis, then, to suppose that this tradition functioned to proscribe such reverent behavior, so that the criticism levelled at a seer may actually have been projected at an intended reader as well? Initially, this explanation might seem compulsory. In exploring this question, it is necessary to examine the context and significance of the seer's behavior which is then prohibited.

---

[92] E.g., (1) "Do not fear" as a prohibition is at times hard to distinguish from an expression intended as encouragement or comfort (e.g., *2 En.* 1:4-8; *Jos. and Asen.* 14:9-11; Tob 12:16); (2) the angel's attempt to direct the seer's attention toward God could be independent of the motif of a seer's inappropriate veneration (see II.A.2.b.ii, pp. 87-92 below).

Most obviously, angelophanic proscriptions express how a posture deemed fitting in one setting must be denied in another. The seer's behavior before an angelic figure is portrayed as inappropriate in such narratives because it has assumed a form which occurs in texts describing encounters with the divine. This includes reactions such as trembling (*2 En* 20:1; *Apoc.Paul*; *3 En* 16:2), terror/"fear" (Tob 12:16; *2 En* 20:1; 21:2; *3 En* 16:2), and "worship" (προσκύνησις)/prostration (*Apoc.Gosp.Mt.* 3:3-*adorans*; *Apoc.Zeph.* 6:5,14; Rev 19:10; 22:8; *Asc.Isa.* 7:21; *2 En* 21:2; cf. *3 En* 1:7). Each of the passages referred to here leaves an unmistakable impression of, to borrow Rudolf OTTO's expression, an encounter with the "numinous".[93] At the core, from which these terminologically different reactions emanate, is a basic disposition of fear (see pp. 87-92 below).

Furthermore, if the angelic refusal is to be understood as a response to a seer's behavior, it becomes a matter of relevance to reflect on the following distinction. As BAUCKHAM rightly observes, the fear of the visionary in such an encounter may take on either voluntary or involuntary qualities.[94] Of special interest for the question of religious praxis would, of course, be volitional responses since they could be expected to provide the most suitable indicator of a religious posture. In this sense, it might be useful to speak of an author's wish to express a seer's *intention*, generated by a sense of awe, to worship the angelic figure, a posture which can often be distinguished from responses which are forced upon the seer (such as terror, trembling, or falling down "as though dead"). This distinction might then lead one to expect that the communicative import behind the angel's exhortation that the seer worship God should reflect the degree of the seer's volition, while otherwise--when the seer has been overwhelmed by the fear--an intentionality in such an exhortation is less conspicuous. Despite these foregoing deliberations, the texts themselves often do not harbor the transparency that such a distinction is supposed to bring. Indeed, it is sometimes quite difficult to identify precisely the nature of a seer's response; correspondingly, it may in fact be that the involuntary-voluntary categories are not mutually exclusive. For this reason, OTTO reasoned that an experience of the "numinous" may involve the two contrasting, yet complementary and simultaneous, aspects of terror (=involuntary reactions, depicted by the expressions *myster-*

---

[93] *The Idea of the Holy*, translated by John W. HARVEY (London/Oxford/New York: Oxford Univ., 1950²) 5-11.

[94] "The Worship of Jesus" 323.

ium tremendum, majestas) and entrancement (=voluntary reactions, depicted by the expression *fascinans*).[95]

Hence, for all the potential significance of terming a given reaction to an angelophany as "voluntary" or "involuntary," the narration of the visionary's disposition alone cannot suffice as a reason for the angelic censure. Indeed, in biblical and early Jewish writings *any one of the above-mentioned reactions to the presence of an angel or human superior* (p. 82) *is frequently not deemed an act which runs at all counter to the worship of one God*.[96] Such behavior was of course probably acceptable within a monotheistic framework on the grounds that the one being honored was thought to be God's instrument or that the venerative action somehow accorded with divine purpose.[97]

Whether it be a matter of voluntary or involuntary response, the refusal seems to presuppose an allusion to or description of the angel's elaborate

---

[95] See *ibid.*, pp. 12-40. It is therefore precarious to explain reprehensible behavior as voluntary alone; see, e.g., Mt 28:4-5 and *3 En* 1:7.

[96] Some of the more notable examples are listed here, in which the there is no effort of any kind to counter these reactions. *Trembling*: 1 Sam 16:4 (before Saul), 21:1 (David); Dan 10:10-11 ("a certain man"/angel); Acts 16:9 (Paul and Silas). *Terror/"fear"*: *2 En* 1:7 (two angels; esp. Rec. J); Ex 34:30 (Moses); Acts 16:29 (Paul and Silas). *"Worship"* (προσκύνησις)/ *prostration*: Gen 18:2 (3 visitors; cf. v. 1); 19:1 (two angels); 23:7 (sons of Heth); 33:6-7 (Esau); 42:6 (Joseph); 43:26 (Joseph); 48:12 (Jacob); Jos 5:14 ("captain of the Lord's host"); Judg 6:19 (angel of the Lord; LXX Cod. Alex.- προσεκύνησεν); Ruth 2:10 (Boaz); 1 Sam 20:41 (Jonathan); 24:6 (Saul); 25:23 (David); 28:14 (Samuel); 2 Sam 9:8 (David); 14:22,33 (David); 24:20 (David); 1 Kgs 1:23 (David), 53 (Solomon); 2:19 (Bathsheba); 2 Kgs 2:15 (Elisha); 4:37 (Elisha); 1 Chr 21:21 (David); Dan 8:17-18 (Gabriel); Rev 3:9 (those belonging to the church at Philadelphia); *Jos.Asen.* 5:7 (Joseph); 15:11-12 (longer recension; the "man" from heaven); 22:5 (Joseph); 22:8; 28:2,9 (Aseneth); 29:6 (Levi); *T.Abr.* 3:5-6 (angel; Rec. A); 9:1-2 (Michael; Rec. A); PHILO, *Jos.* 164 (Joseph; cf. Gen 42:6); *Somn.* 2.90 (sons of Heth; cf. Gen 23:7); and *3 Bar* 11:6 (Slav-an angel before Michael; Grk-the accompanying angel before Michael).

Note, in particular, the passage in JOSEPHUS (*Ant.* 11.331-333) in which Alexander the Great explains to Parmenion, the Macedonian general, why he prostrated himself before the high priest in Jerusalem: "I did not worship (προσεκύνησα) this one (i.e., the high priest), but God for whom he is honored [to serve] as high priest."

[97] See H. GREEVEN on προσκυνέω, προσκυνητής in *TDNT* v. 6, pp. 761-63; Joachim BECKER, *Gottesfurcht im Alten Testament* (AnBib, 25; Rome: Pontifical Biblical Institute, 1965) 39-41,43.

appearance within the narrative.[98] The context is, above all, *angelophanic*.[99] The vision of a prominent angel, as narrated in the texts, might not only inspire fear and admiration for God's angel, but could also yield an unhealthy speculative fascination which, in turn, could be condemned by being associated with idolatry. In other words, those documents employing the *refusal* tradition at the same time often contain elements which represent an underlying

---

[98] This obtains in the following texts: (1) Tob 12:15-16--the prostration and fear of Tobit and Tobias follows immediately upon Raphael's declaration of his name and that he was "one of the seven angels who stand ready and enter before the glory of the Holy One/Lord (v. 15-Cod. Sin.: ἡ δόξα τοῦ ἁγίου; A,B: ἡ δόξα τοῦ κυρίου)"; see also 11:14, where God's "holy angels" are praised alongside God: Εὐλογητὸς εἶ ὁ θεὸς καὶ εὐλογητὸν τὸ ὄνομά σου εἰς τοὺς αἰῶνας καὶ εὐλογημένοι πάντες οἱ ἅγιοί σου ἄγγελοι. The connection between Raphael's appearance and their venerative reaction is reflected in both recensions: the men are prostrate during the encounter, but when they finally stand after the angel's exhortation, the angel is no longer in sight (v. 21-Cod. Sin.: καὶ ἀνέστησαν καὶ οὐκέτι εἶδον [A,B: ἠδύναντο ἰδεῖν] αὐτόν). See also 4Q200+4Q196 to 12:22, in which the accent on the angel's appearance may be even more pronounced than in the Grk recensions: "...praising] his great work and marvelling (ptc.; Grk A,B-adj.) at how the angel of God had appeared to them." (2) *Apoc.Zeph.* 6:11-12--the seer reacts (v. 13) to the angel's "face shining like the rays of the sun in its glory...like that which is perfected in its glory. And he was girded as if a golden girdle were upon his breast. His feet were like bronze which is melted in a fire" (trans. WINTERMUTE, *OTP* 1.513). (3) *Asc.Isa.* 7:2 (and "Greek Legend" 2:6)--the "glorious angel" who leads Isaiah to the seventh heaven appears with such glory that Isaiah "cannot describe the glory of this angel." (4) *2 En* 1:4-5 (Rec.'s J and A)--Enoch prostrates before the "two huge men" (v. 7) after their splendorous appearance is described (variously in the recensions). (5) *2 En* 20:1 (J and A) --Enoch apparently reacts to the "great light" emanating from the heavenly creatures at God's throne in the seventh heaven. (6) *3 En* 1:7--R. Ishmael's trembling and falling is linked to "the radiant appearance of their [the princes of the chariot] eyes and the bright vision of their faces." (7) *3 En* 16:2--Aḥer reacts to Metatron's royal appearance. (8) C. Gen. Hekh. A/2, 14-- the admonition not to bow to the "youth" is followed by an explanation of the real nature of his appearance. Cf. Mt 28:3 and *Apoc.Abr.* 11:1-5. The angel's appearance, on the other hand, does not seem to have been an immediate factor in Rev 19:10; 22:8-9; and *Apoc.Gosp.Mt.* 3:3.

[99] This postulate may be supplemented by the observation that, except in Tobit (earliest extant angelic refusal) and *Apoc.Gosp.Mt.* (late adaptation), the refusal in heavenly journey accounts occurs alongside, and sometimes in conjunction with, the seer's observation of and/or participation in angelic worship (in which the appearance of angels is noted or implied); see *Apoc.Zeph.* 8:1-4 (and the citation in CLEMENT of ALEXANDRIA, *Strom.* 5.11.77); *Apoc.Paul* 11(?); *Asc.Isa.* 7:15-17,19-20,29-30,36-37; 8:3,17-22; (the degree of angels' glory corresponds to the relative quality of their praise); Rev 19:1-8; 22:3; *2 En* 20:1-4 (J,A); 21:1-3 (J,A); *3 En* 1:10-12;15:1; and, of course, throughout the Hekhalot texts. The concurrence of the rejection of angel worship with a vision of angelic worship of God discourages the assumption that these are unrelated alternatives; see n. 184 below.

special interest in prominent angels *per se*. How are these conflicting attitudes to be understood?

In discussing the passages containing the refusal tradition, BAUCKHAM offers a possible explanation for the polemic against improper reverence to angels as follows: since "the glory of all angels to some extent resembles the glory of their Maker...the danger of idolatry was always present in circles which devoted as much attention to angels as apocalyptic and *Merkabah* mysticism."[100] A venerative response to glorious angelic figures is in itself, however, no guarantee that the writer of a given narrative would have the seer understand it that way. In some of the refusal texts a visionary's response to the divine resemblance of angels is simply portrayed as a matter of genuine confusion or mistaken identity.[101] In this case, there would be nothing which reflects a real danger of angelolatry; in actuality, the seer is depicted as one who at all times has harbored a monotheistic devotion towards God. In such cases the angel's refusal of worship would merely function to specify the precise purpose and content of the apparition.

The interpretation of a seer's (inappropriate) response to angelophanies can be an even more complex matter.[102] Though the possibility of attributing to seers a confusion of identity cannot be discounted in some instan-

---

[100] "The Worship of Jesus" 327. Though BAUCKHAM's immediate point of reference is the visions of Metatron in the Hekhalot literature, his comment appears to be a general explanation for the association of angelolatry with idolatry reflected in the other texts (discussed on pp. 323-26). See also p. 324, where BAUCKHAM argues that "the divine glory" emanating from prominent angels evokes a reaction that comes "very close to the essentially religious response to the numinous."

[101] See esp. *Apoc.Zeph.* 6:4 (the angelic "accuser"),13 (Eremiel; cf. n. 77 above); perhaps *3 En* 16:2 (Metatron); and C. Gen. A/2 Recto ll. 14-16 (Metatron). In *Somn.* 1.232, PHILO entertains the possibility of confusion arising when God appears in an angelic form which bears a resemblance (δόξα) to and is yet distinguishable from God. Here, however, this confusion is considered normal and is not expressly censured.

[102] For instance, though the visionary in the *Apoc.Zeph.* confuses Eremiel with "the Lord Almighty" (6:13-*pchaeis pantokratōr*), the narrative itself (in the first person) introduces him as "a great angel" (6:11). Thus the genuine confusion is mitigated by the literary context. While the angel announces the error to the seer, the reader--who has no doubt about the figure's angelic identity--is allowed from the start to see the dangerous implications of the seer's actions, implications which the seer, as represented in the narrative, knows through hindsight. On the other hand, Zephaniah's confusion of the "accuser" with God is not qualified in such a way. Nevertheless, this figure's emergence from a sea of fire and slime (originally mistaken for "a sea of water"; 6:1-3), as well as the repeated phrase "I thought" (6:2,4; see v.13), may have been elements which would have sufficiently raised the suspicions of readers.

ces,[103] it remains that the polemics against an unwarranted form of veneration in these visions (with or without descriptions of the angels)--to the extent that they are represented as encounters with the "numinous"--may have represented a way of coming to terms with a potential or real danger inherent in the application of language customarily used to describe God to *another* heavenly being. If this is the case, then the *mode of the seer's reaction*, if understood as a reaction to the grandeur of a heavenly angel, takes on a special import after all. A posture reminiscent of theophanies, however appropriate, nevertheless indicates a disturbing ambiguity which led some authors to provide for a further clarification within the narrative.

Thus the refusal tradition cannot be explained on the basis of what the narrative communicates about *either* the angel's characteristics *or* the seer's reaction alone. The symbiosis of both elements, the angelic appearance or action provoking an ensuing reaction, are indispensable to the scene and provide it a basis for its rhetorical thrust. Once this combination of motifs is further supplemented with language castigating idolatry, the encounter assumes a polemical tone which corresponds to an author's specific emphasis.

The rejection of venerative behavior towards angels through the application of language proscriptive of idolatry will be discussed below (pp. 91-92). For now, we may infer that the equivocation of an angel with an idol

---

[103] In attempting to explain the element of danger in the passage concerning entry into *pardes* (b.Ḥag. 14b), SCHOLEM cited a passage from the Mün. ms 22 of the so-called *Hekhalot Zutrati* (i.e., the "Lesser Hekhalot"), which speaks of gate-keepers (=angels) confusing "one who is not worthy of seeing the King in his Beauty" (*Major Trends*, pp. 52-53, text on p. 361 n. 47: שאינו ראוי לדאות מלך ביפיו היו נוחצין בלבו). The confusion here, as in *Apoc.Zeph.* 6:1-3, has to do with the perception of water in the vision. The passage as a whole, presented in synopsis by SCHÄFER (*Synopse*, par. 407), is preserved in mss in New York (Jewish Theological Seminary="N8128"), Philadelphia (Dropsie="D436"), Munich ("M40"), and Oxford ("O1532"), but the confusion motif is absent in D436 and M40; concerning problems in establishing a clear literary context for the vision, see SCHÄFER, "Aufbau und redaktionelle Identität der *Hekhalot Zutrati*," in idem, *Hekhalot-Studien* (TSAJ, 19; Tübingen: J.C.B. Mohr [Paul Siebeck], 1988) 50-62, esp. pp. 56-62. HIMMELFARB (*Tours of Hell*, pp. 153-55) relates this motif of confusion to the general notion of "the visionary's inability to perceive accurately in the heavenly realm," and therefore associates it with the mistaken identification of an angel in the *Apoc.Zeph*. However parallel the structures of the *Apoc.Zeph.* 6:1-17 and b.Ḥag. 15a-b (confusion of water followed by confusion of an angelic figure) may be, it is more suitable to argue that the refusal tradition itself represents an independent development (see below). A distinction needs to be made between confusion and danger, on the one hand, and the origin and development of the refusal tradition, on the other. Whereas the latter may have been taken up in the former, it would be misleading to assume that writers assumed a seer's confusion whenever they made use of the refusal tradition.

could not have been achieved without some degree of conscious reflection. Of course, as far as the question of idolatry is concerned, any show of reverence towards other deities, whether because they were simply alien or fashioned by human hands, is condemned throughout Jewish literature. Moreover, it is not surprising to find that a posture such as προσκύνησις is consistently avoided before figures who were either associated with such deities or who themselves were thought to pose a threat to the well-being of the Jewish people.[104] However, in order to safeguard a strict monotheistic belief from unacceptable reverence *toward angelic beings*, it would have been necessary to adjust the biblical injunctions against idolatry to fit a more comprehensive application. While the idolatrous association of foreign monarchs or persons of prominence with alien gods is, given the inimical overtones, comprehensible, a further logical step would have been necessary before certain forms of reverence could be prohibited in relation to angels subordinate to--that is, aligned with--the purposes of God. In order to trace this traditio-historical development, we turn to the angelic prohibition itself.

ii. Fear: The Seer's Veneration and the Angel's Prohibition

At the heart of the tradition is the declaration by the angel which dissuades the seer from an inappropriate show of veneration. In the sources this could take one of several forms: "Do not fear" (Tob 12:17); "Do not worship" (*Apoc.Zeph.* 6:15; *Asc.Isa.* 7:21); "Do not bow down to him" (C. Gen. A/2 R l. 14); and "Do not see (to do it)" (Rev 19:10; 22:9). The most basic form of this rejection is "Do not fear" (as in Tob 12:17), from which the other, more specific formulations, may be said to have derived. Verbal roots for "to fear," as in early Semitic usage, could either simply denote "to be frighten-

---

[104] GREEVEN ("προσκυνέω, προσκυνητής, pp. 761-62) and BAUCKHAM ("The Worship of Jesus" 337 n. 14) both cite the LXX addition to Esth 13:12-14 as the "first" instance of protest against προσκύνησις. Their claim is true insofar as Mordecai's refusal to bow before Haman amounts to a monotheistic confession of loyalty to God. Their claim, however, should not be misconstrued to mean that the refusal to prostrate oneself out of loyalty to God was non-existent before then; the refusal to do so is already implied in 1 Kgs 19:18 (LXX-ἐπροσκύνησεν αὐτῷ for MT לוֹ נָשַׁק). Indeed, the renderings of the LXX, and especially the Second Tg. to Esth 3:3 may be understood as elaborations of the biblical strictures against idolatry (e.g., Ex 23:24; Lev 26:1; Deut 5:9; Jos 23:7). Cf. also PHILO, *Gaium*, 114-116: προσκύνησις (before Gaius) is "a barbarous custom" (116) which the Jews reject because "there is but one God the Father and Creator of the world" (115).

ed" or carry the further sense of "to revere,"[105] depending upon the context. While not exclusive of the former connotation, the prohibition, in denoting a censurable form of devotion, represents the convergence of two usages of the phrase "Do not fear" in the literatures of ancient Israel and Early Judaism.

First, the expression "Do not fear" was frequently used in biblical and Ancient Near Eastern literature to communicate a message of divine comfort. In uncertain or adverse circumstances, recipients of the message are told not to be afraid and then are assured of God's redemptive activity on their behalf. In the Hebrew scriptures this assurance could be variously expressed through a promise of future progeny, protection from the enemy, victory in battle, or a combination thereof.[106] Here the phrase most often presupposes a "real-life" situation faced by the seer; as such, its meaning does not stand alone within a narrative context, but is linked to a promise which betokens a favorable outcome for the predicament. In the biblical texts, this form of

---

[105] These two senses are well attested for the Semitic roots *yr'* and *sht'/tt'* (Heb, Ugar), *palaḫu* (Akkad) and *dḥl* (Aram) in the Hebrew scriptures and ANE texts. For comprehensive discussions of such occurrences, see FUHS, "ירא, *yare'*," in eds. G. Johannes BOTTERWECK and Helmer RINGGREN, *TDOT* vol. 6, trans. David E. GREEN (Grand Rapids: Wm. B. Eerdmans, 1990) 290-315 and Mayer I. GRUBER, "Fear, Anxiety and Reverence in Akkadian, Biblical Hebrew and Other North-West Semitic Languages," *VT* 40 (1990) 411-22.

[106] See Gen 15:1; 26:24; 28:13 LXX; 46:3 (to patriarchs); Deut 1:21; 3:2 (par. Num 21:34) (to Moses); Deut 31:8; Jos 8:1; 2 Kgs 19:6 (par. Isa 37:6); Hag 2:5; Isa 7:4; 10:24; LXX 13:2; (to monarchs); Deut 20:3; 31:6; Isa 10:24; 35:4; 40:9; 41:10,14; 43:1,5; 44:8; 2 Chr 20:15; Neh 4:8; Jer 30:10; 46:27,28; Zeph 3:16 (to the community of Israel/Judah); Ezek 2:6-7; Jer 1:17 (cf. LXX) (to prophets). In the NT see Acts 18:9 (ὁ κύριος to Paul). The form-critical kernel of these passages has been identified by Edgar W. CONRAD as divine communications to monarchs in "War Oracles" well attested in Ancient Near Eastern literature; see CONRAD, *Fear not Warrior. A Study of 'al tira' Pericopes in the Hebrew Scriptures* (BJS, 75; Chico: Scholars, 1985). CONRAD argues that the original context of exhortation, along with its warrior imagery, was subsequently extended analogically to divine communications in promises to patriarchs, calls narratives of prophets, and in reassurances to Israel as a whole.

The exhortation similarly appears in reassurances mediated or given by humans who have been invested with authority; see, e.g., Gen 43:23 (Joseph to his brothers); Ex 14:13 (Moses to the Israelites); Jos 10:25 (Joshua to Israelites); 1 Sam 23:17 (David to Mephibosheth); 2 Sam 13:28 (Absalom to his servants); 1 Kgs 17:13 (Elijah to the widow); 2 Kgs 6:16 (Elisha to his servant); 25:24 (Gedaliah to the Judeans; par. Jer 40:9-10); 1 Chr 28:20 (David to Solomon); 2 Chr 20:17 (Jahaziel to the Judeans); and 32:7 (Hezekiah to his army commanders). Cf. also the adaptation of Deut 20:2-4 in 1QM 10.3 and 15.8 (high priest to Israel).

reassurance, though often placed directly within a theophany, could also be mediated by a prophet[107] or by an "angel" (מלאך).[108]

By definition, neither a theophany nor a message conveyed through a prophet would have been viewed as a threat to monotheistic belief. This, however, may or may not have been true in the case of angelophanies. While in both the Hebrew scriptures and early Jewish writings it was not uncommon to have messages of reassurance mediated through "angels,"[109] the visionary aspect of such encounters raised a further possibility: Sometimes not only the visionary's human circumstances but also, as in *theo*-phanies of biblical and early Jewish tradition,[110] the angelic vision or encounter could itself become the source of the visionary's alarm.[111] Whereas the use of angels as mediating

---

[107] See instances listed in the previous footnote.

[108] See esp. Gen 21:17 (angel of God) and 2 Kgs 1:15 (angel of the Lord). See also Judg 6:11-24, though here the "angel of the Lord" is difficult to distinguish from "the Lord," to whom the reassurance is attributed (v. 23). It is uncertain whether, at this stage, the angel is being referred to as an independent being or is intended as an angelomorphic *theophany*.

[109] In addition to the biblical passages indicated in the previous footnote, see Gen 16:7-14; Mt 1:20-21; Mk 16:5-7; Lk 1:11-20, 26-35; and 2:8-12. In early Jewish literature, see also Tob 5:15; 6:18; *Jub* 32:24; *2 En* 21:3; *Apoc.Zeph.* 4:9; *3 Bar* 8:5 (Slav); *Apoc.Abr.* 9:3-4 and 16:2; and *T.Jac.* 2:4-27; 3:5. An apparent derivation from "Do not fear" in angelophanies is represented by the common angelic greeting, "Peace to you"; see Judg 6:23 (יהוה="angel of the Lord"; meaning is par. to אל תירא), *T.Is.* 2:2, and *Hist. Rech.* 4:2-3 (meaning par. to "Do not fear"). Similarly, see *Jos.Asen.* 14:11 (and 15:2,4,6); 26:2; and 28:7.

[110] Gen 18:1-2; Isa 6:5; Ezek 3:23; 43:3; 44:4; Dan 7:15,28; *1 En* 14:13-14,24; 71:11; *2 En* 22:4-5; *Vit.Ad.Ev.* 26:1; 27:1; 28:1; *Apoc.Mos.* 22:3; 23:2; and *Apoc.Abr.* 10:1-5.

[111] Hence the significance of the angel's appearance. In addition to passages with the refusal tradition, the seer's fear (here not regarded as reverential) is linked to the appearance of the angelic figure(s) in the following texts: Dan 10:4-14 (vv. 5-6, *a certain man*: "clothed in linen, and his loins girt with a belt of gold from Uphaz, and his body like beryl, and his face as the appearance of lightning, and his eyes like flaming torches, and his arms and legs like burnished bronze, and the sound of his words like the sound of a multitude"), 18-21; *T.Abr.* 3:5-6 (Rec. A: "the face of *the angel*"; cf. 9:1-3, Rec. A); *2 En* 1:4-8 (Rec.'s J and A; *two huge men*: "Their faces were like the shining sun; their eyes were like burning lamps..."); *Apoc. Abr.* 11:3-4 (*Iaoel*: "the appearance of his body was like sapphire, and the aspect of his face was like chrysolite, and the hair of his head like snow. And a kidaris on his head, its look that of a rainbow, and the clothing of his garments purple; and a golden staff in his right hand"); *Jos.Asen.* 14:9-11 (*a man from heaven*: "his face was like lightning, and his eyes like sunshine, and the hairs of his head like a flame of fire of a burning torch, and hands and feet like iron from a fire..."; the longer version is more extensive). In the later *Hist.Rech.* 5:4, the seer (Zosimus) prostrates before the "naked man" whose face looked like that of an angel (5:4); the latter re-

agents may have originally functioned either to certify the divine origin of a communication or to avoid facile assertions about "seeing" God directly, *the angelic vision itself*--and especially the fear engendered by it--*became an obstacle to an appropriate reception of the message*. As a result, in some texts containing the refusal tradition the phrase "Do not fear" is less intended as comfort than as a prohibition; though in a visionary context not entirely inconsistent with the motif of comfort, the expression (or one of its derivatives) could stand alongside or, at times, even supplant the force of an exhortation.[112]

Given such a proscriptive connotation, the expression would then have functioned to divert the seer's focus from the visionary medium and to direct

---

sponds by raising Zosimus and saying "Do not fear," perhaps a mild rejection of this posture (but cf. 6:3!).
   On the necessary distinction between אל־תירא as comfort and reaction to a numinous encounter, see BECKER, *Gottesfurcht*, p. 53.

[112] Two biblical passages illustrate how the motifs of reassurance and prohibition from fear could already be merged or juxtaposed in non-angelophanic traditions: (1) At the conclusion of his vision of the throne, Ezekiel is told twice not to fear (אל תירא + מ-, 2:6 *bis*, LXX once; cf. 3:9) the Israelites to whom he is being sent. The phrase is not used, however, in connection with Ezekiel's reaction to the vision (1:28); he is simply raised to his feet in order to receive the message (2:1; cf. 3:24). Though the element of fear is associated with both the vision and call, the phrase אל תירא is actually reserved for the latter, thus directing attention away from the vision itself and underscoring its purpose in relation to Ezekiel's mission.
   (2) In Gen 50:18-21 the expression appears twice, once as a prohibition and once as a form of reassurance. In the MT the brothers' fear of Joseph bears two dimensions: (a) the fear of punishment after the death of their father Jacob and (b) the reverence they show toward Joseph ("they came and fell before him") as they beg for forgiveness. Joseph's counters both emotional reactions with the phrase "Do not fear" in vv. 19 (followed by the rhetorical התחת אלהים אני, "Am I in the place of God?"; cf. Gen 30:2) and 21 (followed by a promise to provide for them). In v. 19 Joseph regards his brothers' prostrate petition for forgiveness as a posture appropriate to God alone. *Beshallah* 1 on Ex 13:19 in *Mek. de-Rabbi Ishmael* shows how later interpretation embellished the rhetorical question as an indication of the subordinate position of Joseph's coffin to the ark during the wandering in the wilderness. In the LXX tradition, the expression also appears twice, but the motif of reassurance predominates; the brothers' petition and reverence is not viewed as reprehensible in any way. Joseph's response would initially appear to make a point opposite to that of the MT (τοῦ γὰρ θεοῦ εἰμὶ ἐγώ). The gen. case, here without a preposition (τοῦ θεοῦ), could either reflect a later tendency to consider Joseph in exalted terms (cf. *Jos.Asen.* 14:8-11 [the angelic figure resembles Joseph]; 17:8-9; 18:11 [God's "firstborn son" in Syr and Grk mss]; 18:1,2 ["powerful one of God"]) or serve to align Joseph's promise to the brothers with God's purposes for good (vv. 20-21 and Gen 45:1-7,11). Though the determination of a precise meaning is elusive, the absence of any equivalent for ויפל in the LXX argues in favor of the latter possibility; in this sense, see PHILO, *Jos.* 266; *Migr.* 22.160; and *Somn.* 2.107.

it to the purpose of the vision. In this way, unlike contexts in which a message of assurance predominates, "Do not fear" acquired a connotation distinct from the aims of the vision itself. Two developments may be inferred from this shift in function: First, we may assume that the idea of a numinous appearance of chief angelic figures had become an acceptable commonplace among circles in which literature showing an interest in them flourished. Second, such a fascination with the mien of prominent angels necessitated a restructuring of traditional theophanic motifs, sometimes to the extent that any notion of angelic rivalry to God had to be dispelled before the message could be communicated at all. In other words, an undivided devotion to God in these instances could no longer be taken for granted. Thus in some instances the meaning of "Do not fear!" evolved into "Do not fear [me]!".

The second traditional complex containing "Do not fear" offers some insight into the intensity of its prohibitive force. Though less frequently attested in biblical and early Jewish texts than the idea of assurance, "Do not fear"--followed by a direct object (e.g., Heb-אֶת; Grk-accusative) or prepositional phrase (Heb-מִפְּנֵי; Grk-accusative, either as semitizing translation or composition)--also specified a monotheistic stricture forbidding the worship of alien gods and idols.[113] As such, the expression is not found in visionary contexts. Rather, it served as a negative counterpart for the well attested notion in which the root ירא (as verb and noun) denotes an exclusive reverence toward God.[114] Given this meaning, "Do not fear" in angelophanic con-

---

[113] The predominant grammatical construction is the verb "to fear" followed by a prepositional phrase which includes the noun (e.g., verb + מִפְּנֵי). The connotation of reverence is even more pronounced in those instances in which the alien gods constitute a direct object for the verb; see esp. Judg 6:10 and 2 Kgs 17:35,37,38. The influence of the dir. obj. construction is seen in LXX translation of other passages. In this form, the proscription sounds one of the central themes of *Ep.Jer.* (vv. 16,23,29,65,69-μὴ φοβηθῆτε αὐτοὺς αὐτά).

[114] For example, in Deut 6:13 the command to "fear the Lord your God" (אֶת יהוה אֱלֹהֶיךָ תִּירָא; LXX-κύριον τὸν θεόν σου φοβηθήσῃ [A προσκυνήσεις]) is synonymous with the injunction to "serve him" (אֹתוֹ תַעֲבֹד; LXX-αὐτῷ λατρεύσεις); cf. also Jos 24:14 and 1 Sam 12:14,24. In addition, this meaning--with the verb ירא and/or φοβεῖν in the Greek versions taking God as the direct object--is especially frequent in the Psalms (e.g., 14:4; 21:23; 24:12; 30:19; 32:8; 33:7; 59:4; 60:5; 65:16; 66:7; 84:9; 85:11; 101:15; 102:11; 110:5; 111:1; 113:21; 117:4; 118:63; 127:1; 134:20; 144:19; 146:11), wisdom literature (e.g., Prov 3:7; Eccl 5:6; 7:19; 8:12; Sir 1:13; 2:7; 6:16; 7:31; 10:19; 15:1; 21:6; 25:10; 26:3; 31:13; 35:14; 36:1), and exilic and post-exilic prophets (e.g., Hos 10:3; Mic 6:9; Mal 1:6; 3:5,16; 4:2; Jer 5:22; 33:19). See

texts could be made to reinforce the prohibition by underscoring the need to safeguard monotheistic devotion.

Both of these functions--whether to give assurance by announcing divine interventive activity or to warn against idolatry--are presupposed in the refusal tradition. On the one hand, the polemic against foreign deities incompatible with the God of Israel is now directed against angels who, however, are aligned with God. On the other hand, whereas in visionary contexts the phrase "Do not fear" functioned as an exhortation based on the divine promise to act on behalf of the human addressee, it has evolved into a statement that clears the way for a following summons to render the devotion due God alone.

In summary, on the narrative level of the texts themselves, two recurring elements combine to prompt the refusal of worship: (1) the angel's (or angels') countenance and (2) the visionary's subsequent venerative behavior. Traditio-historically, the refusal tradition represents a transformation of announcements of divine reassurance to angelic injunctions within a visionary setting, while the traditional proscription against the worship of alien gods has been imported into this context in order to delineate the bounds of monotheistic belief.

iii. *The Angelic Denial of Superiority over the Seer*

This element in the refusal tradition is only clearly evidenced in writings preserved within Christian circles. In going beyond the mere clarification of the angel's status in relation to God, it marks a secondary development. In Revelation 19:10, 22:9, the *Ascension of Isaiah* 8:5 (also the related "Greek Legend" 2:10-11), and the much later *Apocryphal Gospel of Matthew* 3:3, the *angelus interpres* also rejects the notion that he holds a status superior to that of the seer. This motif is closely related to the understanding of God reflected in the respective documents.

In both Revelation 19:10 and 22:9, the angel responds to John's prostration and intention to worship him by declaring that he is only a "fellow-servant" (σύνδουλός σου εἰμί) and by exhorting John to "worship God." The *Apocryphal Gospel of Matthew* is rather late and reflects the apparent influ-

---

also Gen 22:12; 24:18; Ex 9:30; 14:31; Lev 19:14; 25:17; Dan 3:41; Esth 2:20; Jud 8:8; 16:16; Tob 4:21; 14:2.
    Note that in *Jub* 12:3b, the injunction against idolatry is already coupled here with an exhortation to worship "the God of heaven."

ence of John's Apocalypse:[115] After Joachim "adores" the angel (introduced as an "angel of God" in 3:2) and asks him for a blessing, he presents himself as "your servant" (3:3-*me servum tuum*). To this the angel replies "Do not say 'servant' (*servum*), but 'my fellow-servant' (*conservum meum*) for we are servants of one Lord (*unius enim domini servi sumus*)."

Common to the Apocalypse of John and the *Apocryphal Gospel of Matthew* is a rejection of the seer's "servant" status in relation to the angel. In both cases the seer's servanthood[116] is qualified by a subsequent statement (in the form of a declaration or exhortation) which stresses that devotion belongs to God alone. The seer (and, in the Apocalypse, the faithful among the communities addressed[117]) and the angel are thereby placed on an equal footing. This elevation of the righteous and self-diminution of the angel also functions as a rhetorical device which implies denote the accessibility of a transcendent God. Provisionally, we may observe that the author of the Apocalypse of John shows no apparent interest in depicting the contours of a heavenly hierarchy in which angels and humans are ranked according to importance. The refusal tradition in the Apocalypse collapses any such differences when it comes to the position from which one serves and worships God. By the end of the document, it becomes clear that, despite the frequency with which angelic beings are mentioned, God is no less immanent to the seer, the group of prophets with which he is associated, and the righteous of the communities addressed than God is to the heavenly angels who have been sent as guides and heralds of his vision. The guiding angel's repeated refusal, in its immediate context, thus serves both to legitimate John's activity as a prophet and to link this activity to the status of those who recognize its authority.

As the Apocalypse of John, the *Ascension of Isaiah* is, in its present form, a Christian apocalypse. It also contains two, though more divergent,

---

[115] This document, which achieved a measure of popularity during the Medieval period, draws heavily on the *Prot.Jas.* (or *Book of James*) and the *Gosp.Th.*; see M.R. JAMES, *ANT*, pp. 70 and 79. The refusal tradition in the *Apoc.Gosp.Mt.*, however, is added by the author on the basis of other traditions. The comments below are based on K. von TISCHENDORF's critical edition in *Evangelia Apocrypha* (Leipzig: Hermann Mendelssohn, 1876).

[116] Though in the Apocalypse the seer does not designate himself as the angel's "servant", this is implied by his venerative posture, on the one hand, and the angel's self-designation, on the other. For the designation of John as δοῦλος, see Rev 1:1 (τῷ δούλῳ αὐτοῦ, i.e. *God's* servant).

[117] Καὶ τῶν ἀδελφῶν σου τῶν ἐχόντων τὴν μαρτυρίαν Ιησοῦ (19:10) and καὶ τῶν ἀδελφῶν σου τῶν προφητῶν καὶ τῶν τηρούντων τοὺς λόγους τοῦ βιβλίου τούτου (22:9). See also the identification of John (ὁ δοῦλος αὐτοῦ) and members of his community (οἱ δοῦλοι αὐτοῦ) as "servant(s)" in Rev 1:1.

angelic refusals of worship. During the seer's journey to the seventh heaven, above which God is enthroned, these are placed in the second (7:21-22) and sixth (8:4-5) heavens. In the first instance, the ascending "Isaiah" is inspired to join the angelic praise of an enthroned figure[118] whose precise identity is not given (7:19).[119] The guiding angel dissuades Isaiah from showing such veneration on the grounds that the throne already allotted him (and other righteous ones after death; cf. 7:23; 8:11-14; 9:17-18; and 11:32) is located in the seventh heaven; Isaiah's status will be even more glorious than anything he has seen here. The angel's restriction, then, pertains to any heavenly being in the first six heavens, whether throne[120] or angel (7:21), implying that in the seventh the prohibition to worship will be lifted.[121]

---

[118] The versions are not explicit at this point. It is unclear whether the angels of the second heaven are directing their praise to God or to the enthroned figure in their midst. In favor of the former is the angel's comment in 7:17 that the praise of the first heaven is directed towards God (all texts agree here). Nevertheless, the rejection of Isaiah's attempt to worship the enthroned figure suggests either that he (falsely) supposed that the angels were worshiping this figure or that he was simply joining in the angelic praise which, though ultimately intended for God, was directed towards this figure.

[119] Following the Eth recension: "and a throne in the middle, and the praise of the angels who (are) in the second heaven; and the one who sat upon the throne (*wazashanaber diba manbar*) of the second heaven was exceedingly more glorious than the others." Though this description is absent in Lat^1, Lat^2, and Slav versions (see the text in CHARLES, *The Ascension of Isaiah* [London: Black, 1900], p. 108), the *eum* in Lat^2 (7:21; Lat^1 ends at v. 20) suggests an omission of such an object at an earlier stage (cf. *ibid.*, p. 109). A similar difference between the recensions can be observed in 7:24,29 (but see Lat^2-*gloria vero sedentis*),37; however, in 7:14 Lat^2 and Slav speak of an enthroned angel in the first heaven. In 7:37, the Lat and Slav agree against the Eth mss in having Isaiah marvel, not at the enthroned figure, but at the angels who are praising God in the fifth heaven: *ego miratus sum, tantam multitudinem angelorum videns diversis bonitatibus ordinatorum et singuli gloriam habentes glorificabant existentem in alto* (Lat^2). According to these versions, the angel then reprimands Isaiah: *quare miraris de hoc, quod non sunt unius speciei? non enim vidisti insuperabiles virtutes et millia milium angelorum* (Lat^2). Here, in which the oneness of God is contrasted with the multitude of angels, we have to do with secondary reflection which seeks to ensure the notion of the supremacy of God by appealing to the divine unity. This criterion is not operative elsewhere in *Asc.Isa.*

[120] It is an open question whether the text refers to the one seated on the throne or to a heavenly being. Certainly the term "throne" was frequently used to denote angelic beings; see KNIBB, "Martyrdom and Ascension of Isaiah," in *OTP* 2.166 n. m. In addition to Col 1:16, see *T.Levi* 3:8, Eth *Asc.Isa.* 7:15, 27; 8:8; 11:25; and the "Greek Legend" 2:40--all of which are cited by KNIBB--; in addition, see *2 En* 20:1 (Rec. J); *Apoc.Elij.* 4:10; and the liturgy in *Apost. Const.* 8.12.6.

[121] Reading with the Eth mss: "until I tell you in the seventh heaven".

In the second instance (8:4-5), the angel's stricture in the Ethiopic, Slavonic and Latin versions of the document comes close to the text of the Apocalypse. Michael KNIBB's translation of the Ethiopic recension in *OTP* volume 2 (p. 168) runs as follows:

> (4) And I said to the angel who led me, "What (is) this which I see, my lord?"
> (5) And he said to me, "I am not your lord, but your companion."[122]

In verse 5, which bears a resemblance to Revelation 19:10 and 22:9, the angel's self-disclosure as "your companion" is supplemented by his refusal to be called "my lord" (8:5). The disallowance of this epithet presupposes the visionary's fascination with this angel's appearance in 7:2: "I saw a glorious angel; he was not like the glory of the angels...but he had great (Lat[1], Slav: and holy) glory...I cannot describe the glory of this angel."[123] Nevertheless, as far as worship before God is concerned, the author stresses that, unlike the angelic beings from the first six heavens, the guiding angel is no greater than Isaiah.

The "Greek Legend," a compilation of stories about the martyrdoms of saints preserved in a 12th-century manuscript containing a much abbreviated version of the *Ascension*, preserves these prohibitions in reverse order. Initially, upon entry into the first heaven, Isaiah addresses the guiding angel (2:10-τῷ θείῳ ἀγγέλῳ τῷ μετ' ἐμοῦ ὄντι) as "lord" (κύριε). The angel's answer (2:10-11) is likewise close to the text in Revelation: "I am not 'lord' (κύ-

---

See also the "Greek Legend" 2:22: ἕως ἂν ἐγώ σοι εἴπω. Lat[2], as Slav, tries to eliminate the potential theological problem by focusing Isaiah's worship directly toward God: *sed tantum quem ego dixero tibi.*
    The restriction, qualified by the temporal prep. "until," does not exclude the possibility that in the seventh heaven other angelic figures could be the objects of worship. In fact, upon reaching the seventh heaven, Isaiah is directed to join the angelic praises of Christ who has taken on the appearance of an angel (9:30; see also v. 35). Similarly, the Holy Spirit, whom Isaiah is also directed to worship, is designated "the second angel" (9:35-Eth: *wa-ladagem mal'ak*; Lat[2] [= Slav]: simply *alium*) and "the angel of the Holy Spirit" (9:36-Eth=Lat[2] and Slav).

[122] The Eth *biṣka* ("your companion") corresponds to the Greek σύνδουλός σου (as in the "Greek Legend"), which in the Latin and Slavic versions is corrupted to *consiliator* (from σύμβουλος). In favor of the Eth reading is the self-designation *biṣka* by the same angel in 8:14 (omitted in the other versions) and σύνδουλος in the "Greek Legend" 2:11.

[123] Cf. similarly the "Greek Legend" 2:6 (for text editions used, see the following n.): εἶδον θεοῦ ἄγγελον δεδοξασμένον· οὐ κατὰ τὴν τάξιν δὲ τῶν ἀγγέλων ὧν εἶδον τότε ἐγὼ ἔβλεπον νῦν, ἀλλὰ πλείονα καὶ περισσοτέραν εἶχεν δόξαν.

ριος), but your fellow-servant (ἀλλα σύνδουλός σου εἰμί)."[124] The other stricture, placed in the sixth heaven, is more comprehensive: μὴ προσκυνήσῃς μήτε ἀγγέλους μήτε ἀρχαγγέλους μήτε κυριότητας μήτε θρόνους (2:22).[125] Here the angel reacts to Isaiah's fear and prostration (2:21-ἐφοβήθην καὶ ἔπεσον ἐπὶ πρόσωπον) in the presence of overwhelming light. Isaiah is forbidden to render any form of worship until instructed to do so (2:22-ἕως ἂν ἐγώ σοι εἴπω).

It is difficult to sort out just how the refusal motif has been adapted in the *Ascension of Isaiah*, due to textual uncertainties.[126] In contrast to the Apocalypse of John, the portrayal of the heavenly world in the *Ascension* is stratified into seven heavens through which Isaiah ascends with increasing glory, much in the same way as ascents described in the Hekhalot literature. More than in the Apocalypse, there is an interest in enumerating various degrees of glory for angelic beings, whose assigned positions not only correspond to the seven heavens but are also distinguished within each heaven itself.[127] Included within this stratification is an apparent distinction between angelic beings from the first six heavens and the righteous human beings who are superior to them. This is illustrated when Isaiah is brought to the sev-

---

[124] The citations negotiate between the editions of Oscar von GEBHARDT, "Die Ascensio Isaiae als Heiligenlegende: Aus Cod. Gr. 1534 der Nationalbibliothek zu Paris," *ZWT* 21 (1878) 330-53 and CHARLES (*Ascension*, pp. 141-48), who reedited the text and indicated with in bold type correspondences with the other versions.

[125] In enumerating heavenly beings which will worship Christ, the "Greek Legend" expands the list even more: πάντες ἄγγελοι, ἀρχάγγελοι, θρόνοι, κυριότητες, ἀρχαί, ἐξουσίαι καὶ πᾶσαι τῶν οὐρανῶν αἱ δυνάμεις, καὶ γνώσονται πᾶσαι αἱ τῶν οὐρανῶν στρατιαὶ (2:40). However, this section as a whole, reminiscent of Col 1:16, is probably a secondary development.

[126] In addition to the problem of negotiating between readings in the Eth, Lat, Slav and Greek texts, one should not presume a general priority of these versions as a whole without allowing for certain qualifications. Though the "Greek Legend" seems to be an adaptation of a version similar to the preserved materials of *Asc.Isa.* through truncation and structural changes (e.g., Isaiah's martyrdom is recounted, more logically, *after* the vision), it nevertheless often contains complementary phraseology which may stem from an independent or even earlier version. See BAUCKHAM, "The Worship of Jesus" 340-41 n.'s 72 and 73. One such instance may be detected with respect to angelology. It is arguable that the mention of κυριότητας in 2:22 (cf. *Asc.Isa.* 7:21), in following the κύριε address of the angel, makes good sense in the context of the sixth heaven (according to the order in *Asc.Isa.*) or in the second heaven (according to the "Greek Legend"). If this is correct, then the term ἀρχάγγελοι (nowhere else in the document or in *Asc.Isa.*) was added to provide symmetry to the list.

[127] Within the first through fifth heavens the versions, taken as a whole, distinguish between three classes of angelic beings (listed here in order of rank): the throne in the middle, those angels to the right, and those angels to the left.

enth heaven (9:1-5); at this point, the angel who oversees the worship from the sixth heaven (v. 4) questions the seer's worthiness to enter (v. 1). This obstacle is overcome once Christ overrules this angel's judgment. Christ declares that Isaiah has "a robe" in the seventh heaven (v. 2), a pronouncement which is already anticipated within the context of the refusal tradition in the second heaven, in which the angel announces that the seer will have a "throne," "robes," and a "crown" in the seventh heaven (7:22). While the seven-fold division of heaven and the classes of angels would seem to underscore the notion of a God far removed from humanity, it is adjusted by the writer to the extent that the transcendent God, who is above the seventh heaven, will be more proximate to the righteous than to the angels in the first six heavens. The angelic refusals to be honored (7:21; 8:5) thus function, though less radically than in the Apocalypse, to dismantle any notion that human righteous are inferior to these angels, that is, they modify a differentiated cosmology, shared by the author and his readers, in which angelic beings are given a prominent place.

If the statements "I am not your lord" or "I am your fellow-servant" are taken independently, they would merely seem to diminish the angel's status in relation to the seer. But, though this motif was probably not original to the refusal tradition, it eventually functioned as a substitute or supplement to the expression "Do not fear!"[128] (understood as a stricture), apparently without undermining a concern to protect monotheism. The result is a double signification: (1) to clarify the relation of the human being and angel (as in *Asc.Isa.* 7:21 and 8:4-5) and (2) to safeguard God's preeminence over the angel (as in *Asc. Isa.* 8:4-5 and 9:40-42).

Again, this dual function raises the question of origin and, again, the simple presence of specific terminology does not bring clarity to the matter. In most early Jewish writings, addressing an angel as "(my) lord" and designating one's self as a "servant" of an angel are tolerated, even in visionary contexts,[129] whether they communicated a common show of respect or--as in the

---

[128] In the refusal tradition, the proscriptions against "fear," on the one hand, and those against being a "servant" of the angel or calling the angel "lord," on the other, are never found side-by-side.

[129] For this sense of "lord" see esp. *2 En* 21:3-4 (esp. Rec. J-"my Lord"; see F.I. ANDERSEN, "2 (Slavonic Apocalypse of) ENOCH," in *OTP* 1.136 n. h); CLEMENT of ALEXANDRIA, *Strom.* 5.11.77 (*Apoc.Zeph.*?); *Apoc.Zeph.* 4:8 (Akhm); *4 Ez* 4:38 ("O sovereign Lord"-the referent, whether God or the angel Jeremiel, is not clear); *Quest.Ez.* Rec. A, 1:4,9,22,31; *Apoc.Sedr.* 2:2,4; *3 Bar* 2:7 (Slav), 8:5 (Grk), etc.; *Apoc.Abr.* 13:6; *T.Abr.* Rec. A 2:7; 11:8; 13:1; 14:1; 15:4; Rec. B 7:7,11,18; 8:9; 9:10; 10:1,4,6; 11:1; 12:3; *Jos.*

case of the expression "lord"--derive from a monotheizing diminutive, such as from the plural form in the divine epithet "God of gods and Lord of lords" (Deut 10:17).[130]

On the other hand, clear rejections of superiority are, albeit in other terms, associated with a dismissal of venerative behavior in at least two biblical passages. Already in Genesis 50:19 Joseph reacts to the prostration of his brothers with the phrase, "Am I in the place of God?" The rhetorical question (cf. also Gen 30:2) is an expression of piety which is as concerned with modifying the expectations of his brothers as with making an assertion about God.[131] In Acts 10:25-26 Peter counters Cornelius' prostration (v. 25- πεσὼν ἐπὶ τοὺς πόδας προσεκύνησεν) with the explanation, "I am also a human being." Peter's refusal to accept such hommage serves not only to eliminate the cultic distinction between Jew and Gentile (vv. 28,34), but also underlines the overall purpose of the story, which is to ensure that the reception of the Holy Spirit by Gentiles is continuous with a proper worship of God (v. 46). This passage is probably too late to provide any real background for the motif in which an angel denies superiority. Conversely, however, it is possible that the refusal tradition may in fact underlie Acts 10:25. But the encounter in Genesis, in which there is no allusion to the appearance of Joseph, may represent a form of piety that would later be well suited rhetorically to to play down a superiority which an angel's glorious appearance may have been thought to imply. At the same time, the question as formulated by

---

Asen. 14:7; 15:12,13,14; 16:3,11; 17:4; 4QAmram 2 1.3. Cf. Rev 7:14. In the T.Abr. (Rec. A 2:10; 5:12; 6:4, etc.; Rec. B 4:1; 6:5) and Jos.Asen. (4:3,6, 9; 7:7; etc.), the title is also used as an expression of general respect towards humans; see also Vit.Ad.Ev. 2:1; 3:1, etc. (addressed to Adam). In the Apoc.Zeph. 12:4, in contrast to 4:8, the angel's response to the seer's address ("O lord" = pchaeis) perhaps suggests an uneasiness with the title: "I do not have the authority to show them to you." The designation "Lord Almighty" (pchaeis ppantokratōr) is, however, reserved for God, especially where the author seems to be concerned with distinguishing God from the guiding angel (6:4,13; 12:5). See n. 102 (II.A.2.b.i) above.

In Apoc.Abr. 11:4; 14:1,9 Abraham's being a "servant" to Michael is not countered.

The designations "servant" and "lord" in the context of an angelophany may have been influenced by the earliest such instance in Dan 10:17, in which the seer both addresses the interpreting angel as "lord" (MT-2X אֲדֹנִי; LXX-τοῦ κυρίου αὐτοῦ; Theod.-κύριε, τοῦ κυρίου μου τούτου; see also v. 19; 12:8) while designating himself as "servant" (MT-עֶבֶד; LXX-ὁ παῖς; Theod.-ὁ παῖς σου).

[130] So WINTERMUTE (OTP 1.508, n. a), as explanation for the application of "lords" to heavenly angels in CLEMENT of ALEXANDRIA's citation of Apoc. Zeph.

[131] See further comments on this text in n. 112 above.

Joseph to his brothers, when interpreted as an assertion about God, demonstrates the suitability of this form in angelological contexts where monotheistic belief is being safeguarded. Therefore, in addition to the (angelophanic) visionary context, the refusal passages in the *Ascension of Isaiah* may be said to go beyond the Genesis narrative in two ways: (1) an interest in the angel's appearance (absent in Rev 19:10 and 22:8-9) and (2) an intensification of the significance of the angel's self-deprecation for a devotion to God (especially prominent in Rev).

In Revelation and the *Ascension of Isaiah*, then, the combination of the angelic denial of superiority and ultimate focus on God may represent a development in which a pious commonplace is given renewed meaning within an angelological context. At the same time, it is one expression in apocalyptic literature of a growing interest in defining the relation between faithful human beings and chief angelic figures, a motif further employed by writers to illustrate the nature of the monotheistic belief being advocated. The notion of God's ultimate superiority and transcendance is thus bound together with the assertion of equality between the righteous and angels. This, in turn, enables the authors, each in their own way, to describe the relation between human beings and God in terms of proximity.[132]

iv. The Emphasis on God

In the discussion above (II.A.2.b.ii), we have attempted to demonstrate that, traditio-historically, the angelophanic prohibition was the product of a transformation of a traditional theo- and angelophanic exhortation into a prohibitive statement which drew upon strictures against idolatry. Given the nature and extent of this development, it is hard to escape the conclusion that the angel's refusal to be worshiped reflects a development in which a pure devotion to God *vis-à-vis some angelic beings* could not be assumed. It remains here to consider two further points: (1) the relation between the angel's restriction and the ensuing declaration of God's ultimate superiority and (2) the adaptation of this emphasis within Christian circles.

---

[132] *Contra* Eugène TISSERENT, *Ascension d'Isaie* (Paris: Letouzay, 1909), who did not consider the possibility of the *Asc.Isa.*'s anthropological modification of divine transcendence (p. 7), expressed through the superiority of the righteous over the angels. Cf. 9:28,33,41 (the righteous precede the angels in praising Christ, the Holy Spirit, and God); 9:37 (the angels cannot see God); 9:38 (the righteous can see God); 9:37a,39 (Isaiah is briefly allowed to see God).

First, how were the motifs of God's ultimate superiority and the prohibitive statements coordinated? It would be insufficient merely to suppose that the monotheistic emphasis on God is dependent on the presence of a proscriptive element. Frequently, in visionary narratives which have nothing to say about the danger of angelolatry, a seer is explicitly enjoined to direct his attention toward God.[133] This summons, then, does not so much distinguish the refusal tradition as it is conditioned by it. In combination with the prohibition it attains a level of intensity in which the preeminence of God is (re-)asserted.[134] As observed in the previous section (II.A.2.b.iii), the force of such a declaration was in no way compromised by the further need to clarify the relationship between angels and the human faithful.

Second, it is striking that in some Christian circles, components of the refusal tradition are applied in two directions. The traditional motif of worshiping God is supplemented by expressions of devotion to Christ. In the *Ascension of Isaiah*, the qualified rejection of worship "until the seventh heaven" (7:21) employs the tradition in a way which not only says something about the superiority of the righteous over angels, but which also anticipates Christ and the Holy Spirit as legitimate objects of worship. Thus much less so than in the Apocalypse, *the author's cosmological classification, in which heavenly beings reflect their rank through various degrees of praise, does not result in the use of worship as a general criterion for monotheism.* Rather, the monotheism of the document is expressed in terms of an *ultimate* focus of worship. Christ and the Holy Spirit, to whom even angelic qualities can be ascribed,[135] are worshiped by the righteous and angels in the seventh heaven (9:31-32,36), from where they join with the angels in worshiping God (9:40-42).

In Revelation 1:12-17, there occur some elements of the refusal tradition, but without either a refusal to be worshiped or a formal emphasis on God (see further in Part Three, section IV). After the splendor of "one like a son of man" is described (vv. 13-16), the seer falls at his feet "as though dead" (v. 17). With the words μὴ φοβοῦ, Christ comforts John and identifies *himself* as the one who is "the first and the last" (cf. 1:8). John is here

---

[133] As in passages listed in n. 109 (section II.A.2.b.ii) above.

[134] For various ways the supremacy of God was expressed in the refusal tradition, see column 5 in the Appendix.

[135] The Holy Spirit is more explicitly an angel (9:36,39, and 40-"the angel of the Holy Spirit"; cf. 9:35) than Christ. The latter, normally designated "the Beloved" or "the Lord," is made to resemble an angel in 9:30, and in 9:35 the Holy Spirit alongside him is designated "the second angel."

not forbidden to worship, and Christ does not point the way beyond himself.[136] It is, however, not in the angelomorphicizing epiphany but in the Lamb Christology (Rev 5) that the author sees the worthiness of Christ to be worshiped. In Revelation, and to a lesser degree in the *Ascension of Isaiah*, elements of the refusal tradition are thus used *both* to safeguard devotion to אלהינו אדוני (as in Rev 19:10; 22:8-9; *Asc.Isa.* 8:1-5) and to underscore the prominence of Christ (Rev 1:12-17; 5:6-13; *Asc.Isa.* 9:27-32).

c. Summary

The adjustment of traditional elements in angelophanic encounters to reinforce monotheistic devotion presupposes an speculative interest in angels as such. This interest was accompanied by descriptions of their divine-like appearance, which could be thought to demand some kind of venerative response. In documents preserving the refusal tradition the splendor attributed

---

[136] A similar pattern can be detected in the Gospel of Mt. In addition to retaining the traditional emphasis on worshiping the one God (4:10--from "Q" tradition--citation of Deut 6:13), the author's redaction of material found in Mk employs elements of the refusal tradition to focus attention on Christ. In the ending of Mk the women's failure to report the empty tomb is explained by referring to their fear (16:8-ἐφοβοῦντο γάρ), despite the angel's exhortation (v.6-μὴ ἐκθαμβεῖσθε). Mt transfers the objectionable fear of the angelophany to the guards at the tomb (v. 4-"they quaked...and became as dead") and has the angel exhort the women not to react in the same way: "Do not you (ὑμεῖς) fear [as the guards]" (v. 5). This rearrangement functions in two ways. First, it distinguishes the fear of the guards from the posture which is deemed appropriate for the women. Whereas Mt follows up the guards' response with an account of them making a false report about the events at the tomb (vv. 11-15), the (proper) reverence attributed to the women leads them to submit a true testimony concerning the resurrection to Jesus' disciples (vv. 7,10; cf. v. 16). Whereas μὴ φοβεῖσθε in v. 5 (addressed by the angel to the women) is a prohibition not to react as the guards, the same phrase in v. 10 (by Jesus to the women) is intended as comfort that should not be understood as a reprimand for taking hold of his feet and worshiping him (v. 9). If the contrast between the guards and the women is to be explained on the basis of Matthean redaction of Mk, the movement from an angelophany (Mt 28:2-3) to a christophany (v. 9) suggests that the author has adapted a tradition in which an angel refuses worship, already current in "Christian" circles, using it to recast the content and structure of the narrative in underlying tradition. This tradition has admittedly been suppressed, but traces of it have left their stamp in the Matthean account: When the women see the angel, whose appearance was "like lightning" (as the angel in Dan 10:6) and whose clothing was "white as snow" (as the Ancient of Days in Dan 7:9), they are told not to fear. Though the contrast with the guards' response prevails in the exhortation itself, its original sense as a refusal of worship is suggested by the worship of the resurrected Lord by the women and disciples narrated in vv. 9 and 17. Cf. also Mt 17:6.

to the prominent angels is never questioned, a perspective which both authors and readers may be presumed to have had in common. It would seem only proper that beings thought to have special proximity to the throne of "the Most High" would themselves mirror that glory. At the same time, such splendor is closely linked with a reprehensible show of veneration. Had the apocalyptic writers faulted the majesty of angels in and of itself, they would have risked calling the glory of "the Most High" into question, thereby dismissing a motif which had been woven into the fabric of shared perceptions concerning the nature of cosmological reality. Thus it is not misleading if one assumes that apocalyptic writers who employed the refusal tradition were concerned with dangers which speculation about the function and appearance of angels (a conception shared with their communities) could pose for monotheistic belief.

Against this backdrop, the danger of "pagan" idolatry recedes into the background. The reprimand, put into the mouth of the angel himself, serves to define the devotion to the one God of Israel more precisely: even allied beings who serve God's purposes must not be worshiped. Thus if the aim of a vision was to be realized at all, the seer (and reader) must not be sidetracked by the glory of angelic beings who are encountered.[137] The authors who made use of the tradition betray at least some awareness that without such strictures their message could be jeopardized.

We have seen that in Revelation and the *Ascension of Isaiah* the refusal tradition reflects the degree to which Christology could be absorbed into a monotheistic framework. On the other hand, it is significant to note that the refusal tradition is never used to focus attention on an angelic being in non-Christian Jewish literature. Whatever the venerative attitudes that may have existed towards angelic beings, they never surfaced in the literature to the point that they required an emphasis which a refusal--for example, a rejection of venerative behavior more suitably expressed towards an angel--would have provided.

These observations do not leave much room for a conclusion that the refusal tradition constitutes evidence for a polemic against a veritable angel

---

[137] This point perhaps illuminates why writers were willing to represent their seers, who in the heavenly journeys are depicted as somewhat of an ideal type, as (wrongly) wanting to worship an angelic being. We may assume that the refusal tradition functioned rhetorically; it was less a simple account of an alleged encounter of a visionary than an attempt to assist the reader (through the seer's experience) in overcoming the temptation to venerate inappropriately the heavenly servants of God.

"cult."[138] But it is possible to suggest that it may have functioned as *a critique from within* which recognized a danger of veneration inherent in speculations concerning the prominence of angels thought to be encountered in heavenly journeys.[139] Since the application of the refusal tradition leaves no trace that the notion of an angel's striking appearance is being questioned, we may assume that the author and the position being opposed shared common angelological ideas.[140] At the same time, the intensity of the refusal is hard to explain without positing some form of underlying venerative behavior which may have been deemed appropriate towards God's messengers, an attitude which at least the proponents themselves would probably not have considered destructive to a belief in one God. We may suppose that the refusal tradition found its *Sitz im Leben* as a response to such a posture. Hence in the refusal tradition we encounter a form which--if its use in Revelation, the *Apocalypse of Zephaniah*, and the *Ascension of Isaiah* and its varied adaptation in further early Jewish and Christian writings are any indication--was well-known, indeed, flourishing among various Jewish and Christian circles by the late first-early second century CE.

3. Alleged Allusions to Angel Worship in New Testament Writings and Early Christian Literature

The passages discussed above contain no explicit accusation of angel veneration as a practice within a religious group. If a polemic against a

---

[138] *Contra* BOUSSET and GRESSMANN, *Religion des Judentums*, p. 330 and CHARLES, *Revelation*, 2.224-25.

[139] PERCY argued that an actual practice of worshiping angels would have called for a "more direct polemic" than that represented by the refusal tradition (*Probleme*, p. 152). This argument, which starts with a narrow definition of veneration ("Verehrung"), presumes that a polemic would have been directed towards some group on the "outside." In response, one only needs to affirm that the placement of the refusal in the mouth of an angel may well have been a effective literary device, based on common points of reference, to curb such an attitude. Furthermore, if we are correct in positing that the authors and the communities to and for whom they wrote shared common views concerning the function of angels, then, for the sake of the perception of the original readers, a more "direct" polemic would have been unnecessary.

[140] In this respect it is interesting to note in the later *Hist.Rech.* 6:3-3a a modified form of the refusal tradition (no immediate emphasis on worshiping God)--here, an encounter of "Zosimus" with a "Blessed One" whose face resembles that of an angel (5:4)--can be combined with the seer's subsequent observation of, prostration (before), and "worship" of "the Blessed Ones" (though the author does not consider them "angels" in the proper sense).

actual practices underlies any of the rabbinic passages and writings preserving the refusal tradition, it is ultimately a matter of inference. The texts to be discussed in this section (II.A.3) are likewise difficult to interpret. They have, however, often been regarded as containing accusations of "angel worship," whether observed among Jewish or Christian circles. These traditions, which are extant in writings of the New Testament and early patristic authors, will be examined here to ascertain (1) their connection with known Jewish and Christian motifs, (2) whether they in fact polemicize against either Jews or Christians, and (3) the degree to which, if at all, the claims leveled may have obtained.

a. Galatians 4:3,8-9 (viz. 3:19-20)

The meaning of στοιχεῖα in Paul's letter to the Galatians (4:3 and 9) has been much debated.[141] In 4:9 the term is made the object of the verb δουλεύειν, and an exegetical decision concerning the possibility that Paul is referring to serving "angels" (viz. 3:19) requires consideration of the overriding argument in the passage. The expression τὰ στοιχεῖα τοῦ κόσμου (4:3) surfaces initially in a context in which Paul attempts to convince the Galatians that yielding to the demands of the "Judaizers" is nothing less than a regression from faith (3:3). Though in this respect Paul consistently contends for the superiority of faith over the Jewish Torah, some aspects of his argument remain unclear. How does the discussion in 3:6-29, which focuses almost exclusively on the priority of faith and on the salvation-historical function of the Torah, relate to what Paul wishes to argue concerning the status of his *Gentile* Galatian readers? In other words, to what extent does Paul draw an analogy between the epoch of the Torah--ordained through angels (διαταγεὶς δι' ἀγγέλων, 3:19) and a temporary παιδαγωγός (3:24)--and the Gentiles' former status without Christ (4:8)?

That Paul intended at least some analogy is clear. Both life under the Torah and the Galatians' former life, referred to in 4:3 and 9 respectively, are characterized in relation to στοιχεῖα. Paul's description of his readers' life before Christ as adherence to ἀσθενῆ καὶ πτωχὰ στοιχεῖα would not be entirely unexpected in a non-Jewish context (4:9), but his apparent equivoca-

---

[141] In his *Forschungsbericht* on Pauline studies since 1945, HÜBNER devotes several pages to this issue alone: "Paulusforschung seit 1945. Ein kritischer Literaturbericht," in *ANRW*, II.25.4, pp. 2691-94.

tion of life ὑπὸ τὰ στοιχεῖα τοῦ κόσμου (4:3) with being ὑπὸ τὸν νόμον--despite the extent to which the law has been disparaged in 3:6-26--is more difficult to explain. If in 4:3 Paul is indeed referring to the life of a Jew under the Torah,[142] one may well inquire about the conditions under which Paul could have regarded the Galatians' acceptance of *Judaizing* influences as a lapse into serving στοιχεῖα. An approach to this problem is in large part determined by (1) the meaning one attributes to στοιχεῖα in 4:3 and 9 and (2) the relation between the expressions στοιχεῖα, νόμος, and the ἄγγελοι mentioned in 3:19.

The linguistically parallel constructions with ὑπό in 3:21-4:11[143] have led a number of interpreters to associate the στοιχεῖα with νόμος and, frequently, to draw a further correlation between the former, understood as personal beings, and angels through whom the latter was ordained (3:19). Accordingly, the Judaizing opponents are thought to have been "worshipers of angels"[144] who, as well as exacting legal requirements, were requiring a scrupu-

---

[142] The comparison signaled by οὕτως καὶ in 4:3 leads from the legal image of being "under guardians and trustees" (v. 2) to the more radical claim that "we" were "enslaved under the elements of the world" (v. 3). An attempt to smooth out the difficulty by appealing to different meanings subsumed by Paul under νόμος (so, e.g., G.B. CAIRD, *Principalities and Powers* [Oxford: Clarendon, 1956] and L. GASTON, *Paul and the Torah* [Vancouver: Univ. of British Columbia, 1987] esp. pp. 169-90), so that in 4:3 Paul refers to a natural law rather than to the Torah, does not satisfy the soteriological emphasis of Paul's argument.

[143] The preposition ὑπό appears several times during Paul's attempt to answer the question, "Is the law, then, against the promises of God?" (3:21). Despite according the law a negative anthropological function (v. 21b), Paul attributes to the Torah a historical function in the history of salvation which he describes on the basis of two analogies. First, the age of being "guarded" ὑπὸ νόμον (3:23), which picks up the idea of the scripture "shutting up" all things ὑπὸ ἁμαρτίαν in v. 22, is typified by the notion of being ὑπὸ παιδαγωγόν (v. 25). Second, the introduction of the status of sonship (υἱοὶ θεοῦ, v. 26) possible for Jew and Gentile alike through faith in Christ and the participation in the fulfillment of the Abrahamic promise as "heirs" (κληρονόμοι, v. 29) brings Paul to the notion of inheritance. Thus life before Christ, characterized as enslavement to the "elements" (4:3-with ὑπό; 4:9), is compared in 4:2 to being ὑπὸ ἐπιτρόπους...καὶ οἰκονόμους.

[144] This interpretation is usually taken in two directions: (1) The "angels=στοιχεῖα" are equated as demonic powers; see esp. A. SCHWEITZER, *Die Mystik des Apostels Paulus* (UTB, 1091; Tübingen: J.C.B. Mohr [Paul Siebeck], 1930) 70-74 and Hans HÜBNER, *Das Gesetz bei Paulus* (FRLANT, 199; Göttingen: Vandenhoeck & Ruprecht, 1982⁵) 27-29. (2) The angels, though not demonic, are identified with the στοιχεῖα when Paul wishes to underscore their negative significance; so PERCY, *Probleme*, pp. 157-60; Bo REICKE, "The Law and this World according to Paul," *JBL* 70 (1951) 261-63; J. BLIGH, *Galatians* (London: St. Paul Publications, 1969) 330-31; John J. GUNTHER, *St. Paul's Opponents*

lous observance of calendrical regulations. Is this interpretation defensible in any form?

The RSV translation of στοιχεῖα in 4:3 and 9 as "elemental spirits" does not contradict a possible identification with the angels of 3:19. This rendering, however, has been contested by those who see no evidence for such a meaning before the late second century. E. SCHWEIZER, for example, has argued on the basis of usage in literature up until the second century that the στοιχεῖα are "nothing else than...the four (or five) elements of the universe" and, therefore, cannot refer to personified beings in any sense.[145] The bondage outside of Christ spoken of in Galatians 4:3 and 9 is an "imprisonment of the soul in the ceaseless rotation of the four elements" which was thought to impede a soul's ascent after death.[146] In order to overcome these elements, it would have been necessary to purify the soul by making various legal regulations compulsory. In this way, the imposition of Jewish commandments (in the form of ascetic requirements) would have amounted to a reintroduction of the Galatian Gentiles' former way of life.[147] Interestingly enough, SCHWEIZER, who correlates the religious background for both Galatians and Co-

---

and Their Background (SuppNT, 35; Leiden: Brill, 1973) 172-93; and F.F. BRUCE, "Paul and the Law of Moses," BJRL 57 (1974/75) 265, though he appears less certain about the angels-elements identification in his Commentary on Galatians (NICNT; Grand Rapids: Eerdmans, 1982) 203. Apparently due to the difficulty in making a precise identification, a mediating position is adopted by H.D. BETZ, Galatians (Hermeneia; Philadelphia: Fortress, 1979) 204-205.

SEGAL (Two Powers, p. 211) takes Gal 3:19-20 as evidence to support his general contention that "a polemic against angelology already existed in Jewish circles in the first century" (emphasis my own).

[145] SCHWEIZER, "Slaves of the Elements and Worshipers of Angels: Gal 4:3, 9 and Col 2:8, 18, 20," JBL 107 (1988) 465-66.

[146] Ibid., p. 466.

[147] J. BANDSTRA, The Law and the Elements of the World (Grand Rapids: Eerdmans, 1964) 43-44 had argued similarly, but concluded that the στοιχεῖα-by nature not gods (4:8)-here refer to the "elementary teachings"; see also Ernest D. BURTON, A Critical and Exegetical Commentary on the Epistle to the Galatians (ICC; Edinburgh: T. & T. Clark, 1921) 216 and 219; J. BLINZLER, "Lexikalisches zu dem Terminus τὰ στοιχεῖ τοῦ κόσμου bei Paulus," in Studiorum Paulinorum Congressus Internationalis Catholicus, 1961 (AnBib 18; Rome: Pontifical Biblical Institute, 1963) 429-43; G. DELLING, "στοιχεῖα," in TDNT 7.684-85; Linda L. BELLEVILLE, "'Under Law': Structural Analysis and the Pauline Concept of Law in Galatians 3.21-4.11," JSNT 26 (1986) 67-68; and, most recently, D. RUSAM, "Neue Belege zu den στοιχεῖα τοῦ κόσμου (Gal 4,3.9; Kol 2,8.20)," ZNW 83 (1992) 119-25. SCHWEIZER, citing PHILO and JOSEPHUS, tries to argue the plausibility of his thesis by stressing that such a Pythagorean concern with the the elements had been taken up within Judaism "long before" and, therefore, may be used to explain the position of Paul's Judaizing opponents.

lossians (see below), can speak of a pagan "worship" of heroes and demons and a similar attitude among Jews toward "angels" who were thought to have successfully penetrated the elements and who, therefore, could exercise some control over them. This point, however, cannot in his view be exegetically derived from the term στοιχεῖα.

In the end, SCHWEIZER's hesitation to identify the στοιχεῖα with "elemental spirits," based on his appeal to the religio-historical background, seems questionable for two main reasons. First, his thesis, based primarily on a word study, neglects some important motifs current in Jewish circles around the turn of the era. Even if one grants that his Pythagorean definition for στοιχεῖα, based on Hellenistic and Jewish-Hellenistic sources before the first century, is correct, it is another matter to consider the perception of some Jewish authors concerning the function of the στοιχεῖα among Gentiles.[148] The author of the Wisdom of Solomon (second half of the 1st cent. BCE) commended "genuine knowledge" (7:17-γνῶσις ἀψευδής) concerning "the composition of the world and the operation of the elements" (σύστασις κόσμου καὶ ἐνέργεια στοιχείων), a knowledge which contrasts sharply with what he later describes as the "ignorance of God" (13:1-θεοῦ ἀγνωσία) among the foolish who consider "fire, wind, swift air, the orbit of stars, violent water, and heavenly luminaries as *gods and rulers of the world* (v. 2-πρυτάνεις κόσμου θεούς)." Similarly, PHILO (*Vit. Cont.* 2-4) contrasted the Therapeutai who "worship" (θεραπεύειν) God with "those who revere the elements (οἱ τὰ στοιχεῖα τιμῶντες) earth, water, air, and fire", maintaining that the latter identify these elements with deities whose names had been devised by the sophists.[149] These texts raise the possibility that, however aware Paul may have been of a widespread fear of an elemental imprisonment of souls, in the context of Galatians 4:9 he may have been adapting a traditional Hellenistic Jewish polemic in which the Gentiles were perceived as venerating the στοιχεῖα as if they were deities.[150]

---

[148] So correctly George HOWARD, *Paul: Crisis in Galatia* (SNTSMS, 35; Cambridge: Univ., 1990^2) 67; see already A. SCHWEITZER, *Mystik*, p. 72.

[149] In this passage PHILO retains the essential meaning of στοιχεῖα as material cosmic elements in that they are essentially "lifeless substance and incapable of generating movement" (ἄψυχος ὕλη καὶ ἐξ ἑαυτῆς ἀκίνητος). The association of names of deities with the elements, even if contrived by the sophists, nevertheless for PHILO represents an existing form of religiosity among "those who profess piety" (οἱ ἐπαγγελλόμενοι εὐσέβειαν).

[150] If a situation of Gentile readers attracted to Jewish practices is kept in view, Paul's drawing on such a tradition would have been rhetorically

Second, SCHWEIZER's proposal does not reflect a sufficient consideration of internal progressions within Paul's argument. The rhetorical question in 4:9, in which Paul attempts to objectify for his readers the dimensions of their current predicament (viz. 3:3), follows a caricature of their former way of life: Before they knew God, they served entities "which by nature are not gods" (v. 8–ἐδουλεύσατε τοῖς φύσει μὴ οὖσιν θεοῖς).[151] If they succumb to the Judaizers' requirements, they run the risk of reverting to their life before Christ. This representation of the Galatians' prior life is resumed in the description of their present predicament in several ways: (a) the resumption of δουλεύειν in verse 9, this time in relation to τὰ ἀσθενῆ καὶ πτωχὰ στοιχεῖα; (b) the characterization of their behavior in terms of a "return" (ἐπιστρέφειν); and (c) the use of πάλιν (twice) to modify δουλεύειν (in conjunction with ἄνωθεν) and ἐπιστρέφειν. Thus the argument in verses 8-9 alone makes it difficult to escape an interpretation of στοιχεῖα as deities which Gentiles were thought to have venerated ("served") before Christ.[152]

The relationship between 4:8-9 and the foregoing argument in 3:1-4:7 is more difficult to determine. If, as is arguable, Paul has adapted a polemical Jewish tradition against Gentile στοιχεῖα-religiosity, is it possible that in 4:3 it is specifically directed against life "under the law" as well (viz. Rom 2:1)? The plausibility of this correlation depends upon a consideration of Paul's preceding argument.

The opponents' apparent insistence that the universal offer of salvation to Jews and Gentiles through Christ should accommodate the notion of a universalized Torah leads Paul to enjoin a soteriologically *Christo*-centric

---

more a *propos* than a simple denigration of a common form of religiosity which was less specifically related to a Jewish consciousness *vis-à-vis* paganism.

[151] Here the argument runs strikingly parallel to that of PHILO in *Vit. Cont.* 2-4 insofar as Paul seems aware, on the one hand, that the στοιχεῖα are not actually divinities while, on the other, being able to suggest that they could be "served" as if they were. This nuance is missed in the discussions of SCHWEIZER, "Slaves of the Elements" 460 and 466 and BELLEVILLE, "'Under Law'" 67 and 77 n. 65. In 1 Cor 8:4-6 Paul also denies an actual existence of an εἴδωλον ἐν κόσμῳ (v. 4), while being able to entertain the notion of θεοὶ πολλοὶ καὶ κύριοι πολλοί (v. 5). Paul's admission of the existence of these λεγόμενοι θεοί probably refers to function. Their existence holds "to the extent that they are being worshipped"; so BETZ, *Galatians*, p. 215 and see n. 22.

[152] The term δουλεύειν may be used in vv. 8-9 with a double sense: (1) to denote the "bondage" of their former life and (2) as a term of (religious) devotion rendered to a superior. The passive form in v. 3 (δεδουλωμένοι), on the other hand, evokes more clearly the first meaning.

exclusivism.[153] The law, relegated to the role of a chronological "stop-gap" between the promise to Abraham and its fulfillment in Christ (3:23-25), is denied any positive anthropological function (3:21). In this sense, Paul can imply that the "curse" of the law is applicable to Jews and Gentiles who submit to its demands as conditions for full acceptance (3:10-ὅσοι γὰρ ἐξ ἔργων νόμου εἰσίν). In other words, Gentile participation in the Torah after Christ is soteriologically ineffective; indeed, it would mark a "return" to their former way of life (4:9). Once the Torah's functional impotence is asserted (3:21) in this manner, it follows logically that in Christ, the goal and fulfillment of the Abrahamic promise, any essential difference between "Jew and Greek" is irrelevant (3:26-29).

Is this correlation extended to the religious condition before Christ in 4:1-11? The argument in chapter 3 and in 2:15-16, in which the righteous status of both Jew and Gentile is equally determined by πίστις Ἰησοῦ Χριστοῦ, points toward an answer in the affirmative, though not without qualification.[154] Several interpreters play down this consideration and regard Paul's use of pronouns as a decisive indicator for how the argument in 4:1-11 progresses. In verses 1-5 Paul (except for the opening λέγω in v. 1 and the sing. εἶ in v. 6) restricts himself to first person plural forms, while in verses 6-11 he only refers to his readers in the second person plural. This shift is thought to correspond to references to Jewish Christians ("we, our") and the Galatian Gentiles ("you") respectively. From this it is then argued that Jewish bondage under the law is distinguishable from Gentile service to στοιχεῖα.[155] Thus the analogy between the former life of Jews "under the law" and that of the Galatians would appear to break down in the transition from verses 6-8.

---

[153] Thus, unlike in Rom 4:1-12, Paul cannot even speak of *Abraham's* faith; faith is only a realization *through Christ* of the promise made to Abraham. See J. Christiaan BEKER, *Paul the Apostle: The Triumph of God in Life and Thought* (Philadelphia: Fortress, 1980) 47-57.

[154] As argued below, it seems that an interpretation of Paul's conception of life outside of Christ in 4:1-11 is open to anthropological nuances which are no longer retained after Christ (3:28). The clarity with which Paul argues the Christological "solution" (ch. 3) is not matched by his delineation of the anthropological "problem"; see E.P. SANDERS, *Paul, the Law, and the Jewish People* (Philadelphia: Fortress, 1983) 88 n. 23 (in agreement with H. RÄISÄNEN).

[155] So, e.g., BANDSTRA, *The Law and the Elements*, pp. 43-44; Ferdinand HAHN, "Das Gesetzesverständnis im Römer- und Galaterbrief," *ZNW* 67 (1976) 29-63; and BELLEVILLE, "'Under Law'" 68-69.

Although it is not clear whether Paul would have made such pronominal distinctions merely on the basis of a certain salvation-history priority of the Jewish Torah,[156] a transition from 4:1-5 to 6-11 can be discerned on other grounds. First, the notion of being "under the law" (4:4-5) is not carried over into verses 8-11. This suggests that to the extent Paul can refer to the life of a Jew outside of Christ, he is compelled to speak of a condition in relation to the law. In this association Paul retains, however negatively, the salvation-historical priority of the Jew, while he attempts not to sacrifice the analogical basis which his argument in chapter 3 has produced. Second, whereas the Galatians' past religiosity is represented as one of active engagement (v. 8-ἐδουλεύσατε; v. 9-θέλετε δουλεύειν), the νήπιοι, being under guardians and trustees, find themselves in a state of being "enslaved" (v.3- pass. ptc. δεδουλωμένοι).

It is unlikely, then, that the τὰ στοιχεῖα τοῦ κόσμου in 4:3 refer to deities in precisely the sense taken up in verse 9. Whereas Gentile religiosity could be encapsulated by the description, "we were slaves under the elements of the world" in verse 3, an inclusion of the Jew without Christ under the more specific description, "wishing to serve elemental spirits," cannot be demonstrated. Moreover, were the στοιχεῖα in verse 3 understood primarily as angels or beings in some sense, one would expect ὑπό to have been followed by the genitive case.[157] Instead, the comparison, in which the plural form στοιχεῖα is associated with the ἐπίτροποι καὶ οἰκονόμοι, is centered on the law "which could [not] bring life" (3:21-εἰ γὰρ ἐδόθη νόμος ὁ δυνάμενος ζῳοποιῆσαι...).[158] From this vantage point, Paul's failure to pick up ἄγγελοι from 3:19 suggests that he did not regard the belief in angelic instrumentality in the giving of the law as tantamount to an objectionable venerative attitude.

Hence, the motif of angelic mediation of the law, an interpretation of the Sinai events well-attested in Jewish and Christian literature during Gre-

---

[156] Apart from whether readers would have been able to follow referential distinctions on the basis of a fluctuation in pronouns, the argument in 3:1-4:11 turns so much on the issue of soteriology that such deliberate precision would have risked playing into the distinctions held by Paul's Judaizing opponents.

[157] Thus on internal grounds it seems unlikely that Paul presupposes a background in which angels were identified with natural phenomena; contra CALLAN, "Pauline Midrash in Gal 3:19b" 551 n. 4.

[158] See E.P. SANDERS, *Paul, the Law, and the Jewish People*, pp. 68-69 and Heikki RÄISÄNEN, *Paul and the Law* (Philadelphia/Tübingen: Fortress and J.C.B. Mohr [Paul Siebeck], 1986) 131.

co-Roman antiquity,[159] only serves Paul's argument by distancing the law from the promise-covenant which God had made with Abraham (3:17; cf. v. 20). On the basis of the epistle, it is quite reasonable to argue that Paul is polemicizing against the Torah as conditional for the admission of Gentiles into the community and, further, that he is drawing an analogy between it and the former allegiances of the Galatians to the "elements". It is going too far, however, to include a worship of angels within the analogy.[160]

b. Colossians 2:18

This text alone has played a major role in scholarly discussion concerning the nature of the "Colossian error" opposed in the epistle. In Colossians 2:18 the phrase "worship of angels," which appears within the first of two successive participial phrases (θέλων ἐν ταπεινοφροσύνῃ καὶ θρησκείᾳ τῶν ἀγγέλων, ἃ ἑόρακεν ἐμβατεύων), has been subjected to widely divergent interpretations. It has traditionally been supposed that the author was engaged in a polemic against those who were advocating the veneration of angels within a cultic setting. Many interpreters have often explained this posture (and, hence, the "error" itself) as Jewish, that is, as a practice that they think can be attributed to at least some Jewish groups.[161] In order to substantiate

---

[159] See esp. JOSEPHUS Ant. 15.136 (ἡμῶν δὲ κάλλιστα τῶν δογμάτων καὶ τὰ ὁσιώτατα τῶν ἐν τοῖς νόμοις δι' ἀγγέλων παρὰ τοῦ θεοῦ μαθόντων; though see R. MARCUS and A. WIKGREN, Josephus [LCL, 410; Cambridge, Mass./London: Harvard Univ. and Heinemann, 1980] 8.66-67 n. a); Jub 1:27, 29; 2:1, etc. (transmitted to Moses through the angel of the Presence); and the intro. to the socalled Apoc.Mos. In the NT, see Acts 7:53 (εἰς διαταγὰς ἀγγέλων; cf. v. 38-μετὰ τοῦ ἀγγέλου [sg.] τοῦ λαλοῦντος αὐτῷ) and Hebr 2:2 (ὁ δι' ἀγγέλων λαληθεὶς λόγος).

[160] Were Paul polemicizing against a veneration of angels among the Galatians, one would expect him, esp. in the section following this argumentation, to have avoided commending them for receiving him ὡς ἄγγελον θεοῦ... ὡς Χριστὸν Ἰησοῦν (4:14b)!

[161] See J.B. LIGHTFOOT, Saint Paul's Epistles to the Colossians and to Philemon (London: Macmillan, 1879) 71-111 who, in arguing that the opponents represented an early form of Jewish Gnosticism similar to the Essenes, nevertheless concluded, "In the Colossian epistle we still breathe the atmosphere of Jewish angelology, nor is there any trace of the aeon of later Gnosticism." (p. 108). See further WILLIAMS, "The Cult of Angels at Colossae" 437-38 ("the worship of angels...was only to be found among Jews in a few circles [as those at Colossae] and these removed from more orthodox influences"); T. K. ABBOTT, Epistles to the Ephesians and to the Colossians (ICC; Edinburgh: T. & T. Clark, 1897) 268; S. LYONNET, "Les adversaires de Paul à Colosses," Bib 56 (1956) 27-38 (the mystical motif of seeing angels suggests a veneration of angels); W.D. DAVIES, "Paul and the Dead Sea Scrolls: Flesh and Spirit," in ed. Krister STENDAHL, The Scrolls and the New Testament (New York:

this view, appeals have been made to JOSEPHUS' description of the Essenes,[162] Qumran texts,[163] the Κήρυγμα Πέτρου (2nd cent. CE)[164] and later patristic writers who, in commenting on this passage, are thought to have argued that the polemic of the epistle was directed against just such a practice.[165] This appeal to a Jewish background, however, has been dismissed by those scholars who are

---

Harper, 1957) 167; J. MICHL, "Engel II (jüdisch)," in *Reallexikon für Antike und Christentum* (Stuttgart: Anton Hiersemann, 1962) 75; SIMON, *Verus Israel*, pp. 345 and 367; Herbert BRAUN, *Qumran und das Neue Testament* (Tübingen: J. C.B. Mohr [Paul Siebeck], 1966) I.232; GUNTHER, *St. Paul's Opponents*, pp. 173-77 (though see p. 183); and, by implication, FITZMYER, "Qumran Angelology and 1 Cor 11:10," in *Essays on the Semitic Background of the New Testament* (SBLSBS, 5; Missoula: Scholars, 1974) 203.

[162] For the similarity of the opponents with the Essenes, LIGHTFOOT (*Colossians*, p. 88; similarly, LYONNET, "Les adversaires" 36) emphasized the latter's interest in preserving the names of angels (see JOSEPHUS *Ant.* 2.142: ὅμνυσιν [οἱ Ἐσσηνοί]...συντηρήσειν ὁμοίως τά τε τῆς αἱρέσεως αὐτῶν βιβλία καὶ τὰ τῶν ἀγγέλων ὀνόματα); LIGHTFOOT termed this feature an "esoteric doctrine" which linked "Essenism to the religion of Zoroaster" (*ibid.*).

[163] E.g., DAVIES, BRAUN, and LYONNET (see previous two n.'s) referred to 1QM 10.10-11; see, however, section II.B.1.a below.

[164] As cited in CLEMENT of ALEXANDRIA, *Strom.* 6.5.41 and ORIGEN, *Comm. Jn.* 13.17.104; see SIMON, "Remarques sur l'Angélolâtrie Juive," pp. 456-57 and *Verus Israel*, pp. 345-46. See section II.A.3.d below.

[165] E.g., JEROME (*Ep. ad Algasiam* 10; MPL 22, col. 1032-the *religio angelorum* of Col 2:18 is explained by referring to Acts 7:42: *deus tradidit eos* [the Jews] *ut colerent militiam coeli*); CHRYSOSTOM on Col 2:18 (MPG 62-ἦσαν τινες οἱ λέγοντες· Οὐ δεῖ ἡμᾶς διὰ τοῦ Χριστοῦ προσάγεσθαι, ἀλλὰ διὰ τῶν ἀγγέλων...[col. 514]; δι' ἀγγέλων προσήγοντο τῷ θεῷ, εἶχον πολλὰς καὶ Ἰουδαϊκὰς καὶ Ἑλληνικάς [col. 301: the occasion prompting the epistle]); THEODORE of MOPSUESTIA (MPG 66, cols. 929,932-ἐπειδὴ δι' ἀγγέλων ὁ νόμος ἐλέγετο δεδόσθαι...ὡς ἂν δὲ τῆς τοῦ νόμου φυλακῆς οὐκ ἐξιστάμενοι τῷ μηδὲ τοὺς ἀγγέλους περιορᾶν τοῦ νόμου τὴν καταφρόνησιν. Μὴ τοίνυν, φησί, τοῖς τὴν μετριότητα ταύτην ἐπιδεικνυμένοις καὶ βουλομένοις τοὺς ἀγγέλους προβαλέσθαι προσέχητε; THEODORE cites Hebr 2:2 for support); and THEODORET (MPG 82, col. 613-οἱ τῷ νόμῳ συνηγοροῦντες, καὶ τοὺς ἀγγέλους σέβειν αὐτοῖς εἰσηγοῦντο, διὰ τούτων λέγοντες δεδόσθαι τὸν νόμον). THEODORET's testimony resists a simple identification with Jews contemporary to the writing of Col (*contra* ABBOTT's suggestion in *Epistles*, p. 268). THEODORET was less interested in specifying the original opponents behind Col than in identifying the reference to angel worship in the epistle with a cult of the angel Michael--practiced in Phrygia and Pisidia during his own time (τὸ τοῖς ἀγγέλοις προσεύχεσθαι· καὶ μέχρι δὲ τοῦ νῦν εὐκτήρια τοῦ ἁγίου Μιχαὴλ παρ' ἐκείνοις καὶ τοῖς ὁμόροις ἐκείνων ἔστιν ἰδεῖν) and which had been condemned by the Council of Laodicea (360 CE)--, which he considered a consequence of a belief in God's transcendence: λέγοντες ὡς ἀόρατος ὁ τῶν ὅλων θεὸς ἀνέφικτός τε καὶ ἀκατάληπτος, καὶ προσήκει διὰ τῶν ἀγγέλων τὴν θείαν εὐμένειαν πραγματεύεσθαι.

On the other hand, ORIGEN (*c.Cels.* 5.8) cites Col 2:18-19 in order *to defend Jews* against Celsus' charge of angelolatry, since the instructions here were given by Paul, "who was accurately trained in matters of the Jews" (GCS 2/2-ἀκριβῶς τὰ Ἰουδαίων παιδευθέντι).

not convinced that there is any clear evidence attesting the existence of an angel "cult" among Jews during the Greco-Roman period.[166]

Other scholars have tried to account for the polemic in Colossians 2:18 by referring to specifically non-Jewish influences. In this connection, Martin DIBELIUS' analysis took the term ἐμβατεύων ("to enter") as the interpretive point of departure. On the basis of inscriptions excavated at the Claros temple of Apollo in Asia Minor, DIBELIUS--and independently, four years earlier, William RAMSEY--contended that ἐμβατεύειν functioned there as a *terminus technicus* within the context of a mystery cult.[167] More specifically, the proximity of this verb to expressions associated with the initiation (μυηθέντες or παραλαβὼν τὰ μυστήρια) into priestly rites performed at the sanctuary gave DIBELIUS reason to suspect an equation which could explain the other elements attributed to the opponents in the verse. While he identified ταπεινοφροσύνη with the ascetic requirements listed in 2:21, DIBELIUS concluded from ἐμβατεύων that θρησκεία τῶν ἀγγέλων refers to an initiate's worship of "cosmic deities" (2:8,20-τὰ στοιχεῖα τοῦ κόσμου).[168]

Critics of DIBELIUS' thesis have, however, rightly questioned whether ἐμβατεύειν, the meaning of which depends on its association with more specific terminology than that of Colossians, could have functioned at all as a technical expression in the inscriptions. Furthermore, it remains uncertain to what degree the Claros inscriptions, which date to the second century CE (132-163 CE), can be expected to supply information with such precision about

---

[166] See esp. PERCY, *Probleme*, pp. 149-55 and W. CARR, *Angels and Principalities* (SNTSMS, 42; Cambridge: Univ., 1981) 69-71.

[167] Martin DIBELIUS, "Die Isisweihe bei Apuleius und verwandte Initiations-Riten," *Sitzungsberichte der Heidelberger Akademie der Wissenschaften, Philosophisch-historische Klasse* 8 n. 4 (1917), reprinted in idem, *Botschaft und Geschichte. Gesammelte Aufsätze von Martin Dibelius* (Tübingen: J.C.B. Mohr [Paul Siebeck] 1956) 2.30-79, esp. pp. 59-64 (citations below refer to this reprint) and William RAMSEY, *The Teaching of Paul in Terms of the Present Day* (London: Hodder & Stoughton, 1913) 283-305.

[168] "Isisweihe," pp. 63-64: "Diese Beziehung der Paulus-Worte auf visionäres Schauen empfiehlt sich um so mehr, als wir auch hier annehmen dürfen, daß die Räume [= ἃ ἑόρακεν], die der Myste 'betritt', kosmische Bezirke darstellen. Denn kosmische Gottheiten sind es, die in der θρησκεία τῶν ἀγγέλων verehrt werden: die στοιχεῖα (2,8)" (p. 63); see also DIBELIUS and H. GREEVEN, *An die Kolosser Epheser und Philemon* (HNT, 12; Tübingen: J.C.B. Mohr [Paul Siebeck] 1953³) 35. According to DIBELIUS, such a cult existed outside the church at Colossae. DIBELIUS' interpretation of ἐμβατεύειν as pointing to a local mystery cult is still essentially followed by J. GNILKA, *Der Kolosserbrief* (HThKNT, 10/1; Freiburg/Basel/Wien: Herder, 1980) 153 and Peter POKORNY, *Der Brief des Paulus an die Kolosser* (THNT, 10/1; Berlin: Evangelische Verlagsanstalt, 1987) 95-101.

developments in the previous century.¹⁶⁹ In addition to DIBELIUS' interpretation within the context of mystery religions, others have linked the Colossian errorists with Pythagorean ideas¹⁷⁰ and Bacchic practices.¹⁷¹ These efforts at contextualization have in common the concern to illuminate local factors behind the controversy.¹⁷²

---

¹⁶⁹ As recognized, e.g., by A.D. NOCK, "The Vocabulary of the New Testament," *JBL* 52 (1933) 131-33; E. LOHMEYER, *Die Briefe an die Philipper, an die Kolosser und an Philemon* (MeyerK; Göttingen: Vandenhoeck & Ruprecht, 1961) 124 n. 2; H. PREISKER, "ἐμβατεύω," in *TDNT* 2.535-36; Fred O. FRANCIS, *A Re-examination of the Colossian Controversy* (Yale Univ.: Ph.D. Diss., 1965) 39-47; and Roy YATES, "'The Worship of Angels' (Col 2:18)" *ExT* 97 (1985) 14.

¹⁷⁰ E. SCHWEIZER, *Der Brief an die Kolosser* (EKKNT; Neukirchen-Vluyn / Zürich: Neukirchener and Benziger, 1976) 122-23: "Vor allem ist die Verehrung der zum Himmel aufsteigenden Seelen, die im Judentum mit den Engeln, im Hellenismus mit den Heilanden der Mysterien gleichgesetzt werden, in der pythagoreisch beeinflußten Philosophie belegt"; see also idem, "Christianity of the Circumcised and Judaism of the Uncircumcised: Background of Matthew and Colossians," in eds. Robert HAMMERTON-KELLY and Robin SCROGGS, *Jews, Greeks and Christians: Religious Cultures in Late Antiquity. Essays in Honour of W.D. Davies* (SJLA, 21; Leiden: Brill, 1976) 250 and 254 and "Slaves of the Elements" 456-68.

¹⁷¹ CARR, *Angels and Principalities*, pp. 68-69 and 191 n. 73, drawing upon the work of E.R. DODDS, *Euripides' Bacchae* (Oxford: Univ., 1960) and Martin P. NILSSON, *The Dionysiac Mysteries of the Hellenistic and Roman Age* (Lund: Gleerup, 1957), relates ἐμβατεύειν to ecstatic excesses of a Phrygian form of Bacchism. CARR (*ibid.*, p. 70), however, assumes a position (similar to that of PERCY, *Probleme*, pp. 158-60) that, as in Judaism, there is no direct evidence for an angel cult in paganism of the first century; see also idem, "Two Notes on Colossians," *JTS* 34 (1973) 500.

¹⁷² In an important recent study on "Mediator Figures in Asia Minor: Epigraphic Evidence" (paper prepared for the consultation on Jewish and Christian Mediator Figures in Greco-Roman Antiquity, SBL Meeting 1992 in San Francisco) Clinton E. ARNOLD, on the basis of pagan, Jewish, and Christian inscriptions, explains θρησκεία τῶν ἀγγέλων as "a rhetorically powerful way of shocking the readers into viewing their own practice less favorably" (manuscript, p. 28). The phrase, which would have been reminiscent of pagan "angel cults"--which ARNOLD understands as having been devoted to the goddess Hekate--known through inscriptions from Stratonikeia, Temrek, and Didyma, was actually leveled against the tendency of the readers to invoke angels in special circumstances, a practice attested in the Jewish inscriptions. ARNOLD's synthesis of pagan and Jewish evidence from Asia Minor thus advances the discussion concerning the phenomenological background of Colossians in a way which is not inconsistent with the polemical texts found in rabbinic, early patristic, and apocalyptic literature (discussed in sections II.A.1 and II.A.2). Furthermore, ARNOLD's study demonstrates how problematic it is to assume that the "local" background for Colossae must be restricted to non-Jewish sources. The main difficulty with his religio-historical explanation, however, may be, from the Jewish end, a tendency to emphasize elements of magic to the exclusion of other forms of Judaism and, within the Colossians passage, its almost complete focus on the phrase θρησκεία τῶν ἀγγέλων while neglecting its association with the terms ταπεινοφροσύνη and ἑόρακεν. It

Many scholars, while maintaining that the possibility of such local influences at Colossae cannot be dismissed, have nevertheless insisted, in view of the general nature of Christianity during this time, that it would be wrong to ignore categorically a Jewish background for the heresy.¹⁷³ Therefore, most interpreters who hold to the idea that the writer was referring to an existing angel cult, have been content to speak of some kind of religious "syncretism" composed of a certain combination of Jewish and pagan (often "Gnostic") elements.¹⁷⁴ Two tenets have regularly accompanied this outlook: (1) the interpretation of τῶν ἀγγέλων as an objective genitive (as is the case with all views discussed thus far) and (2) the necessarily non-Jewish character *of the cult* itself.

Both contentions were called into question by Fred O. FRANCIS in his influential article on "Humility and Angelic Worship in Col. 2:18."¹⁷⁵ Like

---

therefore remains to be seen whether "invocation" alone can account for the practice against which the expression was directed; see pp. 181-91 below.

¹⁷³ Günther BORNKAMM ("Die Häresie des Kolosserbriefes," *TLZ* 73 [1948] 15 defended a Jewish background, albeit a limited one, by appealing to (1) the antithesis between σκία των μελλόντων and σῶμα τοῦ Χριστοῦ (Col 2:17), which presupposes some continuity in salvation history; (2) the use of the term ἄγγελοι in 2:18 instead of στοιχεῖα; and (3) the characterization of baptism as περιτομή. ROWLAND (*The Open Heaven*, pp. 409 and 513 n. 26), referring to Col 2:16ff., emphasizes the presence of Jewish communities which were flourishing in Asia Minor.

¹⁷⁴ See BORNKAMM, "Häresie" 15 (a mystery religion mixed with a Jewish form of Gnosis); already E.F. SCOTT, *The Epistles of Paul to the Colossians, to Philemon and to the Ephesians* (MNTC; London: Hodder and Stoughton, 1930) 8 and 53 (the angel cult was essentially pagan, but was mixed with Jewish "syncretism"); SIMON, "Remarques sur l'Angélolâtrie Juive," pp. 456-58 (p. 457: "... d'une hérésie syncrétisante, combinant des observances juives avec une angélologie et une angélolâtrie dont les racines sont à la fois juives et païennes..."); *Verus Israel*, p. 345; F.F. BRUCE, *Commentary on the Epistle to the Colossians* (NICNT; Grand Rapids: Eerdmans, 1957) 247-48 ("...this cult ...an ingredient of non-Jewish provenience in the amalgam of Jewish legalism and Gnostic asceticism"); Johannes LÄHNEMANN, *Der Kolosserbrief* (SNT, 3; Gütersloh: Mohn, 1971) 138 ("nicht ganz auf die Gedankenwelt des spätjüdischen Schrifttums beschränken können...sondern die ganze Breite der synkretistischen Hintergründe beachten müssen"); Ralph P. MARTIN, *Colossians and Philemon* (NCBC; Grand Rapids: Eerdmans, 1973) 94 ("the Colossian situation is thoroughly syncretistic and [besides Jewish features] included pagan elements"); Eduard LOHSE, *Die Briefe an die Kolosser und an Philemon* (MeyerK, 9/2; Göttingen: Vandenhoeck & Ruprecht, 1977) 175 n. 2 ("Verehrung der Engel [ist] innerhalb des Judentums nicht denkbar.... Doch will der synkretistische Charakter der φιλοσοφία beachtet sein, der einem Engelkult kein Hindernis entgegensetzt."); and LONA, *Eschtologie*, p. 207 ("[Man kann] schließen, daß die jüdische Tradition von der Fürsprache der Engel bei Gott in Phrygien auf fruchtbaren Boden fiel...").

¹⁷⁵ Originally published in *ST* 16 (1962) 109-134.

Ernst PERCY before him, FRANCIS did not find any evidence of a pagan or Jewish angel cult that could illuminate "the Colossian error"; instead, he preferred to regard the heresy as an expression of "ascetic-mystic piety [which] obtained generally in the Hellenistic world-not specifically gnostic, not entirely Jewish."[176] Against this general background, he argued that the elements ταπεινοφροσύνη and θρησκεία τῶν ἀγγέλων, picked up in the following relative clause (ἃ ἑόρακεν ἐμβατεύων), function grammatically as the object of what the errorists were claiming to *see* during a visionary ascent or "entrance" (ἐμβατεύων) into heavenly realms. As a result, the polemic may have been more concerned with religious practices than with a doctrinal (i.e. christological) dispute. Objectionable in the situation at Colossae was the apparent requirement that one's identity in Christ should be augmented by a rigorous asceticism, expressed in the errorists' technical term ταπεινοφροσύνη, as well as by a mystical ascent of which *participation in the angels' worship of God* must have been a primary component. In appealing to a variety of passages from early Jewish literature (1QSb 4.25-26; 1QH 3.20-22; *4 Ez* 5:13,20, etc.; *2 Bar* 5:7; 9:2, etc.; *Jos.Asen.* 10-14; PHILO, *Somn.* 1.33-37; *Vit. Mos.* 2.67-70; *Quaes.Ex.* 2.39; *Ebr.* 148-52; *Asc.Isa.* 7:37; 8:17, etc.; *T.Job* 48-50; *3 En* 1:12; *Apoc.Abr.* 17), the *Shepherd of Hermas* (*Sim.* 5.3.7; *Vis.* 3.10.6), TERTULLIAN (*Ieiun.*12), and the *Corpus Hermeticum* (1.26; 13.6-7), FRANCIS tried to show how both "humility" (broadly defined as rigorous ascetic practices) and "angelic worship" are recorded as featured elements in visions of heaven.

FRANCIS' hypothesis, though in some ways not without earlier proponents, offered a comprehensive argumentation which not only treated the individual components of 2:18 but also related them to an understanding of the epistle as a whole. As a result, this interpretation has won considerable, though not universal, support in recent years.[177] A connection between motifs

---

[176] *Ibid.*, p. 134.

[177] See esp. YATES, "The Worship of Angels"; ROWLAND, *Influence*, pp. 238-72 and "Apocalyptic Visions and the Exaltation of Christ in the Letter to the Colossians," *JSNT* 19 (1983) 73-83; Craig A. EVANS, "The Colossian Mystics," *Bib* 63 (1982) 188-205; CARR, "Two Notes" 496-500 and *Angels and Principalities*, pp. 70-71; Andrew T. LINCOLN, *Paradise Now and Not Yet. Studies in the role of the heavenly dimension in Paul's thought* (SNTSMS, 43; Cambridge: Univ., 1981) 111-113 and p. 223 n. 9; Harold W. ATTRIDGE, *The Epistle to the Hebrews* (Hermeneia; Philadelphia: Fortress, 1989) 51 (despite a caution to the contrary, Attridge draws an analogy between the problems underlying Col and Hebr); HURTADO, *One God, One Lord*, pp. 32-33; and Thomas J. SAPPINGTON, *Revelation and Redemption at Colossae* (JSNTSS, 53; Sheffield: JSOT, 1991) 150-70.

of "humility" and "worshiping with angels" with visionary accounts is indeed well attested in the literature he cites, and further support may be drawn from internal considerations of grammar and syntax. Compelling is the parallel structure between verses 18 and 17, in which the relative particle ἅ follows a list of antecedent referents. Thus whereas DIBELIUS considered the relative clause ἃ ἑόρακεν to be the object of ἐμβατεύων (which functions in the same way as the foregoing θέλων),[178] FRANCIS convincingly renders ἐμβατεύων as a temporal modifier, so that the relative particle ἅ, the object of the verb "to see," has its antecedents in ταπεινοφροσύνῃ and θρησκείᾳ τῶν ἀγγέλων. The resulting translation by FRANCIS of verse 18 is as follows: "Let no one disqualify you, being bent on humility and the worship of angels–which he has seen upon entering–being vainly puffed up by his mind of flesh."[179] If this thesis is correct, the problem at Colossae does not have any bearing on the question of the veneration of angels among Jewish groups.

There is good reason, however, to think that the customary alternative posed between a subjective and objective interpretation of τῶν ἀγγέλων is misleading. If DIBELIUS' reading is suspect because the other components of the text are made to serve his almost exclusive focus on ἐμβατεύειν in the Claros inscriptions, FRANCIS' analogous treatment of ταπεινοφροσύνῃ and τῶν ἀγγέλων as the subject matter of visionary experiences does not do justice to a necessary distinction between literature that records visions and the substance of what is seen in visions proper (see below).[180] FRANCIS seems to have been aware of the potential problem in making, by way of "an arithmetical [grammatical] judgment," ταπεινοφροσύνῃ *as practiced by the angels* the object of ἑόρακεν. Nevertheless, wishing to retain the visionary context of ascetic rigors, he was content to conclude that "instruction in humility for the purpose of obtaining visions is itself the subject of visions."[181] To support this

---

[178] "Isisweihe," p. 62.

[179] "Humility and Angelic Worship" 113.

[180] Thus SAPPINGTON (*Revelation and Redemption*, p. 160) goes one step further than FRANCIS by insisting that, given the non-repetition of ἐν before θρησκείᾳ, "the visions of the errorists included 'humility *and* worship performed by angels'," a view which FRANCIS himself explicitly rejected ("Humility and Angelic Worship" 130). This interpretation forces SAPPINGTON to relate only ἐθελοθρησκίᾳ καὶ ταπεινοφροσύνῃ καὶ ἀφειδίᾳ σώματος in v. 23 to the actions of the opponents, actions which seek to "emulate the behavior of the heavenly beings" mentioned in v. 18.

[181] "Humility and Angelic Worship" 130. On this point, FRANCIS is cited approvingly and uncritically by LINCOLN, *Paradise*, p. 223 n. 9 (also p. 112).

notion he cited numerous documents in which ascetic practices are thought to have just such a function.[182]

In considering FRANCIS' proposed reading, two points may be raised. First, the only definition for ταπεινοφροσύνη which he suggests as being observed in visions is "ascetic instruction." In this way, FRANCIS can justify the association of asceticism with the didactic contents of a vision; the "seeing" is, then, not to be taken literally, but would refer to the literary medium in which visions are recorded. With respect to θρησκεία, however, the connotation of ἑόρακεν is, in accordance with FRANCIS' scheme, more direct: "to observe (the worship of angels)." Whatever the semantic range attributable to ἑόρακεν at this point, FRANCIS' interpretation requires that the term refer to visions as a literary form in the first instance and then to the activity of "seeing" or "observing" in the second. Second, it is one thing to show that ταπεινοφροσύνη is *linked* with visionary experiences recorded in literature from antiquity--on this point FRANCIS' presentation is convincing--, but it is another to account for the language of 2:18 itself. Overwhelmingly, the texts cited by FRANCIS primarily refer to ascetic practices in a context of *preparation* for visionary experiences.[183] Even when ascetic practices or instructions are given as part of a vision, the practice as such is often not "seen."

Both comments suggest that, although FRANCIS has successfully demonstrated a connection between ascetic acts and heavenly encounters, the sense which he ascribes to ἑόρακεν requires a strained bifurcation in meaning. A better solution may lie in interpreting this verb less in its literary or literal sense ("to see") than in a derived connotation of "to experience by

---

[182] *Ibid.* 130 n. 64: "IV Ez., Syr. Bar., Apoc. Ez., Apoc. Abr., Herm., Tert. de ieiun., Dan., Philo, Som. I, Mos. II [cited in more detail earlier in the article] ... Philo, Sac. 59-63."

[183] *4 Ez* 5:20 and 6:35 (before prayer and vision of an angel), 9:23-25 (before a prayer and vision); *2 Bar* 5:7-6:4 (before a vision), 9:2-10:1 and 12:5-13:2 (before an auditory communication), 21:1-3 (before a prayer), 43:3 (intructions for preparation to hear from God), 47:2-48:1 (narrative of preparation); *Apoc.Ezek.* 1:5 (fasting before seeing "the mysteries of God and his angels"); *Apoc.Abr.* 9:7-10 and 12:1-2 (before a vision; in 12:2, seeing the "angel" is described as Abraham's "food"); *Shep.Herm. Vis.* 3.10.6 (instruction and narrative of preparation before vision), *Sim.* 5.1.1-5 (before instructions on fasting in a vision), 5.3.5-8 (instructions on fasting and ταπεινοφροσύνη within vision); TERTULLIAN *ieiun.* 12 (ταπεινοφροσύνη practiced before reception of revelations); Dan 9:3 (before a prayer and vision of Gabriel), 10:2 (before a vision); PHILO *Somn.* 1.36 (Moses heard preparatory ascetic instructions from "heavenly hymns" before encountering God), *Vit.Mos.* 2.67-70 (Moses before encountering God), and *Sacr.* 59-63.

means of seeing." If this meaning obtains, then it is no longer necessary to decide whether the writer intended the genitive phrase to denote either the activity of angels or human behavior in which angels are venerated. Indeed, both motifs are found side by side in a number of early Jewish texts,[184] and it is certainly possible that the notion of participating in angelic worship is regarded as dangerous not only on account of its superfluity for the believer, but also, and perhaps especially, because it posed a context in which a seer may be tempted to venerate angelic beings who are encountered during the ascent.[185]

In this light, it would be misleading to dismiss the possibility that the problem at Colossae, as represented in 2:18, involved dimensions which had both practical (3:1-17) *and* christological (1:15-20; 2:9-10) consequences. Thus we may suggest that in 2:18 the opponents are said to emphasize "humility and worship of angels," which they have "experienced within a visionary medium while entering (heavenly realms)."

c. Hebrews 1:5-2:18

As argued in section II.A.3.a above, the argument in Galatians is too laconic to allow for an interpretation which integrally connects the Torah given through angels and an "enslavement" to the στοιχεῖα. The themes of angelic mediation of the law and worship are, however, linked in the first two chapters of the "Epistle" to the Hebrews (1:6-7,13; 2:2). Though, similar to Colossians, the author of Hebrews clearly and radically distinguishes the nature and function of "angels" from categories of Christology, it is more difficult than in either Galatians or Colossians to ascertain whether he was ac-

---

[184] See n. 99 (section II.A.2.b.i) above and the analysis of the Qumran *ShirShabb*, 4Q400 2.1-2 and 4Q403 1 i.32-33 in section II.B.1.b.i (pp. 156-61) below. FRANCIS ("Humility and Angelic Worship" 129) allows for this connection when he acknowledged that "a subjective genitive referring to angelic worship is further confirmed and not contradicted by the derivative possibility of worship directed to angels"; this association is missed by HURTADO, *One God, One Lord*, pp. 32-33.

[185] If the angel veneration at Colossae is to be related to a visionary context, its form may be conceived in at least two ways: (1) The exemplary nature of angelic worship may have led to a certain veneration accorded angels themselves (as in 4QShirShabb; see II.B.1.b.i, pp. 156-61 below), or (2) the dangers associated with a mystical ascent, during which the seer is accompanied and encountered by angelic beings of various classes, may have tempted the seer to petition angels for assistance along the way (an idea which is apparently rejected in *Asc.Isa.*; see BAUCKHAM, "The Worship of Jesus" 332 and 340 n. 71).

tually engaging in a polemic against angel-related beliefs which were either adhered to by the intended readers or which posed a threat within their environment. An overview of the argument in Hebrews 1-2 will be followed by an in-depth analysis of the angel-Son comparison.

Already in the exordium a motif of the exaltation-enthronement, cast in language alluding to Psalm 110:1 (Hebr 1:3e), expresses a clear distinction between the Son and *angels* (v. 4). In the following verses (vv. 5-13) this contrast is developed further through a series of explicit scriptural citations. The appeal to Psalm 2:7 and 2 Samuel 7:14 (v. 5; both passages, LXX= MT), which stresses that Christ is both "Son" and "begotten," is produced in response to the rhetorical question, "For *to which of the angels* (τίνι... τῶν ἀγγέλων) did he ever say... ?" In verse 6 it is the citation itself which depicts the subservience of angels; at the introduction of the "firstborn"[186] in-

---

[186] In Greek Jewish literature, the notion of being "firstborn" is applied to σοφία (who functions as "the architect of all things" and teacher; WisdSol 7:22-μονογενές), λόγος (= πρωτόγονος-PHILO, *Conf.ling.* 146; *Somn.* 1. 215; *Agr.* 51), and to the patriarchal figure Jacob (*Pr.Jos.* preserved in ORIGEN, *Comm.Jn.* 12.189 [*GCS* 2/4-πρωτόγονος παντὸς ζῷου]). None of these passages, however, furnishes an intelligible background for the *contrast* between the "Son" and angels: in WisdSol 7:7 and 22 σοφία is associated with the term πνεῦμα (cf. 1:7, 14); in *Conf.ling.* 146 and *Agr.* 51 PHILO identifies λόγος as both υἱὸς θεοῦ and ἀρχάγγελος or ἄγγελος; and in the *Pr.Jos.* Jacob is the embodiment of a preeminent angelic being. A specific allusion here to Christ's resurrection (as in Rom 8:29 and Rev 1:5) is also unlikely since it is nowhere mentioned in the context.

If anything, the term may have been chosen as a complementary designation for "Son" appointed to rule in v. 5. The term carries such a royal connotation in LXX Ps 88:28 (κἀγὼ πρωτότοκον θήσομαι αὐτὸν ὑψηλὸν παρὰ τοῖς βασιλεῦσιν τῆς γῆς), a psalm which shares other catchwords with the context (ὑψηλός, cf. 1:3e; the comparative παρά, cf. 1:4; on LXX Ps 88:7, see n. 228 below). The appointment motif in LXX Ps 88:28 fits in well with the citations in v. 5, and the passage was at least later found suitable among the rabbis for messianic interpretation (*Exod.R.* 19:7). Most likely, then, the term πρωτότοκος was applied as an explication of Ps 110:1 (v. 3) in conjunction with the "Son" citations in v. 5; in this manner, it was understood as a designation appropriate to Christ's exalted status. The verb with πρωτότοκος is, however, not τίθημι (as in LXX Ps 88), but εἰσάγειν. The temporal construction in v. 6 which contains this verb (ὅταν... εἰσαγάγῃ τὸν πρωτότοκον εἰς τὴν οἰκουμένην) recalls the formula in Deut 6:10 and 11:29 which refers to Israel's entry into the promised land: καὶ ἔσται ὅταν κύριος ὁ θεός σου εἰσαγάγῃ σε εἰς τὴν γῆν. Thus in its present form, the introduction to the citation forges a link between the exaltation of the "firstborn" and the destiny of those who belong to him; "Israel" is designated πρωτότοκος in LXX Ex 4:22; see P. ANDRIESSEN, "La teneur judéo-chrétienne de Hé I 6 et II 14B-III 2," *NT* 18 (1976) 293-97 and L.D. HURST, "The Christology of Hebrews 1 and 2," in eds. HURST and N.T. WRIGHT, *The Glory of Christ in the New Testament. Studies in Christology in Memory of George Bradford Caird* (Oxford: Univ., 1987) 159.

to the world, "all *angels* of God" (=LXX Ps 96:7-πάντες ἄγγελοι θεοῦ; cf. MT 97:7-כל אלהים) are to "worship" (=LXX Deut 32:43-προσκυνησάτωσαν) him.[187] In verses 7-9 the contrast between Christ and angels is further elaborated on the basis of two passages in the Psalms. Whereas Psalm 104(103):4 variously depicts the inferior nature of *angels* as only "spirits" (πνεύματα), "his ministering servants" (οἱ λειτουργοὶ αὐτοῦ, *parallelismus membrorum* with ἄγγελοι), and "a firey flame" (πυρὸς φλόγα; LXX tradition-πῦρ φλέγον), Psalm 45 (44):7-8 (=LXX tradition) functions to underscore the exalted status of "the Son": addressed as ὁ θεός (vv. 8,9), he possesses an eternal throne and has been anointed above his companions" (παρὰ τοὺς μετόχους σου).[188] After the enduring character of Christ as κύριος (v. 10) is reaffirmed through a citation of Psalm 102(101):26-28 (vv. 10-12),[189] the argument returns to Psalm 110:1 (v.

---

[187] If the basis of the citation cannot be restricted to LXX Ps 96:7, several possibilities concerning the use of Deut 32:43 may be entertained: (1) Deut 32:43, which reads πάντες οἱ υἱοὶ θεοῦ (from בני אלים; 4QDeut [=4Q44] to 32:43 has כל אלהים; absent in MT), has been altered ; (2) both LXX Ps 96:7 and Deut 32:43 have been conflated; or (3) the specific wording (with οἱ ἄγγελοι θεοῦ) reflects rather the Grk version of the Song of Moses in a psalter appended to Cod. Alex.; see ATTRIDGE, *Hebrews*, p. 57 n. 78 and bibl. cited there. If the citation made use of Deut 32:43 at all, then a shift to or choice of the reading "angels" could have served both to underline the focus of the comparison and perhaps to avoid possible confusion with the emphasis in v. 5 on Christ's "Son"-ship; see James W. THOMPSON, *The Beginnings of Christian Philosophy* (CBQMS, 13; Washington, D.C.: CBA, 1982) 132 n. 17. This interpretation has recently been challenged by HURST in *The Epistle to the Hebrews. Its background of thought* (SNTSMS, 65; Cambridge: Univ., 1990) 45-46, who argues that "In *his* [the author's] Bible angels were never called 'sons.'" However, HURST's wish to interpret ἐν υἱοῖς θεοῦ in Ps 88:6 LXX--which, significantly, also speaks about the appointment of a πρωτότοκος "exalted above (ὑψηλὸς παρά) the rulers of the earth" (v. 28)--as human beings is strained; the parallel expressions οἱ οὐρανοί (v. 6) and ἐν νεφέλαις (v. 7) indicate rather a worship by heavenly beings (MT-בני אלים). In any case, in αὐτῷ of the citation the author interprets an original reference to God as Christ, who is considered worthy of angelic worship.

[188] In the context of Hebr 1 the μέτοχοι almost certainly refer to angels; so correctly William R.G. LOADER, *Sohn und Hoherpriester* (WMANT, 53; Neukirchen-Vluyn: Neukirchener, 1981) 25; Louis DUSSANT, *Synopse structurelle de l'Epitre aux Hebreux* (Paris: Cerf, 1981) 24; and William L. LANE, *Hebrews 1-8* (WBC, 47A; Dallas: Word Books, 1991) 30. The comparative παρ' τοὺς μετόχους σου picks up παρ' αὐτούς (= angels) in v. 4. A further or even exclusive reference to Christ's followers, as argued by ATTRIDGE (*Hebrews*, p. 60 and further bibl. in n. 117) and emphasized by BRUCE (*Hebrews*, p. 21), is not as immediately apparent. The term itself logically suggests some analogy between Christ and the angels, but this aspect of the comparison is not elaborated by the author.

[189] These verses do not contain any clear references to angels (*contra* ATTRIDGE, *Hebrews*, pp. 60-61); as in the Psalm itself, antecedents for the 3rd pers. pronoun αὐτούς (v. 12) are the earth and heavens (v. 10). The cita-

13). This time the application of the psalm takes the form of a citation, introduced by the rhetorical question adapted from verse 5: "And *to which of the angels* has he ever said,[190] 'Sit at my right hand, until I make your enemies a footstool under your feet'?" In verse 14 the author concludes, not with a statement about Christ, but with another rhetorical question summarily referring to the angels' proper function as λειτουργικὰ πνεύματα (drawn from Ps. 103:4 LXX cited in v. 7). Here, however, a new element is introduced; angels are not only servants of God and thus subject to Christ, but also render service (διακονία) for the sake of the believing community.

The reference to "those who are about to inherit salvation" in verse 14 introduces an exhortation not to neglect the message associated with Christ.[191] In 2:1-4, however, no real comparison is undertaken between "the word spoken through angels" (v. 2-ὁ δι' ἀγγέλων λαληθεὶς λόγος) and "the salvation which is spoken through the Lord" (v. 3-σωτηρίας ἥτις...λαλεῖσθαι διὰ τοῦ κυρίου). Instead, the stated difference serves as the basis for emphasizing the responsibility on the part of the author's readers.[192] An argued comparison is resumed in 2:5: "for *not to angels* did he subject the world to come." The following phrase, "concerning which we are speaking," indicates that the salvation events which have already dawned in Christ (vv. 3-4) are eschatologi-

---

tion functions rather to aggrandize further the cosmic-protological supremacy of Christ, here in relation to creation (cf. 1:2b). Accordingly, the conjunction δέ (instead of γάρ; see following n.), which opens v. 13, suggests a return to the comparison; see the traditio-historical considerations below.

[190] The wording is slightly different: δέ instead of γάρ; the verb and adverb before instead of after τῶν ἀγγέλων; and the verb in the perf. (εἴρηκεν) instead of in the aor. (εἶπεν). The perf. form may imply that the exaltation of Christ to the right hand of God remains in effect *vis-à-vis* the angels.

[191] The logical connection expressed by διὰ τοῦτο (2:1) is unclear. That the recipients of salvation mentioned in 1:14 are picked up by the 1st pers. plur. pronoun in 2:1-4 is apparent enough, but does the warning not to fall away stem (1) from the angels' διακονία on behalf of believers, (2) from the idea that angels are inferior (i.e., an elevated view of angels is tantamount to neglecting "so great a salvation"), or (3) from the general argument of Christ's superiority? The emphasis on Christ in vv. 3-4 suggests that the author wished to make the latter point (see ATTRIDGE, *Hebrews*, pp. 63-64). Nevertheless, the possibility of (2) suggests that the foregoing argument concerning angelic inferiority (insofar as it is such) is not entirely consonant with the ensuing exhortation.

[192] Thus the comparison is not merely a matter of expressing the superiority of Christ over angels as it is the focus of the argument. Here angels play a role that allows for salvation-historical continuity; whereas βέβαιος (v. 2a) expresses the validity (however inferior) of the *law* spoken through angels, ἐβεβαιώθη (v. 3b) refers to the confirmation of the *salvation* brought through Christ.

cal; hence, for the author any notion of a present rule of angels in the cosmos is excluded. A further basis for Christ's superiority over the angels is presented in the citation and interpretation of Psalm 8:5-7 (citation in vv. 6-8a). This time, however, the coronation of Christ and the subjection of all things "under his feet" is linked with his being made "a little while lower than the angels,"[193] an event to which the author attaches decisive soteriological significance (vv. 9-18).[194] Finally, toward the end of chapter 2 the author states that Christ's redemptive activity was obviously (δήπου) not carried out for the sake of angels, but in behalf of Abraham's seed (v. 16). Thus the soteriological alignment between Christ and human beings, who have both shared the same nature (v. 14-αἵματος καὶ σαρκός... παραπλησίως μετέσχεν τῶν αὐτῶν; cf. vv. 10-13), bypasses angels who are neither the source nor objects of salvation.

To sum up thus far, the relation between angels and Christ is, in the text as it stands, expressed by four negative formulations: (1) no angel has ever been addressed by God as "Son" (1:5); (2) no angel has ever been invited to sit at God's right hand until his enemies are subjected (1:13); (3) the world to come has not been subjected to angelic rule (2:5a); and (4) angels are not beneficiaries of the deliverance achieved by Christ.[195] The functions attributed to angels, formulated positively, are the worship of Christ (1:6), assistance to those who will inherit salvation (1:14), and the mediation of the old covenant (2:2). Whereas the argument allows for some ambiguity in the

---

[193] The argument at this point is not clear. How is the author's rejection of angelic rule "in the world to come" (2:5) related to Christ's temporary status as lower than the angels (vv. 7,9)? Though Christ's suffering and death (v. 9) is, from the author's perspective, a past (and determinative) event, it is nevertheless recognized that "now we do not yet see (νῦν δὲ οὔπω ὁρῶμεν) all things subjected to him (αὐτῷ)." If this statement may be taken as a reference to paradoxical (simultaneously "already" and "not yet") conditions under Christ, does the author leave room for the possibility that angelic rule does obtain to some degree until the eschaton is fully consummated (cf. 8:13)? If so, this idea is hardly being emphasized; there is otherwise no hint of enmity between angels and Christ in the argument.

[194] Hence the citation of Ps 8:5-7, in the text as it stands, redefines Christ's exaltation above the angels in terms of his death.

[195] The exclusion of angels as objects of salvation, formulated negatively, does not allow for an inference that they are inferior to human beings; the statement simply reflects the belief that they are spiritual, not corporeal, beings (1:7 and 14-πνεύματα). See the following n.

relationship between human beings and angels,[196] there is a clear distinction between the latter and Christ.

Why does the author engage in an argument in which Christ and angels are so clearly differentiated? Possible interpretations may be listed as follows: (1) the community addressed was somehow attracted to a veneration of angels;[197] (2) the community addressed perceived Christ as an intermediary whom they understood as an angelic figure;[198] (3) the community was interested in

---

[196] The relationship between humans and angels in Hebr is not the focus of the author's comparisons and, hence, would have to be inferred. Whereas 1:14 may leave an impression that angels, on the basis of their "service," are inferior to believers, according to cosmological hierarchy they are considered superior (2:7-9). Finally, a certain equality may be implied in 12:22-23 in which angels and Christians in the present alike share in heavenly worship; on this, see C. SPICQ, *L'Epitre aux Hebreaux* (Paris: J. Gabalda, 1953) 2.58-59 and Ronald WILLIAMSON, *Philo and the Epistle to the Hebrews* (ALGHJ, 4; Leiden: Brill, 1970) 191-93. In this light THOMPSON's argument that the author makes as clear a *metaphysical* distinction between "Christ in the heavenly world" and "angels in the physical world" (*Beginnings*, p. 134) is not persuasive.

[197] For early proponents of this position, see bibl. in John REUMANN, "Martin Werner and 'Angel Christology'," *TLQ* 8 (1956) 357 n. 29. See further BOUSSET-GRESSMANN, *Die Religion des Judentums*, pp. 329-30; Hans WINDISCH, *Der Hebräerbrief* (HNT, 14; Tübingen: J.C.B. Mohr [Paul Siebeck], 1931) 17 (refers to Col 2:18; Rev 19:10; 22:8-9; 1 Clem 56:1; and JUSTIN, *Apol.* I.6); T.W. MANSON, "The Problem of the Epistle to the Hebrews," *BJRL* 32 (1949) 1-17, esp. pp. 12-13 (Col 2:18); Jean HÉRING, *L'Epitre aux Hebreux* (CNT, 12; Paris/Neuchatel: Delachaux and Niestlé, 1954) 24 (the author was contending against influence of "gnostic, 'spiritualizing' movements"); Y. YADIN, "The Dead Sea Scrolls and the Epistle to the Hebrews," in ed. C. RABIN, *Aspects of the Dead Sea Scrolls* (ScrHier, 4; Jerusalem: Magness/Hebrew Univ., 1965^2, repr. from 1958) 39-40 and 45-48 (1QS 3.21; 11.7-8; 1QH 10.8; 3.21-22; 1QM 13.9-10; 17.6-8; a particular emphasis on Michael, identified as the "Prince of Light"); H. KOSMALA, *Hebräer-Essener-Christen. Studien zur Vorgeschichte der frühchristlichen Verkündigung* (SPB, 1; Leiden: Brill, 1959) (the readers were as yet unconverted Jews who held beliefs very close to those of the Essenes); BORNKAMM, "Das Bekenntnis im Hebräerbrief," in idem, *Studien zu Antike und Urchristentum. Gesammelte Aufsätze* (2 vols.; BEvT, 16 and 28; München: Kaiser, 1958-1963) 198 n. 23 (the readers' views, as those of the communities at Colossae and Galatia, were endangered by an "angel cult"); WILLIAMSON, *Philo and the Epistle to the Hebrews*, p. 194 (as in Col 2:18); Philip E. HUGHES, *A Commentary on the Epistle to the Hebrews* (Grand Rapids: Eerdmans, 1977) 51-53 (follows YADIN); and Robert JEWETT, *Letter to Pilgrims. A Commentary on the Epistle to the Hebrews* (New York: Pilgrim, 1981) 5-13, esp. p. 6 (the *Sitz im Leben* behind Hebr and Col is analogous). BRUCE, *The Epistle to the Hebrews* (NICNT; Grand Rapids: Eerdmans, 1964) 9, considers a "doctrine of angel-worship" (see 13:9) as a possible, but uncertain, explanation for the argument behind chapters 1-2; see also *ibid.*, p. 376 on 12:22.

[198] J. Rendel HARRIS, *Josephus and his Testimony* (Cambridge: Heffer, 1931) esp. p. 18 (the Slav JOSEPHUS, as Hebr, argues against the identification of Christ as an angel); Adolphine BAKKER, "Christ an Angel?," *ZNW* 32 (1933) 255-65, esp. pp. 258-63 (builds on HARRIS' thesis); Martin WERNER, *Die*

worship with angels;[199] (4) the author and/or readers were aware of contemporary Jewish angelological traditions, and the author attempts to discourage his readers from showing an active interest in such ideas;[200] and (5) the inferiority of angels to Christ is a rhetorical or literary foil through which the author argues the superiority of the new Covenant over the old.[201]

Entstehung des christlichen Dogmas (Bern/Leipzig: Haupt, 1941) 344-45 (appeal to *Asc.Isa.* 7-9); SPICQ, *L'Epître aux Hebreaux*, 2.60 and n. 5, but who later thinks that the author "réagit contre une estime exagérée du ministère des anges" as found at Qumran ("L'Épître aux Hébreux, Apollos, Jean-Baptiste, les Hellénistes et Qumran," *RQ* 1 [1958] 377-78); H.W. MONTEFIORE, *A Commentary on the Epistle to the Hebrews* (New York/London: Harper and Black, 1964) 35, 40-47; Otto MICHEL, *Der Brief an die Hebräer* (MeyerK, 13; Göttingen: Vandenhoeck & Ruprecht, 1966) 131-32 (appeals esp. to JUSTIN, *Dial.* 34.2 and *Shep.Herm.*, the ideas of which have roots in Jewish thought); Albert VANHOYE, *Situation du Christ. L'epître aux Hébreux 1-2* (LD, 58; Paris: Cerf, 1969) 98-99 (the situation assumed in Hebrews, an angel-Christology, is analogous to that countered in Colossians; DEY, *The Intermediary World and Patterns of Perfection in Philo and Hebrews* (SBLDS, 25; Missoula: Scholars, 1975), pp. 145-49, 154 (polemic against a perception of Christ as an angelic "intermediary" Logos-figure such as is found in PHILO); R.G. HAMMERTON-KELLY, *Pre-existence, Wisdom, and the Son of Man* (SNTSMS, 21; Cambridge: Univ., 1973) 244; Ronald H. NASH, "The Notion of Mediation in Alexandrian Judaism and the Epistle to the Hebrews," *WThJ* 40 (1977) 89-115 (as DEY); DUNN, *Unity and Diversity in the New Testament* (Philadelphia: Westminster, 1977) 260-61 ("a polemic against Ebionite christology"); and HENGEL, *Der Sohn Gottes*, pp. 131-36 and "Christological Titles in Early Christianity," p. 438.

[199] FRANCIS, "Visionary Discipline and Scriptural Tradition at Colossae," *LexThQ* 2 (1967) 77 (associates his view on Colossians with Hebrews). ATTRIDGE (*Hebrews*, p. 51) is attracted to FRANCIS' thesis as a "more likely" explanation for Hebr 1-2 than a polemic against "a worship that had angels as its object," but ultimately rejects this possibility.

[200] See especially James MOFFATT, *Epistle to the Hebrews* (ICC; Edinburgh: T. & T. Clark, 1924) 9, who is content with the general suggestion that the author "is developing his argument in the light of *some contemporary belief* about angels and revelation" (emphasis my own). A similar impression is left by the discussion of GUNTHER (*St. Paul's Opponents*, pp. 182-83).

[201] In addition to bibl. in REUMANN ("Martin Werner" 357 n. 31), see Ernst KÄSEMANN, *The Wandering People of God*, trans. by R.A. HARRISVILLE and I.L. SANDBERG (Minneapolis: Augsburg, 1984) 100; Andreas STRADELMANN, "Zur Christologie des Hebräerbriefes in der neueren Diskussion," *ThBer* 2 (1973) 174; Otto KUSS, *Der Brief an die Hebräer und die Katholischen Briefe* (RNT, 8/1; Regensburg: Pustet, 1966) 47 (despite referring with approval to the general conclusions concerning Judaism by BOUSSET-GRESSMANN); Franz LAUB, *Bekenntnis und Auslegung. Die paränetische Funktion der Christologie im Hebräerbrief* (BU, 15; Regensburg: Pustet, 1980) 52-53; THOMPSON, *Beginnings*, esp. p. 140; ATTRIDGE, *Hebrews*, p. 52; HURST, "The Christology of Hebrews 1 and 2," p. 156; Claus-Peter MÄRZ, *Hebräerbrief* (NEBib, 16; Würzburg: Echter, 1989) 24; E. GRÄBER, *An die Hebräer* (EKKNT, 17/7; Neukirchen-Vluyn/ Zürich: Neukirchener and Benziger, 1990) 72; O. HOFIUS, *Der Christushymnus Philipper 2,6-11* (WUNT, 17; Tübingen: J.C.B. Mohr [Paul Siebeck], 1991) 88; B. LINDARS, *The Theology of Hebrews* (NTT; Cambridge: Univ., 1991) 37-38; LANE, *Hebrews 1-8*, pp. 19-33; Hans-Friedrich WEIß, *Der Brief an die Hebräer* (MeyerK, 15/1;

Of these alternatives, (3) is hardly convincing. If the author was trying to curb an interest in participating in angelic liturgy, it is hard to explain why in Hebrews 12:22-24 the readers are consoled by the image that they have come to "Mount Zion" (i.e., "the heavenly Jerusalem") where angels (v. 22-μυριάσιν ἀγγέλων), "the assembly of the firstborn" (v.23-ἐκκλησίᾳ πρωτοτόκων),[202] and saints (v. 23-πνεύμασι δικαίων τετελειωμένων) are associated in just such a context.[203] Moreover, a specific polemic against a reprehensible veneration of angels (1) or against an angelological understanding of Christ (2) is difficult to establish since there is no indication of such a practice or belief in the epistle.[204] Explanation (4) seems to be a rather axiomatic attempt at asserting a general continuity between the author's valuations and traditions known from his Hellenistic Jewish environment, without being obligated to venture--as do (1) and (2)--that any particular teaching or practice held among the readers was being addressed. Even if one grants, and correctly, that the author shows himself to be aware of contemporary traditions concerning angels, it is by no means clear why he would engage in such a thoroughgoing argumentation merely to dissuade his readers from a generally-known posture. Again, if the author has such a general concern in this section of the epistle, why is it altogether absent in the paraenesis of 2:1-4?

Instead of warning against or pointing out the danger of granting angelic beings an unwarranted religious preeminence, the author actually seems in chapter 2 to tone down the contrast in chapter 1 with a *minores ad maiores* argument which calls for posture of greater adherence (v. 1-περισσοτέρως προσέχειν ἡμᾶς) to "the things heard" in view of "so great a salvation" (v. 3a). In this light, an analysis which seeks to understand *the author's intention* in the epistle is on safest ground by focusing on the literary argument (5). Thus, although explanations (1-2, 4) and (5) are not mutually exclusive and the possibility that angelological ideas held by or known to the commu-

---

Göttingen: Vandenhoeck & Ruprecht, 1991) 158-60; and MACH, *Entwicklungsstadien*, p. 287 n. 22.

[202] Since the supplementary description of this group as "enrolled in heaven" (ἀπογεγραμμένων ἐν οὐρανοῖς) is not applied to angels in extant literature from antiquity, a reference to human beings quite likely; see ATTRIDGE, *Hebrews*, p. 375 and BRUCE, *Hebrews*, pp. 376-77.

[203] The term πανήγυρις (12:22) almost certainly refers to cultic worship in the new Jerusalem; see H. SEESEMANN on "πανήγυρις" in *TDNT* 5.722.

[204] The substance of the warning against adherence to various and strange teachings (διδαχαῖς ποικίλαις καὶ ξέναις) in 13:9a is not immediately apparent; the following statements (13:9b-10), however, go no further than to associate these ideas with eating regulations.

nity addressed are being combated by the author cannot be disproved, the presence of a direct polemic on the part of the author is most unlikely.[205]

The possibility of a polemic in some form is, however, less easy to preclude when one examines the evolution of the traditional materials preserved in Hebrews 1-2.[206] Given the almost thorough interweaving of traditional motifs, allusions to and citations of scripture, any attempt to separate layers of tradition from redactional appropriation must remain, to a large degree, hypothetical. This is particularly the case in Hebrews 1-2, in which the thought of the author and that of any putative traditions is closely aligned. Nevertheless, certain observations suggest that the author has affirmed, expanded, and even altered the emphasis of some transmitted material. For one thing, the function of angelic mediation within the hortatory argument in 2:1-4 does not readily follow upon the impression left by the foregoing catena. Whereas the appeal to scriptural traditions in chapter 1 draws a clear line of discontinuity between Christ's exalted status and the angel's subservient nature, the ensuing paraenesis presupposes a more positive role by angels (the mediation of the law) within a salvation-historical continuum than even the preceding argument would seem to have allowed. In fact, the persuasiveness of the warning against neglecting the salvation "first spoken by the Lord" (v. 3) depends on the degree to which the consequences of disobedience to "the word spoken through angels" (v. 2) could be said to have been in force. To be sure, Christ's superiority over angels in chapter 1 provides the essential assumption behind the idea of the supercessionary nature

---

[205] So, e.g., William R.G. LOADER, *Sohn und Hoherpriester*, p. 28: "Es muß mindestens gesagt werden, daß das [here, a polemic against an angel christology] nicht das Hauptmotiv ist, was ja nicht ausschließt, daß diese Absicht auch verfolgt sein könnte." That the author presupposes an angelology among the readers is apparent in 13:2, in which he exhorts them to hospitality on account of the possibility that they have hosted "angels unawares."

[206] While rejecting HARRIS' thesis that the author drew on an early Christian "testimony-book" containing prophetic texts about Christ, some commentators have maintained that 1:5-14 is based on a traditional catena (such as that found in *1 Clem* 36) formulated to undergird and express the belief in Christ's exalted status; see esp. F.C. SYNGE, *Hebrews and the Scriptures* (London: SPCK, 1959) 3-6; MONTEFIORE, *Hebrews*, p. 43; Gerd THEISSEN, *Untersuchungen zum Hebräerbrief* (SNT, 2; Gütersloh: Mohn, 1969) 33-37; David M. HAY, *Glory at the Right Hand. Psalm 110 in Early Christianity* (Nashville: Abingdon, 1973) 38-39. The existence of proof texts at Qumran (4QFlor and 4QTest) related to messianic events attests that such collections were made among Jewish groups before the common era. This fact, however, does not allow for generalizations concerning a "purpose" of such florilegia (such as baptism); as is the case in Hebr 1-2, an inquiry into the purpose and function of each collection must rely primarily on internal considerations.

of the new covenant over the old. But the force of the contrast in chapter 1 is not sustained in the tenor of the exhortation. The contrary categories of chapter 1, reflected in the exclusion of angels from both "Sonship" (vv. 5-9) and an exalted position "at the right hand" of God (vv. 3e-4,13), give way to a paraenesis in which such differences are simply taken for granted. Such implies a certain logical distance between the argument of Christ's superiority over angels, on the one hand, and accountability to the new covenant, on the other.[207]

It has long been recognized that the exordium (1:1-4), in which the author articulates the Christ event as both continuous with and superior to all previous revelation, is satiated by traditional motifs. In addition, interpreters have affirmed the programmatic significance of these verses for themes which are treated in the epistle as a whole, including the argumentation in chapters 1-2 that immediately follows. Thus 1:3d-4, by means of the allusion to Psalm 110:1, not only embodies a concise statement about the nature of Christ's salvific activity and exaltation, but also introduces a complex of tradition that extends well into 1:5-2:18, in which the same Psalm passage is cited in 1:13 and alluded to again in 2:8c. Since the scriptural citations in 1:5-12 derive their particular function in relation to the affirmation of Christ's exaltation, the delineation of the material adapted may initially begin with Psalm 110:1 and associated motifs.

The significance of Psalm 110:1 for early Christian formulations depicting Christ's exaltation is well documented.[208] The use of this passage from

---

[207] In this vein, LANE (*Hebrews 1-8*), who allows for the possibility that the author of Hebr drew on a "traditional testimony collection" (p. 24), notes that "Although in vv 5 and 13 the supporting quotations are introduced with a rhetorical question, the writer's concern is not to set forth a formal proof in any strict sense of the word. The absence of logical argument, together with the observable fact that much of the content of 1:5-14 is not closely related to the further development of the address, provides evidence that the quotations serve another purpose" (p. 33). LANE does not, however, attempt to delineate the purpose of such a collection.

[208] In Hebrews see further the allusions in 8:1;10:12-13; and 12:2. The classic discussion of the use of Psalm 110 in early Christian writings (with further bibliography) is by HAY, *Glory at the Right Hand*. Apart from Hebrews we may note the following allusions to and citations of Ps. 110:1 in early Christian writings: Mt 22:44/Mk 12:36/Lk 20:42 (cit.); Mt 26:64/Mk 14:62/Lk 22:69 (with Dan 7:13); Mk 16:19; Acts 2:33,34-35 (cit.); 5:31; 7:55,56; Rom 8:34; 1 Cor 15:25; Eph 1:20; 2:6(?); Col 3:1; 1 Pet 3:22; Rev 3:21(?); *1 Clem* 36:2-5; *Ep.Barn.* 12:10; *Asc.Isa.* 10:14; 11:32; *Sib.Or.* 2.243 (Christian interpolation). The frequent combination of Ps 110:1 with either Ps 8:7 or Dan 7:13 is discussed by LOADER, "Christ at the Right Hand-Ps. CX.1 in the New Testament," *NTS* 24 (1977) 199-217 and CALLAN, "Psalm 110:1 and the Origin of

the psalter in early Christian writings demonstrates that it flourished independently of Hebrews.[209] In all probability, then, elements shared by both Hebrews 1-2 and the other passages in Christian literature applying Psalm 110:1 suggest at several points the adaptation in Hebrews of a common tradition. These affinities may be listed as follows:

(A) the adaptation of Psalm 110:1 in conjunction with Psalm 8:7 (Mk 12:35/Mt 22:44[210]; 1 Cor 15:27-28[211]; Eph 1:22; 1 Pet 3:22;

---

the Expectation that Jesus Will Come Again," *CBQ* 44 (1982) 622-36 respectively. Less clear is a messianic use of Ps 110:1 in early Jewish literature. Concerning its possible application to the "elect one"/"son of man" figure in *1 En* 37-71 see further Johannes THEISOHN, *Der auserwählte Richter* (SUNT, 12; Göttingen: Vandenhoeck & Ruprecht, 1975) 95-99 and 154-55, with reference to *1 En* 45:3; 51:3; 55:4; 62:3,5; 69:29; and 84:2. For other uses see *T.Job* 33:3 and *T.Benj.* 10:6, in which the "right hand" is referred to the special proximity to God enjoyed by the righteous. On the other hand, in *2 En* 24:1 the right side of God's throne remains empty, while the left is to be occupied by Enoch along with Gabriel; see HENGEL, "Psalm 110 und die Erhöhung des Auferstandenen," p. 61 (influence of a Christian redactor?). Finally, a possible allusion (though vague) may be found in WisdSol 9:4 the petitioner petitions for "the wisdom seated beside your thrones" (τὴν τῶν σῶν θρόνων πάρεδρον σοφίαν), though the plur. form presupposes another tradition (such as Dan 7:9).

[209] Among the early Christian texts referred to in the previous note, only *1 Clem* 36:2-5 may show signs of dependence on Hebrews.

[210] Both Mk and Mt cite Ps 110:1, substituting ὑποπόδιον with ὑποκάτω, the *lectio difficilior* among the textual witnesses (see Ps 8:7; corrected in Lk 20:43 to ὑποπόδιον) see HAY, *Glory at the Right Hand*, pp. 35-37. The common theme of subjection as well as the phrase τῶν ποδῶν σου created conditions for such a synthesis of these passages.

[211] In order to demonstrate the validity of Christ's resurrection (1 Cor 15:20-28), Paul draws on tradition which stresses the reality of Christ's reign in anticipation of the eschaton. Here the idea of a proleptic subjugation over enemies in Ps 110:1 modifies the factual subjection of "all things" in Ps 8:7 (vv. 25, 28). In achieving this modification, the comprehensive "all" of Ps 8:7 is interposed within the citation of Ps 110:1 (v. 25). Though the argument is considerably different in Hebrews, the provisionary reign in Ps 110:1 performs a similar function after the citation of Ps 8:5-7 in Hebr 2:8c (οὔπω ὁρῶμεν αὐτῷ τὰ πάντα ὑποτεταγμένα), which is probably derived from the citation of Ps 110:1 in 1:13-ἕως ἂν θῶ...).

Phil 2:6-11[212])--cf., in particular, Hebrews 1:3d-e[213],13; and 2:8c[214];

---

[212] No clear allusions to Pss 8:7 and 110:1 are apparent in this christological hymn. The use of Ps 8:7, which represents the position of humanity as part of a given within the created order, may have been counterproductive for a context which stresses that Christ's assumption of human form was a deliberate act (Phil 2:7-ἑαυτὸν ἐκένωσεν; v. 8-ἐταπείνωσεν ἑαυτόν). Concerning Ps 110:1 as a presupposition for the comprehensive presentation of Christ's superiority in Phil 2:10, see e.g. Reginald FULLER, *The Foundations of New Testament Christology* (New York: Scribner, 1965) 213; MARTIN, *Carmen Christi. Philippians ii. 5-11* (SNTSMS, 4; Cambridge: Univ., 1967) 259 n. 3; and HENGEL, "Christological Titles," pp. 441-42. The dual motifs of Christ's humiliation and exaltation were, of course, conceived independently of the Psalm passages. A comparison here is, however, warranted since Christ's assumption of human form (v. 7c,d-ἐν ὁμοιώματι ἀνθρώπων [P^{46}-ἀνθρώπου]...σχήματι εὑρεθεὶς ὡς ἄνθρωπος; cf. Ps 8:5-6), together with the resulting exaltation (v. 9a-διὸ καὶ ὁ θεὸς αὐτὸν ὑπερύψωσεν; cf. Ps 109:7 LXX-διὰ τοῦτο ὑψώσει κεφαλήν) and title (v. 11-κύριος; cf. Ps 109:1 LXX-εἶπεν ὁ κύριος τῷ κυρίῳ μου), reflects Christ's humiliation and exaltation in a way that could easily be given expression by means of both passages. A related nexus of tradition (built upon additional explication through Pss 110:1 and 8:5-7) is especially compelling, given the elaboration of Christ's exalted status in terms of his superior name (vv. 9b-10-τὸ ὄνομα τὸ ὑπὲρ πᾶν ὄνομα...ἐν τῷ ὀνόματι Ἰησοῦ πᾶν γόνυ κάμψῃ ἐπουρανίων; cf. Hebr 1:4).

[213] The "cleansing of sins" in 1:3d, an allusion to the salvific nature of Christ's death, belongs to the exaltation in the same way that the citation of Ps 8:5-7 in 2:6-8a lays the groundwork for defining Christ's exaltation through his death (2:8b-18), in which connection Jesus' function as the perfect "high priest" becomes apparent. This death-exaltation scheme culminates again in the allusions to Ps 110:1 in 7:27b-8:2 (the Son is ἀρχιερεύς), 10:11-13 (priestly function), and 12:2. Whereas the motif in 1:3d is traditional, the language itself is possibly that of the author (see 10:2).

[214] Some interpreters who think that the author understood the subjection in Ps 8:5-7 as referring to humanity (=NRSV's translation of αὐτῷ as "them") tend to overlook the allusion to Ps 110:1; see, e.g., BRUCE, *Hebrews*, pp. 36-37 and esp. HURST, "Christology," pp. 153-54. HURST (*ibid.*, p. 154) does argue that Christ's humiliation is spoken of in a representative role (v. 9-ὑπὲρ παντός; v. 10-πολλοὺς υἱοὺς εἰς δόξαν ἀγαγόντα taking up Ps 8:6's δόξῃ καὶ τιμῇ ἐστεφάνωσας αὐτόν in v. 7). If this view is correct, there is no need to distinguish so sharply between Christ and humanity as the referents in the statements of 2:8, thereby driving a wedge between vv. 8c (=humanity) and 9 (=Jesus); see LOADER, *Sohn und Hoherpriester*, pp. 31-38. The subjection of all things to humanity is not in effect because the consummation of Christ's subjection of his enemies is not yet consummated; see ATTRIDGE, *Hebrews*, p. 72. The addition of "all" to the allusion, which here derives from Ps 8:7, has its analogy in 1 Cor 15:25 (see n. 211).

(B) the assertion of Christ's superiority over heavenly beings²¹⁵ (1 Cor 15:24, 26; Eph 1:21; 1 Pet 3:22-includes ἄγγελοι; Phil 2:10; cf. further Rom 8:38-ἄγγελοι; Col 2:8,10,15,18-ἄγγελοι, 20; cf. 1:16)--cf. Hebrews 1:4²¹⁶;

(C) the superiority of Christ's "name" (Eph 1:21-ὑπεράνω... παντὸς ὀνόματος ὀνομαζομένου; Phil 2:9-τὸ ὄνομα ὃ ὑπὲρ πᾶν ὄνομα)--cf. Hebrews 1:4 (διαφορώτερον παρ' αὐτοὺς κεκληρονόμηκεν ὄνομα²¹⁷);

(D) occurrence of the phrase ἐν δεξιᾷ in the allusion to Psalm 110:1 instead of ἐκ δεξιῶν²¹⁸ (viz. Rom 8:34; Eph 1:20; Col

---

²¹⁵ The heavenly beings subordinate to Christ are variously conceived. In 1 Cor 15:24-26 the apocalyptic powers to be destroyed (πᾶσα ἀρχή, πᾶσα ἐξουσία καὶ δύναμις, and "the last enemy" ὁ θάνατος) are understood as the "enemies" mentioned in Ps 110:1 (109:1 LXX-οἱ ἐχθροί). A similar interpretation of Ps 110:1 is implicit in Eph 1:22 (cf. 6:12-"not a contention against flesh and blood but against the rulers [τὰς ἀρχὰς], against the authorities [τὰς ἐξουσίας]...). In Hebrews, on the other hand, there is no trace of an identification of ἄγγελοι as inimical (so correctly HOFIUS, Christushymnus, pp. 34-35), and it is misleading to suppose that the author is specifically referring to Christ's "triumph over the powers"; contra e.g. BORNKAMM, "Das Bekenntnis im Hebräerbrief," p. 198 n. 23 (an angel-cult "unter dem Einfluß jüdischer Gnosis"); R. DEICHGRÄBER, Gotteshymnus und Christushymnus in der frühen Christenheit (SUNT, 5; Göttingen: Vandenhoeck & Ruprecht) 189; FULLER, Foundations, p. 221; and THOMPSON, Beginnings, p. 139. Angels are simply compared with Christ in terms of nature and status. Finally, in the remaining passages (Eph 1:21; 1 Pet 3:22; Phil 2:10; Col 2:18; cf. 1:16; Rom 8:38-39) the subordinate beings are listed in neutral terms, with the emphasis on Christ's cosmological superiority.

A further indication of a shared tradition is the tendency to choose either ἄγγελοι or ἀρχαί (followed by ἐξουσία) without listing the terms together: 1 Cor 15:24 (πᾶσαν ἀρχὴν καὶ πᾶσαν ἐξουσίαν καὶ δυναμιν); Eph 1:21 (πάσης ἀρχῆς καὶ ἐξουσίας καὶ δυνάμεως...; cf. 6:12); 1 Pet 3:22 (ἀγγέλων καὶ ἐξουσιῶν καὶ δυνάμεων); cf. also Col 1:16 (ἀρχαὶ εἴτε ἐξουσίαι) and 2:10 (πάσης ἀρχῆς καὶ ἐξουσίας). The interchangeability of these two terms within the tradition is underscored by the exception in Rom 8:38 (οὔτε ἄγγελοι οὔτε ἀρχαί [mss D C 81.104 and syr^h**, bo^mss conform the latter with ἐξουσία -αι]), in which they appear within a series of pairs.

²¹⁶ Though here the comparative adjectives (κρείττων and διαφορώτερον), which bear a qualitative connotation, seem to reflect the language of the author (κρείττων-Hebr 6:9; 7:7; 11:40; and, as advb. in 12:24; διαφορώτερον-8:6), who applies them to the superiority of the new covenant over the old; see HOFIUS, Christushymnus, p. 87 n.'s 49-50. The other passages, in drawing out implications of Christ's position at the right hand of God, use at this point more spatial terms to denote his position of supremacy (Eph 1:21-ὑπεράνω [cf. Ps 8:2 LXX]; Phil 2:9-ὑπέρ; Col 3:1-ἄνω).

²¹⁷ See previous n. In addition, the verb κληρονομεῖν may reflect the author's vocabulary (cf. v. 14).

²¹⁸ In the NT writings the citations of Ps 110:1 all agree in the phrase ἐκ δεξιῶν μου (Mk 12:36 parr.; Acts 2:34; Hebr 1:13), while among the allusions to this phrase the preposition ἐν with the sing. δεξιᾷ predominates (the exceptions are confined to Acts: 2:33-τῇ δεξιᾷ τοῦ θεοῦ; 5:31-τῇ δεξιᾷ; 7:55-ἐκ δεξιῶν; 7:56-ἐκ δεξιῶν). This agreement over against preserved tex-

3:1; and 1 Pet 3:22)-- cf. Hebrews 1:3e; 8:1; 10:12; and 12:2;

(E) the elaboration of Christ's position "at the right hand" in terms of heavenly location (Eph 1:20-ἐν τοῖς ἐπουρανίοις; 2:6 (ἐν τοῖς ἐπουρανίοις); Col 3:1-τὰ ἄνω...οὗ; 1 Pet 3:22 (πορευθεὶς εἰς οὐρανόν)--cf. Hebrews 1:3e (ἐν ὑψηλοῖς[219]) and 8:1 (ἐν τοῖς οὐρανοῖς);

(F) the emphasis on Christ's superiority in and/or over the world "to come" (Eph 1:21-οὐ μόνον ἐν τῷ αἰῶνι τούτῳ ἀλλὰ καὶ ἐν τῷ μέλλοντι; cf. 2:7-ἐν τοῖς αἰῶσιν τοῖς ἐπερχομένοις; Col 2:17-σκία τῶν μελλόντων; Rom 8:38-οὔτε ἐνεστῶτα οὔτε μέλλοντα)--cf. Hebrews 2:5 (οὐ γὰρ ἀγγέλοις ὑπέταξεν τὴν οἰκουμένην τὴν μέλλουσαν);

(G) an allusion to or mention of Christ's overcoming death[220] (1 Pet 4:1; Phil 2:8; Col 2:20; Rom 8:34; Rev 3:21)--cf. Hebrews 2:9c (ὑπὲρ παντὸς γεύσηται θανάτου); and

(H) a statement or phrase that expresses the comprehensive nature of God's or Christ's nature and work (1 Cor 15:28-God, τὰ πάντα ἐν πᾶσιν; Eph 1:23-Christ, τὸ πλήρωμα τοῦ τὰ πάντα ἐν πᾶσιν πληρουμένου; cf. Col 1:17-Christ)--cf. Hebrews 2:10a (God-δι' ὃν τὰ πάντα καὶ δι' οὗ τὰ πάντα).

One cannot, of course, assume that all of the language and motifs which appear in conjunction with Psalm 110:1 are to be distinguished from the author's use of this tradition.[221] It is thus quite possible that during later stages of transmission, expansions may reflect an affirmation and, hence, an awareness of the larger network of elements known to be associated with the received tradition. Nevertheless, the comparison above furnishes enough rudiments to attempt a reconstruction of an initial framework upon which the (re-)interpretation of Psalm 110:1 may have taken place.

The earliest, formative stage of tradition may be said to have included at least the following features from the above categories: a combined citation of Psalms 110:1 and 8:7 (A) which was applied to Christ's subjection of "enemies" (Hebr 1:13b; 2:8a) and the identification of these "enemies" as heavenly powers (B). Whereas Psalm 110(109):1 was made to emphasize that

---

tual tradition (MT Ps 110:1 לימיני) speaks strongly for a persistent interpretive tradition.

[219] The language here, as well as the introductory questions in vv. 5 and 13, is reminiscent of Ps 112:5 LXX: τίς ὡς κύριος ὁ θεὸς ἡμῶν ὁ ἐν ὑψηλοῖς κατοικῶν (113:5 MT: מי כיהוה אלהינו המגביהי לשבת).

[220] To some extent this shared motif overlaps with the joint use of Pss 110 and 8. Nevertheless, the possibility remains that Hebrews, as well as other passages using Ps 110:1, makes reference to Christ's death without recourse to Ps 8, but on the basis of generally known kerygmatic traditions. See, in addition, n. 212 on Phil 2:6-11 above.

[221] See, e.g., n. 216 on Hebr 1:4.

Christ will eventually defeat such powers (1:13-ἕως ἂν θῶ; 2:8c-οὔπω ὁρῶμεν), the citation of Psalm 8:7 (πάντα ὑπέταξας) served to assure the certitude and comprehensiveness of this subjugation.[222] To the extent that ἄγγελοι were included among these beings (cf. 1 Pet 3:22), they were potentially (if not actually) hostile. Similar to the argument in 1 Corinthians 15, this eschatological adaptation of Psalm 110:1 attributed present evil to apocalyptic powers whose potency is only temporary. Hence this stage of the tradition would likely have included a reference to the age or world "to come" (F; Hebr 2:5a) in which Christ's or God's rule would be fully established (H; Hebr 2:10a).

The next stage would have involved a major shift in both emphasis and focus. If a specific concern with angelological ideas cannot be ascribed to the author on the level of the text,[223] it is here--we may suppose--that the tradition surrounding Psalm 110:1 was both expanded and altered in this direction. Another aspect of Christ's exaltation is introduced through a contrast with ἄγγελοι, this time not understood as hostile forces but as heavenly beings aligned with the purposes of God.[224] While the tension in the tradition between the present and eschatological rule of Christ is essentially retained (1:13c; Ps 110:1b), the accent falls on the first part of Psalm 110:1, which is now given a further application. Christ's exaltation "at the right

---

[222] This presupposes that the ἄνθρωπος and υἱὸς ἀνθρώπου in Ps 8:5, perhaps on account of its association with Ps 110:1, were very early interpreted in relation to Christ.

[223] Similarly, H.M. SCHENKE, "Erwägungen zum Rätsel des Hebräerbriefes," in eds.H.D. BETZ and L. SCHOTTROFF, Neues Testament und christliche Existenz. Festschrift für H. Braun (Tübingen: J.C.B. Mohr [Paul Siebeck], 1973) 429-32 and Mathias RISSI, Die Theologie des Hebräerbriefs (WUNT, 41; Tübingen: J.C.B. Mohr [Paul Siebeck], 1987) 48-52 and 54. While SCHENKE argues that the author is rejecting his own previous "Jewish" view which understood angels as "Priestern des himmlischen Heiligtums" ("Erwägungen," p. 430), RISSI maintains that the author of Hebrews adapted a "Testimoniensammlung" which was intended to counter an angel Christology. Though the latter's thesis is not accompanied by a thorough argument, the positing of a tradition, the function of which can in part be distinguished from the author's own purpose, merits further consideration; see below.

[224] The basis for such a contrast between aligned figures may have already been present in the combination of Ps 110:1 with Ps 8:7; in Ps 8:5-7 LXX, however, the "all things" subjected (explicated by animals in vv. 8-9) does not include "angels." The association of these psalms, with their emphasis on the eschatological subjection of enemy powers of the cosmos (derived from Ps 110:1), no doubt allowed for the occasional inclusion of angels through Ps 8:6 (ἠλάττωσας αὐτὸν βραχύ τι [understood temporally] παρ᾽ ἀγγέλους; are the angels assimilated to τῶν ἐχθρῶν σου in v. 3?). But the ambiguity of the text itself could have allowed for a realignment of the role of "angels."

hand of God" defines his position as such, and thus may be conceived without mere recourse to the inimical powers.

On the assumption that the ἄγγελοι are essentially aligned with God, the contrast with Christ is carried through in two areas: nature and function. The singularity of Christ's position "at the right hand" is illustrated through a series of citations which underscore his two-fold appointment by God as "Son" and as the one who is to subject the hostile powers. Both of these aspects of Christology categorically exclude angels (vv. 5-9,13; 2:5a) which merely exist as "a fiery flame" and "spirits" and which have no higher rank than that of "servants" (v. 7).[225] It is quite likely, then, that at this stage the received tradition around Psalm 110:1 was expanded by elements (C), (D), and (E). Perhaps through further reflection on Psalm 8:5-7, the exaltation language from Psalm 110:1 was preceded by an allusion to Christ's death or redemptive work (as an accomplished fact). Moreover, the citation of Psalm 8 would have been expanded here--if not already--to include verses 5-6 which speaks of "angels."[226] To underscore the essential difference between Christ and angels, the new material was added in the form of five further scriptural citations (vv. 5a,5b,6,7,8-10). Thematically, the outline of materials put together at this stage may have resembled a chiastic structure framed by the appeals to Psalm 110:1 (and, at the end, to Ps 8):[227]

---

[225] THOMPSON (*Beginnings*, p. 134) draws on the distinction (attested in Middle Platonism and PHILO) between divine transcendence and the heavenly world, on the one hand, and angelic beings (of substantial corporeality), on the other, as a framework for the author's understanding of the latter. This point makes it possible for THOMPSON to eventually associate the ἄγγελοι with the "enemies" of Ps 110:1. Though the author may have such a *metaphysical* contrast in mind (vv. 10-12), in the argument it is related more to the Son's function (*vis-à-vis* the angels) in the act of creation. Despite the angels' mediation of the law (2:2), it is not clear to what extent angels as such, whose function in the heavenly cultus (v. 6; cf. 12:22-23) is presumably not temporary, can be classified in accordance with the author's theological contrast between the "earthly" (=the old covenant) and the "heavenly" (=Christ and the new covenant).

[226] If Ps 8's combination with Ps 110:1 had ever presupposed an identification between the ἄγγελοι in Ps 8:5 and the "enemies" mentioned in v. 3 (2X-κατηρτίσω αἶνον ἕνεκα τῶν ἐχθρῶν σου τοῦ καταλῦσαι ἐχθρὸν καὶ ἐκδικητήν), it is no longer in view. The comparison is between allied, not opposing, powers, and the point at issue is the activity of subjecting.

[227] Similar structural patterns have frequently been observed for at least vv. 5-12; see A. VANHOYE, *La structure littéraire de l'Epître aux Hebreux* (StudNeot, 1; Paris/Bruges: Brouwer, 1962) 69-74, 85 and RISSI, *Theologie des Hebräerbriefs*, p. 50.

Thesis: Christ is greater than the angels

A¹-- *He* is exalted above the angels to "the right hand of God."
(1:3-4: allusion to Ps 110:1)

A²-- *He* is addressed as "Son."
(1:5: combined citation of Ps 2:7 and 2 Sam 7:14)

B -- *Angels* will worship him.
(1:6: citation of Deut 32:43/Ps 97:7)

B -- *Angels* are but "spirits," "a fiery flame," and "ministers."
(1:7: citation of Ps 104:4)

A²-- *He*, addressed as "God," possesses an eternal throne, of which he is worthy; because of loving righteousness and hating wickedness he is anointed beyond his companions.
(1:8-9: citation of Ps 45:7)

A¹-- *He*, not angels, is exalted to the right hand of God until the subjection of the inimical powers.
(1:13; 2:6-8a: combined citation of Pss 110:1 and 8:5-7)

The junctures A^{1-2} and A^{2-1}, at which the inherited materials around Psalm 110:1 are joined to the added catena, are marked by rhetorical questions concerning the status of angels which anticipate a negative answer. Although it is unlikely that their origin in tradition or redaction can be ascertained with any measure of probability, it is not impossible that they were introduced at this (pre-Hebrews) stage.[228] The final citation from Psalm 8:5-7 was understood as a christological statement which redefined Christ's

---

[228] The common assumption that these questions were originally composed by the author (because they correspond to his style) is open to debate. They may be Christo-centric rhetorical reformulations of comparative questions which frequently appear in the Pss. See in particular Pss 88:7 LXX (τίς ὁμοιωθήσεται τῷ κυρίῳ ἐν υἱοῖς θεοῦ) and 112:5 LXX (τίς ὡς κύριος ὁ θεὸς ἡμῶν ὁ ἐν ὑψηλοῖς κατοικῶν [MT-המגביהי לשבת]). The emphasis on the Son's eternal *enthronement* in vv. 8-9 *vis-à-vis* the angels' function as "ministers" in v. 7 is underlined by the introductory question in v. 13, which excludes angels as addressees in the request to "sit."

Similarly, in *3 En* 10:1-6 Metatron's elevation above the other heavenly beings (who "stand"; see 18:24) is expressed by his being *seated* by God on a throne near the door to the seventh palace (cf. also *3 En* 16:1 and 48C:8). The "standing" position of angels is otherwise emphasized in *b.Ḥag.* 15a ("...there is no sitting on high..."); *j.Ber.* 1:1; and *Ber.R.* 65:21. Furthermore, in contrast to the angels Moses is permitted to sit during the giving of the Torah in *Exod.R.* 34:4 and *Tanḥ. Buber beshallaḥ* 13 to Ex 15:1 (texts listed by HENGEL, "Christological Titles," p. 439 n. 43).

exaltation in terms of his humiliation, thus providing an *inclusio* which returns to an opening allusion to Christ's redemptive death (see 1:3d).

If one assumes that the author was entirely responsible for an adaptation which realigned an interpretive traditions of Psalm 110:1 in order to accentuate a contrast between Christ and angels as allied beings, then it becomes difficult to explain why he does not apply them more directly in his exhortation (2:1-4) or why they do not play a major thematic role in the remainder of the epistle. At the same time, the author clearly agrees with the argument of the traditional material.[229] Thus in his appropriation he affirms,[230] adjusts,[231] and augments[232] it in line with his own hortatory intentions.

---

[229] So, correctly, LINDARS, *Theology of Hebrews*, p. 38: "...at this early stage in the letter Hebrews is recalling agreed positions." There is no indication that the author held a view essentially different from what he received through the traditional material. The only substantial modification introduced may have been a tendency to demythologize the personified inimical powers originally associated with Ps 110:1; cf. 1 Cor 15:26 and Hebr 2:9, 14-15 ("death" is distinguished from ὁ διάβολος).

[230] Affirmative commentary by the author is discernible in 1:14. However much the author may have been aware of contemporary motifs according to which angels were "spirits" (e.g., Acts 23:8?-μήτε ἄγγελον μήτε πνεῦμα; 1 En 37-71 *passim*-"Lord of spirits"; 4QShirShabb 20X-רוח/רוחי) and "ministers" (PHILO, *Virt.* 74-ἄγγελοι λειτουργοί), the immediate antecedent to the description of them as λειτουργικὰ πνεύματα is the citation of Ps 104:4 in v. 7. Moreover, *if not* already part of the traditional material, the rhetorical questions of 1:5 and 13 would have been supplied by the author. If, however, the author has taken over the rhetorical questions from tradition, a possible shift to the perf. form in 1:13 (εἴρηκεν) may reflect a minor adjustment which emphasizes the continuing reality of Christ's superiority over the angels.

[231] We note here: (1) The terms κρείττων, διαφωρότερον, and κληρονομεῖν in 1:4, which appear throughout the epistle (see n.'s 216 and 217 above), reflect the author's accommodation of the traditional complex to his comparisons between the old and new covenants. They anticipate the superiority of the new covenant assumed in 2:1-4. (2) The tradition's allusion to Christ's humiliation and exaltation in Ps 8 is now explicitly bound up with the proper role of humanity in the created order. Christ's solidarity with humanity serves, then, as a basis for the author's soteriological argument (2:9-18 and 4:14-5:10; 7:1-28; 8:1-7; 10:11-18) in which Christ is a "merciful and faithful high priest" (2:17).

[232] To the author's expansions may be ascribed: (1) 1:10-12 (Ps 102:25-27), which adds to the citation from Ps 45:6-7 introduced as words addressed to the Son. These verses, which interrupt the contrast between Christ and angels in vv. 9 and 13, contain no such contrasting statements and elaborate on Christ's eternal nature in terms of creation (cf. 1:2c). (2) 1:14b-2:4, in which the summary concerning angels, whose function includes serving those who will inherit salvation, leads into the exhortation to pay special attention to "the things heard." (3) The author elaborates on the humiliation implied in the citation of Ps 8:5-7 in a way that underscores the solidarity between Christ's subjection of all things and the proper destiny for human

The identification of a polemical source behind Hebrews 1-2 leads to a consideration of the problem being addressed. It is impossible to decide between argument against a veneration of angels and an "angel Christology."[233] Both ideas are not exclusive of each other; to some extent, a rejection of the latter presupposes the view that angels themselves are not worthy of veneration. As indicated above,[234] the connection between the designations "Son" and "angel" or "archangel," as made by PHILO (in relation to the λόγος, see *Conf.ling.* 146),[235] was already brought to expression within the Jewish diaspora before Hebrews was written.[236] Whereas it is not clear whether PHILO thought

---

beings described in the psalm. In this connection, it is also possible, though not certain, that the tradition in 1:6, which originally referred to πρωτότοκος (on the basis of LXX Ps 88), was recast in language from Deut 6:10 and 10:29 in order to suggest an analogy between the Son's coming to the οἰκουμένη and Israel's entrance into the promised land, an analogy which would have prepared for the solidarity between the Jesus the high priest and believers in ch. 2.

[233] On the problem of using this expression, see n. 3 in Part Three.

[234] See n. 186.

[235] PHILO's application of the term υἱός to λόγος is relatively rare, and never occurs without πρωτόγονος (*Conf.Ling.* 146; cf. 62-63; *Agr.* 51). Thus he seems to have preferred the terms πρωτόγονος and πρεσβύτερος, which also corresponded to his view of the λόγος as an archetype of the universe and as a pre-eminent expression of God's activity; on this, see the helpful discussion by Takeshi NAGATA, *Philippians 2:5-11: A Case Study in the Contextual Shaping of Early Christology* (Princeton Theological Seminary: Ph.D. Diss., 1981) 308-309 n. 265.

[236] These designations form part of a larger network of traditions (e.g., Wisdom, Word/Logos, Archangel, Spirit, Son) which were frequently merged in various forms in Greek-speaking Jewish circles around the turn of the common era; see TALBERT, "The Myth of a Descending-Ascending Redeemer in Mediterranean Antiquity" *NTS* 22 (1976) 426-27. Such combinations are reflected esp. in *1 En* 42:2 (Wisdom took her seat among the angels); WisdSol 9:1-2 (ἐν λόγῳ σου...ἐν σοφίᾳ σου); 9:17 (σοφία...τὸ ἅγιόν σου πνεῦμα); and 10:6 (wisdom rescued Lot; in Gen 19:15-16, ἄγγελοι-נהאלים). Within the framework of such a configuration, PHILO identifies λόγος λόγοι with ἀρχάγγελος ἄγγελος; see *Cher.* 3 (ἀγγέλου ὥς ἐστι θεῖος λόγος "the angel of the Lord" who encountered Hagar in Gen 16:11), 35 (θεοῦ λόγον ἐνωπλισμένον ἄγγελον="the angel of God" who confronted Balaam in Num 22:22-35); *Fug.* 5 (ἄγγελον, θεῖον λόγον; as *Cher.* 3); *QuodDeus* 182 (λόγος...θεῖος, ἄγγελος=angel in Num 22:22-35); *Leg. All.* 3.177 (ἄγγελον ὅς ἐστι λόγος...τοὺς ἀγγέλους καὶ λόγους αὐτοῦ; interpretation of Jacob's prayer at Gen 48:15-16); *Conf.ling.* 28 (τῶν θείων καὶ ἱερῶν λόγων...οὓς καλεῖν ἔθος ἀγγέλους), 62-63 (πρεσβύτερον υἱόν...πρωτόγονον...ὁ γεννηθείς); *Quis rer.div.her.* 205 (τῷ δὲ ἀρχαγγέλῳ καὶ πρεσβυτάτῳ λόγῳ); *Mut. Nom.* 87 (ἄγγελος ὑπηρέτης τοῦ θεοῦ λόγος=the "man" who renamed Jacob in Gen 32:25b-33); *Abr.* 173 (λόγοις οὓς ὀνομάζειν ἔθος ἀγγέλους=the three "men" who visited Abraham in Gen 18:1-22); *Post.Cain* 91 (θεοῦ λόγοι...τῶν ἀγγέλων αὐτοῦ); *Somn.* 1.115 (ἀθανάτοις λόγοις οὓς καλεῖν ἔθος ἀγγέλους); 238 (τὴν τοῦ θεοῦ εἰκόνα, τὸν ἄγγελον αὐτοῦ λόγον); *Agr.* 51 (τὸν ὀρθὸν αὐτοῦ λόγον καὶ πρωτόνονον υἱόν...ἄγγελόν μου the guiding angel in Ex 23:20).

of his Logos-Angel as a fully independent being or as metaphorically conceived divine attribute,[237] it is well known that at least by the end of the first century CE such a pattern of thought was, to a limited degree, being assimilated into christological ideas of some Christian circles.[238] Since there is

---

[237] The alternative between the Logos as an independent personal being and a metaphorical concept (spoken of in personalized form) in PHILO is misleading since there is no evidence that on this score PHILO himself sought to systematize his views. His highly nuanced characterization of the Logos, which attempts to bring together a transcendent view of God with God's activity in the physical universe, cannot be simplified in either direction. Thus it is precarious simply to assume that PHILO conceived of his Logos as a separate "hypostasis," as emphasized, e.g., by DUNN, *Christology in the Making*, pp. 220-30; Samuel SANDMEL, "PHILO, the Man, His Writings, His Significance," in *ANRW* II.21.2; D.T. RUNIA, *Philo of Alexandria and the Timaeus of Plato* (PhAnt, 44; Leiden: Brill, 1986); and HURTADO, *One God, One Lord*, pp. 46-47. PHILO's blending of Middle Platonist metaphysical categories with interpretive traditions of the Jewish scriptures almost inevitably resulted in an ambiguity which was ripe for further reinterpretation.

When the Logos is identified by PHILO as a theophanic manifestation in the form of an "archangel" (see the previous n.), the interpretive problem concerning the nature of the Logos may be carried over. This is particularly the case if PHILO has blended contemporary "archangel" speculations (the term "archangel" does not appear in the Jewish scriptures) into his understanding of the Logos.

[238] FOSSUM, "Kyrios Jesus as the Angel of the Lord in Jude 5-7," *NTS* 33 (1987) 226-43, argues that already Jude 5 (end of the 1st cent.) identifies the pre-existent Christ with the "Angel of the Lord"; the likelihood of such a meaning for κύριος would be enhanced if the reading Ἰησοῦς (the *lectio difficilior* attested in A B 33.81) is original. In relation to the end of the 1st century, *OdesSol* may be of particular importance; in 36:4 Christ is angelomorphically represented as "praised (*mshbḥ*)...among those who praise, and great...among those who are great." For *mshbḥ* as a pa'al pass. ptc. see J. BARTH, "Zur Textkritik der syrischen Ode Salomos" *RSEHA* 19 (1911) 264, who appealed to *parallelismus membrorum* and CHARLESWORTH's translation in *OTP* 2.765; *contra* Michael LATTKE, *Die Oden Salomos in ihrer Bedeutung für Neues Testament und Gnosis* (OBO, 25/1; Fribourg/Göttingen: Editions Universitaires and Vandenhoeck & Ruprecht, 1979) 50, 170-71.

Elsewhere, and more definitively in the second century, explicit attestation for an angel-Christology occurs frequently in JUSTIN, *Apol.* 6; 63 (2X); *Dial.* 34; 61; 126; and 128 (cf. also 56; 58; 60). For JUSTIN the identification of Christ as "angel" functioned both as an argument for Christ's pre-existence (see esp. *Apol.* 63) and, insofar as the Christ-Logos is represented as a messenger in human form, as a safeguard to protect the monotheistic belief in the one transcendent God. Despite the comparable nature attributed to "the Son" and "angels" (*Apol.* 6; 63), JUSTIN's references indicate that they are clearly distinguished. In *Shep.Herm.* the situation is more complicated; cf. *Vis.* 5.2; *Mand.* 5.1.7; *Sim.* 5.4.4; 7.1-5; 8.1.2-18; 8.2.1; 8.3.3; 9.1.3; 10.1.1; and 10.3.1. The relationship of a prominent angel figure(s) (*Sim.* 7.5; 8.1.2,5; 8.2.1-ἄγγελος τοῦ κυρίου; *Sim.* 9.1.3-ἔνδοξος ἄγγελος) to "the Son of God" (*Sim.* 9.12.8) is never clarified systematically. Moreover, the angel Michael, though distinguished from Christ, could in similar fashion be called ὁ ἄγγελος μέγας καὶ ἔνδοξος in *Sim.* 8.3.3 (here, clear-

otherwise scant trace of an explicit representation of Christ as an "angel" in writings which are undisputably dated to the first century,[239] it is difficult to know to what degree and how widespread the linguistic association expressed by PHILO was already being integrated into christological reflection during this period. Nevertheless, with respect to the contrast preserved in Hebrews 1-2, both the lack of any explicit reference to a veneration of angels and the appeal to scriptural traditions and motifs (already in use for some time among Christian circles) to distinguish angels from the nature and function of "the Son" may at the very least suggest a polemic against a *Zeitgeist* in which the fluid ideas about angels and preeminent heavenly figures, however metaphorically conceived, were perceived as a threat to a belief in a surpassing exaltation of Christ. The author of Hebrews takes over this polemic to sharpen his readers' perception of the message given through Christ, through whom God has spoken "in these last days" (1:2).

---

ly distinguished from ὁ υἱὸς τοῦ θεοῦ=ὁ νόμος). See BAKKER, "Christ an Angel?" 257-58 and Joseph BARBEL, *Christos Angelos* (Theophaneia, 3; Bonn: Peter Hanstein, 1949, with appendix, 1964) pp. 47-50, 196-98, and 230-33; *contra* Norbert BROX, *Der Hirt des Hermas* (MeyerK, 7; Göttingen: Vandenhoeck & Ruprecht, 1991) 362-65, 490-92, and n.'s 14-15. Such views are attributed to Jewish-Christian groups during this period by EPIPHANIUS (*Pan.* 30.3.1-6) and HIPPOLYTUS (*Ref.* 9.13.1-3); concerning the problem of identifying these groups and the traditions on which they were dependent, see Gerard P. LUTTIKHUIZEN, *The Revelation of Elchasai* (TSAJ, 8; Tübingen: J.C.B. Mohr [Paul Siebeck], 1985). Finally, see *T.Sol.* 6:8 (the angel which subdues Beelzeboul), 22:20.

[239] See n. 238. In *Gosp.Th.* Logion 13 the identifications of Jesus by Simon Peter as "a righteous angel" (Copt=Grk, δίκαιος ἄγγελος) and by Matthew as "a wise philosopher" are rejected in favor of Thomas's admission that he is incapable of saying what Jesus is like. This may be a mild polemic against an angel Christology, if ἄγγελος, which could denote a human "messenger" (e.g., a prophet; cf. Mk 8:28//Mt 16:14//Lk 9:19), actually refers to a heavenly angel; on ἄγγελος=prophet, see Stevan DAVIES, "The Christology and Protology of the *Gospel of Thomas*," *JBL* 111 (1992) 675 n. 21. The date of composition for *Gosp.Th.* is, of course, currently the subject of a lively debate, that is, whether it may be assigned to sometime during the mid- to late second century or to the latter part of the first; for a summary of the various views, see Francis T. FALLON and Ron CAMERON, "The Gospel of Thomas: A Forschungsbericht and Analysis," in *ANRW* II.25.6, esp. pp. 4213-24. Even if one were to concede that the original composition behind the document is as late as the early second century, one might speculate whether the *tradition* of Jesus "as a righteous ἄγγελος" derives from an earlier period. In the end, however, it remains impossible on the basis of *Gosp.Th.* to draw any conclusions about the polemic in the tradition underlying Hebrews.

The Slavic version of JOSEPHUS' account of Jesus (see n. 198 above) also contains a polemic against the view of Jesus as an angel. This recension, heavily influenced by the transmission of Christian scribes and dependent on earlier "tainted" versions of *Ant.* 18.63-64, is too late to be of any relevance.

d. Second Century Accusations: Kerygma Petrou, Aristides,
and Celsus (Origen, c.Cels. 1.26; 5.6)

In these sources the accusation of "angel worship" is unambiguously directed against Jews. In the Κήρυγμα Πέτρου and the Syriac version of ARISTIDES' *Apology* 14 these charges are formulated in similar fashion, as shown in the synopsis below (additions in ARISTIDES are in *italics*):

Kerygma Petrou	Aristides
(in CLEMENT of ALEXANDRIA, Strom. 6.5.41.2-3)[240]	
Μηδὲ κατὰ Ἰουδαίους σέβεσθε	But they [Jews] too have wandered away from the accurate truth,
καὶ γὰρ ἐκεῖνοι μόνοι οἰόμενοι τὸν θεὸν γινώσκειν οὐκ ἐπίστανται	supposing [sbryn] in their minds that they are serving [plḥyn] God, *but in the nature of their actions [bzny' dyn dsw'rnyhwn]*
λατρεύοντες ἀγγέλοις καὶ ἀρχαγγέλοις	their service [plḥynhwn] is to angels *and not to God [wl' l'lh']*
μηνὶ καὶ σελήνῃ· καὶ ἐὰν μὴ σελήνη φανῇ σάββατον οὐκ ἄγουσι τὸ λεγόμενον πρῶτον, οὐδὲ ἄζυμα οὔτε ἑορτὴν οὔτε μεγάλην ἡμέραν.	*when [kd]* they keep the sabbath and new moon and the passover and the great fast and the feast *and circumcision and cleanness of meats.*[241]

---

[240] Text in GCS 2/15. The line divisions are provided to aid the comparison.

[241] The Syr ms, dated to the 7th cent., was edited by HARRIS and translated into English by J. Armitage ROBINSON in *The Apology of Aristides* (TS, 1/1; Cambridge: Univ., 1891); ROBINSON's translation is adapted here. Though the original apology was written in Grk, the Syr text contains a more original version than the more compact Grk evidence, which says nothing about Jews serving angels. The Grk version (3 mss are collated on pp. 110-112), which is preserved in mss of "Life of Barlaam and Josephat" by St. JOHN of DAMASCUS, has been adjusted considerably (shortened) to fit its new context. Due to signs of expansion in the Syr, HARRIS (*ibid.*, p. 80) does conclude that the Grk version "will as a rule give us the actual words of ARISTIDES, except in very few places in which modification was obviously needed." Two reasons suggest the priority of the Syr in the section on Jewish worship: (1) First, the likelihood that ARISTIDES drew on the *Kerygma Petrou*; see ROBINSON, *ibid.*, pp. 86-99 and W. SCHNEEMELCHER, "Das Kerygma Petrou," in *NTA* 2.35 (with further bibl.). (2) Second, the Grk version, unlike the Syr, criticizes Jewish worship of God because "they deny Christ the Son of God": σέβονται γὰρ καὶ

(in ORIGEN, Comm.Jn. 13.17)²⁴²
...μηδὲ κατὰ ᾿Ιουδαίους σέβειν
τὸ θεῖον
ἐπείπερ καὶ αὐτοὶ μόνοι οἰόμενοι
ἐπίστασθαι θεὸν
ἀγνοοῦσιν αὐτόν,
λατρεύοντες
ἀγγέλοις
καὶ μηνὶ καὶ σελήνῃ.

In scholarly discussion these two texts are frequently cited and interpreted together.²⁴³ In choosing similar language which not only speaks of "serving" angels but also mentions other Jewish practices, they both give expression to unsympathetic perspectives towards "Jews" leveled from the "outside." Thus HURTADO,²⁴⁴ drawing largely upon the observations of Marcel SIMON,²⁴⁵ maintains that *both* sources (1) "are not directed against marginal Jewish groups" and (2) "appear to be concerned primarily with the ritual practices, ... [i.e.] the statements in *Aristides* and in the *Kerygma Petrou* both list examples of Jewish ritual occasions as illustrations of the things being criticized."²⁴⁶ Clinton E. ARNOLD relates the texts similarly, but ventures a dif-

---

νῦν τὸν θεὸν μόνον παντωκράτορα, ἀλλ᾽ οὐ κατ᾽ ἐπίγνωσιν· τὸν γὰρ Χριστὸν ἀρνοῦνται τὸν υἱὸν τοῦ θεοῦ, καὶ εἰσὶ παρόμοιοι τῶν ἐθνῶν, κἂν ἐγγίζειν πῶς τῇ ἀληθείᾳ δοκῶσιν, ἧς ἑαυτοὺς ἐμάκρυναν (p. 110). It should be further noted that this emphasis does not serve well the argument of ARISTIDES' apology.

²⁴² Text in GCS 2/2; cf. also A.E. BROOKE, *The Fragments of Heracleon* (TS, 1/4; Cambridge: Univ., 1891) 77-79. ORIGEN is citing a version preserved in the commentary on John by Heracleon (of the 2nd-cent. Valentinian "gnostic" school). In the context, ORIGEN mentions that Heracleon had appealed to the *Kerygma*--which castigates both Gentile and Jewish worship--when he referred the "you" in Jn 4:2 (ὑμεῖς προσκυνεῖτε ὃ οὐκ οἴδατε) to Jews and Gentiles. As in *c.Cels*. 1.26 and 5.6-9 (see below), ORIGEN rejects any suggestion that Jews worship angels.

²⁴³ In addition to those mentioned below, see GOODENOUGH, *Jewish Symbols*, 2.161 and Howard M. TEEPLE, *How Did Christianity Really Begin? A Historical-Archaeological Approach* (Evanston, Illinois: Religion and Ethics Institute, 1992) 420-21.

²⁴⁴ *One God, One Lord*, pp. 33-34.

²⁴⁵ "Remarques de l'Angelolâtrie Juive," pp. 456-57. Whereas for SIMON these charges of angelolatry are ultimately traceable to magical practices in "syncretizing Jewish circles" (*Verus Israel*, p. 345), HURTADO sees in them no such connection. The groundlessness of the claims in ARISTIDES and *Kerygma Petrou* was, with apologetic interests, already argued by J. BERGMANN, rabbi in Frankfurt, in *Jüdische Apologetik im neutestamentlichen Zeitalter* (Berlin: Reimer, 1908) 73, 82 and 161-62.

²⁴⁶ *One God, One Lord*, p. 34; HURTADO sees here a characterization which is similar to the argumentation in Gal 4 and Col 2. Even more so, see Henning PAULSEN, "Das Kerygma Petri und die urchristliche Apologetik," *ZKG* 88 (1977) 18-19 and MACH, *Entwicklungsstadien*, p. 297.

ferent analysis; he ponders (1) why these traditions choose the worship of angels to describe Jewish practices and suggests (2) that the authors "were probably familiar with Jewish circles which gave undue attention to angels (from their perspective) such that they felt justified in describing this practice as 'worship' or 'service'."[247] What HURTADO considers as a critique of Judaism as a whole (which, then, must have had little basis in reality), ARNOLD regards as an accusation which may well presuppose an awareness of such practices among some Jewish groups. Despite their different conclusions, HURTADO and ARNOLD have interpreted these accusations together. Which of these interpretations is correct?

When the versions of the *Kerygma* and ARISTIDES are compared, certain differences can be detected. Most conspicuous is the additional material in ARISTIDES (given in *italics* above), which emphasizes "the nature of their actions" and includes "circumcision and cleanness of meats" in the list of observances. Furthermore, the rituals in ARISTIDES are placed in a subordinate clause (introduced by *kd*, "when"), so that the list functions as an *elaboration* of the worship of angels. On the basis of ARISTIDES alone, then, it is difficult to escape the conclusion that the accusation amounts to a theologically motivated caricature which labels the whole of Jewish religious life--that is, observance of the Torah--as the "worship of angels."[248] The statement, "supposing in their minds that they are serving God," serves as a rhetorical device in support of the author's claim to veracity. In this manner, the apology betrays an admission that the accusation contradicts what may otherwise be known about contemporary Judaism. The particular form is thus fertile soil for a critique which, in its comprehensiveness, can portray Jewish angel "worship," circumcision and meat regulations (absent in the *Kerygma*), and observance of the calendar as but varied expressions of the fact that Jews have "wandered from the truth." According to the author the Jews, despite appearance, "serve angels" without being aware of it. The charge of

---

[247] "Mediator Figures in Asia Minor," p. 23 n. 93.

[248] So correctly, LUEKEN, *Michael*, p. 5 WILLIAMS, "The Cult of Angels at Colossae" 426; and HURTADO, *One God, One Lord*, p. 34. Whether the statement assumes a knowledge of the tradition of angelic mediation of the Torah, in which the listed observances are prescribed, is not immediately clear. Whatever the case, this description, as it stands, forges links which can only be taken either as a deliberate misrepresentation (so that continuity with reality is highly suspect) or as a misunderstanding of Jewish observances.

angel worship is placed within an amalgam of *topoi* in a way that renders any basis in reality incredulous.

The difference in arrangement and sentence structure in the *Kerygma*, however, suggests that the motif of angel worship is not as integrated into the list which follows. The point of departure for further elaboration is the charge that Jews serve "month and moon."[249] The degree to which a veneration of angels can be linked with common Jewish observances depends on the extent to which the angelic figures[250] mentioned are thought to be synonymous with the following phrase. In any case, the link between the charge of angelolatry and the remainder of the description is more loosely connected than in ARISTIDES. The actual observation of the sabbath, Passover, and Day of Atonement is associated with the appearance of the moon, not angels.[251] If considered in this way, it is precarious to assume a simple identification of the ἄγγελοι with what follows. Consequently, the way is opened for a reference to something else.

Despite its fragmentary nature, the purpose of the *Kerygma*, as in the case of ARISTIDES' *Apology*, was clearly apologetic: to represent the piety of Christians as superior to pagan and Jewish worship. In the effort to demonstrate the Jewish religion as inferior, the *Kerygma* author's claim that Jews "serve angels" may be understood either as a fabrication or as reflecting some knowledge, though no doubt distorted, of Jewish ideas or practices involving angels. The former possibility is improbable; it reflects an unlikely assumption that the author of the *Kerygma*, in drawing on *topoi*, could not have had any knowledge of Jewish attitudes toward angels.[252] It is thus more

---

[249] The supposition that here the Jews are being accused of worshiping the astral deity "Meis" is, in the absence of any evidence which specifically links this Asia Minor cult with Jewish thought, unlikely; contra WILLIAMS, "The Cult of Angels at Colossae" 426; Cécile BLANC, *Origene. Commentaire sur saint Jean* (SC, 222; Paris: Cerf, 1975) 3.288-90; and A.R.R. SHEPPARD, "Pagan Cults of Angels in Roman Asia Minor," *Tal* 12-13 (1980-81) 92-94, who regards the accusations of the *Kerygma* as paralleled by a pagan misunderstanding of Judaism--reflected in the Lydian inscription (text given on p. 92)--, according to which Jews were thought to worship "a supreme 'One' god of the moon" (p. 93).

[250] In this respect, the difference between the versions in CLEMENT of ALEXANDRIA ("angels and archangels") and ORIGEN ("angels") is immaterial. It seems that on literary grounds the phrase "and archangels" in CLEMENT, which creates two pairs, is more likely a later addition.

[251] It is not clear whether one can ascribe to the author the knowledge of the tradition in *Jub* 2:17 in which the sabbath is observed by the angels.

[252] Thus the significance of distinguishing between the motif of angel worship in the *Kerygma* and ARISTIDES, already recognized by Ernst VON DOB-

pertinent to inquire concerning the basis for the mention of angels at all. One possibility is that here the author derived his mention of angels from the belief among some Jews in angelic mediation of the Torah, a notion which could be interpreted negatively in the New Testament.[253] Again, however, this seems more likely in the case of ARISTIDES than in the *Kerygma*, given the latter's emphasis on the specific association of the "moon" with what follows.

Whether or not Jews could be thought to "serve angels" is a matter of definition, especially in a polemical context. As noted above, ARISTIDES emphasized a contradiction between a Jewish intention to worship God and what is to be inferred from their actions. In the *Kerygma*, however, this contradiction is understood differently. The phrase οὐκ ἐπίστανται, which may be translated "they do not give attention to," does not necessarily dismiss the possibility of *any* knowledge of God among Jews and hence may reflect the opinion that they do worship God, but insufficiently. Understood in this way, what the *Kerygma* describes from the "outside" as reprehensible may betray the knowledge of a practice of invoking angels alongside God.[254] What from the "inside" may have been thought to be within the bounds of a monotheistic framework would have easily been interpreted as just such a compromise.[255]

Celsus' depiction of Jewish worship, preserved in two citations by ORIGEN, is likewise hard to delineate, but offers more detail: (1) "...they worship angels and are devoted to sorcery [γοητείᾳ], concerning which Moses was their instructor" (*c.Cels.* 1.26[256]) and (2) "...they worship both heaven and

---

SCHÜTZ, *Das Kerygma Petri* (TU, 11/1; Leipzig: Hinrichs, 1893) 36-41, continues to be overlooked. In addition to HURTADO and SIMON, see PAULSEN, "Das Kerygma Petri" 16-19.

[253] See n. 159 above. For rabbinic texts, see CALLAN, "Pauline Midrash in Gal 3:19b."

[254] See esp. the two Jewish burial inscriptions from Rheneia near Delos (2nd cent. BCE) discussed below in section II.B.3.a (pp. 183-85).

[255] ARNOLD ("Mediator Figures in Asia Minor," p. 23) argues similarly, but, as do SIMON (*Verus Israel*, p. 345) and GOODENOUGH (*Jewish Symbols*, 2. 161) wishes to locate the invocation of angels specifically within magical practices. Since not all the evidence for calling upon angels shows specific affinities with the magical traditions, such as the Rheneia inscriptions, it is preferable, in the case of the *Kerygma*, to refer to invocation in general. See sections II.B.2.d (pp. 173-79), II.B.3.d (pp. 188-91) and the Excursus on Jewish invocation of angels in magical sources (pp. 192-200) below.

[256] GCS 2/2-... αὐτοὺς σεβεῖν ἀγγέλους καὶ γοητείᾳ προσκεῖσθαι ἧς ὁ Μωϋσης αὐτοῖς γέγονεν ἐξηγήτης.

the angels who dwell within" (c.Cels. 5.6²⁵⁷). Again, any veracity to Celsus' claim is quickly dismissed by those who argue that his accusations are distorted by polemical intentions. Furthermore, ORIGEN himself, through whom Celsus' charges are preserved, emphatically rejects angel worship as a Jewish practice.²⁵⁸

In the context of Celsus' charge in contra Celsum 5.6, Jews are accused of being inconsistent in that they can worship heaven and angels, while failing to worship the most prominent parts of heaven, such as the sun, moon, stars, and planets. In countering this claim, ORIGEN accuses Celsus of "confusion" and attempts to defend Jewish monotheism by appealing to the First and Second Commandments (Ex 20:3-5): any law-observant Jew would not worship heaven or angels. Thus ORIGEN, more so than Celsus, defines the "Jewish" practice from the biblical record.²⁵⁹ This observation is closely connected to a further point. Despite ORIGEN's dismissal of Celsus' claim, he actually comes close to admitting it himself in the way he alludes to contemporary practices. In 5.9 ORIGEN suggests that Celsus could have represented matters more clearly had he either (1) not ascribed angel worship to the Jews to begin with or, if he had done so, (2) "he should have shown that Jews *who transgress the law* were doing such things."²⁶⁰ ORIGEN goes on to speak of such transgressors as "those who through sorcery (ἐκ γοητείας) worship beings concealed somewhere in darkness." In other words, Celsus attributed to Judaism on the basis of contemporary reports what ORIGEN, on the basis of the Jewish law, regarded as an aberration. This gives reason to suspect the veracity of ORIGEN's defense as well.

---

²⁵⁷ GCS 2/2-... τὸν μὲν οὐρανὸν καὶ τοὺς ἐν τῷδε ἀγγέλους σέβουσι.

²⁵⁸ WILLIAMS, "The Cult of Angels at Colossae" 426-27; SIMON, "Remarques sur l'Angélolâtrie Juive," p. 455; and HURTADO, *One God, One Lord*, p. 33: "Given his polemical purpose, it is likely that Celsus either deliberately exaggerated the Jewish interest in angels for the purpose of trying to make Jews seem inconsistent or clumsily misunderstood their interest in angels as the worship of them."

²⁵⁹ See also 5.8 (GCS 2/2-... Κέλσου νομίζοντος Ἰουδαϊκὸν εἶναι τὸ προσκυνεῖν οὐρανῷ καὶ τοῖς ἐν αὐτῷ ἀγγέλοις, οὐκ Ἰουδαϊκὸν μὲν τὸ τοιοῦτον, παραβατικὸν δὲ Ἰουδαϊσμοῦ ἐστιν); 5.9 (appeal to Lev 19:31). The accusation attributed to Celsus, on the other hand, seems to refer less to scriptures than to practices. ARNOLD ("Mediator Figures in Asia Minor," p. 23) correctly calls attention to the proscriptive nature of ORIGEN's argument.

²⁶⁰ GCS 2/2-... παραστῆσαι ὅτι τὰ τοιαῦτα οἱ παρανομοῦντες Ἰουδαῖοι ἐποίουν.

Celsus is portrayed by ORIGEN as one who took marginal or "unorthodox" views and unjustly transferred them into his critique of the whole.[261] If he was interested in demonstrating the inconsistency of Jewish devotion (c.Cels. 5.6), "it is possible that he capitalized on *the variety of practices* he witnessed in Judaism, i.e. he tried to make a point based on some groups who venerate angels knowing full well that this was not representative of all of Judaism" (emphasis my own).[262]

4. Summary

Neither the polemical nor varied nature of the texts reviewed in this section allows for any firm or general conclusions concerning Jewish practices or beliefs in relation to the veneration of angels. A reading of this literature is immediately confronted by the probability that such traditions, if they refer to religious praxis at all, may have been the product of hypothetical reasoning, distortion, or generalization. At the same time, we are in a better position to determine the sorts of attitudes and activities which were *perceived* as dangerous.

(1) Our study of various interpretive traditions in the rabbinic texts suggests that the danger of venerating angels instead of God was perceived in relation to several overlapping complexes of tradition: (a) speculation in the context of mystical ascents to the Merkabah; (b) the notion of angelic rule over nations, which could lead to the association of angels with idolatry; and, more generally, (c) the notion of angelic mediation. Can anything be said about possible practices addressed in the rabbinic injunctions? It is admittedly difficult to see how the prohibitions against sacrificing to and making images of angels could have obtained among groups which defined themselves as Jewish. Though the midrashic passages do betray a measure of apprehension that seems to extend beyond exegetical interests, they leave little room for inferences concerning specific activities or ideas being rejected. In this respect, the text in *Exodus Rabbah* 32:4 is likewise not much help, since there the notion of "serving" the guiding angel in the wilderness is only vaguely associated with obtaining forgiveness. Thus, aside from sacri-

---

[261] See *c.Cels.* 6.27-30: Celsus attributes to Christians the belief in seven "archontic angels" the head of which is the demiurge. ORIGEN restricts this charge to the Ophite sect which he argues is not Christian.

[262] So ARNOLD, "Mediator Figures in Asia Minor," p. 23 n. 93.

fices and image-making, the only *human activity* explicitly condemned in the texts reviewed is the invocation of angels, as demonstrated especially in *j. Berakoth* 9:13a-b. Significantly, the rejection of such invocation is not accompanied by a categorical dismissal of angelic mediation as such. This suggests a debate among rabbinic circles concerning the proper understanding of angels as mediators, in the context of which a praying through angels could be labelled (by one side) as a corruption of monotheistic belief.

(2) The refusal tradition, which is attested in both Jewish and Christian writings roughly contemporaneous to the Apocalypse of John, depicts and rejects venerative behavior towards angelic figures. Here the angelophanic encounter is placed within a narrative framework which purportedly records a seer's visions frequently during an ascent to the divine throne. The objectionable behavior, usually presented as a seer's response to the angel's overwhelming appearance, could variously take the form of "fear," "prostration," "worship," or a combination thereof. With the possible exception of the *Ascension of Isaiah*--in which legitimate worship includes Christ and the Holy Spirit and the motif of rivalry between the righteous and angels is accentuated--, the clearest adaptations of this tradition show a concern to define proper venerative behavior as the worship of God alone. Furthermore, the incorporation of language prohibiting idolatry into this motif assumes some reflection on the application of the First and Second Commandments. It is hence possible, though by no means clear, that the refusal's prohibition has a background in the kind of midrashic proscriptions found in the later rabbinic texts.

(3) The analysis of passages from Galatians, Colossians, Hebrews, and polemical traditions from the second century has yielded divergent results.[263] Paul's argument in Galatians does not draw the analogy between life in bondage to the στοιχεῖα and Jewish life under the Torah to the extent that the latter is thought to consist of subservience to angels. The author of Colossians, however, is convinced that the faith of his readers is endangered by those who participate in ταπεινοφροσύνῃ καὶ θρησκείᾳ τῶν ἀγγέλων ἃ ἑόρακεν ἐμβατεύειν. A consideration of Jewish and Christian apocalyptic sources suggests that the Colossian "error" should be neither confined to the aspiration

---

[263] These passages, then, cannot be regarded equally as references to "ideas and worship of angelic mediators" without a considerable degree of nuancing as suggested, e.g., George JOHNSTON, *The Spirit-Paraclete in the Gospel of John* (SNTSMS, 12; Cambridge: Cambridge University Press, 1970) 122.

to participate in angelic worship (subjective genitive) of God nor be satisfied with an explanation which posits an angel "cult" (objective genitive). This interpretation is corroborated by the refusal tradition, which frequently appears in the context of observation of or participation in heavenly angelic liturgy.

The analysis of Hebrews 1-2 produces a different kind of picture. A polemic against beliefs associated with angelology is not apparent from the author's emphases in the epistle itself. Such, however, is more likely to have obtained at an intermediate stage of tradition in which the use of Psalm 110:1 was readjusted to form a comparison between Christ, on the one hand, and complementary angelic beings, on the other. Whereas the problem at Colossae seems to have involved behavior directly associated with angels, the tradition taken up in Hebrews was targeted against cosmological ideas in which the fluidity of Hellenistic-Jewish speculation concerning angels and ideas about intermediary figures threatened to undermine the soteriological significance of Christ's exaltation. The tradition hence represents an early rejection of a comparison which, by and during the second century CE, would be favorably attested in Christian writings (Jude?, JUSTIN, *Shepherd of Hermas*, *Ascension of Isaiah*).

Neither in Colossians nor in Hebrews is there any trace of an attempt to protect monotheistic belief as such. The overriding concern, rather, is to safeguard Christology from an accommodation to veneration of angels (Colossians) or from an amalgamation into angelological ideas (Hebrews). In both cases, we are not confronted by traditions which go back to the earliest developments in Christology, but by problems which were encountered well after Christ's exalted status was firmly established within Christian communities. This emphasis on protecting Christ's exalted status may be taken as an indicator of the degree to which Christology had been absorbed into a monotheistic framework. At the same time, developments in speculation concerning angels reached a point that angelology and Christology could be merged in a way that could be thought to threaten monotheistic belief.

The second-century traditions polemicizing against angelolatry involve caricatures which presuppose the previous existence of such accusations. Thus the sharp tone in *Apology* of ARISTIDES, which depends and elaborates on earlier tradition, makes it difficult to draw any lines of continuity with actual Jewish practices. On the other hand, the *Kerygma Petrou*, in which the references to angel worship and Jewish rituals are expressed more independently, may reflect some knowledge of an interest in angels among Jews. Nev-

generalization and amplification of some known practice (such as, for instance, the inclusion of angels in invocations).

Celsus' accusations against Jews and ORIGEN's attempt to exonerate them suggest some form of angel veneration within a context of magical practices. Whether such activity could be ascribed to "Jews" depends largely on Celsus' relatively wide or on ORIGEN's much narrower definition.[264] In any case, it is significant that Celsus' charge of angel veneration in the context of magical practices is admitted by ORIGEN who, however, can only attribute it to Jews who have deliberately transgressed the Torah.

What, then, did various writers consider to be an improper veneration of angels? The polemical texts suggest several areas in which an examination of venerative language in relation to angels requires further examination: (1) invocation of angels (including magical practices); (2) participation in angel worship; and (3) attitudes perceptible through venerative language or physical posture. These categories will be addressed in the section on non-polemical sources (II.B) below.

B. NON-POLEMICAL SOURCES

The following discussion is focused on Jewish sources which point toward human venerative attitudes towards angelic beings from the third century BCE through the second century CE. The analysis itself remains, to some degree, heuristic; what actually constitutes an expression of "veneration" or "worship" is difficult to define on the basis of polemical traditions alone (as discussed above). Moreover, the determination of what was and was not thought to compromise monotheistic belief, in all probability, varied from group to group. One can say that at different times, among different groups, and in different circumstances invocation of angels, venerative language and posture towards angels, and an intense interest in angelic worship could be met by various forms of mild or explicit rejection. Thus, as already indicated, it may be preferable to distinguish between various degrees of veneration before considering possible backgrounds for the interrelation of angelology, Christology, and monotheistic belief in the Apocalypse of John. If we cannot assume that the polemical statements were accurate reflections of religious behavior, it is important to examine the existing "evidence" to see if there might be any lines of correlation at all.

---

[264] On the problem of defining "magic" see below, pp. 188-90.

150   *Angelic and Heavenly Figures: Veneration and Monotheism*

1. *Qumran Documents*[265]

It lies outside the scope of this study to present an overview of angelological ideas in the texts from Qumran.[266] Clearly, in the area of angelology these materials have provided a significant amount of data for early Jewish thought[267] in relation to classification of angels, dualistic patterns, and, in particular, forms of human participation in angelic functions. Despite the abundance of evidence in the Qumran materials, it is conspicuous that relatively little is said which seems to have a direct bearing on the problem of human veneration of angels.[268] Nevertheless, a discussion of several

---

[265] For the sake of consistency, unless otherwise indicated, the citations of published Qumran documents (in the order of fragment, column, and line numbers) correspond to those included in ed. CHARLESWORTH, *Graphic Concordance to the Dead Sea Scrolls* (Tübingen/Louisville: J.C.B. Mohr [Paul Siebeck] and Westminster-John Knox, 1991).

[266] The most comprehensive studies of angelology at Qumran to date are S.F. NOLL's unpublished dissertation, *Angelology in the Qumran Texts* (Univ. of Manchester: Diss., 1979) and Maxwell J. DAVIDSON, *Angels at Qumran. A Comparative Study of 1 Enoch 1-36, 72-108 and Sectarian Writings from Qumran* (JSPS, 11; Sheffield: JSOT, 1992) esp. pp. 132-285. See also SCHÄFER's review of Qumran and other early Jewish sources in *Rivalität*, pp. 9-40 and Paul KOBELSKI, *Melchizedek and Melchiresa'* (CBQMS, 10; Washington, D.C.: CBA, 1981) 3-83. With the exception of DAVIDSON's work, these treatments must now be supplemented by data from the *Shirot 'Olat ha-Shabbat*; see Carol NEWSOM, *Songs of the Sabbath Sacrifice. A Critical Edition* (HSS, 27; Atlanta: Scholars, 1985) 23-38. In addition, further materials will be provided by the as yet unpublished texts.

[267] The analysis of the scrolls' contents should, of course, not proceed too facily to the identification of a sociological context (e.g. the Qumran community). Though some of the "sectarian" materials from the 11 caves may be said to reflect the thought of the community during various stages of its existence (e.g. 1QS, 1QSa, 1QSb, 1QM, the *pesharim*, and of CD), the sociological contextualization of other texts remains far from clear (e.g. 11QTemple, the *New Jerusalem* fragments, 1QapGen, 3Q15). When taken together, the diversity of the texts is striking. Qumran provenance for a text, then, should not be taken for granted, but is a matter to be weighed in each case.

[268] For instance, none of the available DSS texts unambiguously associate language of worship with the figures Melchizedek or Michael. Though Melchizedek is designated אלוהים in 11QMelch 2.10 and, as a heavenly figure, embodies royal (2.9-16; cf. esp. Ps 82:1 with 2.10) and perhaps priestly (2.8?) functions, preserved materials provide no information on whether he could be the object of veneration. In short, the question of angel "worship" is not suitable to the characterization of "Melchizedek" in 11QMelch. In 1QM Michael is said to have a "rule" (משרה; 17.7) which will be established when the eschatological war ends in triumph over "the prince of evil reign" (רשעה שר ממשלת; 17.5-6). Nothing here, however, portrays Michael as an object of reverence by the human community. The special position accorded an angelic figure seems less understood as a matter of honor or devotion given by the human community than as a function of a stratified conception of the heavenly

passages is warranted and may contribute in two ways. First, in some cases it should be stressed that what some scholars may previously have taken as evidence for the veneration of angels is highly suspect. Such instances will be briefly mentioned (II.B.1.a). Second, there are some pertinent texts which merit special attention (II.B.1.b).

a. Purported Evidence

In connection with "worship of angels" in Colossians 2:18, W.D. DAVIES, Herbert BRAUN, and S. LYONNET[269] have appealed to 1QM 10.10-11, calling attention to the phrase ודואי מלאכי קדוש ("and who see the angels of holiness") in line 10. Indeed, a parallel to Colossians may obtain insofar as the angels in

---

world. Such would seem further confirmed, if the interpretation of 4Q491 as a poem concerning Michael by M. BAILLET (*DJD VII*, pp. 26-29) is correct. In this ms, which contains portions which overlap thematically with 1QM, a (heavenly?) figure speaks of himself as being singularly "exalted" (l. 13- ולוא ידונכם זולתי), "reckoned among the אלים" (l. 14-אתחשב אלים עם; l. 18- עם אלים אחשוב], unequaled in dispensing judgment (l. 17- מיא יועדני איא) and "established in the holy congregation" (l. 14-בעדת ומכוני במשפטי וידמה) קודש). The exaltation referred to is probably more a matter of classification in the heavenly spheres than a human act of veneration of an angel; see similarly the angelomorphic self-characterization attributed to Christ in *OdesSol* 36:4 (*kd mshbḥ 'n' bmshbḥ'* [HARRIS' text: *bmshbḥn'*] *wrb 'n' brwrbn'*. For an altogether different interpretation of the 4Q491 fragment, that the figure is a self-aggrandizing mystic "with an exaggerated notion of his own sanctity," see Morton SMITH, "Two Ascended to Heaven," in *Jesus and the Dead Sea Scrolls*, pp. 295-99. A literary context of this fragment of 4Q491 within the *War Scroll*, if correct, undermines the plausibility of SMITH's hypothesis.
   Finally and significantly, DAVIDSON (*Angels at Qumran*, pp. 310-13) observes that, in comparison to the *1 En* texts, there is a conspicuous lack of any explicit mention among the texts attributable to the Qumran community concerning angelic intercession or mediation of revelation. DAVIDSON (*ibid.*, pp. 275-76 and 311) is aware that the *New Jerusalem* materials constitute a possible exception for an angelic mediator, though their relation to the Qumran community is not clear. Here an an unidentified (angelic) figure guides a seer through the heavenly Jerusalem, as can be inferred from the following: (1) the repeated phrases ואעלני ("and he brought me," as in 5QJN 1 1.18, 1 2.6; 4Q554 PAM 43.564 2.6; 4Q555 PAM 43.610 3.4) and אחזי(א)ני ("and he showed me," as in 5QJN 1 2.2,6; 2QJN 1 1.4, 8 1.7) and (2) phrases indicating conversational interaction between the seer and guide (11QJN PAM 43.996 rt. frgt. 1.4-ואמר לי; PAM 43.998 rt. frgt. l. 5- ואמר לי]. הוא אגרה; and PAM 43.999 lt. frgt. ll. 5-6- ...אחוא לי כתב / למקרא שרי[לי. For 2Q and 5Q see M. Baillet and J.T. MILIK in *Les 'Petites Grottes' de Qumrân* (DJD, 3; Oxford: Clarendon, 1962) 84-89 and 184-93 respectively. The JN texts from 4 and 11Q are as yet unpublished; for a precursory text and translation of the 4Q fragments, see EISENMAN and WISE, *The Dead Sea Scrolls Uncovered*, pp. 41-46. Ultimately, however, JN preserves nothing which associates the angel's mediary role with an attitude of venerative devotion on the part of the seer.

[269] See n.'s 161-163 (section II.A.3.b).

the epistle (2:18) can be conceived as the object of ἑόρακεν. There is, however, no mention of veneration here, and it is going too far to draw an association with Colossians.[270] Two further considerations seem to undergird this point. First, the clause is one of a series of participial constructions describing the privileges accorded to Israel as God's chosen people. These privileges are framed by a hymn devoted to praising the "God of Israel" (10.8).[271] In this connection, it is important to consider the opening question (1.8- "Who is like you, O God of Israel...") which is reformulated in the following encomium on Israel (1.9-"Who is like your people Israel...").[272] This construction makes clear that the unique status of Israel among the nations is derived from the incomparable status of אל ישראל. Given this context, it is misleading to attribute too much to Israel's vision of "the angels of holiness." Second, it is not evident whether the "seeing" of angels refers to some aspect of the community's eschatological self-understanding[273] or whether it is but part of a summary interpretation of salvation-historical events at Sinai.[274] It is also possible that both concepts are intended since the interpretation of present and future condition of "Israel" depended to some extent on drawing lines of continuity with decisive salvific events in the past. None of these alternatives, however, suggest a point of departure for attributing to the Qumran community a veneration of angels.

The significance of another passage for angel veneration is likewise problematic: 1QSb 4.28-ויכבד שמו וקודשיו. At issue is how to interpret the linguistically difficult קודשיו. Given the plural suffix, several translators

---

[270] This misinterpretation is a good example of how the desire to find parallels can lead to the association of extraneous elements. Hence the importance of examining context.

[271] From 10.8 until at least 12.13 the governing pronoun is the 2nd pers. sg.

[272] מיא כעמכה ישראל אשר בחרתה (1. 8); מיא כמיכה אל ישראל בשמים ובארץ לכה מכול עמי הארצות (1. 9).

[273] Cf. 1QM 7.6: For the eschatological battle, ritual purity is to be maintained "because angels of holiness together with their hosts numbering in the thousands are among them" (כיא מלאכי קודש עם צבאותם כאלפים באמה). YADIN, in *The Scroll of the War of the Sons of Light against the Sons of Darkness* (Oxford: Univ., 1962), apparently understood the seeing of angels in 10.10-11 as a "privilege of the elect, often alluded to in the Pseudepigrapha" (p. 306); cf. also Jürgen BECKER, *Das Heil Gottes* (SUNT, 3; Göttingen: Vandenhoeck & Ruprecht, 1964) 77.

[274] So J. CARMIGNAC, *La Regle de la Guerre* (Paris: Letouzey et Ané, 1958); J. VAN DER PLOEG, *Le Rouleau de la Guerre* (STDJ, 2; Leiden: Brill, 1959) p. 137; and B. JONGELING, *Le Rouleau de la Guerre* (Assen: Van Gorcum, 1962) p. 249.

have rendered the term as "his holy ones (beings)."[275] If the conjunction before קודשיו does not introduce a new thought,[276] the blessing for the high priest[277] may be translated, "for you sa]nctify him and glorify his name and his holy ones." The immediate problem with this rendering is conspicuous: the *qutl* form קודש nowhere (in either Qumran literature or biblical Hebrew) refers to angels.[278] An alternative explanation is, however, also elusive. J.T. MILIK, for whom the form means "his holiness," had attempted to explain the form in the *editio princeps* by pointing out the use of a plural suffix in place of the singular in the large Isaiah scroll (1QIs^a).[279] If MILIK's explanation is correct, this is the only such usage of the suffix among the published non-biblical materials. Another possible explanation for MILIK's translation is to take the form as a majestic plural, such as appears in Proverbs 9:10, but it is not entirely convincing.[280] An interpretation is, however, possible on internal grounds. The clause, introduced by כיא, is preceded on the same line by a reference to the high priest's consecration to the "holy of holies" (נזר לקודש קודשים) [[281]. This suggests an elaboration of the high priest's function in the "holy of holies" for which he has been consecrated;

---

[275] See E. LOHSE, *Die Texte aus Qumran* (Darmstadt: Wissenschaftliche Buchgesellschaft, 1971) 58-59 ("seine Heiligen"); Johann MAIER and Kurt Schubert, *Die Qumran-Essener* (UTB, 224; München/Basel: Ernst REINHARD, 1973) 300 ("Seine Heiligen"); and T.H. GASTER, *The Dead Sea Scriptures* (Garden City, NY: Doubleday, 1976^3) 98 ("His Holy Beings").

[276] קודשיו is the last word of the column; the beginning of col. 5 is not preserved. Gaster's translation apparently led him to separate קודשיו from the foregoing תכבד: "... showest forth the glory of His name. And may His Holy Beings [wait upon thee]."

[277] This identification rests on the phrase earlier in l. 28 (נזר [לקודש קודשים), which connects the Holy of Holies with an allusion to the diadem made for "Aaron" in Ex 39:30; see Jacob LICHT, סרך המרכים (Jerusalem: Bialik, 1965) 285.

[278] Of course the *qatol* adjectival form (קדוש(ים)) is frequently equivocal to angelic beings in the Dead Sea Scrolls; see s.v. in CHARLESWORTH, *Graphic Concordance*.

[279] *Discoveries in the Judaean Desert I: Qumran Cave I* (Oxford: Clarendon, 1955) 127. MILIK cites 23 examples from 1QIs^a; the same form for "his holiness" occurs only in the text of Isa 50:6.

[280] "The beginning of wisdom is the fear of YHWH, and knowledge of the Holy One (קדשים) is understanding." Though the pointing of MT derives "Holy One" from קדוש, the form is ambiguous. For analogous parallels, see E. KAUTZSCH, *Gesenius' Hebrew Grammar*, translated by A.E. COWLEY (Oxford: Clarendon, 1910^{28}) par. 124 h.

[281] The restoration of a jussive form with 2nd ms. sg. dir. obj. suff. such as ישימכה (as in l. 27) is all but certain; so MILIK, *DJD I*, p. 126.

the plural form may, then, be a resumption of קוֹדֶשׁ קָדָשִׁים, so that the entire line may be translated as follows: "May he make (in) you] a consecration for the holy of holies, so that you may sanctify him and bring glory (to) his name and (to) his holy place." It is hence, in the final analysis, improbable that 1QSb 4.28 provides evidence for a veneration towards angels.

b. "Fellowship" with Angels and Veneration

As noted above, the Qumran writings provide further evidence for the notion of communion with angels in early Jewish thought. This motif, taken up in a number of the documents, seems to have been applied within several contexts. The presence of angels in the community is formulated in relation to (1) help in the eschatological holy war against the forces of evil;[282] (2) the community's participation in heavenly worship;[283] (3) the exclusion of the rit-

---

[282] See esp. 1QM 1.14-15-"and the might of God strength[ens] the he[art of the sons of ligh]t and with the seventh lot (בגורל) the great hand of God humbles..."; 12.4-5-"and to appoint h[osts of] your [el]ect in thousands and myriads together with (יחד עם) your holy ones [...] your angels to lead in the battle [... the ve]ngeful of the earth by your great judgments, and together with (עם) the elect of heaven [...]"; 12.7- "the congregation of your holy ones is in our midst as an eternal help (בתוכנו לעזר עולמ[ים)"; 12.8-9- "the migh[ty of] the angelic host is among our appointed men (בפקודינו), and the Hero of wa[r] is in the midst of our congregation (בעדתי) and the host of his spirits is with our infantry and cavalry (עם צעדנו ופרשינו)"; 13.10- "and a Prince of Light you have appointed from aforetime to be our help (לעזרנו)"; 17.6- "and he will send an eternal help (עזר) to the lot (לגורל) of his redemption by the might of the splendorous angel for the princely domain of Michael." The terms גורל, עזר, and prep. עם here express a solidarity with angels within a dualistic framework.

[283] The most characteristic element of this aspect is the preposition עם and further by the expressions גורל, התיצב במעמד, יחד. See 1QS 11.8-"he has allowed them to inherit the lot of the holy ones (וינחילם בגורל) and with the sons of heaven (עם בני שמים) he has joined their council"; 1QSb 3.6?-עם מלאכי קודש; 4.26-"and let fall (your) lot together with the angels of presence (פניכם מלאכי) and (your) council in common [with...] (ועצה [יחד)"; 1QH 3.21-23-"in order to take position (במעמד להתיצב) with (עם) the host of holy ones, and in order to enter into community with (ביחד עם) the congregation of the sons of heaven; for you have allotted to man an eternal lot together with (עם) the spirits of knowledge to praise your name in common (ביחד) ..."; 6.13-"to all the men of your council, (those) in the common lot together with (ובגורל יחד עם) the angels of presence"; 11.11-12-"that he might be united with (להיחד) [...] the sons of your truth, and (be) in the lot together with (בגורל עם) your holy ones"; 11.13-"and that he might take position (ולהתיצב במעמד) before you together with (עם) the everlasting host"; 11.14-"and rejoicing in common (ביחד) with (עם) those who know"; 1QH frgt. 2.10-"to be united with (עם) (להיחד להיחד) the sons of heaven"; 2.14-"se]rving together with (עם) your host"; 5.3- "together with (עם) the congregation of your holy ones"; 7.11-"and to take position [with (]במעמד ולהתיצב; 10.6-7-

ually unclean from war camps[284] or from the present and future worshiping community;[285] and (4) the guarantee of the community's physical and religious well-being.[286] These functions lend credence to H.-W. KUHN's conclusion that "one cannot speak of *one* concept of communion with the angels" at Qumran.[287] Among these distinctions, human reflection on the significance of angels is most explicit in relation to the community's participation in the heavenly cult.

"and into a community (ביחד) we have been assembled, and together with (עם) thos[e] who [k]now [...] together with (עם) your mighty ones"; 1Q36-"eternal [...] together with (עם) your holy ones and in the l[ot ...; 4Q181 frgt. 1 1.3-4-"e]lim as a holy congregation in the position of eternal life together with (עם) your holy ones"; 1 1.4-"and in the lot together with (עם ובגורל) his holy ones"; 4Q491 (=4QM^a) 24 1.4-"and by psal[m] in common with (עם יחד) the sons of *elim*; 4Q511 2 1.8:-"]lot of the *elohim* together with (עם) the an[gels of]his glorious lights". Cf. also 1QM 12.1-2 and 4Q511 8 1.9.

[284] 1QM 7.6- "because (כיא) the holy angels are with their hosts as a community (עם צבאותם יחד)," corroborated by 4Q491 (=4QM^a) 1-3 1.10- "because (כיא) the holy angels are in their arrangements together (במערכותמה יח]ד)."

[285] 1QSa 2.8-9-exclusion from "entering to take position" (...[יבו]או להתיצב) in the eschatological community's assembly "because (כיא) holy angels are [in] their [congrega]tion"; CD 15.15-17=4QD^b 17 1.8-9 (see Benjamin Zion WACHOLDER and Martin G. ABBEGG, *A Preliminary Edition of the Unpublished Dead Sea Scrolls* [2 fascicles; Washington, D.C.: BAS, 1991] 1.16-17)-exclusion from the community "because (כיא) the hol[y] angel[s..."; and 4QFlor 1.4-exclusion from the eschatological temple "because (כי) my holy ones are there." The purity of the heavenly temple is similarly underscored in the *Shirot* (4Q400 1 i 14); see n. 306 below.

[286] See 11QBer 1.6-14, published by A.S. VAN DER WOUDE, "Ein neuer Segensspruch aus Qumran (11 Q Ber)," in ed. S. WAGNER, *Bibel und Qumran. Festschrift für Hans Bardtke* (Berlin: Evangelische Haupt-Bibelgesellschaft, 1968) 253-58.

[287] KUHN, *Enderwartung und Gegenwärtiges Heil* (SUNT, 4; Göttingen: Vandenhoeck & Ruprecht, 1966) 66-73 (translation from German on p. 70) and Hermann LICHTENBERGER, *Studien zum Menschenbild in Texten der Qumrangemeinde* (SUNT, 15; Göttingen: Vandenhoeck & Ruprecht, 1980) 224-27 (n. 155), whose discussions are critical of unsatisfactory attempts to derive one aspect from another; so, e.g., P. VON DER OSTEN-SACKEN, *Gott und Belial* (SUNT, 6; Göttingen: Vandenhoeck & Ruprecht, 1969) 222-32 (worship with angels goes back to a context of holy war) and B. GÄRTNER, *The Temple and the Community* (SNTSMS, 1; Cambridge: Univ., 1965) 93 (the assistance of angels in the holy war reflects the Qumranites' more general conviction that they embody "a line of communication...between the 'temple' (community) on earth and the dwelling place of God in heaven"). Regardless of what one decides, the extant passages show an overlap of some technical terms (i.e., גורל, עם, יחד, מעשה in 1QM and the *Shirot*), suggesting a considerable inter-appropriation among the traditions.

156   *Angelic and Heavenly Figures: Veneration and Monotheism*

i. The Songs of the Sabbath Sacrifice

This brings us to a consideration of the angelic sabbath-liturgy (*Shirot 'Olat ha-Shabbat*), which was not fully published and edited until 1985 by Carol NEWSOM.[288] The document is preserved in numerous fragments from ten manuscripts, eight from Cave 4 (4Q400-407), one from Cave 11 (11QShirShabb), and one from Masada.[289] Nevertheless, internal formal indicators as well as the reconstructive methods applied by NEWSOM have resulted in virtual agreement concerning its reconstruction: The *Shirot* consists of 13 songs corresponding to each sabbath within a period of three months in a 364-day reckoning of the solar calendar. Within this structure the seventh song seems to occupy a central position,[290] framed on either side by songs with which it shares a thematic emphasis and literary structure based on the number seven.[291] The relative clarity obtained with regard to structure is offset, however, by problems in interpreting its language. Though the document does not contain a very rich vocabulary, its syntax--characterized by a frequency of participial forms, paucity of verbs, and chains of nouns in construct state[292]--leaves us, as we shall see, with a text which is often difficult to divide into meaningful clauses and phrases.

Despite strong arguments for regarding the *Shirot* as a work of the Qumran community,[293] it is striking that in the extant portions none of the formal

---

[288] *Songs of the Sabbath Sacrifice*. Partial publications had been prepared by STRUGNELL "The Angelic Liturgy at Qumran" (fragments of the sixth and twelfth songs) and A.S. VAN DER WOUDE, "Fragmente einer Rolle der Lieder für das Sabbatopfer aus Höhle XI von Qumran (11QŠirŠabb)," in eds. W.C. DELSMAN et al., *Von Kanaan bis Kerala* (AOAT, 211; Neukirchen-Vluyn: Neukirchener, 1982) 311-37.

[289] Published separately by NEWSOM with YADIN, "The Masada Fragment of the Qumran Songs of the Sabbath Sacrifice," *IEJ* 34 (1984) 77-88.

[290] See NEWSOM, *Songs of the Sabbath Sacrifice*, p. 13. Whereas the other songs open with brief summons to praise, the seventh contains seven in extended form (see 4Q403 1 i 30, 31, 32, 33, 36, 38, and 39).

[291] See *ibid.*, pp. 13-17. The sixth song contained distinct summons to seven ראשי נשיא ("head princes"-4Q403 1 i 17, 18-19, 21, 23-24; 4Q405 3 ii 6; 13 2-3, 4-5=נשיא[י] בשמני and 7=נשיא משנ[י] instead) to pronounce blessings with seven words (4Q403 1 i 1-29). In the eighth song are mentioned seven priesthoods (כהונות; 4Q403 1 ii 22; 4Q405 8-9 5), seven holy councils (סודי קודש; 4Q403 1 ii 22), seven mysteries of knowledge (רזי דעת; 4Q403 1 ii 27) corresponding to seven holy domains (גבולי קוד[ש]; 4Q403 1 ii 27), and seven tongues, each being seven-fold more powerful than the next (4Q403 1 ii 27-29).

[292] As summarized by STRUGNELL, "Angelic Liturgy" 342-43.

[293] *Contra* E.G. CHAZON, "Review of Newsom, *Songs of the Sabbath Sacri-*

features associated with communion with angels--for example, the preposition עם, the noun עזר, גורל, hitp. of יצב, יחד)--is applied to the notion of angelic presence *in the human community*.[294] Yet the whole document is a construction predicated on the community's belief to partake in the angelic worship of the heavenly cultus. Here we find the most significant materials that have a bearing on the problem of the veneration of angels.

Anna-Marie SCHWEMER has raised the possibility of angel veneration in relation to two fragments:[295] 4Q400 2 (ll. 1-2=4Q401 14 i 7-8) and 4Q403 1.[296] An analysis of each text will be preceded by a translation. Primarily on the basis of codicology, NEWSOM has assigned fragment 4Q400 2 to the second song.[297] The following translation from 4Q400 2 lines 1-9 is, where possible, provided with divisions:

¹to praise (להלל) Your glory,
  a wonderful thing among the *elim* of knowledge (פלא באלי דעת)

---

fice," *IEJ* 36 (1986) 282-84, who, in criticizing NEWSOM's ascription of the *Shirot* to Qumran, fails to distinguish between the problems of origin and use (i.e., at Masada). NEWSOM and YADIN ("The Masada Fragment" 81) demonstrate that the association of creation and predestination in this fragment, which preserves the end of the 5th sabbath song and the beginning of the 6th, shows a close affinity to CD 2.9-10; 1QS 3.15; 1QH 1.19-20 and 13.11-12. In addition, NEWSOM calls attention to terminological and motif similarities between the *Shirot* and 4QBerakhot (=4Q286), the latter now in EISENMAN and WISE, *The Dead Sea Scrolls Uncovered*, pp. 222-30; both documents share the otherwise rare expressions such as אלוהות, היכלי מלך, and רוקמת רוח (cf. s.v. in CHARLESWORTH, *Graphic Concordance*) and contain angelic blessings and descriptions of worship in the heavenly temple. Another feature shared uniquely with other Qumran documents is the *technical* use of the phrase "to/for the instructor" (למשכיל) at the beginning of each song (NEWSOM, *Songs of the Sabbath Sacrifice*, pp. 2-3; for the formula למשכיל שיר see esp. 4Q511 2 1.1 and 8 1.4).

[294] The terms themselves do occur in the *Shirot* (see s.v. in *Songs of the Sabbath Sacrifice*), but not with the more technical usage found elsewhere.

[295] SCHWEMER ("Gott als König in den Sabbatliedern," pp. 81-82 and 99-100), whose discussion of the *Shirot*, aside from that of NEWSOM, is the most thorough one to date.

[296] Paleographical analysis leads NEWSOM (*Songs of the Sabbath Sacrifice*, pp. 86, 126, 186-87) to the following conclusions: 4Q400 (late Hasmonean script-ca. 75-50 BCE), 4Q401 (very early Herodian script-ca. 25 BCE), and 4Q403 (early Herodian-25-1 BCE). The script of the largest copy, 4Q405, can likewise be assigned to the 2nd cent.: ca. 50 BCE (*ibid.*, pp. 258-59). To the extent that these considerations are reliable, the *Shirot* may be dated, at the latest, to the first half of the 1st cent. BCE.

[297] *Songs of the Sabbath Sacrifice*, pp. 86-88 (photo on Plate I). The placement of this fragment, as NEWSOM admits, is by no means certain. At the very least, it belongs to Col. 5 (so NEWSOM) or later in the manuscript (that is, second song or later).

158   Angelic and Heavenly Figures: Veneration and Monotheism

   and (to praise) the praiseworthiness of Your kingdom,
    (a wonderful thing) among the most holy ones (בקדושים).
² They are honored (הדמה נכבדים) among all the camps of the *elohim*
   and revered (ונוראים) by human councils (למוסדי אנשים),
   a [wonder] ³(greater) than the *elohim* and human beings
        alike (מאלוהים>ם< ואנשים),
   for they recount (ויספרו) the splendor of His kingdom
    according to their knowledge
  and ₄they exalt [His ... in all]
     the heavens of His kingdom,
   and in all the exalted heights wonderful psalms
    according to all [their insight ...
  ...] ⁵the glory of the King of the *elohim* they recount (יספרו)
   in the dwellings of their (assigned) position. *VACAT*
  An[d ...,]
    ⁶how can we be reckoned [among] them,
   and our priesthood,
    how (can it be reckoned) among their dwellings?
  And [our] ho[liness,
    how can it compare with] ⁷the[ir] ho[li]ness?
  [And what] is the offering of our tongue of dust
    (in comparison) with the knowledge of the *elim/elohim*?
   ₈...] our resounding,
  ₉let us exalt the God of knowledge [...
  ... ho]liness,
   and his understanding is beyond all who [have eternal]
    knowledge.

  In this passage several motifs are combined: (1) praise of God by angels (2nd pers.-l. 1; 3rd pers.-ll. 3-5); (2) statement concerning the superiority of some angels (l. 2); (3) statement of the human worshipers' unworthiness in comparison to the angels (1st pers.-ll. 5-7); and (4) praise of God by the community (1st pers.-ll. 8-9). How are these aspects related in the text?

  The content immediately preceding line 1 of 4Q400 2 may be supplemented by 4Q401 14 i 6 which refers to "chiefs of realms" (לראשי ממשלות).²⁹⁸ The subject of להלל, then, seems to be an elite group of angels probably equivalent to the נשיאים ("princes") mentioned in the other *Shirot*.²⁹⁹ Their function in praising God is characterized in 4Q400 2 1 as "a wonderful thing" (פלא) among the "elim" and "most holy ones."³⁰⁰ What is implied by the פלא clause in line 1 concerning the superiority of the "chiefs" finds an elaboration in line 2.³⁰¹

---

  ²⁹⁸ For the text, see *ibid.*, p. 136 (cf. Plate II).
  ²⁹⁹ On the synonymity between ראשים and נשיאים in Num and the *Shirot*, see *ibid.*, pp. 32-33.
  ³⁰⁰ The common structure (ב-) as well as the non-repetition of להלל before תשבוחות argues in favor of supplying פלא before קדושים בקדוש.
  ³⁰¹ This seems likely, given the apparent resumption of פלא at the end

The ראשים themselves, taken up in the pronoun המה, are characterized by two passive participial forms in predicate position; they are "glorified" and "revered." Though these participles are elsewhere applied to angels as attributes,[302] the syntax suggests something more; both angelic and human beings are represented as acknowledging the chief angels' superiority.

The reason for the chief angels' venerative position is clear: "they recount[303] the splendor of His kingdom according to their knowledge" (l. 3). They possess an understanding of the God's מלכות which manifests itself in a superior form of praise. In lines 3-5[304] this worship (for example, in the form of "wonderful psalms" in l. 4), is briefly described.[305] As the remainder of the column suggests, the angels' superiority represents something to which the community aspired.[306]

In the following lines (6-7) the recognition of angelic superiority is underscored by a confession (in the first pers. plur.) of the human worshipers' own poverty. This self-deprecation is expressed through three rhetorical questions (introduced by מה) which draw several comparisons in which it is no longer clear whether the chief angels are still in view.[307] The community's priesthood, holiness, and knowledge do not compare with that of the angels,

---

of l. 2 (פ[לא]) in a comparative construction (מ־) in which the elements אנשים and אלוהים are repeated.

[302] נכבדים (1QH 10.8-מלך נכבדים); נוראים (11QShirShabb 5 3-אלוהים נוראי כוח).

[303] The conjunction before ספרו may be explicative.

[304] An *inclusio* in l. 5 is formed by the resumption of the verb ספר.

[305] This is perhaps done preliminarily. Songs six and eight contain a fuller version of the blessings and praises by the נשיאי רוש and נשיאי משנה.

[306] See n. 308 below. If in the 2nd song angels are accorded an exemplary worship and a superior knowledge, in the 1st song they play a role in the inclusion of humans into the heavenly cultus (4Q400 i): "they (the angels) do not give support (לוא יכלכלו) to any who are [pervert]ed of way, and there [is] no impurity (טמא) in their holy places" (l. 14); "they propitiate (וכפרו) his good will for all who turn from sin" (l. 16).

[307] The תרומת לשון עפרנו in l. 8 are contrasted with בדעת אלוהים/ים, whereas in l. 1 the באלי דעת seem to have been distinguished from the ראשים. The self-effacing rhetoric is reminiscent of 1QH 3.24 (3-fold self-effacing rhetorical questions introduced by מה) in which the writer's confession follows a thanksgiving for being brought into "the congregation of the sons of heaven" (3.22) and for being allowed to participate with the "spirits of knowledge" (רעת רוחות) in praising God's name and declaring (ולספר) God's wonderful works (3.22-23); see already the well-known passage in Ps 8:5-6, in which the human low-estate is contrasted with the position of angels (מה אנוש...ותחסרהו מעט מאלהים), and 4 Ez 8:34-36. The adaptation of this confessional *topos* here may explain why the *chief* angels are not explicitly referred to in the comparison.

that is, any human contribution to heavenly worship pales next to the grandeur of the angels' priestly function. From the cohortative "let us exalt" in lines 8-9, however, one may infer that despite a sense of unworthiness, the worshipers are nevertheless able to participate in the heavenly cult.[308]

A second passage near the beginning of the seventh song (4Q403 1 i 31b-33a) may also give expression to a venerative posture towards angels. Given the difficulty in translating some of the terms, the full Hebrew text is provided as well as possible translations:[309]

[31]... O chiefs of the praises/
O praiseworthy chiefs,
ראשי תושבחות
[32]praise the God of splendorous praises/
praise the splendorously praiseworthy God,
שבחו לאלוה]י ת[שבחות הוד
for in/through majesty of praises is/exists the glory of His rule/
for in/through praiseworthy majesty is the glory of His rule,
כי בהדר תשבחות כבוד מלכותו
in it/through it are the praises of all [33]elohim/
in it/through it is the praiseworthiness of all [33]elohim
בה תשבחות כול אלוהים
together with the majesty of [his] whole king[dom.
עם הדר כול מלכו]תו

NEWSOM comments appropriately that in this passage "the language has become abstract almost to the point of incomprehensibility."[310] The noun ת(ו)שבחות can either be a plural form (-ōt) or an abstract noun (-ūt). A simple choice of one interpretation over the other is unsatisfactory. Whereas the abstract meaning associated with God at the beginning of l. 32 (="praiseworthy God") is suitable to the context,[311] the following phrase, which is elaborative (כי) of the active summons to praise, may be (here idiomatically) translated "for the glory of His kingdom is reflected in the majesty of praises."

---

[308] Similarly, the contrast with angels in Ps 8 functions rhetorically to underline the importance accorded to humanity within creation. In 1QH 3. 21-23, in which the writer's mention of a privileged status among angels precedes his self-deprecatory statements, the purpose of the rhetoric is to emphasize that despite this position the destructive activity of Belial can only be overcome by God.

[309] The format is adapted from SCHWEMER, "Gott als König in den Sabbatliedern," p. 99.

[310] *Songs of the Sabbath Sacrifice*, p. 215.

[311] NEWSOM's translation (*ibid.*, p. 212) only uses the abstract meaning here.

More open to debate is the term in lines 31 (ראשי תושבחות) and 32 (3rd occurrence; בה תשבחות כול אלוהים). In the latter case, SCHWEMER prefers to see a reference to the praiseworthiness of the angels "which is ascribed to them by the earthly community," arguing that the second song has already attached such a notion to the chief angels.[312] Thus the feminine suffix in בה, which picks up the preceding מלכותו, would then suggest that the angels' venerative status is grounded in *God's* glorious rule. On the other hand, one could argue that the writer of the text wished to stress that God's rule manifests itself or is brought to expression through the angels' praises. This interpretation, however, squares neither with the parallelism between הדר and תשבחות in lines 32b-33a nor with the strong emphasis on God's transcendence in the following parts of the song.[313]

ii. 11Q Berakhot

In relation to the presence of angels, another document merits discussion. In 11Q Berakhot, published by A.S. VAN DER WOUDE in 1968,[314] "all his holy angels" are the final predicate of a brief four-fold blessing to be recited by a (high-)priestly figure:[315] (ll. 4-5- וברוכים כול מלאכי קודשו). The first three parts of the formula consist of (1) a blessing (plur.) with an uncertain predicate (l. 2-?] ברוכים א), but probably referring to "you" (plur.), that is, the community; (2) a blessing of God's holy name (l. 3-

---

[312] "Gott als König in den Sabbatliedern," p. 100 and n. 153.

[313] SCHWEMER (*ibid.*) does not sufficiently clarify her argument concerning the latter point. In ll. 33-35 God's exalted status, which is stressed through a conglomeration of words derived from רום (ורומם רום מרום[, רומם לנדום...מעל לכול) is grounded in divine titles ([?]אל אלים]; מלך) and in God's creation of the angels (מלכים). If this emphasis on God's categorical transcendence is in any way anticipated in ll. 31-33, it is at least clear that the writer does not wish to imply that the manifestation of divine rule somehow depends on angelic praises. A statement concerning the angels' (albeit limited) worthiness is thus more in line with what follows.

[314] "Ein neuer Segensspruch," pp. 253-58 (text, photo, and brief commentary).

[315] The top line of the largest fragment (no. 2; left) preserves וברכם בשם [, which may be read (with VAN DER WOUDE) prescriptively (through a *waw*-conversive): "and he shall bless them in the name of [the God] of [I]srael" (ll. 1-2). The blessings appear on the second of 2 preserved columns. Only a few letters from the 1st col. (right part of frgt.'s 2 and 3) remain, preventing further observations concerning the context of the blessing. The instructive element in l. 1, however, is reminiscent of 1QSb, though there are important differences (see the following discussion).

[וברוך שם קודשו]); and (3) a blessing (plur.), the predicate of which is unfortunately lost (l. 4-וב[12 letters]וברוכים.[316]

The combination of these blessings raises the question of genre. It is one thing for human members of the community to be "blessed" and another to call God "blessed." In the text, the former gives expression to the belief that the community's "blessed" status depends on "the name of the Most High" (ll. 2-3),[317] while the latter formula functions as a form of praise. Whereas predicative blessings involving human beings and God are abundant in the Hebrew Bible, Dead Sea Scrolls, and early Jewish literature, only rarely are angelic beings ever included (Gen 48:15-16;[318] Tob 11:14[319]).[320] This makes the formula in 11Q Berakhot conspicuous. In which sense is the "blessed"-ness of "his holy angels" to be understood?

Lines 6-14 of the joined fragments 1 and 2 provide some clue. Line 6, which in the fragment begins a new section, opens with a jussive blessing formula derived from the Aaronic blessing in Numbers 6:24-26 and reminiscent of 1QSb:[321] "May God Most High (יברך אתכם אל עליון) bless you and make his face to shine upon you and open for you his good treasure which is in heaven...". This formulation, then, introduces a section which elaborates the first formula in l. 2. We cannot know whether the lost portions of 11Q Berakhot con-

---

[316] It is possible, that the lost text also referred to angels; the blessing would then run parallel to the next, ות[being read "his[..." analogous to קודש "his holiness." If the rest of the column was intended as an elaboration of the blessings in ll. 1-5, the resumption of only two elements in ll. 13-14 (God and angels) may point in this direction. In the end, this matter must remain uncertain.

[317] In this sense the blessing (and esp. that in ll. 6-14) comes close to what is preserved in 1QSb, in which blessings (from God) are pronounced upon various classes or figures (present and eschatological) of the sect.

[318] See section II.A.1.b n. 58 (though here the "angel" is called upon to bless).

[319] The correspondence between 11Q Berakhot and Tobit (esp. as preserved in the Sinaitic recension) is close. The combination of blessing humans and praising God is implied in Tobit (Cod. Sin.). See below, section II.B.2.a (pp. 165-66).

[320] See *Jos.Asen.* 5:12 (pp. 169-70). Such a formulation is remarkably scarce in the later Hekhalot literature. Thus far, the present author has been able to find only one independent example, in which the predicate is Metatron; see SCHÄFER, *Synopse* (par. 704), the mss from München (M40) and New York (N8128): (עלמ]י -M40 ;זכרי+N8128) שלום (M40-שלו) ברוך מטטרון עד כאן ראיתי רום ידידיה עלמא.

[321] 1QSb- "may the Lord bless you (sg.; 1.3- יברככה>רככה אדוני; 3.25- יברככה אדוני"; "may the Lord lift his countenance upon you/all your congregation" (3.1- כול עדתכה יש]א פניו אל; 3.2-3- ישא אדוני פניו אליכה).

tained any further elaborations of the other formulae. Nevertheless, in ll. 7b-13a the community's enjoyment of God's "good treasure"--here expanded in terms of favorable weather, good harvest, and protection from a variety of mortal and unclean dangers--is grounded in a belief in the presence of God and that of his holy angels (ll. 13-14).[322] Here the angels' function in behalf of the community is analogous to, though not independent from, that of God. God's holy angels are praiseworthy as protectors whose presence, like that of God, is thought to guarantee the community's well-being.[323]

c. Summary

The foregoing observations on the *Shirot* and 11Q Berakhot lead to several conclusions. A qualified veneration involving angels, expressed by the predicative blessing formula (ll. 4-5), is implied in 11Q Berakhot. The grounds for this inclusion seems to be elaborated in the following section (ll. 6-14), in which both angels and God, because they are present to the congregation, are the source of the community's welfare in its earthly existence. The mention of angels, however, does not detract from the emphasis on God, from whose "good treasure" the blessings are experienced.

More significant for the Apocalypse of John are the two passages from the *Shirot*, which may be said to give expression to the human veneration of angels. This veneration, however, is not understood as contradictory to the worship of God; indeed, recognition of the angelic superiority derives at least partly from their exemplary worship of God. The description of the chiefs as "glorified" and "revered" and the confession of inadequacy together function to express the community's aspiration to participate in the heavenly cultus.[324] Though unlike apocalyptic writings the *Shirot* do not describe angel-

---

[322] "For God is with you (עמכם אל כיא) and [his holy] angels ar[e positioned] in your congregation" (בערתכם מתיצבי[ם קודשו]ומלאכי; traces of a final *mem* after the lacunae can be detected in the photo opposite p. 253 in VAN DER WOUDE, "Ein neuer Segensspruch").

[323] Hence, though it is possible that the praise-formula of angels in 11Q Ber reflects known tradition (see Tob 11:14), in this context it has been integrated into ideas concerning the community.

[324] Hence NEWSOM's thesis that the *Shirot* served primarily to legitimate the Qumranites' priesthood (*Songs of the Sabbath Sacrifice*, pp. 71-72) may require modification. See Joseph M. BAUMGARTEN, "The Qumran Sabbath Shirot and Rabbinic Merkabah Traditions," *RQ* 13 (1988) 206 who, on the basis of this passage argues that "It is the heavenly priesthood which is glorified in the *Angelic Liturgy*. As far as human worshipers are concerned...their aspira-

ic worship within the narrative framework of an ascent, they preserve a similar convergence of motifs: an interest in angelic worship and a corresponding venerative posture.

The difference is, of course, that whereas the refusal tradition emphatically rejects the desire to venerate a prominent angel, the author(s) of the *Shirot* do(es) not see therein a contradiction with the worship of God. To be sure, the veneration of angels in the *Shirot* is qualified: (1) the angels' status is ultimately derived from their exemplary worship; (2) their knowledge is limited (emphasized esp. in the Masada frgt. i 4-6); and (3) they are created beings (Mas*ShirShabb* i 2-3; cf. 1QS 3.15, CD 2.9-10, 1QH 1. 19-20). The notion of the special status of angels played an important role in the community's self-understanding. Within a monotheistic framework certain honor could be given them because the function of angels as priests in the heavenly temple represented a worship both to which members of the community aspired and into which they understood themselves to have been admitted.

2. Other Early Jewish Texts

In section II.A.2 (pp. 75-103), we have reviewed evidence for a refusal tradition which functioned rhetorically in a narrative setting to prevent a seer from worshiping an angelic figure. In addition, it was suggested that this and some rabbinic traditions (II.A.1.b, pp. 63-73) may be understood as a critique which presumes a common traditional heritage among authors and readers or betweem tradents and opponents. Nevertheless, no single instance of the kind of outright worship forbidden in the refusals turns up in early Jewish literature. It remains possible, if not likely, that some authors made use of polemical traditions in order to paint a dark picture of milder tendencies to venerate angels or to protect against a potential misunderstanding of something within their own or similar writings. The question explored below is whether there is anything in early Jewish texts (outside Qumran) which explains the use of the polemic in its various forms.

a. *A Doxology in Tobit 11:14-15*

The date of composition for the legend contained in "The Book of the Words of Tobit" (so Grk mss) is not certain, but is probably to be placed

---

tions are fulfilled by merely being permitted to descriptively approach the splendors of the angelic realm."

within the 3rd or early-2nd century BCE.[325] In this writing, a four-fold doxology expresses Tobit's response to his son's return home and the restoration of his sight. The formulaic praise is in 11:14, followed in 11:15 by a description of the divine act which occasioned it. The recension in Codex Sinaiticus (Sin.), which preserves the doxology in the 3rd person, includes the angels twice in the predicative position:

> 14 Blessed (εὐλογητός) God,
> and blessed (εὐλογητός) his great name,
> and blessed (εὐλογημένοι) all his holy angels;
> may his great name be upon us,
> and blessed (εὐλογητοί) all the angels unto all ages,
> 15 for he (ὅτι αὐτός) has afflicted me,
> but (καί) now I see my son Tobias![326]

There are good reasons for arguing that this text is earlier than the type which appears in the other Greek manuscripts. Unlike this recension, Codices Alexandrinus and Vaticanus (Alex. and Vat.) contain a blessing which is both shorter[327] (only one blessing of angels) and more fully integrated into the story (2nd person).[328] In addition, verse 15 of these manuscripts contains

---

[325] See e.g. NICKELSBURG on Tobit, "Stories of Biblical and Early Post-Biblical Times," in ed. Michael E. STONE, *Jewish Writings of the Second Temple Period. Apocrypha, Pseudepigrapha, Qumran Sectarian Writings, Philo, Josephus* (CRINT, 2/2; Assen/Philadelphia: Van Gorcum and Fortress, 1984) 45 and *New Schürer*, 3.223-24. The presence of 5 mss of Tobit at Qumran is consistent with this date as a *terminus ad quem*.

[326] The readings here are based on the critical edition of Robert HANHART, *Tobit* (SeptGott, 8/5; Göttingen: Vandenhoeck & Ruprecht, 1983). Cod. Sin.: (14) εὐλογητὸς ὁ θεὸς καὶ εὐλογητὸν τὸ ὄνομα τὸ μέγα αὐτοῦ καὶ εὐλογημένοι πάντες οἱ ἄγγελοι οἱ ἅγιοι αὐτοῦ· γένοιτο τὸ ὄνομα τὸ μέγα αὐτοῦ ἐφ' ἡμᾶς καὶ εὐλογητοὶ πάντες οἱ ἄγγελοι εἰς πάντας τοὺς αἰῶνας· (15) ὅτι αὐτὸς ἐμαστίγωσέν με, καὶ ἰδοὺ βλέπω Τοβιας τὸν υἱόν μου.

[327] Unfortunately, the tiny Heb frgt. at Qumran which MILIK assigned to Tob 11:10-14 ("La patrie de Tobie" 522-30, esp. p. 523 n. 3) does not help clarify the extent of the text; cf. the upper left frgt. in PAM photo no. 43.184 (= Pl. 1239 in Robert H. EISENMAN and James M. ROBINSON, *Facsimile Edition* [Washington, D.C.: BAS, 1991] vol. 2). Given the uneven size and arrangement of the letters on each l., it is difficult to reach any conclusion concerning either an approximate line length in the col. or how to evaluate the partly visible letters at the bottom (l. 6) which MILIK apparently takes as]בני[, "my son" (v. 15). Should this reading be correct, it is possible to infer that the Heb frgt. contained a shorter form of the blessing which is closer to, though likewise shorter than, Cod.'s Alex. and Vat. The form, however, could also be בנו ("his son"-beg. of v. 13), which would avoid the difficulty of having to posit a shorter version of the blessing. Perhaps a fuller evaluation will be made possible by the publication of the fragment with a better photographic print.

[328] Cod.'s Alex. and Vat.: (14) εὐλογητὸς εἶ ὁ θεός, καὶ εὐλογητὸν τὸ ὄνομά σου εἰς τοὺς αἰῶνας, καὶ εὐλογεμένοι πάντες οἱ ἅγιοί σου ἄγγελοι (15)

an added phrase in Tobit's account of what God has done: "and you have shown me mercy" (καὶ ἠλέησάς με).[329] Finally, unlike Codex Sin., which has angels follow both the forms εὐλογητός (as before God) and εὐλογημένος, Alex. and Vat. retain only the latter, thereby placing the distinction into sharper relief.[330] The text in Sin. to 11:14-15, then, may have contained a form and content which later editors thought rendered excessive praise to angels for the story's happy resolution.[331]

The observation of special measures in Alex. and Vat., which ensure that the emphasis on the activity of God within the narrative is preserved, does not mean that no such measures were already taken in Sin. In section II.A.2 we have seen that the author made use of a milder form of the refusal tradition in 12:17-22.[332] It is significant that Raphael's exhortation to praise God (12:17-18) follows several first-person statements revealing the identity of Raphael and his accomplishments on Tobit and Tobias' behalf: "I

ὅτι ἐμαστίγωσας καὶ ἠλέησάς με, ἰδοὺ βλέπω Τοβιας τὸν υἱόν μου. At this point, the Vulgate tradition ascribed to JEROME (here, further adumbrated) goes even further; the blessing, formulated in the 1st and 2nd pers., omits the mention of angels entirely: (11:17) *benedico te Domine Deus Israhel quoniam tu castigasti me et tu sanasti me et ecce video Tobiam filium meum.*

[329] The phrase may reflect influence from v. 16 (ἠλέησεν αὐτὸν ὁ θεός). This tendency is further reflected in the blessings in 11:17 and 13:18. In the former, Cod. Sin. contains a four-fold blessing of God (εὐλογητός), Tobit, Tobias, and Sarah (the latter three are predicates to the appropriate form of εὐλογημένος), while in Cod.'s Alex. and Vat. only the first (εὐλογητὸς ὁ θεός) is retained. In 13:18, Sin.'s καὶ εὐλογητοὶ εὐλογήσουσιν τὸ ὄνομα τὸ ἅγιον (following εὐλογητὸς ὁ θεὸς τοῦ Ἰσραήλ) is not taken up in Alex. and Vat.

Significantly, Raphael's exhortation to praise God in 12:6 is longer in Alex. and Vat. (8 expressions of praise) than in Sin. (only 6).

[330] See J. SCHARBERT, "ברך," in *Theologisches Wörterbuch zum Alten Testament* (Stuttgart: Kohlhammer, 1973) 834-35 whose observations, however, do not reflect the differences among the recensions. The special emphasis on the subordination of angels to God in Alex. and Vat. is also apparent in the blessing in 8:15, which is absent in Sin.: εὐλογείτωσάν σε οἱ ἅγιοί σου καὶ πᾶσαι αἱ κτίσεις σου καὶ πάντες οἱ ἄγγελοί σου καὶ οἱ ἐκλεκτοί σου.

[331] Even if the recension in Sin. does not correspond to an "original" form of the text, it does not materially affect the existence of a blessing in which the angels are praised alongside God at an early stage (see *New Schürer*, 3.228-29) in the textual transmission and interpretation of tradition.

[332] In Tob the angel's appearance is not as emphasized as in the later documents using the refusal tradition; see II.A.2.b.i above n. 98. The accent of Cod.'s Alex. and Vat. on God (11:14-15,17; 13:18) as the only proper predicate of εὐλογητός at the expense of angels makes the text more consistent with point of Raphael's own words to Tobit and Tobias (12:16- bless God", 17-18-"bless God...bless him").

brought the record of your prayers before the Holy One" (12:12-ἐγὼ προσήγαγον κτλ.); "I was sent to test you and to heal you" (v. 13-ἀπέσταλμαι κτλ.; Alex., Vat.-ἀπέστειλέν με ὁ θεός κτλ.); and "I am Raphael (ἐγώ εἰμι ʿΡαφαήλ), one of the seven holy angels who are present and enter before the glory of the Lord" (v. 15-Sin.; Alex., Vat.-"who carry up the prayers of the holy ones and enter before the glory of the Holy One"). The refusal in each of the recensions thus guarantees that Raphael's prominence as a divine agent (as protector and counselor) in the story[333] is not allowed to overshadow the fact that the good fortunes of Tobit, Tobias and Sarah are due to God. In 11:14-15, this emphasis is made even clearer in Sin.; the second occurrence of angels in the blessing formula is immediately represented as a reflection on God's own (αὐτός) activity.[334]

In the document, God's angels are praised by Tobit, especially in Codex Sinaiticus.[335] That the blessing was understood as such may be observed in the recensions which moderate this element while laying more exclusive stress on God (Alex., Vat.). This praise, however, only occurs alongside that of God, and there are signs that the author (or the one responsible for the early Greek recension) took measures to ensure that an essentially monotheistic outlook was not being compromised. Such "protective" measures were further developed and intensified during the recension and textual transmission of the story.

---

[333] Succinct summaries of Raphael's mission are given before (foreshadowing in 3:17) and after (12:12-15-in the angel's own words) the actual account of his participation in the plot. Both passages Raphael's mission to heal Sarah (from being afflicted by the demon Asmodeus; see 8:3) and Tobit from his blindness. The choice of language is no doubt related to the etymology of "Raphael" (רפאל="God [El] heals"). In addition, 12:12 and 16 (Alex., Vat.) infers an intercessory function from Raphael's commission. The narrative in 5:4-11:8 places emphasis, however, on his protection of Tobias from harm (5:22; 6:10-18; 8:2-3).

[334] God's affliction of Tobit with blindness (cf. 2:10; 3:2-6) is, however, not associated with the activity of either angels or Raphael in the narrative. If ὅτι...με was constructed in order to avoid a potential misunderstanding of the preceding blessing, it is possible (though speculative) to consider the resulting inconsistency as an early interpolation in either the Semitic or Greek stage of transmission.

[335] On this, see Ronald H. PFEIFFER, *History of New Testament Times. With an Introduction to the Apocrypha* (New York: Harper, 1949) 282, who concludes that Tob 11:14, along with 8:15 and 12:12-15, express "a doctrine about angels more elaborate than in any earlier or contemporary writing."

b. *Joseph and Aseneth 14:1-12 and 15:11-12x*[336]

Despite virtual agreement among scholars that *Joseph and Aseneth* was orignally composed in Greek by a Jew[337] sometime between 100 BCE and the early second century CE,[338] significant divergences among the recensions require caution in interpretation, especially where particular wording is involved.[339] In the narrative, two heavenly figures are mentioned: "Repentance" (15:7-8) and the divine messenger encountered by Aseneth (14:1-17:7). Despite the personifying and venerative language associated with the former,[340] the close relationship between Μετανοία's activity and those who repent (οἱ μετανοιοῦντες)

---

[336] Following the mostly smaller verse numeration introduced (e.g., 15:11,12,12x) introduced in the text of Christoph BURCHARD in "Joseph and Aseneth," *OTP* 2.202-247 (p. 227). Marc PHILONENKO (*Joseph et Aséneth* [SPB, 13; Leiden: Brill, 1968]) offers a variant verse numeration (see parentheses in BURCHARD) which corresponds to larger units in the chapter 15 passage.

[337] That *Joseph and Aseneth*, as a whole, is Christian has not been argued since E.W. BROOKS, *Joseph and Asenath* (TED, 2/7; London/New York: 1918) p. XI. Concerning the Jewish character of the work, see PHILONENKO, *Joseph et Aseneth*, pp. 99-101.

[338] Given the absence of historical allusions, linguistic and cultural considerations have acquired an added importance, though BURCHARD admits that the question of "the date and provenance" still await a thorough examination (*OTP* 2.187; see also *New Schürer*, 3.549 n. 67). The early date would correspond roughly to the time when LXX tradition, which is reflected in the document (for this, see PHILONENKO, *Joseph et Aseneth*, pp. 28-32 and G. Delling, "Einwirkungen der Septuaginta im 'Joseph und Asenath'," *JStJ* 9 [1978] 29-56), began to exert linguistic influence in Jewish Greek literature, while setting a *terminus ad quem* (i.e., before the Second Jewish War in 132-135 CE; in the case of Egyptian provenance, before the Jewish revolt in 115-117) depends on the document's assumption of a milieu within which proselytism to Judaism could be viewed with some favor; see BURCHARD, *OTP* 2.187-88.

[339] PHILONENKO and BURCHARD's texts and translations are based on conflicting assessments of the textual data. PHILONENKO's edition (hereafter *Ph*) in *Joseph et Aseneth* is based on Grk mss of the shortest recension (BURCHARD's "Group d" in *OTP* 2.178-79), from which he maintains the others are derived. BURCHARD questions the assumption of *brevior et potior*, and begins with "Group b" which, though containing four diverging and relatively late Grk mss (15-17th cent.'s), is attested in the earliest ms evidence for the document (Arm and Syr mss) and shows the least signs of editorial activity; see "Zum Text von 'Joseph und Asenath'," *JStJ* 1 (1970) 3-34. BURCHARD offers a Grk text (hereafter *Bu*), 50% longer than *Ph*, reconstructed from the b mss and related translations (unless the other groups furnish a more complete text) in "Ein vorläufiger griechischer Text von Joseph und Asenath," *DBAT* 14 (1979) 2-53 and "Verbesserungen zum vorläufigen Text," *DBAT* 16 (1982) 37-39.

[340] In 15:7-8 "Repentance" is called the "daughter of the Most High," the "mother" (*Ph*) or "overseer" (*Bu*) of virgins, the "sister" of the divine messenger (*Bu*), acts as an intercessor, and is adored by all the angels (*Bu*= *Ph*: πάντες οἱ ἄγγελοι αἰδοῦνται αὐτήν).

in the text leaves little doubt that "Repentance" is ultimately a personification of an idealized human activity. The heavenly "man" (14:4), who descends to converse with Aseneth, is another matter.

The encounter (14:1-17:9), in which the angel confirms Aseneth's conversion, functions as a bridge between Aseneth's prayers of confession (10:1-13:12) and the account of her marriage to Joseph (18:1-21:9). In 14:1-12 Aseneth is told twice (14:7,11) by the "man" to rise from a prostrated position (vv. 4,10) in order that she may receive his message. The second prostration specifically occurs in response to the angel's appearance (v. 9): the angel, whose royal attire resembles that of Joseph, has a face "as lightning, and his eyes were as sunshine, and the hairs of his head as a flame of fire,[341] and his hands and feet as iron from a fire."[342] The angel's response is milder than clearer instances of the refusal tradition; his command not to fear and to rise (μὴ φοβοῦ ἀλλὰ ἀνάστηθι) does not so much single out Aseneth's behavior as it calls attention to the angel's purpose in coming.

One could, of course, argue that in 14:1-12 such a modification of the refusal tradition might imply a limited toleration of venerative behavior;[343] however, such a conclusion, when drawn on the basis of chapter 14 alone, amounts to an over-interpretation.[344] Nevertheless, the interchange between Aseneth and the angel in 15:11-12 suggests a different picture. When the heavenly "man" has finished announcing that Aseneth's repentance has been accepted and that she can now become Joseph's bride (15:2-6, 7-10), the longer version (Bu) reads that she (1) "fell at his feet and prostrated (προσεκύνησεν) before him on (her) face to the ground" (v. 11); (2) uttered a twofold blessing to "the Lord your God the Most High" and to "your[345] name forever" (v. 12); and, in a section lacking in the other textual recensions,[346] (3)

---

[341] Bu adds: "of a burning torch."

[342] Bu adds: "shining forth, and sparks leaping out from his hands and feet."

[343] So CHESTER, "Jewish Messianic Expectations and Mediatorial Figures," pp. 54-55, 64.

[344] A stronger rebuke by the angelic "man" is deliberately avoided since it would have undermined the idealized presentation of Aseneth's conversion. Thus E.W. SMITH, *Joseph and Asenath and Early Christian Literature* (Claremont School of Theology: Ph.D. Diss., 1974) 174 reads the angel's statement as a rejection.

[345] Ph: αὐτοῦ. Bu: εὐλογημένον τὸ ὄνομά σου εἰς τὸν αἰῶνα.

[346] See BURCHARD's text-critical apparatus to 15:12x in *Untersuchungen zu Joseph und Aseneth* (WUNT, 8; Tübingen: J.C.B. Mohr [Paul Siebeck], 1965)

she requested to know the angel's name "in order that I may praise (ὑμνήσω) and glorify (δοξάσω) you forever (v. 12x). It is only verse 12x in which Aseneth makes a request that is denied. Without this addition, the text allows the angel to be praised alongside God. Even with verse 12x, however, the explicit reason for the angel's refusal to divulge his name is *neither* the appropriateness of such worship for God alone *nor* the angel's unworthiness (as in the refusal tradition), but the secrecy of "all names recorded in the book of the Most High," names which are "exceedingly great (μέγαλα) and wonderful (θαύμαστα) and praiseworthy (ἐπαίνετα). In other words, the angel's refusal does not categorically reject Aseneth's venerative behavior.

This interpretation may make sense of the *Bu* recension, but can verse 12x be assigned to a more original version of document? Relative certainty concerning the text can only be argued where the *Bu* and *Ph* recensions overlap: verses 11-12 (without x). But even if it is assumed that verse 12x is later, the *Bu* text--which in verse 12 is not shorter--contains a predicative blessing formula for the angel, a blessing which is left unqualified in the immediate context.[347]

c. Pseudo-Philo 13:6

In the so-called *Liber Antiquitatum Biblicarum*, a haggadic retelling of the biblical history from Adam until David from the first or early second century CE,[348] the mention of "watchers" occurs in relation to the "feast of trumpets," the festival of the New Year. The passage, for which the best textual witnesses are in Latin,[349] reads as follows:

68-73. This text-critical problem is overlooked by HURTADO (*One God, One Lord*, p. 81), who reads v. 12-12x as a textual unity.

[347] Despite a similarity in wording with LXX Ps 71:17 (= ἔστω τὸ ὄνομα αὐτοῦ εὐλογημένον εἰς τοὺς αἰῶνας; see PHILONENKO, *Joseph et Aseneth*, p. 185 n.), there is reason to question the certainty of Ph's application of the second blessing to God. V. 12x (Aseneth's wish to know the angel's name; his name is "in the heavens") presupposes entirely the praise of the angel in *Bu*; if v. 12x is original, then the blessing in the *Bu* text is superior. Moreover, it is possible though uncertain that, as in Alex. and Vat. of Tob 11:14, the forms εὐλογητός and εὐλογημένος in Ph indicate what was originally different predicate objects. If so, the text may have been adjusted early on to remove what was deemed an excessive veneration of the angel.

[348] On the general tendency to date *Pseudo-Philo* within the 1st or early 2nd cent. CE, see CHARLESWORTH, *PMR*, p. 170.

[349] See Daniel J. HARRINGTON, "Pseudo-Philo," in *OTP* 2.298.

13:6[350]

| Nam festivitas psalphingarum in oblationem erit pro speculatoribus[351] vestris. In eo quod prespexi creaturam, memores sitis totius orbis; per initia ostendentibus vobis agnoscam numerum mortuorum et natorum. Per ieiunium misericordie ieiunabitis enim mihi pro animabus vestris, ut compleantur sponsiones patrum vestrorum. | Now the feast of trumpets shall be as an offering for your watchers. In that I watched over creation, may you be mindful of the whole world. At the beginning of your presentation, I will make known the number of those who will die and be born. Through a fast of mercy you you shall fast for me for the sake of your souls, so that the promises to your fathers may be fulfilled. |

The possibility that the text refers to an "offering" for angels has been entertained and dismissed by several commentators who argue that in *Pseudo-Philo* 34:2 such a practice is categorically opposed.[352] The text is indeed obscure at this point, and one should allow for the possibility that in the difficult phrase "offering for your watchers" the author was making a short allusion to something which was more generally known than the text indicates.[353] Thus Christian DIETZFELBINGER has suggested that, given the associ-

---

[350] The text is based on the critical edition by C. PERROT and P.-M. BOGAERT, with HARRINGTON, *Pseudo-Philon. Les Antiquites Bibliques* (SC, 229-230; Paris: Cerf, 1976) 2.134. The minor differences from the edition of G. KISCH, *Pseudo-Philo's Liber Antiquitatum Biblicarum* (Medieval Studies, 10; Notre Dame, 1949) are not significant for the interpretation of the text.

[351] The mss read *prospeculatoribus*. The absence of this word as an attested form, as well as perhaps the wording in the previous verse (v. 5-...*oblationem pro fructibus vestris*, though with a different sense), supports M.R. JAMES' suggestion to separate the word; see JAMES, *The Biblical Antiquities of Philo* (TED, Ser. 1; London: SPCK, 1917, repr. 1971 in New York by Ktav, with a "Prolegomemon" by Louis FELDMAN) 115, accepted by Christian DIETZFELBINGER, *Pseudo-Philo: Antiquitates Biblicae* (JSHRZ, 2/2; Gütersloh: Mohn, 1975) 137 n. 6c.

[352] So FELDMAN, "Prolegomenon," p. xcviii; DIETZFELBINGER, *Pseudo-Philo*, p. 137 n. 6d; HARRINGTON, "Pseudo-Philo" in *OTP*, 2.321 n. e; and MACH, *Entwicklungsstadien*, p. 292 (and n. 38), who supposes that in 34:2 the motif of sacrifice to angels reenforces the negative portrayal of Aod (father of the witch of Endor).
    HARRINGTON's assessment is followed by HURTADO ("'First-Century Jewish Monotheism'," p. 363) in his denial of RAINBOW's contention ("Jewish Monotheism as the Matrix" 83) that this text contains a possible allusion to angel worship.

[353] Aside from a possible word-play with the term *prespexi* in the following phrase, the reference to "watchers" is not explicated any further.

ation of Rosh ha-Shanah with judgment, the text assumes that angels bring Israel to judgment at the New Year.[354]

The exclusion of an "offering for your watchers" on the basis of the passage in 34:1-3, however, does not follow. In the latter passage Aod, a Midianite magician, is said to have been able to do his magic tricks through angels (*angeli*) "because he had been sacrificing to them for a long time" (v. 2).[355] Verse 3 adds a confusing explanatory note in which several points may be reconstructed: (1) there was a time when angels taught magic to humans; (2) this magic, if gone unchecked, would have destroyed "the immeasurable age"; (3) because of their transgression, these angels were stripped of this power; and (4) these angels are still active,[356] though only in a restricted sense, through magicians who render services to humans until "the immeasurable age" comes. Clearly, the passage describes these angels as wicked, and there could be no question of sacrificing to them, much less paying them any honor.

In 13:6 the "watchers" are good angels. Their link to judgment, as proposed by DIETZFELBINGER, finds support within the angelological ideas in *Pseudo-Philo* itself. Though the term (*pro*)*speculatores* does not otherwise occur, the document refers to angels (*custodes*) who protect (59:4-David), testify for or against (11:12-observation of the commandment in Ex 20:16), or intercede (15:5) for God's people. Of particular interest for 13:6 is their function in 15:4-6, a midrashic retelling of Numbers 14:1-12: Because of the Israelites' complaints in the wilderness, God informs Moses that he will afflict them with an angel of wrath, and then

> (5) ...I will command my angels who watch over (*custodiunt*)them not to intercede on their behalf, for I will shut up their souls (*animas eorum*) in dark chambers, and I will say to my servants their fathers (*patribus eorum*): "Behold, this is the seed

---

[354] DIETZFELBINGER, *Pseudo-Philo*, p. 137 6d. See, e.g., m.*Rosh ha-Shanah* 1:2.

[355] Ps-Philo 34:2-*Et abiit et fecit magiciis suis, precipiens angelis qui preerant maleficiis, quoniam immolabat eis multo tempore.*

[356] Whether the subject in *operantur qui ministrant hominibus in maleficiis* is human magicians or the fallen angels is not clear. The reference to angels teaching magic to human beings, probably an allusion to the tradition in *1 En* 6-16, suggests that the text distinguishes between the wicked angels' lot before and after their fall. The phrase, *ut angeli in potestate non essent*, does not mean the total loss of power, but allows for a limited degree of activity; see HARRINGTON, "Pseudo-Philo" in *OTP*, 2.301. The story of Aod, which is only found in *Ps-Philo*, may be a vehicle through which the author polemicizes against contemporary practices of magic; the point is made rhetorically: just as the fallen angels, though still active, actually have no power that is of any consequence.

(of) which I said, 'Your seed will come to a land not its own, and the nation which it will serve I shall judge.' And I fulfilled (*complevi*) my words... (6) And now the days are coming, and I will do to them as they wished,and I will throw away their bodies in the wilderness."

The context here is not the New Year festival. Yet the angels are given the function of interceding as advocates for Israel before God, a function which in this case is removed due to Israel's ingratitude. Without angelic intercession the promises of God to the patriarchs no longer apply and punishment can be exacted. A similar complex of ideas seems to provide a plausible background for 13:6. If so, the author of *Pseudo-Philo* may have preserved an interpretation of the festival of trumpets as an offering to "your watchers" in a sense that presupposes angelic intercession for Israel. The attribution of such a function to the good "watchers" in relation to the festival gave expression to an assurance of good standing in God's judgment "when he considers all their works" (Ps 33:15, cited in *m.Rosh ha-Shanah* 1:2) and ensured the fulfillment of God's promises to the patriarchs.

Nothing in the passage suggests that the watchers' offering conflicts with the worship of God. Though these angels are described as independent beings (15:5), they are fully aligned with, and ultimately subordinate to, God's activity.

d. Angelic Mediation and Prayer: Other Early Jewish Texts

The mediating function of angels in prayer is cast in a positive light in a number of Jewish writings from the Second Temple period through the early part of the second century CE. This material has been reviewed in many of the standard discussions on angelology, and it is not necessary to engage in a full discussion of the texts here. The task here is to list more obvious instances[357] in which this motif occurs and to see whether the materials allow

---

[357] Excluded from the list are passages such as *1 En* 39:5 and 89:76 because it is not clear whether the intercession mentioned refers specifically to that of angels; while in 39:5 the petitioning for humanity may be done by the righteous who now dwell with the angels (and who perhaps have taken over angelic functions), in 89:76 the Eth mss do not allow for the certain identification of the petitioner with either an angel or with Ezra. The angelic conveyance of human prayers to God's throne is featured in *Hist. Rech.* (esp. 16:8), but the present form of this part of the document, though no doubt containing early traditions (see CHARLESWORTH, "History of the Rechabites," in *OTP* 2.445) can be expected to provide more confirmatory than primary evi-

for any distinctions which may define the motif in relation to the problem of veneration.

i. *Enochic Literature*

(a) *1 Enoch* 9:1-11.[358] Four angels (Grk recensions)--Michael, Uriel (4QEn[a+b] שריאל] in 9:1,4), Raphael, and Gabriel--or the "holy ones of heaven" (Aram, Eth)[359] are called upon by "the souls of people" to "bring (Eth=Grk-εἰσαγάγετε) our case (Cod.Pan., Syn[a]-κρίσις; Syn[b]-δέησιν) to the Most High" (v. 3).[360] The angels' prayer to God is contained in verses 4-11. Verse 10 suggests the reason for their intermediary role: the groaning of the human souls "has ascended and[361] is unable to go forth (ἐξελθεῖν)[362] from before the wickedness that is being done upon the earth." Hence the intermediary role of these an-

---

dence for the motif. Zosimus' petition for forgiveness in 7:11 (Syr mss), which CHARLESWORTH assigns to the earliest stage of the work (100 CE?), is not addressed to angels "from heaven" (6:6a), but to the "Blessed Ones"/ "Earthly Angels" who are the "lost" Rechabites. Concerning *4 Macc* 4:10-14 and *Par.Jer.* 3:4-14, see HURTADO, *One God, One Lord*, p. 28.

[358] The Book of Watchers (*1 En* 1-36) is preserved in Aram frgt.'s from Qumran (published in MILIK, *The Books of Enoch*), several partly extant Grk versions (Codex Panopolitanus=Cod.Pan. and citations in Syncellus=Syn[a,b]), and is complete in numerous Eth mss. Except for the Astronomical Book (*1 En* 72-82), this portion of "1 Enoch" is the earliest of extant Enochic works (late 3rd-early 2nd cent. BCE). The Grk texts are provisionally edited by Matthew BLACK, *Apocalypsis Henochi Graece* (PVTG, 3; Leiden: Brill, 1970) 3-44.

[359] A reference to the "holy ones" in verses 2 and 3 are lacking in the Grk traditions. The Eth recensions have the four angels address "holy ones of heaven" (*1 En* 9:3a) to whom the case is being made. The extant Qumran Aram frgt.'s to the passage, 4QEn[a] (*f* and *h*), are closer to the Eth at this point: תרעי שמי[ה...לקדי[שי שמ]וה. See MILIK (*The Books of Enoch*, Pl. IV and pp. 158, 161), who, despite an eclectic reconstruction of the lacunae, proposes a plausible placement for the frgt.'s.

[360] The same petition is already found in Syn[b] to *1 En* 8:4 (indirectly in Syn[a], absent in Eth mss and Cod.Pan.), where it is most likely due to expansional activity constructed from material associated with 9:3 (esp. as given in Syn[a]); see KNIBB, *The Ethiopic Book of Enoch*, 2.84, contra CHARLES, *The Ethiopic Version of the Book of Enoch* (Anecdota Oxoniensia; Oxford: Clarendon, 1906) xiv and, more recently, BLACK, *The Book of Enoch or I Enoch. A New English Edition* (SVTP, 7; Leiden: Brill, 1985) 29.

[361] The καί may derived from an adversative conjunction (-ו).

[362] *Contra* CHARLES, *The Apocrypha and Pseudepigrapha of the Old Testament* (Oxford: Clarendon, 1913) 2.193 who unnecessarily conjectured that ἐξελθεῖν (Cod.Pan., Syn[b]; from Aram למנפק) is corrupt from למפסק "to cease," thus altering the meaning: "their lamentations have ascended: and cannot cease...".

gels is closely associated with the transcendence of God[363] who is not immediately accessible to the human petitions for help.[364]

(b) *1 Enoch* 15:2. This passage expresses the irony of Enoch's intercession for the fallen Watchers since this is actually the proper function of angels. Enoch is told to "Go and say to those who sent you, 'It is proper (Cod.Pan.-ἔδει) that you intercede (ἐρωτῆσαι) for humans and not humans for you.'" The Watchers have forfeited their role as heavenly intercessors by mingling themselves with the human race (vv. 3-10).

(c) *1 Enoch* 40:6, 9.[365] Of the four angels, Gabriel (v. 9) is heard "interceding and praying for those who dwell on the earth and supplicating[366] in the name of the Lord of the Spirits."[367]

(d) *1 Enoch* 47:1-2. In this passage, language reminiscent of 9:1-11 expresses that in response to prayers of the righteous (plur.) the "holy ones...shall supplicate and pray...on behalf of the blood of the righteous ones which has been shed." This intercession results in the execution of divine judgment.[368] The parallelism in verse 1 suggests that the human prayers come before the Lord of the Spirits.

---

[363] The angels' prayer is filled with divine titles that indicate such: In 9:4 God is called "the God of gods" (9:4, all Grk versions), "King of the world" (Cod.Pan. βασιλεὺς τῶν αἰώνων, Syn^a βασιλεὺς τῶν βασιλευόντων καὶ θεὸς τῶν αἰώνων [Syn^b θεὸς τῶν ἀνθρώπων], 4QEn^b מרא עלמא) and "our great Lord" (4QEn^b מרנא רבא, Syn^{a,b} κύριος τῶν κυρίων).

[364] Correctly Henry J. WICKS, *The Doctrine of God in the Jewish Apocryphal and Apocalyptic Literature* (New York: Ktav, 1971 [1915]), 39. HURTADO (*One God, One Lord*, p. 27) seems to interpret all the early Jewish texts on angelic intercession without making any distinctions: "That God employed many angelic servants in carrying out his will did not make God more remote."

[365] From the Similitudes (*1 En* 37-71) which are only preserved in Eth mss. Most scholars date these chapters to sometime during the 1st cent. BCE until the late 1st cent. CE.

[366] CHARLES (*Apocrypha and Pseudepigrapha*, p. 211) observed that most of the mss included in his edition give the verbs in the plural.

[367] Translations of the Eth, unless otherwise indicated, are from E. ISAAC, "1 Enoch," in *OTP* 1.

[368] The precise function of the angels in v. 2b is not clear: Does the text emphasize that angelic intercession insures that the prayers of the righteous are not going to be "in vain before the Lord of the Spirits" (CHARLES) or that the angels do not cease interceding until judgment is executed (Isaac)? If the latter, then a "cause-and-effect" relationship between the angels' intercession and the ensuing judgment is to be ruled out.

(e) *1 Enoch* 99:3.[369] Following a pronouncement of "woes" to the wicked (vv. 1-2), the righteous are told to "make your prayers as a memorial, place them in a testimony before the angels, so that (CB-ὅπως) they may bring the sins of the unrighteous before the Most High as a memorial." Angels guarantee that the complaints of the righteous against the wicked will be heard.

(f) *1 Enoch* 104:1. A description of deeds against the righteous by their oppressors (103:5-15), who cannot remember (CB-οὐκ ἀναμιμνήσκουσιν) their sins (v. 15), concludes in an emphatic assurance that "the angels in heaven will remember (CB- ἀναμιμνήσκουσιν)" the righteous before God (104:1). As in 47:2 and 99:3, the angels make the case of the righteous heard at the eschatological judgment.

ii. *Testaments of the Twelve Patriarchs*

(a) *Testament of Levi* 3:5-7.[370] In the highest heaven with God are angels who function as priests by propitiating God for "sins of ignorance" committed by the righteous (v. 5). Below them are "angels who carry answers for[371] the angels of the presence of the Lord" (v. 7).[372]

(b) *Testament of Levi* 5:5-6. The visionary Levi, after being assisted through an angel in defeating the sons of Hamor, addresses the angel as "Lord" and asks to know the angel's name "in order that I may call upon (ἐπικαλέσομαι) you in a day of tribulation" (ἐν ἡμέρᾳ θλίψεως; v. 5). The an-

---

[369] Chapters 91-107, the so-called "Epistle of Enoch," are generally assigned to the latter part of the 2nd cent. BCE. A Chester BEATTY papyrus preserves an unbroken Grk text (CB) from 97:6 to 104, published by Campbell BONNER, *The Last Chapters of Enoch in Greek* (London: Chatto and Windus, 1937).

[370] Concerning date and the problem of Christian interpolations, see CHARLESWORTH, *PMR*, pp. 212-13. "T12P" was not written by one author. The *T.Levi* is unique among them in its inclusion of a visionary ascent to God's throne. At Qumran, fragments of *T.Levi* (Aram-1Q21, 4Q213-214, partly published) and *T.Naph* (Heb-4Q, unpublished) have been found. The passages of the *T.Levi* discussed here do not overlap with the published Qumran materials, which contain considerable divergences. The Greek text cited negotiates the editions of CHARLES, *Greek Versions of the Testaments* and M. DE JONGE et al., *The Testaments of the Twelve Patriarchs. A Critical Edition of the Greek Text* (Leiden: Brill, 1978), hereafter *Testaments. Critical Edition*.

[371] Since these are presumably angels below those who are closest to God, the dat. should be read "for" rather than "to," as suggested as a possibility by CHARLES, *Apocrypha and Pseudepigrapha*, p. 306 n.

[372] These functions of the angels are found in the Greek mss, but are absent in one of the Armenian recensions (A^a), upon which CHARLES placed considerable value.

gel identifies himself as "the one who makes intercession (παραιτούμενον[373]) for the nation Israel, so that they might not be completely beaten" (v. 6).[374] Levi responds by praising (εὐλόγησα) both God (ὁ ὕψιστος) and, in one family of manuscripts,[375] the angel (ὁ ἄγγελος) "who intercedes for the nation Israel and all the righteous" (v. 7). If verse 7b is original to the text, the author has the intercessory angel praised alongside God for his protective role. If it represents an addition, it is not clear by whom or how early the clause was added. Moreover, it is not clear whether "day of tribulation" is eschatological or, more generally, refers to a time of trouble.[376]

(c) *Testament of Dan* 6:2. "Draw near to God and to the angel who intercedes[377] for you, because he is a mediator between God and humanity, and for the peace of Israel he will take his stand against the kingdom of the enemy." An original text is difficult to certify on the basis of the manuscripts, and the same applies to the problem of Christian redaction. If anywhere, the text may have undergone such editing in a universalizing of the angel's intermediary role (cf. 1 Tim 2:5). The identification of Christian reworking on this basis must remain uncertain. Moreover, "Christian" editing

---

[373] See CHARLES, *Greek Versions of the Testaments*, p. 38 n. 39 concerning the probability of this reading.

[374] MACH (*Entwicklungsstadien*, p. 293 n. 40) considers this passage "die tragfähigste" as evidence for the veneration of angels. He erroneously argues that the tradition must be early because of the absence of the seer's prostration before the angel.

[375] The blessing of the angel is omitted in the translation of Howard Clark KEE in *OTP* 1.790, and included in that of CHARLES, *Apocrypha and Pseudepigrapha*, p. 307. DE JONGE, who considers "T12P" written by a Christian author, retains the clause in his edition, while CHARLES places it, as an eventual addition, in the margin (text families β,A^β,S^1). The text remains uncertain, though there is nothing distinctively Christian in this verse.

[376] See H.W. HOLLANDER and DE JONGE, *The Testaments of the Twelve Patriarchs* (SVTP, 8; Leiden: Brill, 1985) 145 and references cited there, esp. LXX Ps 49:15 and Sir 51:10. Cf., however, *j.Ber.* 9:13a.

[377] The text is uncertain; some mss have the ptc. παρεπόμενος "who follows"; see CHARLES, *Greek Versions of the Testaments*, p. 140 and de Jonge, *Testaments: Critical Edition*, p. 109. The subsequent explanatory clause, however, clearly refers to mediation. HOLLANDER and DE JONGE, *The Testaments of the Twelve Patriarchs*, pp. 291-92, while acknowledging the "very complicated internal structure" of this passage (p. 84), see in this interceding angel "a primitive angel-christology." This interpretation is improbable. The assumption that the σωτήρ = the "angel" can only be considered if the whole section is "Christian," as DE JONGE and HOLLANDER do. Furthermore, while *T.Dan* 6:7 and 9 show clear signs of Christian interpolation (references to σωτήρ of the Gentiles), it is mistaken to assume that universalism can be a criterion for identifying what is "Christian" (as HOLLANDER and DE JONGE do in the case of *T.Levi* 5:7).

may have drawn on Jewish traditions. If an honorable position is assigned to the intercessory angel in verse 2, such an angelology is modified (in the text as it stands) in verses 5-7: "since none of the angels is like him" (v. 6), the *Lord's presence* with Israel which guarantees that Israel will become a nation who seeks to do his will.

iii. Other Writings

(a) Tobit 12:12,15. Raphael, one of the seven angels "before the glory" of God (v. 15) brings "the memorial of your prayer before the glory of the Lord" (v. 12; see II.B.2.a, pp. 166-67 above).

(b) *3 Baruch* 11-16.[378] Both Slavonic and Greek versions agree in describing Michael as a chief angel (Grk-ἀρχιστράτηγος) who descends "to receive the prayers of humanity" (11:4; see also 12:1,7) and conveys them to God (14:2-Slav "prayers", Grk ἀρετάς "virtues"; cf. 11:9 Grk).[379] Below Michael are a group of angels who bring prayers to him (12:6). The angel accompanying Baruch prostrates before Michael (Slav-"bows"; Grk-προσεκύνησεν αὐτόν), acknowledging him as "chief of our whole regiment." The seer is not depicted as sharing this venerative posture.

(c) *Pseudo-Philo* 15:5. The execution of punishment for Israel's wrong-doing in the wilderness takes the form of isolation from God since angelic intercession is commanded to cease. (Cf. II.B.2.c, pp. 170-73 above).

(d) *Vita et Adae et Evae* 9:3.[380] After the expulsion, Satan (disguised as an angel) persuades Eve to leave her purification bath in the Tigris River with an assurance that her repentance has been accepted: "all we angels have entreated for you and interceded with the Lord" (cf. the "Apoc. of Moses" 29:16). This tactic suggests a rhetorical application of the motif; the guarantee of forgiveness normally associated with angelic intercession is

---

[378] See H.E. GAYLORD's translations of the Slav and Grk versions in "3 Baruch," *OTP* 1.652-79. Citations of the Grk are based on edition of the two Grk mss by J.-C. PICARD, *Apocalypsis Baruchi Graece* (PVTG, 2; Leiden: Brill, 1967) 61-96. Most scholars assign *3 Bar* to the first two cent.'s CE; see GAYLORD, "3 Baruch," pp. 656-57.

[379] Michael's role comes close to that of the priestly angel described in Rev 8:3-5.

[380] General agreement among scholars that this writing, preserved in Grk and Lat mss, dates to the 1st cent. CE, rests largely on a conspicuous absence of Christian editing together with the presence of parallels with early Jewish traditions (early rabb., *2 En*, and JOSEPHUS). If the original language was Hebrew, the document may have been composed in Palestine. See M.D. JOHNSON, "Life of Adam and Eve," in *OTP* 2.249-95, esp. p. 250. The citation is based on JOHNSON's translation.

not taken for granted. The reason for the fall of Satan and his angels is his refusal to heed God's command for the angels to "worship *the image of the Lord God*," that is, Adam (12:1-16:1)!

(e) *Testament of Solomon* 5:5.[381] The numerous invocations of named angels by "Solomon" to overpower demons are well known (see esp. 18:1-42).[382] Despite close motif connections with magical practices,[383] venerative *language* is wholly restricted to God.[384] Aside from the function of angels in subduing the demons, in 2:7 Solomon prays "that the archangel Ouriel would come help me" which in the context is unlikely intended as a prayer *to* the archangel. Nevertheless, it is knowledge of the names of angels upon which power over demons depends (2:5; 5:5-demons are worshiped μὴ γινωσκόντων τῶν ἀνθρώπων τὰ ὀνόματα τῶν καθ' ἡμῶν τεταγμένων ἀγγέλων).

e. Summary

Among these texts the intermediary functions of angels cannot be harmonized into one concept of angelic intercession. The angels' relation to (righteous) humans can take several forms. First, in some passages there is no explicit mention of the prayers of humans; angels pray on their behalf (*1 En* 40:6, 9; 47:1-2; *T.Levi* 3:5; *Ps-Philo* 15:5). This function comes close

---

[381] It is impossible to speak of "the date" of the *T.Sol.*, whose textual tradition (in 4 major recensions) shows considerable signs of reworking up until the medieval period. Against F.C. CONYBEARE's earlier contention that it was written by a Jewish author around 100 CE, most scholars since C.C. McCOWN ascribe the document to sometime within the 3rd cent. while the issue of Jewish or Christian authorship is recognized as impossible to determine; see McCOWN, *The Testament of Solomon* (Leipzig: Hinrichs, 1922) 108-109; *New Schürer*, 3.374; and CHARLESWORTH, *PMR*, p. 198. If Jewish, then the *T.Sol.* has undergone Christian reworking; if Christian, the author drew heavily on Jewish tradition. In either case, this writing may reflect magical practices among Jews (and later, Jewish or Gentile Christians) in the late 1st cent. (cf. JOSEPHUS, *Ant.* 8.45-49; Acts 19:13-16). Citation of *T.Sol.* below is based on McCOWN's edition.

[382] The most prominent of these are the four great angels (Michael, Gabriel, Ouriel, and Raphael-their order in 18:4-8), especially "the archangel Michael" who presents Solomon with a ring from God and announces that he will subdue the demons to build the temple (1:6-7). In clearly Christian parts of the document, even Christ is represented as a thwarting angel (6:8; 22:20).

[383] On the problem of defining "magic" see II.B.3.d (pp. 188-90) below.

[384] See 1:6; 2:5 (note the contrast between knowing the angel's name and worshiping God),9; 7:1; 8:1; 12:1; 14:7; 15:1,13; 16:1; 20:21; 22:16; and 25:9.

to,[385] yet may be distinguished from, a second notion, namely, that angels are bearers of human prayer to God (*1 En* 15:2; *1 En* 99:3; *3 Bar* 11-16; Tob 12:12; *T.Levi* 3:7[386]; Rev 8:3-5). Third, the *Testament of Solomon* emphasizes the knowing the names of angels who can be invoked. This does not seem like a matter of prayer either *to* or *through* angels. The significance of angels here is more apotropaic than devotional.[387] Fourth, there are two texts in which the question of prayer *to* angels may be raised: *1 Enoch* 9:3 and *Testament of Levi* 5:5. In the former passage, the position of angels as addressees of the human petition is related to the idea of God's remoteness from the scene (*1 En* 9:10); here the petition to the angels is actually formulated: "Bring our case to the Most High." This appeal is, however, not directed at the angels *instead of* God, but is ultimately concerned with gaining a hearing before God. In the *Testament of Levi* 5:5, though not formulated, prayer to the intercessory angel is entertained as a possibility for "a day of tribulation." Levi's request to know the angel's name is not countered; rather, the angel's function in behalf of Israel is reiterated, and in one (though later) family of manuscripts the visionary praises the angel alongside God.

Angelic intercession, mediation, or involvement in human prayer, then, is rarely a function which in the texts just reviewed results in praise or becomes the object of venerative language by human beings. Three possible exceptions are encountered in the *Testament of Levi* (however, probably through an early interpolation), Tobit (11:14-15), and *Joseph and Aseneth* (15:12). While in the first two the intercessory and protective roles are combined into one angelic figure, in *Joseph and Aseneth* the "blessing" by Aseneth is ultimately formulated in response to the heavenly figure's function as a herald of divine forgiveness. It is thus safe to conclude that the passages of these writings, in presenting human veneration of an angelic figure, do not restrict the angels' respective roles to some future eschatological judgment, but represent (from the visionary's perspective) spontaneous responses to their present activity in behalf of Israel or of righteous individuals.

---

[385] This is esp. clear in *1 En* 104:1, in which the angels' remembrance of the plight of the righteous is emphasized. The plight itself (103:5-15) is not formally expressed through a prayer, but is described in words attributed to the visionary Enoch (see 103:2). That human prayer is somehow involved is nevertheless suggested in CB to 104:2-"your cry will be heard."

[386] Cf. 4Q400 1 i 16 of the *Shirot*, n. 306 above.

[387] On this distinction, see the Excursus below (pp. 192-200) on Jewish invocation of angels in magical sources.

3. Ἄγγελος Inscriptions in Asia Minor

The combination of human petition and angels extends well beyond the genre of literature. A relative abundance of inscriptions, mostly from western Asia Minor, contain invocations or dedications referring to "an angel" or "angels"[388] which are not necessarily to be identified with "gods" or "messenger gods" known from the traditional Greek pantheon.[389] Despite the sometimes

---

[388] Such epigraphic texts from the early to late Hellenistic period have been found in the following locations: (1) *Stratonikeia* (in Caria): 4 dedicatory inscriptions (3 to "Zeus Most High and the good/divine angel"; 1 to "the angelic divinity"). In three of the inscriptions, one (the Angelos) or both deities is/are thanked by means of various formulae: ὑπὲρ σωτηρί[ας]...χαριστήριον, εὐχαριστοῦμεν ὑπὲρ σωτηρίας, εὐχαριστοῦμεν. (2) *Kidrama*: curse calling on punishment "by the fir[e] of angels." (3) *Phrygia* (3rd cent. CE): vow to Holiness (and) Justice by "the association of angel-friends (φιλανγέλων)." (4) *Temrek* (in Lydia): dedication to "the holy and just Angel" erected "through the prophet Alexander of Saittae." (5) *Kölekoy* (in Lydia; 164-65 CE): brief narrative describing "the powers" of the deity "Men" who took vengeance on a thief and brought him to confession after he had stolen a cloak. "Thus the god commanded through an angel that the cloak be sold and his powers inscribed on a stele." (6) *Thera* (island): some 44 tombstones with ἄγγελος + person's name in gen. case, or ἄγγελος/ἀγγέλου alone. (7) *Kalecik* (Galatia; late 2nd-early 3rd cent. CE): clearly Jewish dedicatory inscription; see pp. 185-87. (8) *Rheneia* (island near Delos; late 2nd-early 1st cent. BCE): 2 clearly Jewish inscriptions; see pp. 183-85. (9) Just south of *Smyrna*: apparently Jewish amulets; see p. 191. (10) *Cyzicus* (ca. 90 mi. north of Pergamum; latter half of 3rd cent. CE): invocation of the four great angels; clearly Jewish (pp. 190-91). (11) *Claudiopolis* (in Bythinia; 3rd or 4th cent. CE): malediction invoking κύριοι θεοὶ ἄνγελοι against 42 men and women. (12) *Oenoanda* (in Lycia; late 2nd-early 3rd cent. CE): oracle to Oenoanda by the Clarian Apollo; after a description of θεός the text reads τοῦτο θεὸς μικρὰ δὲ θεοῦ μερὶς ἄγγελοι ἡμεῖς ("such is God, and we are a small portion of God"). (13) *Eumeneia* (ca. 39 mi. north of Colossae): warning against the reuse of a tomb. Jewish or perhaps Jewish-Christian; see pp. 187-88.
Texts under (1-5) and (7) have been recently discussed by SHEPPARD, "Pagan Cults of Angels" 77-101, ed. princ. for (3) and (7) on pp. 87-90 and 94-96, and (1), (3-12) by ARNOLD, "Mediator Figures in Asia Minor." On *editiones princeps* of (1-2), (4-5), and (7) see *Supp.Ep.Gr.* 31 (1981) no. 1689. Further bibl. is cited during the discussion which follows.

[389] This distinction constitutes the main contribution of SHEPPARD, "Pagan Cults of Angels" (listing of ἄγγελος/-οι identified with traditional gods on p. 80 n. 7). In reviving the interpretation of F. SOKOLOWSKI ("Sur le Culte d'Angelos dans le paganisme grec et romain," *HTR* 53 [1960] 225-29), ARNOLD contests SHEPPARD's interpretation of the Stratonikeian inscriptions by arguing that the epithets ἀγαθὸς θεῖος ἄγγελος and θεῖος ἄγγελος ἀγαθός are to be understood as references to Hekate, the feminine deity-messenger of the underworld ("Mediator Figures in Asia Minor," pp. 10-14). Ἄγγελος is in fact considered a feminine deity (τῆς Ἀγγέλου) in a dedicatory inscription (1st cent. CE?) from Didyma which its editor, Theodor WIEGAND, argued refers to Hekate; see *Didyma. Zweiter Teil: Die Inschriften* (Berlin: Gebr. Mann, 1958) 243-44 (no. 406). Nevertheless, the decisive question is whether the form

infelicitous uncertainty of date, these materials may shed further light on the *Zeitgeist* of angelological ideas in the geographical regions proximate to the cities addressed in the Apocalypse of John (Rev 2:1-3:22).

The possible attribution of these inscriptions to Jewish or (Jewish-) Christian groups or individuals constitutes a special problem. The mere reference to angelic or divine names known from Jewish tradition does not demand the identification of an epigraph as "Jewish" (as, for example, in the magical papyri) and thus may only signal a borrowing of Jewish ideas.[390] Similarly, the supposition of "Jewishness" or even specifically "Jewish influence" in an inscription or text cannot depend on the mere occurrence of terms such as "angel,"[391] "holy and righteous" (as attributes for ἄγγελος)[392] or "Theos Hypsistos"[393] since these expressions occur regularly in contemporary inscriptions

---

θείῳ attested in Stratonikeia is a noun or adj. and whether it is masc. or neut. A masc. noun or adj. would exclude the Hekate hypothesis, while a neuter noun could be harmonized with it: "the deity ([τὸ] θεῖον) Angelos (fem.)." Despite the existence of a Hekate cult near Stratonikeia (Lagina), the double function of θείῳ as both an adj. (θείῳ ἀγγέλῳ parallel to ἀγαθῷ ἀγγέλῳ) and noun (θείῳ ἀγγελικῷ) suggests rather a masc. identity of the Angelos; similarly, see Martin P. NILSSON, *Geschichte der Griechischen Religion* (München: Beck, 1961²) 577 n. 1.

[390] From Asia Minor, a good example appears in a magical apparatus from Pergamum published by Richard WÜNSCH in *Antikes Zaubergerät aus Pergamon* (JKDAI, Ergänzungsheft, 6; Berlin: Reimer, 1905). The inscription, which appears three times on three separate stones, mentions ιαεω (ll. 1-2; l. 2 is inverse of l. 1) and the angels Μιχαηλ Γαβριηλ Ραγουηλ Ραφαηλ (l. 5), but is otherwise dominated by pagan magical formulations in which the deities Σθεννω and Μερχουρι occur.

[391] The use of ἄγγελος in the grave inscriptions at Thera are not singularly representative enough for an identification as either Jewish or Christian; so DIBELIUS, *Die Geisterwelt im Leben des Paulus* (Göttingen: Vandenhoeck & Ruprecht, 1909) 215 and ARNOLD, "Mediator Figures in Asia Minor," p. 7. *Contra* J.H. Moulton, "It is His Angel," *JTS* 3 (1902) 519-20 ("Christian tombs"); F. CUMONT, "Les anges du paganisme," *RHR* 72 (1915) 180 (see n. 4) and the impression left in *New Schürer* 3.71.

[392] See SHEPPARD, "Pagan Cults of Angels" 91-92, esp. n. 64.

[393] CUMONT, "Les anges du paganisme," 162 and "Ὕψιστος, in eds. G. WISSOWA et al., *Paulys Realencyklopädie der klassischen Altertumswissenschaft* (Stuttgart: Metzler) 9.1.445, by making the question of provenance determinative for function, was unable to understand "the Most High God/Zeus"--which as a whole he attributed to "Judeo-Syrian influence"--as an expression of *local* religion in Asia Minor. The identification of such inscriptions as Jewish or pagan is esp. raised as a problem by A.D. NOCK, C. ROBERTS, and T.C. SKEAT, "The Guild of Zeus Hypsistos," *HTR* 29 (1936) 39-88; A.T. KRAABEL, "Ὕψιστος and the Synagogue at Sardis," *GRBS* 10 (1969) 81-93; *New Schürer*,

which preserve no further trace of Jewish elements. The identification of Jewish provenance should ultimately rest on clearer indicators such as iconography, typically Jewish personal names or functions, location (for example, synagogue) and *termini technici* known otherwise only from Jewish sources. Hence, though the identification of some materials may be ultimately unattainable, a limited transparency and delimitation can be achieved if the following socio-religious possibilities are considered: inscriptions (1) composed by Jewish groups or individuals, (2) composed by Christians, (3) composed within a pagan context, and (4) influenced by Jewish ideas (as possible in the case of Christian and pagan inscriptions). The "angel" epigraphic materials which in all probability correspond to (1) and (2) will be presently discussed, while attempting not to isolate them from motifs which also occur in pagan inscriptions.

a. Rheneia (near Delos)

The island of Rheneia served inhabitants of Delos, an island commercial center off the southwest coast of Asia Minor, as a burial ground. Here were found two virtually identical grave inscriptions on separate stones, which are now on display in Bucharest and Athens. Both epigraphs, underneath a raised pair of open hands at the top,[394] contain a call for divine retribution against the murderers of two girls. These epigraphs are of particular importance (1) because, on the basis of paleography, they are datable to the late 2nd-early 1st century BCE[395] and (2) because they are decidedly Jewish in origin.[396]

3.68, 72, and 169; and, recently, by Paul TREBILCO, *Jewish Communities in Asia Minor* (SNTSMS, 69; Cambridge: Univ., 1991) 127-33, 142-44.

[394] On the stone in Bucharest the text appears twice (front and back), both times underneath the raised hands.

[395] The questions of provenance and paleography of both inscriptions were not settled until 65 years after the initial publication by P. LE BAS (1836), who had claimed that they date to the 11th or 12th century and are Christian. On the basis of paleography, content, and consultation with colleagues, Adolf WILHELM ("Zwei Fluchinschriften," *JÖAI* 4 [1901] 10) was able to declare confidently that "Mit diesem Ansatze hat der erste Herausgeber ohne Zweifel gewaltig fehlgegriffen."

[396] In addition to paleographical considerations (pre-Christian), decisive are the complete absence of specifically Christian motifs, language reflecting LXX-tradition, and reference to a day in which before God "all souls humble themselves with supplication"), all of which best fit a Jewish context.

The text[397] opens with an appeal (ἐπικαλοῦμαι καὶ ἀξιῶ) to "the Most High God, the Lord of the spirits and of all flesh." After the curse itself, the invocation is resumed, this time with the address, "O Lord who sees all things and angels of God, before whom (sing.) all souls on this day humble themselves with a supplication, that you (sing.) avenge the innocent blood and render account (for it) quickly."[398]

The function of angels within this prayer has been variously interpreted. In his influential discussion of the text Adolf DEISSMANN argued that the inclusion of the "angels of God" does not constitute evidence for an "angel cult." Stressing that the invocation remains within the bounds of biblical thought, he appealed to LXX Psalm 102:20 (=MT) as an analogy.[399] On the other end, a number of early and recent interpreters have regarded the invocation as the reflection of an "angel cult."[400] Against DEISSMANN, it should be noted that in the Psalm passage the appeal to angels is of a different sort: While the psalmist calls upon "(LXX + all) his angels" (v. 20) and "all his hosts" (v. 21) to "bless the Lord," in the text of the inscriptions the "angels of God," together with God, are summoned to take revenge on behalf of Heraclea and Marthina. Though the motif of angelic participation in divine vengeance is in itself not uncommon,[401] their inclusion in the appeal itself

---

[397] The text, in addition to WILHELM's publication (see previous n.), is printed in Adolf DEISSMANN, "Die Rachegebete von Rheneia," in *Licht vom Osten* (Tübingen: J.C.B. Mohr [Paul Siebeck], 1923⁴) 351-62; W. DITTENBERGER, *Sylloge Inscriptionum Graecarum* (Leipzig: Hinrichs, 1915-1924³) no. 1181; Pierre ROUSSEL and Marcel LAUNEY, *Inscriptions de Delos* (Paris: Librairie Ancienne Honoré Champion, 1937) no. 2532 (followed here; the most complete presentation of the three texts); J.-B. FREY, *Corpus Inscriptionum Judaicarum* (New York: Ktav, 1975 repr. 1936, 1952) 1.523-25 (no. 725); and *New Schürer*, 3.70.

[398] Text: κύριε ὁ πάντα ἐφορῶν καὶ οἱ ἄγγελοι θεοῦ, ᾧ πᾶσα ψυχὴ ἐν τῇ σήμερον ἡμέραι ταπεινοῦται μεθ ἱκετείας ἵνα ἐγδικήσῃς τὸ αἷμα τὸ ἀναίτιον ζητήσεις καὶ τὴν ταχίστην (Bucharest stele, ll. 9-13). The Athens text omits the second verb ζητήσεις.

[399] DEISSMANN's assessment is followed by HURTADO, *One God, One Lord*, pp. 28-29, 140 n. 42 and ARNOLD, "Mediator Figures in Asia Minor," pp. 21-22.

[400] So CUMONT, "Les anges du paganisme" 162-63; GOODENOUGH, *Jewish Symbols*, 2.145-46; SIMON, "Remarques sur l'Angélolâtrie Juive," p. 453 (with some reserve); Louis ROBERT, "Épitaphes d'Eumeneia de Phrygie," *Hellenica* 11-12 (1960) 433 n. 3; HENGEL, "Der Alte und der Neue ‚Schürer'" 37; and SCHWEMER, "Gott als König in den Sabbatliedern," p. 100 n. 153.

[401] Given the epithet ὁ κύριος τῶν πνευμάτων κτλ., one thinks of *1 En* 47:1-2 (cf. also *1 En* 99:3 and 104:1) in which, however, the angels' intermediary function is more explicit.

the angels referred to were accorded some honor. For lack of more data, however, this point should perhaps not be pressed too far.[402] The iconography (raised hands) may indicate as much a maledictive posture[403] as it reflects a simple expression of piety.[404] Moreover, the Rheneia inscriptions leave no indication that the angels are viewed as intermediary figures *between* God and the supplicants (unlike *1 En* 9:3). The prayer is ultimately directed towards God "the Most High," and the singular forms immediately following the mention of angels make plain that those who wrote the text were seeking quick exaction from *God*.

b. Kalecik (Galatia)

In 1980 A.R.R. SHEPPARD published an inscription on a broken red marble column with the following text: "To the great God Most High and Heavenly (τῷ μεγάλῳ θεῷ ὑψίστῳ καὶ ἐπουρανίῳ) and to his holy angels (καὶ τοῖς ἁγίοις αὐτοῦ ἀγγέλοις) and for[405] his venerable house of prayer (καὶ τῇ προσκυνητῇ αὐτοῦ προσευχῇ) the works here are set forth...."[406] The precise origin of the epi-

---

[402] The *New Schürer* (3.71), as in SCHÜRER's older *Geschichte* (e.g., par. 31) makes no attempt at assessing this aspect of the inscription.

[403] See another Delos inscription found in the Syrian temple in ROUSSEL and LAUNEY, *Inscriptions de Delos* no. 2531, in which a certain Theogenes αἴρει τὰς χεῖρας τῷ Ἡλίῳ καὶ τῇ Ἁγνῇ Θεᾷ against a woman who has stolen savings he had deposited with her. At the bottom of the inscription is also a pair of open raised hands. See further J.H.M. STRUBBE, "'Cursed be he that moves my bones'," in eds. Christopher A. FARAONE and Dirk OBBINK, *Magika Hiera. Ancient Greek Magic and Religion* (Oxford: Univ., 1991) 42 and n.'s 94, 160 (the volume hereafter cited as *Magika Hiera*) who, while not noting this inscription, observes that this iconographical motif is esp. common in summons for divine vengeance in cases of premature or unjust deaths of children and young people. See further CUMONT, "Ὕψιστος," col. 447.

[404] It is hence difficult in this case to distinguish clearly between a curse and a non-coercive prayer for divine vengeance. In a thorough essay treating instances which contain the latter element, H.S. VERSNEL, "Beyond Cursing: the Appeal to Justice in Judicial Prayers," in *Magika Hiera*, pp. 60-106, makes such a distinction while admitting that judicial "prayer and *defixio*...(are) two opposites on the extreme ends of a whole spectrum of more or less hybrid forms" (p. 92).

[405] The dat. case is rendered differently here in order to stress that the essential difference between respect accorded to the place of prayer and the dedication to God and his angels.

[406] "Pagan Cults of Angels" 94-96. The "first" publication, to which SHEPPARD refers, actually appeared in 1982: S. MITCHELL, *Regional Epigraphic Catalogues of Asia Minor II. The Ankara District. The Inscriptions of North*

graph, which had been brought to Kalecik (ca. 90 mi. northeast of Ankara), is unknown; paleographical considerations have led S. MITCHELL to date the text to sometimes in the 3rd century,[407] while SHEPPARD is inclined toward "the late second or third century AD."[408] The combination of elements virtually certifies the Jewish context of the inscription:[409] the definite article before the epithet "the Most High God," the term προσευχή as a place of prayer,[410] and the reference to "holy angels."

The bottom of the text is, unfortunately, lost. It is possible that "the works here" refers to donations made by a patron or patrons of the venerable house of prayer." In this case, one might speculate that the building was a gathering place for Jewish devotees of both God and angels. This is, however, unlikely: the singular αὐτοῦ makes clear that the προσευχή is identified as a place of God. The form of the inscription suggests rather that "the works here," perhaps to be specified, are presented as a "thank-offering" for some activity attributed to "God the Most High and Heavenly" and "his holy angels."[411] Though it remains uncertain to what extent angels may have been invoked alongside God, the role of angels in the text goes one step beyond the maledictions in Delos, in which the *activity* of retribution is explicitly related to God (sing. forms). The Kalecik inscription, then, proba-

---

Galatia (BIAAnk, 4; Oxford: British Archaeological Reports International Series 135, 1982) 177-78 (no. 209B).

[407] MITCHELL, *Regional Epigraphic Catalogues*, p. 177.

[408] SHEPPARD, "Pagan Cults of Angels in Asia Minor" 94.

[409] So esp. TREBILCO, *Jewish Communities in Asia Minor*, p. 137.

[410] Only one inscription with προσευχή as a religious gathering place can, in all probability, be identified as non-Jewish: a 3rd-cent. dedication (εὐχαριστήριον) from Amastris (northern coast of Asia Minor) "to (the) unconquered deity Asbames (Ασβαμει) and to the prominent house of prayer (τῇ κυρίᾳ προσευχῇ) ; see bibl. and text in HENGEL, "Proseuche und Synagoge. Jüdische Gemeinde, Gotteshaus und Gottesdienst in der Diaspora und in Palästina," in eds. H.-W. KUHN and H. STEGEMANN, *Tradition und Glaube. Das frühe Christentum in seiner Umwelt. Festschrift für K.G. Kuhn* (Göttingen: Vandenhoeck & Ruprecht, 1971) 179 and "Der Alte und Neue ‚Schürer'" 37. SHEPPARD uses this example to interpret the Kalecik inscription ("Pagan Cults of Angels in Asia Minor" 96) and hence is inclined to think of "borrowing from Judaism or else an attempt on the part of pagans to give their cult a Jewish veneer" (pp. 96-97). His argument, however, is ultimately built on an exception which itself may have had remote connections with Jewish influence (HENGEL, "Proseuche und Synagoge," 179).

[411] See the inscription from Amastris (previous n.) for a similar structure. The question of genre can only be settled by a thorough comparison of (εὐ)χαριστήριον inscriptions with those which indicate a gift.

bly reflects some sort of veneration or devotion to angels which was not intended to displace monotheistic belief.

c. Eumeneia (Phrygia)

In 1947 Louis ROBERT[412] copied a tomb inscription from Haydan (4 mi. southeast of Eumeneia, 40 mi. north of Colossae), probably written in the 3rd century CE,[413] which warns against further interment: εἴ τις δὲ ἕτερον θήσει, ἔστε αὐτῷ πρὸς τὸν θεὸν καὶ τὸν ἄγγελον τὸν ʿΡουβῆδος. Here, a certain Lycidas, who has erected the tomb for two sisters, has had the warning formulated in language reminiscent of other grave inscriptions from Phrygia.[414] On the basis of this affinity, ROBERT and SHEPPARD have argued that Lycidas was a Christian.[415] The name ʿΡουβῆς (nominative), a graecized form of ראובן (in LXX tradition mostly ʿΡουβήν or ʿΡουβείν),[416] probably denotes the name of a Jew or least a Jewish convert.[417]

---

[412] ROBERT, "Épitaphes d'Eumeneia," pp. 429-35. The inscription is republished by SHEPPARD in "Jews, Christians and Heretics in Acmonia and Eumeneia," AnatSt 29 (1979) 175-76 (Pl. XXI,b).

[413] See ROBERT, "Épitaphes juives d'Éphèse et de Nicomédie," Hellenica 11-12 (1960) 398-99.

[414] Ibid., pp. 387 and 392 (Nicomedia) 399-400 (Acmonia) and in "Épitaphes d'Eumeneia de Phrygie" (Eumeneia).

[415] SHEPPARD, "Jews, Christians and Heretics," 176; ROBERT, "Épitaphes d'Eumeneia," pp. 423-24 and n.'s 7 and 8. Esp. important for this identification are Christian inscriptions in Eumeneia. It is nevertheless possible --the formula ἔσται αὐτῷ πρὸς τὸν θεόν (Acmonia), ἕξει ἡ πρὸς τὴν κρίσιν and ἔξῃ κρίσιν πρὸς τὸν θεόν do not specifically suggest a Christian context-- that the inscription is Jewish, as ROBERT admits ("Inscriptions juives," p. 400).

[416] See also CIJ no.'s 912, 950 (Joppa: Ρουβη, gen.), 928 (Joppa: Ρωβη, nom.; 781 (Syr. Antioch: Ρουβην, acc./nom.); and 1175 (Jerusalem: ʿΡωβήλ, gen.), cited in ROBERT, "Épitaphes d'Eumeneia," pp. 422-23 n.'s 7-9.

[417] In a contemporary epitaph found 2 km away, a certain Gaius declares he has provided for the burial of himself, his wife Tatia, their deceased children that they might share the grave "with Roubes, worshiper of the great God (σὺν ʿΡούβῃ μεγάλοιο θ[εο]ῦ θεράποντι). Is this the same or a different "Roubes"? Does Lycidas speak of the "angel of Roubes" while the latter is alive, while Gaius speaks of the deceased Roubes who shares the same tomb? For the text see ROBERT, "Épitaphes d'Eumeneia," pp. 414-15 and SHEPPARD, "Jews, Christians and Heretics," 177-78. A Christian identity of Gaius is suggested by what may be a Chi-Rho at the beg. of l. 14 (not clearly visible; see SHEPPARD's Pl. XXII), together with a statement near the end "the righteous (οἱ δίκαιοι) always [p]o[i]nt to resurrection (ἀνάστασιν). See also HENGEL, "Die Synagogeninschrift von Stobi" 156 n. 32.

As in the grave inscriptions from Thera, the ἄγγελος is nameless and followed by the proper name in a genitive construction.[418] Does "the angel" here refer to the soul of the deceased Roubes, as frequently argued concerning the Thera inscriptions?[419] The form of the inscription militates against such an interpretation. The inclusion of "the angel which (is) of Roubes" with ὁ θεός within the warning formula (εἶναι+pers. pron.[dat.]+πρός)[420] makes it more likely that Lycidas is, alongside ὁ θεός, invoking an independent angel to guard the tomb.[421]

Of all published inscriptions from Phrygia bearing this or a similar formula for protection, only this one mentions an "angel." If "Roubes" is still living, then the mention of his "angel" in relation to an active belief in this angel may be significant. If "Roubes" is dead, it is possible that the angel thought to guard his tomb is being, however indirectly, summoned.[422]

d. Jewish Magical Materials from Asia Minor

Beyond concerns reflected in the inscriptions discussed above, a few clearly Jewish materials from Asia Minor preserve invocations expressing apotropaic calls for help with regard to more mundane matters. These sources are usually understood to represent some form of "magic." Allusions to magic have

---

[418] This might be significant if it were possible to establish clearly that the Thera inscriptions are Jewish. Despite NILSSON's apparent assumption to the contrary (*Geschichte der Griechischen Religion*, 2.540 n. 7), this possibility cannot be discounted categorically.

[419] See MOULTON, "It is His Angel," 519-20 and literature cited there.

[420] On the formula see TREBILCO, *Jewish Communities*, pp. 78-79.

[421] The definite article preceding "Roubes" (τόν) prevents an interpretation which would have ὁ θεός specifically refer to the God of Roubes. This leaves the impression that Lycidas is, in effect, summoning the protection of two separate deities.

[422] Another possible case of angelic protection in a Jewish context (3rd cent.?) seems to be an epigraph found in Argos, in which a certain Aurelios Joses summons "the divine and grea[t] powers (δυνάμ<ει>ς) which are of God and th[e] powers (δυνάμ<ει>ς) of the Law (τοῦ Νόμου)" along with the honor (ἡ τιμή) of patriarchs, ethnarchs, and sages to guard against defacement of his tomb; for the text, see *CIJ* no. 719 and HENGEL, "Die Synagogeninschrift von Stobi" 156 n. 32. Of uncertain provenance is a second-century funerary inscription from Achaia (original site not known) which contains an appeal to δύναμις τον ἀγγέλον κὲ χαρακτήρον (-ον = gen. plur.) for protection (διαφυλάξατε...δότε νίκην χάριν...) of the tomb of Ἰωάνου κὲ Γεοργίας; see *CIJ*, no. 717 (only partly given, and with transcriptional inaccuracies) and *Inscriptiones Graeciae Septentrionalis*, Otto KERN ed. (*Inscriptiones Graecae*, 9/2; Berlin: Reimer, 1908) no. 232 (full publication).

already been encountered above in the discussions of the accusations of Celsus (II.A.3.d) and the *Testament of Solomon* (II.B.2.d). Before a brief glance at invocations of angels in magical Jewish materials from Asia Minor, it is first necessary to comment on the understanding of "magic" upon which the following discussion is based, since a precise definition of the term with respect to antiquity is elusive.

Drawing largely on W.J. GOODE's anthropology-based distinctions between "magic" and "religion," David E. AUNE has proposed a two-faceted (social and functional) working definition: (1) "that form of religious deviance whereby individual or social goals are sought by means alternate to those normally sanctioned by the dominant religious institution" and, given this sociological framework, involves (2) "goals (which are)...attained through the management of supernatural powers in such a way that results are virtually guaranteed."[423]

With respect to our texts, the definition is problematic. First, how can concepts such as "religious deviance" and "dominant religious institutions" be delineated? A sociological explanation for magic depends primarily on what one can establish as the relationship of the sources to their immediate environment. As Roy KOTANSKY has noted, AUNE's definition "is valid only for the social-political and historical context in which such dichotomies between 'dominant religious institutions' and 'religious deviance' can flourish."[424] Thus on the basis of AUNE's definition, it would be difficult to discern how the inscriptions from Rheneia, Kalecik and Eumeneia may be said to differ from the "magical" texts treated below; we know too little about their respective contexts to delineate anything concerning the extent to which a form of social "deviation" *could* have been involved.

Second, the functional part of the definition requires more precision if one is to distinguish between coercive invocation of divine powers and petitionary prayer. Indeed, as suggested by our analysis of the Rheneia epigraphs (II.B.3.a), it may be misleading to decide the question without some measure of ambiguity. The possibility of such fluidity may to some degree explain why Celsus, if he was not misrepresenting Judaism entirely, could have

---

[423] "Magic in Early Christianity," in *ANRW*, II.23.2.1515-16 (parenthetical words supplied).

[424] Roy KOTANSKY, "Incantations and Prayers for Salvation on Inscribed Greek Amulets, " in *Magika Hiera*, p. 123 n. 1.

associated venerative attitudes towards angels among some Jews with magical practices (on the latter, see Excursus below).[425]

If these considerations are kept in mind, AUNE's functional definition nevertheless provides a useful theoretical framework which highlights the coercive nature of magical sources, an aspect which is conspicuous in the following texts.

i. Cyzicus (ca. 90 mi. north of Pergamum)

A. Sorlin DORIGNY published the text of a bronze amulet from Cyzicus in 1891.[426] On the reverse side of the amulet Μιχαήλ, Γαβριήλ, Οὐριήλ, ʿΡαφαήλ are called upon to protect (διαφύλαξον; sing.!) its bearer.[427] On the upper-center of this side are randomly placed letters from the *trishagion* plus "RRSSS"(?). On the observe, the rim contains a command that ἄγγελος ʾΑραaφ (further designated μεμισμένη) flee, followed by the warning, "Solomon is pursuing you." The illustration surrounded by the text shows an angelic figure walking ahead of a star and a horseman who is plunging a spear into a snake and a woman below.[428] Apparently the amulet envisions, perhaps alongside God,[429] a variety of

---

[425] In the end, it remains impossible to discern whether Celsus was attributing to "the Jews" the sort of practices reflected in eclectic magical texts such as those collected and edited by Karl PREISENDANZ (*Papyri Graecae Magicae. Die Griechischen Zauberpapyri* [2 vols.; Leipzig/Berlin: Teubner, 1928-1931] or was aware of the practice of invoking angels among some Jews, which he then pejoratively characterized as "magic." The possibility of the former, as can be inferred from the materials discussed below in II.B.3.d. and the Excursus, cannot be ruled out.

[426] "Phylactère Alexandrin," *REG* 4 (1891) 287-96 (drawing on p. 287); DORIGNY (p. 289), on the basis of iconographical features, dated the amulet to the late 3rd cent. CE. For brief discussion and further bibl. see ALEXANDER, "Incantations and Books of Magic," in *New Schürer* 3.376-77.

[427] PETERSON, ΕἿΣ ΘΕΌΣ (FRLANT, n.F., 24; Göttingen: Vandenhoeck & Ruprecht, 1926) 106 explained the order of the angels' names on the basis of astrological texts. The same order, however, is found in the *T.Sol.* 18:5-8; *Sib.Or.* 2.215; and most Eth mss to *1 En* 9:1 (not in the Aram or Grk materials).

[428] Soon after DORIGNY's publication a similar amulet, discovered by M. FONTRIER in Koula near Smyrna, was published by T. HOMOLLE, "Nouvelles et Correspondance: Ionie," *BCH* 17 (1893) 638, in which the horseman and the angelic figure, respectively, tread upon the snake and spear the woman. PETERSON, ΕἿΣ ΘΕΌΣ, pp. 106-107, reproduces drawings of both amulets for comparison. In the talisman from Koula, not angels but "the seal of the living God" (σφραγις του ζοντος θεου) is invoked for protection of its bearer (φυλαξον τον φορουντα).

[429] An explicit reference to God after the *trishagion* is probable. On ΠΙΠΙ as a Greek transcription for יהוה (as already in JEROME, *Epist.* 25), see

guardian figures (Solomon, the angelic figure with him, and the four angels) who, as the divergent formulae on the opposite sides indicate, are accorded different functions. Though there is considerable evidence on the importance of Solomon in magical practices in the ancient world (as early as JOSEPHUS, Ant. 8.45-49),[430] the invocation formulae itself is limited to the angels named on the other side, while the desired efficacy is illustrated by horseman's activity.

ii. The Region of Smyrna

The sighting of numerous stones, one bearing a menorah, was reported by Henry J. VAN LENNEP in 1870.[431] The text on each piece contained an identical, obscure text: θωβαρραβο υλακασακις αβρασας ωαωη ναλη εχεχε. ARNOLD infers from the appearance of a similar word θαυβαρραβαυ in an amulet found in Syria[432] that the inscription must have included angels in the invocation.[433] The date, however, is uncertain.

DORIGNY, "Phylactère Alexandrin" 291; GOODENOUGH, Jewish Symbols, 2.220; and now Erika ZWIERLEIN-DIEHL, Magische Amulette und andere Gemmen des Instituts für Altertumskunde der Universität zu Köln (ARWAWSond, PapCol, 20; Opladen: Der Westdeutsche Verlag, 1993) 62-64. Correspondingly, in the amulet from Koula (see previous n.), the trishagion is predicated by κύριος, followed by the liturgical phrase Σαβαωθ πλιρις ο ουρανος και η γι τις δοξις.

[430] See McCOWN, The Testament of Solomon, pp. 90-104; ALEXANDER, "Appendix: Solomon and Magic," New Schürer 3.375-79; and DULING, "The Testament of Solomon," in OTP 1.944-51.

[431] Travels in Little-Known Parts of Asia Minor (2 vols.; London: John Murray) 1.19-20, cited by GOODENOUGH, Jewish Symbols, 2.221; see also CIJ no. 743.

[432] "Mediator Figures in Asia Minor," pp. 7-8. The amulet was published with analysis by Paul PERDRIZET, "Amulette grecque trouvée en Syrie," REG 41 (1928) 73-82 (text--at least 24 ll.--on pp. 73-74), for whom the orthography indicates a date during the 4th-6th cent.'s CE; l. 8: θαυβαρραβαυ. The text invokes many names, including Ιαω, Μιχαηλ, Γαβριηλ, Ου[ρ]ιηλ, Ελωαι; showing further connection with Asia Minor is the recapitulating epithet κυριοι αρχανγελοι θεοι known in pagan inscriptions from Asia Minor. See ROBERT, "Reliefs votifs et cultes d'Anatolie," Anat 3 (1958) 122 n. 71 with bibl.: κύριοι θεοί άγγελοι in Claudiopolis (Bithynia; see n. 388 above) and Pisidian Antioch.

[433] "Mediator Figures in Asia Minor," pp. 7-8. ARNOLD follows GOODENOUGH's plausible suggestion (Jewish Symbols, 2.221) that ωαωη be read as a transliteration of the tetragrammaton.

Excursus: Jewish Invocation of Angels in Magical Sources from Antiquity

As is well known, magical practices among Jewish circles in antiquity was both early and widespread.[434] In their characterizations of "Jewish magic," scholars such as Marcel SIMON,[435] E.R. GOODENOUGH,[436] and CHARLESWORTH[437] have stressed the importance of three features: (1) a high regard for applying Hebrew phrases which, though often not understood, were thought to possess special powers; (2) the use of names (the names of angels and, especially, variations of the divine name); and (3) a speculative interest in angelology. In elaborating the third of these characteristics, SIMON and GOODENOUGH center almost exclusively on angelolatry and find in Jewish magic the referent in the accusations of Celsus, ARISTIDES, and the *Kerygma Petrou* (see II.A.3.d).[438]

However, the limited focus of SIMON and GOODENOUGH may mislead one to oversimplify what is otherwise a rather varied and complex phenomenon. Thus before some of the pertinent examples can be cited, it is important to emphasize that the invocation of angels in these materials was apparently not considered an indispensable element and, hence, should not be assumed. Though the phenomenon of magic extended well beyond what we know from sparse extant sources, it nevertheless may be significant to note that no "magical" Jewish source from the 1st century CE or earlier preserves any prayer or address made to an angel.[439] Furthermore, within the collection edited by Karl PREIS-

---

[434] See esp. Ludwig BLAU, *Das altjüdische Zauberwesen* (Westmead/Farnborough/Hants., England: Gregg International Publishers, 1970; repr. from 1898) and, further, the influential discussions covering Jewish magic from the Second Temple to the Amoraic periods by SIMON, *Verus Israel*, pp. 339-68; GOODENOUGH, *Jewish Symbols*, 2.153-295; URBACH, *The Sages*, pp. 97-134; and ALEXANDER, "Incantations and Books of Magic," in *New Schürer*, 3.342-79. Concerning magic in Babylonian rabbinism beginning with the late 3rd cent CE, see Jacob NEUSNER, *A History of the Jews in Babylonia* (5 vols.; SPB; Leiden: Brill, 1965-1970) 3.115-27; 4.330-62; and 5.217-43, 174-93.

[435] *Verus Israel*, pp. 343-47.

[436] *Jewish Symbols*, 2.161-62.

[437] "Prayer of Jacob," in *OTP* 2.716.

[438] SIMON, *Verus Israel*, p. 345 and GOODENOUGH, *Jewish Symbols*, 2.161.

[439] See ALEXANDER, "Incantations and Books of Magic," pp. 364-66 (on 4Q186=4QCryptic; 4QMess ar, now more accurately 4QBirth of Noah=4Q534; and 4QBront=4Q318). To these Qumran texts add the fragmentary amulet formula in 4Q560, included in EISENMAN and WISE, *The Dead Sea Scrolls Uncovered*, pp. 265-67. ALEXANDER (*ibid.*, pp. 369-72) disputes CHARLESWORTH's 1st cent. BCE dating for the astrologically oriented *Treatise of Shem* (see *PMR*, pp. 182-84 and *OTP*, 1.474-75); in any case, the document makes no reference to angels.

ENDANZ (PGM), a number of texts which contain specifically Jewish elements preserve traces of a more traditional emphasis on God and stress God's superiority over angels without including the latter in the invocations:[440]

- PGM IV (papyrus, 4th cent. CE[441]), 1167-1226[442]--Prayer-formula for protection: to "Helios" (1182)="the great God...who is radiant at Jerusalem" (1221-22), whose name is "considered sacred (καθηγιασμένον) by all the angels" (1191-93) and who created "gods, archangels, and decans" (1203-1204).

- PGM IV, 1227-1264--Formula in a rite for expelling demons which, in present form, contains Christian elements: invokes "God of Abraham...God of Isaac...God of Jacob; Jesus Chrestos, the Holy Spirit, the Son of the Father, who is above the Seven, who is within the Seven" (1232-36; this portion in Copt).

- PGM IV, 3007-3086--Charm for those who are demonized. Demons are conjured by "the god of Hebrews, Jesus" (3019-20)..."the great god Sabaoth" (3052-53)..."the one in holy Jerusalem" (3069), "whom every heavenly power of angels and of archangels praises" (3050-52). The charm recounts the god's activity by referring to events in Israel's history (e.g., appearance to "Osrael" in a cloud, deliverance from Pharaoh, division of the Jordan River and Red Sea).[443]

- PGM XXIIb (papyrus, 4th cent. CE)--Προσευχὴ Ἰακώβ: addressed to the "Father of the patriarchs" (1-2), "Creator of the angels and archangels" (3)..."Lord God of the Hebrews" (18). The one praying considers himself "a terrestrial angel" (24-ἄγγελον ἐπ[ίγ]ειον).

The magical practices referred to in Jub 10:10-14 and Tob 6:3-9 and 8:1-3 are in the form of remedies mediated by angels rather than cures accomplished by appealing directly to them. Similarly, JOSEPHUS' claim that the Essenes, on the one hand, studied healing of diseases, protective roots and properties of stones (Bell.Jud. 2.136) and, on the other hand, the oath "to preserve...the books of their sect and the names of the angels" (Bell.Jud. 2.142) does not allow for the conclusion that the former was accomplished through appeals to angels.

[440] The well-known lead tablet from Hadrumetum (capital of the Roman province of Africa), a spell adjuring a demon to cause a certain Urbanus to fall in love with and marry Domitiana, likewise draws heavily on traditional Jewish motifs in relation to "the holy Aoth Ab[ao]th the God of Abraan and Iao the (God) of Iakou, Iao Io[th Ab]aoth God of Israma" (ll. 1-3). The text makes no mention of angels. See BLAU, Das Altjüdische Zauberwesen, pp. 96-112.

[441] See ALEXANDER, "Incantations and Books of Magic," p. 358, who argues plausibly that the contents of many recipes found in PGM IV antedate the 4th cent CE.

[442] The citations in English and line numbers follow ed. H.D. BETZ, The Greek Magical Papyri in Translation, Including the Demotic Spells (Chicago/London: Univ. of Chicago, 1992^2), hereafter EPGM, while the Greek, when cited, follows PGM.

[443] See also BLAU, Das Altjüdische Zauberwesen, pp. 112-17.

On the other hand, extant materials which include "angels" in invocation formulae, not all of them by means of Jewish elements, are abundant. Many of these were discussed by GOODENOUGH in volume 2 of his *Jewish Symbols in the Greco-Roman Period* (pp. 153-295) on the basis of various charms and amulets found in the *PGM*, Coptic magical texts,[444] coins, amulets, charms, Aramaic incantations bowls, and various indices in rabbinic literature. A complete re-citation of GOODENOUGH's evidence here would be superfluous. However, the following presentation of examples, drawn primarily from the *PGM* corpus, may provide some indication of the interpretive difficulties in sorting out the motif's religious provenance.[445]

> *PGM* I (papyrus, 4th-5th cent.'s CE), 42-195--Spell of Pnouthis for procuring an assistant (πάρεδρος). In ll. 163-72: "And this is spoken next: 'Hither to me, King,...God of gods, mighty, boundless, undefiled, indescribable, firmly established Aion.' ...Then question him by the same oaths. If he tells you his name, take him by the hand, descend and have him recline..., setting before him part of the foods and drinks which you partake of. And when you release him, sacrifice to him after his departure what is prescribed and pour a wine offering, and in this way you will be a friend of the mighty angel (τῷ κραταίῳ ἀγγέλῳ; l. 180-κραταιῷ παρέδρῳ)." The "ἄγγελος" is frequently designated "θεός" (ll. 77, 86, 88-90, etc.). The spell contains no obvious sign of Jewish influence.
>
> *PGM* I, 262-347-- Ἀπολλωνιακὴ ἐπίκλησις. In the invocation to Apollo proper (297-327), the prayer is also addressed to "the first angel of [God], great Zeus Iao" (300), "you who rule heaven's realm, Michael" (300-301), "you, archangel Gabriel" (301-302), "Abrasax" (303), "Adonai" (304), "Pakerbeth" (305). The formula goes on to adjure, among a number of items, "Aion" (309), "Adonaios" (310), and "Eloaios" (311). Though GOODENOUGH calls the text "possibly a Jewish charm recast by a pagan," he admits that its basic structure is pagan since all the Jewish figures are subordinated to Apollo and Zeus.[446]
>
> *PGM* III (papyrus, 4th cent. CE), 1-164--Cat ritual for a variety of (malicious) purposes. In 71-98 the "powerful and mighty angel of this animal in this place" is conjured to do vengeance against enemies by "Iao, Sabaoth, Adonai, Abrasax, and by the great god

---

[444] See the bilingual (Coptic-German) edition by Angelicus M. KROPP, *Ausgewählte Koptische Zaubertexte* (3 vols.; Brussels: Édition de la Fondation Égyptologique Reine Élisabeth, 1930-1931).

[445] The examples are strictly limited to instances in which an "angel" or "angels" (ἄγγελος or traditional Jewish proper designation) is/are addressed in some form. The names of Jews angels occur in other, distinguishable, contexts; see e.g. *PGM* VII, 927-30 ("the great commander-in-chief Michael" brings the one reciting the formula with the divinit-y/ies listed) and XXIIa, 18-27 (the reciter requests to be endowed with attractive characteristics attributed to Iao, Sabaoth, Lailam, Barbaras, Michael, and Gabriel).

[446] *Jewish Symbols*, 2.194.

Iaeo." In another formula (129-61) the one reciting it, while identifying himself with "Adam," conjures "by the god Iao, by the god Abaoth, by the god Adonai, by the god Michael, by the god Souriel, by the god Gabriel, by the god Raphael, by the god Abrasax..., by the lord god Iaiol, by the god lord Chabra(ch)..."

PGM III, 187-262--Spell for revelation. The hymnic prayer, to be "recited to Helios" (197), calls upon "King Semea" (206), "Titan... flaming messenger (ἄγγελος) of Zeus, divine Iao" (211-12), "you ...who rule heaven's realm, O R[aphael]"[447] (213), "Abrasax" (213), "M[ichael], your helper, who saves..." (214-15).

PGM IV, 1928-2005--Spell of attraction in King Pitys' petition to Helios. The initial invocation begins: "I call upon you, lord Helios, and your holy angels (τοὺς ἁγίους σου ἀγγέλους), on this day, in this very hour: Preserve me (sing. διάσωσόν), NN, for I am Thenor, and you (ὑμεῖς) are holy angels, guardians of the Ardimalecha" (1930-37).

PGM VII (papyrus, 3rd-4th cent.'s CE), 255-59--Demand for dream-oracle ('Ονειραιτητόν; see 250), spoken to a lamp: "Hail, lord, lamp, you who shine beside Osiris and shine beside Osirchentechtha and my lord, the archangel Michael (τῷ κυρίῳ μου, τῷ ἀρχαγγέλῳ Μιχαήλ)...., show (sing. δεῖξον) me..."

PGM VII, 973-80--Love spell of attraction. After performing specified actions, one is to recite twice the following spell: "Thobarrabau Michael Michael Osiris Phor Phorba Abriel Seseggenbarpharagges Iao Sabaoth Adonaie Lailam, compel (ἐπαναγκάσατε) her, NN,...".

PGM VII, 1009-1016--For divination by dream. The formula: "I call upon [you], Sabaoth, Michael, Raphael and you, [powerful archangel] (δυ[νατὲ ἀρχάγγε]λε) Gabriel, do not [simply] pass by me (plur. παρέλ<θ>ατε) [as you bring visions], but let one of you enter (sing. εἰσερχέσθω) and reveal [to me] concerning the NN matter, Aiai Achene Iao."

PGM VII, 1017-1026--Request for strength: "Hail Helios!] Hail, Helios! Hail, [Gabriel (Γα[βριήλ)! Hail Raphael! Hail,] Michael! Hail, whole [universe! Give me] the [authority] and power of Sabaoth, ...Grant (sing. δός) me victory..."

PGM XIII (papyrus, 4th cent. CE), 254-61--Spell to make Helios appear, in which the user is identified with Yahweh: "I am he on the two cherubim, between the two natures, heaven and earth, sun and moon, ... Appear to me, O archangel (ὁ ἀρχάγγελος) of those subject to the cosmos, ruler Helios, set in authority under the One and Only Himself. The Eternal and Only orders you."

PGM XXXV (papyrus, 5th cent. CE), 1-42--Charm for favor and victory: "I call upon you, who sit over the Abyss, Bythath; I also call upon the one who sits in the first heaven, Marmar; ...you, who sit in the 2nd heaven, Raphael; ...you, who sit in the 3rd heaven, Souriel;... you, who sit in the 4th heaven, Iphiaph; ...you, who sit in the 5th heaven, Pitiel; ...you, who sit in the [6th] heaven, Mouriatha." Further invocations follow to Telze, Edanoth, Saeseschel, Tabiym, Bimadam, Chadraoun ("you..., who sit in the midst of Chadrallou, in between the two cherubim and seraphim, as they

---

[447] See *PGM*, I, 40-41: 'Ρ[αφαήλ], not Michael (as in I, 301); cf. *EPGM*, p. 24 and n. 49.

praise you, the lord of the whole host which is under heaven"). All these (ὑμᾶς) are conjured "by the god of Abraham, Isaac, and Jacob" and, later, "by the god Sarachael, Biliam, and the god who made heaven and earth and everything in it."

PGM XXXVI (papyrus, 4th cent. CE), 36-67--Charm for curbing anger and for gaining victory in litigation. Invoked are: "Iao, Sabaoth, Adonai, Eloai, Abrasax, Ablanathanalba, Akrammachamari, Pephtha, Phoza, Phnebennouni, supreme angels (κύριοι ἄγγελοι)" to "give (plur. δότε)" the advantage desired.

PGM XXXVI, 295-311--Love spell of attraction. The spell recounts the events at Sodom and Gomorrah and then invokes the sulfur rained upon these cities to cause a woman to be overwhelmed by attraction. The spell concludes with adjuring the sulfur "by the great Pap Tapheiao Sabaoth Arbathiao Zagoure Ragoure, and by the great Michael Zouriel Gabriel Sesengenbarpharanges Istrael Abraam..."

PGM XLIII (papyrus, 5th cent. CE), 1-27--Amulet against fever. Many, figures, mostly with "Jewish" names, are invoked: Emanouel, Asouel, Marmarel, Melchiel, Ouriel, Thouriel, Marmarioth, Athanael, Aoe..., Sabaoth, Adonai, Eloai, Abo..., Sesengen, Sphranges, Michael, Sabaoth, Lapapa, ...Gabriel, Souriel, Raphael.[448] Cf. further PGM XLIV and XLVIII.

PGM LXXIX (papyrus, 3rd-4th cent.'s CE), 1-7--Charm for curbing anger, the text of which is to be spoken three times: "I am the soul of darkness, Abrasax, the eternal one, Michael, but my true name is Thoouth, Thoouth. Restrain the angel and wrath [of him, NN] toward me, NN, [with] the authority of the great god Neouphneioth."

PGM LXXX (papyrus, 3rd-4th cent.'s CE), 1-5--Same as PGM LXXIX.

Angelicus M. KROPP's collection of Coptic texts, XLVII--A lengthy charm (431 lines), with Christian elements in its present form, summoning assistance from "Father, Only One, Pantokrator" (I,6), "holy angels" (I,19-23 listed by name with functions in II,4-III,6). God--variously designated Iao, Sabath, Adonai, Eloi, Pantokrator, etc., "who has assumed the face of Gabriel"--is praised as "above the angels and archangels" (IV,9). Many of the adjurations or appeals (παρακαλεῖν) are addressed to "Gabriel" the "angel (ἄγγελος) of righteousness (δικαιοσύνη) (IV,10; V,12).[449]

These texts allow for several considerations which may provide the basis for further study. First, it is difficult, if not impossible, to determine in some instances the origin of the Jewish motifs which are attested. Of each of the sources one could ask several questions: Were Jewish magicians responsible, either directly or ultimately, for the use of such material? Does the use of, for example, pagan names exclude the possibility of Jewish

---

[448] It is not clear whether these names represent a plurality of figures or were considered different names for one deity (the imperative. vb. is sing.: δ]ιαφύλαξον.

[449] See KROPP, Koptische Zaubertexte, 1.63-78 (text); 2.176-99 (translation with bibliography) and GOODENOUGH, Jewish Symbols, 2.174-90 (translation with notes).

provenance? Or are we simply dealing with a pagan source, in which non-Jewish magicians have drawn upon traditionally Jewish names (divine and angelic) and motifs in order to enhance the efficacy of their formulations? By what criteria can one be led to such attributions? Is is legitimate at all to inquire after Jewish provenance, given the syncretistic nature of these documents?[450] Whereas GOODENOUGH was often over-optimistic in being able to distinguish between pagan and Christian sources with Jewish influence and Jewish sources with pagan influence,[451] ALEXANDER has argued that "a high or totally Jewish content" may serve as one indicator that a given text can be classified as "Jewish" in its present form.[452] From this vantage point it seems that not only the use of names, but also the recapitulation of motifs from the history of Israel would be significant indicators of a Jewishness, *if not in the present form then just underlying the text as preserved*. If ALEXANDER's criterion is strictly applied, then the texts in *PGM* VII (1009-1016), XXXV, XXXVI (295-311), and KROPP's no. XLVII represent the best claim to preserving apotropaic invocations of angels within a Jewish context.

Second, the use of plural and singular pronouns and verbs may be worth noting. The invocations of angels in *PGM* VII (973-80, 1009-1016), XXXV, and XXXVI (36-67), which contains plural forms of address, betray no conscious effort to preserve a monotheistic tone. In other texts cited above, despite an address to angels and other figures, the authors hold tenaciously to singular forms: IV (1928-2005-to Helios and "your holy angels") and VII (255-59-to Osiris and Michael, 1017-1026-to Helios and Jewish angels). In each instance of the latter case, the invoked names of an angel or angels, much like some of the materials examined above (Tob 11:14; inscriptions from Rheneia and Kalecik) follow upon the mention of a primary deity (who remains, in effect, the one addressed. Moreover, such would accord with our emphasis on the interest in preserving monotheistic framework in materials which likewise show a particular interest in angels. However, this may simply be a formal similarity and the text in *PGM* VII (1017-1026) shows no signs of being Jew-

---

[450] See ALEXANDER, "Incantations and Books of Magic," p. 346: "It is not yet possible to draw a hard and fast line between Jewish and pagan magic in late antiquity; in fact, given the fundamental syncretism of magic, it may be misguided in principle to do so." That syncretism played a role in the invocation of angels in magical texts cannot be excluded from consideration, as the motif in the certainly pagan formula in *PGM* I, 42-195 as cited above suggests; see also KROPP, *Kopitische Zaubertexte*, no.'s 1 and 4.

[451] See esp. GOODENOUGH, *Jewish Symbols*, 2.164-207.

[452] ALEXANDER, "Incantations and Books of Magic," p. 346.

ish. Whether the preservation of singular forms may be explained as Jewish influence remains for now an open question, since it depends on an analysis of similar linguistic features within the magical sources as a whole.

Third, that Jews during the Amoraic period *did* invoke angels within the context of magic seems confirmed by the existence of the Hebrew *Sefer ha-Razim*,[453] a collection of magical spells, parts of which can be confidently dated at least to sometime during the 4th century CE.[454] As SCHÄFER has insisted,

---

[453] We confine our comments to this work since other known Jewish works containing magical materials, such as *Ḥarba de-Moshe* and *Sefer ha-Malbush*, preserve no positive indices suggestive of such an early date. Concerning *Ḥarba de-Moshe*, see ALEXANDER, "Incantations and Books of Magic," p. 351 and, for the two versions, see SCHÄFER, *Synopse*, par. 598-620 (in Heb with Aram title: mss New York 8128 and Oxford 1531) and 640-50 (a shorter version in Aram: New York 8128) and p. VII.

On the basis of numerous appeals to YHWH and traditional angelic names, a connection with Jewish magicians has been assumed for many of the incantation bowls and amulets edited by James A. MONTGOMERY, *Aramaic incantation texts from Nippur* (Publications of the Babylonian Section, 3; Philadelphia: The University Museum, 1913); ISBELL, *Corpus of the Aramaic Incantation Bowls* (see section II.A.1.b, n. 69 above), 72 texts; and Joseph NAVEH and Shaul SHAKED, *Amulets and Magic Bowls. Aramaic Incantations of Late Antiquity* (Jerusalem/Leiden: Magness and Brill, 1985), 36 texts from Palestine, Syria, Mesopotamia and the Cairo Geniza. On the basis of paleography, orthographic features and *Zeitgeist*, these materials have most often dated by scholars since MONTGOMERY to anywhere between the fourth and seventh centuries CE; see ISBELL, *Corpus of the Aramaic Incantation Bowls*, p. 6 and n. 33. Despite the proliferation of designations for Jewish angels and the God of Israel and the frequent allusions to religious events of Israel on the bowls, the conspicuous lack of Jewish names among clients and the relatively small Jewish population in Mesopotamia and Iran suggested for NAVEH and SHAKED that Jewish magicians were often commissioned by pagans and Zoroastrians to provide formulaic spells for curses, cures, or protection (*Amulets and Magic Bowls*, p. 18).

[454] The editor, Mordecai MARGOLIOTH, attempted to argue for a date of composition no later than the 3rd cent CE; see *Sepher ha-Razim, A Newly Recovered Book of Magic from the Talmudic Period, Collected from Genizah Fragments and Other Sources* (Jerusalem: American Academy for Jewish Research, 1966) 23-28 (in Hebrew); at this stage of writing the edition was no longer available and, therefore, some comments must depend upon the observations of others. The statement --"These are the angels who are obedient in each matter during the first and second year of the indiction [=15-year cycle] according to the reckoning of the kings of Greece."--was interpreted by MARGOLIOTH as referring to a cycle already adopted in Egypt in 211 CE; see also SĒD, "Le *Sefer Ha-Razim* et la méthode de 'combinaison des lettres'," *REJ* 130 (1971) 295-304 and Joseph DAN, Review of MARGOLIOTH, *Sefer ha-Razim*, *Tarb* 37 (1967/ 1968) 209. Most scholars, however, seem inclined to follow A.S. ROSENTHAL's suggestion (*ibid.*, pp. 24-25) that the 15-year cycles refer the one either inaugurated by Diocletian in Egypt (297 CE) or by Constantine (312 CE); see e.g. Ch. MERCHAVYA, "Razim, Sefer Ha-," in *Encyclopaedia Judaica*, 13.1595; Johann MAIER, "Das Buch der Geheimnisse," *Jud* 24 (1968) 110; GRUENWALD, *Apoc-*

there are persisting uncertainties concerning the original text and structure of the work,[455] and in these respects Mordecai MARGOLIOTH's edition can only be used with extreme caution.[456] Nevertheless, it seems safe to observe that the manuscripts used for MARGOLIOTH's reconstruction contain (1) invocations to angels in magical incantations and (2) place at least some of them within the ordered framework of seven heavens.[457] Among the invocation of non-Jewish deities such as Aphrodite, the moon and Hermes,[458] there is a short prayer to Helios transliterated from Greek into Hebrew.[459] The absence of conspicuously Jewish motifs in this prayer illustrates well both the syncretistic nature of magic and attests the degree to which a Jewish author could simply take over pagan material. Given the apparent Jewish influence on invocations of Helios in the PGM corpus (III, 187-262; esp. VII, 1017-1026 and XIII, 254-61 [here Helios=ὁ ἀρχάγγελος]), it is reasonable to think that this motif was taken up

---

alyptic and Merkavah Mysticism, p. 226; and ALEXANDER, "Incantations and Books of Magic," pp. 348-49.

[455] See SCHÄFER, Synopse, p. VIII: "Dieser 'klassische' magische Text ...ist ein Musterbeispiel für eine verfehlte Editionspraxis, die einen Originaltext suggeriert." SCHÄFER, in referring to the critical work of J.-H. NIGGEMEYER, calls for an non-homogenizing edition "which represents clearly the state of the different manuscripts and fragments of manuscripts, and which does not promote the illusion of a uniform text"; see "Tradition and Redaction in Hekhalot Literature," in Hekhalot-Studien, p. 15.

[456] See further ALEXANDER, "Incantations and Books of Magic," p. 349 and GRUENWALD, Apokalyptic and Merkavah Mysticism, pp. 226-27 and 234.

[457] Cf. ALEXANDER, "Incantations and Books of Magic," pp. 347-48 who argues for the essential literary integrity of the work.

[458] See ibid., p. 349.

[459] See MARGOLIOTH, Sepher ha-Razim, p. 12 (and p. 98, under IV, 61-63). The text of MARGOLIOTH is, along with the context (oaths formulae addressed to angels, beginning with Abrasax, which accompany the sun [שמש] on its path), cited in extenso by MAIER, "Die Sonne im antiken Judentum," in ANRW II.19.1, pp. 375-76, n. 136 (IV, 25-72; translation, pp. 377-80); see also Morton SMITH, "Helios in Palestine," EI 16 (1982) 210*. For an attempted transliterations back into Greek, see e.g. MARGOLIOTH, Sepher ha-Razim, p. 12, Mary DEAN-OTTING, Heavenly Journeys. A Study of the Motif in Hellenistic Jewish Literature (JU, 8; Frankfurt/Bern/New York: Lang, 1984) 146, and Michael A. MORGAN, Sepher Ha-Razim. The Book of the Mysteries (SBLTT 25, PS 11; Chico, CA: Scholars, 1982) 71 n. 21. The invocation of Helios begins as follows (transcription from MARGOLIOTH and DEAN-OTTING; departures in MORGAN are noted in square brackets): εὐσεβῶ [εὐσεβὴς] ἀνατολικὸν Ἥλιος, ναύτης ἀγαθός, πιστοφύλαξ [πιστὸς ἀκτῶν], κορυφαῖος εὔπιστος (ὕψιστος?), ὅς (sic!) πάλαι τροχὸν ὄβριμον (οὐράνιον?) καθίστης, κοσμητής (κοσμώντης?) ἅγιος, πολοκράτωρ (πολυπράκτωρ?), κύριε, πομπὸς εὔφωτος, τύραννος, ἀστροθητής [στρατιώτης].

by Jewish magicians well before the 4th century.[460] Thus, while it is problematic to assume that prayer to angels in magical texts is an indication of Jewishness, it is equally precarious to suppose that Jews *could not* have used material in such a non-Jewish form (cf. the angels alongside Helios in *PGM* IV, 1928-2005 and VII, 1017-1026).

Fourth, the invocation of angels in these materials should not be taken to constitute a form of veneration. In hardly any of the cases cited above can it be said that angelic beings from Jewish tradition hold a primary position.[461] Thus the matter should not be treated in isolation from the conjunction of angels with other figures, such as the Jewish God and pagan deities. In any case, given the coercive nature of the materials, "veneration" is hardly an appropriate term to describe a posture towards any of the deities invoked.[462] Perhaps a better question would be why angels from Jewish tradition could be included in many of the magical formulae to begin with. In addition to speculation concerning complementary angelic figures within Jewish tradition, developments in the direction of dualistic and gnostic cosmological thought should also undergo examination as sources for underlying presuppositions.[463] A precise analysis of the latter problem would take us far afield from the concerns of the present study.

III. SUMMARY

A. *A Veneration of Angels in Early Judaism?*

The foregoing investigation into the problem of angel veneration in early Jewish sources allows for the following observations. A *veneration of angels* among Jewish (and Jewish-Christian) circles is perceptible in several forms: (1) invocation of angels for assistance, vengeance or protection (Rhe-

---

[460] It is relevant to note the representations of Helios (on his chariot) preserved in mosaics on the floors of several synagogues in Palestine from the 4th to the 6th cent.'s CE; see the discussion by SMITH, "Helios in Palestine" 199*-214*.

[461] This is as true in the incantation bowls as in *PGM*.

[462] *Contra* MARGOLIOTH's conclusion that the posture shown, among others, to Helios (whom the editor considers an angelic being) indicates that the author worshiped angels (*Sefer ha-Razim*, p. 14).

[463] The problem may be formulated as follows: To what extent can the function of angelic figures from Jewish tradition be said to presuppose demonology? Is SIMON (*Verus Israel*, p. 346) correct in maintaining that "Angelology and demonology are inseparable."?

neia-divine vengeance; Eumeneia-protection of tomb; however, calls for protection, vengeance, or help in mundane matters is clearly coercive in the magical texts); (2) reverence of angels whose heavenly worship is exemplary (*Shirot 'Olat ha-Shabbat*); and (3) expressions of thanksgiving in response to various functions or activities attributed to angels. In the last-mentioned category angels are placed alongside God in predicative blessing formulae (11QBer-the presence of angels guarantees the community's well-being; Tob 11:14-15-response to healing by Raphael; *Jos.Asen.* 15:12-after the angel's announcement of divine acceptance of Aseneth's conversion; *T.Levi* 5:5-6-for angel's role as intercessory and protector), while in other texts the reason for such is either unknown or must be inferred (respectively, the Kalecik epigraph-a dedicatory inscription; *Ps-Philo* 13:6-feast of trumpets is an offering to the watchers).

How is this "evidence" to be interpreted? First, the materials are without doubt quantitatively incomplete. Hence we cannot expect them to convey everything or even the bulk of what was thought about the veneration of angels among Jews and Christians during the early part of the common era. Perhaps future finds will augment the extant sources and illuminate areas which cannot be more completely addressed in this study. Second, the analysis above makes it in any case apparent that the magical materials from antiquity by no means exhaust the sources relevant for a consideration of the question of angel veneration in Jewish contexts. Third, though none of these instances can be firmly labelled as "cultic devotion" to angels, some of them seem to apply venerative language to angels *within a cultic context* (*Shirot 'Olat ha-Shabbat*; 11QBer; *Ps-Philo* 13:6). Fourth, the questions of date, provenance, and purpose of the materials reviewed suggest a phenomenon that cannot be confined to one geographical location, or identified as a characteristic practice of a particular group or time. Any attempt to produce an overall assessment should thus proceed with caution. Therefore, on the basis of the texts it would be hasty for one to speak of *the* veneration of angels in Early Judaism. The relevant sources do not allow us to infer a common practice, but rather seem to reflect *specific* contexts within which worship toward angels, in a variety of forms, could find expression.

Despite the variety of genre, date, and context, the texts reviewed (the magical texts aside) have shown a remarkable consistency on one point: Angel veneration is not conceived as a substitute for the worship of God. Indeed, most often the venerative language is followed by an explanation which emphasizes the supremacy of God (*Shirot*-כי clause in 4Q400 2 l. 4; *Ps-Philo*

13:6; Tob 11:15-ὅτι αὐτός) and, in the case of concise liturgical formulations (blessings and invocations), angels frequently appear after God as the second element in the construction (11QBer 11.4-5; Tob 11:14; Jos.Asen. 15:12, 12x; T.Levi 5:6; inscriptions from Rheneia, Kalecik, and Eumeneia).[464] For this reason, it is misleading to link the existence of angel veneration in Early Judaism with a weakened sense of monotheism.[465]

The *polemical texts* direct their warnings against worshiping angels in thematic settings sometimes compatible with those of the "non-polemical" sources. Certain contexts were thought to be capable of breeding an unhealthy posture which threatened monotheistic belief: (1) the invocation of a prominent angel "in a time of distress" (*j.Ber.* 9:13a-עת צרה; cf. *T.Levi* 5:5-ἐν ἡμέρᾳ θλίψεως; Rheneia inscription?); (2) observation of or participation in angel worship (Col 2:18; *Apoc.Zeph.* 8:1-4; *Asc.Isa.* 7:15-37 and 8:3,17-22; Rev 19:1-9; cf. *Shirot*, 4Q400 2 1 and 4Q403 1 i 31-33); (3) angelophany, often during an ascent to the divine throne (Tob 12:16-22; *Apoc.Zeph.* 6:11-15; *Asc.Isa.* 7:18-23, 8:3; *2 En* 1:4-8; 20:1-4; *3 En* 16:1-5; *Apoc.Gosp.Mt.*; cf. *Jos.Asen.* 15:11-12); and (4) in settings with "cultic" overtones (*t.Hull.* 2:18; *b.Hull.* 40a; cf. *Ps-Philo* 13:6; 11QBer; *Shirot*[466]). Nevertheless, it is tenuous to explain any one of these traditions as mere references to a practice of venerating angels. As has been observed in relation to ARISTIDES' *Apology*, the veracity of charges leveled in polemical traditions is suspect by its very nature. If there is any element of truth to the claims made, the actual practice is milder and the problem seen by someone on the "outside" is

---

[464] Whereas the blessing formula arose from Jewish prayer, the mention of God and angels with an intervening καί in the texts from Rheneia, Kalecik, and Eumeneia corresponds in form with the Stratonikeian inscriptions; see n. 388 above.

[465] HURTADO (e.g., *One God, One Lord*, p. 27) and BOUSSET-GRESSMANN (*Religion des Judentums*, p. 329), despite differing definitions and conclusions, closely link the two questions. In "What Do We Mean by 'First-Century Jewish Monotheism'?" (p. 355), HURTADO correctly proposes that "monotheism" in Jewish antiquity be understood primarily in terms of "how they [Jews] describe themselves," so that the "flexibility and variety in forms of monotheistic religion" can be taken into account. However, HURTADO may in the end be drawing the line of a strict monotheism too narrowly when he plays down or ignores evidence for the application of venerative language to angels in the early Jewish texts.

In two inscriptions, one from Stratonikeia and one from Temrek, dedications are only made to an angel; moreover, the tomb epigraphs at Thera, may reflect the invocation of an angel against thieves. None of these materials can, however, is clearly of Jewish or Christian provenance.

[466] The *Shirot* apply here insofar as they were intended for use within the worship context of the Qumran community.

not recognized as such by the ones accused. Thus a better case for correlating a polemic with a specific practice or attitude can be made if both occur in the same document, whether it be a matter held in tension by an author or a phenomenon that can be traced within different extant recensions (*T.Levi*; *T.Dan*; Tob; *Jos.Asen.*).[467]

If it is impossible to forge connections among the scattered references to the veneration of angels, some of the polemical statements may be grouped into interrelated traditions. Such may be observed in midrashic developments of known traditions (extension of proscriptions against idolatry in rabbinic literature) or constitute a new tradition specifically formed in relation to a visionary context (the refusal tradition). In other words, polemics against angel worship as found in various texts sometimes show such an affinity with each other that their character as *a tradition* should be taken seriously (cf. ARISTIDES' *Apol.* 14 and the *Kerygma Petrou*; see also the refusal tradition). This raises the problem of whether in each instance one has to do with a real polemic or with a popular motif adapted into an argument as a literary-rhetorical form. In the latter case, the polemic can function as an author's effort to prevent his message from being misinterpreted or provides a way of legitimizing the medium chosen to communicate to his readers.

As discussed in II.A.2 above, several elements in the refusal tradition suggest that the writer and readers valued common ideas: the glorious appearance of angels, the genre of ascent to the divine throne, and an interest in, among other things, the angelic worship of God. The polemical statements may be easily explained as a critique of ideas based on these shared traditions rather than of idolatrous practices by "outside" individuals or groups. The same may be said of the later polemic against invoking angels in *j.Berakoth* 9:13a, in which angelic mediation is not categorically rejected, as well as of warnings against confusing the angel in Exodus 23:20 with God (*Exod.R.* 32:4; *b.Sanh.* 38b).

B. Angelology and Christology

As the polemicizing statements in Colossians and Hebrews make clear, already within the first century some Christian writers considered angelological ideas and practices to be in conflict with Christ's soteriological and cosmological preeminence. The polemic taken over by the author of Hebrews

---

[467] Section II.B.2 (pp. 164-180).

(1:3b-2:10) presupposes a conflation or comparison of Christ with angels, a tendency which we meet again in late first-century and early second-century Christian literature.

The polemical texts against the veneration of angels and angelological ideas could function to safeguard Christology (in Christian writings) as well as monotheism (in Jewish and Christian writings). Significantly, both the refusal tradition (for instance, in *Asc.Isa.*; *Apoc.Zeph.*; *2 En*; and Rev) and angelological portraits of Christ (Jude?; *Gosp.Th.*; *Rev.Elch.*; JUSTIN MARTYR; Rev) seem to have flowered toward the end of the first and into the second century. In addition, corresponding to the interest in angels generally, a number of documents and recensions which give expression to some form of angel veneration probably took shape during this period (*Ps-Philo*; *Jos.Asen.*; later recension of *T.Levi*), that is, approximately when the Apocalypse of John in its final form was taking shape. Finally, a number of the angelological motifs encountered in the analysis above are also taken up in the Apocalypse itself: various forms of mediation (Rev 8:3-5; 17:1-19:9; 21:9-22:7), heavenly worship (4:8-11; 5:11-12; 7:11-12; 19:1-8; 22:3), the refusal tradition (19:10; 22:8-9), and elements of an angelomorphic Christology (1:12-17; 14:14-16). The significance of angelology for Christology and monotheistic belief in the Apocalypse of John will be explored in Part Three.

PART THREE

ASPECTS OF ANGELOLOGY AND MONOTHEISM IN THE
CHRISTOLOGY OF THE APOCALYPSE OF JOHN

I. INTRODUCTION

The analysis in Part Two has brought us to the following conclusions: Although it is possible to identify several polemical (Jewish and Jewish-Christian) traditions which labeled any form of angel veneration as a breach of monotheistic faith (II.A), those source materials in which veneration toward angels can actually be detected leave no apparent trace of an intention to compromise the worship of God (II.B). Moreover, we have also observed that in some Christian circles, the introduction of Christology into such a traditio-historical complex made the delineation between monotheism and veneration of a being alongside God a more complicated matter. In this context, on the one side, a polemic against angel veneration could be applied to underscore Christ's unapproachable position within God's *oikonomia* (*Asc.Isa.*, Rev, Col). On the other side, the authors of these writings--though sometimes less explicitly--remain concerned to formulate their diverse Christologies within a monotheistic framework. Despite such efforts in antiquity to sort out these categories, an analysis of selected passages in the Apocalypse of John furnishes reason to doubt that *Christ*-ology, *angel*-ology, and *the*-ology were always so clearly distinguished. This thesis will be tested as we examine evidence for the fluidity and retention of these distinctions and examine their function within the Apocalypse of John.

We may note at the start that worship language in the Apocalypse is exclusively directed toward God and Christ (as the Lamb), while "angels" themselves are never venerated. With reference to angelology, this very point finds an emphasis in the refusal tradition in 19:10 and 22:8-9. At the same time, the author's application of the refusal tradition, in which the angel summons the seer to "worship God" instead, raises an apparent contradiction within the Apocalypse: a stress on monotheism, on the one hand, and the worship of Christ, on the other. In attempting to explain this logical tension, it would be possible to argue that the author has absorbed his Christology into a monotheistic framework, so that the angel's exhortation to worship God in the refusal tradition is made to imply that Christ is also considered a legitimate focus of worship.[1] For instance, as is apparent in the opening ci-

---

[1] So BAUCKHAM ("The Worship of Jesus" 329) who, in emphasizing the categorical distinction between Christ and angels in the Apocalypse of John, notes that, "Implicitly the monotheistic prohibition of the worship of angels

tation of this study (p. 1), verbs and pronouns which have both God and the Lamb as possible antecedents are overwhelmingly found in the singular.[2] Yet, as increasingly emphasized in some recent studies on the Apocalypse, Christ--though never explicitly designated as ἄγγελος--can also be portrayed as an angelic figure.[3] If the author made such an association at all, it is significant that an incorporation of angelological elements into Christology does not prevent Christ from being made an object of worship.

---

does not prohibit the worship of Jesus," who "is the source, not the intermediary, of revelation." BAUCKHAM does admit that there are "traces" of an "angel-Christology" in the Apocalypse, but largely delimits their significance to the sphere of terminology (ibid. 338 n. 42).

[2] Most obviously, see the ambiguous antecedents to the forms in 11:15 (βασιλεύσει), 14:1 (γεγραμμένον), 20:6 (μετὰ αὐτοῦ), 21:22 (ἐστίν), and 22:3b-4 (οἱ δοῦλοι αὐτοῦ; λατρεύσουσιν αὐτῷ; τὸ πρόσωπον αὐτοῦ; τὸ ὄνομα αὐτοῦ). It is possible, though unclear, that in 1:1 αὐτοῦ (3X) reflects the same linguistic usage; see HOLTZ, Christologie, p. 202. The only exception to this pattern seems to be 6:17, in which some mss (e.g., ℵ,C) refer to God and the Lamb with αὐτῶν rather than αὐτοῦ (e.g., A M). BAUCKHAM ("The Worship of Jesus" 331) may be correct when he maintains that the origin of the plural form in 6:17 is would be mor explicable than a change (or, correction) to the singular. Even if the plural form were original, however, this should be considered a departure.

[3] As a figure who is made to appear among a series of angels (14:6-20) or as one who incorporates features frequently attributed to angels. Concerning the latter, see esp. ROWLAND, "The vision of the Risen Christ in Rev. i.13ff." 1-11; The Open Heaven, pp. 100-103; "Man Clothed in Linen" 99-110 (also p. 108 n. 1); and YARBRO COLLINS, "The 'Son of Man' Tradition and the Book of Revelation," in The Messiah, pp. 548-51.

The relative novelty of this development in scholarship can be explained by the sharp reaction among scholars during and after World War Two against WERNER's one-sided thesis that as long as early Christian communities held the parousia to be imminent, Christ was primarily regarded as an angel (Entstehung des christlichen Dogmas, pp. 302-321). See esp. W. MICHAELIS, Zur Engelchristologie im Urchristentum. Abbau der Konstruktion Martin Werners (GBTh, 1; Basel: Majer, 1942); W.G. KÜMMEL, "Das Urchristentum," ThRund 17 (1948-1949) 108-111; Georg KRETSCHMAR, Studien zur frühchristlichen Trinitätstheologie (BHT, 21; Tübingen: J.C.B. Mohr [Paul Siebeck], 1956) 220-22; BARBEL, "Anhang" in Christos Angelos, pp. 347-48; H.R. BALZ, Methodische Probleme der neutestamentlichen Christologie (WMANT, 25; Neukirchen-Vluyn: Neukirchen, 1967) 208; and Aloys GRILLMEIER, Christ in Christian Tradition, vol. 1 to From the Apostolic Age to Chalcedon (451), trans. John BOWDEN (Atlanta: John Knox Press, 1975²) 46-48. Similarly, see DUNN, Christology in the Making, pp. 156, 158-59, whose claim is exaggerated: "...the thesis that an angel christology was entertained in some parts of earliest Christianity has little or nothing to sustain it, and the suggestion that any NT author maintained an angel christology runs clearly counter to the evidence." This assessment is correct, if "angel christology" refers to a complex of ideas which play a decisive role in a given author's theological framework. Such, however, does not exclude the possibility that angel speculation could contribute to early Christology. On the problem of the term "angel Christology" see the following note.

Thus we phrase the the problem addressed in Part Three as follows: How are Christology and angelology in the Apocalypse interrelated, and to what extent may angelological motifs in the author's christological presentation[4] be said to account for the combination of worshiping Christ and an insistence on monotheism in the Apocalypse?

II. THE OPENING EPIPHANY IN REVELATION 1:12-20 AND ITS RELATION TO ANGELOLOGY IN THE APOCALYPSE

The first visionary encounter in the Apocalypse (1:12-20) is imbedded within two epistolary frameworks: In 1:4 a letter is commenced with an address by John to "the seven churches in Asia" followed by an extended greeting formula (vv. 4b-5a) and a doxology epitomizing Christ's function as beneficent redeemer (vv. 5b-6). The epistolary opening in 1:4-8 may have been intended to frame the document as a whole, to which the concluding benediction in 22:21 serves as the conclusion. More immediately, the epiphany of "one like a son of man" is related to the seven letters "dictated" by this figure in chapters 2 and 3. Just preceding the vision proper John, who is reintroduced in 1:9, is told to "write what you see" to the seven churches (v. 11). The commission is recapitulated in verse 19 and directly introduces each of the seven letters.[5] Thus the literary context makes it apparent that the vision itself is to be understood as an integral part of what the author wan-

---

[4] The term "angel Christology" is here deliberately avoided; it is often associated with documents in which Christ is actually designated "angel" and in which Christ as "angel" takes a prominent place in christological thought. ROWLAND ("Man Clothed in Linen" 100) is therefore correct to suggest that with reference to NT writings it would be more accurate to speak in terms of an "angelomorphic" or "angelophanic christology." See also BROX (*Der Hirt des Hermas*, pp. 490-92 and n.13), who applies the former term ("angelomorphe") to the unsystematic Christology of the *Shep.Herm.* Whether a flowering of "angelophanic Christology" can be assigned to "the earliest period," as ROWLAND and BROX maintain, remains a matter for further exploration, especially given developments in angelology which do not to occur until literature from the late-1st/early-2nd century.

[5] Note esp. the impv. γράψον in 1:11 and 19 (to the churches); 2:1, 8,12,18; 3:1,7,14. The position of the verb before an obj. relative particle in 1:11 (ὃ βλέπεις εἰς βιβλίον) and 19 (ἃ εἶδες καὶ ἃ εἰσὶν καὶ ἃ μέλλει γενέσθαι μετὰ ταῦτα) alludes to the general substance of the message (which includes the whole book), while in ch.'s 2 and 3 the impv. introduces the specific content of the letters themselves. Because of other common features between the vision and the letters (see below), there is no reason to derive the letters from another hand; *contra* Heinrich KRAFT, *Die Offenbarung des Johannes* (HNT, 16a; Tübingen: J.C.B. Mohr [Paul Siebeck], 1974) 49-50.

ted to communicate to the churches through the letters in chapters 2-3 and, more broadly, to the message of the remainder of the work.

Interpreters have frequently pointed out that a primary function of the epiphany was to legitimate John's commission to write. This observation, however, does not need to presuppose that 1:9-20 constitutes a traditional prophetic call. Unlike prophetic calls in Exodus 3:9-15, Jeremiah 1:4-10, Isaiah 6:1-8,[6] the seer neither tries to disqualify himself[7] nor does he give any indication that the commission has marked a decisive change.[8] Instead, John's status as bearer of a divine message is presupposed,[9] and he is being called *as a prophet* to a specific task.[10] The vision, then, is more than just a preface to the letters or to the rest of the book; its substance may be ultimately regarded as part of the communication itself.

The epiphany is divided into auditory (1:10-12a) and visionary (vv. 12b-20) sections, each containing near the end a commission to write (vv. 11,19). The audition is quickly overshadowed by the visionary part of the encounter. In verse 11 John is already told to write "what you *see*," and in

---

[6] *Contra*, e.g., B.G. CAIRD, *A Commentary on the Revelation of St. John the Divine* (HNTC; New York: Harper & Row, 1966) 9-26 (the first section on 1:1-20 is unreflectingly entitled "The Prophet's Call"); KRAFT, *Offenbarung des Johannes*, p. 38 and Robert T. MOUNCE, *The Book of Revelation* (NICNT, 17; Grand Rapids: Eerdmans, 1977. So E. LOHMEYER, *Die Offenbarung des Johannes* (HNT, 16; Tübingen: J.C.B. Mohr [Paul Siebeck, 1926) 11-12; HARTMANN, "Form and Message," in *L'Apocalypse johannique*, pp. 141-42; Ulrich B. MÜLLER, *Die Offenbarung des Johannes* (ÖTKNT, 19; Gütersloh: Mohn, 1984) 80; and Martin KARRER, *Die Johannesoffenbarung als Brief* (FRLANT, 140; Göttingen: Vandenhoeck & Ruprecht, 1986) 140-41.

[7] As is also the case in Ezek 2:1-3:11.

[8] In the latter sense, the commission differs from accounts of Paul's conversion (Gal 1:13-17; Acts 9:1-6; 22:6-10; 26:9-18).

[9] If correct, this point underscores the credibility that "John," who in 1:9 speaks of himself as "your brother and one who shares in the tribulation, kingdom, and endurance in Jesus," was known to the churches which he addressed.
  To some degree Jewish pseudepigraphal writings--such as the Enoch literature, *4 Ez*, *2* and *3 Bar*--offer a closer analogy than the Hebrew prophetic literature, since they presuppose that the figures are already known (albeit from tradition) as those who have in the past faithfully conveyed God's message.

[10] See, e.g., AUNE, "Social Matrix" 24.

verse 12a he turns expecting to *see* (βλέπειν) the voice[11] addressing him,[12] before seeing (v. 12b-εἶδον) seven golden lampstands with "one like a son of man" in their midst. Nevertheless, the auditory element continues to play an important role; it is repeatedly emphasized as the primary mode of receiving revelation for the churches addressed in the seven letters (2:7,11,29; 3:6, 13,22) which follow. In the first three chapters, then, both author and readers are portrayed as hearers. The author, however, represents himself alone as a *seer*, and it is precisely his seeing which may be indicative of the communicative import with which the opening vision has been invested.

A. A Traditio-historical Comparison

Numerous commentators have noted that the figure whom John encounters in Revelation 1 is described in terms of both divine and angelic attributes. The main biblical sources for the author's language are Daniel 7:9-14 (a throne theophany) and 10:5-6 (an angelophany). Whereas the various recensions of Daniel leave unclear the relationship between "one like a son of man" in 7:13 with either the Ancient of Days (7:9) or one of the chief angels (ch.'s 8-12), in the Apocalypse this figure is comprised of, indeed, elements from both. The extent to which material from both sections of Daniel (and portions of Ezekiel) have been taken over is indicated in the comparison below. The closest correspondences to the text of the Apocalypse are introduced in *italics*.

	Rev 1:13b-16	Dan 7:9	Dan 10:5-6; Ezek 1; 9
A.	V.13-*ἐνδεδυμένον ποδήρη*	(LXX-ἔχων περιβολὴν ὡσεὶ χιόνα λευκήν;	LXX-*ἐνδεδυμένος βύσσινα* (Theod.-βαδδιν) MT-לבוש בדים
		Theod.-τὸ ἔνδυμα αὐτοῦ ὡσεὶ χιὼν λευκόν MT-(לבושה כתלג חור	Ezekiel 9:2[13]- LXX-*ἐνδεδυκὼς ποδήρη* MT-לבש בדים

---

[11] See CHARLESWORTH, "The Jewish Roots of Christology" 19-41, esp. p. 24. The background to φωνή--whether it refer to a "hypostatic being" or not--should, however, be distinguished from the question of how the expression has been made to function within the author's presentation of "one like a son of man."

[12] Though the commission in v. 11 may very well have the entire writing in view, the visionary character of what immediately follows renders problematic the assumption that the vision actually begins in ch. 4.

[13] The text refers to an angelic "man" who acts as God's scribe.

B.	καὶ περιεζωσμένον πρὸς τοῖς μαστοῖς ζώνην χρυσᾶν	NO PARALLEL	LXX-καὶ τὴν ὀσφὺν περιεζωσμένος βυσσίνῳ Theod.-καὶ ἡ ὀσφὺς αὐτοῦ περιεζωσμένη ἐν χρυσίῳ Ωφαζ MT-ומתניו חגרים בכתם אופז
C.	V.14-ἡ δὲ κεφαλὴ αὐτοῦ καὶ αἱ τρίχες λευκαὶ ὡς ἔριον λευκὸν ὡς χιών	LXX-καὶ τὸ τρίχωμα τῆς κεφαλῆς αὐτοῦ ὡσεὶ ἔριον (CB Pap. 967+λευκὸν) καθαρόν Theod.-καὶ ἡ θρὶξ τῆς κεφαλῆς αὐτοῦ ὡσεὶ ἔριον καθαρόν MT-ושער ראשה כעמר נקא	NO PARALLEL
D.	καὶ οἱ ὀφθαλμοὶ αὐτοῦ ὡς φλὸξ πυρός	LXX-ὁ θρόνος ὡσεὶ φλὸξ πυρὸς βαδίζουσα Theod.-ὁ θρόνος αὐτοῦ φλὸξ πυρός MT-כרסיה שביבין די נור	LXX=Theod.-καὶ οἱ ὀφθαλμοὶ ὡσεὶ λαμπάδες πυρός MT-ועיניו כלפידי אש
E.	V.15-καὶ οἱ πόδες αὐτοῦ ὅμοιοι χαλκολιβάνῳ ὡς ἐν καμίνῳ πεπυρωμένης	NO PARALLEL	LXX-καὶ οἱ βραχίονες αὐτοῦ καὶ οἱ πόδες ὡσεὶ χαλκὸς ἐξαστράπτων Theod.-καὶ οἱ βραχίονες αὐτοῦ καὶ τὰ σκέλη ὡς ὡς ὅρασις χαλκοῦ στίλβοντος MT-ודרעתיו ומרגלתיו כעין נחשת קלל Ezekiel 1:7[14]- LXX-καὶ πτερωτοὶ οἱ πόδες αὐτῶν... ὡς ἐξαστράπτων χαλκός MT-רגליהם (= legs) כעין נחשת קלל Ezekiel 40:3[15]- LXX-καὶ ὅρασις αὐτοῦ ἦν ὡσεὶ ὅρασις χαλκοῦ στίλβοντος
F.	καὶ ἡ φωνὴ αὐτοῦ ὡς φωνὴ ὑδάτων πολλῶν	NO PARALLEL	LXX-καὶ φωνὴ λαλιᾶς αὐτοῦ ὡσεὶ φωνὴ θορύβου Theod.-καὶ ἡ φωνὴ τῶν λόγων αὐτοῦ ὡς φωνὴ ὄχλου

---

[14] From the description of the four living creatures.

[15] A feature attributed to the angelic guide (LXX-ὁ ἀνήρ) in Ezekiel's vision of the vision ch.'s 40-48 of the ideal temple and land.

Revelation 1:12-20 and Angelology: A Traditio-historical Comparison

		MT-הָמוֹן וְקוֹל דְּבָרָיו כְּקוֹל Ezekiel 1:24[16]- LXX-τὴν φωνὴν...ὡς φωνὴν ὕδατος πολλοῦ MT-קוֹל...כְּקוֹל מַיִם רַבִּים Ezekiel 43:2[17]- LXX-καὶ φωνὴ...ὡς φωνὴ διπλασιαζόντων πολλῶν MT-וְקוֹלוֹ כְּקוֹל מַיִם רַבִּים
G. V.16-καὶ ἡ ὄψις αὐτοῦ ὡς ὁ ἥλιος φαίνει ἐν τῇ δυνάμει αὐτοῦ	NO PARALLEL	LXX=Theod.-τὸ πρόσωπον αὐτοῦ ὡσεὶ ὅρασις ἀστραπῆς MT-וּפָנָיו כְּמַרְאֵה בָרָק Cf. LXX Judg 5:31[18]- ἡ ἀνατολὴ τοῦ ἡλίου ἐν δυναστείαις αὐτοῦ

Attributes of "one like a son of man" associated in biblical tradition with an angelic figure are as follows: *(a)* "clothed in a long robe" (see esp. Ezek 9:2); *(b)* "girded at the breast by a golden girdle" (cf. Dan 10:5 LXX= MT); *(c)* "his eyes as a flame of fire" (Dan 10:6; but cf. 7:9); *(d)* "his feet as burnished bronze, refined as in a furnace" (Dan 10:6 LXX); *(e)* "his voice as the sound of many waters" (Dan 10:6; Ezek 1:24-living creatures; but cf. Ezek 43:2); and *(f)* "his appearance as the sun" (cf. Dan 10:6). The only characteristic exclusively associated with God in the biblical tradition is "his head and hair white as wool, white as snow" (cf. Dan 7:9). Finally, in two cases the description generally corresponds to the angelophany in Daniel 10, but contains wording which is more exactly paralleled (here in italics) elsewhere in relation to God: "his eyes *as a flame of fire*" (Dan 7:9-God's throne) and "*his voice as the sound of many waters*" (Ezek 43:2-the glory of God).

B. Christ's Divinity: The "Ancient of Days" and the Old Greek Tradition to Daniel 7:13

In Revelation 1:14 the "one like a son of man" is described with elements associated with the "ancient of days" in Daniel 7:9. Some scholarly

---

[16] The text refers to the four living creatures surrounding the divine throne. The MT goes on to liken this sound to "the sound of Shaddai."

[17] The text refers to the "glory of God."

[18] The phrase describes "those who love God" (MT=LXX).

discussion has been devoted to whether Danielic tradition used by the author already contained such an identification. Moreover, it would be significant to inquire into how such a tradition may have been understood among circles in which it was circulated (II.C).

At issue are the differing Greek recensions for Daniel 7:13. The readings within the LXX (or "Old Greek") text-tradition diverge from the more literal Theodotionic recension in that the "one like a son of man" is made to come "*as* the ancient of days" (ὡς παλαιὸς ἡμέρων; Theod.=MT-ἕως παλαίου ἡμέρων, עד עתיק יומיא). Against BOUSSET, who took this reading as evidence for the belief in a pre-existent Messiah within the LXX recension,[19] James A. MONTGOMERY (1921) regarded it as a "pre-Christian" scribal error (ἕως mistaken as ὡς), thus inadvertently producing a version to which Revelation 1:14 attests.[20] In the Göttingen edition of the Greek versions of Daniel (1954), Joseph ZIEGLER, primarily on the basis of patristic citations, apparently concurred with MONTGOMERY's error-hypothesis and proposed that the original text be corrected back to ἕως (against A. RAHLFS' LXX text, based on the Syro-Hexapla [SyH] and Chisianus ms "88" [Chis.]).[21] In 1967, however, the publication of the text to Daniel 7:13 in the Cologne portion of the second-century Papyrus 967 by Angelo GEISSEN[22] (hereafter CP 967)--not included in ZIEGLER's 1954 edition[23]--provided further evidence for an original text with ὡς. The high antiquity of this manuscript makes it necessary to reconsider the ZIEGLER text, since it can no longer be argued that the reading with ὡς reflects a relatively late development in the transmission of the text. For

---

[19] *Religion des Judentums*, pp. 264-65 and *Kyrios Christos*, p. 15.

[20] MONTGOMERY, "Anent Dr. Rendel Harris's 'Testimonies'," *Exp* 22 (1921) 214-17 and *The Book of Daniel* (ICC; Edinburgh: T. & T. Clark, 1927) 304.

[21] Cf. ZIEGLER, *Susanna-Daniel-Bel et Draco* (SVTG, 16/2; Göttingen: Vandenhoeck & Ruprecht, 1954) 169-70 and RAHLFS, *Septuaginta* (2 vols.; Stuttgart: Deutsche Bibelgesellschaft, 1935) 2.914, who based his critical text on Chisianus 88 (88-9th/11th cent.'s CE) and the Syro-Hexapla (SyH-ea. 7th cent. CE; a Syr translation of the LXX column of ORIGEN's Hexapla). For a still helpful description of these mss, see H.B. SWETE in *The Old Testament in Greek* (3 vols.; Cambridge: Univ., 1912[4]) xii-xiii.

[22] *Der Septuaginta-Text des Buches Daniel. Kap. 5-12, zusammen mit Susanna, Bel et Draco, sowie Esther Kap. 1,1a-2,15 nach dem Kölner Teil des Papyrus 967* (PTA, 5; Bonn: Rudolf Habelt, 1968) 108.

[23] ZIEGLER only had available the *recto* portion of Pap. 967 which had been published by Frederic G. KENYON in *The Chester Beatty Biblical Papyri. Ezekiel, Daniel, Esther* (fascicle 7; London: Emery Walker, 1937-1938 for text and plates).

the sake of clarity in the discussion to follow, we present here the above-mentioned textual witnesses to Daniel 7:13 in synoptic format:

MT

חזה הוית בחזוי ליליא
וארו עם ענני שמיא כבר אנש אתה הוה
ועד עתיק יומיא מטה וקדמוהי הקרבוהי

Theodotion (Cod.'s Alex. and Vat.)	RAHLFS (Chis.,SyH)	ZIEGLER	CP 967
ἐθεώρουν ἐν ὁράματι τῆς καὶ ἰδοὺ μετὰ τῶν νεφελῶν τοῦ οὐρανοῦ ὡς υἱὸς ἀνθρώπου ἐρχόμενος καὶ ἕως τοῦ παλαίου τῶν ἡμερῶν ἔφθασε καὶ	ἐθεώρουν ἐν ὁράματι τῆς καὶ ἰδοὺ ἐπὶ τῶν νεφελῶν τοῦ οὐρανοῦ ὡς υἱὸς ἀνθρώπου ἤρχετο καὶ ὡς παλαιὸς ἡμερῶν παρῆν καὶ οἱ παρεστηκότες	ἐθεώρουν ἐν ὁράματι τῆς καὶ ἰδοὺ ἐπὶ τῶν νεφελῶν τοῦ οὐρανοῦ ὡς υἱὸς ἀνθρώπου ἤρχετο καὶ ἕως τοῦ παλαίου ἡμερῶν παρῆν καὶ οἱ παρεστηκότες	ἐθεώρουν ἐν ὁράματι τῆς καὶ ἰδοὺ ἐπὶ τῶν νεφελῶν τοῦ οὐρανοῦ ἤρχετο ὡς υἱὸς ἀνθρώπου καὶ ὡς παλαιὸς ἡμερω(ν) παρῆν καὶ οἱ παρεστηκότες
προσήχθη αὐτῷ (Vat.=ἐνώπιον αὐτοῦ)	παρῆσαν αὐτῷ (SyH mg. προσήγαγον αὐτόν)	προσήγαγον αὐτόν	προσήγαγον αὐτῷ

Given the now early textual evidence, how can the rise of the identification of "one like a son of man" with "Ancient of Days" be explained?

In two recent and detailed examinations of this problem, Share PACE JEANSONNE (1988) and Adela YARBRO COLLINS (1992)[24] have explicated further the scribal error thesis of MONTGOMERY. According to their analysis the error, due to *homoioteleuton* with ὡς in the earlier part of verse 13, led to a series of "hyper-corrections" which, in turn, may adequately account for the differences between the Old Greek and Theodotionic versions. Until certain changes had corrupted the text (already during the first century CE), the existence of a theological interpretive tradition, whether in Jewish or Christian circles, is improbable. Despite the thorough arguments advanced by PACE JEANSONNE and YARBRO COLLINS, a closer look at the error hypothesis, as well as a consideration of the Old Greek version in Daniel 7 as a whole, suggests that an explanation of the text as a theological translation-interpretation is equally plausible.

---

[24] PACE JEANSONNE, *The Old Greek Translation of Daniel 7-12* (CBQMS, 19; Washington, D.C., 1988) 96-98. Her arguments are cited approvingly and further discussed by YARBRO COLLINS in "The 'Son of Man' Tradition," p. 554.

Excursus

PACE JEANSONNE, followed by YARBRO COLLINS, reconstructs the sequence of corruptive changes as follows: (1) as already stated above, the miscopying of εως as ως through influence from the preceding ως; (2) in order to accommodate this inadvertent change, παλαιου underwent a deliberate grammatical "correction" to the nominative παλαιος; (3) at the end of verse 13, προσηγαγον was altered to παρησαν (a secondary corruption based on the preceding form παρην); and, in order to accommodate παρησαν, (4) corresponding to (3), αυτον (as in Cod. Alex.=MT) was altered to αυτῳ.

This text-historical reconstruction is questionable on several points. First, it offers no explanation for the reading παρην (in ως παλαιος ημερων παρην), upon which the change from προσηγαγον to παρησαν (3) is based; is one to suppose that εφθασεν was altered to παρην as an accommodation to ως παλαιος? In this case, we do not have to do with a corruption through confusion through similar spelling; hence, the mere occurrence of παρην (from εφθασεν) already betrays a theological intentionality.

Second, no matter how one interprets the presence of ὡς, it is difficult to conceive of the change from παλαιοῦ to παλαιός apart from any theological intentionality.[25] Thus, contra PACE JEANSONNE and YARBRO COLLINS, who tend to find a theologically useful recension only *after* change (2), theological reflection appears to have been already operative at the level of (1)-(2), that is, very close to the stage at which the Old Greek version emerged. Of course, it remains difficult, if not impossible, to determine exactly when theological reflection influenced the text and at what point a text has been corrupted through copying errors. At stake is ultimately whether the identification of the "one like a son of man" with the "ancient of days" occurred during the process of translation or, as PACE JEANSONNE and YARBRO COLLINS, occurred through an unintentional error which was later put to theological use. In favor of the latter would be the readings in Syro-Hexapla and Codex Chisianus, which contain a recension secondary (v. 13-παρησαν) to that of CP 967 (προσηγαγον, closer to the verb in Aram. MT הקרבוהי), thus allowing one to suppose that with time errors of textual transmission moved the recension further away from the original source.

This notion leads to a third problem: What PACE JEANSONNE and YARBRO COLLINS regard as a sequential corrective change (3-4) presupposes that the text in CP 967 is corrupt. Indeed, παρησαν in the Syro-Hexapla and Codex Chisianus is quite probably secondary (as an attempt at correction) to CP 967's combination of προσηγαγον with αυτῳ, and one might be predisposed to conclude that with time errors of textual transmission moved the Old Greek recension further away from the original source of translation. But does this exclude the possibility that CP 967 itself offers a coherent text? The verb in CP 967 does not necessarily require a direct object and, if one takes προσηγαγον αυτῳ seriously, the mere presence of αυτῳ does not necessarily require παρησαν in the text.

Fourth, the scribal error hypothesis espoused by PACE JEANSONNE and YARBRO COLLINS requires that changes (3)-(4) arose independently of (1)-(2). This supposition does not explain why παρησαν (see change 3) reflects closely the sense of ως παλαιος.

Finally, and perhaps most in favor of the translation hypothesis, is that the identification of the "one like a son of man" with the "ancient of

---

[25] See Chrys C. CARAGONIS, *The Son of Man. Vision and Interpretation* (WUNT, 38; Tübingen: J.C.B. Mohr [Paul Siebeck], 1986) 62.

days" in CP 967 coincides with further details from the surrounding context of Daniel 7 in the Old Greek version (see below).

An effort to take seriously the theological nature of the LXX was attempted by F.F. BRUCE, whose discussion does reflect knowledge of the CP 967 reading,[26] and by J. LUST.[27] The latter has gone so far as to hypothesize that CP 967 follows an original Hebrew *Vorlage* to Daniel 7:13 and that the MT Aramaic and Theodotionic traditions contain the derivative versions.[28] LUST ascribes the identification of "one like a son of man" with the "ancient of days" in the supposed original version of Daniel 7 to the influence of Ezekiel 1:26, in which enthroned figure is described as "human-like." Though LUST's suggestion of an Ezekiel tradition behind the ὡς reading is plausible and his analysis provides a warning against an uncritical assumption that MT must convey the most original version, his own theory too quickly passes over the possibility that the identification of "one like a son of man" and the "ancient of days" may have occurred on the level of translation.[29]

The form of the LXX recension is conceivable as a translation which reflects a theological intention. Several considerations may be noted: (1) The identification may have resulted from the exegesis of the vision in Ezekiel 1:26, in which "a likeness as a human form" (LXX-ὁμοίωμα ὡς εἶδος ἀνθρώπου) is beheld upon "the likeness of the throne," whereas the separation of the figures in MT-Theodotion may ultimately derive from the apparent distinction between the enthroned figure in Ezekiel 1:26 and the humanlike figure distinguished from the divine throne in 8:2.[30] If this reconstruction is correct, then the LXX tradition may reflect an early monotheistic concern to safeguard against a dangerous "interpretation" of the plural "thrones" in Daniel 7:9. Other contextual elements within the Septuagintal recension, which cannot be explained as "hyper-corrections," suggest further this interpretation: (2) In

---

[26] "The Oldest Greek Version of Daniel," in eds. H.A. BRONGERS et al., *Instruction and Interpretation* (OS, 20; Leiden: Brill, 1977) 22-40, esp. pp. 25-26.

[27] "Daniel 7,13 and the Septuagint," *ETL* 54 (1978) 62-69.

[28] *Ibid.* 69: LUST concludes that MT text (=Theod.) "disturbs the parallelism" in LXX between the phrases ὡς υἱὸς ἀνθρώπου ἤρχετο and ὡς παλαιὸς ἡμερῶν παρῆν.

[29] So correctly CARAGONIS, *The Son of Man*, pp. 62-63. The Danielic recensions in the Old Greek and Theodotionic differ considerably in wording and style to the text of Daniel. Whereas the latter shows a tendency to hold rather closely to a *Vorlage*, the LXX version is often freer in style.

[30] See ROWLAND, *The Open Heaven*, pp. 96-97.

Daniel 7:21-22 the outcome of the conflict between "the horn" and "holy ones" is settled when "the ancient of days came" (MT[=Theod.]-עד די אתה עתיק יומיא; LXX-ἕως τοῦ ἐλθεῖν τὸν παλαιὸν ἡμερῶν) to render judgment. The verb "to come" does not describe the "ancient of days" in 7:9 but "one like a son of man" in verse 13.[31] (3) The occurrence of οἱ παρεστηκότες προσήγαγον (SyH, Chis: παρῆσαν) αὐτῷ at the end of verse 13[32] recalls παρειστήκεισαν αὐτῷ in verse 10, where it expresses the worship of the "ancient of days" by the myriads.[33] (4) In verse 14 the LXX manuscripts agree in having λατρεύουσα denote the worship of the "son of man" by "all the nations of the earth according to kind and every glory" (Theod.-δουλεύσουσιν).

That such a translation-interpretation tradition was open to varying interpretations may be evident in the Apocalypse. If known to the author of the Apocalypse, it has been significantly modified. In comparison to the recension of Daniel in the LXX, his identification of "one like a son of man" with the "ancient of days" is less complete. Whereas the LXX tradition tends to coalesce the figures of Daniel 7:9 and 7:13, the author draws extensively on terminology from the angelophany in Daniel 10:5-6 and reflects a knowledge of contemporary angelological motifs.

C. Christ as an Angelomorphic Being: The Tradition

The author's combination of angelic with divine features into one heavenly figure by drawing on Daniel tradition is not unique to the Apocalypse. ROWLAND has pointed out the similarity between Revelation 1:13-16 and the angelophanic encounters described in *Joseph and Aseneth* 14:8-9 and the *Apocalypse of Abraham* 10:1-11:6 (late 1st-early 2nd cent. CE).[34] In the *Apocalypse*

---

[31] Cf. v. 22 with the phraseology of v. 13-כבר אנש אתה הוה ועד עתיק יומיא מטה. The Grk translator LXX, recognizing vv. 17-28a as an interpretation of vv. 1-14, may have found support for his identification in v. 13 from the common elements--עתיק יומיא, עד, אתה--realigned in v. 22, in which עד now functions as part of a temporal expression, and עתיק יומיא becomes the subj. of אתה. It is impossible to determine the extent to which, in v. 22, the LXX version presupposes an Aram *Vorlage* different from MT.

[32] ZIEGLER's emendation to οἱ παρεστηκότες προσήγαγον αὐτόν ("and those standing by *brought him*"), on the basis of a marginal reading in SyH and JUSTIN (προσάγεται), harmonizes with the Theod.-MT recension.

[33] The whole phrase (μύριαι μυριάδες παρειστήκεισαν αὐτῷ), which occurs in all the Greek versions, is in parallel with the preceding ἐθεράπευον αὐτόν (CB 967; SyH; Chis; Theod.-ἐλειτούργουν αὐτῷ).

[34] ROWLAND, *The Open Heaven*, pp. 101-103 and "Man Clothed in Linen" 101-107. The following citations are based on a comparison of the transla-

of Abraham, an "angel...in the likeness of a human" named "Iaoel" is sent to accompany Abraham on his heavenly journey (10:4-5). In 11:2 "the hair of his [the angel's] head (was) like snow," and the mention of his "body," "clothing," and "face" (11:2-3) are all elements found in Daniel 10:5-6. Along with signs of dependence on Daniel 10, in common with Revelation is, of course, the allusion to Daniel 7:9 and 7:13 which may also presuppose the Old Greek recension.[35] The basis of the status accorded to Iaoel is that he is bearer of the divine name (11:8-cf. *b.Sanh.* 38b: Metatron). Nevertheless, this characterization of Iaoel falls short of the divine status accorded to "one like a son of man" in Revelation; in the *Apocalypse of Abraham* 17:1-2 Iaoel, who is distinguished from "a voice of many waters" (17:1; 18:2;[36] cf. Rev 1:15b), bows with Abraham and worships God. However, the portrayal of Iaoel does show that the application of divine attributes, such as "head and hair white as wool, white as snow," are consistent with developments within Jewish angelological tradition.[37]

A further reflection of contemporary angelological tradition is suggested at the close of Christ's self-introduction in 1:17c-18: "Do not fear! I

---

tions from Old Slav (the only extant version) by Gottlieb N. BONWETSCH, *Die Apokalypse Abrahams* (SGTK, 1/1; Aalen: Scientia, 1972, repr. from 1897); R. RUBINKIEWICZ, "Apocalypse of Abraham," in *OTP* 1.681-705; and Belkis PHILONENKO-SAYAR and Marc PHILONENKO, *Die Apokalypse Abrahams* (JSHRZ, 5/5; Gütersloh: Mohn, 1982.

[35] In *Jos.Asen.* 14:8-9 a link between Dan 7:13 and 7:9 is likewise apparent, though which may also presuppose the LXX-tradition. The angelic messenger from heaven seen by Aseneth is introduced as "a man" (ἀνήρ; cf. Dan 7:13), and "the hairs of his head" (αἱ τρίχες τῆς κεφαλῆς αὐτοῦ) are described "like a flame of fire of a burning torch" (ὡς φλὸξ πυρὸς ὑπολαμπάδος καιομένης; a combination of elements from Dan 7:9-"hairs of his head," "flame of fire"-and Dan 10:6-"flaming torch").

[36] It is possible that Iaoel, who has run to make peace between the living creatures (18:9), is the speaker behind the "voice...out of the midst of the fire" in *Apoc.Abr.* 19:1; so Peter KUHN, *Offenbarungsstimmen im Antiken Judentum* (TSAJ, 20; Tübingen: J.C.B. Mohr [Paul Siebeck], 1989) 97. Even were this the case, the text leaves unanswered whether this voice is identical with the "voice of many waters" (17:1) or the "voice like the roaring of the sea" (18:2). The parallel structure between 19:1 and 20:1 suggests that in the former the voice belongs to God.

[37] Thus, unless other such characteristics can be detected, this feature alone does not supply evidence for divinization *vis-à-vis* angelology; contra HOLTZ, *Christologie*, pp. 121-22 and KARRER, *Johannesoffenbarung als Brief*, p. 149 and n. 47. This is especially the case if the *Apoc.Abr.* presupposes the LXX-tradition of Dan 7:9-14. A different direction is taken in *1 En* 46:1, in which feature "his head was white like wool" is reserved for God, the "Head of days" (Eth variants do not significantly diverge; see ISAACS, "1 Enoch," in *OTP* 1.34 n. d), whereas "the Son of Man" has a countenance comparable to that of "one of the holy angels."

am the first and the last, and the living one; I died, and behold I am alive forever, and *I have the keys of death and Hades."* In the *Apocalypse of Abraham,* Iaoel identifies himself as having been commissioned "to loosen Hades and to destroy those who wondered at the dead" (10:11b). Here the elements Hades and death are integrated to suit the author's own concerns. The phrases beginning with "to loosen" and "to destroy" are in parallelism; the latter can be interpreted through 10:12 immediately following, in which Iaoel states he has punished Abraham's father because "he honored the dead." A more traditional version of the motif is preserved in the *Apocalypse of Zephaniah* 6:15. After refusing the seer's worship (6:15) the heavenly figure introduces himself as "the great angel Eremiel, *who is over the abyss and Hades."* Eremiel is invested with caring for the souls imprisoned in Hades,[38] and is contrasted with an accusing angel who tries to condemn them on account of their sins (6:17b). The christophany in Revelation is similar; Christ too is portrayed as having power over Death and Hades. The author, then, is drawing on a motif associated with a principle angel--a motif of which Revelation 20:1 ("an angel descending from heaven holding the key of the abyss") is reminiscent. In 1:17c-18, however, its significance derives from Christ's own death and resurrection. Thus Christ's self-introduction ultimately reaches beyond categories known in Jewish or Jewish-Christian angelology.

Finally, whereas the relationship in Daniel between the בר אנש in 7:13 and the "holy" ones (7:18,21,22,25,27), Gabriel (8:15-16; 9:21; perhaps 10:5, 16,18; 12:7[39]), and Michael (10:13,21; 12:1) is not clearly delineated,[40] the

---

[38] This angel actually announces to the seer, who has pleaded for mercy from God because of his sins, that he may "come up from Hades and the abyss" (7:9).

[39] In 10:5,16,18; and 12:7 "Gabriel" is not mentioned. In ch.'s 8 and 9 Gabriel is introduced as כמראה גבר (8:15-no doubt related to the proper name; LXX-ὡς ὅρασις ἀνθρώπου; Theod.-ὡς ὅρασις ἀνδρός) and referred to as האיש (9:21; LXX, Theod.-ὁ ἀνήρ); the designations איש אחד לבוש בדים (10:5; LXX-ἄνθρωπος εἷς...; Theod.-ἀνὴρ εἷς), כדמות בני אדם (v. 15; LXX-ὡς ὁμοίωσις χειρὸς ἀνθρώπου; Theod.-ὡς ὁμοίωσις υἱοῦ ἀνθρώπου), כמראה אדם (v. 18; LXX-ὡς ὅρασις ἀνθρώπου; Theod.-ὡς ὅρασις ἀνθρώπου), האיש לבוש הבדים (12:7; Theod.-τοῦ ἀνδρός...) and the continued function of this figure as an interpreter for Daniel suggest this identification, though it must remain uncertain. ROWLAND, "The Vision of the Risen Christ" 3, distinguishes too radically between the possibility of influence from Ezek 1 on the angelophany in Dan 10 and connections within the latter's literary context.

[40] Against the corporate interpretation of "one like a son of man," scholars have increasingly begun to identify him with Michael, "the great prince who stands over the children of your people" (Dan 12:1); see, e.g., ROWLAND, *The Open Heaven,* p. 182; John J. COLLINS, *The Apocalyptic Vision of the Book of Daniel* (HSM, 16; Missoula: Scholars, 1977) 144-47, 149 (n. 7) and

author of the Apocalypse more explicitly links his ὅμοιος υἱὸς ἀνθρώπου (Rev 1:13) with the angelic interpreter in Daniel 10:5-6. The designations identifying Gabriel as a human(like) figure in Daniel 8 and 9, as well as those for the angel in chapters 10 and 12, come close to the language of 7:13. The LXX tradition shows over against the Theodotionic recension a preference for ἄνθρωπος terminology, while in 10:16 the latter terms the angel ὡς ὁμοίωσις υἱοῦ ἀνθρώπου. In the Apocalypse the author has chosen an expression (as in 14:14), the form of which approximates, but is not identical with, those applied to the "son of man" in Daniel 7:13 or to angelic interpreters in 8-12. A clear allusion to any one of the passages cannot be determined.[41]

This comparison leaves the impression of a considerable continuity between the author's portrait of Christ in Revelation 1 and angelophanies preserved in biblical and developing traditions. Such may even be observed in relation to "divine" characteristics known from Daniel 7:9. Before an attempt at an explanation can be ventured, it is necessary to consider connections within the Apocalypse of John itself and their possible relation to its communicative *Sitz im Leben*.

D. Christ as an Angelic Being: Affinities Between Angels in the Apocalypse and the Opening Epiphany

The angelic character of the epiphany in Revelation 1:13-16 is underlined further by internal considerations. Some of the features found in the epiphany are associated with angels in remaining passages of the Apocalypse. Whether these traits can be explained as a transference from chapter 1 to other angels, as a transference from angels in the Apocalypse into chapter 1, or as a varying adaptation of traditional motifs depends on a consideration of each instance.

The Apocalyptic Imagination (New York: Crossroad, 1987) 82-83; YARBRO COLLINS, "The 'Son of Man' Tradition," pp. 550-51.

[41] Another possibility is argued by ROWLAND, "Man Clothed in Linen" 104, who argues (as CHARLES, *The Book of Revelation*, 2.35-36) that the identical linguistic form in 1:13 and 14:14 must be interpreted together (ὅμοιον = ὡς). Since the argument does not take into account that the usage in one passage (1:13) could have been carried over to the other, it is not entirely convincing. For the "son of man" in Rev 1:13, Cod. Alex. reads ὁμοίωμα plus dat., which in LXX Ezek 1:26 is applied to the figure on the divine throne: ὁμοίωμα ὡς εἶδος ἀνθρώπου. Taken as an improvement of a more difficult ὅμοιος (a dat. is expected), this reading is probably secondary.

1. The "Voice as the Sound of Many Waters": 14:1-5 and 19:1-8

First, among the divine attributes found in biblical tradition, the motif of a voice "like the sound of many waters" (1:15b) recurs in 14:2 (φωνήν ...ὡς φωνὴν ὑδάτων πολλῶν καὶ ὡς φωνὴν βροντῆς μεγάλης) and 19:6 (φωνήν...ὡς φωνὴν ὑδάτων πολλῶν καὶ ὡς φωνὴν βροντῶν ἰσχυρῶν). An association of these occurrences with angelology is not immediately apparent in each case.

In 14:2 the "sound of many waters" marks a transition to an audition following the seer's vision of the Lamb with the 144,000 redeemed on Mount Zion (v. 1) and refers to heavenly worship. It is not immediately clear, however, how this voice is related to the singing of the "new chant" in verse 3, that is, whether worship heard in verses 2-3 comes from angelic choirs, the 144,000, or both. In interpreting the audition as an extension of the vision (v. 1), several commentators have simply identified the "sound" as worship by the 144,000 redeemed.[42] The primary difficulty with this view is its neglect of the transition from vision to audition in verses 1-2. Moreover, that only the redeemed "were able *to learn* the chant" (v. 3) suggests that their worship is conceived in terms of *participation*,[43] whether still in the future or already actualized. An attempt to resolve the difficulty of the subject by including the redeemed in the subject of ᾄδουσιν ᾠδὴν καινήν (v. 3a) is reflected in the reading καὶ φωνὴν ἤκουσα in verse 2b (P^{47} 2053 M^A), according to which the harp music is distinguished from the foregoing sounds.[44] Even then, this is only a matter of inclusion, and the "sound of many waters..." in verse 2a does not specifically describe the worship of the 144,000. But if in verse 2b one reads καὶ ἡ φωνὴ ἣν ἤκουσα,[45] then the sound "as of harpers

---

[42] Martin KIDDLE, *The Revelation of St. John* (MNTC; London: Hodder & Stoughton, 1940) 266; MOUNCE, *Revelation*, p. 268; YARBRO COLLINS, *The Apocalypse* (NTM, 22; Wilmington, Del.: Michael Glazier, 1979) 99.

[43] Cf. *Apoc.Abr.* 18:1-3, in which "a voice like the roaring of the sea" is identified as the singing of the four living creatures under the divine throne. In 17:8-21 (see also 18:3) the seer participates in this singing, which he has learned from the angel Iaoel.

[44] KRAFT (*Offenbarung des Johannes*, pp. 187-88) takes this variant as the original, arguing that the plur. subj. of ᾄδουσιν "can only be the harp players" (v. 2b-κιθαρῳδῶν, gen.) whom he identifies with the 144,000. It is easier, however, to understand καὶ φωνὴν ἤκουσα as an attempt to resolve a *lectio difficilior* in an otherwise vague transition to the resumption of the 144,000 in v. 3b. Furthermore, it harmonizes with 15:2-3 in which those who have conquered the beast sing "the song of Moses...and the song of the Lamb" with harps.

[45] Concerning the preference of this reading, see the previous note.

playing their harps" is identical to the foregoing "sound of many waters." Thus those who sing a new chant (ᾄδουσιν ᾠδὴν καινὴν) "before the throne and before the four living beings and the elders" would most likely be a nameless angelic choir,[46] while the words to this chant can only be learned, and not yet sung, by the 144,000 (v. 3b; cf. 19:6).[47]

In contrast to the opening vision (1:15) the Lamb is not directly identified in 14:1-5 with the "voice out of heaven as a sound of many waters." The passage is focused much more on the link between the Lamb and his followers and, in this way, marks a stark contrast with the foregoing vision of the beasts. Whereas those who worship the image of the beast are entitled to buy or sell on account of being marked by his name (13:17), "those redeemed from the earth," are privileged to learn "the new chant" (v. 3).[48] The lack of clarity concerning the relationship between the Lamb and angelic choirs is due to another concern, namely, the author's interest in fully aligning the Lamb's position with that of God; the name (sing.!) of each is written on the foreheads of the 144,000 (v. 1) who are first fruits for them (v. 4-ἀπαρχὴ τῷ θεῷ καὶ τῷ ἀρνίῳ). On the basis of this passage all one can say for certain is that human participation in angelic, heavenly worship is made possible by the Lamb and is contingent upon one's status as "redeemed out of the earth."[49] Since 14:1-5 does not furnish any of the content of the new chant, it is un-

---

[46] As maintained by BOUSSET, Offenbarung Johannes (MeyerK; Göttingen: Vandenhoeck & Ruprecht, 1906²) 380-81; CHARLES, The Revelation of St. John, 2.7; Isbon T. BECKWITH, The Apocalypse of John (New York: Macmillan, 1919) 651; LOHMEYER, Offenbarung des Johannes, p. 119; J. MICHL, Die Engelvorstellungen in der Apokalypse des Hl. Johannes. Die Engel um Gott (München: Max Hueber, 1937) 220-26; HOLTZ, Christologie, p. 124; MÜLLER, Offenbarung des Johannes, p. 262; and SCHÜSSLER FIORENZA, "Visionary Rhetoric and Social-Political Situation," p. 189.

[47] See BORNKAMM, "Die Komposition der apokalyptischen Visionen in der Offenbarung Johannes," in Studien zu Antike und Urchristentum, 1.210-212, who is followed by JÖRNS, Das hymnische Evangelium, p. 124.

[48] The phrase presupposes that, as in 7:2-3, the redeemed will be protected from the destruction brought about through God's judgment (as in 7:2-3; cf. 14:13, 15:2). In the context of 14:1-5, the sharpness of this motif is heightened. In 13:11-18 those who refuse to obey the command of the second beast (who is likened to a "lamb", v. 11) to worship the image of the first are to be slain (v. 15). In 14:1-5 this process is reversed; see SCHÜSSLER FIORENZA, "Visionary Rhetoric and Social-Political Situation," p. 189. What follows is the announcement (14:6-15:4) and execution (15:5-16:21) of God's judgment, from which the redeemed are spared (14:13; 15:2).

[49] Contra Eduard LOHSE, Die Offenbarung des Johannes (NTD, 11; Göttingen: Vandenhoeck & Ruprecht, 1971) 82, who maintains that the sounds of many waters and thunderpeals "weisen hin auf die Hoheit des Lammes."

necessary to speculate on the degree to which the Lamb here would figure as the content or object of such worship.

The second instance of a sound "like the sound of many waters" occurs in the audition-vision of heavenly praise in 19:1-8 located at the climax of the vision of God's judgment over "Babylon" (17:1-18:24). The content of this worship, which is emphatically directed towards "God" (19:1,4,5,6,7), expresses thanksgiving for God's triumph over "the great whore" of Babylon (vv. 1-4) and for the establishment of God's reign which finds expression through the marriage of the Lamb with his Bride (vv. 5-8).[50] In verse 6 the seer hears "something like the voice of a great multitude" and describes it "as the sound of many waters and as the sound of strong thunderpeals." It is unclear whether the expression ὄχλος πολύς in verses 1 and 6 is meant to refer to the same group. In the first instance, whether it be angels[51] and/or[52] the redeemed faithful,[53] the worshipers do not yet consist of the living creatures and the elders (cf. 4:3), whose worship functions as a responsorium in verse 4. In verse 6, the expression comprehends "all his servants, those who fear him, the small and the great," who are summoned to praise God. The impression left by the passage is two-fold: (1) The emphasis is placed on the worship by the human faithful who have been slain (18:24; see also 11:18 and 18:20) and (2) their worship does not exclude the notion of a participation in angelic worship.[54]

As in 14:1-5, the Lamb in 19:1-8 is not identified with the "sound of many waters...," which here also specifically characterizes the worship itself. Similarly, it is the Lamb's special relation to the faithful (v. 7-"the

---

[50] The praise formulae is grounded in two parallel ὅτι-clauses which signify the correspondence between God's rule and the consummation of the redemption achieved through the Lamb.

[51] So CHARLES, *The Book of Revelation*, 2.118; LOHMEYER, *Offenbarung des Johannes*, p. 150; KIDDLE, *The Revelation of St. John*, pp. 375-80 (the worship in vv. 5-8 is also that of angels); and HOLTZ, *Christologie*, pp. 124, 167.

[52] Some interpreters leave the question open: BOUSSET, *Offenbarung des Johannes*, p. 426; MICHL, *Engelvorstellungen*, pp. 228-29; KRAFT, *Offenbarung des Johannes*, p. 242; and PRIGENT, *L'Apocalypse de Saint Jean*, p. 278.

[53] E.g., LOHSE, *Offenbarung des Johannes*, 99-100; JÖRNS, *Das Hymnische Evangelium*, p. 145; and MÜLLER, *Offenbarung des Johannes*, p. 315.

[54] On account of the emphasis here on the heavenly worship of the faithful, angelic worship is presupposed, since all the other groups are mentioned. Further, the author may not wish to distinguish angels and the faithful in heaven as before (see 19:10). The latter are, to a certain extent, "angelified"; after this passage angelic worship is no longer portrayed in the Apocalypse.

Bride") which provides the essential grounds for the praise of the great multitude. In this connection, it should not be overlooked that the "many waters" and "thunderpeals" have been placed within the christological part of 19:1-10.

Traugott HOLTZ has commented that the disjuncture between the christological application of ὡς φωνὴ ὑδάτων πόλλων in 1:15, on the one hand, and that in 14:2 (angelological) and 19:6 (anthropological), on the other, makes it difficult to regard it as a divine attribute in 1:15.[55] As noted in the comparison above, the author of the Apocalypse went beyond the angelophanic tradition of Daniel 10 for specific wording to describe Christ. In Ezekiel it is applied to the four living creatures (1:24-esp. MT) and to the glory of God (43:2), but neither association immediately apparent in either Revelation 14:2 or 19:6.

The author's use of this imagery motif is more clearly illumined by a consideration of the *Apocalypse of Abraham* 17:1-18:14. The seer "Abraham" and Iaoel are moved to worship when approached by a voice in a fire "like a voice of many waters, like a voice of the sea in uproar." This worship takes the form of a song which Iaoel teaches the seer. In 18:2-3 this voice is apparently identified with the singing of "the four fiery living creatures." The "voice" inspires the heavenly worship in which the seer, together with the angel, participates. As with the principal angel Iaoel in the *Apocalypse of Abraham*, the author of Revelation distinguishes in 14:1-5 and 19:5-8 the "sound of many waters..." from the Lamb.[56] Yet it is the Lamb, whose voice (as "one like a son of man") in 1:15b bears this characteristic, who makes learning and participating in the heavenly song possible for the faithful. Thus it seems likely that the Apocalypse of John's diverse use of this traditional element presupposes, and ultimately surpasses, a stage in which this sound was being associated with participation of the privileged faithful in angelic worship in heaven. The author adapts this idea, together with Ezekiel tradition, so that for his followers Christ becomes both the basis for and means

---

[55] HOLTZ, *Christologie*, pp. 124-25.

[56] This is done for different reasons. In *Apoc.Abr.* Iaoel is brought to worship, and there is never a question of an identification with the angel. In Rev, on the other hand, the Lamb's achieved redemption provides the essential reason for the singing.

to heavenly worship of God.[57] In this sense, Christ's function extends beyond what the author could have used in Daniel 10.

2. "Clothed" and "Girded at the Breasts with Golden Belts": The Seven Angels in 15:6

The seven angels through whom the seven plagues are unleashed are described in a way that recalls the opening epiphany. As the "one like a son of man" in chapter 1, they are "clothed" (15:6b-ἐνδεδυμένοι; 1:13b-ἐνδεδυμένον), though in "pure bright linen" (λίνον καθαρὸν λαμπρόν), whereas Christ has a long robe (ποδήρη). The clothing assigned to the angels is echoed elsewhere in the Apocalypse through the garments worn by the worshiping 144,000 in 7:9 "before the throne and before the Lamb" (περιβεβλημένους στολὰς λευκάς) and by the "Bride" of the Lamb in 19:8 (ἐδόθη αὐτῇ ἵνα περιβάληται βύσσινον λαμπρὸν καθαρόν καθαρόν), and is attributed to the heavenly armies which follow Christ in 19:14 (ἐνδεδυμένοι βύσσινον λευκὸν καθαρόν). In these passages the clothing, reminiscent of garments attributed to priests (e.g., Lev 6:10), represents the cultic purity of those who are aligned with Christ (viz. also 3:4 and 6:11).

The description of the seven angels' clothing in 15:6 is based largely on Ezekiel 9:2, in which six "men" holding an "instrument of destruction" (MT-כלי מפצו; LXX-πέλυξ) are called to act as agents of God's judgment upon the wicked of Jerusalem.[58] Significantly, the most prominent of these human-

---

[57] This is probably the sense in which the hymn in Rev 15:3b-4 is to be understood as "the song of Moses the servant of God and the song of the Lamb." The apparent incongruity of the figures Moses and the Lamb does not necessitate a hypothesis of interpolation; so already BOUSSET, *Offenbarung des Johannes*, p. 393; JÖRNS, *Das Hymnische Evangelium*, pp. 127-28; and MÜLLER, *Offenbarung des Johannes*, p. 274. Though the hymn contains no christological element, it is sung by "those who have conquered (οἱ νικῶντες) the beast and its image." From this perspective God is praised for the justice and inevitability of God's judgment. The privilege of singing the song thus assumes a position of redemption by those who are excepted (see 14:13) from the last outpouring of God's wrath through the seven plagues to follow. The gen. "of the Lamb" is neither objective (worshiping the Lamb) nor subjective (sung or written by the Lamb), but rather evokes the Lamb's function in achieving the worshipers' redemption. In this passage, the functional difference between Moses and the Lamb is expressed in the epithet "the servant of God" (which is taken from Ex 14:31). The hymn's character as "the song of Moses" stems from the typology suggested by the "glass sea mixed with fire" (= "Red Sea" in Ex 15) and victory over the beast and its image (="the Egyptians" in Ex 14:30-31).

[58] That in fact the Apocalypse has "seven" angels and not "six" (as in Ezek 9) corresponds to the symbolic significance of the number "seven" for

like angelic figures is a man "clothed in linen," for which the extant LXX tradition reads ἐνδεδυκὼς ποδήρη (9:2; see vv. 3,11[59] and cf. 10:2). If the author has adapted Ezekiel 9:2-10:2 in chapters 1 and 15, he has drawn on angelological motifs to describe both the "seven" angels in 15:5-17:1 and has applied the imagery associated with their leader to Christ in 1:13b.[60] In 17:1 it is one of these seven angels who offers to show the seer the destruction of the great harlot Babylon and who subsequently acts as the *angelus interpres* (17:7,15; 19:9). Moreover, one of this group, perhaps the same one, becomes the seer's guide through the New Jerusalem in 21:9.[61] The angelic guide

---

the author, who stresses here (ch.'s 15-16) the comprehensiveness of the divine judgment. Significantly, in Ezek 9 it is not clear whether the principal "man" who marks those to be spared from judgment (Ezek 9:4) is one of the six or is a seventh figure. This ambiguity may have opened the way for a double signification in the Apocalypse. The author could have either (a) appropriated the text as a reference to seven angelic figures, so that the prominent "man" is given a counterpart in the guiding angel in ch.'s 17-18 (19:9-10) and 21:9-22:5 (22:8-9); or (b) accommodated the number "six" to his own interest in "seven," while finding a counterpart in the "one like a son of man" in ch. 1, whose name (as the Lamb), along with that of God, marks the faithful who are to escape judgment (14:1; 22:4). (In the *Shep.Herm.*, *Sim.* 9.12.7-8, the "man" of Ezek 9 is correlated to "the Son of God," while the number of "glorious angels" in whose "midst" he appears is left at "six.") These alternatives are not mutually exclusive and may reflect one way the author used available traditions, namely, by multiplying their referents, so that the principal "man" in Ezek 9 is at once appropriated in the author's christological and angelological presentation. For further elaboration on this use of tradition, see section IV.3 below.

[59] MT-לבוש בדים. Whereas the Heb has this man holding a "writing case on his loins," the Grk refers to "a sapphire belt around his waist" (ἐζωσμένος τῇ ζώνῃ τὴν ὀσφὺν αὐτοῦ). Thus the order of LXX Ezek 9:11--being "clothed" and "girded about the waist"--corresponds to that of Dan 10:5 (=MT, LXX, Theod.) and is taken up in Rev 1:13.

[60] See n.'s 58 and 59 above. It is especially noteworthy that the prominent "man" is assigned the task of placing a "mark" (Ezek LXX 9:4,6-σημεῖον; MT-תו) upon the foreheads (τὰ μέτωπα; cf. Rev 14:1; 22:4) of those excepted from punishment.

[61] This may be implied by the parallel wording in 17:1 and 21:9: καὶ ἦλθεν εἷς ἐκ τῶν ἑπτὰ ἀγγέλων τῶν ἐχόντων τὰς ἑπτὰ φιάλας (21:9 adds, "full of the seven last plauges") καὶ ἐλάλησεν μετ᾽ ἐμοῦ λέγων δεῦρο δείξω σοι; so BOUSSET, *Offenbarung des Johannes*, p. 446 and MOUNCE, *The Book of Revelation*, p. 377 (the similar openings function to identify the angel in 21:9 and 17:1 as well as to contrast Babylon from the heavenly Jerusalem). On the basis of the contrast of the ensuing visions, CAIRD (*Revelation of St. John*, p. 269) has argued that the author wanted to refer to two different angels. The final criterion, however, should not be the visions, but indices within the language (as above), which do not point beyond "one" guiding angel. Perhaps, however, the matter should ultimately be left open. More important is the fact that the refusal tradition makes clear that the angel in 21:9 is made to share the same status as the one in 17:1; see BECKWITH, *The Apocalypse of John*, p. 756.

thus achieves a certain functional prominence in the narrative.⁶² If the Ezekiel 9 passage functioned here as a point of reference for the Apocalypse, the author has very likely made the the chief angelic figure there to serve both christological (1:13b) and angelological ends (15:6; and esp. the *angelus interpres* introduced in 17:1 and 21:9). On the basis of tradition, therefore, one may observe a connection between Christ and the guiding angel, a link which we shall attempt to interpret below (pp. 256-259) in relation to the author's representation on the level of the text.

The prominence implied by the two-fold function associated with the seven angels in Revelation 15 (agency of divine wrath and interpretation of visions) is further underscored in that, similar to the "one like a son of man" in chapter 1, they are "girded around the breasts with golden girdles" (15:6-περιεζωσμένοι περὶ τὰ στήθη ζώνας χρυσᾶς). Aside from the more obvious diferences in 1:13 exhibited by the accusative and singular participle (περιεζωσμένον), the only real verbal divergence (πρὸς τοῖς μαστοῖς) may reflect either a non-theological, stilistic variation or a subtle attempt to distinguish these angels from Christ. Whatever the case, this imagery, which is well-established within angelophanic tradition, is by no means distinctively christological in character.⁶³ Already in Ezekiel 9:2 the "man in the midst of the six" in Ezekiel 9:2 is "girded with a belt at the waist." Even closer to the language of 1:13 is the angel in the MT and Theodotionic versions to Daniel 10:5: "his waist girded about with the gold of Uphaz." The most exact parallel, however, is preserved in the *Apocalypse of Zephaniah* 6:12: "And he was girded as if a golden girdle were upon his breast" (see pp. 257-259).

---

⁶² The activity of the angelic guide is further supplemented by language from Ezek 40; see section IV.A (p. 247 and n. 123) below.

⁶³ Though such descriptions of clothing at the breast, along with the term ποδήρη in 1:13, reflect vestments frequently associated with the priesthood (e.g., Ex 28:4; Lev 6:10; and JOSEPHUS, *Ant.* 3.154,171), in angelophanies such as Dan 10 and *Apoc.Zeph.* 6, they no longer immediately imply a priestly function. HOLTZ (*Christologie*, p. 118) supposes that these features in 1:13 are indicative of Christ's "priestly character," but admits (p. 119) that this aspect is not developed any further in the Apocalypse. This absence of a development of a priestly Christology becomes explicable in part if one presupposes that the author specifically understood the imagery to be angelological.

3. "His Face as the Sun" and the "Cloud": The Angel in 10:1-11

The "strong angel" who descends from heaven incorporates a combination of attributes suggesting the significance of his function. Similar to the Christ in the opening epiphany, "his face (is) as the sun" (10:1-τὸ πρόσωπον αὐτοῦ ὡς ὁ ἥλιος; cf. 1:16c-ἡ ὄψις αὐτοῦ ὡς ὁ ἥλιος φαίνει ἐν τῇ δυνάμει αὐτοῦ). The motif of a shining face occurs in several connections in biblical and early Christian tradition: Moses' face shines after his descent from Sinai (Ex 34:29-35; cf. 2 Cor 3:7); the משכלים will "shine as the brightness of the firmament" (Dan 12:3=Theod.; LXX-"as the stars of heaven"). Though the angel's descent with the little scroll from heaven echoes Moses' descent with the Torah from Sinai, the element "as the sun" links him, on the level of the text, more directly with the opening christophany.

While admitting that the language in 1:16c may have been influenced by the text in Judges 5:31 (LXX-οἱ ἀγαπῶντες αὐτὸν καθὼς ἡ ἀνατολὴ τοῦ ἡλίου ἐν δυναστείαις αὐτοῦ), YARBRO COLLINS ultimately derives the feature in 1:16c from the angelophany in Daniel 10:6 ("his face as the appearance of lightning").[64] This derivation would have particular support if the angel in Revelation 10 was being identified with Gabriel.[65] In the phrase "as the sun," however, it seems that the angel's appearance is accommodated to that of the opening christophany, and hence shows a less immediate dependence on Daniel 10:6.[66] In the *Apocalypse of Zephaniah* 6:11, which like Revelation 1 shows some dependence on the angelophany in Daniel 10, the "great angel" Eremiel has a face "shining like the rays of the sun in its glory." If we are correct in maintaining that the tradition represented in the *Apocalypse of Zephaniah*

---

[64] "The 'Son of Man' Tradition and the Book of Revelation," p. 549.

[65] Esp. since Gabriel may be the angel encountered in Dan 10; see n. 39 on p. 220 above. Many commentators have argued, from a word play with ἰσχυρός=גבור from גבריאל ("El is my strength") and noting the parallel between 10:5-6a and Dan 12:7, that the author had Gabriel in mind; so CHARLES, *The Book of Revelation*, 1.259; LOHMEYER, *Offenbarung des Johannes*, p. 81; LOHSE, *Offenbarung des Johannes*, p. 62; MÜLLER, *Offenbarung des Johannes*, p. 200; and RITT, *Offenbarung des Johannes* (NEB, 21; Würzburg: Echter, 1986) 58. Although CHARLES' linguistic argument itself is unconvincing (ἰσχυρὸς ἄγγελος is not confined to *this* angel; see Rev 5:2 and 18:21), the further allusions to Dan 8:26 (and 12:4) in 10:4 render the inference plausible.

[66] In a similar adjustment of Daniel 12:3, "the righteous will shine as *the sun*" at the conclusion of the judgment (Mt. 13:43-interpretation of the parable of the tares), while the transfigured Jesus is described as having a face which shone like the sun (Matthean redaction in 17:2-ἔλαμψεν τὸν πρόσωπον αὐτοῦ ὡς ὁ ἥλιος; cf. Mk 9:3).

is not dependent on the Johannine Apocalypse,[67] it becomes rather plausible to argue that the similar description of Christ and the "strong angel" reflects a common (Jewish or Jewish-Christian) exegetical tradition which expanded on Daniel 10:5-6 as it continued to be applied within an angelophanic context.[68] Remaining particular to the christophany of the Apocalypse of John is ἡ ὄψις, which perhaps is best translated "appearance" rather than "face."[69]

A possible allusion in chapter 10 to the opening epiphany is the strong angel's association with "a cloud," with which he is arrayed (περιβεβλημένον νεφέλην). The connection here to the christophany proper (1:12-20) is only indirect. Since Christ is unambiguously represented as "one like a son of man" in 1:13, christological allusions to Daniel elsewhere in the Apocalypse may be significant. In 1:7 the mixed citation of Daniel 7:13 (=Theod.) and Zechariah 10:11 heralds that Christ "is coming with the clouds" (ἔρχεται μετὰ τῶν νεφελῶν), while in 14:14 the seer beholds "one like a son of man seated" on a cloud (ἐπὶ τὴν νεφέλην καθήμενον ὅμοιον υἱὸν ἀνθρώπου). Nevertheless, in terms of identification the "cloud" and attendant description of the angel's face in 10:1 should not be overinterpreted.[70] Though, form-critically, Revela-

---

[67] On the problem of literary dependence of *Apoc.Zeph.* on Rev see Part Two, n. 83 (pp. 78-79 above). The parallels between *Apoc.Zeph.* 6:11-15 and Rev 1:13-16,18 (and 19:10; 22:8-9) are indeed striking: Though the *Apoc.Zeph.* presents the features of Eremiel (which are in common with Rev) in a different order and includes a number of minor details not found in Rev (e.g., 6:11b-his face shines "like the rays of the sun in its glory since his face is like that perfected in glory"; v. 14-"I fell upon my face, and I worshiped him"; no allusion to Dan 7:9 or 7:13; v. 14-the seer's confusion of the angel's identity), nowhere do these elements agree with Dan 10 against Rev 1. Outside this passage the overall theology of the *Apoc.Zeph.* shows no feature exclusively shared by Rev; 6:11-15 is so well integrated into narrative that it is hard to posit a conflation of separate elements from Rev. Thus this and other elements of *Apoc.Zeph.* in common with early "Christian" writings presupposes "a common Jewish-Christian heritage" (see WINTERMUTE, "Apocalypse of Zephaniah," in *OTP* 1.501).

[68] ROWLAND ("Man Clothed in Linen" 102-103) includes *Apoc.Zeph.* in his synoptic comparison of Rev 1, *Jos.Asen.* 14, Dan 7 and 10, and *Apoc.Abr.* 11, but does not discuss its position within the exegesis of Dan 10. The *Apoc. Zeph.* though mentioned in KARRER's comparison (*Johannesoffenbarung als Brief*, pp. 143-44 and n. 30), is not integrated into his analysis.

[69] Thus whereas πρόσωπον refers literally to the angelic revealer's "face," ὄψις comprehends Christ's general appearance (the eyes, hair, head, and feet are already described); see BOUSSET, *Offenbarung des Johannes*, pp. 196-97 and esp. HOLTZ, *Christologie*, p. 125 n. 2. Is the use of ὄψις an attempt on the part of the author to show Christ's superiority over angels? If so, then he has done so within the framework of angelological categories.

[70] That is, they do not warrant an identification of the angel with Christ, as first argued by VICTORINUS OF PETTAU (see also bibl. in MOUNCE, *The Book of Revelation*, p. 207 n. 4), nor do they allow for the supposition

tion 10:1-11 corresponds to a commissioning call by a heavenly figure, it is not ultimately modeled on chapter 1.

Both in form and content, chapter 10 is to be understood as an adaptation of the prophet's call in Ezekiel 2:8-3:3 (esp. vv. 8-11), prefaced by an eschatological setting drawing on the interpreting angel's instruction not to disclose his message "until the time of the end" in Daniel 12:4-9 (vv. 4-6). On the level of the text, this means that the previously hidden prophecy (here, the content of what the "seven thunders" say; vv. 3b-4a) concerning the end time may now be disclosed (v. 2a), but not until the seer has eaten the little scroll. Though the combination of traditional motifs results in some infelicitous seams within the narrative,[71] it may at least help explain the combination of traditionally angelic and divine traits in the "strong angel": in addition to those discussed, "a rainbow over his head"[72]; "his feet like pillars of fire"[73]; and his voice "like a lion roaring."[74] Except for the

---

that the angel is "the angel of Jesus Christ" (CAIRD, *The Revelation of St. John*, pp. 125-26). Furthermore, the combination of cloud with a rainbow in v. 1 already describes the divine glory in the throne-theophany of Ezek 1:28 (see Rev 4:3).

[71] E.g., it still leaves unclear how the command not to write (v. 4)--since there is no more delay (v. 6, referring to what the seven thunders have spoken)--is related to the seer's call to prophesy "again" (v. 11; see 1:19), which has to do with the contents of the open βιβλαρίδιον. Whereas the former is made to anticipate the events following the seventh angel's trumpet (11:15), the latter comes to fruition in 11:1-13. Further difficulties are recapitulated by Roland BERGMEIER, "Die Buchrolle und das Lamm," *ZNW* 76 (1985) 236-38.

[72] Ἡ ἶρις ἐπὶ τῆς κεφαλῆς αὐτοῦ. As a feature associated with a heavenly being, see the rainbow in Rev 4:3 (from Ezek 1:28-"around the throne") and *Apoc.Abr.* 11:3 (Iaoel-"a kidaris on his head, its look that of a rainbow). Whereas the wording is close to the angelophany of the *Apoc.Abr.*, the cloud-rainbow combination goes back to Ezek 1:28.

[73] Καὶ οἱ πόδες αὐτοῦ ὡς στῦλοι πυρός; in 1:15 the corresponding description, on the basis of Dan 10:6 is more expansive (οἱ πόδες αὐτοῦ ὅμοιοι χαλκολιβάνῳ ὡς ἐν καμίνῳ πεπυρωμένης; cf. *Apoc.Zeph.* 6:12b-"his feet were like bronze which is melted in a fire"). At the same time, the feature in 10:1 is *linguistically* closest to "pillar of fire" which accompanied Israel in the wilderness as a sign of God's abiding presence at night (LXX Ex 13:21-22, 14:24-στῦλος πυρός). Significantly, the "pillar" took the form of a "cloud" during the day (13:21-22; 14:19, 24-στῦλος νεφέλης). The association between Ezek 1:28 and Dan 12:4-9 is probably made by the author on the basis of elements from Ezek already taken over in Dan 10:5-6 (humanlike figure; waist; fire; description of voice); nevertheless, in Ex 14:19 (MT=LXX) the "pillar of cloud," neither term of which is applied to the angel in Dan 8-12, is said to move in conjunction with ὁ ἄγγελος τοῦ κυρίου.

[74] The only feature in vv. 1 and 3 which in the biblical and Early Judaism is exclusively associated with God (Hos 11:10; Amos 3:8).

description of the angel's face, the verbal links with chapter 1 thus do not betray an attempt on the part of the author to align the description of the angel in 10:1 with the christophany.

Despite the grandeur of his appearance, the angel's function in chapter 10 ends up being rather limited. The narrative constitutes neither a throne-room theophany (as in chapters 4-5) nor an epiphany, in which the heavenly figure does the commissioning (as in chapter 1). The angel merely acts as a divine agent who holds the "open little scroll" (βιβλιαρίδιον) in his hand (vv. 2,9-10; cf. a sealed βιβλίον in 5:2-5,8-9; cf. Ezek 2:9; 3:1-3).[75] Furthermore, the seer receives his primary instructions, not from the angel (cf. Dan 12:4,9), but from the "voice from heaven" (vv. 4,8), while in 10:11 the otherwise problematic λέγουσιν[76] minimizes the angel's role as the one who issues the call to prophesy.

If several angelological texts in Revelation are reminiscent of motifs found in the opening epiphany, this does not occur at the expense of an emphasis that Christ is superior to God's angels. In order to assess how the author's angelomorphic Christology is coordinated here with a superiority over angelic beings, we shall consider the imagery of 1:12-20 as it relates to the letters to "the angels of the seven churches" which follow in chapters 2 and 3.

E. Christ and the Angels of the Seven Churches

After the initial commission to write (1:11), the author refers to the seven churches by name and to seven "golden lampstands" (v. 11-λυχνίας χρυσᾶς), in the midst of which he sees the "one like a son of man" (vv. 11-12). The number seven is picked up again in verse 16a where in the description of the figure's glory it is applied to "stars in his right hand" (ἐν τῇ δεξιᾷ χειρὶ αὐτοῦ ἀστέρας). In verse 20 these stars are interpreted as "angels of

---

[75] This is esp. significant, if the contents of the little book are delimited to 11:1-13.

[76] Are *both* the angel and the voice from heaven the subject? CHARLES (*The Book of Revelation*, 1.269) thus prefers to see therein an indefinite plur. statement (as occurs in Heb and Aram). BERGMEIER, "Die Buchrolle" 239, explains the form source critically; the subj. in the author's *Vorlage* (reconstructed by BERGMEIER from ch.'s 5 and 10) was "the seven thunders" (10:3-4). CHARLES' suggestion is preferable since the same usage appears in 13:16 and 16:15 (as CHARLES notes), an explanation which is not dependent on the correctness of source-critical reconstruction.

the seven churches" (ἄγγελοι τῶν ἑπτὰ ἐκκλησιῶν),[77] while the lampstands of verse 12 are identified with the "seven churches" themselves. The subtle differentiation in this explanatory signification might seem to contrast with the more spatially disparate images of lampstands and stars as initially introduced in verses 12 and 16, leading some earlier commentators to regard the whole of verse 20 as an insertion by a post-authorial editor.[78] This symbolism and its interpretation in verse 20, however, cohere well with the first predication of the risen Christ in 2:1: "Thus says the one who holds the seven stars in his right hand (1:16), who walks in the midst of the seven golden lampstands (1:12)." If 2:1 recalls the images of the epiphany, 1:20 marks a transition which allows lampstands and stars to be interpreted more clearly in light of the author's communicative intention. Whereas 1:20 makes clear that the spatial image of being "in the midst" of the lampstands represents Christ's presence among the churches addressed, the "holding" (1:16-ἔχων, cf. 3:1; 2:1-κρατῶν) in his right hand denotes Christ's superiority over the "angels" of these churches. Since in 1:20 the angels are clearly distinguished from the churches, the author's interest extends beyond a mere assertion of Christ's status among the churches.[79] The "one like a son of man," as one who embodies both divine and angelomorphic characteristics, is thus at the same time unambiguously portrayed as superior to angels which become the addressees of the letters in chapters 2-3.

---

[77] The mention of "seven stars" in 1:16 as an adorning feature within the epiphanic delineation no doubt inhibited the author from leaving traces concerning a specific origin of the image (no definite article!)--whether it derives from fallen stars which have gone astray (see 1 En 18:13-16; 21:3-6; cf. the dream vision in 86:1-6), the most prominent heavenly bodies, i.e. the sun, moon, and five planets created by God (e.g., 2 En 27:3 and 30:3-4 [both Rec. J]), or from a constellation such as the seven stars of Ursa Minor (cf. Job 38:31-33); for a recent summary of the religious historical possibilities see e.g. PRIGENT, *L'Apocalypse de Saint Jean*, p. 30 and Michał WOJCIECHOWSKI, "Seven churches and seven celestial bodies (Rev 1,16; Rev 2-3)," *BibNot* 45 (1988) 48-50 (esp. pp. 48-49). KARRER (*Johannesoffenbarung als Brief*, p. 176 n. 164) is therefore probably correct when he argues that the indefiniteness of 1:16 opens the way for "die Stern-Assoziation von Engeln, die nicht gesamtkosmische, sondern nur Einzelgemeinden betreffende Befugnisse haben."

[78] For bibl. references see BECKWITH, *The Apocalypse of John*, p. 446.

[79] A primary concern with angelology is underscored by grammatical considerations: the term "mystery" (1:20-τὸ μυστήριον) is immediately followed by "the seven stars" in the gen. case--in v. 20b interpreted as angels--, while the phrase referring back to the lampstands (in the acc. case, attracted to the relative pron. οὕς) is separated by καί.

1. The "Angels" of the Seven Churches

Who are these angels? The term ἄγγελος can denote either a *human* or a *heavenly* messenger, and both interpretations are open to further nuancing.[80] On the basis of internal indications alone the assumption of a human "messenger" is unlikely since, if 1:20 and chapters 2-3 are excepted, there is not one instance in the Apocalypse in which the term refers to a human being.[81] However, the assumption of an address to real, heavenly angels is likewise not without difficulty. Consequently, several have been wont to refer back to the thesis that the letters were indeed addressed to human leaders of or messengers to the seven churches. As a proponent of this view, Heinrich KRAFT summed up one of the major difficulties with the postulation of real angels behind the letters: "Wir müssen dann hinnehmen, daß Christus durch die Feder eines Menschen an einen Engel schreibe."[82] More than this, if the distinction between "angels" and the "churches" in 1:20 holds true, one would have to imagine that letters could be sent to "guardian" angels who, contrary to what one would expect, are placed in a position in which they can be reproached (they are not bad angels). These considerations have led a number of scholars to modify the traditional "guardian" or "patron angel" theory by maintaining that the angels are simply being understood as "heavenly doublets or counterparts" to the earthly churches assigned to their arena of responsibility.[83]

---

[80] The different perspectives are reviewed by HOLTZ, *Christologie der Apokalypse des Johannes*, pp. 113-16; Akira SATAKE, *Die Gemeindeordnung in der Johannesapokalypse* (WMANT, 21; Neukirchen-Vluyn: Neukirchen, 1966) 150-55; MÜLLER, *Offenbarung des Johannes*, pp. 87-89; and KARRER, *Johannesoffenbarung als Brief*, pp. 169-86.

[81] As emphasized e.g. by BOUSSET, *Offenbarung des Johannes*, pp. 200-201; CHARLES, *The Book of Revelation*, 1.34; BECKWITH, *The Apocalypse of John*, p. 445; and SATAKE, *Gemeindeordnung*, p. 151. The overwhelming evidence in favor of ἄγγελος as celestial beings should should caution interpreters from proceeding too rashly to demythologize the author's argument.

[82] *Offenbarung des Johannes*, p. 51. See also STRACK-BILLERBECK, *Kommentar zum NT*, 3.791 and R.C.H. LENSKI, *The Interpretation of St. John's Revelation* (Columbus: Lutheran Book Concern, 1935) 68. KIDDLE, *The Revelation of St. John* (pp. 16-17), simply questions the "supreme religious value" of an author addressing the angels.

[83] See CHARLES (*The Book of Revelation*, 1.34-35) who is compelled to this view by "unanswerable objections" to the interpretation in which "Christ is supposed to send letters to superhuman beings through the agency of John, and the letters in question are wholly concerned, not with these supposed angels, but directly with the Churches themselves and their spiritual condition." See also MOULTON, "It is His Angel" 514-16; BECKWITH, *Apocalypse of St. John*, pp. 445-46; LOHMEYER, *Offenbarung des Johannes*, p. 18; KITTEL, "ἄγγελος," in *TDNT* 1.86-87; Kiddle, *Revelation of St. John*, pp. 16-17; William

Because of a resulting logical problem--that is, that one symbol (the stars= angels) is being interpreted by another (the lampstands=churches) in 1:20--a few scholars who reject the "human messenger" theory have, despite the difficulties involved, seen no alternative other than to posit angel guardians for the churches.[84]

Two further nuances of the heavenly "angel" view have appeared in the last twenty years. Before ultimately favoring the angel-doublet theory,[85] Ulrich B. MÜLLER had proposed that the ἄγγελοι are a "literary fiction" which the author, apparently not familiar with the ecclesiological structures of the communities, must have created to avoid having to address the community leaders directly.[86] A more direct link between the ἄγγελοι and the community leadership has been maintained by SCHÜSSLER FIORENZA and AUNE.[87] Appealing to 22:16, SCHÜSSLER FIORENZA argues that the angels are "visionary counterparts of the prophets in the communities."[88]

In common with all of these views is a hesitancy to entertain any literal meaning of ἄγγελοι as celestial beings. Martin KARRER, however, has recently argued convincingly that the notion of an address to angels through a human can no longer be dismissed as a phenomenon without religio-historical plausibility.[89] In the Aramaic *Book of Giants*, portions of which are preserved among the Qumran fragments from Cave 4, a fragment of one of the manuscripts published by J.T. MILIK (4QEnGiants^a frgt. 8[90]) contains a "copy of the s[ec]ond tablet" (1. 3-אנ[י]נה לוחא פרשגן) written by "Enoch the scribe of inter-

---

BARCLAY, *The All-Sufficient Christ* (London: SCM Press, 1963) 39; HOLTZ, *Christologie*, p. 115; SATAKE, *Gemeindeordnung*, p. 154; CAIRD, *The Revelation of St. John*, p. 24; MOUNCE, *The Book of Revelation*, p. 82; and BEASLEY-MURRAY, *The Book of Revelation* (NCB; London: Marshall, Morgan & Scott, 1978, rev. ed.) 69.

[84] E.g., BOUSSET, *Offenbarung des Johannes*, pp. 200-201; LOHSE, *Offenbarung des Johannes*, p. 22.

[85] See MÜLLER, *Offenbarung des Johannes*, p. 88.

[86] So MÜLLER in *Zur frühchristlichen Theologiegeschichte. Judenchristentum und Paulinismus in Kleinasien* (Gütersloh: Mohn, 1976) 34.

[87] SCHÜSSLER FIORENZA, "Apokalypsis and Propheteia," in *The Book of Revelation*, pp. 145-46; AUNE, "Social Matrix" 23.

[88] The order of conveyance in 22:16 is: Jesus-his angel-"you" (plur.)-the churches. However, this theory would expect the plur. "you" to be matched by the plur. form "angels." Thus 22:16 more immediately refers to the mediating angel mentioned in 22:6,8.

[89] *Johannesoffenbarung als Brief*, pp. 57-59 and 172.

[90] An early Herodian hand (late 1st cent. BCE); see MILIK, *The Books of Enoch*, p. 303 (see pp. 314-16 and Pl. XXXII).

pretation"[91] (l. 4-אשרפ רפס ךונה) to the fallen Watchers. The fragment, which contains portions of 15 lines of text, preserves part of a divine communication in lines 5-15. The piece is clearly intended as a letter:[92] it contains a formula of address (ll. 4-5-"the...] and Holy One to Shemiḥazah and all [his] co[mpanions"); a decree formula (l. 6-"let it be known to you t[hat al]l [..."); a recounting of the watchers' and the giants' wrongdoings upon the earth (ll. 7-11); a promise of judgment (ll. 12-13); and, finally, a summons to "loose what binds you...and pray" (ll. 13-15). Given these characteristics, one may conclude that Enoch, acting as a scribe for God or one of the principal angels,[93] writes a letter to the fallen angels.[94] Admittedly, in the *Book of Giants* the figure of Enoch, though human, appears to be otherworldly. Furthermore, unlike the Apocalypse of John, the angels addressed are clearly fallen, and their destruction is irreversible.[95] At the same time, this text

---

[91] MILIK's translation, "scribe of *distinction*," is misleading. Though the verbal root פרש is in Aramaic most frequently attested with the meaning "to divide, separate," two extant passages of the *Book of Giants* closely associate the title with Enoch's function as an interpreter; so this frgt. of 4QEnGiants[a] (cf. l. 4 with 13-"and the interpretation [רשפ] of the matter ...") and 4QEnGiants[b] frgt. 2 (l. 14-"to Enoch] the scribe of אשרפ, that he will interpret [רשויפ] for us..."). For this meaning in Aramaic see the Nabataean inscription edited in *Répertoire d'épigraphie sémitique* (Académie des inscriptions et belles-lettres; Paris: Imprimérie Nationale, 1916-1918) 3. 1792 B, ll. 7-8: "in order to interpret for me the matter" (*lmprsh ly mlt'*). Cf. also BEYER, *ATTM*, p. 264. Enoch thus mediates the petitions of the fallen angels and communicates a divine response to them.

[92] KARRER (*Johannesoffenbarung*, p. 58 and n. 47) wants to follow MILIK, (*The Books of Enoch*, p. 314) in restoring ארגיא ("l[etter") after יד at the end of l. 3. The restoration is doubtful; see especially BEYER, *ATTM* (p. 261), who reads instead יתיא יד ("which i[s"). As KARRER recognizes, however, the question of genre does not depend on the veritude of this reconstruction.

[93] The latter possibility is as likely as a designation for God; see *1 En* 22:6, where in the Aram (4QEn[e]) the interpreting angel "Raphael" is called "the watcher and holy one" (אשידקו אריע); cf. Rev 3:7. Favoring this interpretation would also be *1 En* 12:4-6, in which the good "watchers" commission Enoch to announce judgment to the evil "watchers." However, for "the Holy One" as the latter of two or more epithets for God, see *1 En* 10:1.

[94] Elsewhere, in 4QEnGiants[b] 2.21-23-3.4-11, the giant Mahawai seeks to elicit dream interpretations from Enoch on behalf of the giants, but the text gives no indication that he conveys the letter from Enoch to the watchers. The text in 4QEnGiants[a] 7 2.1, which MILIK takes as a reference to Mahawai, is doubtful:].הכל מ.[(cf. MILIK, *The Books of Enoch*, Pl. XXXI).

[95] At the same time, the *Book of Giants* displays an interest in the plight of the giants *as a plight*, and the tone can at times even be sympathetic (cf. 4QEnGiants[b] 2.20-23 and 3.4-11). The summons to pray (4QEnGiants[a] 8. 15) is unusual. In *1 En* 12-13 and 15, the watchers petition for mercy, but at no time is this elicited. The imperative that they pray may function as a

does offer a background that makes it possible to take seriously the notion of celestial ἄγγελοι as addressees of such communication through a human being. If it is possible to assume the author to have been aware that angels were held in high regard among the churches, then a direct address to "the angel" of each church would have represented a demotion in status.

While an identification of specific angelological ideas held by each of the communities in chapters 2-3 is ultimately a matter of reconstruction, the guardian or patron angel hypothesis gains in probability. From this, however, it would be wrong to assume that each community or individual members thereof must have had espoused an identical angelology.[96] Whereas an awareness of, if not belief in, the protective or intermediary roles of angels may be plausibly attributed to Asia Minor Jews and Christians near the end of the first century CE,[97] the specific one angel-one congregation correspondence is more likely a construction of the author.[98] Taken together with the fact that these

---

literary device to signal that there will be further interchange between the fallen watchers and God or his angels.

[96] This assumption underlies KARRER's otherwise insightful discussion in *Johannesoffenbarung als Brief*, pp. 169-85; see esp. p. 185.

[97] In Part Two, it was observed that limited forms of veneration could be directed towards angelic beings who were thought to act as divine agents in relation to "Israel," a group (such as the Qumranites), or an individual; see the discussions of Tob 11:14-15 (pp. 164-67), *Ps-Philo* 13:6 and 15:5 (pp. 170-73), *T.Levi* 5:5-6 (pp. 176-77), and 11QBer 11. 13-14 (pp. 161-63). This stream of tradition is corroborated by some of the inscriptions from Asia Minor, though, as observed, the exact date and provenance (pagan, Jewish, or Christian) is often not known (pp. 181-91); esp. relevant may be the thanksgiving inscriptions from Stratonikeia (p. 181, n. 388) and the tomb inscriptions invoking protection or vengeance (Delos [pp. 183-85], Thera and Eumeneia [pp. 187-88]).

[98] There is nothing in early Jewish and (Jewish-) Christian literature which corresponds precisely to this conception. The *Asc.Isa.* 3:15 (within the Christian portion in 3:13-4:22) does contain the concept of "an angel of the church which is in the heavens, whom he will summon in the last days," which Isaiah is said to have foretold (trans. KNIBB, *OTP*, 2.160; on a date to the late 1st-early 2nd cent., see *ibid.*, p. 149). The image is not the same as each community-church with its own angel, as in Rev, but could have evolved into such an idea. A more advanced stage is represented in the *Shep.Herm.* in *Sim.* 5.5, in which the parable concerning a vineyard is allegorically interpreted: "the servant"="the Son of God"; "the vines"="the people whom he [God] has planted"; "the fences"="the (holy) angels of the Lord who keep together his people". In *Sim.* 5.6 the Son is said to have placed the angels in charge of God's people "to watch over them." The concept in the *Shep. Herm.* is more general than the one-to-one angel-church correspondence in Rev 2-3. These analogies may explain why the author, for the sake of communicative strategy, could have chosen a medium of writing to an angel of each church. However, *Asc.Isa.* and *Shep.Herm.* do not provide enough of an exact parallel for Rev

angels can be reproved as well as commended, both the admonitory tone associated with the letter-form and known religious historical indications of contemporary attitudes towards angels (among Jewish communities; concerning Asia Minor, see Part Two, pp. 181-91) furnish ample reason to suspect that the author's representation of angels in the seven letters involves a demotion from views of angelic functions held by the intended readers. This postulate is further enhanced by a brief examination of the christological portrait in the letters.

2. The Portrayal of Christ in the Letters and the Epiphany

Once the supposition that the letters addressed to real angels is granted as religio-historically plausible, two primary observations take on significance. First, in substance the letters are targeted at specific circumstances in each community, and despite this, the author, commensurate to a formal address to one angel, retains to a large degree the singular form of the second person within the letters. Of the ninety-one verbs and pronouns in the second person, only ten can be found in the plural.[99] This is, however, only a formality, and the angels addressed are otherwise virtually ignored.

Second, the inclusion of angels in the opening address of the letters is countered by a noticeable absence of symbols associated with angelology within the Apocalypse. As is frequently noted, in the first seven (especially the first five) letters Christ describes himself with terms taken from the opening vision.[100] While features in the christophany associated with angelophanies in tradition are taken up, *in no case does any trait from 1:12-20 occur in Revelation 2-3 which later in the Apocalypse is also descriptive of angelic beings*:

2-3 to posit a widespread belief in a specific patron one angel-one church at the end of the 1st cent. CE.

[99] Most efforts to clarify the author's language have focused on the singular forms, which have been interpreted as "collective" in meaning. But if the address to angels is taken seriously, it is the plural forms which would require explanation. The 2nd pers. plur. forms occur in 2:10(3X),13,23-25(6X). They tend to appear in clusters (2:10,23-25), and occur when the author is making distinctions within the communities.

[100] In addition to observations made in many commentaries, see Birger GERHARDSSON, "Die christologischen Aussagen in den Sendschreiben der Offenbarung (Kap. 2-3)," in ed. A. FUCHS, *Theologie aus dem Norden* (SNTU, A/2; Linz: A. Fuchs, 1976) 142-66.

2:1- "who holds the seven stars in his right hand" (1:16, 20; cf. 3:1)
"who walks in the midst of the seven golden lampstands (1:12, 13)
2:8- "the first and the last, who was dead and came to life" (1:17)
2:12- "who has the two-edged sword" (1:16; cf. 19:15 and 21-Christ)
2:18- "whose eyes (are) as a flame of fire" (1:14)
"whose feet (are) like burnished bronze" (1:14)
3:1- "who has the seven spirits of God" (1:4; cf. 4:5)
"and the seven stars" (1:16, 20; cf. 2:1)
3:7- "the holy one, the true one" (6:10-God; cf.19:11-Christ);
"who has the key of David" (cf. 1:18; 20:1; and 5:5-Christ); and
"who opens and no one will shut, and who shuts and no one opens"
3:14- "the Amen, the faithful and true witness" (cf. 1:5) and
"the beginning of God's creation"

The traces of angelology which remain are such due to angelophanic traditions applied by the author. Such is especially conspicuous in the terminology of 2:18 (=1:14c-15a, except for the acc. case: τοὺς ὀφθαλμοὺς αὐτοῦ ὡς φλόγα πυρὸς καὶ οἱ πόδες αὐτοῦ ὅμοιοι χαλκολιβάνῳ;) which, as in 1:14c-15a, is similar to, but not identical with, the angel's appearance in Daniel 10:6 (cf. Ezek 1:7). From within the Apocalypse itself, the only possible exception to the exclusion of angelological features in the seven letters is "the key of David" in 3:7. In 20:1 an "angel descending from heaven" has "the key of the abyss" into which he throws and imprisons the dragon. The symbolism of this "key" is, however, punitive, while in 3:7 this image is elaborated in terms of hope for the faithful of the church at Philadelphia (3:8). Moreover, the language of 3:7 is taken from Isaiah 22:22 (MT), in which king Hezekiah's steward Eliakim is invested with "the key of the house of David" as a symbol of managing authority. Consequently, more than with 20:1, the "key" in 3:7 is formulated more in continuity with the epiphany in 1:18, according to which "the keys" refer to the living Christ's authority over Death and Hades. Ultimately, traces of angelology in the christological predications, if not entirely absent, remain in the background, especially on the level of the text. Thus the attributes attributed to Christ in the letters serve to reinforce his superiority over the "angels of the churches."[101]

---

[101] So also, but more generally, HOLTZ, Christologie, pp. 137-47.

Unlike the radical disjunction between christological and angelological categories in Hebrews 1-2 (pp. 119-39), the author of the Apocalypse has retained an angelomorphic Christology. As noted in the comparisons above with tradition and the literary symbolism of the Apocalypse (pp. 211-32), a number of the features attributed to the "one like a son of man" in 1:12-20 are explicable within the framework of angelological tradition and continuing developments thereof. On the basis of the passages reviewed thus far, the picture which emerges is, first, that Christ is unambiguously superior to angels and, second, that this does not occur wholly at the expense of angelomorphic features. It is unlikely that a combination of *both* the repression *and* the retention of such elements within the christological presentation can be simultaneously explained as *either* the author's application of known literary traditions *or* as his critique of the recipients' angelological views. The christological portrait, rather, seems to be a function of the author's own revision (initially reflected in the christological predications of the seven letters and ultimately expressed in a non-angelological Lamb Christology) of angelo- and christological conceptions which he nevertheless continued to share with his intended readers. If this hypothesis avails, then it is necessary to explore one more passage in the Apocalypse (14:6-20), within which many interpreters have noted an identification of Christ as an "angel."

III. REVELATION 14:6-20: "ONE LIKE A SON OF MAN" AND THE ANGELS

Between visions of the Lamb's faithful followers on Mount Sion (14:1-5) and of their hymn of triumph in heaven (15:2-4) occurs a series of visions involving six "angels" (each designated ἄλλος ἄγγελος-14:6,8,9,15,17,18) and "one like a son of man" (14:14-16). The activity of the latter, which is described after the first three angels have announced judgment (vv. 6-11), is coordinated with that of the second group of three angels who act as agents carrying out God's wrath over the earth (vv. 14-20).

Who is this "one like a son of man" in 14:14, described as "seated" on a "white cloud" with a "golden crown upon his head and a sharp sickle in his hand"? The nomenclature applied to the angel in the following verse (v. 15), ἄλλος ἄγγελος, might also, however, be taken to imply that the humanlike figure is simply an angelic being. On the other hand, readers already familiar with the epiphany of chapter 1 would undoubtedly have thought of Christ, whether he is understood here as an angelic being or not. Each of these alternative identifications encounters interpretive difficulties. If it turns out that the author intended to identify this figure as an ἄγγελος, then for our purposes it remains unclear whether the vision is concerned with a christophany or with an angelic being; in addition, the latter possibility cannot be assumed to exclude the former.[102] If one proposes that the author considered "one like a son of man" to be an angelic Christ who can take and carry out divine orders through another angel (vv. 15-16), then this vision appears to conflict with the author's apparent efforts elsewhere, by means of symbolism, to distinguish between Christology and angelology (1:20-3:22). Finally, if the ἄλλος ἄγγελος in 14:15 does not have its antecedent in the "one like a son of man" of verse 14,[103] then the text would preserve the distinction of symbolism underscored elsewhere by the author. Even in the latter case, however, it would be logically problematic to modern readers why the author has not attempted to introduce terms which would keep his christological and angelological categories more separate.

Interpreters have attempted variously to come to terms with this knotty exegetical problem. BOUSSET posited an original source in which the "one like a son of man" in 14:14 was overtly identified as Christ; this source was subsequently modified by the author of the Apocalypse, who instead chose to represent this figure as an angel and hence added ἄλλος before ἄγγελος in verse 15.[104] CHARLES also tried, with respect to the author, to separate any identification of Christ with an angel; he ascribed verses 15-17 to the interpolation of a later editor and proposed that ἄλλος ἄγγελος in verse 18 be translated "another one, an angel."[105] Irregardless of how, the solutions of BOUSSET and CHARLES both mark attempts at coming to terms with an angelophanic context which, at the very least, is reminiscent of Christology. Not surprisingly, where such literary-critical solutions have been avoided, interpretations focused on the author's presentation itself have diverged. While a majority of scholars have maintained that "one like a son of man" is Christ who therefore--due to the designation, attending attributes, and placement within the

---

[102] See n. 111 below.

[103] That is, either (1) ἄλλος refers back to the angel in v. 9 or, being applied to all six angels of chapter 14 (even to the first, in v. 6), (2) it is simply a generic attribute which is not to be understood literally.

[104] See BOUSSET, *Offenbarung des Johannes*, pp. 388-89, whose linear reading of the Apocalypse excluded a christophany at this point in the text: "...weil für ihn [the author] das eigentlich messianische Gericht viel später kommt."

[105] CHARLES, *The Book of Revelation*, 2.21,23. Concerning CHARLES' linguistic criteria for excising vv. 15-17, see HOLTZ, *Christologie*, p. 129 n. 2.

context--is clearly set apart from or superior to the angels,[106] others have remained insistent that the humanlike figure is no more than the fourth (and therefore most prominent) of seven angels who carries out an assigned task of "harvesting" the earth.[107]

A christological identity of this figure and his placement and function in the text are difficult to harmonize. On the one hand, he is termed ὅμοιον υἱὸν ἀνθρώπου. The expression as a whole occurs only here and in 1:13, that is, not even in any of the traditional material taken over by the author (Dan 7:13-LXX,Theod. have ὡς). Whether the designation is titular[108] or not,[109] the author's interchangeable use of ὡς and ὅμοιος throughout the Apocalypse suggests in 14:14 an adaptation of ὡς υἱὸς ἀνθρώπου in Daniel 7:13 and clinches the author's identification of the figure in 1:13 and 14:14.[110] There is good reason, then, to interpret the vision of the humanlike figure "seated on a cloud" as a christophany.[111]

---

[106] BECKWITH, Apocalypse of St. John, pp. 661-62; LOHMEYER, Offenbarung des Johannes, pp. 124-25; HOLTZ, Christologie, pp. 128-34; CAIRD, Revelation of St. John, pp. 190-91; LOHSE, Offenbarung des Johannes, p. 86; A.P. VAN SCHAIK, "Ἄλλος ἄγγελος in Apk 14," in L'Apocalypse johannique, 221-28; MOUNCE, The Book of Revelation, p. 279; YARBRO COLLINS, The Apocalypse, p. 105; MÜLLER, Offenbarung des Johannes, pp. 269-70; and PRIGENT, L'Apocalypse de Saint Jean, pp. 233-34.

[107] KIDDLE, Revelation of St. John, pp. 274-77; KRAFT, Offenbarung des Johannes, pp. 197-98; J. COPPENS, "La mention d'un Fils d'homme angélique en Ap 14, 14," in L'Apocalypse johannique, p. 229; and RITT, Offenbarung des Johannes, pp. 77-78.

[108] So CHARLES, The Book of Revelation, 1.27 (and 2.20) who, though correct in seeing no essential difference between ὡς υἱὸς ἀνθρώπου and ὅμοιος υἱὸς ἀνθρώπου, argued that the former expression is equivalent to the articular sense (="the one like...") since it was being interpreted "as a Messianic designation." A specifically messianic function is, however, not apparent in chapter 14.

[109] E.g., correctly, VAN SCHAIK, "Ἄλλος ἄγγελος," in L'Apocalypse johannique, p. 223.

[110] CHARLES, The Book of Revelation, 2.36-37.

[111] Criteria such as a the mere dependence on Dan 7:13 and the attributes assigned to the figure are not as convincing. Though recognizing an essential difference in literary context, both Maurice CASEY (The Son of Man [London: Hodder & Stoughton, 1979] 196) and KARRER (Johannesoffenbarung als Brief, p. 148 n. 41) have observed that beyond Dan 7:13, an equally close formal parallel to a vision of one "sitting on a cloud" can be found in VERGIL's Aeneid 9.638-40 (Apollo). More importantly, if Dan 7:13 is in view in 14:14, then one should note several differences: (a) The figure's function as an agent of divine punishment is constructed variously. The "one like a son of man" is in 14:14 accommodated to Joel 3:13, whereas 1:7 is combined with an allusion to Zech 12:10-14 and 1:13 associates the allusion to Dan 7:13 with the angelophany in Dan 10:5. (b) The preposition and number are differ-

A christological interpretation should not be advanced at the expense of the literary context of chapter 14 in which the analogies to angels are conspicuous. First, as already noted above (p. 241), the depiction of his appearance is followed immediately in verse 15 by the arrival of "another angel." Does the adjective ἄλλος refer, then, to the figure in verse 14 or to the "other" angels which have heralded divine judgment in verses 6 and 8-9? Perhaps not too much should be made of this linguistic argument since the first of the group of angels in verse 6 is already introduced as ἄλλος ἄγγελος. Nevertheless, were the author concerned to distinguish Christ from angels, one would expect an avoidance of such ambiguity. Second, in verse 15 the ἄλλος ἄγγελος gives "the one seated on the cloud" (repeated from v. 14!) a command to put forth (πέμψον) his sickle and reap (θέρισον), to which "the one who was sitting on the cloud" immediately responds (v. 16). The common explanation for the notion of an angel commanding Christ has been to assert either that the angel was acting on God's behalf (the command actually derives from God)[112] or that the "loud voice" is in reality the voice of God.[113] Even if the command ultimately comes from God--the angel comes out of the temple (v. 15)--, these considerations do not account for why the angel is still placed in a mediating role *between* God and the "one like a son of man." Finally, this humanlike figure performs an task analogous to that of the final "other angel" in verses 19-20. Without doubt the repetition of the har-

---

ent (14:14-ἐπὶ νεφέλη λευκή; 1:7-μετὰ τῶν νεφελῶν), and (c) the figure in question is "sitting" (14:14) instead of "coming" (1:7).
     As for the attributes, a "crown" is also worn by the conquering rider of a white horse in the first seal (6:2; probably a christophany-cf. Christ, who wears "many diadems," as the rider of a white horse in 19:11-13). However, since "golden crowns" are worn by the twenty-four elders (4:4-στεφάνους χρυσοῦς; 14:14-στέφανον χρυσοῦν; cf. also the "crown" promised to those who overcome in 2:10), this attribute cannot be understood as a christological feature. See further, HOLTZ, *Christologie*, p. 130 n. 1. In 10:1 the "other strong angel" is also associated with "a cloud," in which he is wrapped (περιβεβλημένον); if Dan 7:13 lies in the background, it has only contributed in imagery, and the author is not attempting to identify the "one like a son of man."

[112] So esp. MÜLLER, *Offenbarung des Johannes*, p. 270: "... Überbringer eines göttlichen Befehls, da er [the angel] aus dem Bereich Gottes kommt; deshalb liegt keine Unterordnung des Menschensohngleichen unter den Engel vor."

[113] HOLTZ, *Christologie*, pp. 132-33 and emphasized by VAN SCHAIK, "Ἄλλος ἄγγελος," pp. 224-25, for whom the angel's command operates "hypostatically" as an introductory formula intended to denote the urgency and imminence of divine judgment. Such an interpretation is rendered improbable by the fact that the verb ἐξῆλθεν, not applied to the "one like a son of man," denotes a separation from the source.

vesting of verse 16 in verses 17-20, where it is likewise follows an angel's command (v. 18), is explicable from the use of Joel 3:15 (MT); LOHMEYER has accurately observed that "Was hier als poetischer Parallelismus erscheint, ist als sachliche Doppelheit aufgefaßt; so schien das Wort von zwei Ernten, von mindestens zwei Erntenden und zwei Sicheln zu reden."[114] Yet, would the author, in applying this biblical tradition, have created a difficulty for his Christology gratuitously?

The structure of 14:6-20, in which "one like a son of man" is preceded and followed by three angels, is noteworthy. Since he appears in the middle of the group and is given attributes not applied to *these* angels,[115] there is little question that this figure is cast in a superior role.[116] And yet, it is doubtful whether this prominence warrants HOLTZ's conclusion that in this passage the position given to Christ is "weit über sie [the angels] hinaus."[117] To the extent that the author is either responsible for or a tradent of the muddied boundaries between Christ and the angels, the most satisfactory solution is simply to take the analogies of this passage seriously.[118] Because of the contextual proximity to angelic beings, Christ as "one like a son of man" takes on angelic *functions*, and even more so than in 1:13-16. This angelic representation of Christ becomes understandable if seen within the framework of growing speculative interest in angels (even to the point of veneration) and of developing angelomorphic Christologies at the turn of the second century CE.[119]

---

[114] LOHMEYER, *Offenbarung des Johannes*, p. 125.

[115] See n. 111 above.

[116] The closest analogy to the notion of 6 heavenly beings plus 1 superior is Ezek 9:2, already considered above (pp. 226-28) relation to ch. 15. If this model already underlies the organizational conception of 14:6-20, it does so only in a formal sense.

[117] *Christologie*, p. 131.

[118] Cf. *1 En* 61:10 in which "the Elect One," alongside several classes of heavenly beings, can be *summoned* to "bless" the Lord of the Spirits (v. 11). However, the one summoning is either the Lord of the Spirits or the Elect One himself and, in any case, clearly not an angel.

[119] Similarly, KARRER, *Johannesoffenbarung als Brief*, p. 148 and YARBRO COLLINS, "The 'Son of Man' Tradition and the Book of Revelation," p. 566, who, however, posits "a very early christological tradition" that "has its roots in Palestinian Christianity" (p. 568). YARBRO COLLINS argues that the ὡς-indefinite form of the "son of man" must have preceded the definite form in the Gospels. But, given the close correspondence between the author's "son of man" language and the traditions of Ezek, Dan, and contemporary apocalypses, as well as the author's own style (see p. 242 and n. 108 above), it is not necessary to resort to such an early dating.

This examination of Revelation 14:6-20 raises two problems with respect to the Apocalypse author's presentation: (1) The portrait of Christ in chapter 14 acquires a different emphasis than what is found in the christological predications opening the letters to the seven churches, in which, on the narrative level of the Apocalypse, an avoidance of categories attached elsewhere to angels can be observed (pp. 238-39). Moreover, (2) to what degree, if any, could something like an angelomorphic Christology such as in Revelation 1:12-16 and 14:14-20, whether taken over from tradition or creatively formulated by the author, have served his theological interests? An approach to these questions may be suggested by an analysis of the place and function of the refusal tradition within the Apocalypse of John.

IV. THE REFUSAL TRADITION IN THE APOCALYPSE OF JOHN

In the discussion of the refusal tradition in section II.A.2 above (pp. 75-103), we have tried to show that in 19:10 and 22:8-9 the author of Revelation adapted a motif well and variously attested in early Jewish and Jewish-Christian writings. Furthermore, though the angel's refusal in this literature often reflects an attempt to safeguard monotheistic belief, the tradition could take a variety of forms, thus serving further particular interests of a given author. Given this flexibility, the tradition lent itself especially to rhetorical uses which sometimes reflect a shared *Vorstellungswelt* which served as a communicative among authors and their readers. Finally, we have also observed that, in the materials preserved, the prohibitions--or, "refusal" proper--most characteristically follow the narration of an angelophany (pp. 81-87),[120] because of which the seer is moved to bow before the angel.

In view of our traditio-historical comparison of the angelophanic refusal tradition, two emerging features suggest distinctive interests of the author in the Apocalypse of John: (1) the author has made use of this tradition

---

[120] As in *Asc.Isa.* 7:2,19; *Apoc.Zeph.* 6:11-15; *2 En* 1:4-8; *3 En* 16; and the C. Gen. frgt. Though the primary reason for the attempt to venerate Raphael in Tob 12:15-16 is the series of acts by which he, as God's agent, has protected Tobias on his journey (see also 11:14-15), his appearance cannot be dismissed as a factor; see p. 84 n. 98 above.

twice in the same form[121] and (2) the refusal by an angel in 19:10 and 22:8-9 does *not* follow an angelophanic epiphany.

A. The Angel in 19:10 and 22:8-9

As we have noted above (section II.D.2, pp. 226-28) the angel or angels which show and interpret the visions of Babylon's destruction (17:1-19:8) and the New Jerusalem (21:9-22:5) are taken from the group of seven angels who, commissioned to pour our the seven bowls of wrath, are initially introduced in 15:1. In 15:5-6 the seer beholds these angels emerging from the heavenly temple wearing "pure bright linen" and "golden girdles around their breasts." Despite the reminiscence of these features both to the opening epiphany (esp. 1:13) and to "the man clothed in linen" in Ezekiel 9-10, their appearance plays no further role in the Apocalypse. It seems clear, therefore, that the seer's desire to worship the angel in 19:10 and 22:8-9 has little or nothing to do with the features attributed to the angels in 15:6; an angelophany proper has not prompted John's *proskunesis*. In the author's presentation, this would appear to bring the *function* of the angel as mediator and interpreter of the visions into sharper relief (p. 247 below).

Indeed, until chapter 17 the seer's interaction with angelic beings is minimal. At several points in the narrative the seer is addressed by or himself addresses one of the heavenly beings, but such interaction is momentary.[122] By contrast, in both 17:1 and 21:9 the guiding angel summons the seer to view the fall of Babylon and "the Bride of the Lamb" respectively with the words, δεῦτε δείξω σοι. From this point on, the language describes an interactive activity between the angel and seer which is more sustained. The con-

---

[121] In the *Asc.Isa.* the two occurrences of the angelic refusal respond to different forms of impropriety (7:21-inappropriate worship of an enthroned figure; 8:4-address of the *angelus interpres* as "my lord"). In Rev both instances of the tradition retain elements from both occurrences in *Asc.Isa.* (i.e., the seer's attempt to worship the angel and the angel's self-identification as a "fellow servant"; see p. 95 above) and, therefore, is more homogenous.

[122] Before ch. 17 such interaction has occurred in three passages: (1) *5:5*-One of the elders tells the seer not to weep. (2) *7:13-17*-One of the elders questions the seer concerning the identity of those clothed in white robes (v. 13); the seer does not know (v. 14a), and the elder gives the answer (v. 14b-17). (3) *10:9-10*-The seer takes and eats the little scroll from the "strong angel" and is commissioned to prophesy. Of these instances the commissioning in ch. 10 is the most significant; however, in its present form, the angel's active role in relation to the seer is overshadowed by the "voice from heaven." See further section II.D.3 above (pp. 229-32).

trast with previous the narrative of the Apocalypse is highlighted by the listing below of such instances in each vision:

17:1-19:10: Punishment of Babylon

17:1-   "Come, I will show you..." (δεῦτε δείξω σοι 21:9).

17:3-   "And he carried me away in spirit (ἀπήνεγκέν με ἐν πνεύματι) into the wilderness." (cf. 21:10)

17:6-14-   In response to the seer's bewilderment (v. 6b-ἐθαύμασα...θαῦμα μέγα), the angel offers to explain "the mystery of the great woman and the beast": "And the angel said to me, 'Why do you marvel? I will tell you...' (v. 7a-καὶ εἶπέν μοι ὁ ἄγγελος διὰ τί ἐθαύμασας; ἐγὼ ἐρῶ σοι...).

17:15-18-   The angel interprets for the seer the meaning of "the waters" (v. 15a-καὶ λέγει μοι).

19:9-   The angelic guide speaks to the seer (καὶ λέγει μοι) at the conclusion of the vision of heavenly worship: he (1) tells the seer to write a makarism and (2) affirms to the seer (καὶ λέγει μοι) that "These [the substance of the foregoing vision; cf. 22:6] are the true words of God."

21:9-22:9: New Jerusalem

21:9-   "Come, I will show you..." (δεῦτε δείξω σοι 17:1).

21:10-   "He carried me away in spirit (ἀπήνεγκέν με ἐν πνεύματι) to a great and high mountain, and he showed me (ἐδειξέν μοι) the holy city Jerusalem descending from heaven from God..." (Ezek 40:3[123]; cf. 17:3)

21:15-17-   The angel who measures the city (cf. Ezek 40-48) is designated "he who was speaking with me" (v. 15a-ὁ λαλῶν μετ' ἐμοῦ).

22:1-   "And he [the angel] showed me (καὶ ἔδειξέν μοι) the river of the water of life...."

22:6-   The angelic guide speaks to the seer (καὶ εἶπέν μοι) at the conclusion of the vision of the New Jerusalem. He (1) affirms again that "These words are trustworthy and true" (cf. 19:9) and (2) describes to him his mission: "the Lord, the God of the spirits of the prophets, has sent his angel to show his servants (ἀπέστειλεν τὸν ἄγγελον αὐτοῦ δεῖξαι τοῖς δούλοις αὐτοῦ) what must happen soon." (cf. 1:1 and 22:16)

Within the narrative of the Apocalypse, the angel's role as interpretive guide for the climactic visions of the book is conspicuous. We may summarize the functions attributed to the angel in both sections as follows: (1) The angel has mediated the vision to the seer (17:1; 21:9); (2) the angel has put the seer in a position to see the vision (17:3; 21:10); and (3) the angel

---

[123] The transfer of Ezekiel to the "very high mountain" is ascribed to "the hand of the Lord" (Ezek 40:1).

has acted as the seer's interpreter (17:7,15; 21:15); (4) the angel has enabled the seer to participate in that which he has heard (19:9); and (5) the angel is prominent because he is one of the seven angels in 15:6 (17:1; 21:9) whose clothing resembles Christ in chapter 1 (see section II.D.2, pp. 226-28). Thus the reason for attaching the refusal tradition to *this* angel is, from within the narrative, transparent enough.

Moreover, as the comparative references above indicate, the respective literary contexts concluded by the refusal tradition in 19:9-10 and 22:8-9 is analogous. Both sections are anticipated by short units which include a narration of what the visions presuppose: 16:17-21 (the seventh bowl: the divine destruction of Babylon) and 21:1-8 (the descent of the New Jerusalem). Taken together with the angelic refusal, a proximate linguistic correspondence between the beginning and close of these sections underlines the antithetical contrast between the visions,[124] the structurally complementary nature of which is underscored by the increased significance of the *angelus interpres* in the narrative. The resulting impression is that the author has attempted to provide the concluding visions of the Apocalypse with a structural symmetry, which leaves no doubt as to the primary importance within the narrative attached to the angel's refusal to be worshiped.

Considered traditio-historically, however, the motivation behind the visionary's *proskunesis* remains puzzling.[125] In none of the Jewish and Jewish-

---

[124] See e.g. YARBRO COLLINS, *The Combat Myth in the Book of Revelation* (HTRHDR, 9; Missoula: Scholars, 1976) 19 and "Revelation 18: Taunt-Song or Dirge?," in *L'Apocalypse johannique*, pp. 188-89, who sets off the visions of "Babylon" and "Jerusalem" from the foregoing seven bowls (15:1-16:20) and "seven unnumbered visions." YARBRO COLLINS, however, ends the Jerusalem "appendix" at 22:5 (see also her commentary, *The Apocalypse*, p. 148), which provides no parallel of substance to the end of the section on Babylon. SCHÜSSLER FIORENZA's emphasis on concentric patterns posits a structure which at this point is very similar, but which also takes into account the conclusive nature of the refusal tradition in each section: 15:1,5-19:10; 19:11-22:9; see her essay on "The Composition and Structure of Revelation" in *The Book of Revelation*, pp. 174-76 and BAUCKHAM, "The Worship of Jesus" 329.

[125] The materials studied in Part Two does not provide much clarification for the Apocalypse seer's desire to worship the angel, esp. as concerns 19:10. (a) Insofar as functions (2) and (4) listed on p. 247 above are operative, there may be some analogy with the *Shirot* from Qumran (Part Two, II.B.1.b.i, pp. 156-61), in which the community's venerative recognition of the chief angels' ability to "recount the splendor of his kingdom" (4Q400 2 ll. 2-3) leads the human community to reflect on its unworthiness to participate in the angelic worship (ll. 6-7) and then to praise God for this admittance (ll. 8-9). The *Shirot*, however, are liturgical and, unlike the Apocalypse, do not narrate a mystical ascent to or guided tour in heaven with an angelic guide. Furthermore, the language of the songs emphasize more the participation of the *earthly* community in heavenly worship, rather than offering

Christian materials preserving an angelic refusal does an angel's mere function as interpreter of and guide through a heavenly journey ever produce such a reaction.[126] This suggests that, for the author, the refusal tradition is invested with a significance within the Apocalypse which extends beyond the literary boundaries marked by the final two visions. To ascertain this import it therefore becomes necessary to take into account some further aspects of the author's literary and theological design.

B. A Double Refusal

Behind the double use of the tradition and the analogous literary context of both passages, interpreters have frequently been disposed to recognize some form of intentionality. However, the nature and scope of this purpose and the literary level to which they ought to be assigned (such as author, redaction of a written tradition by author, interpolation by a later editor, or addition by a later scribe) has been subject to considerable debate.

Among earlier commentators in this century, BOUSSET, CHARLES, and BECKWITH considered the double use of the refusal tradition as sufficient grounds for questioning the literary unity of the text.[127] For them, the interpretive

---

a momentary glimpse or audition. (b) If Col 2:18 refers to angel veneration in a visionary context (Part Two, II.A.3.b, pp. 111-19), it would offer a more contemporary and geographically proximate history of religions explanation for the setting of the Apocalypse. The parallelism between 2:18 and 2:16 and the emphasis on "humility" (v. 18; 2:23) suggest that the rejected form of veneration was linked with the observance of ascetic practices. However, if one supposes that the author of Revelation was concerned with such a problem among the communities, it is hard to explain why in the letters the criticism is emphatically levelled against those who advocate a laxness of ethical behavior (2:14-teaching of Balaam; 2:20-21-teachings of the "prophetess" Jezebel). (c) Finally, since the angel is one of the seven who came out of the heavenly temple in 15:6, might in itself be reason enough for the seer's high esteem. Indeed, the angel Raphael in Tob (12:15-22) appears to reject Tobit and Tobias' posture before him after revealing that he is one of the *seven* "holy angels" who stand in the presence of God. In the Apocalypse, the angel's status as one of the seven with the bowls of wrath does contribute to the fact that he is chosen in the narrative as an interpreting guide. However much the author may have known of the tradition in Tobit, the seer's venerative posture in 19:10 is narrated more as a spontaneous act which the the angel curtly rejects (ὅρα μή); in contrast to Rev, the angel's acts of protection (and possibly appearance; see p. 84 n. 98) account for the visionaries' worshipful posture.

[126] See p. 245 n. 120 above.

[127] BOUSSET, *Offenbarung des Johannes*, pp. 429-30; CHARLES, *The Book of Revelation*, 2.130, 224-25; BECKWITH, *The Apocalypse of John*, pp. 742 and 773.

difficulties encountered are mainly associated with 19:9-10: (1) The speaker at the opening in 19:9a is not indicated (who is the subject of λέγει?); (2) the conclusive "these words are true" are more suitable to the end of this writing (such as in 22:8-9) than after a penultimate vision; (3) the reason for the seer's desire to worship in 22:8 seems logically unintelligible if it has already been rejected in 19:10; and (4) the two passages contain apparent inconsistencies with respect to the representation of "the prophets."[128] These problematic features have led to a number of attempts at literary-critical solutions, most of which have regarded part or all of the version in 19:10 as a secondary interpolation.[129] This approach remains viable insofar as no reason for authorial intention can be found.

A number of exegetes have, however, recognized that the double refusal reflects the Apocalypse author's redaction of traditional material. An intention of the author is most clearly seen in the angel's self-identification as a "fellow servant" (19:10; 22:9). In summoning the seer to worship God, the angel places himself on the same level as the seer (and his prophetic group); hence the *repetition* of the refusal tradition may correspond to the author's interest in legitimating his prophetic status and message.[130] These literary-

---

[128] Whereas in 22:9 the angel demotes himself to the status of three groups (the seer; his "brothers the prophets"; and "those who hold the words of the prophecy of this book"), in 19:10, according to which "brothers" and "those who hold" are listed together, only two groups are mentioned (the seer; his "brothers who hold the testimony of Jesus").

[129] If one assumes that all of 19:10 is secondary, then the inconsistencies enumerated above become even more conspicuous. Would a later editor have created such incongruities gratuitously? It might be possible that the end of v. 10--"For the testimony of Jesus is the Spirit of prophecy"--, the latter part of which is a singular formulation in the Apocalypse, represents an addition intended to harmonize 19:10 with the mention of "prophets" in 22:9; so, e.g., MÜLLER, *Offenbarung des Johannes*, p. 320 and BAUCKHAM, *The Theology of the Book of Revelation* (Cambridge: Univ. Press, 1993) 120-21, whose respective views on 19:10b largely follow that of CHARLES (*The Book of Revelation*, 2.130). Against a later interpolation, however, is the consistency of the christological assertion of v. 10b with the way *theo-* and Christology are functionally related in the foregoing verses (vv. 7 and 9); see p. 251 below.

[130] E.g., KRAFT, *Offenbarung des Johannes*, p. 245 and SCHÜSSLER FIORENZA, "Apokalypsis and Propheteia," pp. 145-46. This emphasis is not altogether denied by BOUSSET (*Offenbarung des Johannes*, pp. 429-30) and BECKWITH (*The Apocalypse of John*, p. 773), but is limited to 19:10. A wider intention behind 19:10 is attributed to a final editor by CHARLES (*The Book of Revelation*, 2.225), for whom the refusal in 19:10 places more emphasis than 22:8-9 on the importance of prophets, while preserving (with 22:8-9) a polemic directed against the worship of angels.

and redaction-critical interpretive options will be presently be evaluated as both passages are further analyzed.

1. Revelation 19:9-10

Though the presence of the angel has to be inferred from as far back as chapter 17 (vv. 1,3,7,15),[131] 19:9 is thematically continuous with the jubilation of 19:4-8, in which the seer has heard the great multitude proclaim the reign of "the Lord our God the Almighty" (κύριος ὁ θεὸς [ἡμῶν-ℵ*,ℵ² P] ὁ παντοκράτωρ). This divine nomenclature and the phrase δώσωμεν τὴν δόξαν αὐτῷ are reminiscent of the wording in 4:11, 14:7, and 15:4, hymns of portions thereof which focus exclusively on God.[132] This emphasis is in line with the summons to praise God in verses 6-7 and the ascriptive acclamation and depiction of worship in verses 1 and 4. At the same time, the *theo*-logical statements here have been integrally assimilated into the author's christological and ecclesiological interest. In verse 7, the glory to be ascribed to God is grounded both in the coming of the Lamb and in the prepared status of "the Bride" (v. 7b), that is, the saints who remain faithful (v. 8b). In this way the worship of God, insofar as linked to "the Bride," presupposes the accomplished act of the advent (v. 7b-ἦλθεν) of the "marriage supper of the Lamb." This interrelation is picked up again in the angel's address to the seer (v. 9) who is told to record a makarism (echoing v. 7b) declared to be "the true words of God." The angel's declaration in verse 9b serves as a concluding pronouncement, not only for the makarism but also for the entire preceding visionary unit (17:1-19:8).[133] The *theo*-logical statements of 19:1-10, then, embody a christological undercurrent from which they are inseparable.

The audition, at the conclusion of which the seer himself is invited to record the makarism (v. 9a) and is addressed with the angel's pronouncement confirming the veritude of the vision (v. 9b), breaks off when the seer falls

---

[131] The indefinite καὶ λέγει μοι (twice in v. 9) repeats the same formula in 17:15, in which the referent is clearly the guiding angel in vv. 1,3, and 7.

[132] The terms θεός with a possessive pronoun and παντοκράτωρ are reserved for God in the Apocalypse. Even Christ, as the dictator of the seven letters refers to "my God" (never to "your" God!) or to "my Father": 2:27; 3:2,5,12, and 21. The designation "our God" occurs only in the hymns: 4:11; 7:12; 11:15; and 19:1,5,6.

[133] See LOHMEYER, *Offenbarung des Johannes*, p. 153. In addition to being recapitulative of v. 7, the makarism, as those in 14:13 and 22:14-15, also has an exhortative character.

at the angel's feet. In rejecting the seer's venerative posture, the angel places himself on the same level as "you and your brethren who hold the testimony of Jesus" and summons the seer to "worship God" (v. 10). Here, as in verse 9a--which alludes to verse 7b--, language about "God" betrays a christocentric orientation. True worship of God presupposes an identification of the faithful with the Lamb or Jesus, which, in turn, marks the criterion for true prophecy.[134] The pervasiveness of this theological pattern within the passage thus places the burden of proof on attempts to solve the presence of the refusal tradition in 19:10 by literary-critical means. If instead we suppose some sort of redactional activity, an explanation for the remaining interpretive difficulties must be found on other grounds.

If in the present text chapter 19 the seer's intention to worship the angel is the result of the latter's mediary role in the visions, it is pertinent at this point to consider the chain of mediation indicated in 1:1, 22:6, and 22:16. These passages imply the angel's subordinate role to God (22:6) and to Christ (1:1 and esp. 22:16). Though in 1:1 and 22:16 the angel's subordinate status as a mediary figure is apparent enough, the mention of this function in 22:6--that is, just preceding the refusal tradition--implies that the author considered it necessary to delineate further the nature and origin of this mediation. This necessity is all the more obvious, since the commission entrusted to the guiding angel "to show his servants what must happen soon" (22:6-δεῖξαι τοῖς δούλοις αὐτοῦ ἃ δεῖ γενέσθαι ἐν τάχει) describes, in precisely the same terminology, a function of *Christ* at the opening of the Apocalypse (1:1).[135] Consequently, given the relative prominence of the angel's activity in relation to the seer in 17:1-19:9, on the one hand, and ambiguity in the chain of mediation implicit in statements at the beginning and near the end of the Apocalypse (1:1; 22:6), on the other, it would be reasonable to suppose that the refusal tradition was directed against a possible misconstrual of the significance of angelic mediation.[136]

---

[134] The genitive in μαρτυρία Ἰησοῦ is probably objective (the testimony about Jesus), esp. if μαρτυρία ἣν εἶχον (6:9) is interchangeable with the phrase; see HOLTZ, *Christologie*, p. 23.

[135] Further, the portrayal of God and the Lamb in the New Jerusalem as inseparable (22:3-4; see the citation on p. 1) may be thought to conflict with the application of mediatory language to Christ in 1:1. As in 19:10, the refusal tradition of 22:8-9, with the summons to "worship God," thus implies a christological component.

[136] This application of the refusal tradition would thus be similar to that of Tobit, in which the significance of Raphael's protective activity-- brought to expression in Tobit and Tobias' doxology to "angels" alongside God

2. Comparison Between Revelation 22:8-9 and 19:10

In drawing attention to the angel's mediary function, we have already made some observations concerning the literary context of 22:8-9 in the preceding section. This angelic refusal does not present the contextual problems raised by the presence of the tradition in 19:10 and is well suited to this part of the Apocalypse. Here we may note the primary reasons: First, as already suggested, given its clarifying function within the narrative (p. 252), the placement of the refusal after the final vision of the Apocalypse and, more specifically, after the statement concerning mediation in 22:6, poses little difficulty. Second, the author situates his desire to worship the angel as a response to what he has "heard" and "seen" (v. 8-twice ἀκούειν and βλέπειν); lacking in 19:10, this first-person statement of "John" possesses a comprehensiveness which may extend beyond the final vision into the foregoing work as a whole.[137] Finally, the mediary role of the angel--not expressly mentioned in 19:10--is emphasized in a participial relative clause added to the description of the visionary's response: "I fell down to worship before the feet of the angel *who showed me these things* (τοῦ δεικνύοντός μοι ταῦτα; cf. v. 6). Even more so than in 19:10, then, the author gives expression to the prominence of the angel's function, only to have the angel's rejection of his attempt to worship downplay its significance. Is this a matter of an authorial attempt to explain to readers potential incongruities in the narrative, or does may the refusal, in its double appearance, be thought to have communicated something further to the intended readership?

The emphasis in this discussion has thus far turned on the role of the angel and on clues within the narrative which suggest why the seer would have wanted to worship the angel at all. This, in turn, makes the exhortation to worship God understandable. Rather than expressing a pious commonplace which is simply to be taken for granted, such a call to monotheistic devotion in a context of angelic mediation could take on a significance on his own. The remaining question is, however, to what degree, if any, might the author have had religious attitudes of his readers in mind?

The self-identification of the angel as a "fellow servant" is worded similarly in 19:10 and 22:9 with a few differences:

(11:14-15)--is modified by Raphael's mild rejection of their prostration before him; see pp. 164-67 above.

[137] In addition, the seer otherwise only mentions his own name at the beginning of the Apocalypse (1:1,4, and 9).

19:10	22:9
σύνδουλός σού εἰμι	σύνδουλός σού εἰμι
καὶ τῶν ἀδελφῶν σου	καὶ τῶν ἀδελφῶν σου
	τῶν προφητῶν
τῶν ἐχόντων	καὶ τῶν τηρούντων
τὴν μαρτυρίαν Ἰησοῦ	τοὺς λόγους
	τοῦ βιβλίου τούτου
...ἡ γὰρ μαρτυρία Ἰησοῦ	
ἐστιν τὸ πνεῦμα τῆς προφετείας	

Whereas in 19:10 the angel's status is made equivalent to that of the seer and his "brothers who hold the testimony of Jesus," in 22:8-9 his position is compared to three groups: the seer, his "brothers the prophets," and "those who keep the words of this book." In 19:10 the angel says nothing explicitly about prophets; those who "hold the testimony of Jesus" are not defined any further.[138] In 22:8-9 the prophets are singled out and distinguished from those who "keep the words of this book." In both passages the angel makes himself is equivalent in status to the seer and a larger, less well defined group; in 19:10 this group presumably would have included the prophets, while in 22:9 they are distinct. Thus there is no compelling reason to suppose with, for instance, SCHÜSSLER FIORENZA and KRAFT that the author, even in 19:10, wishes to emphasize an equality between angels and prophets alone, thereby reinforcing the divine commission of the latter group.[139] If "brothers who hold the testimony of Jesus" (19:10) and "brothers who keep the words of this book" (22:9) are equivocal and refer to Christians beyond a smaller prophetic circle,[140] then 19:10 and 22:8-9 can be interpreted, even more emphatically, as a

---

[138] That this group cannot be limited to a prophetic circle is apparent from the makarism in 19:9 which refers generally to those invited to the marriage supper of the Lamb. Similarly, the subject of the makarism in 22:7b is picked up in 22:9 in relation to the faithful.

[139] See bibl. in n. 130 above. To argue that 19:10 emphasizes the status of prophets more than 22:8-9 is to read the latter passage, with its more explicit interest in prophets (cf. 22:6) into the former. The explanatory statement 19:10b, which identifies "the spirit of prophecy" with "the testimony of Jesus," says nothing specific about a prophetic circle. As a general assertion, it may simply have its most immediate reference to the author's understanding of his own role as a prophet. Concerning the integrity of 19:10b see n. 129 above.

[140] This is suggested in several passages of the Apocalypse. In 1:9, "John" addresses his readers as "your brother (ὁ ἀδελφὸς ὑμῶν) and companion in suffering and the kingdom and endurance in Jesus; in 12:17 the dragon wages war "on the rest of her [the woman's] children, who keep the commandments of God (τῶν τηρούντων τὰς ἐντολὰς τοῦ θεοῦ; cf. 22:9) and have the testimony of Jesus (ἐχόντων τὴν μαρτυρίαν Ἰησοῦ; cf. 19:10); and in 20:4 authority to judge is given to the martyrs beheaded "on account of their testimony to Jes-

comprehensive, clarion call for to monotheistic devotion. What the seer has seen in the visions of judgment and the New Jerusalem is true because these visions ultimately come from God. The angel's summons, then, underscores the worship of God emphasized specifically in the preceding sections (19:1-8-in the hymns; 22:1-5-as described)[141] and, generally, throughout the Apocalypse.[142]

The emphasis in 22:6-9 on prophets does call attention to their special role as bearers, alongside John, of the divine message. The angel is an emissary from "the Lord, God of *the spirits of the prophets*" sent to "*his servants*" (v. 6; cf. 1:1). From this and 22:16, it is clear that John includes himself within a circle of prophets. His role as seer in the Apocalypse marks him as a prophet of distinction among them, who lays claim to a special prophetic authority.[143] It is reasonable, therefore, to maintain that within 22:6-9 the refusal tradition functions to legitimate John's prophetic message by situating him as a leading figure among contemporary early Christian prophetic circles. Implicit therein is also the authoritative claim of his message over the larger Christian community; nevertheless, as far as his status before God and in relation to the angel is concerned, no distinctions are maintained.[144]

As a result, it is possible to detect in the refusal tradition of the Apocalypse a dual concern: (1) to safeguard monotheism over against an exal-

---

us and on account of the word of God (διὰ τὴν μαρτυρίαν Ἰησοῦ καὶ διὰ τὸν λόγον τοῦ θεοῦ)," "who worshiped neither the beast nor its image..."

[141] See MÜLLER, *Offenbarung des Johannes*, p. 320.

[142] Summarily, see e.g. BAUCKHAM, "The Worship of Jesus" 329.

[143] The makarism in verse 7b commends faithfulness to "*the prophecy of this book*," and keeping "*the words of this book*" (v. 9) qualifies one to a status no less inferior to that of the angel.

[144] The angel's self-designation, σύνδουλός σου... (in 19:10 and 22:9), rhetorically breaks down the distinctions implied among the groups listed; despite the existence of a distinct class of "servant prophets" in tradition (cf. here 10:7) and among Christian communities (22:9), every one who is faithful is, in effect, a "servant" of God (*contra* SCHÜSSLER FIORENZA, "Apokalypsis and Propheteia," in *The Book of Revelation*, p. 151: "In choosing this title [δοῦλος] John characterizes his authority as similar not only to that of the OT prophets but also to that of Paul."). Worship in the New Jerusalem is envisaged, for example, as carried out by "his servants" (22:3; οἱ δοῦλοι αὐτοῦ), who "shall see his face and his name (is) upon their foreheads" (22:4). Through the angel's self-demotion the author thus "democratizes" angels and humans alike insofar as only "God" is to be worshiped (cf. also 11:18-οἱ δοῦλοι are identified as "the prophets" *and* "the saints" and "those who fear" God's name), while the essential distinction, as among different groups, remains; see AUNE, *Prophecy in Early Christianity and the Ancient Mediterranean World* (Grand Rapids: Wm. B. Eerdmans, 1983) 206.

ted view of angelic mediation and (2) to legitimate his prophetic message. The double use of the refusal tradition served him in underscoring both intentions. That these aspects are not distributed through the two passages, but occur together in each, indicates the importance which the author associated with them. As we have attempted to show (above, pp. 251-255), the respective contexts of the two passages can account for most of their differences. Whereas 19:10 concludes the vision of judgment, 22:8-9 concludes not only the vision of the New Jerusalem but also the Apocalypse as a whole, in which emphasis is placed on the prophetic status of "this book" as well as on John's status as a prophet.

It has been noted that despite an angelic guide's increased interaction with and activity on behalf of the seer, the refusal tradition in each case remains awkward. This is most conspicuously the case in 19:10, while the tradition in 22:8-9 has been integrated more completely into its literary context. But even in the latter passage, the attempt at integration is not entirely smooth. If in 19:10 the seer's worship appears to be spontaneous, in 22:8 it amounts to a more deliberate reaction: "I am John who heard and saw these things, and when I heard (ἤκουσα) and saw (ἔβλεψα), I fell down to worship at his feet." While the tradition here is conditioned by its placement at the conclusion of the whole book and by the more explicit emphasis on angelic mediation, the angel's functional role is no different than what is narrated before 19:10, and the seer's second attempt at worshiping the angel looks much like a repeated mistake!

While the double use of the refusal tradition is in itself explicable enough, the form given to the tradition seems to presuppose something which is missing in the immediate literary context. Therefore, the author's use of this tradition is not satisfactorily described as a rhetorical way for the author to explain a possible misunderstanding of his narrative. We have argued above for situation-related factors underlying the author's christological and angelological presentation (see pp. 232-239), especially in the opening vision and letters to the seven churches. Our consideration of the refusal tradition above places us in a position to question whether, if at all, it may have been directed against attitudes of angelology which were knwon the author among the churches he addressed.[145]

---

[145] *Contra* LOHMEYER, *Offenbarung des Johannes*, p. 153: "Der Seher hat Mißstände in den Gemeinden in den Sendschreiben gerügt; hier ist für Erörterung von Gegenwartsverhältnissen nicht der Ort." So also CAIRD, *The Revelation of St. John*, p. 237; MÜLLER, *Offenbarung des Johannes*, pp. 319-20; and BAUCKHAM, "The Worship of Jesus" 327-28. In limiting the author's critique to what

C. The Refusal Tradition and the Opening Vision of the Apocalypse

It is appropriate here to bring together several observations we which have made throughout this study. In Part Two a form-critical analysis (section II.A.2, pp. 75-103) made it possible to observe that, in extant literature from antiquity, the most common literary setting for an angel's rejection of worship was that of an angelophany (see pp. 81-87, esp. p. 84 n. 98). We have also noted that the opening epiphany was modelled significantly on biblical angelophanic tradition (esp. Dan 10:5-6; pp. 211-213), while reflecting later developments in angelology in early Jewish and Jewish-Christian thought (pp. 213-221). Furthermore, we have seen how the author could bifurcate symbols attached to a received tradition reading *seven* "men" in Ezekiel 9 by applying them both to Christ in Revelation 1:13b and to the seven angels in 15:6, the latter group from which the *angelus interpres* associated with the refusal tradition (pp. 226-228). Finally, a correspondence in symbolism between the opening christophany in Revelation 1:12-20 and the angelophany-refusal tradition preserved in the *Apocalypse of Zephaniah*, along with signs indicating their literary independence,[146] suggests that both documents have drawn upon a common tradition (pp. 220,228,229-230). In addition, we recall here that the *Ascension of Isaiah* (8:5), preserves the refusal tradition in a form, which perhaps also underlies the Apocalypse, that emphasized that the *angelus interpres* is not superior to the seer (pp. 92-99).

In the *Apocalypse of Zephaniah*, the angelophany of "the great angel" Eremiel constitutes the first part of the refusal tradition narrative (6:11-12). In Revelation, the vision of the "one like a son of man" stands alone; a rejection of worship by Christ would, of course, have run counter to the author's wider understanding of Christology (cf. 5:9-11-the hymn to God and to the Lamb). At the same time, unlike the *Apocalypse of Zephaniah* (cf. 6:13-15), the desire to worship an angel and its sharp rejection in Revelation 19:10 and 22:8-9 are not narrated as subsequent to an epiphanic encounter. This comparison provides sufficient grounds for asking whether the author of the Apocalypse of John was aware of and adapted a refusal tradition in a fuller form. If so, this may, for instance, explain why the refusal tradition in

---

is explicitly stated in the seven letters, the communicative import of the author's symbolism and any coherence between this symbolic representation and the refusal tradition is thereby underestimated.

[146] See Part Two (section II.A.2.a), p. 78 n. 81 and Part Three (section II.D.3), p. 230 n. 67.

19:10 and, even more clearly, in 22:8-9 could be invested with redactional activity, while the severing of the refusal proper from its epiphanic context would account for the awkwardness of the seer's unexpected desire to worship the angel in 19:10.

In what form may the refusal tradition known to and adapted by the author of Revelation have had? On the basis of our form-analysis, we may posit that the underlying tradition was circulating in a form in which more speculative attention was being devoted to the mien of a prominent angel than what the text of the Apocalypse preserves. An angelophany, in which an *angelus interpres* was described with terminology shaped by the Daniel 10 and subsequent traditions (such as Dan 7:9; 7:13 [the Old Greek recension]; and angelophanic literature-cf. *Apoc.Zeph.*), was linked with a rejection of a visionary's inappropriate worship. Use of or allusion to such a tradition may not have begun the refusal actually occurs (at the end of Revelation), but at the beginning. In formulating the inaugural *christophany*, the author supplemented a largely angelophanic tradition with his own wording for "one like a son of man"--such a figure was already present in the tradition--and by embellishing the description of his appearance with christological motifs (vv. 17c-18a), cosmological symbolism (v. 16a), and imagery associated with principal angels known through apocalyptic writings (e.g., vv. 14a, 16c, 18c; cf. *Apoc. Abr.* 11 and *Jos.Asen.* 14). Having merged these elements in 1:12-20, the writer presented the "one like a son of man" as a heavenly being superior to the angels of the seven churches. If a rejection of worship formed part of this angelophanic tradition,[147] then it has been separated out and applied more strictly to the angel at the conclusion of the work.[148] If, however, there was no such connection in the tradition known to the author, then we may at least observe that the opening vision and the angel's rejection of worship, given their substantive overlap and complementary effect, frame the Apocalypse with a contrastive theological statement which emphasizes an essential distinction between Christ and angels.

The angelophanic form of the seer's tradition, on the one hand, and a refusal to be worshiped frequently associated with it, on the other, thus both served the author's emphasis on Christ's superiority, only in a way that marks a formal departure from tradition. Similar to 19:10 and 22:8-9, the

---

[147] See n. 149 below.

[148] On a similar, though less conspicuous, bifurcation of symbolism alluding to Ezek 9, applied to Christ and the seven angels with seven plagues (from which the *angelus interpres* is taken), see pp. 226-228 above.

seer in 1:17 falls at the feet of Christ,[149] but unlike the refusal, this revering posture is neither interpreted as "worship" nor rejected as an inappropriate form of behavior. Contrary to the mediating angel, Christ does not reject the seer's prostrate behavior. In other words, the encounters in 1:13-17, 19:10, and 22:8-9 all include formal elements which, if combined, would constitute a refusal tradition in one of its characteristic forms (angelophany, revering reaction, and refusal). While a worshipful posture occurs in all three passages (and a commission to write in both 19:10 and 1:11,19), the opening vision consists of an epiphany lacking at the close of the final two visions, while the latter contain a refusal to be worshiped lacking in the christophany.

If the version of the tradition in the Christian part of the *Ascension of Isaiah* reflects an earlier use of the form, it is also possible that the author was aware that the tradition could function as an exhortation to the faithful and used it accordingly. In the *Ascension of Isaiah* the superiority of the faithful righteous over angels is depicted as a heavenly reward to be granted because of their belief in "the words" of Christ (9:26). Their place is in the seventh heaven--above the six heavens where the angels dwell--and there they worship God, Christ (the Beloved), and the Holy Spirit (see pp. 96-97,100). In Revelation, the refusal tradition is not placed within the context of visions related to a heavenly ascent. Instead of using the tradition exclusively as a promise of and exhortation toward future or heavenly bliss, the author more clearly has the angel define an existence in the present for "those who keep the words of this book."[150] In chapter 22, therefore, before the promised eschatological rewards and punishments of faithfulness and wickedness respectively are described (vv. 14-15; cf. 21:6-8), the refusal tradition is more immediately followed by an exhortation[151] concerned with activity in the present (v. 11). Since the eschatological events are immanent, the angel's instruction not to seal up "the words of the prophecy of

---

[149] Traces of a possibly original common tradition may be detected behind (1) the seer's reaction to Christ and to the two angels (1:17-ἔπεσα πρὸς τοὺς πόδας αὐτοῦ; 19:10-ἔπεσα ἔμπροσθεν τῶν ποδῶν αὐτοῦ προσκυνῆσαι αὐτῷ; 22:8-ἔπεσα προσκυνῆσαι ἔμπροσθεν τῶν ποδῶν τοῦ ἀγγέλου) and (2) the negative formulation of the angel's words (1:17b-μὴ φοβοῦ; 19:10,22:9-ὅρα μή).

[150] The status of σύνδουλος with the angel in both 19:10 and 22:9 is to be understood as a consequence of faithfulness as expressed in the foregoing makarisms (19:9; 22:7b).

[151] "Let the evildoer continue to do evil and the filthy one continue to be filthy, and the righteous one continue to do right, and the holy one continue to be holy!"

this book" culminates in a summons exhorting readers to take decisive action. This, in turn, brings into sharper relief the importance of the angel's exhortation to "worship God!," out of which faithfulness *to God* finds expression. The practical religious significance of angelic mediaries is thereby diminished. The true worship of God and a proper understanding of the role of angels as heavenly beings in God's service are, in Revelation, not moot religious points to be taken for granted, but constitute part of the message itself. By resuming the makarism in 22:7b within the refusal (22:9), the author, in legitimizing his message, communicates that "keeping the words of the prophecy of this book" involves the recognition that the visions granted him are ultimately an act of divine (not angelic) communication.

The categorical rejection of venerating an angelic mediary in 19:10 and 22:8-9 contrasts sharply with 1:17, in which the seer's prostration before "one like a son of man" is not turned away.[152] Christ, after all, is not merely a mediary of revelation or a "fellow servant," but "the living one" who is "holding" the angels of the seven churches in his right hand (1:20). In dictating the letters to the seven churches, Christ, in contrast to angels, is portrayed the source of the seer's message as well. The author has thus used both parts of the refusal tradition (epiphany and the refusal scene) to underscore that the author's message is derived from both God *and* Christ *vis-à-vis* angels. Whereas, however, the angelic refusal scenes reach a climax in the exhortation to "worship God," the opening epiphany does not result in a scenario in which Christ is explicitly worshiped. The corresponding demotion of angelic beings implies a critique by the author, who has recast a tradition in order to sort out more clearly attributes and functions associated with both Christ and angels than the received perceptions had previously allowed. A situation which the writer perceived as a crisis thus contributed to the formulation of a "higher" Christology for which angelomorphic categories could not suffice.

If it was so important for the author to distinguish between angels and Christ, why did he not simply remove the analogies between his Christology and angelology (as attempted in Heb 1-2) altogether? Here the answer seems to

---

[152] Unlike Dan 10:10 Christ does not raise the seer from this position. In 1:17b the phrase "Do not fear!" is neither prohibitive (i.e., "Do not worship") nor, in the context of chapter 1, is it intended to alleviate the visionary's fear of the vision. Instead, similar to Dan. 10:12,19, it (1) comforts the seer in his circumstances (cf. 1:9a)--the encountered figure is "the living one" who "died...and is alive for ever" (vv. 17c-18a)--and (2) thus prepares him to receive the commission to write.

be clear: an angelomorphic Christology comprised part of the writer's (and readers') *Vorstellungswelt* (see above, pp. 240,244). It was a motif bound up with visionary experiences which served to legitimate prophetic messages addressed to early Christian communities.[153] Such a conception could not be dispensed without attenuating the glory of "the Enthroned One," from whom majestical qualities of angels are derived.

V. CHRISTOLOGY AND MONOTHEISM IN THE APOCALYPSE

The Apocalypse of John contains two opening scenes: the initial vision in chapter 1 and the throne-room vision in chapters 4 and 5. In both scenes Christ is introduced, in chapter 1 as a heavenly being with angelomorphic characteristics, and in chapter 5 as the Lamb. These images are as contrastive as the purpose of the chapters. As "one like a son of man," Christ, while neither denying nor explicitly receiving worship, commissions John to write (1:12,19). As "Lamb standing as one slain" (5:6), Christ is found worthy to open the scroll with the seven seals. The opening vision stresses that Christ is the source of John's message, especially to the angels of the seven churches. As such, he appears essentially as an angelic figure overlaid with divine attributes which ensure his superiority over angels. In chapter 5, the Lamb and angels are more radically distinguished. A "strong angel" asks, "Who is worthy to open the scroll and break its seals?," and the seer weeps "because no one"--is an angel here implied?--"was found worthy" (v. 3). Once the Lamb takes the scroll, he becomes an object of worship expressed in three acclamations, each spoken by a larger group: "Worthy are you..." (v. 9-by the four living creatures and twenty-four elders); "Worthy is the Lamb..." (v. 12-many angels); and "To him who sits upon the throne and to the Lamb..." (v. 13-every creature in the cosmos).[154] It is the Lamb, himself worshiped by angels, who becomes the centerpiece of the author's Christology.

In 5:9 and 5:12 the worship of Christ *alone* reaches its high point.[155] The Lamb is worthy because he was slain and can open the seals contained in the scrolls. In 5:13, however, the worship, which includes earthly as well as heavenly beings, is directed towards both "the one seated on the throne and

---

[153] HURTADO, *One God, One Lord*, pp. 119-20.

[154] HOLTZ, *Christologie*, p. 29.

[155] For another summation of monotheistic sensitivities in the Apocalypse, see BAUCKHAM, "The Worship of Jesus" 330-31.

the Lamb." From this point on, when Christ is worshiped or mentioned alongside God, such a two-pronged formula, in various forms, resurfaces:

6:16-	"Hide us from (ἀπό) the face of him who is seated on the throne and from (ἀπό) the wrath of the Lamb!"
7:9-	..."there was a great multitude...standing before (ἐνώπιον) the throne and before (ἐνώπιον) the Lamb..."
7:10-	"Salvation belongs to (ἐπί) our God who sits upon the throne and to the Lamb!"
11:15-	"The kingdom of the world has become the kingdom of (gen.) our Lord and of (gen.) his Messiah, and he will reign forever and ever."
12:10-	"Now have come the kingdom of (gen.) our God and the authority of (gen.) his Messiah..."
14:4-	"They have been redeemed from humankind as first fruits for (dat.) God and for (dat.) the Lamb..."
20:6-	"...they will be priests of (gen.) God and of (gen.) the Messiah, and they will reign with him a thousand years."
21:22-	"I saw no temple in the city, for the Lord God Almighty (nom.) is its temple and the Lamb (nom.)."
21:23-	"And the city has no need of sun or moon to shine on it, for the glory (nom.) of God lightens it and its lamp is the Lamb (nom.)."
22:1-	"...the water of life...flowing out from (ἐκ) the throne of (gen.) God and of (gen.) the Lamb"
22:3-	"And the throne of (gen.) God and of (gen.) the Lamb shall be in it, and his servants will worship him."

A monotheistic thrust behind this phraseology[156] is apparent from the language of the respective contexts of these passages: As already observed (p. 208 n. 2), with possibly one exception (6:17), God and the Lamb are at no point in the Apocalypse clearly referred to with a plural pronoun or are they the subject of a plural verb; among the texts just cited, this phenomenon avails in 14:1; 20:6; 21:22; and 22:3. Thus, although the author has Christ worshiped alongside God, he strove to retain language which maintains a monotheistic framework.

In conclusion, the author's choice of traditional motifs and language in retaining an emphasis on God encourages several reflections. First, though

---

[156] The repetition of a preposition and/or case before the second element indicates the close relationship between the God and the Lamb (as does the propensity to use sing. forms where they are mentioned together), while retaining them as essentially distinct. Apart from this combination, three other passages listing groups or heavenly beings contain a similar grammatical instruction: (1) 3:5-"If you conquer...I will confess your name before (ἐνώπιον) my Father and before (ἐνώπιον) his angels"; (2) 7:11-"And all the angels stood about (κύκλῳ) the throne (gen.) and the elders (gen.) and the four living creatures (gen.)"; and (3) 14:10-"... and they [those who worship the beast] will be tormented by fire and sulfur before (ἐνώπιον) the holy angels and before (ἐνώπιον) the Lamb."

the "one like a son of man" in chapter 1 is given divine traits and represented as superior to angels, this imagery would not have been as appropriate to the throne-room theophanic scene in chapter 5. The specific interests of the author in his Lamb Christology aside, a "manlike" figure closely related to God's throne, as ROWLAND has recently suggested, may have posed theological difficulties for the author in a way that the Lamb imagery would not.[157] Had in fact such been the case, it would have been more difficult to maintain a monotheistic emphasis on worshiping God without giving the impression of a ditheism.

Second, the description of Christ as "one like a son of man," though placed in the inaugural vision, is not a central motif in the Christology of the Apocalypse. This form of christological representation, as found in chapters 1 and 14, was prone to an association with attributes commonly ascribed to angels, a point borne out by features applied to angels as they appear in the document (pp. 221-232) and by angelological interpretations among early Jewish and Jewish-Christian circles of biblical tradition (Ezek 9-10; 40; Dan 7; 8-12; cf. *Apoc.Abr.* and *Jos.Asen.*; pp. 218-221). If the "angels of the seven churches" are correctly understood as being or representing real heavenly beings, it seems likely that the author implicitly rejected angelological ideas which he perceived among the communities he addressed. Hence an "angel-Christology" or an angelomorphic portrayal of Christ would ultimately have been counterproductive in presenting his prophetic communication as divine--and not angelic--in origin. Christ is worthy of worship, not because of angelic characteristics which are ascribed to him, but because he is the victorious "Lamb standing as slaughtered" through whom redemption for a responsive humanity has been achieved (5:6,9).

Third, the juxtaposition of Christ and God in the author's language has been variously interpreted. While some think that the language of the Apocalypse seems at certain places to add Christological statements as an "afterthought,"[158] others have derived this pattern from biblical tradition (Psalm

---

[157] See ROWLAND, "The Parting of the Ways: the Evidence of Jewish and Christian Apocalyptic and Mystical Material," in ed. James D.G. DUNN, *Jews and Christians. The Parting of the Ways A.D. 70 to 135* (WUNT, 66; Tübingen: J.C.B. Mohr [Paul Siebeck]) 218 n. 16.

[158] Most obviously, EDWARDS, "Christological Perspectives in the Book of Revelation," pp. 139-50 and WHEALON, "New Patches on an Old Garment" 56. JÖRNS (*Das hymnische Evangelium*, pp. 170-75) explains the added christological phraseology as the author's incorporation of Christ into theocentric traditional material concerned with God's redemptive activity; see p. 24 n. 66 above.

2:2-κατὰ τοῦ κυρίου καὶ κατὰ τοῦ χριστοῦ αὐτοῦ).[159] In Part Two, we have reviewed sources which give expression to limited forms of the veneration of angels among Jewish or Jewish-influenced circles (section II.B, pp. 149-204). With the exception of a number--though not all!--of the magical texts (pp. 192-200), nothing transparent emerges that would reflect an intention to compromise the notion of monotheistic belief.[160] As seen, several of these texts bring this monotheistic juxtaposition of angels alongside God to linguistic expression. This phenomenon is conspicuous since, unlike many of the magical sources,[161] singular forms are retained even though the context might allow for otherwise:

> Tobit 11:14-15 (Cod. Sin.) - "...blessed (be) his [God's] great name and blessed be all his holy angels for ever, because he (αὐτός)..."; (Cod.'s Alex. and Vat.: "because you" [sg.]...) (II.B.2.a, pp. 164-167).
>
> Rheneia (Delos) inscription - "O Lord who sees all things and angels of God, before whom (ᾧ) all souls on this day humble themselves with a supplication that you (sg.) avenge..." (II.B.3.a, pp. 183-185).
>
> Kalecik inscription - "To God the Most High and Heavenly, and to his holy angels, and for his (αὐτοῦ) venerable house" (II.B.3.b, pp. 185-187).

While this evidence is not abundant, it does attest a conscious preservation of a monotheistic framework within a Jewish context, in which angelic beings are mentioned, if not to some degree venerated, alongside God. One may well raise the question whether the Apocalypse author's language reflects or shows an awareness of this usage as it was widely applied with reference to angelic beings in Jewish circles. If so, then there may be some analogy between the veneration of angels and the worship of Christ, insofar as a deliberate retention of the monotheistic emphasis is concerned.

This thesis, of course, seems to be further supported by the double use of the widespread and apparently well-known angelic refusal tradition; here the concern to safeguard the worship of God is linked directly with the demotion of the *angelus interpres*, while numerous symbols applied to Christ remain composed of features which were at home in contemporary angelological

---

[159] E.g. Marinus DE JONGE, "The Use of the Expression ὁ χριστός in the Apocalypse of John," in *L'Apocalypse johannique*, p. 272.

[160] These diverse materials are summarized on pp. 201-202.

[161] For important exceptions see the sing. frame of reference preserved in the Cyzicus amulet (pp. 190-191); *PGM* IV, 1928-2005; VII, 255-59; and VII, 1017-1026 (p. 195).

tradition. The author's possible bifurcation of his traditional motifs and material (e.g., the refusal tradition and Ezek 9-10) presupposes a background in which Christology and angelology were more tightly interwoven (as esp. in 14:14-20) than is ultimately underlined by the Apocalypse of John in its extant form. In this manner, the angelomorphic portrayal of Christ as superior to the angels may have functioned in the author's communicative situation to clear the path for a Lamb-Christology in which Christology and angelology were more clearly sorted out. The criterion underscoring this difference is worship. Nevertheless, though the heavenly worship of Christ in the Apocalypse is far more comprehensive and exclusive than anything attested about angelic beings among Jewish and Jewish-Christians in antiquity, it was accommodated to the worship of one God in like manner. This leads us at the end to propose the following possibility: Attempts to safeguard monotheism from potential problems arising from the veneration of angels most likely provided a formative religio-historical development behind the way the author found it possible to merge the heavenly worship of Christ, on the one hand, with his emphasis that only God be worshiped, on the other.

PART FOUR

CONCLUSION

I. Angels and Monotheistic Devotion

What can be said about angelological antecedents in Early Judaism to the worship of Jesus? There is little existing evidence in early Jewish literature which supports the notion of an "angel cult" which could have provided a basic religio-historical explanation for this development. A number of texts, however, suggest that, to a lesser degree, angels could be made objects of veneration as beings aligned with and subordinate to God. It is impossible to say whether there was any direct link between such attitudes towards angels and the origin of devotion to the exalted Christ. Nevertheless, the authors of most of these sources seem to have reflected consciously concerning possible implications of venerative language towards angels and, in the midst of expressing such honor, made attempts to preserve a monotheistic framework.

The invectives against "angel worship" in rabbinic and early Jewish and Jewish-Christian literature most often regarded an unhealthy interest in angels--whether as a real practice or a potential problem--as a threat to monotheism. Indeed, magical sources from antiquity which are either Jewish or show signs of Jewish influence might be thought to provide evidence that angels were frequently invoked along with the God of Israel and other deities, that is, within a polytheistic-syncretistic context. For the most part, however, the names of such angels, as the names of the God of Israel or the other deities, were invoked as coercive means to mundane ends. While it is possible that some accusations of angel worship presupposed the existence of such practices, it is misleading to think that these polemics were only concerned with "magic." Indeed, as we have seen, a "veneration" of angels--or, for that matter, of any deity--is in the strict sense quite alien to many of the magical sources. A number of other texts, in which angels are praised, addressed, or invoked, leave little room (if any) to infer that a devotional posture towards angels was intended as an affront to monotheistic belief. Language expressing praise towards angels could even be rooted in the exemplariness attributed to their heavenly worship, as in the *Shirot 'Olat ha-Shabbat* of Qumran. Moreover, descriptions of the awesome appearance of a given angel or angels may have ultimately derived from an interest in underscoring the incomparable glory of the one transcendent God. These traditions, however, could easily be made the object of polemics or misunderstanding, as among distant observers, or required further clarification, as among circles in which they were formulated.

II. Traditions Against Worshiping Angels

The sources for polemical statements by Jews and Christians against the worship of angels are many and could serve a variety of purposes. While in Colossians the author was very likely denouncing "the worship of angels" as a practical problem being imposed upon his readers, other polemical statements do not provide enough information to make such an inference.

At the beginning of Part Two, we posed the question whether polemical statements may be expected to provide any evidence for religious praxis. During the course of the investigation, it has become apparent that an approach to this problem can only be gained by analyzing the particular features of and concerns behind each document and tradition. Nevertheless, a number of these texts show signs of cohesion in emphasis and literary context; hence it is possible to speak of some polemical accusations in *groups of traditions*: (1) rabbinic prohibitions against sacrificing to angels; (2) against making images of angels; (3) against "two powers"; (4) second-century apologetic accusations of angelolatry among Jews; and (5) the "refusal tradition." These affinities make it clear that in a given denunciatory statement, the interpreter is not only be confronted by the complicated issue of whether there is any truth behind them, but needs also to take seriously that many polemical texts against angel worship reflect a tradition in their own right. Such is clearly the case in texts which we have ascribed to the refusal tradition, the adaptation of which reveals a variety of literary-rhetorical and practical purposes.

In the refusal tradition, the primary actors are the *seer* and the *angel*. The choice of the seer, who wants to worship an angel (most often because of his dazzling appearance), and of the angel, who rejects such a revering posture, provided an effective form for rhetorical communication which presupposed a shared cosmology between author and intended readers. In this respect, the angel's refusal could function several ways: as an interpretive tool within the text to prevent the reader from misunderstanding the text (so esp. Tob 11:14-15 and 12:12, 15-22), as a means of exhortation (*Asc.Isa.*), or as a subtle critique of possible or real proclivities among an author's readers (Rev). To the degree that these functions availed, a specific invective against "outsiders," while not impossible, becomes less likely. Said in other terms, the refusal tradition is often "at home" in a literary context which combines a prohibition to safeguard monotheism, on the one hand, with a common interest in angelology, on the other (Tob, *Asc.Isa.*, *Apoc.Zeph.*, *2 En, 3 En, Apoc.Gosp.Mt.*, and Rev). This traditio-historical background provides a basis for exploring its function within the Apocalypse of John.

III. A Polemic Against "Worshiping" Angels in the Apocalypse of John

In the Apocalypse of John, the refusal tradition is applied in connection to the merger of several thematic elements: (1) angelic mediation (esp. 17:1-19:10; 21:9-22:9); (2) angelomorphic Christology (1:12-20; 14:14-20); (3) worship of Christ (esp. 5:8-12; 22:1-5); and (4) a sensitivity to a monotheistic outlook (esp. 19:10; 22:8-9). In order to assert the preeminence of both God *and* Christ over angels, the author may have split what was originally a refusal tradition consisting of (a) an angelophany, (b) the seer's venerative response, and (c) an angel's refusal which consisted of a self-demotion to the level of the seer and his community and an exhortation to worship God. The *epiphanic element* (and, implicitly, the seer's prostrate position) of the tradition comprises the opening vision; in this case, have been embellished with further motifs to stress that the angelic-divine figure of the christophany, here "one like a son of man," is superior to the "angels of the seven churches." Correspondingly, Christ does not reject the seer's venerative posture. The emphasis of God and Christ over angels may take on an added contingent significance if the conspicuous address to "angels" in the seven letters represent an interest in angelology among the communities addressed. The other elements of the refusal tradition, the *seer's attempt to worship the angel* and *the angel's refusal* (in 19:10; 22:8-9), are placed outside the context of an angelophanic vision. This in itself further underlines the demotion to which the opening vision, coupled with the letters to the seven churches, points.

IV. Angelomorphic Christology in the Apocalypse of John

While in its immediate literary context the opening vision embodies a prophetic commission to write, and describes Christ as superior to the angels of the churches (and therefore to the churches themselves), its function in relation to the overall Christology of the Apocalypse is problematic. That there *is* an analogy between Christology and angelology is apparent from 1:12-20, from attributes shared with some of the angels (e.g., 10:1 and 15:6), and especially from 14:14-20. At the same time, this association seems to be severed emphatically in the vision of the Lamb in chapter 5. Was the angelomorphic aspect of the author's Christology merely a retention of tradition, or did it, as such, serve a constructive purpose?

In terms of salvation history, the seer's commission by Christ in chapter 1 presupposes the heavenly throne-room scene in chapter 5, in which the Lamb--not any other being--is found worthy to open the scroll. Christ's superiority over angels is, however, not taken for granted. If we may assume that the author was concerned with what he considered to be an unhealthy fascination of angels among his readers, it becomes possible to argue that the angelomorphic traits of Christ reflect a shared tradition (and thus function as an underlying communicative link), while the author's creative modification of the refusal tradition functioned as a rhetorical--clear, but subtle-- way of criticizing such a posture. Christ is not to be worshiped as a *primus inter pares angelorum*, but as the Lamb who, because he is slaughtered, has brought God's redemptive activity to bear on communities faced with societal estrangement.

V. Christology and Monotheism: A Pattern of Accommodation?

The exalted status of Christ as an object of worship alongside God was not intended as a breach of monotheism. While the Apocalypse of John may have been read by "outsiders" as a writing with a ditheistic theology, linguistic and thematic considerations suggest that the author took deliberate measures to impede such an idea. Christ the Lamb, who is portrayed as worshiped by the myriadic thousands in heaven and by the creatures of the entire cosmos, is still cast as subordinate to God. Perhaps the closest analogy to the veneration of an independent figure coupled with an express retention of a monotheistic framework is evident in some of the sources in which angels are honored alongside God as aligned and yet subordinate beings. If this is true, then we may be faced with a religio-historical discontinuity as to the kind and intensity of worship between angels and Christ, while we do not go far astray in positing a certain traditio- and religios-historical continuity as to the accommodation as to how such venerative attitudes were reconciled to monotheistic belief. Thus, while without question the worship of and devotion to Christ in the Apocalypse of John presupposes a number of internal developments within Christian circles, the veneration of angels in Early Judaism may ultimately have provided a siginificant underlying model behind the author's way of placing this religious outlook alongside the indispensable primacy in devotion to the one unique and transcendent God "who sits upon the throne."

APPENDIX

TEXTS FORM-CRITICALLY COMPARED FOR THE REFUSAL TRADITION

Abbreviations:

    Ang   Angelophany
    Mer   Vision of the Merkabah
    Th   Theophany
    Chr   Christophany
    Hum   Human (monarch, apostle)

Texts A through K are representative of an angelic refusal tradition. The remaining passages (L through CC), which contain comparable elements, are listed in alphabetical order.

Passage	Setting	Type of Venerative Posture	Negative Directive	Theocentric or Christocentric Emphasis
1	2	3	4	5
A) Tob 12:16-22 (B,ℵ)	Ang	Prostration (v.16-ἔπεσο/αν ἐπὶ πρόσωπον) FEAR (v.16-ἐταράχθησαν, ἐφοβήθησαν)	"Do not fear" (v.17-μὴ φοβεῖσθε)	"Bless God forever." (B,v.17-τὸν θεὸν δὲ εὐλογεῖτε εἰς τὸν αἰῶνα; ℵ,v.17-τὸν θεὸν εὐλογεῖτε εἰς πάντα τὸν αἰῶνα) (cf. also B-v.18; ℵ,B-v.20)
B) Apoc. Zeph. 6:11-15 (OTP tr. from Akh.)	Ang	Prostration (v.14-I fell on my face...) (v.14-...and I worshiped him)	"Do not worship me" (v.15)	"I am not the Lord Almighty" (v.15)
C) 2 En 1:4-8[1]	Ang	Fear Prostration	"Be brave, Enoch! In truth, do not	"The eternal God has sent us to

---

[1] The passage as it is, is not strictly a *refusal*; "Do not fear!" may be interpreted as comfort in the face of the vision (the phrase is preceded by an exhortation to "Be brave!"), as a rejection of the seer's prostration, or both. On the ambiguity inherent in this terminology, see p. 81 and n. 92. In his *OTP* translation, F.I. ANDERSEN apparently opts for the first alternative, reading the seer's reaction to the vision in 1:7 as "homage" which the men apparently accept (*OTP*, 1.107 n. u). If ANDERSEN is correct, this passage should

(1)	(2)	(3)	(4)	(5)
(OTP tr. from Slav. recensions J,A)		(J,v.7-Then I bowed down to them [2 huge men] and I was terrified; and the appearance of my face was changed because of fear.) (A,v.7-Then I hurried and stood up and bowed down to them; and the appearance of my face was glittering because of fear.)	fear!" (J,v.8) "Be brave, Enoch! Do not fear!" (A,v.8)	you. And behold, you will ascend with us to heaven today." (J,v.8) "The eternal Lord has sent us to you. And behold, today you will ascend with us to heaven." (A,v.8)
D) *Asc. Isa.* 7:18-23 (*OTP* tr. from Lat., Eth., Slav.)	Ang	Prostration (v.21-I fell on my face to worship him)	"Worship neither throne, nor angel from the six heavens" (v.21)	
E) *Asc. Isa.* 8:1-10; 8:15 (*OTP* tr. from Lat., Eth., Slav.)	Ang	Manner of Address (v.4-"What [is] this which I see, my lord?") see, my lord?")	"I am not your lord" (v.5)	"but your companion" (v.5)
F) *Apoc. Gosp. Mt.* 3:3	Ang	Worship (*adorans eum*)	"Do not say servant" (*servum*)	"but my fellow-servant (*conservum*) for we are servants of one Lord (*domini*)."

have been treated in section II.B.2 of Part Two as evidence for the veneration of angels. It is included here as part of the refusal tradition, given (1) the possibility of ambiguity in the men's response and (2) the text's close *formal* correspondence with the other occurrences of the tradition (angelophanic appearance, revering posture, negative directive, theocentric emphasis).

G) Rev 19:10	Ang (no vision of appearance)	Prostration Worship (ἔπεσα ἔμπροσθεν τῶν ποδῶν αὐτοῦ προσκυνῆσαι αὐτῷ)	"Do not see (to do it)" (ὅρα μή)	"I am a fellow-servant (σύνδουλος) with you and your brothers" "Worship God" (τῷ θεῷ προσκύνησον)
H) Rev 22:8-9	Ang (no vision of appearance)	Prostration Worship (v.8-ἔπεσα προσκυνῆσαι ἔμπροσθεν τῶν ποδῶν τοῦ ἀγγέλου)	"Do not see (to do it)" (v.9-ὅρα μή)	"I am your fellow-servant (v.9-σύνδουλος) and of your brothers the prophets" "Worship God" (v.9-τῷ θεῷ προσκύνησον)
I) 3 En 1:6-10 (OTP tr.)	Mer	Fear (v.7-But as soon as the princes of the chariot looked at me [R. Ishmael] and the fiery seraphim fixed their gaze on me, I shrank back trembling, and fell down, stunned by the radiant appearance of their eyes and the bright vision of their faces, ...)	...until the Holy One, blessed be he, rebuked them and said, "My servants, my seraphim, my cherubim, my ophanim, hide your eyes from Ishmael my beloved son and honored friend, so that he does not shrink and tremble so." (vv.7-8)	At once Metatron, Prince of the Divine Presence, came and revived me and raised me to my feet, but still I had not strength enough to sing a hymn before the glorious throne of the glorious King, the mightiest of kings, ...until an hour had passed. (vv.9-10) (vv.11-12: description of heavenly worship)
J) 3 En 16:1-5 (OTP tr.; par. in b.Hag. 15a) Synopsis of mss. mss in SCHÄFER, Synopse zur He-	Ang (Metatron)	FEAR (v.2-But when Aḥer [Ms. Mün 40 adds: 'lysh' bn rwkzyh] came to behold the vision of the chariot and set eyes upon me, he was afraid and trembled before me. His soul was alarmed to the	Immediately a divine voice came out from the presence of the Shekinah and said, "Come back to me, apostate sons—apart from 'Aḥer!" (v.4)	Then 'Anapi'el YHWH...came at the command of the Holy One... and struck me with sixty lashes of fire and made me stand to my feet. (v.5)

Appendix

(1)	(2)	(3)	(4)	(5)
khalot-Literatur, par.856		point of leaving him because of his fear, dread, and terror of me, when he saw me seated upon a throne like a king, with ministering angels standing beside me as servants and all the princes of kingdoms crowned with crowns surrounding me.) Worship (v.3-Then he opened his mouth and said, "There are indeed two powers in heaven!"		
K) C. Gen. Hekh. A/2 R, ll.13-16 (*Tarbiz* 38 [1968] 362-63) (*OTP* tr.)	Ang (Metatron)	Response not narrated (l.13-And when a youth [n'r] comes out to meet you from behind the throne of glory, ...)	"...Do not bow down to him..." (l.14-'*l tshthwh lw*)	(Metatron only *resembles* the Lord: ll.14-16- ...for his crown is as the crown of his king and his sandals as the sandals of his king and the robe which is upon him as the robe of his king. ...His eyes b[urn as t]orches and his eyeballs burn as candlesticks. His splendor is as the splendor of his king and his glory as the glory of his creator.
L) *Apoc. Paul* (tr. in BUDGE, *Coptic Texts*)	Ang	Prostration (I fell on my face) Fear (I trembled in all my members)	"Do not fear"	

M) Acts 10:25-46	Hum	Prostration Worship (v.25-πεσὼν ἐπὶ τοὺς πόδας προσεκύνησεν)	"Stand up" (v.25-ἀνάστηθι)	I also am a man" (v.25-καὶ ἐγὼ αὐτὸς ἄνθρωπος εἰμί) (v.46-for they heard them speaking in tongues and extolling God)
N) Dan 10:4-21	Ang	Prostration Fear (v.9-w'ny hyyty nrdm 'l pny wpny 'rsh; v.11-'mdty mr'yd; v.15-ntty pny 'rsh wn'lmty) (LXX-v.9-ἐγὼ ἤμην πεπτωκὼς ἐπὶ πρόσωπόν μου ἐπὶ τὴν γῆν [Th. omits ημ. πεπτ.]; v.11-ἔστην τρέμων [Th. ἀνέστην ἔντρομος]; v.15=MT [LXX-ἐσιώπησα; Th.-κατενύγην]	"Do not be afraid" (vv.12,19-'l tyr') (MT=LXX,Th.-μὴ φοβοῦ)	"from the first day that you set your mind to understand and to humble yourself before God, your words have been heard" (v.12)
O) 1 En 14:8-15:2	Th	Prostration Fear (4QEn ms. c,v.14-].nplt [) (Cod.Pan.,v.14-ἤμην σειόμενος καὶ τρέμων καὶ ἔπεσον; v.24-κἀγὼ ἤμην ἕως τούτου ἐπὶ πρόσωπόν μου βεβλημένος καὶ τρέμων)	"Do not fear, Enoch, righteous man, scribe of righteousness..." (Cod.Pan.,15:1-μὴ φοβηθῇς, Ἐνώχ, ἄνθροπος ἀληθινὸς καὶ νὸς καὶ γραμματεὺς τῆς ἀληθείας)	"Come near!" (Cod.Pan.,v.24-πρόσελθε ὧδε) "Hear my [God's] word." (cf. also 15:1) (Cod.Pan.,v.24-τὸν λόγον μου ἄκουσον; cf. 15:1)
P) 2 En 20:1-4 (OTP tr. from Slav. recensions J,A)	Ang	Fear (J,v.1-And I was terrified and trembled with great fear) (A,v.1-And I was terrified, and I trembled.)	"Be brave, Enoch! Don't be frightened!" (angels) (J,A,v.2)	They showed (me) the Lord from a distance sitting on his very high throne...all the heavenly armies...did obeisance to the Lord. (J,v.3) They showed me from a distance

280   Appendix

(1)	(2)	(3)	(4)	(5)
				the Lord, sitting on his throne...all the heavenly armies...and doing obeisance to the Lord. (A,v.3)
Q) 2 En 21:1-6 (OTP tr. from Slav. recensions J,A)	Ang	Prostration Fear (J,v.2-I became terrified; and I fell on my face, and I said in myself, "Woe to me! What has happened to me?") (A,v.2-I became terrified; I fell on my face.)	"Be brave, Enoch! Don't be frightened!" (angels) (J,A,v.3)	"Stand up...in front of the face of the Lord forever." (J,A,v.3)
R) 2 En 22:1-11 (OTP tr. from Slav. recensions J,A)	Th	Prostration Worship (v.4-I fell down flat and did obeisance to the Lord)	"Be brave, Enoch! Don't be frightened!" (God) (v.5)	"Stand up in front of my face forever" (God) (v.5)
S) Gen 50:19,21	Hum	Prostration (v.18-...*wylkw wyplw lpnyw wy'mrw hnnw lk l'bdym*) (cf. LXX-no equivalent for *wyplw*) (MT=Onk.,Neof., Tg.Ps.Jon.)	"Do not be afraid" (vv.19,21-*'l tyr'w*) (LXX-μὴ φοβεῖσθε) (MT=Onk.,Neof.,Tg. Ps.Jon.)	"Am I in the place of God?" (v.19-*htht 'lhym 'ny*) (LXX-not interr.: τοῦ γὰρ θεοῦ εἰμι ἐγώ; viz. also Tg.Ps.Jon.) (MT=Onk.) (Neof.-omits; cf. Neof. Gen. 44:14)
T) Jos. Asen. 14:9-11 (OTP tr.)	Ang (man-like angel)	Prostration Fear (v.10-And Aseneth saw and fell on her face at his feet on the ground. And Aseneth was	"Courage, and do not be afraid" (v.11)	"but rise and stand on your feet, and I will tell you what I have to say" (v.11)

Appendix

(1)	(2)	(3)	(4)	(5)
		filled with great fear, and all of her limbs trembled)		
U) Josh 5:13-15	Ang	Prostration Worship (v.14-*wypl yhwsh'h 'l pnyw 'rsh wyshthw*) (cf. LXX-no equivalent for *wyshthw*) (MT=Tg.Ps.Jon.)		
V) Judg 6:11-23	Ang (but Gideon also communicates with the Lord *via* the angel)	Worship (LXX,A: v.19-προσεκύνησεν; LXX,B-προσήγγισεν=MT) (Ambiguity as to who is worshiped in Cod. Alex) Fear (v.22-"Alas, Lord God, for I have seen an angel of of the Lord face to face!")	And the Lord said to him, "Peace be to you! Do not fear; you will not die." (v.23) (MT-*'l tyr' l' tmwt*; =LXX)	And Gideon built there an altar to the Lord (v.24)
W) Mk 10:17-18	Jesus	(Prostration) Manner of Address (v.17-καὶ γονυπετήσας αὐτὸν ἐπηρώτα αὐτόν· διδάσκαλε ἀγαθέ...)	"Why do you call me good?" (v.18-τί με λέγεις ἀγαθόν;)	"There is no one good except for one, God." (v.18-οὐδεὶς ἀγαθὸς εἰ μὴ εἷς ὁ θεός)
X) Mt 17:5-8 (par. Mk 9:2-10 and Lk 9:28-36	Chr Moses Elijah	Prostration Fear (v.6-ἔπεσαν ἐπὶ πρόσωπον αὐτῶν καὶ ἐφοβήθησαν σφόδρα) (Mk 9:6-ἔκφοβοι γὰρ ἐγένοντο; Lk 9:34-ἐφοβήθησαν; and in Mt as response to the exhortation to listen to the Son)	"Rise, and do not be afraid" (v.7-ἐγέρθητε καὶ μὴ φοβεῖσθε) (omitted in Mk and Lk)	And when they lifted up their eyes they saw no one but Jesus only. (v.8-ἐπάραντες δὲ τοὺς ὀφθαλμοὺς αὐτῶν οὐδένα εἶδον εἰ μὴ αὐτὸν Ἰησοῦν μόνον)

Υ) Mt 28:2-7	Ang	Fear (guards) (v.4-ἀπὸ δὲ τοῦ φόβου αὐτοῦ ἐσείσθησαν οἱ τηροῦντες καὶ ἐγενήθησαν ὡς νεκροί)	(to the women) "Do not be afraid" (v.5-μὴ φοβεῖσθε ὑμεῖς)	"for I know that you seek Jesus who was crucified" (v.5) "he is going before you to Galilee; there you will see him" (v.7)
Ζ) Mt 28:9-10	Chr	Prostration Worship (v.9-αἱ δὲ προσελθοῦσαι ἐκράτησαν αὐτοῦ τοὺς πόδας καὶ προσεκύνησαν αὐτῷ; cf. v.17)	"Do not be afraid" (v.10-μὴ φοβεῖσθε)	"go and tell my brethren to go to Galilee, and there they will see me" (v.10; cf. v.18)
ΑΑ) Rev 1:13-20	Chr	Prostration (v.17-ἔπεσα πρὸς τοὺς πόδας αὐτοῦ ὡς νεκρὸς)	"Do not be afraid" (v.17-μὴ φοβοῦ)	"I am the first and the last..." (v.17-ἐγὼ εἰμὶ ὁ πρῶτος καὶ ὁ ἔσχατος; cf. v.8)
ΒΒ) Test Abr. 9:1-3[2] (OTP tr. from Rum. to recension A)	Ang (Michael)	Fear Prostration (vv.1,2-When the righteous man [Abraham] saw him [Michael] he fell on his face on the ground as one dead...with many tears he fell at the feet		... and the Commander-in-chief told him everything which he had heard from the Most High... (v.2)

---

[2] The prostration before Michael in the longer recension A of *Test. Abr.* is not rejected (as in *2 En* 1:4-8; see p. 275 n. 1 on the question of inclusion in Part Two, section II.B.2 above), a posture which is absent in the shorter recension (B). The text-critical development of the writing is complex, and the problem of determining which recension at which point preserves a more original version of *Test.Abr.*, though the subject of numerous hypotheses, remains ultimately unsolved; see esp. DELCOR, *Le Testament d'Abraham* (SVTP, 2; Leiden: Brill, 1973); NICKELSBURG, ed., *Studies on the Testament of Abraham* (SCS, 6; Missoula: Scholars, 1976, rev. ed.); and E.P. SANDERS, "Testament of Abraham," in *OTP*, 1.872-73. Concerning some of the differences in the angelological presentation of the two recensions--which, however, does not consider veneration--, see Anitra Bingham KOLENKROW, "The Angelology of the Testament of Abraham," in *Studies on the Testament of Abraham*, pp. 153-62.

Appendix 283

(1)	(2)	(3)	(4)	(5)
		of the incorporeal one...) (Rec. B does not contain such acts of reverence)		
CC) *Test Abr.* 3:5-6[3] (*OTP* tr. from Rum., Grk. to recension A)	Ang	Prostration (vv.5-6-And when Isaac saw the face of the antel he said to Sarah his mother, "... The man sitting with my father Abraham is no son of the face which dwells upon the earth." And Isaac did obeisance [ἐμπροσεκύνησεν] to him and fell at the feet of the incorporeal one.) (Rec. B: does not contain such acts of reverence; cf. 4:4-6, which emphasizes angels' worship of God.)		And the incorporeal one blessed him and said, "The Lord God will bestow upon you his promise which he gave to your father Abraham and to his seed..." (v.6)

---

[3] See previous note.

Selected Bibliography

I. Primary Sources and Reference Works

ALBECK, E., ed. סדר קדשים שישה סדרי משנה, revised by E. ELON. Jerusalem/Tel Aviv: Bailik Institute and Debir, 1958.

BAILLET, Maurice, ed. *Qumrān Grotte 4 III (4Q482-4Q520)*. DJD, 7. Oxford: Clarendon Press, 1982.

BAILLET, M., J.T. MILIK, and R. DE VAUX, eds. *Les 'Petites Grottes' de Qumrān*. DJD, 3. Oxford: Clarendon Press, 1962.

BARTHÉLEMY, D. and J.T. MILIK, eds. *Qumran Cave I*. DJD, 1. Oxford: Clarendon Press, 1955.

BETZ, Hans Dieter, ed. *The Greek Magical Papyri in Translation, Including the Demotic Spells*. 2nd ed. Chicago/London: University of Chicago Press, 1992.

BEYER, Klaus. *Die aramäischen Texte vom Toten Meer*. Göttingen: Vandenhoeck & Ruprecht, 1984.

_____. *Die aramäischen Texte vom Toten Meer. Ergänzungsband*. Göttingen: Vandenhoeck & Ruprecht, 1994.

BLACK, Matthew, ed. *Apocalypsis Henochi Graece*. PVTG, 3. Leiden: E.J. Brill, 1970. Pp. 3-44.

_____. *The Book of Enoch or I Enoch. A New English Edition*. SVTP, 7. Leiden: E.J. Brill 1985.

BLANC, Cécile. *Origène. Commentaire sur saint Jean*. SC, 222. Paris: Cerf, 1975.

BONNER, Campbell, ed. *The Last Chapters of Enoch in Greek*. London: Chatto and Windus, 1937.

BONWETSCH, Gottlieb N. *Die Apokalypse Abrahams*. SGTK, 1/1. Aalen: Scientia, 1972. Repr. from 1879.

BOTTERWECK, G. Johannes, Helmer RINGGREN, H.J. FABRY, eds. *Theological Dictionary of the Old Testament*. Translated by John T. WILLIS, Geoffrey W. BROMILEY, and Davie E. GREEN. Grand Rapids: Wm. B. Eerdmans, 1974-.

BROOKE, A.E. *The Fragments of Heracleon*. TS, 1/4. Cambridge: Cambridge University Press, 1891.

BROOKS, E.W. *Joseph and Asenath*. TED, 2/7. London/New York: 1918.

BUDGE, E.A.W. *Miscellaneous Coptic Texts in the Dialect of Upper Egypt*. Oxford: Oxford University Press, 1915.

BURCHARD, Christoph. *Untersuchungen zu Joseph und Aseneth*. WUNT, 8. Tübingen: J.C.B. Mohr (Paul Siebeck), 1965.

BUTTRICK, George A., gen. ed. *Interpreter's Dictionary of the Bible*. 4 vols. and suppl. Nashville: Abingdon Press, 1962-1975.

CARMIGNAC, Jean. *La Règle de la Guerre*. Paris: Letouzey et Ané, 1958.

CHABOT, J.-B, ed., et al. *Répertoire d'épigraphie sémitique*. 8 vols. Académie des inscriptions et belles-lettres. Paris: Imprimérie Nationale, 1900-1968.

CHARLES, R.H, ed. *The Apocrypha and Pseudepigrapha of the Old Testament in English*. 2 vols. Oxford: Clarendon Press, 1913.

_____. *The Ascension of Isaiah*. London: Black, 1900.

_____. *The Ethiopic Version of the Book of Enoch*. AnOx. Oxford: Clarendon Press, 1906.

_____. *The Greek Versions of the Testaments of the Twelve Patriarchs*. 2nd ed. Oxford: Oxford University Press, 1908.

CHARLESWORTH, James H, ed., et al. *Graphic Concordance to the Dead Sea Scrolls*. Tübingen/Louisville: J.C.B. Mohr (Paul Siebeck) and Westminster-John Knox Press, 1991.

_____. *The Old Testament Pseudepigrapha*. 2 vols. Garden City, NY: Doubleday. 1983-1985.

_____. *The Pseudepigrapha and Modern Research with a Supplement*. SCS, 7. Chico, CA: Scholars Press, 1981.

COLSON, F.H. and G.H. WHITAKER. *Philo*. 10 vols., LCL. Cambridge, Mass./London: Harvard University Press and Heinemann, 1929-1943.

DE JONGE, Marinus et al., eds. *The Testaments of the Twelve Patriarchs. A Critical Edition of the Greek Text*. PVTG, 1/2. Leiden: E.J. Brill, 1978.

DELCOR, M., ed. *Le Testament d'Abraham: Introduction, traduction du texte grec et commentaire de la recension grecque longe, suivie de la traduction des Testaments d'Abraham, d'Isaac et de Jacob d'après les versions orientales*. SVTP, 2. Leiden: E.J. Brill, 1973.

DENIS, Albert-Marie, ed. *Fragmenta Pseudepigraphorum quae supersunt graeca*. PVTG, 3. Leiden: E.J. Brill, 1970.

DIETZFELBINGER, Christian. *Pseudo-Philo: Antiquitates Biblicae*. JSHRZ, 2/2. Gütersloh: Gerd Mohn, 1975.

DITTENBERGER, W., ed. *Sylloge Inscriptionum Graecarum*. 4 vols. 3rd ed. Leipzig: J.C. Hinrichs, 1915-1924.

EISENMAN, Robert H. and James M. ROBINSON, eds. *Facsimile Edition*. 2 vols. Washington, D.C.: Biblical Archaeology Society, 1991.

ELIADE, Mircea, gen. ed. *The Encyclopedia of Religion.* 16 vols. New York: Macmillan, 1987.

ELLIGER, K. and W. RUDOLPH, eds., *et al. Biblia Hebraica Stuttgartensia.* Stuttgart: Deutsche Bibelgesellschaft, 1984.

EPSTEIN, I., ed. *Hebrew-English Edition of the Babylonian Talmud.* London: The Soncino Press, 1960-.

_____, ed. *The Babylonian Talmud.* 18 vols. London: The Soncino Press, 1935-1952.

FREEDMAN, David Noel, gen. ed. *The Anchor Bible Dictionary.* 6 vols. Garden City, NY: Doubleday, 1992.

FREEDMAN, H. and M. SIMON, eds. *Midrash Rabbah.* London: Soncino, 1939.

FREY, Jean-Baptiste, ed. *Corpus Inscriptionum Judaicarum.* 2 vols. New York: Ktav, 1975. Repr. from 1936, 1952.

GASTER, T.H. *The Dead Sea Scriptures.* 3rd ed. Garden City, NY: Doubleday, 1976.

GEBHARDT, Oscar von. "Die Ascensio Isaiae als Heiligenlegende: Aus Cod. Gr. 1534 der Nationalbibliothek zu Paris." *ZWT* 21 (1878), pp. 330-53.

GIESSEN, Angelo, ed. *Der Septuaginta-Text des Buches Daniel. Kap. 5-12, zusammen mit Susanna, Bel et Draco, sowie Esther Kap. 1,1a-2,15 nach dem Kölner Teil des Papyrus 967.* PTA, 5. Bonn: Rudolf Habelt, 1968.

GLATZER, N.N., ed. *The Passover Haggadah.* New York: Schocken Books, 1953.

GODLEY, A.D. *Herodotus.* Vol. 1. LCL. Cambridge, Mass. and London: Harvard University Press and William Heinemann, 1966.

GRUENWALD, Ithamar. קטעים חדשים מספרות ההיכלות. *Tarbiz* 38 (1968), pp. 354-72.

HANHART, Robert, ed. *Tobit.* SVTG, 8/5. Göttingen: Vandenhoeck & Ruprecht, 1983.

HARNACK, Adolf von. *Bruchstücke des Evangeliums und der Apokalypse des Petrus.* 2nd ed. Leipzig: J.C. Hinrichs, 1893.

HARRIS, J. Rendell, ed. and J. Armitage ROBINSON. *The Apology of Aristides.* TS, 1/1. Cambridge: Cambridge University Press, 1891.

HOFFMANN, D., ed. *Midrasch Tannaim zum Deuteronomium.* Berlin: Poppelauer, 1908-1909.

JAMES, M.R. *The Apocryphal New Testament.* Oxford: Oxford University Press, 1924.

_____. *The Biblical Antiquities of Philo.* TED, Ser. 1. New York: Ktav, 1971. Repr. from 1917.

JONGELING, B. *Le Rouleau de la Guerre.* Assen: Van Gorcum, 1962.

KAUTSCH, E. *Gesenius' Hebrew Grammar*. 28th edition. Translated by A.E. COWLEY. Oxford: Clarendon Press, 1910.

KENYON, Frederic G, ed. *The Chester Beatty Biblical Papyri. Ezekiel, Daniel, Esther*. Fascicle 7. London: Emery Walker, 1937-1938.

KISCH, G. *Pseudo-Philo's Liber Antiquitatum Biblicarum*. Medieval Studies, 10. Notre Dame, 1949.

KLAUSER, Theodor, ed., et al. *Reallexikon für Antike und Christentum. Sachwörterbuch zur Auseinandersetzung des Christentums mit der antiken Welt*. 13 vols., 5 fasc.'s, and 4 suppl.'s. Stuttgart: Anton Hiersemann, 1950-1988.

KRAUSE, Gerhard and Gerhard MÜLLER, eds. *Theologische Realenzyklopädie*. 16 vols. Berlin/New York: Walter de Gruyter, 1977-1987.

KROPP, Angelicus M., ed. *Ausgewählte Koptische Zaubertexte*. 3 vols. Brussels: Édition de la Fondation Égyptologique Reine Élisabeth, 1930-1931.

KÜMMEL, Werner G., ed. *Jüdische Schriften aus hellenistisch-römischer Zeit*. 5 vols. (in fasc.'s). Gütersloh: Gerd Mohn, 1973-1984.

LATTKE, Michael. *Die Oden Salomos in ihrer Bedeutung für Neues Testament und Gnosis*. OBO, 25/1-3. Fribourg/Göttingen: Editions Universitaires and Vandenhoeck & Ruprecht, 1979.

LAUTERBACH, Jacob Z. *Mekilta de-Rabbi Ishmael*. 3 vols. The Schiff Library of Jewish Classics. Philadelphia: The Jewish Publication Society of America, 1933-1935.

LEHRMAN, S.M., trans. *Midrash Rabbah. Exodus*. London: Soncino, 1939.

LICHT, Jacob. סרך הסרכים. Jerusalem: Bialik, 1965.

LIEBERMAN, S., ed. *Midrash Debarim Rabbah*. 2nd ed. Jerusalem: Wahrmann Books, 1964.

LOHSE, Eduard. *Die Texte aus Qumran*. Darmstadt: Wissenschaftliche Buchgesellschaft, 1971.

MAIER, Johann and Kurt SCHUBERT. *Die Qumran-Essener*. UTB, 224. Munich/Basel: Ernst Reinhard, 1973.

MARGOLIOTH, Mordecai, ed. *Sepher ha-Razim, A Newly Recovered Book of Magic from the Talmudic Period, Collected from Genizah Fragments and Other Sources*. Jerusalem: American Academy for Jewish Research, 1966. In Hebrew.

McCOWN, C.C. *The Testament of Solomon*. UNT, 9. Leipzig: J.C. Hinrichs, 1922.

MEAGHER, Paul Kevin, Thomas O'BRIEN, and Consuelo Maria AHERNE, eds. *Encyclopedic Dictionary of Religion*. 3 vols. Washington, D.C.: Corpus Publications, 1979.

MILIK, J.T. *The Books of Enoch. Aramaic Fragments of Qumrān Cave 4*. Oxford: Clarendon Press, 1976.

MIGNE, J.-P., ed. *et al. Patrologia graecae*. 161 vols. and 1 Index. Paris: Petit-Montouge and Garnier.

_____, ed. *et al. Patrologia latinae*. 221 vols. and 5 suppl.'s. Paris: Petit-Montouge and Garnier.

MIRAKIN, Moshe A. *Midrash Rabbah*. 11 vols. Tel-Aviv: Yavneh, 1956-1967.

MITCHELL, S. *Regional Epigraphic Catalogues of Asia Minor II. The Ankara District. The Inscriptions of North Galatia*. British Institute of Archaeology at Ankara, 4. Oxford: British Archaeological Reports International Series 135, 1982.

MONTGOMERY, James A. *Aramaic incantation texts from Nippur*. Publications of the Babylonian Section, 3. Philadelphia: The University Museum, 1913.

MORGAN, Michael A. *Sepher Ha-Razim. The Book of the Mysteries*. SBLTT 25, PS 11. Chico, CA: Scholars Press, 1983.

NAVEH, Joseph and Shaul SHAKED. *Amulets and Magic Bowls. Aramaic Incantations of Late Antiquity*. Jerusalem/Leiden: Magness Press and E.J. Brill, 1985.

NESTLE, Eberhard, *et al*, eds. *Novum Testamentum Graece*. 27th ed. Stuttgart: Deutsche Bibelgesellschaft, 1993.

NEWSOM, Carol. *Songs of the Sabbath Sacrifice: A Critical Edition*. HSS, 27. Atlanta: Scholars Press, 1985.

ODEBERG, H. *3 Enoch or The Hebrew Book of Enoch*. 2nd ed. LBS. New York: Ktav, 1973. Repr. from 1928.

PERROT, C. and P.-M. BOGAERT, with Daniel H. HARRINGTON. *Pseudo-Philon. Les Antiquités Bibliques*. 2 vols. SC, 229-230. Paris: Cerf, 1976.

PHILONENKO, Marc, ed. *Joseph et Aséneth*. SPB, 13. Leiden: E.J. Brill, 1968.

PHILONENKO-SAYAR, Belkis and Marc PHILONENKO. *Die Apokalypse Abrahams*. JSHRZ, 5/5. Gütersloh: Gerd Mohn, 1982.

PICARD, J.-C., ed. *Apocalypsis Baruchi Graece*. PVTG, 2. Leiden: E.J. Brill, 1967. Pp. 61-96.

PREISENDANZ, Karl, ed. *Papyri Graecae Magicae. Die Griechischen Zauberpapyri*. 2 vols. Leipzig/Berlin: B.G. Teubner, 1928-1931.

RAHLFS, Alfred, ed. *Septuaginta*. 2 vols. in 1. Stuttgart: Deutsche Bibelgesellschaft, 1935.

ROUSSEL, Pierre and Marcel LAUNEY, eds. *Inscriptions de Delos*. Paris: Librairie Ancienne Honoré Champion, 1937.

ROTH, Cecil and Geoffrey WIGODER, eds. *Encyclopaedia Judaica*. 16 vols. Jerusalem: Keter, 1971-1972.

SCHÄFER, Peter, ed. *Geniza-Fragmente zur Hekhalot-Literatur*. TSAJ, 6. Tübingen: J.C.B. Mohr (Paul Siebeck, 1984).

_____. *Synopse zur Hekhalot-Literatur*. TSAJ, 2. Tübingen: J.C.B. Mohr (Paul Siebeck), 1981.

_____. *Übersetzung der Hekhalot-Literatur*. Vols. 2-4. TSAJ, 17,22, and 29. Tübingen: J.C.B. Mohr (Paul Siebeck), 1987-1991.

SCHÄFER, Peter and Hans-Jürgen BECKER. *Synopse zum Talmud Yerushalmi*. Tübingen: J.C.B. Mohr (Paul Siebeck), 1991. Vol. I/1-2.

SCHNEEMELCHER, Wilhelm. *Neutestamentliche Apokryphen*. 2 vols. 5th ed. of Edgar HENNECKE's original collection. Tübingen: J.C.B. Mohr (Paul Siebeck), 1987-1989.

SPERBER, Alexander, ed. *The Bible in Aramaic*. 4 vols. Leiden: E.J. Brill, 1959-1973.

STEINDORFF, G. *Die Apokalypse des Elias, eine unbekannte Apokalypse und Bruchstücke der Sophonias-Apokalypse*. TU, n.F. 2/3a. Leipzig: J.C. Hinrichs, 1899.

STRACK, H.L. and P. BILLERBECK. *Kommentar zum Neuen Testament aus Talmud und Midrasch*. 6 vols. Munich: C.H. Beck, 1922-1956.

STRACK, H.L. and G. STEMBERGER. *Einleitung in Talmud und Midrasch*. 7th ed. Nördlingen: C.H. Beck, 1982.

STRUGNELL, John. "The Angelic Liturgy at Qumran--4QSerek Šîrôt 'Olat Haššabbat." In *Congress Volume: Oxford 1959*. VTS, 7. Leiden: E.J. Brill, 1960. Pp. 318-45.

SWETE, Henry Barclay. *The Old Testament in Greek*. 3 vols. 4th ed. Cambridge: Cambridge University Press, 1912.

THACKERAY, H.S.J. et al. *Josephus*. 10 vols., LCL. Cambridge, Mass./London: Harvard University Press and Heinemann, 1926-1965.

TISCHENDORF, K. von. *Evangelia Apocrypha*. Leipzig: Hermann Mendelssohn, 1876.

TISSERENT, Eugène. *Ascension d'Isaie*. Paris: Letouzay, 1909.

VAN DER PLOEG, J. *Le Rouleau de la Guerre*. STDJ, 2. Leiden: E.J. Brill, 1959.

VAN DER WOUDE, A.S. "Ein neuer Segensspruch aus Qumran (11 Q Ber)." In *Bibel und Qumran. Festschrift für Hans Bardtke*, edited by S. WAGNER. Berlin: Evangelische Haupt-Bibelgesellschaft, 1968. Pp. 253-58.

_____. "Fragmente einer Rolle der Lieder für das Sabbatopfer aus Höhle XI von Qumran (11QŠirŠabb)." In *Von Kanaan bis Kerala*, edited by W.C. DELSMAN et al. AOAT, 211. Neukirchen-Vluyn: Neukirchener Verlag, 1982. Pp. 311-37.

WACHHOLDER, Benjamin Zion and Martin G. ABBEGG. *A Preliminary Edition of the Unpublished Dead Sea Scrolls*. 2 fascicles. Washington, D.C.: Biblical Archaeology Society, 1991-.

WEBER, Robert. *Biblia Sacra iuxta Vulgata Versionem*. 2nd ed. Stuttgart: Württembergische Bibelanstalt, 1975.

WIEGAND, Theodor. *Didyma. Zweiter Teil: Die Inschriften.* Berlin: Gebr. Mann, 1958.

WISSOWA, Georg, ed. et al. *Paulys Real-Encyclopädie der classischen Altertumswissenschaft.* Neue Bearbeitung. 19 vols. with 15 suppl.'s and a Register. Stuttgart: J.B. Metzler; Munich: Alfred Druckenmüller, 1839-1980.

YADIN, Yigael. "The Masada Fragment of the Qumran Songs of the Sabbath Sacrifice." *IEJ* 34 (1984), pp. 77-88.

_____. *The Scroll of the War of the Sons of Light against the Sons of Darkness.* Oxford: Oxford University Press, 1962.

ZIEGLER, Joseph, ed. *Susanna-Daniel-Bel et Draco.* SVTG, 16/2. Göttingen: Vandenhoeck & Ruprecht, 1954.

ZUCKERMANDEL, M.S., ed. *Tosephta.* Jerusalem: Wahrmann Books, 1963.

II. Secondary Sources

ABBOTT, T.K. *Epistles to the Ephesians and to the Colossians.* ICC. Edinburgh: T. & T. Clark, 1897.

ALBRIGHT, William F. *From Stone Age to Christianity.* Garden City, NY: Doubleday, 1957.

ALEXANDER, P.S. "3 Enoch and the Talmud." *JStJud* 18 (1987), pp. 40-68.

_____. "Appendix: 3 Enoch." In Emil SCHÜRER, *The history of the Jewish people in the age of Jesus Christ*, edited by Geza VERMES, Martin GOODMAN, and Fergus MILLAR. Edinburgh: T. & T. Clark, 1986. Vol. 3, Part 1, pp. 269-77.

_____. "Incantations and Books of Magic." In Emil SCHÜRER, *The history of the Jewish people in the age of Jesus Christ*, edited by Geza VERMES, Martin GOODMAN, and Fergus MILLAR. Edinburgh: T. & T. Clark, 1986. Vol. 3, Part 1, pp. 342-79.

_____. "The Historical Setting of the Hebrew Book of Enoch." *JJS* 28 (1977), pp. 156-80.

ALTMANN, Alexander. "Sacred Hymns in Hekhaloth Literature." *Melilah* 2 (1946), pp. 1-24.

ANDERSEN, F.I. "2 (Slavonic Apocalypse of) ENOCH." In *The Old Testament Pseudepigrapha*, edited by James H. CHARLESWORTH. 2 vols. Garden City, NY: Doubleday, 1983-1985. Vol. 1, pp. 91-213.

ANDRIESSEN, P. "La teneur judéo-chrétienne de Hé I 6 et II 14B-III 2." *NT* 18 (1976), pp. 293-313.

ARNOLD, Clinton E. "Mediator Figures in Asia Minor: Epigraphic Evidence." Paper presented at the Consultation on Jewish and Christian Mediator Figures in Greco-Roman Antiquity, SBL Meeting 1992 in San Francisco. Manuscript, 29 pp.

ATTRIDGE, Harold W. *The Epistle to the Hebrews*. Hermeneia. Philadelphia: Fortress Press, 1989.

AUNE, David E. *Prophecy in Early Christianity and the Ancient Mediterranean World*. Grand Rapids: Wm. B. Eerdmans, 1983.

_____. "The Apocalypse of John and the Problem of Genre." *Semeia* 36 (1986), pp. 65-96.

BAKKER, Adolphine. "Christ an Angel?" *ZNW* 32 (1933), pp. 255-65.

BALZ, H.R. *Methodische Probleme der neutestamentlichen Christologie*. WMANT, 25. Neukirchen-Vluyn: Neukirchener Verlag, 1967.

BANDSTRA, J. *The Law and the Elements of the World*. Grand Rapids: Wm. B. Eerdmans, 1964.

BARBEL, Joseph. *Christos Angelos*. 2nd ed. Theophaneia, 3. Bonn: Peter Hanstein, 1964.

BARCLAY, William. *The All-Sufficient Christ*. London: SCM Press, 1963.

BARKER, Margaret. *The Great Angel. A Study of Israel's Second God*. London: SPCK, 1992.

BARR, David L. "The Apocalypse as a Symbolic Transformation of the World: A Literary Analysis." *Int* 38 (1984), pp. 39-50.

BARTH, J. "Zur Textkritik der syrischen Ode Salomos." *RSEHA* 19 (1911), pp. 261-65.

BAUCKHAM, Richard. "Jesus, Worship of." In *The Anchor Bible Dictionary*, gen. ed. David N. FREEDMAN. 5 vols. Garden City, NY: Doubleday, 1992. Vol. 3, cols. 812-19.

_____. "The Worship of Jesus in Apocalyptic Christianity." *NTS* 27 (1980-1981), pp. 322-41.

BAUMGARTEN, Joseph M. "ShirShabb and Merkabah Traditions." *RQ* 13 (1988), pp. 199-213.

BEALE, Gregory K. "The Problem of the Man from the Sea in IV Ezra 13 and its Relation to the Messianic Concept in John's Apocalypse." *NT* 25 (1983), pp. 182-88.

BEASLEY-MURRAY, G.R. "How Christian is the Book of Revelation?" In *Reconciliation and Hope. New Testament Essays on Atonement and Eschatology*, edited by Robert BANKS. Grand Rapids: Wm. B. Eerdmans, 1974. Pp. 275-84.

_____. *The Book of Revelation*. NCB. London: Marshall, Morgan & Scott, 1978. Rev. ed. from 1974.

BECK, Dwight Marion. "The Christology of the Apocalypse of John." In *New Testament Studies*, edited by E.P. BOOTH. New York/Nashville: Abingdon-Cokesbury Press, 1942.

BECKER, Joachim. *Gottesfurcht im Alten Testament*. AB, 25. Rome: Pontifical Biblical Institute, 1965.

BECKER, Jürgen. *Das Heil Gottes*. SUNT, 3. Göttingen: Vandenhoeck & Ruprecht, 1964.

BECKWITH, Isbon T. *The Apocalypse of John*. New York: Macmillan, 1919.

BEKER, J. Christiaan. *Paul the Apostle: The Triumph of God in Life and Thought*. Philadelphia: Fortress Press, 1980.

BELLEVILLE, Linda L. "'Under Law': Structural Analysis and the Pauline Concept of Law in Galatians 3.21-4.11." *JSNT* 26 (1986), pp. 53-78.

BERGMAIER, Roland. "Die Buchrolle und das Lamm." *ZNW* 76 (1985), pp. 225-42.

BERGMANN, J. *Jüdische Apologetik im neutestamentlichen Zeitalter*. Berlin: Georg Reimer, 1908.

BETZ, Hans Dieter. *Galatians*. Hermeneia. Philadelphia: Fortress Press, 1979.

_____. "The Problem of Apocalyptic Genre in Greek and Hellenistic Literature: The Case of the Oracle of Trophonius." In *Apocalypticism in the Mediterranean World and the Near East*, edited by David HELLHOLM. Tübingen: J.C.B. Mohr (Paul Siebeck), 1983. Pp. 577-97.

BIETENHARD, H. *Die himmlische Welt im Urchristentum und Spätjudentum*. WUNT, 2. Tübingen: J.C.B. Mohr (Paul Siebeck), 1951.

BLACK, Matthew. "The Twenty Angel Dekadarchs at I Enoch 6,7 and 69,2." *JJS* 33 (1982), pp. 227-35.

BLAU, Ludwig. *Das altjüdische Zauberwesen*. Westmead/Farnborough/Hants., England: Gregg International Publishers, 1970. Repr. from 1898.

BLIGH, J. *Galatians*. London: St. Paul Publications, 1969.

BLINZLER, J. "Lexikalisches zu dem Terminus τὰ στοιχεῖ τοῦ κόσμου bei Paulus." In *Studiorum Paulinorum Congressus Internationalis Catholicus, 1961*. AnBib, 17-18. Rome: Pontifical Biblical Institute, 1963. Vol. 18, pp. 429-43.

BOCCACCINNI, Gabriella. *Middle Judaism*. Minneapolis: Augsburg-Fortress Press, 1991.

BORING, M. Eugene. "The Theology of Revelation: 'The Lord Our God the Almighty Reigns'." *Int* 40 (1986) 257-69.

BORNKAMM, Günther. "Das Bekenntnis im Hebräerbrief." In *Studien zu Antike und Urchristentum. Gesammelte Aufsätze*. 2 vols. BEvT, 16 and 28. Munich: Chr. Kaiser, 1958-1963. Vol. 1, pp. 188-203.

_____. "Die Häresie des Kolosserbriefes." *TLZ* 73 (1948), cols. 11-20.

_____. "Die Komposition der apokalyptischen Visionen in der Offenbarung Johannes." In *Studien zu Antike und Urchristentum. Gesammelte Aufsätze*. 2 vols. BEvT, 16 and 28. Munich: Chr. Kaiser, 1959. Vol. 2, pp. 204-222.

BOUSSET, Wilhelm. *Die Offenbarung Johannis*. Göttingen: Vandenhoeck & Ruprecht, 1906.

_____. *Die Religion des Judentums im späthellenistischen Zeitalter*. Revised by Hugo GRESSMAN. HNT, 21. 3rd ed. Tübingen: J.C.B. Mohr (Paul Siebeck), 1926.

_____. *Jesus der Herr. Nachträge und Auseinandersetzungen zu Kyrios Christos*. Göttingen: Vandenhoeck & Ruprecht, 1916.

_____. *Kyrios Christos. Geschichte des Christusglaubens von den Anfängen des Christentums bis Irenaeus*. 5th ed. Göttingen: Vandenhoeck & Ruprecht, 1965.

BRAUN, Herbert. *Qumran und das Neue Testament*. 2 vols. Tübingen: J.C.B. Mohr (Paul Siebeck), 1966.

BROX, Norbert. *Der Hirt des Hermas*. MeyerK, 7. Göttingen: Vandenhoeck & Ruprecht, 1991.

BRUCE, F.F. *Commentary on Galatians*. NICNT. Grand Rapids: Wm. B. Eerdmans, 1982.

_____. *Commentary on the Epistle to the Colossians*. NICNT. Grand Rapids: Wm. B. Eerdmans, 1957.

_____. "Paul and the Law of Moses." *BJRL* 57 (1974/1975), pp. 259-79.

_____. *The Epistle to the Hebrews*. NICNT. Grand Rapids: Wm. B. Eerdmans, 1964.

_____. "The Oldest Greek Version of Daniel." In *Instruction and Interpretation*, edited by H.A. BRONGERS et al.. OS, 20. Leiden: E.J. Brill, 1977. Pp. 22-40.

BULTMANN, Rudolf. *Theology of the New Testament*. Translated by Kendrick GROBEL. 2 vols. New York: Charles Scribner's Sons, 1951-1955.

BURCHARD, Christoph. "Ein vorläufiger griechischer Text von Joseph und Aseneth." *DBAT* 14 (1979), pp. 2-53.

_____. "Joseph and Aseneth." In *The Old Testament Pseudepigrapha*, edited by James H. CHARLESWORTH. 2 vols. Garden City, NY: Doubleday, 1983-1985. Vol. 2, pp. 202-247.

_____. "Verbesserungen zum vorläufigen Text." *DBAT* 16 (1982), pp. 37-39.

_____. "Zum Text von 'Joseph und Aseneth'." *JSJ* 1 (1970), pp. 3-34.

BURTON, Ernest D. *A Critical and Exegetical Commentary on the Epistle to the Galatians*. ICC. Edinburgh: T. & T. Clark, 1921.

CAIRD, G.B. *A Commentary on the Revelation of St. John the Divine*. HNTC. New York: Harper & Row, 1966.

_____. *Principalities and Powers*. Oxford: Clarendon Press, 1956.

CALLAN, Terrance. "Pauline Midrash: The Exegetical Background of Gal 3:19b." *JBL* 99 (1980), pp. 549-67.

_____. "Psalm 110:1 and the Origin of the Expectation that Jesus Will Come Again." *CBQ* 44 (1982), pp. 622-36.

CARMIGNAC, Jean. "Roi, Royauté et Royaume dans la Liturgie Angélique." *RQ* 12 (1986), 178-86.

CARNEGIE, David R. "Worthy is the Lamb: The Hymns in Revelation." In *Christ the Lord. Studies in Christology Presented to Donald Guthrie*, edited by H.H. ROWDON. Leicester: Inter-Varsity Press, 1982. Pp. 243-56.

CARR, W. *Angels and Principalities*. SNTSMS, 42. Cambridge: Cambridge University Press, 1981.

_____. "Two Notes on Colossians." *JTS* 34 (1973), pp. 492-500.

CASEY, Maurice. *The Son of Man*. London: Hodder & Stoughton, 1979.

CASPAR, Robert. "Der Monotheismus des Islams und seine bleibende Bedeutung." *Conc* 21 (1985), pp. 46-54.

CHARLES, R.H. *Studies in the Apocalypse*. Edinburgh: T. & T. Clark, 1913.

_____. *The Revelation of St. John*. 2 vols. ICC. New York: Charles Scribner's Sons, 1920.

CHARLESWORTH, James H. "History of the Rechabites." In *The Old Testament Pseudepigrapha*, edited by James H. CHARLESWORTH. 2 vols. Garden City, NY: Doubleday, 1983-1985. Vol. 2, pp. 443-61.

_____. "Prayer of Jacob." In *The Old Testament Pseudepigrapha*, edited by James H. CHARLESWORTH. 2 vols. Garden City, NY: Doubleday, 1983-1985. Vol. 2, pp. 715-23.

_____. "The Apocalypse of John--Its Theology and Impact on Subsequent Apocalypses." In *The New Testament Apocrypha and Pseudepigrapha*, edited by James H. CHARLESWORTH with James R. MUELLER. Metuchen, NJ/London: American Theological Library Association and Scarecrow Press, 1987. Pp. 19-51.

_____. "The Jewish Roots of Christology: The Discovery of the Hypostatic Voice." *ScJTh* 39 (1985), pp. 19-41.

_____. "The Significance of the New Edition of the Old Testament Pseudepigrapha." In *La littérature intertestamentaire. Colloque de Strasbourg (17-19 octobre 1983)*, edited by M. PHILONENKO. Bibliothèque des Centres d'Études Supérieures Spécialisés. Paris: Presses Universitaires de France, 1985. Pp. 11-25.

_____. "Treatise of Shem." In *The Old Testament Pseudepigrapha*, edited by James H. CHARLESWORTH. 2 vols. Garden City, NY: Doubleday, 1983-1985. Pp. 473-86.

CHAZON, E.G. "Review of Newsom, *Songs of the Sabbath Sacrifice*." *IEJ* 36 (1986), pp. 282-84.

CHERNUS, Ira. *Mysticism in Rabbinic Judaism. Studies in the History of Midrash.* SJ, 11. Berlin/New York: Walter de Gruyter, 1981.

_____. "Visions of God in Merkabah Mysticism." *JStJud* 13 (1983), pp. 123-46.

CHESTER, Andrew. "Jewish Messianic Expectations and Mediatorial Figures and Pauline Christology." In *Paulus und das antike Judentum*, edited by Martin HENGEL and Ulrich HECKEL. WUNT, 58. Tübingen: J.C.B. Mohr (Paul Siebeck), 1991. Pp. 17-89.

COLLINS, Adela Yarbro. "Dating the Apocalypse of John." *PCSBR* 26 (1981), pp. 33-45.

_____. "Revelation 18: Taunt-Song or Dirge?" In *L'Apocalypse johannique et L'Apocalyptique dans le Nouveau Testament*, edited by J. LAMBRECHT. BETL, 53. Leuven: Leuven University Press, 1980. Pp. 185-204.

_____. *The Apocalypse.* NTM, 22. Wilmington, Delaware: Michael Glazier, 1979.

_____. *The Combat Myth in the Book of Revelation.* HTRHDR, 9. Missoula: Scholars Press, 1976.

_____. "The Social Situation - Perceived Crisis." In *Crisis and Catharsis: The Power of the Apocalypse.* Philadelphia: Westminster Press, 1984. Pp. 84-110.

_____. "The 'Son of Man' Tradition and the Book of Revelation." In *The Messiah. Developments in Earliest Judaism and Christianity*, edited by James H. CHARLESWORTH et al. Minneapolis: Fortress Press, 1992. Pp. 536-68.

_____. "When Was Revelation Written?" In *Crisis and Catharsis: The Power of the Apocalypse.* Philadelphia: Westminster Press, 1984. Pp. 54-83.

COLLINS, John J. *The Apocalyptic Imagination.* New York: Crossroad, 1987.

_____. *The Apocalyptic Vision of the Book of Daniel.* HSM, 16. Missoula: Scholars Press, 1977.

COMBLIN, Joseph. *Le Christ dans l'Apocalypse.* Tournai, Belgium: Desclée, 1965.

_____. "Monotheismus und Volksreligion." *Conc* 21 (1985), pp. 61-67.

CONRAD, Edgar W. *Fear not Warrior. A Study of 'al tira' Pericopes in the Hebrew Scriptures.* BJS, 75. Chico, CA: Scholars Press, 1985.

COOK, D.E. *The Christology of the Apocalypse.* Duke University: Ph.D. Dissertation, 1962.

COPPENS, J. "La mention d'un Fils d'homme angélique en Ap 14, 14." In *L'Apocalypse johannique et l'Apocalyptique dans le Nouveau Testament*, edited by J. LAMBRECHT. BETL, 53. Leuven: Leuven University Press, 1980. P. 229.

COURT, John. *Myth and History in the Book of Revelation*. Atlanta: John Knox Press, 1979.

CREECH, Richard Robert. *Christology and Conflict. A Comparative Study of Two Central Themes in the Johannine Literature and the Apocalypse (Lamb of God, Logos, Ego Eimi, Revelation, I Am)*. Baylor University: Dissertation, 1984.

CULIANU, Ioan P. "The Angels of the Nations and the Origins of Gnostic Dualism." In *Studies in Gnosticism and Hellenistic Religions. Festschrift for G. Quispel*, edited by R. VAN DEN BROEK and M.J. VERMASEREN. EPRO, 91. Leiden: E.J. Brill, 1981. Pp. 78-91.

CUMONT, Franz. "῞Υψιστος." In *Paulys Realencyklopädie der klassischen Altertumswissenschaft*, edited by August PAULY et al. 6 vols. in 8 (1st Series), 19 vols. (n.F.) with 15 suppl.'s and Register. Munich: Alfred Druckenmüller, 1839-1980. Vol. 9, Part 1, cols. 444-50.

_____. "Les anges du paganisme." *RHR* 72 (1915), pp. 159-82.

DAHL, Nils A. "Sources of Christological Language." In *Jesus the Christ. The Historical Origins of Christological Doctrine*, (essays by Dahl) edited by Donald H. JUEL. Minneapolis: Fortress Press, 1991. Pp. 113-36.

DAN, Joseph. *Gershom Scholem and the Mystical Dimension of Jewish History*. New York/London: New York University, 1988.

_____. Review of Margolioth, *Sefer ha-Razim*. *Tarbiz* 37 (1967/1968), pp. 208-214.

DAVIDSON, Maxwell J. *Angels at Qumran. A Comparative Study of 1 Enoch 1-36, 72-108 and Sectarian Writings from Qumran*. JSPS, 11. Sheffield, JSOT, 1992.

DAVIES, Stevan. "The Christology and Protology of the *Gospel of Thomas*." *JBL* 111 (1992), pp. 663-82.

DAVIES, W.D. "Paul and the Dead Sea Scrolls: Flesh and Spirit." In *The Scrolls and the New Testament*, edited by Krister STENDAHL. New York: Harper, 1957.

DEAN-OTTING, Mary. *Heavenly Journeys. A Study of the Motif in Hellenistic Jewish Literature*. JU, 8. Frankfurt/Bern/New York: Peter Lang, 1984.

DEICHGRÄBER, R. *Gotteshymnus und Christushymns in der frühen Christenheit*. SUNT, 5. Göttingen: Vandenhoeck & Ruprecht).

DEISSMANN, Adolf. "Die Rachegebete von Rheneia." In *Licht vom Osten*. 4th ed. Tübingen: J.C.B. Mohr (Paul Siebeck), 1924. Pp. 351-62.

DE JONGE, Marinus. "The Use of the Expression ὁ χριστός in the Apocalypse of John." In *L'Apocalypse johannique et l'Apocalyptique dans le Nouveau Testament*, edited by J. LAMBRECHT. BETL, 53. Leuven: Leuven University Press, 1980. Pp. 267-81.

DELLING, G. "Einwirkungen der Septuaginta im 'Joseph und Asenath'." *JSJ* 9 (1978), pp. 29-56.

_____. "στοιχεῖον." In *Theological Dictionary of the New Testament*, edited by Gerhard KITTEL and Gerhard FRIEDRICH. Translated by Geoffrey W. BROMILEY. 10 vols. Grand Rapids: Wm. B. Eerdmans, 1964-1976. Pp. 666-67.

DEY, Lala Kalyan Kumar. *The Intermediary World and Patterns of Perfection in Philo and Hebrews*. SBLDS, 25. Missoula: Scholars Press, 1975.

DIBELIUS, Martin. *Die Geisterwelt im Leben des Paulus*. Göttingen: Vandenhoeck & Ruprecht, 1909.

_____. "Die Isisweihe bei Apuleius und verwandte Initiations-Riten." In *Botschaft und Geschichte. Gesammelte Aufsätze von Martin Dibelius*. 2 vols. Tübingen: J.C.B. Mohr (Paul Siebeck), 1956. Repr. from 1917. Vol. 2, pp. 30-79.

DIBELIUS, Martin and Huck GREEVEN. *An die Kolosser Epheser und Philemon*. 3rd ed. HNT, 12. Tübingen: J.C.B. Mohr (Paul Siebeck), 1953.

DIMANT, Devorah and John STRUGNELL. "4Q Second Ezekiel (4Q385)." *RQ* 13 (1988), pp. 45-58.

_____. "The Merkabah Vision in *Second Ezekiel* (*4Q385* 4)." *RQ* 14 (1990), pp. 331-48.

DOBSCHÜTZ, Ernst von. *Das Kerygma Petri*. TU, 11/1. Leipzig: Hinrichs, 1893.

DORIGNY, A. Sorlin. "Phylactère Alexandrin." *REG* 4 (1891), pp. 287-96.

DULING, D.C. "Testament of Solomon." In *The Old Testament Pseudepigrapha*, edited by James H. CHARLESWORTH. 2 vols. Garden City, NY: Doubleday, 1983-1985. Vol. 1, pp. 935-87.

DUNN, James D.G. *Christology in the Making*. Philadelphia: Westminster Press, 1980.

_____. "Let John be John." In *Das Evangelium und die Evangelien. Vorträge zum Tübinger Symposium 1982*, edited by Peter STUHLMACHER. WUNT, 28. Tübingen: J.C.B. Mohr (Paul Siebeck), 1983. Pp. 309-339.

_____. *The Partings of the Ways*. London/Philadelphia: SCM Press and Trinity International Press, 1991.

_____. *Unity and Diversity in the New Testament*. Philadelphia: Westminster Press, 1977.

_____. "Was Christianity a Monotheistic Faith from the Beginning?" *ScJTh* 35 (1981), pp. 303-336.

DUSSANT, Louis. *Synopse structurelle de l'Épître aux Hébreux*. Paris: Cerf, 1981.

EDERSHEIM, Alfred. *The Life and Times of Jesus the Messiah*. 2 vols. 3rd ed. London: Longman, Green & Co., 1890.

EDWARDS, Sarah Alexander. "Christological Perspectives in the Book of Revelation." In *Christological Perspectives. Essays in Honor of Harvey K. McArthur*, edited by Robert F. BERKEY and Sarah A. EDWARDS. New York: Pilgrim Press, 1982. Pp. 139-54.

EISENMAN, Robert and Michael WISE. *The Dead Sea Scrolls Uncovered*. Rockport, Maine: Element, 1992.

ENGELBRECHT, Johannes Jacobus. *The Christology of the Revelation to St. John*. University of South Africa: Ph.D. Dissertation, 1981. In Afrikaans.

EVANS, Craig A. "The Colossians Mystics." *Bib* 63 (1982), pp. 188-205.

FALLON, Francis T. and Ron CAMERON. "The Gospel of Thomas: A Forschungsbericht and Analysis." In *Aufstieg und Niedergang der römischen Welt*, edited by Wolfgang HAASE. Series II, Part 25, vol. 6. Berlin/New York: Walter de Gruyter, 1988. Pp. 4195-251.

FAUTH, Wolfgang. "Tatrosjah-Totrosjah und Metatron in der jüdischen Merkabah-Mystik." *JStJud* 22 (1991), pp. 40-87.

FINKELSTEIN, Louis. "The Oldest Midrash: Pre-Rabbinic Ideals and Teachings in the Passover Haggadah." *HTR* 31 (1938), pp. 306-309.

FISHER, Karl Martin. "Die Christlichkeit der Offenbarung Johannes." *TLZ* 102 (1981), pp. 165-72.

FITZMYER, Joseph A. "Qumran Angelology and 1 Cor 11:10." In *Essays on the Semitic Background of the New Testament*. SBS, 5. Missoula: SBL and Scholars Press, 1974. Pp. 187-204.

_____. "The Semitic Background of the New Testament *Kyrios*-Title." In *A Wandering Aramean. Collected Aramaic Essays*. SBLMS, 25. Missoula: Scholars Press, 1979.

Ford, J. MASSYNGBERDE. *Revelation. Introduction, Translation and Commentary*. AB, 38. Garden City, NY: Doubleday, 1975.

FOSSUM, Jarl E. "Jewish-Christian Christology and Jewish Mysticism." *VigChr* 37 (1983), pp. 260-87.

_____. "Kyrios Jesus as the Angel of the Lord in Jude 5-7." *NTS* 33 (1987), pp. 226-43.

_____. *The Name of God and the Angel of the Lord*. WUNT, 36. Tübingen: J.C.B. Mohr (Paul Siebeck), 1985.

_____. "The New *Religionsgeschichtliche Schule*: The Quest for Jewish Christology." In *SBL 1991 Seminar Papers*, edited by Eugene H. LOVERING, Jr. Atlanta: Scholars Press, 1991. Pp. 638-46.

FRANCIS, Fred O. *A Re-examination of the Colossian Controversy*. Yale University: Ph.D. Dissertation, 1965.

_____. "Humility and Angel Worship in Col. 2:18." *ST* 16 (1962), pp. 109-134.

_____. "Visionary Discipline and Scriptural Tradition at Colossae." *LexThQ* 2 (1967), pp. 71-81.

FRANCIS, R.T. "The Worship of Jesus: A Neglected Factor in Christological Debate?" In *Christ the Lord. Studies in Christology presented to Donald Guthrie*, edited by H.H. ROWDON. Leicester: Inter-Varsity Press, 1982. Pp. 17-36.

FRIESEN, Steven John. *Ephesus, Twice Neokoros*. Harvard University: Ph.D. Dissertation, 1990.

FUHS, H.F. "ירא, yare'." In *Theological Dictionary of the Old Testament*, edited by G. Johannes BOTTERWECK and Helmer RINGGREN. Translated by David E. GREEN. Grand Rapids: Wm. B. Eerdmans, 1974-. Vol. 6, pp. 290-315.

FULLER, Reginald. *The Foundations of New Testament Christology*. New York: Scribner, 1965.

GAGER, John. *Kingdom and Community*. Englewood Cliffs, NJ: Prentice-Hall, 1975.

GÄRTNER, B. *The Temple and the Community*. SNTSMS, 1. Cambridge: Cambridge University Press, 1965.

GASTON, Lloyd. *Paul and the Torah*. Vancouver: University of British Columbia, 1987.

GAYLORD, H.E. "3 Baruch." In *The Old Testament Pseudepigrapha*, edited by James H. CHARLESWORTH. 2 vols. Garden City, NY: Doubleday, 1983-1985. Pp. 653-79.

_____. "Speculations, Visions, or Sermons." *JStJud* 13 (1982), pp. 187-94.

GERHARDSSON, Birger. "Die christologischen Aussagen in den Sendschreiben der Offenbarung (Kap. 2-3)." In *Theologie aus dem Norden*, edited by Albert FUCHS. SNTU, A/2. Linz: A. Fuchs, 1976. Pp. 142-66.

GNILKA, J. *Der Kolosserbrief*. HThK, 10/1. Freiburg/Basel/Wien: Herder, 1980.

GOLDIN, J. "Not by Angel and not by a Messenger." In *Religions in Antiquity. Essays in Memory of Erwin Ramsdell Goodenough*, edited by J. NEUSNER. SHR, 14. Leiden: E.J. Brill, 1968. Pp. 412-24.

GOODENOUGH, E.R. *Jewish Symbols in the Greco-Roman Period*. 13 vols. Bollingen Series, 27. New York: Pantheon Books, 1953-1968.

GRÄßER, Erich. *An die Hebräer*. EKK, 17/7. Neukirchen-Vluyn/Zürich: Neukirchener and Benziger Verlag, 1990.

GRILLMAIER, Aloys. *Christ in Christian Tradition*. Vol. 1, *From the Apostolic Age to Chalcedon (451)*. Translated by John BOWDEN. 2nd ed. Atlanta: John Knox Press, 1975.

GRÖZINGER, Karl Erich. "Engel III. Judentum." In *Theologische Realenzyklopädie*, edited by Gerhard KRAUSE and Gerhard MÜLLER. Berlin/New York: Walter de Gruyter, 1982. Vol. 9, cols. 586-96.

GRUBER, Mayer I. "Fear, Anxiety and Reverence in Akkadian, Biblical Hebrew and Other North-West Semitic Languages." *VT* 40 (1990), pp. 411-22.

GRUENWALD, Ithamar. *Apocalyptic and Merkavah Mysticism*. AGAJU, 14. Leiden: E.J. Brill, 1980.

_____. *From Apocalypticism to Gnosticism. Studies in Apocalypticism, Merkavah Mysticism and Gnosticism*. Frankfurt am Main: P. Lang, 1988.

GUNTHER, John J. *St. Paul's Opponents and their Background*. SNT, 35. Leiden: E.J. Brill, 1973.

HAHN, Ferdinand. *Christologische Hoheitstitel. Ihre Geschichte im frühen Christentum*. 3rd ed. Göttingen: Vandenhoeck & Ruprecht, 1966.

_____. "Das Gesetzesverständnis im Römer- und Galaterbrief." *ZNW* 67 (1976), pp. 29-63.

HALPERIN, David. *The Faces of the Chariot. Early Jewish Responses to Ezekiel's Vision*. TSAJ, 16. J.C.B. Mohr (Paul Siebeck), 1988.

_____. *The Merkabah in Rabbinic Literature*. AOS, 62. New Haven: American Oriental Society, 1980.

HAMMERTON-KELLY, R.G. *Pre-existence, Wisdom, and the Son of Man*. SNTSMS, 21. Cambridge: Cambridge University Press, 1973.

HANSON, Paul D. "Apocalypticism." In *Interpreter's Dictionary of the Bible*, edited by George A. BUTTRICK. 4 vols. and suppl. Nashville: Abingdon Press, 1962-75. Suppl., cols. 28-34.

_____. *The Dawn of Apocalyptic. The Historical and Sociological Roots of Jewish Apocalyptic Eschatology*. Philadelphia: Fortress Press, 1975.

HARRINGTON, Daniel J. "Pseudo-Philo." In *The Old Testament Pseudepigrapha*, edited by James H. CHARLESWORTH. 2 vols. Garden City, NY: Doubleday, 1983-1985. Vol. 2, pp. 297-377.

HARRIS, J. Rendel. *Josephus and his Testimony*. Cambridge: Heffer, 1931.

HARTMANN, Lars. "Form and Message." In *L'Apocalypse johannique et l'Apocalyptique dans le Nouveau Testament*, edited by J. LAMBRECHT. BETL, 53. Leuven: Leuven University Press, 1980. Pp. 129-49.

_____. "Johannine Jesus-Belief and Monotheism." In *Aspects of the Johannine Literature*, edited by Lars HARTMANN and Birger OLSSON. CBNTS, 18. Uppsala: Almqvist & Wiksell Internaional, 1987. Pp. 85-99.

HAY, David M. *Glory at the Right Hand. Psalm 110 in Early Christianity*. Nashville: Abingdon, 1973.

HAYES, John H. and Frederick Prussner. *Old Testament Theology. Its History and Development*. Atlanta: John Knox Press, 1985.

HAYMAN, Peter. "Monotheism - A Misused Word in Jewish Studies?" *JJS* 42 (1991), pp. 1-15.

HELLHOLM, David. "The Problem of Apocalyptic Genre and the Apocalypse of John." *SBL 1982 Seminar Papers*, edited by Kent H. RICHARDS. Chico, CA: Scholars Press, 1982. Pp. 157-98.

HEMER, Colin. *The Letters to the Seven Churches of Asia in Their Local Setting*. JSNTSS, 11. Sheffield: JSOT, 1986.

HENGEL, Martin. *Between Jesus and Paul. Studies in the Earliest History of Christianity*. Philadelphia: Fortress Press, 1983.

_____. "Christological Titles in Early Christianity." In *The Messiah. Developments in Earliest Judaism and Christianity*, edited by James H. CHARLESWORTH, et al. Minneapolis: Fortress Press, 1992. Pp. 425-48.

_____. "Christology and New Testament Chronology." In *Between Jesus and Paul*, pp. 30-47.

_____. "Der alte und der neue Schürer." *JSS* 35 (1990), pp. 1-54.

_____. *Der Sohn Gottes. Die Entstehung der Christologie und die jüdisch-hellenistische Religionsgeschichte*. 2nd ed. Tübingen: J.C.B. Mohr (Paul Siebeck), 1977.

_____. "Die Synagogeninschrift von Stobi." *ZNW* 57 (1966), pp. 145-83.

_____. "Hymns and Christology." In *Between Jesus and Paul*, pp. 78-96.

_____. *Judaism and Hellenism*. Translated by John BOWDEN. 2 vols. Philadelphia: Fortress Press, 1974.

_____. "Proseuche und Synagoge. Jüdische Gemeinde, Gotteshaus und Gottesdienst in der Diaspora und in Palästina." In *Tradition und Glaube. Das frühe Christentum in seiner Umwelt. Festschrift für K.G. Kuhn*. Göttingen: Vandenhoeck & Ruprecht, 1971. Pp. 155-84.

_____. "Psalm 110 und die Erhöhung des Auferstandenen zur Rechten Gottes." In *Anfänge der Christologie. Festschrift für Ferdinand Hahn*, edited by Cilliers BREYTENBACH and Henning PAULSEN. Göttingen: Vandenhoeck & Ruprecht, 1991. Pp. 43-73.

_____. *The 'Hellenization' of Judaea in the First Century after Christ*. Translated by John BOWDEN. Philadelphia/ London: Trinity International Press and SCM Press, 1989.

HÉRING, Jean. *L'Épître aus Hébreaux*. CNT, 12. Paris/Neuchatel: Delachaux and Niestlé, 1954.

HIMMELFARB, Martha. *Tours of Hell*. Philadelphia: University of Pennsylvania Press, 1983.

HOFIUS, O. *Der Christushymnus Philipper 2,6-11*. WUNT, 17. Tübingen: J.C.B. Mohr (Paul Siebeck, 1991.

HOLLANDER, H.W. and Marinus DE JONGE. *The Testaments of the Twelve Patriarchs. A Commentary*. SVTP, 8. Leiden: E.J. Brill, 1985.

HOLTZ, Traugott. *Die Christologie der Apokalypse des Johannes*. TU, 85. 2nd ed. Berlin: Akademie-Verlag, 1971.

_____. "Gott in der Apokalypse." In *L'Apocalypse johannique et l'Apocalyptique dans le Nouveau Testament*, edited by J. LAMBRECHT. BETL, 53. Leuven: Leuven University Press, 1980. Pp. 247-65.

HOMOLLE, T. "Nouvelles et Correspondance: Ionie." *BCH* 17 (1893), p. 638.

HOWARD George. *Paul: Crisis in Galatia.* SNTMS, 35. 2nd ed. Cambridge: Cambridge University Press, 1990.

HÜBNER, Hans. *Biblische Theologie des Neuen Testaments.* Vol. 1. Göttingen: Vandenhoeck & Ruprecht, 1990.

_____. *Das Gesetz bei Paulus.* 5th ed. FRLANT, 199. Göttingen: Vandenhoeck & Ruprecht, 1982.

HUGHES, Philip E. *A Commentary on the Epistle to the Hebrews.* Grand Rapids: Wm. B. Eerdmans, 1977.

HURST, L.D. "The Christology of Hebrews 1 and 2." In *The Glory of Christ in the New Testament. Studies in Christology in Memory of George Bradford Caird*, edited L.D. HURST and N.T. WRIGHT. Oxford: Oxford University Press, 1987. Pp. 151-64.

_____. *The Epistle to the Hebrews. Its background of thought.* SNTSMS, 65. Cambridge: Cambridge University Press, 1990.

HURTADO, Larry W. "New Testament Christology: A Critique of Bousset's Influence." *TS* 40 (1979), pp. 306-317.

_____. *One God, One Lord. Early Christian Devotion and Ancient Jewish Monotheism.* Philadelphia: Fortress Press, 1988.

_____. "The Binitarian Shape of Early Christian Devotion and Ancient Jewish Monotheism." *SBL 1985 Seminar Papers*, edited by Kent H. RICHARDS. Atlanta: Scholars Press, 1985. Pp. 377-91.

_____. "What Do We Mean by 'First-Century Jewish Monotheism'?" *SBL 1993 Seminar Papers*, edited by David LULL. Atlanta: Scholars Press, 1993. Pp. 348-68.

ISAAC, E. "1 (Ethiopic Apocalypse of) ENOCH." In *The Old Testament Pseudepigrapha*, edited by James H. CHARLESWORTH. 2 vols. Garden City, NY: Doubleday, 1983-1985. Vol. 1, pp. 5-89.

ISBELL, Charles D. *Corpus of the Aramaic Incantation Bowls.* SBLDS, 17. Missoula: SBL and Scholars Press, 1975.

JEWETT, Robert. *Letter to Pilgrims. A Commentary on the Epistle to the Hebrews.* New York: Pilgrims Press, 1981.

JOHNSON, M.D. "Life of Adam and Eve." In *The Old Testament Pseudepigrapha*, edited by James H. CHARLESWORTH. 2 vols. Garden City, NY: Doubleday, 1983-1985. Vol. 2, pp. 249-95.

JOHNSTON, George. *The Spirit-Paraclete in the Gospel of John.* SNTSMS, 12. Cambridge: Cambridge University Press, 1970.

JONES, Donald L. "Christianity and the Roman Imperial Cult." In *Aufstieg und Niedergang der römischen Welt*, edited by Wolfgang HAASE. Series II, Part 23, vol. 2. Berlin/New York: Walter de Gruyter, 1980. Pp. 1023-54.

JÖRNS, Klaus-Peter. *Das hymnische Evangelium*. SNT, 5. Gütersloh: Gerd Mohn, 1971.

KARRER, Martin. *Die Johannesoffenbarung als Brief*. FRLANT, 140. Göttingen: Vandenhoeck & Ruprecht, 1986.

KÄSEMANN, Ernst. *The Wandering People of God*. Translated by R.A. Harrisville and I.L. SANDBERG. Minneapolis: Augsburg, 1984.

KAUFMANN, Yecheskel. *History of the Religion of Israel. From the Babylonian captivity to the end of prophecy*. Translated by C.W. EFROYMSON. New York: Ktav, 1977.

_____. *The Religion of Israel. From its Beginnings to the Babylonian Exile*. Original Heb., 4 vols. Abridged and translated by Moshe GREENBERG. Chicago: University of Chicago Press, 1960.

KENYON, Kathleen and Thomas A. HOLLAND. *Excavations at Jericho*, vol. 3. Jerusalem: British School of Archaeology, 1981.

KIDDLE, Martin. *The Revelation of St. John*. MNTC. London: Hodder & Stoughton, 1940.

KITTEL, Gerhard. "ἄγγελος." In *Theological Dictionary of the New Testament*, edited by Gerhard KITTEL and Gerhard FRIEDRICH. Translated by Geoffrey W. BROMILEY. 10 vols. Grand Rapids: Wm. B. Eerdmans, 1964-1976. Vol. 1, pp. 74-87.

KNIBB, Michael A. "Martyrdom and Ascension of Isaiah." In *The Old Testament Pseudepigrapha*, edited by James H. CHARLESWORTH. 2 vols. Garden City, NY: Doubleday, 1983-1985. Vol. 2, pp. 143-76.

_____. "Prophecy and the Emergence of the Jewish Apocalypses." In *Israel's Prophetic Heritage. Essays in Honour of Peter R. Ackroyd*, edited by R.J. COGGINS, A. PHILLIPS and M.A. KNIBB. Cambridge: Cambridge University Press, 1982. Pp. 155-80.

_____. *The Ethiopic Book of Enoch*. 2 vols. Oxford: Clarendon Press, 1978).

KOCH, Klaus. *Ratlos vor der Apokalyptik*. Gütersloh: Gerd Mohn, 1970.

KOLENKROW, Anitra Bingham. "The Angelology of the Testament of Abraham." In *Studies on the Testament of Abraham*, edited by George W.E. NICKELSBURG. SCS, 6. Missoula: Scholars Press, 1976. Rev. ed. Pp. 153-62.

KOSMALA, H. *Hebräer-Essener-Christen. Studien zur Vorgeschichte der frühchristlichen Verkündigung*. SPB, 1. Leiden: E.J. Brill, 1959.

KOTANSKY, Roy. "Incantations and Prayers for Salvation on Inscribed Greek Amulets." In *Magika Hiera. Ancient Greek Magic and Religion*, edited by Christopher A. FARAONE and Dirk OBBINK. Oxford: Oxford University Press, 1991. Pp. 107-137.

KRAABEL, A.T. "Ὕψιστος and the Synagogue at Sardis." *GRBS* 10 (1969), pp. 81-93.

KRAFT, Heinrich. *Die Offenbarung des Johannes*. HNT, 16a. Tübingen: J.C.B. Mohr (Paul Siebeck), 1974.

KRETSCHMAR, Georg. *Studien zur frühchristlichen Trinitätstheologie*. BHT, 21. Tübingen: J.C.B. Mohr (Paul Siebeck), 1956.

KUHN, Harold B. "The Angelology of the Non-Canonical Jewish Apocalypses." *JBL* 67 (1948), pp. 217-32.

KUHN, H.-W. *Enderwartung und Gegenwärtiges Heil*. SUNT, 4. Göttingen: Vandenhoeck & Ruprecht, 1966.

KUHN, Peter. *Offenbarungsstimmen im Antiken Judentum*. TSAJ, 20. Tübingen: J.C.B. Mohr (Paul Siebeck), 1989.

KÜMMEL, Werner Georg. "Das Urchristentum (Fortsetzung)." *ThRund* 17 (1948-1949), pp. 103-142.

KUSS, Otto. *Der Brief an die Hebräer und die Katholischen Briefe*. RNT, 8/1. Regensburg: Pustet, 1966.

LÄHNEMANN, Johannes. *Der Kolosserbrief*. SNT, 3. Gütersloh: Gerd Mohn, 1971.

LANE, William L. *Hebrews*. 2 vols. WBC, 47A-B. Dallas: Word Books, 1991.

LANG, Bernhard. "Zur Entstehung des biblischen Monotheismus." *TQ* 166 (1986), pp. 135-42.

LENSKI, R.C.H. *The Interpretation of St. John's Revelation*. Columbus: Lutheran Book Concern, 1935.

LÉVI-STRAUSS, Claude. *Structural Anthropology*. Translated by Claire JACOBSON and Brooke GRUNDFESTT SCHOEPF. New York/London: Basic Books, 1963.

LEWIS, Theodor J. *Cults of the Dead in Ancient Israel and Ugarit*. HSM, 39. Atlanta: Scholars Press, 1989.

LICHTENBERGER, Hermann. *Studien zum Menschenbild in Texten der Qumrangemeinde*. SUNT, 15. Göttingen: Vandenhoeck & Ruprecht, 1980.

LIEBERMAN, S. "Mišnat Šir haššîrîm." Appendix D in Gershom SCHOLEM, *Jewish Gnosticism, Merkabah Mysticism, and Talmudic Tradition*. 2nd ed. New York: Jewish Theological Seminary, 1965. Pp. 118-26.

_____. "Metatron, the meaning of his name and his functions." In *Apocalyptic and Merkavah Mysticism*, by Ithamar GRUENWALD. AGAJU, 14. Leiden: E.J. Brill, 1980. Pp. 235-41.

LIGHTFOOT, J.B. *Saint Paul's Epistles to the Colossians and to Philemon*. London: Macmillan, 1879.

LINCOLN, Andrew T. *Paradise Now and Not Yet. Studies in the role of the heavenly dimension in Paul's thought*. SNTSMS, 43. Cambridge: Cambridge University Press, 1981.

LINDARS, B. *The Theology of Hebrews*. NTT. Cambridge: Cambridge University Press, 1991.

LOADER, William R.G. "Christ at the Right Hand-Ps. CX.1 in the New Testament." *NTS* 24 (1977), pp. 199-217.

_____. *Sohn und Hoherpriester*. WMANT, 53. Neukirchen-Vluyn: Neukirchener Verlag, 1981.

LOHMEYER, E. *Christuskult und Kaiserkult*. Tübingen: J.C.B. Mohr (Paul Siebeck), 1919.

_____. *Die Briefe an die Philipper, an die Kolosser und an Philemon*. KEK. Göttingen: Vandenhoeck & Ruprecht, 1961.

_____. *Die Offenbarung des Johannes*. HNT, 16. Tübingen: J.C.B. Mohr (Paul Siebeck), 1926.

LOHSE, Eduard. *Die Briefe an die Kolosser und an Philemon*. MeyerK, 9/2. Göttingen: Vandenhoeck & Ruprecht, 1977.

_____. *Die Offenbarung des Johannes*. NTD, 11. Göttingen: Vandenhoeck & Ruprecht, 1971.

_____. "Wie christlich ist die Offenbarung des Johannes?" *NTS* 34 (1988), pp. 321-38.

LONA, Horacio E. *Die Eschatologie im Kolosser- und Epheserbrief*. FB, 48. Würzburg: Echter Verlag, 1984.

LUDWIG, Theodore M. "Monotheism." In *The Encyclopedia of Religion*, edited by Mircea ELIADE. New York: Macmillan, 1987. Vol. 10, pp. 68-76.

LUEKEN, Wilhelm. *Michael*. Göttingen: Vandenhoeck & Ruprecht, 1898.

LUNT, H.G. "Ladder of Jacob." In *The Old Testament Pseudepigrapha*, edited by James H. CHARLESWORTH. 2 vols. Garden City, NY: Doubleday, 1983-1985. Vol. 2, pp. 401-411.

LUST, J. "Daniel 7,13 and the Septuagint." *ETL* 54 (1978), pp. 62-69.

LUTTIKHUIZEN, Gerard P. *The Revelation of Elchasai*. TSAJ, 8. Tübingen: J.C.B. Mohr (Paul Siebeck), 1985.

LYONNET, S. "Les adversaires de Paul à Colosses." *Bib* 56 (1956), pp. 27-38.

MACH, Michael. *Entwicklungsstadien des jüdischen Engelglaubens in vorrabbinischer Zeit*. TUAJ, 34. Tübingen: J.C.B. Mohr (Paul Siebeck), 1992.

MAGIE, David. *Roman Rule in Asia Minor*. 2 vols. Princeton: Princeton University Press, 1950.

MAIER, Johann. "Das Buch der Geheimnisse." *Jud* 24 (1968), pp. 98-111.

_____. "Die Sonne im antiken Judentum." In *Aufstieg und Niedergang der römischen Welt*, edited by Wolfgang HAASE. Series II, Part 19, vol. 1. Berlin/New York: Walter de Gruyter, 1979. Pp. 346-412.

MANSON, T.W. "The Problem of the Epistle to the Hebrews." *BJRL* 32 (1949), pp. 1-17.

MARTIN, Ralph P. *Carmen Christi. Philippians ii. 5-11.* SNTSMS, 4. Cambridge: Cambridge University Press, 1967.

_____. *Colossians and Philemon.* NCBC. Grand Rapids: Wm. B. Eerdmans, 1973.

MÄRZ, Claus-Peter. *Hebräerbrief.* NEB, 16. Würzburg: Echter, Verlag 1989.

MAUSER, Ulrich W. "One God Alone: A Pillar of Biblical Theology." *PSB* 12 (1991), pp. 255-65.

MAZZAFERRI, Frederick David. *The Genre of the Book of Revelation from a Source-critical Persective.* BZNTWKK, 54. Berlin/New York: Walter de Gruyter, 1989.

MERCHAVYA, Ch. "Razim, Sefer H-." In *Encyclopaedia Judaica*, edited by Cecil ROTH and Geoffrey WIGODER. Jerusalem: Keter, 1971. Vol. 13, cols. 1594-95.

MICHAELIS, Werner. *Zur Engelchristologie im Urchristentum. Abbau der Konstruktion Martin Werners.* GBTh, 1. Basel: Majer, 1942.

MICHEL, Otto. *Der Brief an die Hebräer.* MeyerK, 13. Göttingen: Vandenhoeck & Ruprecht, 1966.

MICHL, J. *Die Engelvorstellungen in der Apokalypse des Hl. Johannes. Die Engel um Gott.* Munich: Max Hueber, 1937.

_____. "Engel." In *Reallexikon für Antike und Christentum*, edited by Ernst DASSEMANN et al. Stuttgart: Anton Hiersemann, 1962. Vol. 5, cols. 53-258.

MILIK, J.T. "La patrie de Job." *RB* 73 (1966), pp. 522-30.

MOFFATT, James. *Epistle to the Hebrews.* ICC. Edinburgh: T. & T. Clark, 1924.

MONTEFIORE, H.W. *A Commentary on the Epistle to the Hebrews.* New York/London: Harper and Black, 1964.

MONTGOMERY, James A. "Anent Dr. Rendel Harris's 'Testimonies'." *Exp* 22 (1921), pp. 214-17.

_____. *The Book of Daniel.* ICC. Edinburgh: T. & T. Clark, 1927.

MOORE, George Foot. "Christian Writers on Judaism." *HTR* 14 (1921), pp. 197-254.

_____. "Intermediaries in Jewish Theology." *HTR* 15 (1922) 41-85.

MOULTON, J.H. "It is His Angel." *JTS* 3 (1902), pp. 514-22.

MOUNCE, Robert T. *The Book of Revelation.* NICNT, 17. Grand Rapids: Wm. B. Eerdmans, 1977.

MORRAY-JONES, C.R.A. "Hekhalot Literature and Talmudic Tradition: Alexander's three Test Cases." *JStJud* 22 (1991), pp. 1-39.

_____. *Merkabah Mysticism and Talmudic Tradition.* Cambridge University: Ph.D. Dissertation, 1988.

_____. Review of *The Faces of the Chariot*, by David Halperin. *JTS* 41 (1990), pp. 585-89.

_____. "Transformational Mysticism in the Apocalyptic-Merkabah Tradition." *JJS* 43 (1992), pp. 1-31.

MÜLLER, H.P. "Mantische Weisheit und Apokalyptik." In *Congress Volume. Uppsala, 1971.* VTS, 22. Leiden: E.J. Brill, 1972. Pp. 268-93.

MÜLLER, Klaus W. "König und Vater." In *Königsherrschaft Gottes und himmlischer Kult im Judentum, Urchristentum, und in der hellenistischen Welt*, edited by M. HENGEL and A.M. SCHWEMER. WUNT, 55. Tübingen: J.C.B. Mohr (Paul Siebeck), 1991. Pp. 21-43.

MÜLLER, Ulrich B. *Die Offenbarung des Johannes.* ÖTKNT, 19. Gütersloh: Gerd Mohn, 1984.

_____. *Messias und Menschensohn in Jüdischen Apokalypsen und in der Offenbarung des Johannes.* SNT, 6. Gütersloh: Gerd Mohn, 1972.

_____. *Zur frühchristlichen Theologiegeschichte. Judenchristentum und Paulinismus in Kleinasien.* Gütersloh: Gerd Mohn, 1976.

NAGATA, Takeshi. *Philippians 2:5-11: A Case Study in the Contextual Shaping of Early Christology.* Princeton Theological Seminary: Ph.D. Dissertation, 1981.

NASH, Ronald H. "The Notion of Mediation in Alexandrian Judaism and the Epistle to the Hebrews." *WThJ* 40 (1977), pp. 89-115.

NEUSNER, Jacob. *A History of the Jews in Babylonia*, vols. 3: *From Shapur I to Shapur II*, 4: *The Age of Shapur II*, and 5: *Later Sasanian Times.* SPB, 12, 14, and 15; Leiden: E.J. Brill, 1968-1970.

NEWSOM, Carol and Yigael YADIN. "The Massada Fragment of the Qumran Songs of the Sabbath Sacrifice." *IEJ* 34 (1984), pp. 77-88.

NICKELSBURG, George W.E. "Stories of Biblical and Early Post-Biblical Times." In *Jewish Writings of the Second Temple Period. Apocrypha, Pseudepigrapha, Qumran Sectarian Writings, Philo, Josephus*, edited by Michael E. STONE. CRINT, 2/2. Assen/Philadelphia: Van Gorcum and Fortress Press, 1984. Pp. 33-87.

_____, ed. *Studies on the Testament of Abraham.* SCS, 6. Missoula: Scholars Press, 1976. Rev. ed.

NILSSON, Martin P. *Geschichte der Griechischen Religion.* 2nd ed. Handbuch der Altertumswissenschaft, 5/2. Munich: C.H. Beck, 1961.

NOCK, A.D. "The Vocabulary of the New Testament." *JBL* 52 (1933) 131-33.

NOCK, A.D., E. ROBERTS, and T.C. SKEAT. "The Build of Zeus Hypsistos." *HTR* 29 (1936), pp. 39-88.

NOLL, S.F. *Angelology in the Qumran Texts*. University of Manchester: Ph.D. Dissertation, 1979.

OTTO, Rudolf. *The Idea of the Holy*. Translated by John W. HARVEY. 2nd ed. London/Oxford/New York: Oxford University Press, 1950.

PACE JEANSONNE, Sharon. *The Old Greek Translation of Daniel 7-12*. CBQMS, 19. Washington, D.C.: CBA, 1988.

PAULSEN, Henning. "Das Kerygma Petri und die urchristliche Apologetik." *ZKG* 88 (1977), pp. 1-37.

PERCY, Ernst. *Die Probleme der Kolosser- und Epheserbriefe*. Lund: Gleerup, 1946.

PERDRIZET, Paul. "Amulette grecque trouvée en Syrie." *REG* 41 (1928), pp. 73-82.

PETERSEN, David L. "Israel and Monotheism: The Unfinished Agenda." In *Canon, Theology, and Old Testament Interpretation*, edited by Gene M. TUCKER, David L. PETERSEN, and Robert R. WILSON. Philadelphia: Fortress Press, 1988. Pp. 92-107.

PETERSON, Erik. "Der Monotheismus als politisches Problem." In *Theologische Traktate*. Munich: Kösel, 1951. Pp. 49-147.

_____. ΕΙΣ ΘΕΌΣ. FRLANT, n.F., 24. Göttingen: Vandenhoeck & Ruprecht, 1926).

PFEIFFER, Ronald H. *History of New Testament Times. With an Introduction to the Apocrypha*. New York: Harper, 1949.

PLÖGER, Otto. *Theokratie und Eschatologie*. 3rd ed. WMATNT, 2. Neukirchen-Vluyn: Neukirchener Verlag, 1968.

POKORNY, Peter. *Der Brief des Paulus an die Kolosser*. THNT, 10/1. Berlin: Evangelische Verlagsanstalt, 1987.

PORTON, Gary G. "Diversity in Postbiblical Judaism." In *Judaism and Its Modern Interpreters*, edited by Robert A. KRAFT and George W.E. NICKELSBURG. Philadelphia/Atlanta: Fortress Press and Scholars Press, 1986.

PREISKER, H. "ἐμβατεύω. In *Theological Dictionary of the New Testament*, edited by Gerhard KITTEL and Gerhard FRIEDRICH. Translated by Geoffrey W. BROMILEY. 10 vols. Grand Rapids: Wm. B. Eerdmans, 1964-1976. Vol. 2, pp. 535-36.

PRICE, S.R.F. *Rituals and Power. The Roman imperial cult in Asia Minor*. Cambridge: Cambridge University Press, 1984.

PRIGENT, P. *L'Apocalypse de Saint Jean*. CNT, 14. Geneva: Labor et Fides, 1988.

_____. "Le temps et le Royaume dans l'Apocalypse." In *L'Apocalypse johannique et l'Apocalyptique dans le Nouveau Testament*, edited by J. LAMBRECHT. BETL, 53. Leuven: Leuven University Press, 1980. Pp. 231-45.

QIMRON, Elisha. "A Review Article of *Songs of the Sabbath Sacrifices: A Critical Edition*, by Carol Newsom." *HTR* 79 (1986), pp. 349-71.

RAINBOW, Paul A. "Jewish Monotheism as the Matrix for New Testament Christology: A Review Article." *NT* 33 (1991), pp. 78-91.

RÄISÄNEN, Heikki. *Paul and the Law*. Philadelphia/Tübingen: Fortress Press and J.C.B. Mohr (Paul Siebeck), 1986.

RAMSEY, William. *The Teaching of Paul in Terms of the Present Day*. London: Hodder & Stoughton, 1913.

REDDISH, Mitchell G. "Martyr Christology in the Apocalypse." *JSNT* 33 (1988), pp. 85-95.

REICKE, Bo. "The Law and this World according to Paul." *JBL* 70 (1951), pp. 259-76.

REUMANN, John. "Martin Werner and 'Angel Christology'." *TLQ* 8 (1956), pp. 349-58.

RINGGREN, H. *The Faith of Qumran*. Philadelphia: Fortress Press, 1963.

RISSI, Mathias. *Die Theologie des Hebräerbriefs*. WUNT, 41. Tübingen: J.C.B. Mohr (Paul Siebeck), 1987.

RITT, Hubert. *Offenbarung des Johannes*. NEB, 21. Würzburg: Echter Verlag, 1986.

ROBERT, Louis. "Épitaphes d'Eumeneia de Phrygie." In *Hellenica. Recueil d'Épigraphie de Numismatique et d'Antiquites Grecques*, vols. 11-12. Paris: Adrien-Maisonneuve, 1960. Pp. 414-39.

_____. "Épitaphes juives d'Éphèse et de Nicomédie." In *Hellenica. Recueil d'Épigraphie de Numismatique et d'Antiquites Grecques*, vols. 11-12. Paris: Adrien-Maisonneuve, 1960. Pp. 381-413.

_____. "Reliefs votifs et cultes d'Anatolie." *Anat* 3 (1958), pp. 103-136.

ROBINSON, John A.T. *Redating the New Testament*. Philadelphia: Westminster Press, 1976.

RODGERS, Bill Wilson. *The Christ of the Apocalypse. A Study in the Origin and Nature of the Christology of the Book of Revelation*. The General Theological Seminary: Ph.D. Dissertation, 1965.

ROWLAND, Christopher E. "A Man Clothed in Linen." *JSNT* 24 (1985), pp. 99-110.

_____. "Apocalyptic Visions and the Exaltation of Christ in the Letter to the Colossians." *JSNT* 19 (1983), pp. 73-83.

_____. Review of *Paul the Convert*, by Alan Segal. *JJS* 42 (1991), 269-70.

_____. *The Influence of the First Chapter of Ezekiel on Judaism and Early Christianity*. University of Cambridge: Ph.D. Dissertation, 1975.

_____. *The Open Heaven. A Study of Apocalyptic in Judaism and Early Christianity*. New York: Crossroad, 1982.

_____. "The Parting of the Ways: the Evidence of Jewish and Christian Apocalypse and Mystical Material." In *Jews and Christians. The Parting of the Ways A.D. 70 to 135*, edited by James D.G. DUNN. WUNT, 66. Tübingen: J.C.B. Mohr (Paul Siebeck). Pp. 213-37.

_____. "The Vision of the Risen Christ in Rev. i.13 ff.: The Debt of an Early Christology to an Aspect of Jewish Angelology." *JTS* 31 (1980), pp. 1-11.

ROWLEY, H.H. *The Relevance of Apocalyptic. A Study of Jewish and Christian Apocalypses from Daniel to Revelation*. London: Lutterworth, 1947.

RUBINKIEWICZ, R. "Apocalypse of Abraham." In *The Old Testament Pseudepigrapha*, edited by James H. CHARLESWORTH. 2 vols. Garden City, NY: Doubleday, 1983-1985. Vol. 1, pp. 681-705.

RUNIA, D.T. *Philo of Alexandria and the Timaeus of Plato*. PhAnt, 44. Leiden: E.J. Brill, 1986.

RUSAM, D. "Neue Belege zu den στοιχεῖα τοῦ κόσμου (Gal 4,3.9; Kol 2,8.20)." *ZNW* 83 (1992), pp. 119-25.

RUSSELL, D.S. *The Method and Message of Jewish Apocalyptic 200 B.C.-A.D. 100*. OTL. Philadelphia: Fortress Press, 1964.

SANDERS, Ed Parish. *Paul, the Law, and the Jewish People*. Philadelphia: Fortress Press, 1983.

_____. "Testament of Abraham." in *The Old Testament Pseudepigrapha*, edited by James H. CHARLESWORTH. 2 vols. Garden City, NY: Doubleday, 1983-1985. Vol. 1, pp. 871-902.

SANDMEL, Samuel. "Philo Judaeus: An Introduction to the Man, His Writings, and His Significance." In *Aufstieg und Niedergang der römischen Welt*, edited by Wolfgang HAASE. Series II, Part 21, vol. 1. Berlin/New York: Walter de Gruyter, 1983. Pp. 3-46.

SAPPINGTON, Thomas J. *Revelation and Redemption at Colossae*. NSNTSS, 53. Sheffield: JSOT Press, 1991.

SATAKE, Akira. *Die Gemeindeordnung in der Johannesapokalypse*. WMANT, 21. Neukirchen-Vluyn: Neukirchener Verlag, 1966.

SCHABERG, Jane. "Mark 14.62: Early Christian Merkabah Imagery?" In *Apocalyptic and the New Testament. J.L. Martyn Festschrift*, edited by Joel MARCUS and Marion L. SOARDS. JSNTSS, 24. Sheffield: JSOT Press, 1989. Pp. 69-94.

SCHÄFER, Peter. "Engel und Menschen in der Hekhalot-Literatur." *Kairos* 22 (1980), pp. 201-225.

_____. "Aufbau und redaktionelle Identität der *Hekhalot Zutarti.*" In *Hekhalot-Studien.* TSAJ, 19. Tübingen: J.C.B. Mohr (Paul Siebeck), 1988. Pp. 50-62.

_____. "New Testament and Hekhalot Literature: The Journey into Heaven in Paul and in Merkavah Literature." *JStJud* 35 (1984), pp. 19-35.

_____. "Tradition and Redaction in Hekhalot Literature." In *Hekhalot-Studien.* TSAJ, 19. Tübingen: J.C.B. Mohr (Paul Siebeck), 1988. Pp. 8-16.

_____. Review of *Apocalyptic and Merkavah Mysticism* by I. Gruenwald, *The Faces of the Chariot* by D. Halperin, and *Mysticism in Rabbinic Judaism* by I. Chernus. *JAOS* 104 (1984), pp. 537-41.

_____. *Rivalität zwischen Engeln und Menschen.* SJ, 8. Berlin: Walter de Gruyter, 1975.

_____. "Tradition and Redaction in Hekhalot Literature." *JStJud* 14 (1983), pp. 172-81.

SCHARBERT, J. "ברך." In *Theologisches Wörterbuch zum Alten Testament*, edited by G. Johannes BOTTERWECK, Helmer RINGGREN, and H.J. FABRY. Stuttgart: W. Kohlhammer, 1970-. Vol. 1, cols. 808-841.

SCHENKE, Hans-Martin. "Erwägungen zum Rätsel des Hebräerbriefes." In *Neues Testament und christliche Existenz. Festschrift für Herbert Braun*, edited by H.D. BETZ and L. SCHOTTROFF. Tübingen: J.C.B. Mohr (Paul Siebeck), 1973. Pp. 421-37.

SCHENKER, A. "Der Monotheismus im ersten Gebot, die Stellung der Frau im Sabbatgebot und zwei Sachfragen zum Dekalog." *FZPhTh* 32 (1985), pp. 323-41.

SCHIFFMAN, Lawrence H. "Merkavah *Speculation at Qumran*: The 4Q Serekh Shirot 'Olat ha-Shabbat." In *Mystics, Philosophers, and Politicians*, edited by Jehuda REINHARZ and Daniel SWETSCHINSKI. Durham: Duke University Press, 1982. Pp. 15-47.

SCHLIER, Heinrich. *Der Brief an die Galater.* MeyerK, 7/11. Göttingen: Vandenhoeck & Ruprecht, 1951.

SCHNACKENBURG, Rudolf. "Christologie des Neuen Testament." In *Mysterium Salutis*, Part 3, vol. 1: *Das Christusereignis*, edited by Johannes FEINER and Magnus LÖHRER. Einsiedeln/Zürich/Köln: Benziger Verlag, 1970. Pp. 227-388.

SCHOLEM, Gershom. *Jewish Gnosticism, Merkabah Mysticism, and Talmudic Tradition.* 2nd ed. New York: Jewish Theological Seminary, 1965.

_____. *Major Trends in Jewish Mysticism.* 3rd ed. New York: Schocken Books, 1974.

_____. "Metatron." In *Encyclopaedia Judaica*, edited by Cecil ROTH and Geoffrey WIGODER. Jerusalem: Keter, 1971. Vol. 11, cols. 1443-46.

SCHÜRER, Emil. *The Literature of the Jewish People in the Time of Jesus.* Translated by Peter CHRISTIE and Sophia TAYLOR. New York: Schocken Books, 1972.

_____. *The history of the Jewish people in the age of Jesus Christ.* 3 vols. Edited by Geza VERMES, Martin GOODMAN, and Fergus MILLAR. Edinburgh: T. & T. Clark, 1973-1987.

SCHÜSSLER FIORENZA, Elisabeth. "Apokalypsis and Propheteia." In *The Book of Revelation. Justice and Judgment.* Philadelphia: Fortress Press, 1985. Pp. 133-56.

_____. "Research Perspectives on the Book of Revelation." In *The Book of Revelation. Justice and Judgment.* Philadelphia: Fortress Press, 1985. Pp. 12-32.

_____. "The Composition and Structure of Revelation." In *The Book of Revelation. Justice and Judgment.* Philadelphia: Fortress Press, 1985. Pp. 159-80.

_____. "Visionary Rhetoric and Social-Political Situation." In *The Book of Revelation. Justice and Judgment.* Philadelphia: Fortress Press, 1985. Pp. 181-203.

SCHWEITZER, Albert. *Die Mystik des Apostels Paulus.* UTB, 1091. Tübingen: J.C.B. Mohr (Paul Siebeck), 1930.

SCHWEIZER, Eduard. "Christianity of the Circumcised and Judaism of the Uncircumcised: Background of Matthew and Colossians." In *Jews, Greeks and Christians: Religious Cultures in Late Antiquity. Essays in Honour of W.D. Davies*, edited by Robert HAMERTON-KELLY and Robin SCROGGS. Leiden: E.J. Brill, 1976. Pp. 245-60.

_____. *Der Brief an die Kolosser.* EKK. Neukirchen-Vlug/Zürich: Neukirchener and Benziger Verlag, 1976.

_____. "Slaves of the Elements and Worshipers of Angels: Gal 4:3, 9 and Col 2:8, 18, 20." *JBL* 107 (1988), pp. 455-68.

_____. "The Background of Matthew and Colossians." In *Jews, Greeks and Christians. Religious Cultures in Late Antiquity. Essays in Honor of William David Davies*, edited by Robert HAMMERTON-KELLY and Robin SCROGGS. SJLA, 21. Leiden: E.J. Brill, 1976. Pp. 245-60.

SCHWEMER, Anna Marie. "Gott als König in den Sabbatliedern." In *Königsherrschaft Gottes und himmlischer Kult im Judentum, Urchristentum und in der hellenistischen Welt*, edited by M. HENGEL and A.M. SCHWEMER. WUNT, 55. Tübingen: J.C.B. Mohr (Paul Siebeck), 1991. Pp. 45-118.

SCOTT, E.F. *The Epistles of Paul to the Colossians, to Philemon and to the Ephesians.* MNTC. London: Hodder and Stoughton, 1930.

SÉD, Nicolas. "Le *Sefer Ha-Razim* et le méthode de 'combinaison des lettres'," *REJ* 130 (1971), pp. 295-304.

_____. "Les Traditions Secrètes et les Disciples de Rabban Yohanan ben Zakkai." *RHR* 184 (1973), pp. 49-66.

SEESEMANN, H. "πανήγυρις. In *Theological Dictionary of the New Testament*, edited by Gerhard KITTEL and Gerhard FRIEDRICH. Translated by Geoffrey W. BROMILEY. 10 vols. Grand Rapids: Wm. B. Eerdmans, 1964-1976. Vol. 5, p. 722.

SEGAL, Alan F. "Heavenly Ascent in Hellenistic Judaism, Early Christianity and their Environment." In *Aufstieg und Niedergang der römischen Welt*, edited by Wolfgang HAASE. Series II, Part 23, vol. 1. Berlin/New York: Walter de Gruyter, 1980. Pp. 1334-94.

_____. *Paul the Convert. The Apostolate and Apostasy of Saul the Pharisee*. New Haven: Yale University Press, 1990.

_____. "Ruler of This World: Attitudes about Mediator Figures." In *Jewish and Christian Self-Definition*, edited by E.P. SANDERS. 3 vols. Philadelphia: Fortress Press, 1989. Vol. 2, pp. 245-69 and 403-413.

_____. "The Risen Christ and Angelic Mediator Figures in Light of Qumran." In *Jesus and the Dead Sea Scrolls*, edited by James H. CHARLESWORTH. Garden City, NY: Doubleday, 1992. Pp. 302-328.

_____. *Two Powers in Heaven. Early Rabbinic Reports About Christianity and Gnosticism*. SJLA, 25. Leiden: E.J. Brill, 1977.

SHEPPARD, A.R.R. "Jews, Christians and Heretics in Acmonia and Eumeneia." *AnatSt* 29 (1979), pp. 169-80.

_____. "Pagan Cults of Angels in Roman Asia Minor." *Tal* 12-13 (1980-81), pp. 77-101.

SIMON, Marcel. "Remarques sur l'Angélolâtrie Juive au Début de l'Ère Chrétienne." In *Le Christianism antique et son contexte religieux*. WUNT, 23. Tübingen: J.C.B. Mohr (Paul Siebeck), 1981). Pp. 450-64.

_____. *Verus Israel. A study of the relations between Christians and Jews in the Roman Empire (135-425)*. Translated by H. McKEATING. LLJC. Oxford: Oxford University Press, 1986.

SMITH, E.W. *Joseph and Asenath and Early Christian Literature*. Claremont School of Theology: Ph.D. Dissertation, 1974.

SMITH, Jonathan Z. "The Prayer of Joseph." In *Religions in Antiquity. Essays in Memory of Erwin Ramsell Goodenough*, edited by J. NEUSNER. SHR, 14. Leiden: E.J. Brill, 1968. Pp. 253-93.

_____. "Wisdom and Apocalyptic." In *Visionaries and Their Apocalypses*, edited by P.D. HANSON. Philadelphia: Fortress Press, 1983. Pp. 101-120.

SMITH, Morton. "Helios in Palestine." *EI* 16 (1982), pp. 199*-214*.

_____. "Observations on *Hekhaloth Rabbati*." In *Biblical and Other Studies*, vol. 1: *Studies and Texts*, edited by A. ALTMANN. Cambridge, Mass.: Harvard University Press, 1963. Pp. 142-60.

_____. "Two Ascended to Heaven." In *Jesus and the Dead Sea Scrolls*, edited by James H. CHARLESWORTH. New York: Crossroad, 1992. Pp. 290-301.

SOKOLOWSKI, F. "Sur le Culte d'Angelos dans le paganisme grec et romain." *HTR* 53 (1960), pp. 225-29.

SORDI, Marta. *The Christians and the Roman Empire*. Norman/London: University of Oklahoma Press, 1986.

SPICQ, C. *L'Épître aux Hébreaux*. 2 vols. Paris: J. Gabalda, 1953.

_____. "L'Épitre aux Hébreux, Apollos, Jean-Baptiste, les Hellénistes et Qumran." *RQ* 1 (1958), pp. 365-90.

STAUFFER, Ethelbert. *Christ and the Caesars*. Translated by K. and R. GREGOR SMITH. Philadelphia: Westminster Press, 1955.

STONE, Michael E. "Lists of Revealed Things in the Apocalyptic Literature." In *Magnalia Dei. The Mighty Acts of God. Essays in the Bible and Archaeology in Memory of G. Ernest Wright*, edited by F.M. CROSS, W.E. LEMKE and P.D. MILLER. Garden City, NY: Doubleday, 1976. Pp. 141-52.

STRADELMANN, Andreas. "Zur Christologie des Hebräerbriefes in der neueren Diskussion." *ThBer* 2 (1973), pp. 135-221.

STRUBBE, J.H.M. "'Cursed be he that moves my bones'." In *Magika Hiera. Ancient Greek Magic and Religion*, edited by Christopher A. FARAONE and Dirk OBBINK. Oxford: Oxford University Press, 1991. Pp. 33-59.

SYNGE, F.C. *Hebrews and the Scriptures*. London: SPCK, 1959.

TATUM, W. Barnes. "The LXX Version of the Second Commandment (Ex. 20,3-6 = Deut. 5,7-10): A Polemic Against Idols, not Images." *JStJud* 17 (1986), pp. 177-95.

TEEPLE, Howard M. *How Did Christianity Really Begin? A Historical-Archaeological Approach*. Evanston, Illinois: Religion and Ethics Institute, 1992.

THEISON, Johannes. *Der auserwählte Richter*. SUNT, 12. Göttingen: Vandenhoeck & Ruprecht, 1975.

THEISSEN, Gerd. *Biblischer Glaube in evolutionärer Sicht*. Munich: Chr. Kaiser, 1984.

_____. *Untersuchungen zum Hebräerbrief*. SNT, 2. Gütersloh: Gerd Mohn, 1969.

THEOBALD, Michael. "Gott, Logos und Pneuma." In *Monotheismus und Christologie. Zur Gottesfrage im hellenistischen Judentum und im Urchristentum*. Freiburg/Basel/Wien: Herder, 1992. Pp. 41-87.

THOMPSON, James W. *The Beginnings of Christian Philosophy*. CBQMS, 13. Washington, D.C.: CBA, 1982.

THOMPSON, Leonard. "A Sociological Analysis of Tribulation in the Apocalypse of John." *Semeia* 36 (1986), pp. 147-74.

_____. *The Book of Revelation. Apocalypse and Empire*. New York/ Oxford: Oxford University Press, 1990.

TREBILCO, Paul. *Jewish Commmunities in Asia Minor*. SNTSMS, 69. Cambridge: Cambridge University Press, 1991.

TRIBBLE, H.W. "The Christ of the Apocalypse." *RevEx* 40 (1943), pp. 167-76.

URBACH, Ephraim E. "The Traditions about Merkabah Mysticism in the Tannaitic Period." In *Studies in Mysticism and Religion presented to Gershom G. Scholem*. Jerusalem: Magness Press, 1967. Pp. 1-28. In Hebrew.

_____. *The Sages. Their Concepts and Beliefs*. Translated by I. ABRAHAMS. 2nd ed. Jerusalem: Magness Press, 1989.

VAN DER HORST, Peter W. "De Joodse toneelschrijver Ezechiel." *NTT* 36 (1982), pp. 97-112.

_____. "Moses' Throne Vision in Ezekiel the Dramatist." *JJS* 34 (1983), pp. 21-29.

VANDERKAM, James C. "The Prophetic-Sapiential Origins of Apocalyptic Thought." In *A Word in Season. Essays in Honour of William McKane*, edited by James D. MARTIN and Philip R. DAVIES. JSOTSS, 42. Sheffield: JSOT Press, 1986. Pp. 63-76.

VANHOYE, Albert. *La structure littéraire de l'Épître aus Hébreux*. StudNeot, 1. Paris/Bruges: Brouwer, 1962.

_____. *Situation du Christ. L'épître aus Hébreaux 1-2*. LD, 58. Paris: Cerf, 1969.

VAN LENNEP, Henry J. *Travels in Little-Known Parts of Asia Minor*. 2 vols. London: John Murray, 1870.

VAN SCHAIK, A.P. "Ἄλλος ἄγγελος in Apk 14." In *L'Apocalypse johannique et l'Apocalyptique dans le Nouveau Testament*, edited by J. LAMBRECHT. BETL, 53. Leuven: Leuven University Press, 1980. Pp. 217-28.

VERSNEL, H.S. "Beyond Cursing: the Appel to Justice in Judicial Prayers." In *Magika Hiera. Ancient Greek Magic and Religion*, edited by Christopher A. FARAONE and Dirk OBBINK. Oxford: Oxford University Press, 1991. Pp. 60-106.

VIELHAUER, Philipp. *Geschichte der urchristlichen Literatur*. 2nd ed. Berlin/New York: Walter de Gruyter, 1978.

VIELHAUER, Philipp and Georg STRECKER. "Apokalypsen und Verwandtes: Einleitung." In *Neutestamentliche Apokryphen*, edited by Wilhelm SCHNEEMELCHER. 5th ed. of Edgar HENNECKE's original collection. Tübingen: J.C.B. Mohr (Paul Siebeck), 1989. Pp. 491-515.

VOGEL, Manfred H. "Monotheism." In *Encyclopaedia Judaica*. 16 vols. Jerusalem: Keter, 1971. Vol. 12, cols. 260-63.

VON DER OSTEN-SACKEN, P. *Die Apokalyptik in ihrem Verhältnis zu Prophetie und Weisheit*. TEH, 157. Münich: Chr. Kaiser, 1969.

_____. *Gott und Belial*. SUNT, 6. Göttingen: Vandenhoeck & Ruprecht, 1969.

VON RAD, Gerhard. *Old Testament Theology*. Translated by D.M.G. STALKER. 2 vols. New York/Hagerstown/San Francisco/London: Harper & Row, 1965.

_____. *Wisdom in Israel*. Translated by James D. MARTIN. London/Nashville/ New York: SCM and Abingdon, 1970.

WEBER, Ferdinand. *System der Altsynagogalen Palästinischen Theologie aus Targum, Midrasch, und Talmud*. Leipzig: Dörffling & Franke, 1886.

WEIß, Hans-Friedrich. *Der Brief an die Hebräer*. MeyerK, 15/1. Göttingen: Vandenhoeck & Ruprecht, 1991.

WERNER, Martin. *Die Entstehung des christlichen Dogmas*. Bern/Leipzig: Haupt, 1941.

WHEALON, John F. "New Patches on an Old Garment: The Book of Revelation." *BThBull* 11 (1981), pp. 54-59.

WICKS, Henry J. *The Doctrine of God in the Jewish Apocryphal and Apocalyptic Literature*. New York: Ktav, 1971. Repr. from 1915.

WILHELM, Adolf. "Zwei Fluchinschriften." *JOAT* 4 (1901), cols. 9-18.

WILLIAMS, A. Lukyn. "The Cult of Angels at Colossae." *JTS* 10 (1909), pp. 413-38.

WILLIAMSON, Ronald. *Philo and the Epistle to the Hebrews*. ALGHJ. Leiden: E.J. Brill, 1970.

WINDISCH, Hans. *Der Hebräerbrief*. HNT, 14. Tübingen: J.C.B. Mohr (Paul Siebeck), 1931.

WINTERMUTE, O.S. "Apocalypse of Zephaniah." In *The Old Testament Pseudepigrapha*, edited by James H. CHARLESWORTH. 2 vols. Garden City, NY: Doubleday, 1983-1985. Vol. 1, pp. 509-515.

WOJCIECHOWSKI, Michał. "Seven churches and seven celestial bodies (Rev 1,16; Rev 2-3)." *BibNot* 45 (1988), pp. 48-50.

WÜNSCH, Richard. *Antikes Zaubergerät aus Pergamon*. JKDAI, Ergänzungsheft, 6. Berlin: Georg Reimer, 1905.

YADIN, Yigael. "The Dead Sea Scrolls and the Epistle to the Hebrews." In *Aspects of the Dead Sea Scrolls*, edited by C. RABIN. 2nd ed. ScrHier, 4. Jerusalem: Magness Press and Hebrew University Press, 1965. Repr. from 1958. Pp. 36-55.

YATES, Roy. "'The Worship of Angels' (Col 2:18)." *ExT* 97 (1985), pp. 12-15.

INDEX OF PASSAGES

Page numbers in *italics* represent citations which occur in footnotes. The italics fall out when a passage occurs on more than one consecutive page.

A. OLD TESTAMENT

Genesis
15:1	88
16:7-14	89
16:11	*137*
18:1-2	89
18:1-22	*137*
18:2	83
19:1	83
19:15-16	*137*
21:17	89
22:12	92
23:7	83
24:18	92
26:24	88
28:13(LXX)	88
30:2	90,98
32:25-33	*137*
33:6-7	83
42:6	83
43:23	88
43:26	83
45:1-7	90
45:11	90
46:3	88
48:12	83
48:15-16	67,*137*
48:15-16(LXX)	67
50:18	280
50:18(LXX)	280
50:18-21	90
50:19	90,98,280
50:19(LXX)	90,280
50:21	90,280
50:21(LXX)	90,280

Exodus
3:9-15	210
4:22(LXX)	120
9:30	92
13:19	90
13:21	69
13:21-22(LXX)	231
14:13	88
14:19	*231*
14:19(LXX)	*231*
14:24(LXX)	*231*
14:30-31	226
14:31	92,226
15	226
15:1	*135*
20:3-5	145
20:4	54,56-58,*61,63,69*
20:4(LXX)	*58*
20:4-5	57
20:16	172
20:20	54,63
20:23	56-59
23:20	69,*137*
23:21	68-70
23:21(LXX)	*68,68*
23:24	87
24:1	69-70,*72*
28:4	228
33:15	70
34:29-35	229
34:30	83
39:30	*153*

Leviticus
6:10	226,228
19:14	92
19:31	145
25:17	92
26:1	87

Numbers
6:24-26	162
14:1-12	172
20:6	52
21:34	88
22:22-35	*137*

Deuteronomy
1:21	88
3:2	88
4:19	57,*57*
5:9	87
6:4	62
6:10	120,*137*
6:13	91,*101*
6:13(LXX)	*91*
10:17	98

10:29	*137*	7:14(LXX)	120
11:29	*120*	9:8	*83*
17:3	*57*	13:28	*88*
18:9-12	*61*	14:22	*83*
20:2-4	*88*	14:23	*83*
20:3	*88*	24:20	*83*
26:8	*52*		
26:14	*61*	1 Kings	
31:6	*88*	1:23	*83*
31:8	*88*	1:53	*83*
32:8(LXX)	*63*	2:19	*83*
32:8-9(LXX)	*62*	17:13	*88*
32:9	*66*	17:35	*91*
32:43	*121,135*	17:37	*91*
32:43(LXX)	121	17:38	*91*
33:2(LXX)	56	19:18	*87*
33:2(Vulg)	*56*	19:18(LXX)	*87*
33:4	*56*		
		2 Kings	
Joshua		1:15	*89*
5:13-15	281	2:15	*83*
5:14	*83,*281	4:37	*83*
5:14(LXX)	281	6:16	*88*
8:1	*88*	19:6	*88*
10:25	*88*	23:5	*57*
23:7	*87*	25:24	*88*
24:14	*91*		
		1 Chronicles	
Judges		21:12	*52*
5:31	213,*213*	21:12(LXX)	*52*
5:31(LXX)	229	21:21	*83*
6:10	*91*	28:20	*88*
6:11-23	281		
6:11-24	*89*	2 Chronicles	
6:19	*83,*281	20:15	*88*
6:19(LXX)	*83,*281	20:17	*88*
6:22	281	32:7	*88*
6:23	*89,*281		
6:23(LXX)	281	Nehemiah	
6:24	281	4:8	*88*
Ruth		Esther	
2:10	*83*	2:20	*92*
		3:3	*87*
1 Samuel		13:12-14(LXX)	*87*
12:14	*91*		
12:24	*91*	Psalm	
16:4	*83*	2:2(LXX)	263-264
20:41	*83*	2:7	120,*135*
21:1	*83*	2:7(LXX)	120
23:17	*88*	8	132,134,*134,136,*
24:6	*83*		*160*
25:23	*83*	8:2(LXX)	*131*
28:14	*83*	8:3	133-134
		8:5	133-134
2 Samuel		8:5-6	*130,159*
7:14	120,135		

8:5-7	122-123,129-130, 133,134-136	*Ecclesiastes*	
8:6	*130,133*	5:6	*91*
8:7	128-130,132-133	7:19	*91*
8:8-9	*133*	8:12	*91*
14:4	*91*		
21:23	*91*	*Song of Songs*	
24:12	*91*	1:3-4	*73*
30:19	*91*	3:24	*62*
32:8	*91*		
33:7	*91*	*Isaiah*	
33:15	173	6:1-8	*210*
44:7-8(LXX)	121	6:5	*89*
45:6-7	*136*	7:4	*88*
45:7	135	10:24	*88*
45:7-8	121	13:2(LXX)	*88*
49:15(LXX)	*177*	22:22	*239*
59:4	*91*	35:4	*88*
60:5	*91*	37:6	*88*
65:16	*91*	40:9	*88*
66:7	*91*	41:10	*88*
71:17	*170*	41:14	*88*
82:1	*150*	43:1	*88*
84:9	*91*	43:5	*88*
85:11	*91*	44:8	*88*
88(LXX)	*120*	50:6(1QIs^a)	*153*
88:6(LXX)	*121*	63:9	*52*
88:7(LXX)	120-121,*135*	63:9(LXX)	*52*
88:28(LXX)	120-121		
96:7(LXX)	121,*121*	*Jeremiah*	
97:7	121,135	1:4-10	*210*
101:15	*91*	1:17(LXX)	*88*
102:11	*91*	5:22	*91*
101:26-28(LXX)	121	8:2	*57*
102:20(LXX)	184	30:10	*88*
102:21(LXX)	184	33:19	*91*
102:25-27	121,*136*	40:9-10	*88*
103:4(LXX)	121-122	46:27	*88*
104:4	56,121,135-136	46:28	*88*
109:1(LXX)	130-132		
110	*128,132*	*Ezekiel*	
110:1	120-121,128-136,148	1	59,211,*220*
110:5	*91*	1:5-21	*57*
111:1	*91*	1:7	212,239
112:5(LXX)	*132,135*	1:7(LXX)	212
113:5	*132,135*	1:24	213,225
113:21	*91*	1:24(LXX)	213
117:4	*91*	1:26	217
118:63	*91*	1:26(LXX)	221
127:1	*91*	1:28	*90,231*
134:20	*91*	2:1	*90*
144:19	*91*	2:1-3:11	*210*
146:11	*91*	2:6	*90*
		2:6(LXX)	*90*
Proverbs		2:6-7	*88*
3:7	*91*	2:8-3:3	231
9:10	153	2:9	232
		3:1-3	232

3:9	90	8	220,221
3:23	89	8-12	211,221,231,263
3:24	90	8:15	220
8:2	217	8:15(LXX)	220
9	211,226-228,257-258	8:15(Th.)	220
9-10	246,263,265	8:15-16	220
9:2	211,213,226,228,244	8:17-18	83
9:2(LXX)	211,226-227	8:26	229
9:2-10:2	227	9	220-221
9:3	227	9:3	118
9:4	227	9:21	220,220
9:4(LXX)	227	9:21(LXX)	220
9:6	227	9:21(Th.)	220
9:6(LXX)	227	10	219-221,226,228-230,258
9:11	227,227		
9:11(LXX)	227	10:1	231
10:2	227	10:2	118
40	228,263	10:4	229,231
40-48	212,247	10:4-14	89
40:1	247	10:4-21	279
40:3	247	10:5	213,220,220,227-228,242
40:3(LXX)	212,212		
43:2	213,213,225	10:5(LXX)	220,227
43:2(LXX)	213	10:5(Th.)	220,227
43:3	89	10:5-6	89,211-212,218-219,221,229-230,257
44:4	89		
		10:5-6(LXX)	211-212
Daniel	118	10:5-6(Th.)	211-212
3:41	92	10:6	101,213,219,229,239
7	215,217,230,263		
7:1-14	218	10:6(LXX)	213,231
7:9	71,80,101,129,211,213,217-221,230,258	10:9	279
		10:9(LXX)	279
7:9(LXX)	211	10:9(Th.)	279
7:9(Th.)	211	10:10	260
7:9-14	211,219	10:10-11	83
7:10(LXX)	218	10:12	260,279
7:13	128,211,213-221,230,230,242-243	10:13	63,220
		10:15	220
7:13(LXX)	214-215,217-218,242,258	10:15(LXX)	220
		10:15(Th.)	220
7:13(Th.)	214-215,217,217,230,242	10:16	220,220
		10:17	98
7:14(LXX)	218	10:17(LXX)	98
7:15	89	10:17(Th.)	98
7:17-28	218	10:18	220,220
7:18	220	10:18(LXX)	220
7:21	220	10:18(Th.)	220
7:21-22	218	10:18-21	89
7:21-22(LXX)	218	10:19	98,260
7:21-22(Th.)	218	10:20-21	63
7:22	218,220	10:21	220
7:22(LXX)	218	12	221
7:25	220	12:1	220,220
7:27	220	12:3	229,229
7:28	89	12:3(LXX)	229

Index of Passages

12:3(Th.)	229		*Micah*	
12:4	229,232		6:9	*91*
12:4-9	231,*231*		7:8	68
12:7	220,*220*,229			
12:7(LXX)	*220*		*Zephaniah*	
12:7(Th.)	220		3:16	*88*
12:8	*98*			
12:8(LXX)	*98*		*Haggai*	
12:8(Th.)	*98*		2:5	*88*
12:9	232			
			Zechariah	
Hosea			10:11	230
10:3	*91*		12:10-14	*242*
11:10	*231*			
			Malachi	
Joel			1:6	*91*
3:5	64,67		3:5	*91*
3:13	*242*		3:16	*91*
3:15	*244*		4:2	*91*
Amos				
3:8	*231*			

B. NEW TESTAMENT

Matthew			9:2-10	281
1:20-21	89		9:3	*227*
4:10	*101*		9:6	281
13:43	229		9:8	77
16:14	*139*		10:17	281
17:2	229		10:17-18	76,281
17:5-8	281		10:18	281
17:6	*101*,281		12:35	129
17:6-8	77		12:36	*131*
17:7	281		12:36	128
17:8	281		14:62	128
22:44	128-129		16:3-8	77
26:64	*128*		16:5-7	89
28:2-3	*101*		16:6	*101*
28:2-7	282		16:8	*101*
28:2-10	77		16:19	*128*
28:3	84			
28:4	*101*,282		*Luke*	
28:4-5	83		1:11-20	*89*
28:5	*101*,282		1:26-35	*89*
28:7	*101*,282		2:8-12	*89*
28:9	*101*,282		9:19	*139*
28:9-10	282		9:28-36	281
28:10	*101*,282		9:34	281
28:11-15	*101*		12:42	*128*
28:16	*101*		20:43	*129*
28:17	*101*,282		22:69	*128*
28:18	282			
			John	
Mark			4:2	*141*
8:28	*139*			

Acts		3:6-29	104
2:33	128,131	3:10	109
2:34	131	3:17	111
2:34-35	128	3:19	10,56,104-106
5:31	128,131	3:19-20	104,106
7:42	112	3:20	111
7:53	111	3:21	105,109-110
7:55	128,131	3:21-4:11	105
7:56	128,131	3:22	105
9:1-6	210	3:23	105
10:25	76,98,279	3:23-25	109
10:25-26	98	3:24	104
10:25-46	279	3:25	105
10:28	98	3:26	105
10:34	98	3:26-29	109
10:46	98,279	3:28	109
16:9	83	3:29	105
16:29	83	4	141
18:9	88	4:1	109
19:13-16	179	4:1-5	109-110
22:6-10	210	4:1-11	109,109
23:8	136	4:2	105
26:9-18	210	4:3	104-106,108,108,110
Romans		4:4-5	110
2:1	108	4:6	109
4:1-12	109	4:6-8	109
8:29	120	4:6-11	109-110
8:34	128,131-132	4:8	104,106,108,110
8:38	131-132	4:8-9	104,108,108
8:38-39	131	4:8-11	110
		4:9	10,104-110
1 Corinthians		4:14	111
8:4	108		
8:4-6	108	Ephesians	
8:5	108	1:20	128,131-132
8:5-6	5	1:21	131-132
15	133	1:22	129,131
15:20-28	129	1:23	132
15:24	131,131	2:6	128,132
15:24-26	131	2:7	132
15:25	128-130	6:12	131
15:26	131,136		
15:27-28	129	Philippians	
15:28	129,132	2:6-11	130,132
		2:7	130
2 Corinthians		2:8	130,132
3:7	229	2:9	130-131
		2:9-10	130
Galatians		2:10	130-131
1:13-17	210	2:11	130
2:15-16	109		
3	109-110	Colossians	
3:1-4:7	108	1:15-20	119
3:1-4:11	110	1:16	94,96,131,131
3:3	104,108	1:17	132
3:6-26	105	2	141

Index of Passages

2:8	*10*,113,*113*,131	1:14-2:4	*136*
2:9-10	119	2	123,125,*137*
2:10	131,*131*	2:1	*122*,125
2:15	131	2:1-2	125
2:16	*249*	2:1-4	122,*122*,125,127,
2:16ff.	*115*		136,*136*
2:17	115,117,132	2:2	*111*,119,122-123,
2:18	*10*,*54*,111-113,115-		127,*134*
	119,*124*,131,*131*,	2:3	122,*122*,127
	147,151,202,*249*	2:3-4	122,*122*
2:18-19	*112*	2:4	125
2:20	113,131-132	2:5	122-123,132-134
2:21	113	2:6-8	123,*130*,135
2:23	*117*,*249*	2:7	*123*,*130*
3:1	*128*,*131*,131-132,	2:7-9	*124*
3:1-17	119	2:8	128-130,132-133
		2:8-18	*130*
1 Timothy		2:9	*123*,*130*,132,*136*
2:5	*177*	2:9-18	*123*,*136*
		2:10	*130*,132-133
Hebrews		2:10-13	123
1	121,125,127-128	2:14	123
1-2	120,124-125,127-	2:14-15	*136*
	129,137,139,148,	2:16	123
	240,260	2:17	*136*
1:1-4	128	4:14-5:10	*136*
1:2	122,*136*,139	6:9	*131*
1:3	120,*120*,130,*130*,	7:1-28	*136*
	132,136	7:7	*131*
1:3-4	128,135	7:27-8:2	*130*
1:3-2:10	203-204	8:1	128,132
1:4	120-121,130-132,	8:1-7	*136*
	132,*136*	8:6	*131*
1:5	120-123,*128*,*132*,	8:13	123
	134-136	10:2	*130*
1:5-6	134	10:11-13	*130*
1:5-9	128,134	10:11-18	*136*
1:5-12	128	10:12	132
1:5-13	120,*134*	10:12-13	*128*
1:5-14	127-128	11:40	*130*
1:5-2:18	119,128	12:2	128,*130*,132
1:6	134-135	12:22	125,*125*
1:6-7	119	12:22-23	124,*134*
1:7	56,*120*,122-123,	12:22-24	125
	134-135	12:23	125
1:7-9	121	12:24	*131*
1:8	121	13:2	*127*
1:8-9	135,*135*	13:9	124-125
1:8-10	134	13:9-10	*125*
1:9	121,*136*		
1:10	121,*121*	**1 Peter**	
1:10-12	121,*134*,*136*	3:22	128-129,131-133
1:12	*121*	4:1	132
1:13	119,121-123,128-		
	136	**Jude**	
1:14	120,122-124,*131*,	5	*138*
	136		

Index of Passages

Revelation
1	221,227-228,230-231,240,248,260-261,263,272
1:1	93,*208*,247,252-253,255
1:4	209,239,*253*
1:4-5	209
1:4-8	209
1:5	31,*120*,239
1:5-6	209
1:7	230,242-243
1:8	41,100,282
1:9	209,*210*,*253*,*254*,260
1:9-20	210
1:10-12	210
1:11	209-211,232,259
1:11-12	232
1:12	211,233,239,261
1:12-16	245
1:12-17	100-101,202
1:12-20	209-210,230,232,238,240,257-258,271-272
1:13	221,*221*,226-228,230,239,242,*242*,246,257
1:13-16	100,211,*230*,244
1:13-17	3,259
1:13-20	282
1:14	*80*,212-213,239,258
1:14-15	239
1:15	212,219,222-223,225,*231*
1:16	213,229,232-233,239,258
1:17	100,239,259-260,*260*,282
1:17-18	219-220,258,*260*
1:18	*230*,239,258
1:19	209-210,*231*,259,261
1:20	232-235,239,260
1:20-3:22	241
2	209,*209*,232
2-3	210,233-234,237,237-238
2:1	*209*,233,239
2:1-3:22	182
2:7	33,211
2:8	*209*,239
2:10	238,*243*
2:11	33,43,211
2:12	*209*,239
2:13	37,41,*238*
2:14	*249*
2:17	33
2:18	*209*,239
2:20-21	*249*
2:23-25	238
2:26	33
2:27	*251*
2:29	211
3	209,*209*,232
3:1	*209*,233,239
3:2	*251*
3:4	226
3:5	33,*251*,*262*
3:6	211
3:7	*209*,236,239
3:8	239
3:9	*83*
3:12	33,*251*
3:13	211
3:14	31,*209*,239
3:21	33-34,43,*128*,132,*251*
3:22	211
4	*211*,261
4-5	232
4:2	41
4:3	224,*231*
4:4	41,*243*
4:5	239
4:8	41
4:8-11	204
4:11	*251*,*251*
5	101,*232*,261,263,272
5:2	*229*
5:2-5	232
5:3	261
5:5	33,239,*246*
5:6	261,263
5:6-13	101
5:6-14	*3*,43
5:8-9	232
5:8-12	271
5:9	261,263
5:9-11	257
5:10	33
5:11-12	204
5:12	261
5:13	261
6:2	*243*
6:9	33,*252*
6:9-17	37
6:10	239
6:11	33,226
6:16	262
6:17	208,262
7:1-17	24

7:2-3	37,*223*	14:6-11	240
7:9	226,262	14:6-20	37,*208*,240,244-245
7:9-12	*3*	14:6-15:4	*223*
7:9-17	43	14:7	251
7:10	24,262	14:8	240
7:10-17	43	14:8-9	243
7:11	37,*262*	14:8-15:1	37
7:11-12	204	14:9	240-241
7:12	*251*	14:10	*262*
7:13	*246*	14:13	*223,226,251*
7:13-17	*246*	14:14	*221,221*,230,240-243
7:14	98,*246*	14:14-16	204,240
7:14-17	*246*	14:14-20	3,240,265,271-272
8:2	37	14:15	240-241,243
8:3-5	*178*,180,204	14:15-16	241
9:5	41	14:15-17	241
10	229,231-232,*246*,	14:16	243-244
10:1	229-232,*243*,272	14:17	240
10:1-10	37	14:17-20	244
10:1-11	229,231	14:18	240-241,244
10:2	231-232	14:19-20	243
10:3	*231*	15	227-228,*244*
10:3-4	231	15-16	*227*
10:4	232	15:1	37,*248*
10:4-6	231	15:1-16:20	*248*
10:6	*231*	15:2	33,*223*
10:7	255	15:2-3	*222*
10:8	232	15:2-4	240
10:8-11	231	15:3-4	*226*
10:9-10	232,*246*	15:4	251
10:11	231-232	15:5	37
11:1-13	231-232	15:5-6	246
11:15	24,*208*,*231,251*,262	15:5-16:21	*223*
11:15-18	*3*	15:5-17:1	227
11:18	224,*255*	15:5-19:10	*248*
12:7-9	37	15:6	33,226,228,246,
12:10	24,262		248-249,257,272
12:10-12	*3*	16:15	*232*
12:11	33	16:17-21	248
12:17	254	17	246,*246*
13:2	37,43	17-18	*227*
13:7	33	17:1	227-228,246-248,
13:11	41,*223*		251
13:11-18	*223*	17:1-18:24	224
13:15	*223*	17:1-19:8	246,251
13:16	*232*	17:1-19:9	204,252
13:17	223	17:1-19:10	247,271
14	242-243,245,263	17:3	247,251
14:1	*208*,222-223,*227*,	17:6	247
	262	17:6-14	247
14:1-4	*3*	17:7	226,247-248,251
14:1-5	222-225,240	17:8	37
14:2	222,*222*,225	17:13	33
14:2-3	222	17:14	31
14:3	222-223	17:15	226,247-248,251,
14:4	223,262		*251*
14:6	240-241,243		

17:15-18	247	19:9-10	227,249-251
18:1	37	19:10	3,75-76,82,84,87,
18:20	224		92-93,95,99-101,
18:21	*229*		124,204,207,*224*,
18:24	224		*230*,245,246,248-
19	252		250,252-259,271,
19:1	224,251,*251*		277
19:1-4	224	19:11	239
19:1-8	*84*,204,222,224,255	19:11-13	*243*
19:1-9	202	19:11-22:9	*248*
19:1-10	225,251	19:14	226
19:1-16	1	19:15	239
19:3	*251*	19:16	31
19:4	224,251	19:17	37
19:4-8	251	19:21	239
19:5	224,*251*	20:1	220,239
19:5-8	224-225	20:4	33,43,*254*
19:6	222-225,*251*	20:6	1,33,*208*,262
19:6-7	251	21:1-8	248
19:7	224,250-252	21:1-22:5	36,*227*,246
19:8	226,251	21:6-8	259
19:9	227,247-248,250-	21:9	227-228,246-248
	252,*254*,*259*	21:9-22:7	204
19:9-10	227,249-251	21:9-22:9	247,271
19:10	1,75-76,82,84,87,	21:10	247
	92-93,95,99-101,	21:15	247-248
	124,204,207,*224*,	21:15-17	247
	230,245,246,248-	21:22	*208*,262
	250,252-259,271,	21:23	262
	277	22	259
19:11	239	22:1	37,43,247,262
19:11-13	*243*	22:1-5	255,271
19:11-22:9	*248*	22:3	24,37,43,*84*,204,
19:14	226		255,262
19:15	239	22:3-4	3,*208*,*252*
19:16	31	22:4	*227*
19:17	37	22:5	*248*
19:21	239	22:6	*235*,247,252-255
20:1	220,239	22:6-9	255
19:1-8	*84*,204,222,224,255	22:7	*254*,*255*,*259*-260
19:1-9	202	22:8	75,82,*235*,*249*,
19:1-10	225,251		250,253,256,277
19:1-16	*3*	22:8-9	1,75,*84*,99,101,
19:3	*251*		124,204,207,*227*,
19:4	224,251		*230*,245-246,248-
19:4-8	251		250,252-254,256-
19:5	224,*251*		260,271,277
19:5-8	224-225	22:9	76,87,92-*93*,95,
19:6	222-225,*251*		250,*250*,254-255,
19:6-7	251		259-260,277
19:7	224,250-252	22:11	259
19:8	226,251	22:14-15	*251*,259
19:9	227,247-248,250-	22:16	*235*,247,252,255
	252,*254*,*259*	22:21	209

C. Apocryphal Jewish Writings of the Septuagint

Paralipomena Jeremiae
3:4-14	174

Judith
8:8	92
16:16	92

Tobit
2:10	167
3:2-6	167
3:17	167
4:21	92
5:4-11:8	167
5:15	89
5:22	167
6:3-9	193
6:10-18	167
6:18	89
8:1-3	193
8:2-3	167
8:3	167
8:15	167
12:12-15	167,248
12:13(A,B)	167
12:15	84,165,165,167, 178,202
12:15-16	84,245
12:15-22	270
12:16	81-82,166,275
12:16(A,B)	167
12:16-22	75,75,78,202,275
12:17	87,275
12:17-18	76,166,166
12:17-22	166
12:18	275
12:20	275
12:21	84
12:22	84
13:18(A,B)	166
13:18(ℵ)	166
14:2	92

3 Maccabees
2:2	19

4 Maccabees
4:10-14	174

Wisdom of Solomon
7:7	120
7:17	107
8:15(ℵ)	166
8:15(A,B)	166
11:10-14	165
11:13(4Q200)	165
11:14	84,163,165,197
11:14(A,B)	170
11:14-15	162,164-167,180, 201,237,245,253, 270
11:14-15(ℵ)	165-166,264
11:14-15(A,B)	165-166,264
11:15(4Q200)	165
11:15(A,B)	166
11:16(A,B)	166
11:17(ℵ)	166
11:17(A,B)	166
11:17(Vulg.)	166
12:6(ℵ)	166
12:6(A,B)	166
12:12	167,167,178,180, 270
12:12(A,B)	167
7:22	120
9:1-2	137
9:4	129
9:17	137
10:6	137
13:1	107
13:2	107

Wisdom of Sirach (Jesus Sirach)
1:13	91
2:7	91
6:16	91
7:31	91
10:19	91
15:1	91
17:17	62-63
21:6	91
25:10	91
26:3	91
31:13	91
35:14	91
36:1	91
51:10	177

Epistle of Jeremiah
16	91
23	91
29	91
69	91

D. OLD TESTAMENT PSEUDEPIGRAPHA

Apocalypse of Abraham
                      18,263
9:3-4   89
9:7-10   *118*
10:1-5   89
10:1-11:6   218
10:4-5   219
10:11   220
10:12   220
11   230,258
11:1-4   *80*
11:1-5   76,81,84
11:2   219
11:2-3   219
11:3   *231*
11:3-4   89
11:4   98
11:8   219
12:1-2   *118*
12:2   *118*
13:6   97
14:1   98
14:9   98
16:2   89
17   116
17:1   219,*219*
17:1-2   77,81,*219*
17:1-18:14   225
17:2   *79-80*
17:8-21   222
18:1-3   222
18:2   219,*219*
18:2-3   225
18:3   222
18:9   *219*
19:1   *219*
20:1   *219*

Apocalypse of Elijah
4:10   94

Apocalypse of Ezekiel
1:5   *118*

Apocalypse of Moses
introduction   *111*
22:3   89
23:2   89
29:16   178

Apocalypse of Sedrach
2:2   97
2:4   97

Apocalypse of Zephaniah
2:1-4   78

4:8   97-98
4:9   89
6   *228*
6:1-3   85-86
6:1-10   76
6:1-17   86
6:2   85
6:4   76,85,*98*
6:5   82
6:7   76
6:8   76
6:11   85,229-230
6:11-12   84,257
6:11-15   76,78,78,202,*230*,
                   245,275
6:12   228,*231*
6:13   84-85,*98*
6:13-15   257
6:14   82,*230*,275
6:15   76,87,220,275
6:17   76,220
7:9   76
8:1-4   84,202
10:9   78
12:4   *98*
12:5   *98*

Ascension of Isaiah
3:13-4:22   *237*
3:15   *237*
7-9   125
7:2   76,84,95,*245*
7:2(Lat1)   95
7:2(Slav.)   95
7:14   94
7:15(Eth.)   94
7:15-17   84
7:15-37   202
7:17   94
7:18-23   76,202,276
7:19   94,*245*
7:19-20   84
7:20(Lat1)   94
7:21   82,87,94,96-97,
                   100,*246*,276
7:21(Eth.)   94
7:21(Lat2)   94-95
7:21(Slav.)   95
7:21-22   78,94
7:22   97
7:23   94
7:24   94
7:27(Eth.)   *94*
7:29   94
7:29-30   84
7:36-37   84

7:37	116	11-16	178,180
7:37(Lat.)	94	11:4	178
7:37(Slav.)	94	11:6(Slav.)	83
7:37(Eth.)	94	11:6(Grk.)	83
8:1-5	101	11:9	178
8:1-10	76,276	12:1	178
8:3	84,202	12:6	178
8:4	246,276	12:7	178
8:4-5	94-95,97	14:2	178
8:5	76,92,95,97,257,276		
		1 Enoch (Ethiopic)	
8:5(Eth.)	95	1-36	174
8:8(Eth.)	94	6-16	172
8:11-14	94	6:7(4QEn^a)	56-57
8:14(Eth.)	95	6:7(4QEn^c)	56
8:15	76,276	8:3	56
8:17	116	8:4	174
8:17-22	84,202	9:1	190
9:1	97	9:1(4QEn^a)	174
9:1-5	97	9:1(4QEn^b)	174
9:2	97	9:1-11	174-175
9:4	97	9:2	174
9:17-18	94	9:3	174,180,185
9:26	259	9:3(4QEn^a)	174
9:27-32	101	9:4	175
9:28	99	9:4(4QEn^a)	174
9:30	95,100	9:4(4QEn^b)	174-175
9:31-32	100	9:4-11	174
9:33	99	9:10	174,180
9:35	100	10:1	236
9:35(Eth.)	95	12-13	236
9:36	100,*100*	12:4-6	236
9:36(Eth.)	95	14:8-15:2	279
9:36(Lat2)	96	14:13-14	89
9:37	99	14:14	279
9:38	99	14:24	89,279
9:39	99,*100*	15	236
9:40	100	15:1	279
9:40-42	97,100	15:2	175,180
9:41	99	15:3-10	175
10:14	128	18:13-16	233
11:25(Eth.)	94	21:3-6	233
11:32	94,128	22:6	236
		32:3	73
2 Baruch (Syriac)		37-71	129,136,175
5:7	116	39:5	173
5:7-6:4	118	40:6	175,179
9:2	116	40:9	175,179
9:2-10:1	118	42:2	137
12:5-13:2	118	45:3	129
21:1-3	118	46:1	219
43:3	118	47:1	175
47:2-48:1	118	47:1-2	175,*175*,179,184
		47:2	175-176
3 Baruch		51:3	129
2:7(Slav.)	97	55:4	129
8:5(Grk.)	97	60:11-22	56
8:5(Slav.)	89	60:15-21	63

61:10	244	3 Enoch (Hebrew)	
62:3	129	1:6-10	277
62:5	129	1:7	76,82-84,277
69:2	56	1:7-8	277
69:29	129	1:9-10	277
71:11	89	1:10-12	84
72-82	174	1:11-12	277
84:2	129	1:12	116
86:1-6	233	10:1	80
89:70-76	63	10:1-6	135
89:76	173	15:1	84
91-107	176	16	80,245
97:6	176	16:1	135
99:1-2	176	16:1-5	71,76,202,277
99:3	176,180,184	16:2	82,84-85,277
103:2	180	16:2-5	79
103:5-15	176,180	16:3	278
103:15	176	16:4	277
104	176	16:5	277
104:1	176,180,184	18:18	80
104:2	180	18:24	80,135
		24:7a	80
2 Enoch (Slavic)		26:7a	80
1:4-5	84	28:3a	80
1:4-8	76,81,89,202,245, 275,282	48C:8	135
1:7	83-84,275	4 Ezra	
1:7(A)	276	4:38	97
1:7(J)	276	5:13	116
1:8	76	5:20	116,118
1:8(A)	276	6:35	118
1:8(J)	276	8:34-36	159
20:1	82,84	9:23-25	118
20:1(A)	94,279		
20:1(J)	279	"Greek Legend"	
20:1-3	76	(of Ascension of Isaiah)	
20:1-4	84,202,279	2:6	84,95
21:1-3	84	2:10	95
21:1-6	280	2:10-11	92,95
21:2	82	2:11	95
21:2(A)	280	2:21	96
21:2(J)	280	2:21-22	9
21:2-3	76	2:22	95-96
21:3	89	2:40	94,96
21:3(A)	279-280		
21:3(J)	279-280	History of the Rechabites	
21:3-4	97	4:2-3	89
21:3-4(J)	97	5:3b-6:3	76
22:1-11	280	5:4	89,103
22:4	280	6:3	89
22:4-5	89	6:3-3a	103
22:5	280	6:6a	174
24:1	129	7:11	174
27:3(J)	233	16:8	173
30:3-4(J)	233		
39:8(J)	64	Joseph and Aseneth	
46:1-3(J)	64	4:3	98

4:6	98	12:3b	92
4:9	98	15:31-32	62
5:7	83	32:24	89
5:12	162	35:17	63
7:7	98		
10-14	116	*Ladder of Jacob*	
10:1-13:12	169	3	77,79
14	*230,258*	3:3	80
14:1-12	168-169		
14:1-17:7	168	*Liber Antiquitatum Biblicarum*	
14:1-17:9	169	(see *Pseudo-Philo*)	
14:4	169		
14:7	97-98,169	*Prayer of Joseph*	
14:8-9	218-219		120
14:8-11	90		
14:9	169	*Pseudo-Philo*	
14:9-11	76,*81*,89,280	11:12	172
14:10	169,280	13:5	*171*
14:11	89,169,280	13:6	170-173,201,202,
15:2	89		237
15:2-6	169	15:4-6	172
15:4	89	15:5	172-173,178-179,
15:6	89		237
15:7-8	168,*168*	15:5-6	172-173
15:7-10	169	34:1-3	172
15:11	168-169	34:2	171-172
15:11-12	76,*83*,169-170,202	34:3	172
15:11-12x	81,168	59:4	172
15:12	98,168-169,180,		
	201-202	*Questions of Ezra*	
15:12-12x	*170*	Recension A	
15:12x	168-170,202	1:4	97
15:13	98	1:9	97
15:14	98	1:22	97
16:3	98	1:31	97
16:11	98		
17:4	98	*Sibylline Oracles*	
17:8-9	90	2.215	190
18:1	90	2.243	128
18:1-21:9	169	3.11	19
18:2	90	3.704	19
18:11(Syr.,Gk.)	90		
18:20-21	90	*Testament of Abraham*	
22:5	83		
22:8	83	Recension A	
26:2	89	2:7	97
28:2	83	2:10	98
28:7	89	3:5-6	83,89,283
28:9	83	3:6	283
29:6	83	5:12	98
		6:4	98
Jubilees		9:1	282
1:27	*111*	9:1-2	'83
1:29	*111*	9:1-3	89,282
2:1	*111*	9:2	282
2:2	56	11:8	97
2:17	*141*	13:1	97
10:10-14	*193*	14:1	97

15:1	97	18:1-42	179
Recension B	283	18:4-8	*179*
4:1	98	18:5-8	*190*
4:4-6	283	20:21	*179*
6:5	98	22:16	*179*
7:7	97	22:20	*139,179*
7:11	97	25:9	*179*
7:18	97		
8:9	97	*Testaments of the Twelve Patriarchs*	
9:10	97		
10:1	97	Levi	
10:4	97	3:5	176,179
10:6	97	3:5-7	176
11:1	97	3:7	176,180
12:3	97	3:8	*94*
		5:5	176,180,202
Testament of Jacob		5:5-6	176,201,*237*
2:4-27	89	5:6	177,202
3:5	89	5:7	177,*177*
Testament of Job		Dan	
33:3	*129*	6:2	177-178
48-50	116	6:5-7	178
		6:6	178
Testament of Isaac		6:7	*177*
2:2	89	6:9	*177*
Testament of Solomon		Benjamin	
1:6	*179*	10:6	*129*
1:6-7	*179*		
2:5	*179,179*	*Treatise of Shem*	
2:7	*179*		192
2:9	*179*		
5:5	*179*	*Vitae Adae et Evae*	
6:8	*139,179*	2:1	98
7:1	*179*	3:1	98
8:1	*179*	9:3	178
12:1	*179*	12:1-16:1	*179*
14:7	*179*	26:1	89
15:1	*179*	27:1	89
15:13	*179*	28:1	89
16:1	*179*		

E. PHILO

De Abrahamo		*De confusione linguarum*	
98	*19*	28	*137*
173	*137*	62-63	*137*
		146	*120,137,137*
De agricultura			
51	*120,137*	*De Decalogo*	
		31	*19*
De cherubim		51	*19*
3	*137*	61	*19,65*
35	*137*	64	*65*

65	65	*Quis rerum divinarum Heres sit*	
66	66	205	137
75-76	66		
178	65	*Quod deus immutabilis sit*	
		182	137

De ebrietate
148-152   116

De sacrificiis Abelis et Caini
59-63   118

De fuga et inventione
5   137

De Somniis
1	118
1.33-37	116
1.36	118
1.115	137
1.215	120
1.232	85
1.238	137
2.90	83
2.107	90

De Iosepho
164	83
266	90

Legatio ad Gaium
114-116	87
115	87
116	87

De specialibus legibus
1.12,13-31	19
2.224	19

Legum Allegoriae
3.172-178	68
3.177	137

De virtutibus
74   136

De migratione Abrahami
22.160   90

De vita contemplativa
2-4   107-108

De mutatione nominum
87   137

De vita Mosis
2	118
2.67-70	116,118

De posteritate Caini
91   137

Quastiones et solutiones in Exodum
2.39   116

F. JOSEPHUS

Antiquitates Judaicae
2.142	112
3.154	228
3.171	228
8.45-49	179,191
11.331-333	83
15.136	111
18.63-64	139

Bellum Judaicorum
2.136	193
2.142	193

Testimonium Flavianum
124,139

G. QUMRAN

1Q36 (Liturgical Fragment)
155

4Q511 (Wisdom Canticles)
2 1.1	157
2 1.8	155
8 1.4	157
8 1.9	155

4Q181 (The Wicked and the Holy)
1 1.3-4	155
1 1.4	155

Index of Passages

4Q560 (Amulet Formula)

4Q'Amram (4Q548)
2 1.3   198

4QBirth of Noah (4Q534)
    198

4QBrontologion (4Q318)
    198

4QCryptic (4Q186)
    192

4QDeut (4Q44)
    121

4QFlorilegium (4Q174)
    127
1.4   155

4QTestimonium (4Q175)
    127

11QMelchizedek (11Q13)
2.9-16   150
2.10   150

Berakhoth (1QSb=1Q28b)
    150, 161
1.3   162
3.1   162
3.2-3   162
3.6   154
3.25   162
4.25-26   116
4.26   154
4.27   153
4.28   152-154
5   153

Berakhoth (4Q286)
    157

Berakhoth (11Q14)
    161, 201-202
1.1   161
1.1-5   162
1.2   161-162
1.2-3   162
1.3   161-162
1.4   162
1.4-5   161, 163, 202
1.6   162
1.6-14   155, 162-163
1.7-13   163
1.13-14   162, 237

Book of Giants
4QEnG^a (4Q203)   236
7 2.1   *236*
8   235
8 1.3   235-236
8 1.4   236, *236*
8 1.4-5   236
8 1.5-15   236
8 1.6   236
8 1.7-11   236
8 1.12-13   236
8 1.13   *236*
8 1.13-15   236
8 1.15   *236*
4QEnG^b (4Q530)
2.14   *236*
2.20-23   *236*
2.21-23–
3.4-11   *236*
3.4-11   *236*

Book of Watchers (1 Enoch 1-36)
4QEn^a (4Q209)
to 6:7   56-57
to 9:1   *174*
to 9:3   *174*
to 9:4   *174*
4QEn^b (4Q208)
to 9:1   174
to 9:4   174-175
4QEn^c (4Q210)
to 6:7   56

Community Rule (1QS=1Q28)
    150
3.15   157, 164
3.21   124
11.7-8   124
11.8   154

Copper Scroll (3Q15)
    150

Damascus Document
CD   *150*
2.9-10   157, 164
15.15-17   155
4QD^b=4Q267
17 1.8-9   155

Genesis Apocryphon (1QapGen=1Q20)
    150

Isaiah Scroll (1QS^a)
    153, *153*

Index of Passages

New Jerusalem
                                  151
2QJN=2Q24
    1 1.4   *151*
    8 1.7   *151*
4Q554 (PAM 43.564)
    2.6   *151*
4Q555 (PAM 43.610)
    3.4   *151*
5QJN=5Q15
    1 1.18   *151*
    1 2.2   *151*
    1 2.6   *151*
11QJN=11Q18
    4 (PAM 43.996, rt.)
                                    151
    5 (PAM 43.998, rt.)
                                    151
    5-6 (PAM 43.999, lt.)
                                    151

Rule of the Congregation (1QSa=1Q28a)
                                      150
    2.8-9   *155*

Songs of the Sabbath Sacrifice
4QShirShabb=4Q400-407
                             30,119,136,156
4Q400   *157*
    1 i 14   *155,159*
    1 i 16   *159,180*
    2   *157*
    2.1   *158-159,202*
    2.1-2   *119,157*
    2.1-9   *157-158*
    2.2   *158-159*
    2.2-3   *248*
    2.3   *159*
    2.3-5   *158-159*
    2.4   *159,201*
    2.5-7   *158*
    2.6-7   *159,248*
    2.8   *159*
    2.8-9   *158,160,248*
4Q401   *157*
    14 i 6   *158*
    14 i 7-8   *157*
4Q403   *157*
    1   *157*
    1 i 17   *156*
    1 i 18-19   *156*
    1 i 21   *156*
    1 i 23-24   *156*
    1 i 1-29   *156*
    1 i 30   *156*
    1 i 31   *156,161*
    1 i 31-33   *160-161,202*
    1 i 32   *156,160-161*
    1 i 32-33   *119,161*
    1 i 33   *156*
    1 i 33-35   *161*
    1 i 36   *156*
    1 i 38   *156*
    1 i 39   *156*
    1 ii 22   *156*
    1 ii 27   *156*
    1 ii 27-29   *156*
4Q405   *157*
    3 ii 6   *156*
    8-9 5   *156*
    13 2-3,4-5   *156*
    13 7   *156*
Masada Fragment   *30,156*
    i 2-3   *164*
    i 4-6   *164*
11QShirShabb (11Q17)
                                    30,156
    5 3   *159*

Temple Scroll (11QTemple=11Q19)
                                  150

Testament of Levi
    1Q21ar   *176*
    4Q213ar   *176*
    4Q214ar   *176*
    4Q215heb   *176*

Thanksgiving Hymns (1QH)
    1.19-20   *157,164*
    3.20-22   *116*
    3.21-22   *124*
    3.21-23   *154,160*
    3.22   *159*
    3.22-23   *159*
    3.24   *159*
    6.13   *154*
    10.8   *124,159*
    11.11-12   *154*
    11.13   *154*
    11.14   *154*
    13.11-12   *157*
Fragments
    2.10   *154*
    2.14   *154*
    5.3   *154*
    7.11   *154*
    10.6-7   *154*

Tobit
    4Q196=papTob ar[a]   *75,84*
    4Q200=Tob heb   *75,84,165*
    6   *165*

War Scroll		13.9-10	124
1QM	150,155	13.10	154
1.14-15	154	15.8	88
7.6	152,155	17.5-6	150
10.3	88	17.6	154
10.8	152,152	17.6-8	124
10.9	152,152	17.7	150
10.10	151	4Q491(4QM^a)	151
10.10-11	112,151-152	1-3 1.10	155
12.1-2	155	11.13	151
12.4-5	154	11.14	151
12.7	154	11.17	151
12.8-9	154	11.18	151
12.13	152	24 1.4	155

H. RABBINIC AND HEKHALOT LITERATURE

Babylonian Talmud

Abodah Zarah			
3b	71		
42b	52,54		
43a	52,54		

Hagigah	
14b	73,86
15a	71,79,135,277
15a-b	73,86

Hullin	
40a	52,59-60,202

Pesah	
118a	68

Rosh Hashanah	
24b	52

Sanhedrin	
38b	52,63,69-71,74-75,219

Sota	
33a	68

Yoma	
52a	52,66

Bereshith (Gen) Rabbah	
65:21	135
78:1	68

Cairo Genizah Hekhalot Fragment	
A/2,13	278
A/2,13-16	76,79,278
A/2,14	80,87,278
A/2,14-16	85,278

Debarim (Deut) Rabbah	
2:34	54,62,62

Harba de-Moshe	
	198

Hekhalot Zutrati	
	86

Jerusalem Talmud

Berakoth	
1:1	135
9:1	52
9:13a	147,177,202-203
9:13a-b	63-66,74

Hagigah	
2:1	73
2:77b	73

Lamentations Rabbah	
3:8	62

Mekhilta de-Rabbi Ishmael

BaHodesh	
6	52
6,242-243	57-58
10	52,59
10,276-277	58

Beshallah	
1	90

Midrash Kohelet Zuta	
107	54

Mekhilta (Sg of Sgs) Shirah	
3	73

Midrash Tannaim
190-191   52,62,62,66

Midrash Tehillim
4:3   52

Mishnah

Hullin
2:8   52,54,59-60

Rosh ha-Shanah
1:2   173

Sefer ha-Malbush
198

Sefer ha-Razim
198,198

Shemoth (Exod) *Rabbah*
19:7   120
32:1   69
32:2   69

32:3   69
32:4   52,63,70,70,74,146
32:7   69
34:4   135

Sifre (Deut) *Debarim*
343   73

Tanhuma (ed. Buber)

Bashallah
13   135

Testament of Nephtali
62

Tosephta

Hagigah
2:3-4   73

Hullin
2:18   52,54,59-60,202

I. TARGUMIC LITERATURE

Neofiti

Genesis
44:14   280
48:15-16   67
50:18   280
50:19   280

Exodus
21:23   68

Onkelos

Genesis
48:15-16   67
50:18   280
50:19   280
50:21   280

Second Targum to Esther
3:3   87

Targum Pseudo-Jonathan

Genesis
48:15-16   67
50:18   280
50:19   280
50:21   280

Exodus
20:23   52,54,58

Joshua
5:14   281

J. EPIGRAPHICAL COLLECTIONS

(Other epigraphical materials are listed under place names provided in the subject index.)

Corpus Inscriptionum Iudaicorum
717   188
719   188
781   187

950   187
1175   187
912   187
928   187

Répertoire d'épigraphie sémitique, v.3
1792.7-8   236

K. Magical Texts

Incantation Bowls
(numeration follows
C. Isbell's *Corpus*)
   49.11   72
   56.12-13   72

Papyri Graecae Magicae
(Preisendanz edition)
   I,40   *195*
   I,42-195   194,*197*
   I,77   194
   I,86   194
   I,88-90   194
   I,163-172   194
   I,180   194
   I,262-347   194
   I,297-327   194
   I,300   194
   I,300-301   194
   I,301   *195*
   I,301-302   194
   I,303   194
   I,304   194
   I,305   194
   I,309   194
   I,310   194
   I,311   194
   III,1-164   194
   III,71-98   194
   III,129-61   195
   III,187-262 195,199
   III,197   195
   III,206   195
   III,211-212 195
   III,213   195
   III,214-215 195
   IV,1167-1226 193
   IV,1182   193
   IV,1191-1193 193
   IV,1203-1204 193
   IV,1221-1222 193
   IV,1227-1264 193
   IV,1232-1236 193
   IV,1928-2005 195,197,200,*264*
   IV,1930-1937 195
   IV,3007-3086 193
   IV,3019-3020 193
   IV,3050-3052 193
   IV,3052-3053 193
   IV,3069   193
   VII,250   195
   VII,255-259 195,197,*264*
   VII,927-930 *194*
   VII,973-980 195,197
   VII,1009-1016 195,197
   VII,1017-1026 195,197,199-200, *264*
   XIII,254-261 195,199
   XXIIa,18-27 *194*
   XXIIb   193
   XXIIb,1-2   193
   XXIIb,3   193
   XXIIb,18   193
   XXIIb,24   193
   XXXV,1-42   195,197
   XXXVI,36-67 196-197
   XXXVI,295-311 196-197
   XLIII,1-27   196
   XLIV   196
   XLVIII   196
   LXXIX,1-7   196
   LXXX,1-5   196

Coptic Magical Texts
(Kropp edition)
   XLVII   197
   XLVII.I,6   196
   XLVII.I,19-23   196
   XLVII.II,4-III,6 196
   XLVII.IV,9   196
   XLVII.IV,10   196
   XLVII.V,12   196

L. Christian and Gnostic Writings

Apocalypse of Paul
   77-79,82,84,278

Apocryphal Gospel of Matthew
   79,84,92,202,271
   3:2   93

   3:3   75,78,82,84,92-93,276

Aristides
   Apology   140-144,148,192, 202

14(Grk.)	140-141			
14(Syr.)	140-141			

Apostolic Constitutions
8.12.6   94

Barnabas, Epistle of
12:10   128

1 Clement
36   127
36:2-5   128-129
56:1   124

Clementine Recognitions
2.52   63
8.50   63

Clement of Alexandria

Stromata
5.11.77   78,84,97
6.5.41   112
6.5.41.2-3   140,143

Epiphanius

Panarion
30.3.1-6   139

Eusebius

Praeparatio evangelica
9.27.5   19

Historia ecclesiastica
3.17-20   32
4.26.9   32

Gospel of Peter
10:39-40   79

Gospel of Thomas
     139,204
13   139

Hippolytus

Refutatio
9.13.1-3   139

Jerome

Epistula ad Algasiam
10   112

John of Damascus

Life of Barlaam and Josephat
     140

Justin Martyr

Apology
1.6   124
6   138
63   138

Dialogue with Trypho
34   138
34.2   125
56   138
58   138
60   138
61   138
126   138
128   138

Kerygma Petrou
     10,53,112,140-144,148,192

Odes of Solomon
36:4   138,151

Origen

Commentary on John
12.189   120
13.17   141,143
13.17.104   112

Contra Celsum
     189,192
1.26   141,144
5.6   145-146
5.6-9   141
5.8   112,145
5.9   145
6.27-30   146

Revelation of Elchasai
     139,204

Shepherd of Hermas
     125,148,237
Visions
3.4.1-2   63
3.10.6   116,118
5.2   138

Mandates
5.1.7	*138*

Similitudes
5.1.1-5	*118*
5.3.5-8	*118*
5.3.7	*116*
5.4.4	*138*
5.5	*237*
5.6	*237*
7.1-5	*138*
7.5	*138*
8.1.2	*138*
8.1.2-18	*138*
8.1.5	*138*
8.2.1	*138*
8.3.3	*138*
9.1.3	*138*
9.12.7-8	*227*
9.12.8	*138*
10.1.1	*138*
10.3.1	*138*

Tertullian

De ieiunio
	118
12	*116,118*

Theodore of Mopsuestia
	112

Theodoret
	112

M. GREEK AND ROMAN LITERATURE

Aeschylus

Agamemnon
43-44	*64*

Persae
532-536	*64*
762-764	*64*

Apuleius

Liber de Mundo
346-351	*64*

Aristotle

Nichomachean Ethics
8.10.3	*65*
8.10.4-11.3	*65*

Politica
3.9.3	*65*

Artapanus
	19

Corpus Hermeticum
	118
1.26	*116*
13.6-7	*116*

Dio Cassius

Historia Roma
67-68	*32*

Herodotus

Historia
1.98-99	*64*

Pliny the Younger

Panegyricus
2.3	*32*

Pseudo-Aristotle
	65
De Mundo	
398a-b	*64*

Suetonius

Vitae Ceasarorum
8	*32*

Tacitus

Agricola
39-45	*32*

Vergil

Aeneid
9.638-640	*242*

INDEX OF SUBJECTS

Abaye 60-61
Ablanathanalba 196
Abraam 197
Abraham *62,67,80,118*,123,*137*,219-220
 - as angel 196
Abrahamic promise *105*,109,111
Abrasax 194-196,*199*
Abriel 195
Absalom *88*
Accusing angel 76,*85*,220
Achaia, inscription *188*
Achene 195
Acmonia, inscription *187*
Adam *98*,170,179
Adam, reciter of magical formula 195
Adonai (or Adonaie) 194-196
Adonaios 194
Aiai 195
Akiba, R. *71*,73
Akrammachamari 196
Alexander the Great *83*
Amastris, inscription *186*
Amulet(s) *181*,190,*190*,194,196,*198*
Amoraic period 53,62,*68*,70,75,*192*,198
Ancient of Days 71,211,213,215-218
Angelology, angel(s), ἄγγελοι 3, 21, 30,37,41-43,47,51,53,*67*,103, 119, 125,148-149,173,182,204,207, 209, 220,237-238,241,256,260,265, 270-272
 - aids in mystical ascents 9, 93-94, 96-97,*119*,*248*
 - angel "cult," angelolatry 10, *50*, 53,102-103,111,112-115, *124*, 148, 184,201,269
 - ἄν/γγελος inscriptions (Asia Minor) 181-188
 - *angelus interpres* 92,*151*,221,227, 231,*246*,248,257-258,264
 - appearance (see angelophany) 81-87,89-90,95,203,229,239,*245*, *249*, 258,270,276
 - archangel 79-80,96,*138*, *143*, 179-180,193,195-196,199
 - as "fire" 56,*56*,121,135
 - as human messengers *139*,234-235
 - as mediaries in Revelation 246-248,252-253,256-260
 - as "ministers" / "servants" 121, 135-136
 - as "powers" *181*,*188*

 - as "spirits" 121-123,134
 - association with natural phenomena 56-57
 - bad 37,172
 - "chief angels" (Qumran) 158-159
 - communion with (Qumran) 154-155, 201
 - divine emissaries 63,89,103,180
 - *elim* 157-158
 - *elohim* 158
 - fallen *56*,63,172,*172*,176,236
 - guardian/patron 234,237-238
 - guardians of individuals 188
 - guardians of/rulers over nations 19,62,*63*,66,74
 - in human appearance 89,169, *211*, 219,*219*,*231*
 - intercession of *151*,172-173,175-177,179,201
 - invocations of 9,49,67, 74, 114-115,*119*,144,*144*,147,149,180-181, 184,190-200,202,*202*,*237*,269
 - mediation in Revelation 252,256
 - mediators of prayer 64, 66-68, 173-180
 - name(s) of *112*,170,176, 179-180, 269
 - "of holiness" 152,*152*
 - Philo *137*,*137*
 - "praiseworthiness" of 160-161
 - propitiation of *159*,176
 - protection 163,167,177,180, 188, *188*,190,*190*,200-201,237,*237*,*245*, *249*,*252*
 - Qumran 150,*150*
 - rule in world to come 123
 - sacrificing to *52*,59-60, 62, 74, 146-147,270
 - self-demotion 80,92-99,250, *250*, 254-255,260,271
 - servants of Satan 37
 - superior knowledge 158-159
 - teachers of magic to humans 172
 - veneration of *8*,*11*,13,47,49, 51-204,249-250,264,269,*276*
 - visionary's interaction with in the Apocalypse of John 247
Angelophany 75-77,79,81-87,89,91,92, 202,211,213,218,*220*,229,241-242, 246,256,258-259,271
Ankara 186

"Another angel" 241,243
Aod 171,*171*
Aoe 196
Aphrodite 199
Apocalypse
  - genre *26*,40
  - social function of 27,39
Apocalypse of John
  - date 31,*31*,50,103,204
  - eschatology 26-31
  - Jewishness 23-26
  - socio-historical situation 31-35, 38
  - symbolic world 35-41
Apocalypse
  - *of Elijah 78*
  - *of Ezekiel 118*
  - *of Paul* 77-79,82,*84*,278
  - *of Zephaniah* 78-79,*103*, 204, *230*, 257-258,271
Apocryphal Gospel of Matthew 79, *84*, 92,204,271
Apocalypticism 39-40
Apollo 194,*242*
  - Clarian *181*
  - temple of (Claros) 113
Araaph 190
Aramaic, language unknown to angels 68
Arbathiao 196
Argos, inscription *188*
Asbames *186*
Ascent
  - mystical *9*,54,72-73, *76*, 96, 116, 119,*119*,146-147,164,202-203, *248*, 259
  - of soul after death 106
Ascetic requirements 106,113,118,*249*
Asceticism 116,118
  - gnostic form of *115*
Aseneth 76,168-170,180,201,*219*
Asia Minor 31-35,38,113-115,*143*, 181-183,188-189,*191*,237-238
Asmodeus *167*
Asouel 196
Athanael 196
Attributes
  - angelic, see Christology, angelomorphic
  - divine 49,213
Aurelios Joses *188*

Balaam
  - in Numbers (ch. 22) *137*
  - in Revelation *249*
Babylon 70-72
  - in Revelation 224,227,246-248

Bacchism 114,*114*
  - Phrygian *114*
Barbaras *194*
Baruch 178
Baruch, Syriac Apocalypse of 118,*210*
Baruch, Third 178,*210*
Bathsheba *83*
Beast(s) in Revelation 31,37,40,222-223,*226*,247
Beelzeboul *139*
Belial *160*
Ben Azzai 73
Ben Zoma 73
Berakhoth (1QSb) *150*
Biliam 196
Bimadam 195
Binitarian, binitarianism *11*,13,20-21
Bithynia *181*,*191*
Blessing 67,*137*,153,*156*,161-163,165-167,169-170,177,180,201-202,264
  - Aaronic 162
Boaz *83*
Book of Giants 235-237
"Bride" of the Lamb 224,226,246,251
Bronze *89*,213,239
Bythath 195

Cairo Genizah 7,*198*
  - Fragment *245*
Calendar, Jewish 142
  - solar 156
  - 15-year indiction (Greece) *198*
Caria *181*
Celsus *112*,144-146,149,189
Chadrallou 195
Chadraoun 195
Cherubim 57-59,195
Chisianus, Codex 214-216,*218*
Christ
  - as mediator 252,*252*
  - death of *123*,*130*,132,134,136,220
  - divine attributes of 211, 213-218,221,233
  - exaltation of 4-5,11,18,120-121, *123*,127-128,*130*,133-134,139,148, 272
  - resurrection *120*,220
  - subjection of enemies 129-135
  - superiority over angels 120-124, 127-128,131,*131*,135-136,*230*,232-233,239-240,258,265,271
  - superiority over the world to come 132
  - throne of 121,135
  - worship of 3,100, 123, 135, 207, 257,259,261,264-265,269,272

Christology 3-5,7-12,17,19-21, 22-43, 50,79,102,119, 148-149, 204, 207-209,241,257,260,263,265,271-272
- angel 124-125, 127, 133, 137-139, 177,204,208-209,263
- angelomorphic 35,100,100,151,204, 208,208-209,211,227,232-233, 240, 244-245,260-261,263,265,271-272
- "god of the Hebrews" 193
- High Priest 130,136
- in Revelation 22-41
- Lamb 3,18,24,31,35-36,41,101,207-208,222-227,240,246,251-252, 254, 257,261-263,265,272
- priestly 228
- Son (of God) 120-121,123,128,134-140,193,227,237
- "one like a son of man" 129, 209, 211,213,215-221,226-227,230, 233, 240-245,257-258,261,263,271
Chrysostom 112
Church, see ecclesiology
Circumcision 140,142
Claros, inscriptions 113
Claudiopolis, inscription 181,191
Cloud 229-231,240,242-243
Coercive invocation 189,200-201,269
Cologne Papyrus 967 214-217
Colossae 111,113-117,119,124,148,181, 187
Colossian error 111-119,147
Commandment
- First 66,147
- Second 57-59,61,69,73-74,145,147
Community Rule (1QS) 150
Confusion 145
- between an angel and God 68-70, 76,85-86,203,230
Constantine 198
Copper Scroll (3Q15) 150
Cornelius 98
Crisis 33,37-40,260
Crown(s) 41,69,97,240,243
Cult(ic) 13-14,47,49
- imperial 31-32,38
- mystery 113
Curse(s) 181,185-186,198
Cyzicus, amulet 181,190-191,264

Damascus Document 150
Danger 86
Daniel 27,220
David 71,83,88,170,172,239
Day of Atonement 140
Death 136,220,239
Decalogue 54
Deioces 64

Delos, see also Rheneia
- inscription 185-186
Demon(s),demonic, demonology 6, 43, 167,179,193,200
Didyma, inscription 114,181
Diocletian 198
Distress, time of 52,63,66,177,202
Ditheistic, ditheism 11,272
Domitian 31,33
Doxology 165-166,209,252
Dualistic,dualism 5-6,11,19, 19, 57, 63,150,200

Ebionite(s) 125
Ecclesiology 25
- angelic 237
Edanoth 195
Egypt(ian) 4,7,19,198
Eleazar, R. b. Azariah 71
Elders, twenty-four 41,223-224, 243, 246
Elements of the universe 106
- Pythagorean view of 106-107
Elephantine papyri 7
Eliakim 239
Elijah 88
Elisha 83,88
Elisha b. Abuyah (A@er) 73,79,79,84
Eloai 191,196
Eloaios 194
Eloi 196
Emanouel 196
Enoch 27,73,129,175,180,210,236,236
Enoch literature
- Ethiopic or 2 Enoch 210
- Hebrew or 3 Enoch 55,271
- Slavic or 2 Enoch 178, 204, 210, 271
Ephesus 33
Ephraim 67
Eremiel 76,76,85,220,229-230,257
Esau 83
Eschatology, eschatological 23, 26-31,122-123
- judgment 176-177,180,259
Essenes 111-112,124,193
Eumeneia, inscription 181, 187-189, 201-202,237
Ezekiel 90
Ezra 27

Faith 23,104,109
Fasting 118,171
Fear
- as reaction to an angelophany 82-84,147
- in prohibitive statements 80,87-

92,97,97,*260*
- in statements offering assurance 88-90,*260*,275
"Fellow-servant" 92-93,96-97,*246*,250, 253,*255*,259-260
Feast of Trumpets 170-171,201
Fire 79,107,169,*89*,213,*219*, *226*, *231*, 239
"Firstborn" *90*,*120*
- assembly of 126
Five
- planets *233*
Forgiveness 68-69,146,*174*,180
Four
- elements 106
- living creatures *213*,222-223,225
- rabbis in the *pardes* tradition 72

Gabriel 64,66-67,*83*,*129*,174-175, *179*, *182*,190-191,194-196,220,*220*, 229, *229*
Gaius *187*
Galatia(n) 104-105,109,*124*,*181*,185
Gamaliel, R. *59*
Gedaliah *88*
Genesis Apocryphon (Qumran) *150*
Gentiles *59*,98,104-107,109,*177*,*179*
Giants 236
Gnostic, Gnosticism 4, *12*, *53*, 71-72, *111*,115-116,*124*,*141*,200
God 41
- as distant 6,64-67,97,175
- as judge, divine judgment 24, *64*, 172-173,175-176,180,223-224, *226*, 236,240,*243*,*243*,256
- as King *62*,64-65,73,75,*86*,158,*175*
- as "Lord God of the Hebrews" 193
- as "Lord of spirits" 175,*175*,184, *184*
- as near 63-64,66-67,93,99,*129*
- as one 5,15,17-19,42,47,65,69,76, 79,*83*,*94*,103,265,273
- as "the Lord Almighty" (Pantocrator) 76,*85*,*98*
- as the one who forgives sin 69
- "has assumed the face of Gabriel" 196
- divine punishment 69
- metaphorical language for 48
- "my God" *251*
- of Abraham 193,196
- of Isaac 193,196
- of Jacob 193,196
- redemptive activity of 88
- throne of *12*,*18*,*30*,*37*, *57*, 71-72, 80-81,*84*,102,*129*,147,*173*,202-203, 211,217,226,*231*,261-262

- transcendence, transcendent *12*, 79,93,97,99,*99*,*112*,*138*,*161*, 175, 269,273
Gold(en)
- belt(s), girdle(s) *89*, 213, 226, 228,246
- calf *57*
- crown 41,240,*243*
- lampstands 232-233,239
- staff *89*
Gospel of Thomas 139,204
Greek Legend (*Ascension of Isaiah*) 9,95-96

Hades 220,239
Hadrumetum, tablet *193*
Hagar *137*
Haman *87*
Hamor *176*
Harba de-Moshe 198
Heaven
- fifth *96*
- first 95
- second 94,97
- seventh *84*,94-97,259
- sixth 94,96-97
Hebrew, language of prayer 68
Hekate *114*,181-182
Hekhalot literature 9-10, 54-55, *80*, 84-85,96,*162*
Helios 193,195,197,199-200
Henotheism 16-18
Heraclea 184
Heracleon *141*
Hermes 199
Heth *83*
Hezekiah *88*,239
High Priest *66*,*83*,*88*,153,161
History of religions school 4-5,*11*
Holy of Holies 154
Holy Spirit *95*,98,100,147,193,259
Horseman 190-191
"Humility" 116-119,*249*
Hypostatic beings 6,*6*,10-11,*138*,*211*, *243*

Iao *191*,194,194-196
Iaoel *80*,*89*,219-220,*222*,225,*225*,*231*
Idith, R. 69-72
Idolatry 57-59,63,66,74,74,84-87,91- 92,99,102,146-147,203
Image-making 52,57-58,*61*,74,146-147, 270
Incantion bowls *198*
Inscriptions
- dedicatory *181*,185-186,201

- tomb 181-182,187-188
Iphiaph 195
Iran *198*
Iron *89*
Isaac *67*
Isaiah 94-96
  - *Ascension of Isaiah* 77,93-94, 96, *96*,*103*,*119*,147-148,204, 259, 270-271
  - Scroll(1QIs^a) 153,*153*
Ishmael, R. 58-59,*84*
Islam *15*,17
Israel, as angel *67*,*120*,196

Jacob 67-68,*83*,*90*,*137*
  - as angel *120*
  - *Ladder of Jacob* 81
Jahaziel *88*
Jerome *112*,*166*
Jerusalem 193
  - heavenly 126,*151*
  - new, see New Jerusalem
Jesus, historical 7-9
"Jezebel," the prophetess *249*
Joachim 93
John, of Revelation 209-210,253-256
Jonathan *83*
Jose, R. *66*
Joseph *83*,*88*,*90*,98,169
Joseph and Aseneth 11,204,263
Joshua *88*
Judan, R. 63-67
Justin Martyr 148,*218*

Kalecik, inscription *181*,185-186,189, 197,201-202,264
Kerygma Petrou 10,*53*,112,140-144,148, 192
Key(s) 220,239
Kidaris *89*,*231*
Kidrama, inscription *181*
Kingship
  - Aristotelian 65,*65*
  - divine 64-65
  - Persian ideal 64-65,67
Köleköy (Lydia), inscription *181*
Koula, amulet 190-191

Lailam 195
Lamp(s)
  - burning *89*
Laodicea *34*
  - Council of *112*
Lapapa 196
Letter(s) 35,209,236,*236*
  - epistolary framework of Revelation 209-210

- to the seven churches 209-211, 232-240,*257*,*260*,271
Levi 176-177
Lightning 56,*89*,229
Linen *89*,226-227,246
Liturgy *14*,*248*
  - angelic 126,156
  - sabbath 156
Living creatures 57,*213*,222-225
"Logos"
  - in Philo *125*,137,137-138
"Lord"
  - prohibited as form of address 95, 97-98,*246*
Lycidas 187-188
Lycia *181*
Lydia(n) *143*,*181*

Magic, magical *10*,*74*, 114, *141*, *144*, 149,*172*,*179*,*179*,188-193,264,269
  - definition of 188-190
  - Jewish, in Judaism 192,196-200
  - materials from Asia Minor 188-191
Magical apparatus (Pergamum) *182*
Magical papyri *10*,*180*, 182, 193-198, 201
Magical texts from Qumran *192*
Magician(s) 171-172,196,*198*
Mahawai *236*
Malediction, see curse
Manasseh *67*
Marmar 195,196 (Marmarel), 196 (Marmarioth)
Marthina 184
Matthew (apostle) *139*
Meats, cleanness of 140,142
Meis (astral deity) *143*
Melchiel 196
Melchizedek *150*
"Men" *181*
Mephibosheth *88*
Merkabah (Mysticism) 9-10,*12*, 29-30, 54-55,*59*,71-72,*75*,*85*,146
Mesopotamia *61*,*198*
Metatron 9,69-72,79-80,84-85,*135*,219
Michael 57,*59*-62,64,66-67,74,*83*, *98*, *98*,*112*,*124*,*138*,150-151,*154*, 174, 178-179,*182*,190-191,194-197,220, *220*,*282*
Middle Platonism *134*,*138*
Min (heretic) 69-70,72
Mishnah 60-62
Monarchism *11*,16,19
Monolatry 15-18
Monotheistic, monotheism 3-5, 7, *10*, *10*,*12*,*14*,*25*,*42*-*43*,*47*-*48*, *63*, 74-

75,77,79-80,83,85,87,89,91-92,97,
99-100,102,*138*, 144-145, 147-149,
197,202,*202*,204,207,209,217, *245*,
253,255,261-265,269,271-272
- defined 15-21
Moon 54,57-60,62,142-143,145,195,199,
233,262
- new 140
Mouriatha 195
Mordecai 87
Moses 69-70,*83*,*88*,*118*, 135, 144, 172,
226,229
"Most High"
- God (of Israel) 102,169,174, 176-
177,180,184-186,264
- θεός Ὕψιστος 182,*182*,184
- Zeus 181-182
Mystery religions 113-114
Myth 36

Nabatean 4,*236*
Nag Hammadi 7
Nahman, R. 69-70
Nathan, R. *59*
Neouphneioth 196
Nero *31*
New chant 222-223
New Jerusalem (Qumran) 150-151
New Jerusalem 36,*227*,246-248,*252*,255-
256

Oenoanda (Lycia), inscription *181*
Ophanim 57-59
Ophites *146*
Origen 141,143-146,149
Osirchentechtha 195
Osiris 195,197
Oxyrhynchus 7

Pakerbeth 194
Palace *64*
- seventh *135*
Palestine, Palestinian 7-8,18,64, 67-
68,*70*
Palmyra *61*
Pantokrator 196
Pap 196
Pardes tradition 72-73,*86*
Parthia(n) 4
Passover 140
Passover Haggadah 52
Paul (in *Apocalypse of Paul*) *83*,*88*
Pephtha 196
Pergamum *181*,190
- magical apparatus *182*
Persecution 31-33,38
- Domitianic 31-32

- Neronian *31*,33
Persian influence 7
Pesharim (Qumran) *150*
Peter 98,*139*
Philadelphia *83*,239
Phor 195
Phorba 195
Phoza 196
Phnebennouni 196
Phrygia *112*,*115*
- inscription *181*,187-188
Pisidia *112*,*191*
Pitiel 195
Planets 54,57-60,62,145,*233*
Polytheistic, polytheism 7,15-17
Prayer *118*
- apotropaic 180,197
- house of (προσευχή) 185-187
- petitionary 66,74,173-179,189
Prayer of Joseph 120
Prophecy, spirit of *250*,*254*
Prophet(s)
- Alexander *181*
- in Hebrew scriptures 28,*88*,89
- in Revelation 93, 210, 235, 247,
250,*250*,254-256
Prophetic call 210
Prostration 80,*83*,87,*87*,103,147,177,
246,248,251-252,259-260,271,275
Protection from enemy 88
Pseudo-Philo 204
Pythagorean 106-107,114,*114*

Qumran
- community *150*, 154-159, 161-164,
201-202,*237*
- writings from 150-164

Ragoure 196
Raguel *182*
Rainbow *89*,231,*231*
Raphael 75,*84*,166,*166*, 174, 178-179,
182,190,195-196,201,*236*,*245*,249,
252-253
Rechabites 174
Red Sea *57*,*226*
"Referential history" 33-34
Refusal tradition 75-103, 147-148,
164,166,*166*,169-170,203,207,*227*,
245-261,270-271,275-278
- double use in one writing 249-
256
"Repentance" 168-169
Resurrection accounts
- Gospel of Matthew 77,*101*
- *Gospel of Peter* 79
Revelation of Elchasai 204

Rheneia,
- inscriptions 10,144,181, 183-185, 189,197,200-202,264
Rhetoric, rhetorical 38-39,48,69, 78, 86,90,102,114,125, 135, 160, 164, 178,256,270,272
Rhetorical questions (in Hebrews 1) 120,122,128,135-136
Robe(s) 97,213,226,246
Rosh ha-Shanah 170,172-173
Roubes 187-188
Rule of the Congregation (1QSa) 150

Sabbath 140,156
Sabath 196
Sabaoth 193-194,195 (Abaoth),196
Sacrifice 52,59-61
- to the dead 60-62
Saesechel 195
Salvation 122-123,126
Samuel 83
Sapphire 89,227
Sarachael 196
Sarah (in Tobit) 167,167
Sariel 79-80
Satan 37,41
Saul 83
Seer 28,211
- in the refusal tradition 75-103
- involuntary reaction to an epiphany 82-83
- voluntary reaction to an epiphany 82-83
Sefer ha-Malbush 198
Sefer ha-Razim 198-199
Seraphim 195
"Servant" 93,93,97-98,224
Seseg/ngenbarpharagges, Sesengen, or Sphranges 195-196
Seven 156,232
- angels 167,193,226-227, 246, 248-249,257
- "archontic angels" 146
- bowls of wrath 246
- churches 35,209,232-240,245, 260, 263,271
- golden lampstands 233,239
- holy councils 156
- head princes 156
- heavens 96,199
- holy domains 156
- letters, see Letters
- mysteries of knowledge 156
- plagues 226
- priesthoods 156
- seals 261
- spirits of God 239
- stars 233,233,239
- thunders 231-232
- tongues 156
- words 156
Shemihazah 236
Silas 83
Sinai 57,62-63,69-70,110,152,229
Sitting 135,243
Six
- heavens 94-95,259
- "men" (Ezekiel 9) 226-227,244
Smyrna 181,190-191
- amulets 181,190-191
Snake 190,190
Snow, white as 89,213,219
Sodom and Gomorrah 196
Solomon 83,88,179,179,190-191
"Son" (see also Christology)
- in Philo 120
Song
- learned by the faithful 223
- learned from Iaoel 225
Song of the Lamb 222,226
Song of Moses
- in Revelation 222,226
- in Codex Alexandrinus 121
Songs of the Sabbath Sacrifice 14, 30,155-156,201-202,248
- first 159
- second 159
- seventh 156,160
- sixth 156
Sophists 107
"Sorcery" 144-145
Soteriology 25
Sound 89,219
- "of many waters" 213,219,222-226
Standing 135
Star(s) 54,57-60,62,107,145,190,232, 233,239
Στοιχεῖα 104-108, 110-111, 113, 115, 119,147
- enslavement to 108,110
Stratonikeia 114
- inscriptions 181-182,202,237
"Strong angel" 229-231,246,261
Structuralism 36-37
Sun 54,57-60,62,145,195,199,233,262
- appearance as 89,213,229,229-230
"Symbolic world" 23,35-42
Symbolism, symbols 30,34,37-42, 226, 233,238,240,257-258,264
Syncretism 54,115,115,141, 197, 197, 199,269
Syria(n) 4,191
Syro-Hexapla 214-216,218

Tabiym 195
Talmud,
- Babylonian 60-61,*68*,73
- Jerusalem 73
Tannaim 55
Tannaitic period *12*,53,57,*70*,72,74-75
Tapheiao 196
Tatia *187*
Telze 195
Temple cult 53
Temple, heavenly 155,*155*,157,243,246, 249
- not in the New Jerusalem 262
Temple Scroll (Qumran) *150*
Temrek (Lydia) *114*,*181*,202
Terror 82-83
Testament
- *of Abraham* 282
- *of Levi* 204
- *of Solomon* *179*,189
Testimony-book 127-128,*133*
Testimony of Jesus *250*,252, *252*, 254, *254*
Tetragrammaton *191*
Thenor 195
Theodicy 57
Theodore of Mopsuestia *112*
Theodoret *112*
Theogenes *185*
Theophany 86,89,91,211,231-232,261
Θεὸς Ὑψιστός, see "Most High"
Thera, inscriptions 181-182,188, *202*, *237*
Therapeutai 107
Thobarrabau 195
Thoouth 196
Throne(s) 37-38,40,42-43, 71, 94,96-97,*129*,217
Thomas *139*
Tobias *84*,166-167,*245*,*249*,*252*
Tobit *84*,165-167,*249*,*252*
Tobit, Book of 75-76,*84*,*165*,*271*
Torah 62,73-75,104-105, 108-110, *135*, 142,147,149,229
- angelic mediation of 104-105,110-111,119,122-123,127,*134*,*142*,144
- anthropological function *105*,109
- as a legal guardian *105*
- in salvation history *105*,110
Tosephta 60-61
Transfiguration 77
Trishagion 190,*190*
Trouble, see Distress

"Two powers" 4,70-71,79,270

Uriel (Ouriel) 174,179-180, 190-191, 195;196 (Suriel); 196 (Zouriel); 196 (Thouriel); 196(Souriel)
Ursa Minor 233

Veneration 13,*48*,*103*,149,200
- as distinguished from "worship" 50
- of saints *17*
Venerative language 21, *21*, 48, 149, 179,201,269
Vengeance, divine 37, 174-178, 180, 183-185,201,*237*
Victorinus of Pettau 230
Visionary, see Seer
Voice, see also Sound
- from heaven 232,*232*,243,*246*
- hypostatic *211*

War, holy 154-155
War Scroll (1QM) *150*
Watchers (good) 170-173,201,*236*
White linen 213
Wilderness 68-69,172,178,*231*,247
Wisdom *129*,*137*
- literature *91*
- relation to apocalyptic literature 27-29
Witch of Endor *171*
Wool, white as 219
Worship
- angelic worship of God *78*, *84*, 100,116,121,*121*,156-161,163-164, 201,219,222,269
- cultic, see also "angel cult" in Angelology 6-7,*10*,13,20,47-49
- definition 49-50
- heavenly 48-49,*134*,154-155, 157, 160,204,222-226,*248*,259
- in prohibitions 80
- of natural phenomena 54,73-74

"Youth" 84

Zagoure 196
Zehobadyah 79
Zenoid dynasty 34
Zeus, see also "Most High" 294
Zion, Mount 126,222
Zoroastrian, Zoroaster *112*,*198*
Zosimus 76,89-90,103,*174*

Wissenschaftliche Untersuchungen zum Neuen Testament

*Alphabetical index
of the first and the second series*

APPOLD, MARK L.: The Oneness Motif in the Fourth Gospel. 1976. *Volume II/1.*
BACHMANN, MICHAEL: Sünder oder Übertreter. 1991. *Volume 59.*
BAKER, WILLIAM R.: Personal Speech-Ethics. 1995. *Volume II/68.*
BAMMEL, ERNST: Judaica. 1986. *Volume 37.*
BAUERNFEIND, OTTO: Kommentar und Studien zur Apostelgeschichte. 1980. *Volume 22.*
BAYER, HANS FRIEDRICH: Jesus' Predictions of Vindication and Resurrection. 1986. *Volume II/20.*
BETZ, OTTO: Jesus, der Messias Israels. 1987. *Volume 42.*
– Jesus, der Herr der Kirche. 1990. *Volume 52.*
BEYSCHLAG, KARLMANN: Simon Magnus und die christliche Gnosis. 1974. *Volume 16.*
BITTNER, WOLFGANG J.: Jesu Zeichen im Johannesevangelium. 1987. *Volume II/26.*
BJERKELUND, CARL J.: Tauta Egeneto. 1987. *Volume 40.*
BLACKBURN, BARRY LEE: 'Theios Anēr' and the Markan Miracle Traditions. 1991. *Volume II/40.*
BOCKMUEHL, MARKUS N. A.: Revelation and Mystery in Ancient Judaism and Pauline Christianity. 1990. *Volume II/36.*
BÖHLIG, ALEXANDER: Gnosis und Synkretismus. Part 1. 1989. *Volume 47* – Part 2. 1989. *Volume 48.*
BÖTTRICH, CHRISTFRIED: Weltweisheit – Menschheitsethik – Urkult. 1992. *Volume II/50.*
BÜCHLI, JÖRG: Der Poimandres – ein paganisiertes Evangelium. 1987. *Volume II/27.*
BÜHNER, JAN A.: Der Gesandte und sein Weg im 4. Evangelium. 1977. *Volume II/2.*
BURCHARD, CHRISTOPH: Untersuchungen zu Joseph und Aseneth. 1965. *Volume 8.*
CANCIK, HUBERT (Ed.): Markus-Philologie. 1984. *Volume 33.*
CAPES, DAVID B.: Old Testament Yaweh Texts in Paul's Christology. 1992. *Volume II/47.*
CARAGOUNIS, CHRYS C.: The Son of Man. 1986. *Volume 38.*
– see FRIDRICHSEN.
CARLETON PAGET, JAMES: The Epistle of Barnabas. 1994. *Volume II/64.*
CRUMP, DAVID: Jesus the Intercessor. 1992. *Volume II/49.*
DEINES, ROLAND: Jüdische Steingefäße und pharisäische Frömmigkeit. 1993. *Volume II/52.*
DOBBELER, AXEL VON: Glaube als Teilhabe. 1987. *Volume II/22.*
DUNN, JAMES D. G. (Ed.): Jews and Christians. 1992. *Volume 66.*
EBERTZ, MICHAEL N.: Das Charisma des Gekreuzigten. 1987. *Volume 45.*
ECKSTEIN, HANS-JOACHIM: Der Begriff der Syneidesis bei Paulus. 1983. *Volume II/10.*
EGO, BEATE: Im Himmel wie auf Erden. 1989. *Volume II/34.*
ELLIS, E. EARLE: Prophecy and Hermeneutic in Early Christianity. 1978. *Volume 18.*
– The Old Testament in Early Christianity. 1991. *Volume 54.*
ENNULAT, ANDREAS: Die ›Minor Agreements‹. 1994. *Volume II/62.*
FELDMEIER, REINHARD: Die Krisis des Gottessohnes. 1987. *Volume II/21.*
– Die Christen als Fremde. 1992. *Volume 64.*
FELDMEIER, REINHARD and ULRICH HECKEL (Ed.): Die Heiden. 1994. *Volume 70.*
FORNBERG, TORD: see Fridrichsen.
FOSSUM, JARL E.: The Name of God and the Angel of the Lord. 1985. *Volume 36.*
FREY, JÖRG: Eugen Drewermann und die biblische Exegese. 1995. *Volume II/71.*
FRIDRICHSEN, ANTON: Exegetical Writings. Ed. by C. C. Caragounis and T. Fornberg. 1994. *Volume 76.*
GARLINGTON, DON B.: The Obedience of Faith. 1991. *Volume II/38.*
– Faith, Obedience, and Perseverance. 1994. *Volume 79.*
GARNET, PAUL: Salvation and Atonement in the Qumran Scrolls. 1977. *Volume II/3.*
GRÄSSER, ERICH: Der Alte Bund im Neuen. 1985. *Volume 35.*
GREEN, JOEL B.: The Death of Jesus. 1988. *Volume II/33.*
GUNDRY VOLF, JUDITH M.: Paul and Perseverance. 1990. *Volume II/37.*
HAFEMANN, SCOTT J.: Suffering and the Spirit. 1986. *Volume II/19.*
HECKEL, THEO K.: Der Innere Mensch. 1993. *Volume II/53.*

Wissenschaftliche Untersuchungen zum Neuen Testament

HECKEL, ULRICH: Kraft in Schwachheit. 1993. *Volume II/56.*
- see FELDMEIER.
- see HENGEL.
HEILIGENTHAL, ROMAN: Werke als Zeichen. 1983. *Volume II/9.*
HEMER, COLIN J.: The Book of Acts in the Setting of Hellenistic History. 1989. *Volume 49.*
HENGEL, MARTIN: Judentum und Hellenismus. 1969, ³1988. *Volume 10.*
- Die johanneische Frage. 1993. *Volume 67.*
HENGEL, MARTIN und ULRICH HECKEL (Ed.): Paulus und das antike Judentum. 1991. *Volume 58.*
HENGEL, MARTIN und HERMUT LÖHR (Ed.): Schriftauslegung. 1994. *Volume 73.*
HENGEL, MARTIN und ANNA MARIA SCHWEMER (Ed.): Königsherrschaft Gottes und himmlischer Kult. 1991. *Volume 55.*
- Die Septuaginta. 1994. *Volume 72.*
HERRENBRÜCK, FRITZ: Jesus und die Zöllner. 1990. *Volume II/41.*
HOFIUS, OTFRIED: Katapausis. 1970. *Volume 11.*
- Der Vorhang vor dem Thron Gottes. 1972. *Volume 14.*
- Der Christushymnus Philipper 2,6 – 11. 1976, ²1991. *Volume 17.*
- Paulusstudien. 1989, ²1994. *Volume 51.*
HOLTZ, TRAUGOTT: Geschichte und Theologie des Urchristentums. Ed. by Eckart Reinmuth and Christian Wolff. 1991. *Volume 57.*
HOMMEL, HILDEBRECHT: Sebasmata. Volume 1. 1983. *Volume 31.* – Volume 2. 1984. *Volume 32.*
KÄHLER, CHRISTOPH: Jesu Gleichnisse als Poesie und Therapie. 1995. *Volume 78.*
KAMLAH, EHRHARD: Die Form der katalogischen Paränese im Neuen Testament. 1964. *Volume 7.*
KIM, SEYOON: The Origin of Paul's Gospel. 1981, ²1984. *Volume II/4.*
- »The›Son of Man‹« as the Son of God. 1983. *Volume 30.*
KLEINKNECHT, KARL TH.: Der leidende Gerechtfertigte. 1984, ²1988. *Volume II/13.*
KLINGHARDT, MATTHIAS: Gesetz und Volk Gottes. 1988. *Volume II/32.*
KÖHLER, WOLF-DIETRICH: Rezeption des Matthäusevangeliums in der Zeit vor Irenäus. 1987. *Volume II/24.*
KORN, MANFRED: Die Geschichte Jesu in veränderter Zeit. 1993. *Volume II/51.*
KOSKENNIEMI, ERKKI: Apollonios von Tyana in der neutestamentlichen Exegese. 1994. *Volume II/61.*
KUHN, KARL G.: Achtzehngebet und Vaterunser und der Reim. 1950. *Volume 1.*
LAMPE, PETER: Die stadtrömischen Christen in den ersten beiden Jahrhunderten. 1987, ²1989. *Volume II/18.*
LIEU, SAMUEL N. C.: Manichaeism in the Later Roman Empire and Medieval China. 1992. *volume 63.*
LÖHR, HERMUT: see HENGEL.
MAIER, GERHARD: Mensch und freier Wille. 1971. *Volume 12.*
- Die Johannesoffenbarung und die Kirche. 1981. *Volume 25.*
MARKSCHIES, CHRISTOPH: Valentinus Gnosticus? 1992. *Volume 65.*
MARSHALL, PETER: Enmity in Corinth: Social Conventions in Paul's Relations with the Corinthians. 1987. *Volume II/23.*
MEADE, DAVID G.: Pseudonymity and Canon. 1986. *Volume 39.*
MELL, ULRICH: Die »anderen« Winzer. 1994. *Volume 77.*
MENGEL, BERTHOLD: Studien zum Philipperbrief. 1982. *Volume II/8.*
MERKEL, HELMUT: Die Widersprüche zwischen den Evangelien. 1971. *Volume 13.*
MERKLEIN, HELMUT: Studien zu Jesus und Paulus. 1987. *Volume 43.*
METZLER, KARIN: Der griechische Begriff des Verzeihens. 1991. *Volume II/44.*
NIEBUHR, KARL-WILHELM: Gesetz und Paränese. 1987. *Volume II/28.*
- Heidenapostel aus Israel. 1992. *Volume 63.*
NISSEN, ANDREAS: Gott und der Nächste im antiken Judentum. 1974. *Volume 15.*
NOORMANN, ROLF: Irenäus als Paulusinterpret. 1994. *Volume II/66.*
OKURE, TERESA: The Johannine Approach to Mission. 1988. *Volume II/31.*
PHILONENKO, MARC (Ed.): Le Trône de Dieu. 1993. *Volume 69.*
PILHOFER, PETER: Presbyteron Kreitton. 1990. *Volume II/39.*
PÖHLMANN, WOLFGANG: Der Verlorene Sohn und das Haus. 1993. *Volume 68.*
PROBST, HERMANN: Paulus und der Brief. 1991. *Volume II/45.*
RÄISÄNEN, HEIKKI: Paul and the Law. 1983, ²1987. *Volume 29.*

Wissenschaftliche Untersuchungen zum Neuen Testament

REHKOPF, FRIEDRICH: Die lukanische Sonderquelle. 1959. *Volume 5.*
REINMUTH, ECKART: Pseudo-Philo und Lukas. 1994. *Volume 74.*
– see HOLTZ.
REISER, MARIUS: Syntax und Stil des Markusevangeliums. 1984. *Volume II/11.*
RICHARDS, E. RANDOLPH: The Secretary in the Letters of Paul. 1991. *Volume II/42.*
RIESNER, RAINER: Jesus als Lehrer. 1981, ³1988. *Volume II/7.*
– Die Frühzeit des Apostels Paulus. 1994. *Volume 71.*
RISSI, MATHIAS: Die Theologie des Hebräerbriefs. 1987. *Volume 41.*
RÖHSER, GÜNTER: Metaphorik und Personifikation der Sünde. 1987. *Volume II/25.*
ROSE, CHRISTIAN: Die Wolke der Zeugen. 1994. *Volume II/60.*
RÜGER, HANS PETER: Die Weisheitsschrift aus der Kairoer Geniza. 1991. *Volume 53.*
SALZMANN, JORG CHRISTIAN: Lehren und Ermahnen. 1994. *Volume II/59.*
SÄNGER, DIETER: Antikes Judentum und die Mysterien. 1980. *Volume II/5.*
– Die Verkündigung des Gekreuzigten und Israel. 1994. *Volume 75.*
SANDNES, KARL OLAV: Paul – One of the Prophets? 1991. *Volume II/43.*
SATO, MIGAKU: Q und Prophetie. 1988. *Volume II/29.*
SCHIMANOWSKI, GOTTFRIED: Weisheit und Messias. 1985. *Volume II/17.*
SCHLICHTING, GÜNTER: Ein jüdisches Leben Jesu. 1982. *Volume 24.*
SCHNABEL, ECKHARD J.: Law and Wisdom from Ben Sira to Paul. 1985. *Volume II/16.*
SCHUTTER, WILLIAM L.: Hermeneutic and Composition in I Peter. 1989. *Volume II/30.*
SCHWARTZ, DANIEL R.: Studies in the Jewish Background of Christianity. 1992. *Volume 60.*
SCHWEMER, A. M.: see HENGEL.
SCOTT, JAMES M.: Adoption as Sons of God. 1992. *Volume II/48.*
SIEGERT, FOLKER: Drei hellenistisch-jüdische Predigten. Part 1. 1980. *Volume 20.* – Part 2. 1992. *Volume 61.*
– Nag-Hammadi-Register. 1982. *Volume 26.*
– Argumentation bei Paulus. 1985. *Volume 34.*
– Philon von Alexandrien. 1988. *Volume 46.*
SIMON, MARCEL: Le christianisme antique et son contexte religieux I/II. 1981. *Volume 23.*
SNODGRASS, KLYNE: The Parable of the Wicked Tenants. 1983. *Volume 27.*
SOMMER, URS: Die Passionsgeschichte des Markusevangeliums. 1993. *Volume II/58.*
SPANGENBERG, VOLKER: Herrlichkeit des Neuen Bundes. 1993. *Volume II/55.*
SPEYER, WOLFGANG: Frühes Christentum im antiken Strahlungsfeld. 1989. *Volume 50.*
STADELMANN, HELGE: Ben Sira als Schriftgelehrter. 1980. *Volume II/6.*
STROBEL, AUGUST: Die Stunde der Wahrheit. 1980. *Volume 21.*
STUCKENBRUCK, LOREN: Angel Veneration and Christology. 1995. *Volume II/70.*
STUHLMACHER, PETER (Ed.): Das Evangelium und die Evangelien. 1983. *Volume 28.*
SUNG, CHONG-HYON: Vergebung der Sünden. 1993. *Volume II/57.*
TAJRA, HARRY W.: The Trial of St. Paul. 1989. *Volume II/35.*
– The Martyrdom of St. Paul. 1994. *Volume II/67.*
THEISSEN, GERD: Studien zur Soziologie des Urchristentums. 1979, ³1989. *Volume 19.*
THORNTON, CLAUS-JÜRGEN: Der Zeuge des Zeugen. 1991. *Volume 56.*
TWELFTREE, GRAHAM: Jesus the Exorcist. 1993. *Volume II/54.*
VISOTZKY, BURTON L.: Fathers of the World. 1995. *Volume 80.*
WAGENER, ULRIKE: Die Ordnung des ›Hauses Gottes‹. 1994. *Volume II/65.*
WEDDERBURN, A. J. M.: Baptism and Resurrection. 1987. *Volume 44.*
WEGNER, UWE: Der Hauptmann von Kafarnaum. 1985. *Volume II/14.*
WELCK, CHRISTIAN: Erzählte ›Zeichen‹. 1994. *Volume II/69.*
WILSON, WALTER T.: Love without Pretense. 1991. *Volume II/46.*
WOLFF, CHRISTIAN: see HOLTZ.
ZIMMERMANN, ALFRED E.: Die urchristlichen Lehrer. 1984, ²1988. *Volume II/12.*

For a complete catalogue please write to
J. C. B. Mohr (Paul Siebeck), P. O. Box 2040, D-72010 Tübingen

www.ingramcontent.com/pod-product-compliance
Lightning Source LLC
Chambersburg PA
CBHW021815300426
44114CB00009BA/196